AF559650

ENTERPRISE INFORMATION SYSTEMS IN 21ST CENTURY

Opportunities and Challenges

ENTERPRISE INFORMATION SYSTEMS IN 21ST CENTURY

Opportunities and Challenges

Editors

DR. BALRAM DOGRA
Director
Apeejay Institute of Management
Jalandhar (Punjab)

KULWANT KAUR
Head, Department of Computer Application
Apeejay Institute of Management
Jalandhar (Punjab)

DEEPAK KAUSHIK
Faculty
Apeejay Institute of Management
Jalandhar (Punjab)

DEEP & DEEP PUBLICATIONS PVT. LTD.
F-159, Rajouri Garden, New Delhi - 110 027

ENTERPRISE INFORMATION SYSTEMS IN 21ST CENTURY
Opportunities and Challenges

ISBN 978-81-8450-183-4

Typeset by RAHUL COMPOSERS
358, Pocket-B, Phase-II, Sector-16B, Dwarka, New Delhi - 110 078

Printed in India at MAYUR ENTERPRISES
WZ Plot No. 3, Gujjar Market, Tihar Village, New Delhi - 110 018

Published by DEEP & DEEP PUBLICATIONS PVT. LTD.,
F-159, Rajouri Garden, New Delhi - 110 027 • Phone : 25435369, 25440916
E-mail : ddpbooks@yahoo.co.in • ddpubs@gmail.com
Showroom :
2/13, Ansari Road, Daryaganj, New Delhi - 110 002 • Telefax : 23245122

Contents

SECTION III

E-LEARNING IN EDUCATION

SECTION IV

DATABASES INTEGRATION

SECTION V

SOFTWARE AGENTS AND INTERNET COMPUTING

Section VI

SECURITY AND PRIVACY

Section VII

MANAGING A WORLD CLASS IT DEVELOPMENT

Acknowledgements

This book owes its origin to the AICTE sponsored National Seminar on Enterprise Information Systems in 21st Century organized at Apeejay Institute of Management, Jalandhar during May 2008. The conference received an overwhelming response from the academia as well as the industry. A large number of papers were submitted on the theme during the course of the conference.

The editors wish to acknowledge with thanks the financial support provided by All India Council of Technical Education, which made it possible to organize the event. We also appreciate the encouragement and support provided by Apeejay Education Society in making the conference a grand success. In particular we would like to express our sense of gratitude and sincere thanks to Dr. Stya Paul, Chairman; Ms. Sushma Berlia, Vice-President and Sh. Yash Raj Aggarwal, General Secretary, Apeejay Education Society for their valuable guidance and support in all academic endeavors including this conference.

We have benefited from the help of many people during the evolution of this book. We express our thanks to Ms. Kamana Raj Aggarwal, Joint Secretary, Apeejay Education Society and Chairperson, All India Fasteners Panel of Engineering Export Promotion Council; Mr. Naresh Nagpal, Additional Director, Technical Education and Industrial Training, Government of Punjab; Dr. Nasib Singh Gill, Head of Department of Computer Science, Maharishi Dayanand, Rohtak; Mr. Satish Kumar Dhanda, Vice-Chairman of Medium Industries Development Board, Government of Punjab; Dr. Moin Uddin, Director, Dr. B.R. Ambedkar National Institute of Technology, Jalandhar; Dr. Kawaljeet Singh, Director, University Computer Centre, Punjabi University, Patiala; Dr. Hardeep Singh, Professor, Department of Computer Science and Engineering, Guru Nanak Dev University, Amritsar; Dr. Seema Bawa, Professor, Department of Computer Science and Engineering, Thapar University, Patiala; Dr. A.S. Pandey, Professor, Institute of Technology and Science, Ghaziabad; Mr. A.L. Sangal, Registrar, Dr. Ambedkar National Institute of Technology; Jalandhar.

Many persons have contributed time, energy, ideas and suggestions for realization of this project. The strength of this book is largely attributed to collective wisdom, work and experiences of academia, researchers, students and practitioners. We also appreciate the unflagging support and huge amount of efforts put in by the members of the faculty and the staff of Apeejay Institute of Management, Jalandhar. The book would not have been possible without the unflinching dedication of one and all.

BALRAM DOGRA
KULWANT KAUR
DEEPAK KAUSHIK

List of Contributors

A.S. Pandey, Professor, Institute of Technology and Science, Ghaziabad.

Abhilasha Singh, Lecturer, Department of Computer Applications, Apeejay Institute of Management, Jalandhar.

Achin Tyagi, Department of Computer Science, Engineering and Information Technology, Jaypee Institute of Information Technology University, Noida.

Achintya Das, Professor and Head, Department of Electronics Communication and Engineering, Kalyani Government Engineering College, Durgapur.

Ajay Bansal, Sr. Lecturer, Department of Computer Applications, Apeejay Institute of Management, Jalandhar.

Ajay Goel, Sr. Lecturer, K.I.T.M Engineering, Kurukshetra.

Akhilesh Kumar Bhardwaj, Lecturer, Department of Computer Science and Engineering, Shri Krishan Institute of Engineering and Technology, Kurukshetra, Haryana.

Aliza Tanwir, Lecturer, Department of Information Technology, Apeejay College of Engineering, Sohna.

Amandeep Kaur, Lecturer, Department of Computer Applications, Apeejay Institute of Management, Jalandhar.

Amar Arora, Department of Computer Science and Engineering, Dr. B.R. Ambedkar National Institute of Technology, Jalandhar.

Amit Jain, Lecturer, Department of Computer Science and Engineering, Shri Krishan Institute of Engineering and Technology, Kurukshetra, Haryana.

Amit Sharma, Lecturer, Department of Computer Applications, Apeejay Institute of Management, Jalandhar.

Anil Kumar, Department of Information Technology, H.C.T.M., Kaithal, Haryana.

Aradhna Mehta, Lecturer, Department of Computer Science and Engineering, JCD College of Engineering, Sirsa.

Arun Jain, Department of Computer Science and Engineering, H.C.T.M., Kaithal.

Ashu Gupta, Senior Lecturer in Computer Applications, Apeejay Institute of Management, Jalandhar.

Ashwani Kumar, Sr. Lecturer, PG Department of Commerce, Government Bikram College of Commerce, Patiala.

Avnip Deora, Lecturer, Department of Computer Applications, Apeejay Institute of Management, Jalandhar.

Balraj Kumar, Asst. Professor, Department of Computer Applications, Lovely Professional University, Phagwara.

Balram Dogra, Director, Apeejay Institute of Management, Jalandhar.

Bharti Rao, Department of Computer Science and Engineering, Apeejay College of Engineering, Sohna.

Biswarup Neogi, Lecturer, Department of Electronics Communication and Engineering, Institute of Advanced Technology and Management, Durgapur.

Chanderkant Verma, Lecturer, Department of Computer Science and Engineering, Kurukshetra University, Kurukshetra.

Daljeet Singh Matharu, Lecturer, Department of Computer Applications, Apeejay Institute of Management, Jalandhar.

Deepak Kaushik, Senior Lecturer, Department of Computer Applications, Apeejay Institute of Management, Jalandhar.

Deepika Thakur, Lecturer, Department of Computer Applications, Apeejay College of Fine Arts, Jalandhar.

Deepshikha, Department of Computer Science and Engineering, Guru Jambheshwar University of Science and Technology, Hisar.

Dharminder Kumar, Professor, Department of Computer Science and Engineering, Guru Jambheshwar University of Science and Technology, Hisar.

Dinesh Kumar, Lecturer, Department of Computer Applications, Apeejay Institute of Management, Jalandhar.

Ganesh Chandra Deka, Assistant Director of Training Section, DGE & T, Ministry of Labour Employment, Delhi.

Geeta Sikka, Lecturer, Department of Computer Science and Engineering, National Institute of Technology, Jalandhar.

Gopal Singh, Lecturer, Department of Computer Science and Engineering, Chaudhary Devi Lal University, Sirsa.

Gurvinder Singh, Reader, Department of Computer Science and Engineering, Guru Nanak Dev University, Amritsar.

Hardeep Singh, Professor, Department of Computer Science and Engineering Computer Science, Guru Nanak Dev University, Amritsar.

Hardeep Singh, Senior Lecturer, Department of Management, C.T. Institute of Management and I.T., Jalandhar.

Harjot Singh, Lecturer, Department of Computer Applications, Apeejay Institute of Management, Jalandhar.

Harprit Kaur, Lecturer, Department of Electronic Engineering, SBBS College of Engineering and Technology, Jalandhar.

Harsh Kumar Verma, Reader, Department of Computer Science and Engineering, Dr. B.R. Ambedkar National Institute of Technology, Jalandhar.

Indu Bala Grover, Department of Computer Science and Engineering, Apeejay College of Engineering, Sohna.

Jagjit Singh, Asst. Professor, Lovely Institute of Management, Jalandhar.

Jaiteg Singh, Senior Lecturer, Department of Computer Science, RIMT-IMCT, Mandi Gobindgarh.

Jaswinder Singh, Department of Computer Science and Engineering, Guru Jambheshwar University of Science and Technology, Hisar.

Jaswinder Singh, Lecturer, Department of Computer Applications, Apeejay Institute of Management, Jalandhar.

Jesmin Zakaria, Lecturer, Department of Electronics Communication and Engineering, Institute of Advanced Technology and Management, Durgapur.

Kanika Lakhani, Lecturer, Department of Computer Applications, Apeejay College of Engineering, Sohna.

Kanwal Garg, Assistant Professor, MMICT and BM, Mullana, Ambala.

Kawaljeet Singh, Director, University Computer Centre, Punjabi University, Patiala.

Kuljit Kaur, Lecturer, Department of Computer Science and Engineering, Guru Nanak Dev University, Amritsar.

Lakwinder Kaur, Sr. Lecturer, Department of Computer Applications, Apeejay Institute of Management, Jalandhar.

M.C. Garg, Reader, Haryana School of Business, Guru Jambheshwar University of Science and Technology, Hisar.

Mahesh Paramjit Kumar, Director, Punjab Institute of Management and Technology, Mandi Gobindgarh.

Malaya Dutta Borah, Lecturer, Department of Computer Engineering, Delhi College of Engineering, Bawana Road, Delhi.

Mandip Saini, Department of Management, Lovely Professional University, Phagwara.

Manu Sood, Department of Computer Science, Himachal Pradesh University, Shimla.

Meghna Sharma, Asst. Professor, Department of Computer Applications, ITM, Gurgaon.

Minakshi Seth, Asstt. Professor, Punjab Institute of Management and Technology, Mandi Gobindgarh.

Nancy Mehta, Lecturer, Department of Computer Science and Engineering, JCDV College of Engineering, Sirsa.

Nasib Singh Gill, Head, Department of Computer Science and Applications, Director, Public Relations, M.D. University, Rohtak.

Navdeep Kaur, Asst. Professor, Chandigarh Engineering College, Landran, Mohali.

Navjote Khara, Sr. Lecturer, Department of Management, Apeejay Institute of Management, Jalandhar.

Navneet Kaur, Lecturer, Department of Computer Applications, Apeejay Institute of Management, Jalandhar.

Neelam, Department of Computer Science and Engineering, Guru Jambheshwer University of Science and Technology, Hisar.

Neera Bawa, Lecturer, Department of Computer Science and Engineering, JCDV College of Engineering, Sirsa.

Pallavi Mehta, Lecturer, Department of Computer Applications, Apeejay College of Fine Arts, Jalandhar.

Paramvir Singh, Lecturer, Department of Computer Science and Engineering, National Institute of Technology, Jalandhar.

Parminder Kaur, Lecturer, Department of Computer Science and Engineering, Guru Nanak Dev University, Amritsar.

Parveen Kumar, Department of Computer Science and Engineering, Kurkushetra University, Kurukshetra.

Pawan Kumar, Sr. Lecturer, Department of Computer Applications, Lovely Professional University, Phagwara.

Pooja Dhand, Lecturer, Department of Computer Applications, Apeejay College of Fine Arts, Jalandhar.

Poonam, Department of Electronics and Communication Engineering, Guru Jambheshwar University of Science and Technology, Hisar.

Pradeep Kumar Bhatia, Lecturer, Department of Computer Science, Guru Jambheshwar University of Science and Technology, Hisar.

Pradeep Kumar Sharma, Sr. Lecturer, Department of Computer Applications, Banasthali Vidayapith, Rajasthan.

Preeti, Department of Computer Science and Engineering, Guru Jambheshwer University of Science and Technology, Hisar.

Priyanka Arora, Lecturer, Department of Computer Science and Engineering, Apeejay College of Engineering, Sohna.

Punit Soni, Lecturer, H.C.T.M., Kaithal.

R.K. Chauhan, Chairman, Department of Computer Science and Applications, Kurukshetra University, Kurukshetra.

Rajbeer Mann, Department of Computer Science, Guru Jambheshwar University of Science and Technology, Hisar.

Rajesh Verma, Assistant Professor, Lovely School of Business, Lovely Professional University, Phagwara.

Rajesh Verma, Asstt. Professor and HOD, GNKITMS, Yamuna Nagar, Haryana.

Rajiv Kumar Bhardwaz, Lecturer, Department of Computer Applications, Apeejay Institute of Management, Jalandhar.

Rajni Mittal, Lecturer, Department of Computer Applications, Apeejay College of Fine Arts, Jalandhar.

Rajwinder Singh, Asst. Professor, Chandigarh Engineering College, Landran, Mohali.

Rakesh Sharma, Department of Computer Science and Engineering, Guru Jambheshwer University of Science and Technology, Hisar.

Raman Kumar, Department of Computer Science and Engineering, Dr. B.R. Ambedkar National Institute of Technology, Jalandhar.

Ramanpreet Kaur, Lecturer, Department of Management, C.T. Institute of Management and I.T., Jalandhar.

Ramu Tanguturi, Department of Computer Science and Engineering, Dr. B.R. Ambedkar National Institute of Technology, Jalandhar.

Rekha Handa, Lecturer, Department of Management, Apeejay Institute of Management, Jalandhar.

Renu Dhir, Sr. Lecturer, Department of Computer Science and Engineering, Dr. B.R. Ambedkar National Institute of Technology, Jalandhar.

Rinku Sanjeev, Asst. Professor, Department of Business Administration, Manav Rachna College of Engineering, MREI Campus, Faridabad.

Roopali Sood, Head, Department of Computer Applications, Apeejay College of Fine Arts, Jalandhar.

S. Banerjee, Professor, Head, Department of Business Administration, Manav Rachna College of Engineering, MREI Campus, Faridabad.

S.K. Bansal, Dean, Punjab School of Management Studies, Punjabi University, Patiala.

S.N. Panda, Professor, Department of Computer Applications, RIMT, Mandi Gobindgarh.

Sanjay Goel, Department of Computer Science, Engineering and Information Technology, Jaypee Institute of Information Technology University, Noida.

Sanjeev Singh, Assistant Professor, Career Institute of Technology and Management, Faridabad.

Saroj, Department of Computer Science and Engineering, Guru Jambheshwer University of Science and Technology, Hisar.

Satbir Rupal, Lecturer, Lyallpur Khalsa College of Education for Women, Jalandhar.

Seema Kailey, Lecturer, Department of Management, Apeejay Institute of Management, Jalandhar.

Shilpy Sharma, Sr. Lecturer, Department of Computer Applications, ITM, Gurgaon.

Shiv Kumar Modgil, Lecturer, Department of Computer Applications, Apeejay Institute of Management, Jalandhar.

Shreemathi S. Mayya, Associate Professor, University of Statistics, Manipal University, Manipal.

Shweta Mongia, Lecturer, Department of Computer Science and Engineering, Apeejay College of Engineering, Sohna.

Sukhdev Singh, Department of Computer Science and Applications, K.U., Kurukshetra.

Sukhmeet Singh, Department of Management, Apeejay Institute of Management, Jalandhar.

Surender Kumar, Department of Information Technology, HCTM, Kaithal.

Suresh Verma, Lecturer, Department of Computer Applications, Apeejay Institute of Management, Jalandhar.

Sureshramana Mayya, Professor of Commerce, MGM College, Udupi, Karnataka.

Vijay Nehra, Department of Electronics and Communication Engineering, Guru Jambheshwar University of Science and Technology, Hisar.

Vikram Singh, Reader and Chairman, Department of Computer Science and Engineering, Chaudhary Devi Lal University, Sirsa.

Yogesh Chaba, Chairman and Reader, Department of Computer Science and Engineering, Guru Jambheshwer University of Science and Technology, Hisar.

Yogita Sharma, Lecturer, Department of Business Administration, Manav Rachna College of Engineering, Delhi, Surajkund Road, MREI Campus, Faridabad.

Yudhvir Singh, Lecturer, Department of Computer Science and Engineering, Guru Jambheshwer University of Science and Technology, Hisar.

Introduction

Information technologies have had a profound influence on how modern organizations operate. Information technologies support information systems, which in turn support the decision-making in various organizations. New technologies are constantly emerging, which are enabling new business models and new types of services. Information technologies are no longer a functional area within an organization, but are integral to the functioning of an organization. Integration improves exposure and, by extension, the value and quality of information to facilitate workflow and reduce business risk. It is an important element of the way organization's business process operates. Data integration technology is the key to pulling organization data together and delivering an information infrastructure that will meet strategic business intelligence initiatives.

Effective, accurate and timely application integration is fundamental to the successful operation of today's organizations. The success of every business initiative relies heavily on the integration between existing heterogeneous applications and databases. For this reason, when companies look to improve productivity, reduce overall costs, or streamline business processes; integration should be at the heart of their plans.

Enterprise-wide information system integrates various functionalities within an enterprise. The target is 'knowledge in an enterprise environment', and the key to the success of the enterprise is the information systems and technologies 'in place' to support the enterprise.

The five major categories of Enterprise Information Systems in 21st Century that have evolved in past and could emerge in future—the economic tracking systems with no overall organizing; the accounting systems that are organized; the application software suites; the enterprise-oriented software packages and models and inter-organizational systems which record transactions in one centralized fashion and make the data available to all parties (inter-enterprise and intra-enterprise) participating in economic exchanges.

Internet is a critical enabler for e-business as it requires defense in depth, multiple and cohesive components, integration into e-business infrastructure, compatibility with technology initiatives and requires comprehensive blueprint.

Integration of information systems can be done at three levels like manufacturing (local purchasing, invoice verification, inventory management, internal sales, shipping and billing, profit/loss, capacity utilization); headquarters (information systems, project management, inventory, purchasing, sales, budget, cash management) and marketing/ sales (sales, shipping and billing, purchasing of trading goods, inventory management, customer service).

Business Intelligence is a tool which enables people to make better decisions and thus improve their business processes. It includes Decision Support Systems (DSS), Executive Information Systems (EIS), reporting, data mining, early warning systems (robots).

Increased globalization and ever escalating costs have placed continuous pressure on manufacturers to optimize resources, meet tighter delivery schedules, and improve overall responsiveness. These demands are driving change and forcing many companies to consider ERP strategies. Almost all organizations are turning to ERP package as a solution to their information management problems. Evolution of ERP includes Manufacturing Integration (MRP), Enterprise Integration (ERP), Customer-Centric Integration (CRP) and Inter-enterprise Integration (XRP).

Enterprise Information Systems in 21st Century have been the central focus of researchers and practitioners worldwide for almost last two decades. This book presents a well-integrated collection of 61 research papers that were presented in the AICTE sponsored National Seminar and brings together the collective wisdom from prominent IT and management scholars and practioners in analyzing Enterprise Information Systems in 21st Century. All the contributions in this book have a practical slant, showing how technology has been or can be innovatively applied to a wide spectrum of domains and tasks for the economic growth of the country.

The book is divided into seven sections that reveal the main concepts examined in the book.

Section I throws light on aspects related to Information Systems Analysis and its specification, e.g. Enterprise Information Systems in 21st Century; Information Management; Software Development Lifecycle; Software Maintainability and Reliability; Software Metrics; Mobile Information Systems and Case Study—Version Control.

Section II provides an insight in to Intelligent Systems, in which the different chapters discuss in detail about the Artificial Intelligence; Intelligent Systems; Fuzzy Approach; Intrusion Detection System and Augmented Reality with various applications.

Section III of the book deals with how technology can be used for e-learning in education. This section deals with issues like use of multimedia in e-learning; e-learning in India; platform for teaching large classrooms and academic enterprise establishment.

Section IV provides details of one of the very important aspect of today's scenario, i.e. Databases Integration which includes techniques of Data Mining; Data Warehousing; Empirical Study of Data Warehouse Development and Case Study—Life Insurance Sector.

Section V deals with very important aspect of today's Internet Computing scenario wherein it discusses issues about Intelligent Software Agents; Transmission Protocol; Online Banking and e-Commerce and various applications in India.

Section VI talk about one of the revolutionary innovations of this age—Security and Privacy. As the new technology comes to use the issue of security has to be addressed. This section also puts forward different security measures for Mobile Systems; Secure Communication; Distributed Service and Wi-Fi Deployment.

Section VII deals with the application of technology to different sectors of the society like Business Process Reengineering; Customer Relationship Management; Information Security; Enterprise Resource Planning; ICT in Indian SMEs and Rural Development; Case Study—Cement Industry.

With the advent of information technology industry, the information is growing at the exponential rate and has been contributing substantially towards country's development. India, home to one of the world's most advanced computing and engineering sectors, is at the forefront of many such efforts; national and state governments, private concerns, and civil societies are all involved in extending what they see as the promise of rapid development to their rural and urban areas.

The strength of this book lies in the comprehensiveness of the treatment of this topic as no other single source contains as many different research papers. This book offers an integrated perspective on the vast body of information available in the IT & Management field. It presents in clear and accessible language a coherent integration of the different quality research papers starting from conceptual to applied research. The resulting synthesis of experience and concepts will be of significant value not only to executives and managers, attempting to implement Enterprise Information Systems in 21st Century within their own firms, but also to the academicians and researchers working on this emerging field.

BALRAM DOGRA
KULWANT KAUR
DEEPAK KAUSHIK

SECTION I

Information Systems Analysis and Specification

1

Enterprise Information Systems in 21st Century: Opportunities and Challenges

NASIB SINGH GILL

ABSTRACT

Technological breakthroughs have not only revolutionized communications and the spread of information but have strongly influenced all aspects of life. The economy and business environment are forced to use advanced technology to survive in the competitive global market. The digital age began when digital computers and related technologies were developed in the second-half of the 20th Century. The present age is variously known as the Digital Age, the Wireless Age and the Information Age.

Information technology refers to the use of computer-based information systems to convert, store, protect, process, transmit and retrieve information. Technological advances in this field have changed lifestyles around the world and spawned new industries around controlling and providing information. Information age in the present economic era has shifted the global economy by means of exploiting the full potential of information technology.

Technical developments continue to enable great changes in organizations. Securing benefits, however, requires more than technology. Every enterprise needs an efficient and customized information system. Specific enterprise business needs demand specific software solutions which drive information systems.

Enterprise Information System (EIS) is a 21st century information system that has enterprise wide focus. Fulfilment of business requirements is the main purpose of such a system. Business requirements must directly determine functionality of an enterprise information system.

Enterprise Information Systems have brought both opportunities as well as challenges. Business data and information comes from multiple sources. The challenge for a business is to capture and use information that is relevant and reliable. For running a business effectively, managers need insights in all kinds of aspects, such as inventory, costs, profits and return, staffing or performance. Business Intelligence (BI) can offer a solution by making this information available. Business intelligence is a broad category of applications and technologies for gathering, storing, analyzing, and providing access to data to help enterprise users make better business decision.

This Chapter discusses the basic concept of information system and enterprise information system in the First Section. Their types, benefits, threats and remedial solutions have been discussed in the following sections of this Chapter.

1. ENTERPRISE INFORMATION SYSTEM

An *Information System* is a system that collects, processes, stores, analyzes and disseminates information for a specific purpose. Like any other system, an information system includes input (data, instructions) and outputs (reports, calculations). It processes the inputs and produces outputs that are sent to the user or to other systems.

Enterprise Information System is a new generation of information system that has enterprise wide focus. The Enterprise Information System (EIS) provides web-based information and reporting service. An *Enterprise Information System* is generally any kind of computing system that is of "enterprise class". This means typically offering high quality of service, dealing with large volumes of data and capable of supporting some large organization. Enterprise Information Systems provide a technology platform that enable organizations to integrate and coordinate their business processes.

It continues to grow in the number of users and ease of use. Increased use of technology has changed the way customers and partners interact with enterprises. Presently, the customers expect an enterprise to provide services and products in the shortest possible time anywhere in the world. Information system has become the major business driver for an enterprise and it enables an enterprise to efficiently use all available resources according to current needs so as to successfully respond to desirable business opportunities.

They provide a single system that is central to the organization and ensure that information can be shared across all functional levels and management hierarchies. Enterprise systems are invaluable in eliminating the problem of information fragmentation caused by multiple information systems in an organization, by creating a standard data structure.

Enterprise information system integrates all data and processes of an organization into a unified and integrated system. A key ingredient of most information systems is the use of a unified database to store data for the various system modules. There are various activities of an oganisation which used to be stand-alone applications, but with the arrival of advanced software, hardware and communication technology, all these have been integrated into a unified and single solution. Few major activities include the following:

- *Financials*
  - General Ledger, Cash Management, Accounts Payable, Accounts Receivable, Fixed Assets.
- *Manufacturing*
  - Engineering, Bills of Material, Scheduling, Capacity, Workflow Management, Quality Control, Cost Management, Manufacturing Process, Manufacturing Projects, Manufacturing Flow.
- *Project Management*
  - Costing, Billing, Time and Expense, Activity Management.
- *Supply Chain Management*
  - Inventory, Order Entry, Purchasing, Product Configurator, Supply Chain Planning, Supplier Scheduling, Inspection of goods, Claim Processing, Commission Calculation.
- *Customer Relationship Management (CRM)*
  - Sales and Marketing, Commissions, Service, Customer Contact and Call Center support.
- *Human Resources*
  - Human Resources, Payroll, Training, Time & Attendance, Benefits.
- Data Warehouse and various *Self-Service* interfaces for Customers, Suppliers, and Employees.

2. TYPES OF INFORMATION SYSTEM FOR AN ENTERPRISE

There are a variety of requirements for information in an enterprise required by different people at different levels, therefore, different types of information systems within an enterprise are needed. For example, senior managers need information to help with their business planning, middle management need more detailed information to help them monitor and control business activities and so on.

Major types of information systems for an enterprise include the following:

- Executive Support Systems
- Management Information Systems
- Decision-Support Systems

- Knowledge Management Systems
- Transaction Processing Systems
- Office Automation Systems
- Expert Systems

A brief outline of these systems is provided below:

(a) Executive Support Systems

An Executive Support System is designed to help senior management make strategic decisions. It collects analyses and summarizes the key internal and external information used in business. It typically involves lots of data analysis and modeling tools such as "what-if" analysis to help strategic decision-making.

(b) Management Information Systems

Management information system is mainly concerned with internal sources of information. It usually receives data from transaction processing systems and summaries it into a series of management reports, which are used by middle management and operational supervisors.

(c) Decision-Support Systems

- A Decision-Support System is an integrated set of computer tools that allows a decision maker to interact directly with computers to create information useful in making semi-structured and unstructured decisions.
- Decision-Support Systems are designed to help management make decisions in situations where there is uncertainty about the possible outcomes of decisions. These systems comprise tools and techniques to help gather relevant information and analyze the options and alternatives.
- The software components for Decision-Support Systems are a language system which enables the user to interact with the decision-support system, a problem-processing system which is made-up of several components that perform various processing tasks and a knowledge system which provides data and artificial-intelligence capabilities to the decision-support system.

(d) Knowledge Management Systems

Knowledge Management Systems help businesses create and share information. These are normally used in a business where employees create new knowledge and expertise—which can then be shared by other people in the organization to create further commercial opportunities. Few good examples include firms of lawyers, accountants and management consultants.

(e) Transaction Processing Systems

Transaction Processing Systems are designed to process routine transactions efficiently and accurately. Few examples of transaction processing systems include the following:

- Billing systems to send invoices to customers,
- Systems to calculate the weekly and monthly payroll and tax payments,
- Production and purchasing systems to calculate raw material requirements, and
- Stock control systems to process all movements into, within and out of the business.

(f) Office Automation Systems

Office Automation Systems improves the productivity of employees who need to process data and information. The best example is the wide range of software systems that exist to improve the productivity of employees working in an office (e.g. Microsoft Office XP) or systems that allow employees to work from home or whilst on the move.

(g) Expert Systems

Expert system is a computer system or program that uses artificial intelligence techniques to solve problems that ordinarily require a knowledgeable human. The method used to develop such systems, knowledge engineering, extracts a set of rules and data from an expert or experts through extensive questioning. Expert systems imitate human experts in many different fields of expertise. Such systems contain rules that help human answer expert questions.

3. BENEFITS OF ENTERPRISE INFORMATION SYSTEMS

Development and deployment of an enterprise information system is not an easy task. For successful implementation of an enterprise information system, the organisation needs to identify all processes so as to integrate the same with people and technology.

(a) Costs

The organisation needs to pay a heavy cost in its successful implementation and making it fully operational. Few of the major elements of cost include the following:

- Hardware
- Telecommunications
- Software
- Services
- Personnel
- Training
- Integration and installation
- Support
- Maintenance
- Storage backup infrastructure

(b) Benefits

The benefits of Enterprise Information Systems may be classified into tangible and non-tangible benefits. Some major benefits are listed below:

Tangible Benefits

- Reduced workforce
- Enhanced productivity
- Reduced operational costs
- Reduced clerical and professional costs
- Reduced facility costs
- Reduced computer expenses
- Lower rate of growth in expenses
- Reduced outside vendor costs
- Central access
- Easy backup
- Easy record-keeping

Intangible Benefits

- More timely information
- Increased job satisfaction
- Improved decision-making
- Improved operations
- Improved asset utilization
- Improved resource control
- Legal requirements attained
- Enhanced employee goodwill
- Higher client satisfaction
- Better corporate image
- Increased organizational flexibility, planning and learning

4. THREATS TO ENTERPRISE INFORMATION SYSTEMS

Information is the blood for any business organisation. Information is the end product of data. When voluminous data is stored in electronic form, it is sensitive and vulnerable to several kinds of risks and challenges. Few of the most common threats against such computerized Enterprise Information Systems include the following:

- Computer crimes
- Software quality problem
- Hardware problems
- Theft of data, service, equipment
- Hardware failure
- Personnel action
- System access penetration
- Disaster
- Telecommunication problems
- Electrical problems
- User errors

There are three important issues regarding information systems which need to be addressed properly. These include the following:

- Accuracy
- Usability
- Time

The most important attribute of the Enterprise Information System is the accuracy of the information. Accuracy is a must when it comes to information that is provided to make decisions of any kind. Another major issue involving information systems is the information's usability. If the enterprise uses software to access the information it has to be easy to use and understand for the end-user as well as the executives. The third most significant attribute of Enterprise Information System is the time factor. As time progresses the enterprise information system scales up and the information needs to be received at a faster rate, which may not be guaranteed always.

4.1. Computer Crimes

A computer crime is a crime in which a computer, or computers, plays a significant role. Computer and Internet plays a large part in the following crimes:

- Unauthorized Access
- Extortion
- Theft
- Sabotage
- Espionage
- Computer Fraud

- Embezzlement
- Copyright Violation
- Forgery and Counterfeiting
- Internet Fraud—"Imposter Sites"
- SEC Fraud and Stock Manipulation
- Child Pornography
- Stalking and Harassment
- Credit Card Fraud and Skimming
- Racketeering
- Fencing stolen goods
- Loan sharking
- Drug trafficking
- Union infiltration
- Illegal gambling
- Money laundering
- Hate message propagation

4.2. External Computer Crimes

There are several crimes which are committed outside the organization and few of these crimes are discussed below:

(a) Denial-of-Service

Many organizations have been hit with Denial-of-Service attack and it floods a website with too many requests for service that it slows down or crashes. The objective is to prevent legitimate customers from getting into the site to do business.

(b) Virus Hoaxes

Virus hoaxes are e-mails sent intending to frighten people about a virus threat, that is in fact bogus. People who get such an alert will usually tell others who react in the same way. The virus is non-existent, but the hoax causes people to get scared and lose time and productivity.

(c) Web Defacing

Web defacing is a favourite sport of hackers who break into computer system. They replace the site with a substitute that is neither attractive nor complimentary or perhaps they convert the website to a mostly blank screen with an abusive and obscene message.

(d) Cyber Terrorists

A cyber terrorist is one who seeks to cause harm to people or destroy critical systems or information. Couple of years back, the opposition leader has got an e-mail threat.

(e) Hackers

A hacker is a person who succeeds in making unauthorized access to a computer network for profit, criminal mischief or personal pleasure. Hackers plant a kind of software that can hide in a system or network until executing at a specified time. Hackers also propagate computer viruses.

(f) Computer Virus

Computer virus is a software program that spreads rampantly from system to system clogging computer memory or destroying programs or data. Many thousands of viruses are known to exist today. Present day viruses are spread through Internet, from files of downloaded software or from files attached to e-mail transmissions. Viruses can also invade information systems from other computer networks as well as from infected diskette or pen-drives.

(g) Disaster

A disaster may cause financial loss, loss of customers, loss of competitive positions, erosion of industry image, reduce market share, loss of confidence, etc. Computer hardware, programs, data files, and other equipments within an enterprise can be destroyed by fires, power failures, or other disasters. The fully digital firms will suffer a lot if these happen. An organization (which hugely depends on computer systems) must have duplicate database system, duplicate network pathways, duplicate terminals, and duplicate power supply.

(h) Security

Security refers to the policies, procedures, and technical measures used to prevent unauthorized access, alteration, theft, or physical damage to information systems. Security can be promoted with an array of techniques and tools to safeguard computer hardware, software, telecommunication networks, and data.

(i) Errors

Computers can also serve as instruments of error, severely disrupting or destroying an enterprise information system. Errors in an automated system can occur at many points in the processing cycle:

- through data entry,
- software error,
- computer operations, and
- hardware.

Because of these errors, system fails very considerably. Each cause has to be taken in isolation and examined, to see where it has gone wrong in the past or is starting to go wrong at present. It is essential to predict likely problems that may arise or accurately recognize failure symptoms when they occur. It is important to identify what is really going on and when these facts have been established, to be able to select a suitable means of handling the situation.

(j) *Defective Software and Data Error*

Defective software and data also pose a constant threat to information systems, causing untold losses in productivity. An undiscovered error in company's credit software or erroneous financial data can result in heavy losses. A major problem with software is the presence of hidden bugs or programs code defects.

(k) *Data Quality Problem*

The most common source of information system failure is poor data quality. Data those are inaccurate, untimely or inconsistent with other sources of information can create serious operational and financial problems for business.

5. SOME REMEDIAL SOLUTIONS OF THREATS

Addressing to the threats and their remedial solutions has come up as a challenge for technocrats. Generally, security of Enterprise Information Systems consists of a combination of measures such as backup procedures, antivirus software, firewalls, access authentication, encryption, intrusion detection software and system auditing.

(a) Backup and Recovery

The easiest and most basic way to prevent information is to make backups of all information. A backup is the process of making a copy of the information stored on a computer. A recovery is the process of reinstalling the backup information in the event that the information was lost. Millions of dollars are lost every year because a system crashes and there is no back up for lost information.

(b) Antivirus Software

Antivirus software detects and removes or quarantines computer viruses. New viruses are created every day and each new generation is more deadly than the previous one. Antivirus software is a must for any organization.

(c) Firewalls

A firewall protects a computer or network from intruders. Any competent network administrator will have at least one firewall on the network to keep out unwanted guests. A firewall will also detect your computer communication with the Internet without your approval, as spyware on your computer may be attempting to do.

(d) Passwords and Biometrics

One of the ways to protect computer systems is authentication systems. Passwords are very popular and have been used since long but these are not a perfect way to protect a computer system because people forget their passwords, so someone has to get them new passwords or find them old one. Another cutting-edge technology to access control is biometrics. Biometrics is the use of physical characteristics—such as your fingerprints, the blood vessels in the retina of your eye, the sound of your voice, or perhaps even your breath—to provide identification. A lot of different types of biometric devices are available these days to control the unauthorized access to information systems.

(e) Encryption

Encryption may be used to protect your messages, files and hide them. Encryption scrambles the contents of a file so that it can't be read without having the right decryption key. There are several ways of encrypting messages.

(f) Cyber Laws

IT Act 2000 has already been enforced by Government of India and it facilitates provisions for some major cyber crimes. Cyber Crimes Covered in IT Act 2000 includes the following:

- Tampering with computer source documents,
- Hacking with computer system,
- Publishing of information which is obscene in e-form,
- Not to obey the direction of Controller,
    - Directions of Controller to a subscriber extend facilities to decrypt information,
    - Intrusion into protected system,
    - Penal action for misrepresentation,
    - Breach of confidentiality and privacy,

- Publishing digital signature certificate false in certain particular etc.
- Act to apply for offence or contravention committed outside India, and
- Confiscation.

6. SUMMARY

This chapter discusses the changing scenario of information systems with the changing technological breakthrough. The essence of enterprise information systems has also been discussed at length along with its costs and benefits. Types of information systems along with their applicability have also been outlined. At last the threats to enterprise information systems and their possible remedial solutions have also been discussed.

REFERENCES

1. O'Brien, J. (1999). *Management Information Systems—Managing Information Technology in the Internetworked Enterprise* (in English). Irwin McGraw-Hill.
2. Berkshire Information Systems Inc., http:www.berkshire-is.comindex.htm, January 12, 2001.
3. Management Information Systems Quarterly. <http:www.misq.orgarchivistvolno 10issue1vol10no1mason.html >. March, 1986.
4. http://www.websiteblitz.net/Articles/ROI.htm
5. http://www.wattpad.com/84165-Types-of-Information-System
6. Bonnett, T. (2000): Competing in the New Economy, Xlibris Corporation.
7. Brynjolfsson, E. (2000): Understanding the Digital Economy: Data, Tools, and Research, MIT Press.
8. Fingar, P., *et al.* (2001): The Death of "e" and the Birth of the Real New Economy : Business Models, Technologies and Strategies for the 21st Century, Meghan-Kiffer Press.
9. O'Brien, James A. Management Information Systems. Irwin McGraw-Hill; 1999.
10. Haag. 'Management Information Systems for the Information Age'.
11. http://www.echeat.com/essay.php?t=33113
12. http://tutor2u.net/business/ict/intro_information_sources.htm
13. Osterle, H. (1995): Business in the Information Age: Heading for new Processes, Springer-Verlag.
14. Leffingwell, D. (2000): Managing Software Requirements: A Unified Approach. Addison Wesley.
15. http://www.few.vu.nl/stagebureau/werkstuk/werkstukken/werkstuk-braams.doc
16. http://java.sun.com/blueprints/guidelines/designing_enterprise_applications_2e/eis-tier/eis-tier.html
17. http://en.wikipedia.org/wiki/Management_information_systems
18. http://www.networkdictionary.com/software/ERP-System-Components.php
19. http://tutor2u.net/business/ict/intro_information_system_types.htm
20. Fowler, M. (2002): Patterns of Enterprise Application Architecture, Addison Wesley Professional, New York.
21. Harrington, J. (1991): Business Process Improvement, McGraw Hill.

2

Information Management : The Right Information at the Right Time

INDU BALA GROVER AND BHARTI RAO

ABSTRACT

As technology advances, the variety, types and source of information multiply exponentially. Deep capabilities in business intelligence; portals and content management; and data management and architecture helps businesses and governments implement comprehensive information management strategies. A successful information strategy requires a vision. Information management services take an integrated, holistic approach to manage all the diverse information assets to plan and run a high performance organization. This paper is focusing on the variety of technology solutions that can address our data needs, issues of ERP, SCM, CRM and the comparative analysis of status of various ERP packages available.

1. INTRODUCTION

Objectives of any implementation are to enable Organization to consolidate efficiency and to synchronize information all across Organization on a single platform by using the proven best practices. Following are the main organization project objectives:

1. Optimization and standardization of business processes to enable availability of integrated information.
2. Availability of information on real time basis.
3. Elimination of duplication of activities across business processes by capturing data at source point.
4. Facilitate information consolidation at corporate level.
5. Availability of information at the right time, at the right place, thereby, enhancing managerial control.
6. Integrating all business applications under single ERP platform with minimum interfaces.
7. Improved responsiveness to changing global market scenario by adopting new and improved technology solutions.

2. ENTERPRISE INFORMATION SYSTEM

Enterprise Information Systems collect data across the entire enterprise. Data may be taken from many different databases and presented in a common way. Report writers will print reports based on a template specifying the fields to be included in the report and the fields which are to be totaled. The user can produce reports without recourse to programming. Data mining can be used to find hidden trends and other previously unknown information within the data. The true goal of an Enterprise Information System (EIS), or Enterprise Resource Planning (ERP) system, is to integrate functions and information across whole enterprise. The benefits are sharing of information, consistency, informational accuracy as well as easy and affordable maintenance of the application.

ERP (Enterprise Resource Planning) is a strategic tool helping an organization to gain an edge over its competitors by helping in integrating its key business operations successfully, synchronizing, planning and optimizing the resources available in the existing extremely competitive environment. Its use has a much broader scope in today's world rather than of just planning the use of the enterprise resources.

Organizations, especially those which expand globally, face many difficulties in quickly setting out the information required. The integration of the business processes improves coordination between bodies, streamlines workflows and processes and, benefits them in terms of satisfying and retaining customers by delivering their orders "just-in-time" and keeping them well informed about their orders' current status rather than keeping them waiting for just a small piece of information. ERP has the effect of making an enterprise more time-sensitive. Another benefit is of better marketing opportunities. ERP penetrates one segment after the other and addresses solutions to many debacles existing in an enterprise.

To implement such a demanding software one needs high performance computing, high availability of systems, large, high speed and high availability of on line storage and high speed, high reliable networks, all at affordable cost. Though many ERP software vendors have been around for

FIG. 2.1
Material Resource Planning

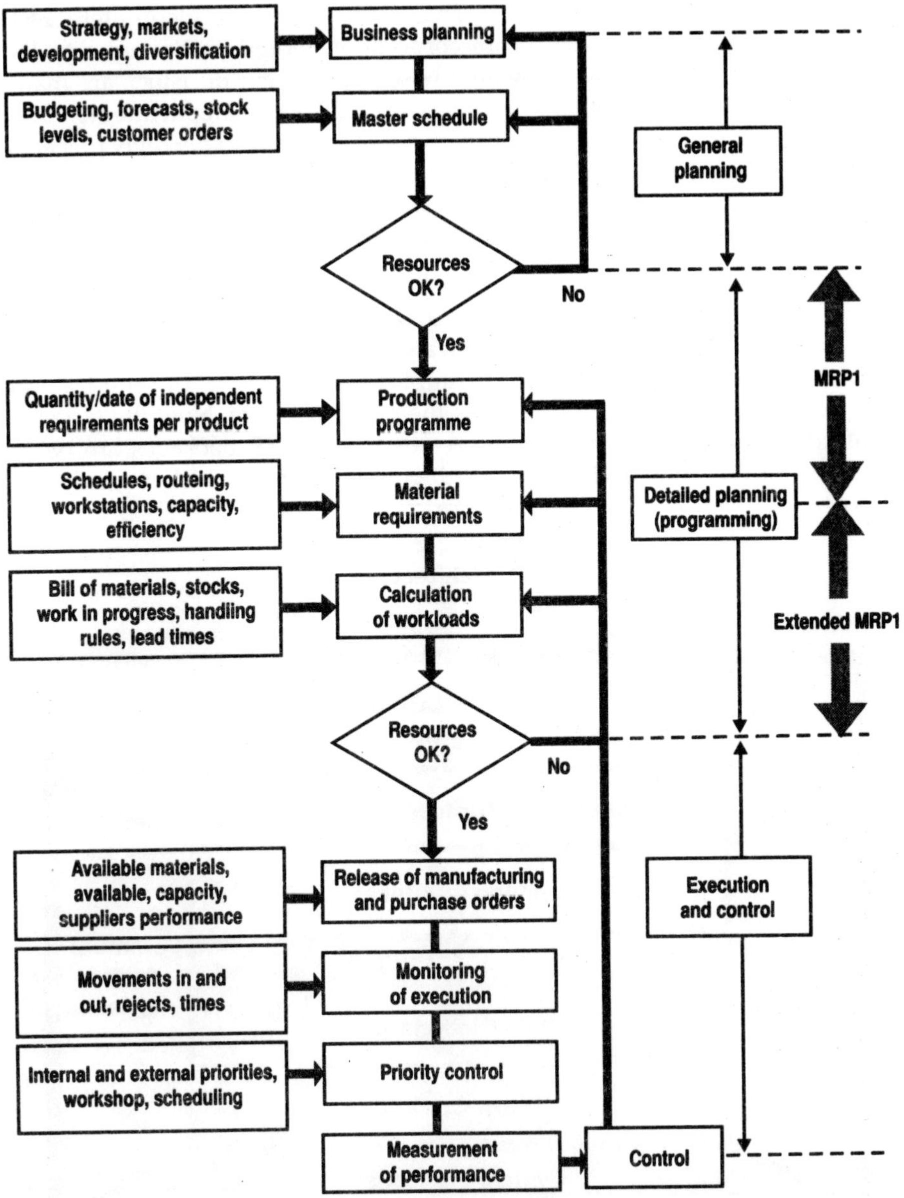

Around 1980, over-frequent changes in sales forecasts, entailing continual readjustments in production, as well as the unsuitability of the parameters fixed buy the system, led MRP (Material Requirement Planning) to evolve into a new concept : Manufacturing Resource Planning or MRP2.

Source : "CIM: Principles of Computer Integrated Manufacturing". Jean-Baptiste Waldner, John Wiley & Sons, 1992. Reproduced with author's authorization.

more than two decades, ERP software started to make major inroads into the corporate world only in the last couple of years. Interestingly Indian corporate houses are taking the ERP route exceptionally fast, even by world standards in the past two years. The investments on a complete ERP implementation for a Rs. 100+ core corporation would easily run into Rs. 10+ crores. ERP is the only software whose deployment decisions are made in the corporate boardrooms and not by EDP/MIS departments. ERP software today represents possibly the single most expensive piece of general-purpose software.

2.1 Current Status and Comparative Analysis

Different ERP systems have been made to facilitate organizations in Enterprise Resource Planning. Leading ERP giants making ERP systems are Microsoft, Oracle, People Soft JD Edwards, SAP AG, etc. Approx. 32% of Indian top companies have already implemented ERP and around about 60% campanies are employing SAP as their ERP package. Now the target is small and medium size companies. A number of ERP packages are being available for the same. ERP B1 is a product in this range, which has only one

Fig. 2.2
SAP Architecture

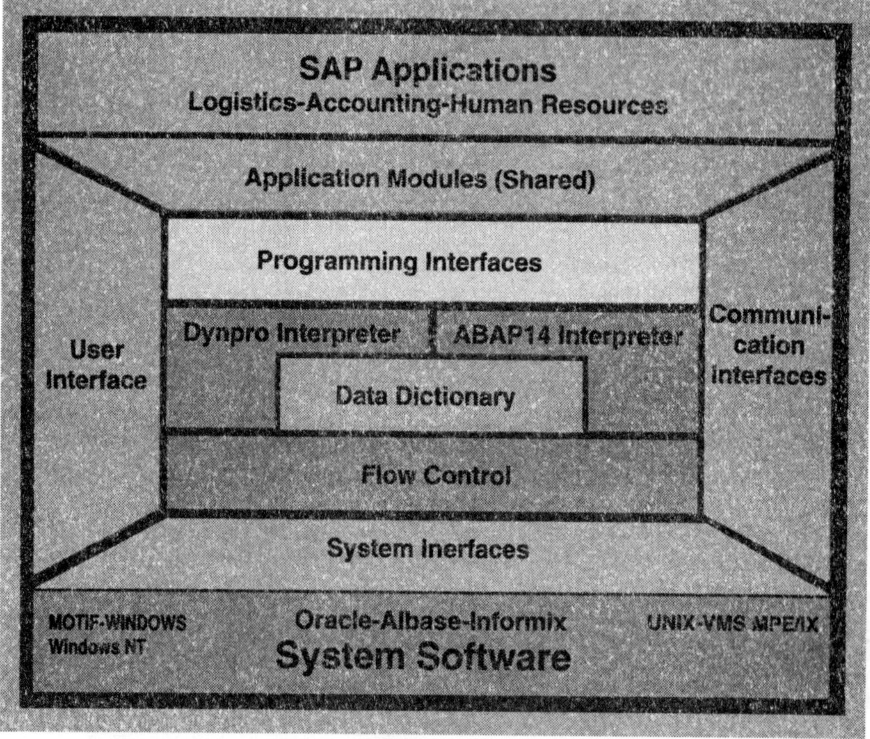

server. It is much cheaper and smaller than SAP R/3. It has simple architecture and hence reduced implementation cost. ERP can boost the business of any company as well as can do the otherway round depend upon the design of the ERP package and data given for the implementation which is provided by the company. The three important things for the success of any ERP package are Data, Data and Data. So this itself puts much stress on the role of data in success of any ERP package. It is not mandatory that we need to implement all the modules of an ERP package. ERP package is customized according to size and business of the company. For example, AIRCON is a company which is using only finance module while GAIL, Pepsi, Indian Oil are the major giants, which are using almost all the modules.

2.2 A Fit between Organization and ERP Software

Above mentioned scenario point to a very critical step, i.e., the right choice of an ERP for your enterprise. There is no precise algorithm that can measure the fit for particular ERP software to an organization. One generally goes by experiences of similar organizations which have implemented ERP. In general, ERP software has exceptional strengths in some areas. It is better to stay with the ERP software which has special strengths for the enterprise. The choice depends upon the structure and type of the organization, e.g. financial, manufacturing, etc. That is why some organizations experience higher benefits as compared to others because they made the right choice and are able to make the right use of their system. For example, BaaN & Oracle have outstanding manufacturing modules; JD Edwards have designing module; SAP has outstanding Integration and reporting module; People Soft and Marshall have outstanding HR modules. If our core business centers around one of these modules, the choice becomes easier. An academic way to evaluate the fit is to carefully study all the business processes that characterize our business and to look for matching business processes that are supported by particular ERP software. Often such an exercise would call for several man-years of effort. The skill set needed for such an exercise may not be easily available within the organization. Getting an outside consulting group to do this exercise may be very expensive. Often most organizations decide the ERP software vendor based on the broad needs of the industry in which they operate and the support offered by particular ERP software for that industry.

2.3 SAPs (System and Applications Products)

An international provider of comprehensive, enterprise-class information systems with proven success, supporting large global manufacturing and distribution enterprises—SAP provides best results in Integration as all the modules are interrelated. For example, if we want to add something in inventory, then, it only increases the stock of the material but in the background it automatically stores relevant accounting documents.

Likewise, if we go for Billing, it not only generates the bill but also generates relevant debit and account entries. *Fiat*, one of the major Europe-based company, was previously using BaaN as its ERP package but now it has decided to implement SAP.

2.4 Challenges of ERP Introduction in India

The challenges of introduction of ERP in India are, in general, the same as in other countries. This includes change management, organizational intervention, shifting from function view to process view and faith in package software in the place of custom-built software. The special challenges in India arise from the existence of large IS shops inside many Indian corporations who may view ERP as a threat to their very existence. The Indian software companies also see a threat to their project-based software business in ERP. Traditionally, organizations in India depended more on IS professionals rather than business professionals for commercial software developments. ERP places more value on domain knowledge of the functions than IT skills. This calls for a mind-set change, which is a challenge. Last, but not the least, is the lack of communication infrastructure, which is often necessary to implement ERP.

3. SUPPLY CHAIN MANAGEMENT

Supply Chain Management (SCM) is the oversight of materials, information and finances as they move in a process from supplier to manufacturer to wholesaler to retailer to consumer. Supply Chain Management involves coordinating and integrating these flows both within and among companies. It is said that the ultimate goal of any effective Supply Chain Management System is to reduce inventory (with the assumption that products are available when needed). As a solution for successful supply chain management, sophisticated software systems with Web interfaces are competing with Web-based Application Service Providers (ASP) which promises to provide part or all of the SCM service to companies that rent their service.

In fact, the need for supply chain management is felt to benefit both customer and enterprise. While it enhances customer delight by satisfying the customer need for better products, lower costs and fastest supply, it improves enterprise plight by improving its productivity. In a nutshell, the benefits derived by applying SCM are:

1. Reduced operational costs.
2. Improved flow of supplies.
3. Reduction of delays in distribution and increased customer satisfaction.
4. Brings compelling bottom line benefits to enterprise.

The corporate profitability can be linked to the deliverables of a supply chain with the help of following equation:

Profit = Revenue + Customer service/Cost + Capital employed

Use of Internet has enabled companies to realize several supply chain-related benefits. These are following:

1. More collaborative and timely product development through enhanced communication among functional departments, suppliers, customers and even regulatory agencies.
2. Reduction of channel inventory and product obsolescence owing to closer linkage across the supply chain and better insights into demand signals to drive products schedule and ultimately achieve build-to-order capability.
3. Reduction in communication costs and customer support costs with more interactive, tailored support capability inherent in Internet technologies.
4. New channel capability to reach different customer segments and further exploit current market.
5. Ability to enhance traditional products and customer relationships through customization driven by Internet connectivity and interactivity.

Figure 2.3 gives a more accurate description of a demand network.

4. CUSTOMER RELATIONSHIP MANAGEMENT

CRM is a multifaceted process, mediated by a set of information technologies, that focuses on creating two-way exchanges with customers so that firms have an intimate knowledge of their needs, wants, and buying patterns. In this way, CRM helps companies understand as well as anticipate the needs of current and potential customers. Functions that support this business purpose include sales, marketing, customer service, training, professional development, performance management, human resource development, and compensation. Many CRM initiatives have failed because implementation was limited to software installation without alignment to a customer-centric strategy.

4.1 Bridging the CRM Analysis Gap

A new type of analytic application, known as Customer Value Management (CVM) answers the increasing need to identify, analyze and predict evolving customer behaviour. Using CVM enables companies to shift from campaign-centric to customer-centric analysis and develop more individualized and profitable customer relationships.

4.2 Beyond CRM and ERP: eBusiness to Optimize Customer and Partner Sales

The key differentiator in today's market is customer satisfaction. Those customers who receive the best quality of service, products, pricing and

FIG. 2.3
Integration of all the Elements of a Demand Network in SCM Approach

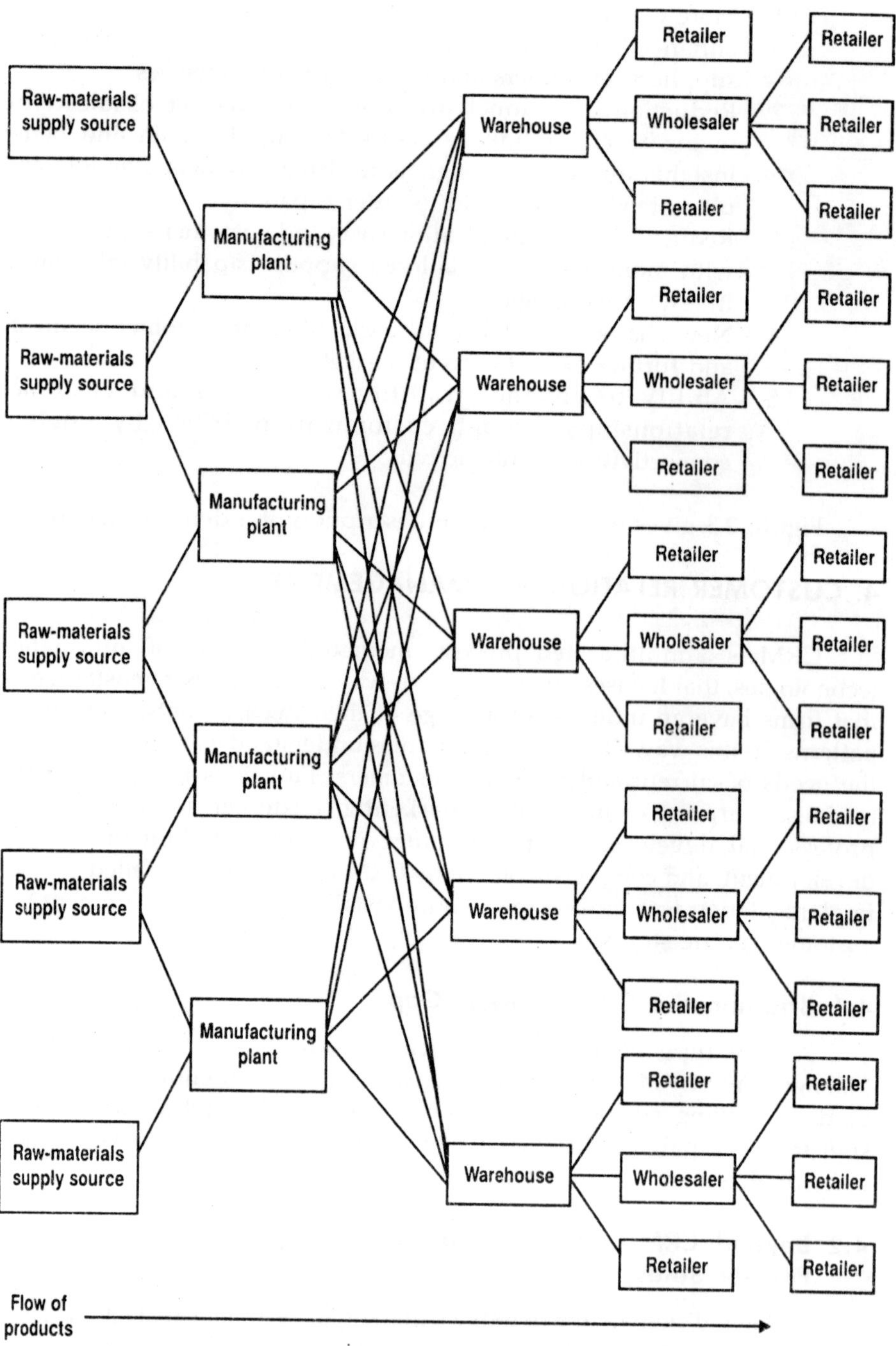

brand experience are most likely to become an organization's most profitable clients. During the last decade, many organizations have made significant investments in ERP and CRM systems to optimize business processes and get a single view of their customers. However, neither ERP nor CRM systems have provided the external-facing, consistent, cross-channel "single face to the customer" that today's eBusiness-savvy partners and customers demand. The Customer Relationship Management (CRM) industry is approaching a ten year anniversary. Despite its longevity, there continues to be a pervasive sense of dissatisfaction within the end user community relative to CRM's perceived delivered value. A next-generation Information Management System consisting of hardware and software components integrated to form an easy-to-administer appliance that can store, retrieve, and analyze all types of structured, semi-structured, and unstructured information. We first summarize the trends that will shape information management for the foreseeable future. Those trends imply three major requirements:

1. to be able to store, manage, and uniformly query all data, not just structured records;
2. to be able to scale out as the volume of data grows; and
3. to be simple and robust in operation.

We, then, describe four key ideas that are uniquely combined in Impliance to address these requirements, namely the ideas of:

(a) integrating software and off-the-shelf hardware into a generic information appliance;
(b) automatically discovering, organizing, and managing all data—unstructured as well as structured—in a uniform way;
(c) achieving scale-out by exploiting simple, massive parallel processing; and
(d) virtualizing computing and storage resources to unify, simplify, and streamline the management of impliance. Impliance is an ambitious, long-term effort to define simpler, more robust, and more scalable information systems for tomorrow's enterprises.

4.3 Business Challenges in the Future

Given the growing information age competition, the business is to face some unique challenges in future. The major ones are described below:

1. *Managing uncertainty*: Business environment is becoming uncertain and complex day-by-day. In the face of such uncertainty, companies are finding it difficult to predict likely changes that take place in their competitive environment. In fact, an altogether new but unconventional competition is emerging as customers are

turning into competitors, the erstwhile competitors are becoming partners and alike. Nonetheless, businesses are bound to cope up with future uncertainty.

2. *Understanding complex customer*: Customer requirements are becoming more and more complex, understanding his taste, preferences, and likings and disliking, is a must for a company to delight its customers though unique value added business mission.
3. *Understanding globalization of business*: With continuous globalization of business, world is shrinking day-by-day. In the globalization of business, the distinction between large and small companies is breaking down with the information technology breaking down the barriers of time and location. Added to this is the emergence of Internet, a powerful global communication vehicle having its profound impact on business processes. E-Commerce, the buzzword of the day, is perhaps the most striking example of the changes occurring in business—be it globalised one or within national boundaries.

5. CONCLUSION

Enterprise-wide information management strategy is required to seek high performance. Though customer has been dictated in the market for long, of late, customer has become supreme in the context of global competitiveness intensifying on an unabated manner. Obviously, only those companies are going to be successful that are able to provide goods and services to customer in time and in a cost effective manner to provide customer delight. This requires competitive advantage. Evidences indicate that every link in supply chain adds to competitive advantage. The new developments such as the proliferation of Internet Technology, World Wide Web, Electronic Commerce, etc. will change the way a company is required to do business and, for that matter, adapt an appropriate supply chain to acquire competitive advantage in future.

ERP has a great importance and ERP systems have become the biggest need of today's organizations to survive. They provide tremendous benefits provided the critical success factors of ERP system implementations are kept in mind.

References

1. James, C. Brancheau, Brian, D. Janz, James, C. Wetherbe, "Key Issues in Information Systems Management", 1994-95 SIM Delphi Results, http://www.jstor.org/pss/249479
2. http://www.compinfo-center.com/tpeis-t.htm#newsg
3. LiteBreeze, "Enterprise Information System/Enterprise Resource Planning", Infotech Pvt. Ltd., http://www.litebreeze.com/Solutions_Enterprise-Information-Systems.php
4. "Bulletin of Applied Computing and Information Technology", Vol. 2, Issue 1, (March 2004). ISSN 1176-4120, Mathew Nicho, http://www.naccq.ac.nz/bacit/0201/2004Nicho_CRM.html

5. "Supply Chain Management from Search CIO.com Definitions", http://searchcio.tech target.com/sDefinition/0, sid182_gci214546, 00.html
6. "Customer Relationship Management from Wikipedia", http://en.wikipedia.org/wiki/Customer_relationship_management
7. "Accenture Information Management Services", http://www.accenture.com/Global/Technology/Information_Mgmt
8. Indu Bala Grover and Kusum Saluja, "ERP: A Rising Need of Enterprises and Key to Operational Efficiency".
9. Dr. S. Sadagopan, "ERP Study Center", http://www.iiitb.ac.in/ss/erp-faq/main 5pg1.htm
10. S.S. Khanka, "From Logistics to SCM", http://www.iimm.org/knowledge_bank/1_from- logistics-to-scm.htm

3

Analyzing the pros and cons of various Software Development Life Cycle (SDLC) Models used for Software Development

AJAY BANSAL, SURESH VERMA AND PRADEEP KUMAR SHARMA

ABSTRACT

The purpose of this paper is to give an understanding of the Software Development Lifecycle (SDLC) models available to software developers. You will also see examples of where each model is most appropriate for various types of software development projects.

In many cases, a decision is made to purchase or outsource the software and associated hardware and network systems needed to implement a new application. This is often referred to as the "buy or build" decision. This paper focuses on the Software Development Life Cycle models, but most of the phases, terms, and issues discussed apply to both the "buy" and "build" process.

1. INTRODUCTION

To help readers understand and implement the SDLC phases [Project Initiation, Requirement Analysis, System Design, Implementation

(Programming and Testing), Installation, Maintenance, and Destruction], various SDLC models have been developed by software development experts, universities, and standards organizations. New SDLC models are being introduced on a regular basis as new technology and new research requires new SDLC techniques. Recent new SDLC models include Extreme Programming and Agile Development. This paper looks at the most commonly known and used model and describes situations where the model is an appropriate choice.

1.1 The General Model

Software life cycle models describe phases of the software cycle and the order in which those phases are executed. There are number of models, and many companies adopt their own, but all have very similar patterns. The general, basic model is shown below:

FIG. 3.1
General Model

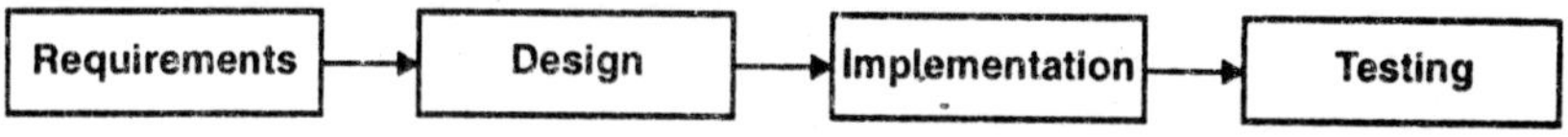

Requirements → Design → Implementation → Testing

Each phase produces deliverables required by the next phase in the life cycle. Requirements are translated into design Code is produced during implementation that is driven by the design. Testing verifies the deliverable of the implementation phase against requirements.

1.2 Requirements

Business requirements are gathered in this phase. This phase is the main focus of the project managers and stakeholders. Meetings with managers, stakeholders and users are held in order to determine the requirements. Who is going to use the system? How will they use the system? What data should be input into the system? What data should be output by the system? These are general questions that get answered during a requirements gathering phase. This produces a nice big list of functionality that the system should provide, which describes functions the system should perform, business logic that processes data, the data stored and used by the system, and an outline of how the user interface should work. The overall result is the system as a whole and how it performs, not how it is actually going to work.

1.3 Design

The software system design is produced from the results of the requirements phase. Architects have the ball in their court during this phase and this is the phase in which their focus lies. This is where the details of how the system will work are produced. Architecture, including hardware and software, communication, software design are all part of the deliverables of a design phase.

1.4 Implementation

Code is produced from the deliverables of the design phase during implementation, and this is the longest phase of the software development life cycle. For a developer, this is the main focus of the life cycle because this is where the code is produced. Implementation may overlap with both the design and testing phases. Many tools (CASE tools) exist to actually automate the production of code using information gathered and produced during the design phase.

1.5 Testing

During testing, the implementation is tested against the requirements to make sure that the product is actually solving the needs addressed and gathered during the requirements phase. Unit tests and system/acceptance tests are done during this phase. Unit tests act on a specific component of the system, while system tests act on the system as a whole.

1.6 Past Testing Activities

After Software is tested as complete unit, it is ready for use for the end user. Software has to be installed and configured. Other activities, hereafter, may be end user training, software maintainance (which involes further enhancements to the software as well as adapting to user environment) and finally destruction (if enhancements and changes to the software generally after long use are costly than the benefits being realized by the use of software).

So in a nutshell, this is a very basic overview of the general software development life cycle model. Now let us develop into some of the traditional and widely used variations.

2. SDLC MODELS

2.1 Waterfall Model

The origin of the term "waterfall" is often cited to be an article published in 1970 by *Winston W. Royce* (1929–1995). Ironically, Royce was presenting this model as an example of a flawed, non-working model. His paper explored how the initial model could be developed into an iterative model, with feedback from each phase influencing subsequent phases. It is only the initial model that received notice; his own criticism of this initial model has been largely ignored. The phrase "waterfall model" quickly came to refer not to Royce's final, iterative design, but rather to his purely sequentially ordered model.

FIG. 3.2
Phases in the Waterfall Model

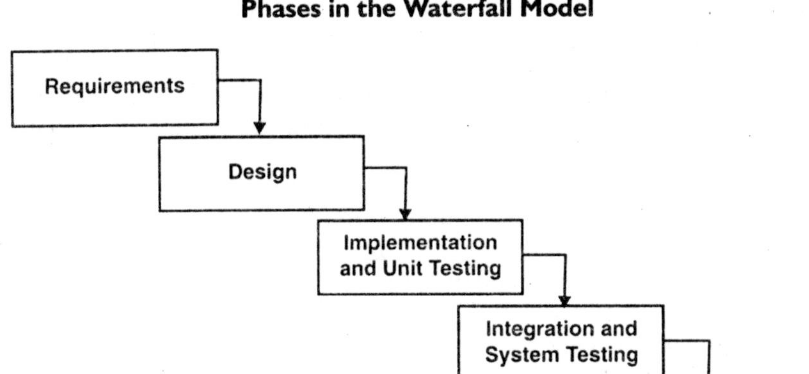

This is the most common and classic of life cycle models, also referred to as a linear-sequential life cycle model. In a waterfall model, each phase must be completed in its entirety before the next phase can begin. At the end of each phase, a review takes place to determine if the project is on the right path and whether or not to continue or discard the project. Unlike what is mentioned in the general model, phases do not overlap in a waterfall model.

The major strength of the waterfall model is its simplicity in understanding and implementation. The product developed will meet the requirements specifications perfectly. It is simple and arguably more disciplined approach. Rather than what the waterfall adherent sees as chaos, the waterfall model provides a structured approach; the model itself progresses linearly through discrete, easily understandable and explainable phases and thus is easy to understand; it also provides easily markable milestones in the development process. It is perhaps for this reason that the waterfall model is used as a beginning example of a development model in many software engineering texts and courses.

- There will be no loss of money, effort and time put in later phases, due to bugs in the preceeding phases, as this model make sure that each phase is 100% complete and absolutely correct before proceeding to the next phase of program creation.
- It places emphasis on documentation (such as requirements documents and design documents) as well as source code. In less designed and documented methodologies, when the team members leave, much knowledge is lost and may be difficult for a project to recover from. When a fully working design document is presented (as is the intent of Big Design Up Front and the waterfall model) new team members or even entirely new teams should be able to familiarize themselves by reading the documents?

The major *weakness* of the Waterfall Model is that after project requirements are gathered in the first phase, there is no formal way to make changes to the project as requirements change or more information becomes available to the project team. Because requirements almost always change during long development cycles, often the product that is implemented at the end of the process is obsolete as it goes into production. The Waterfall Model is a poor choice for software development projects where requirements are not well-known or understood by the development team. It might not a good model for complex projects or projects that take more than a few months to complete. Think about doing a home improvement project (such as new hardwood floors) for the first time and only being allowed to go the hardware store one time. The risk the project will fail is high. Additional criticisms of a non-iterative development approach (such as the waterfall model) include:

- Unless those who specify requirements and those who design the software system in question are highly competent, it is difficult to know exactly what is needed in each phase of the software development process before some time is spent in the phase following it. That is, feedback from following phases is needed to complete preceding phases satisfactorily. For example, the design phase may need feedback from the implementation phase to identify problem design areas. The counter-argument for the waterfall model is that experienced designers may have worked on similar systems before, and so may be able to accurately predict problem areas without spending time in prototyping and implementing.
- Constant testing from the design, implementation and verification phases is required to validate the phases preceding them. Constant prototype design work is needed to ensure that requirements are non-contradictory and possible to fulfil; constant implementation is needed to find problem areas and inform the design process; constant integration and verification of the implemented code is necessary to ensure that implementation remains on track. The counter-argument for the waterfall model here is that constant implementation and testing to validate the design and requirements is only needed if the introduction of bugs is likely to be a problem. Users of the waterfall model may argue that if designers follow a disciplined process and do not make mistakes then there is no need for constant work in subsequent phases to validate the preceding phases.
- Frequent incremental builds (following the "release early, release often" philosophy) are often needed to build confidence for a software production team and their client.
- It is difficult to estimate time and cost for each phase of the development process without doing some "recon" work in that phase, unless those estimating time and cost are highly experienced with the type of software product in question.

- The waterfall model brings no formal means of exercising management control over a project and, planning control and risk management are not covered within the model itself.
- Very specific skill sets are required for each phase, thus, there is a requirement for multiple projects to run in sequence to optimize resource use if all members stay through the course of a given project, or to suffer skill levels by using "jack of all trades" resources throughout each stage.

What are good candidate software development projects for the Waterfall Model?

Waterfall software development model may be applicable to projects where:

- Software requirements are clearly defined and known.
- Software development technologies and tools are well known.
- New versions of the existing software system are created.

For instance, a military system aiming an artillery shell is a system with a single, simple requirement; put the shell on the target. This also assumes that the developers have worked on similar systems in the past and are experts in the application domain (artillery fire control systems). To follow the home improvement example, after a visit to a home to get specifications, an experienced flooring contractor could install new hardwood floors with only one trip to the hardware store. In this case, the risk of project failure is low.

Its advantages and disadvantages are as follows:

Advantages

- Simple and easy to use.
- Easy to manage due to the rigidity of the model—each phase has specific deliverables and a review process.
- Phases are processed and completed one at a time.
- Works well for smaller projects where requirements are very well understood.

Disadvantages

- Adjusting scope during the life cycle can kill a project.
- No working software is produced until late during the life cycle.
- High amounts of risk and uncertainty.
- Poor model for complex and object-oriented projects.
- Poor model for long and ongoing projects.
- Poor model where requirements are at a moderate to high risk of changing.

2.2 V-Shaped Model

The V-model can be said to have developed as a result of the evolution of software testing. Various testing techniques were defined and various kinds of testing were clearly separated from each other which led to the waterfall model evolving into the V-model. Just like the waterfall model, the V-Shaped life cycle is a sequential path of execution of processes. Each phase must be completed before the next phase begins. Testing is emphasized in this model more than the waterfall model. The testing procedures are developed early in the life cycle before any coding is done, during each of the phases preceding implementation. The tests in the ascending (Validation) hand are derived directly from their design or requirements counterparts in the descending (Verification) hand. The 'V' can also stand for the terms Verifications and Validations.

Verfication Phases are:

2.2.1 Requirements Analysis

In this phase, the requirements of the proposed system are collected by analyzing the needs of the users. This phase is concerned about establishing what the ideal system has to perform. However, it does not determine how the software will be designed or built. Usually, the users are interviewed and a document called the user requirements document is generated. The user requirements document will typically describe the system's functional, physical, interface, performance, data and security requirements, etc. as expected by the user. It is one which the business analysts use to communicate their understanding of the system back to the users. The users carefully review this document as this document would serve as the guideline for the system designers in the system design phase. The user acceptance tests are designed in this phase.

2.2.2 System Design

System engineers analyze and understand the business of the proposed system by studying the user requirements document. They figure out possibilities and techniques by which the user requirements can be implemented. If any of the requirements are not feasible, the user is informed of the issue. A solution is found and the user requirement document is edited accordingly.

The software specification document which serves as a blueprint for the development phase is generated. This document contains the general system organization, menu structures, data structures, etc. It may also hold example business scenarios, sample windows and reports for the better understanding. Other technical documentation like entity diagrams and data dictionary will also be produced in this phase. The documents for system testing is prepared in this phase.

2.2.3 Architecture Design

This phase can also be called as high-level design. The baseline in selecting the architecture is that it should realize all which typically consists of the list of modules, brief functionality of each module, their interface relationships, dependencies, database tables, architecture diagrams, technology details, etc. The integration testing design is carried out in this phase.

2.2.4 Module Design

This phase can also be called as low-level design. The designed system is broken up into smaller units or modules and each of them is explained so that the programmer can start coding directly. The low level design document or program specifications will contain a detailed functional logic of the module in pseudocode, database tables with all elements including their type and size, all interface details with complete API references, all dependency issues, error message listings, complete input and outputs for a module. The unit test design is developed in this stage.

2.2.5 Coding

The implementation phase is, again, where all coding takes place, Once coding is complete, the path of execution continues up the right side of the V where the test plans developed earlier are now put to use.

FIG. 3.3
Phases of V-Shaped Model

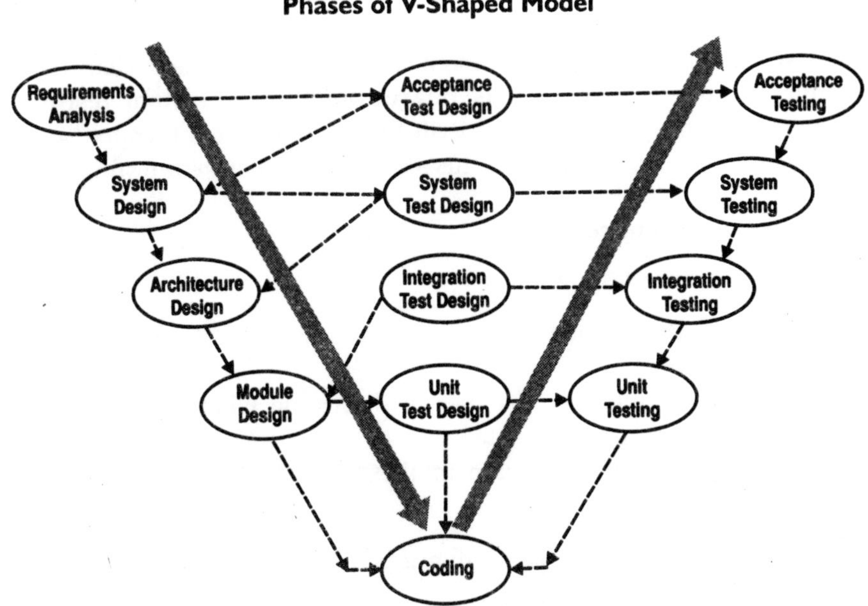

Source : http://en.wikipedia.org

Validation Phases are:

2.2.6 Unit Testing

In the V-model of software development, unit testing implies the first stage of dynamic testing process. According to software development expert Barry Boehm, a fault discovered and corrected in the unit testing phase is more than hundred times cheaper than if it is done after delivery to the customer.

It involves analysis of the written code with the intention of eliminating errors. It also verifies that the codes are efficient and adheres to the adopted coding standards. Testing is usually white box. It is done using the unit test design prepared during the module design phase. This may be carried out by software testers or software developers or both.

2.2.7 Integration Testing

In integration testing the separate modules will be tested together to expose faults in the interfaces and in the interaction between integrated components. Testing is usually black box as the code is not directly checked for errors. It is done using the integration test design prepared during the architecture design phase. Integration testing is generally conducted by software testers.

2.2.8 System Testing

System testing will compare the system specifications against the actual system. The system test design is derived from the system design documents and is used in this phase. Sometimes system testing is automated using testing tools. Once all the modules are integrated several errors may arise. Testing done at this stage is called system testing.

2.2.9 User Acceptance Testing

- Acceptance testing aims:
  - To determine whether a system satisfies its acceptance criteria or not.
  - To enable the customer to determine whether to accept the system or not.
  - To test the software in the "real world" by the intended audience.
- Purpose of acceptance testing is :
  - To verify the system or changes according to the original needs.

2.2.10 Procedures for Conducting the Acceptance Testing

- Define the acceptance criteria:
  - Functionality requirements.
  - Performance requirements.
  - Interface quality requirements.
  - Overall software quality requirements.
- Develop an acceptance plan:
  - Project description.
  - User responsibilities.
  - Acceptance description.
  - Execute the acceptance test plan.

Advantages

- Simple and easy to use.
- Each phase has specific deliverables.
- Higher chance of success over the waterfall model due to the development of test plans early during the life cycle.
- Works well for small projects where requirements are easily understood.

Disadvantages

- Very rigid, like the waterfall model.
- Little flexibility and adjusting scope is difficult and expensive.
- Software is developed during the implementation phase, so no early prototypes of the software are produced.
- Model doesn't provide a clear path for problems found during testing phases.

2.3 Incremental Model

The incremental model is an intuitive approach to the waterfall model. Multiple development cycles take place here, making the life cycle a "multi-waterfall" cycle. Cycles are divided up into smaller, more easily managed iterations. Each iteration passes through the requirements, design, implementation and testing phases.

A working version of software is produced during the first iteration, so developer have working software early on during the software life cycle. Subsequent iterations are build on the initial software produced during the first iteration.

Incremental software development model may be applicable to projects where:

- Software Requirements are well defined, but realization may be delayed.
- The basic software functionalities are required early.

Fig. 3.4
Phases of the Incremental Model

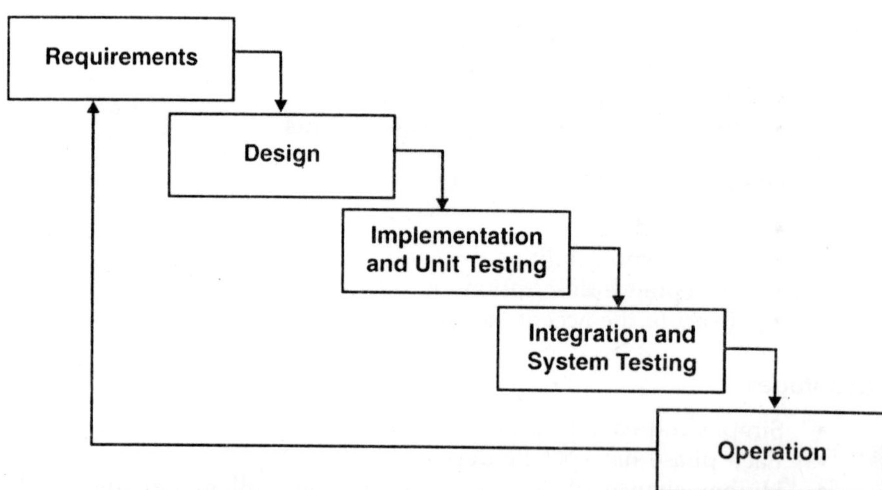

Advantages

- Generates working software quickly and early during the software life cycle.
- More flexible-less costly to change scope and requirements.
- Easier to test and debug during a smaller iteration.
- Easier to manage risk because risky pieces are identified and handled during its iteration.
- Each iteration is an easily managed milestone.

Disadvantages

- Each phase of an iteration is rigid and do not overlap each other.
- Problems may arise pertaining to system architecture because not all requirements are gathered up front for the entire software life cycle.

2.4 Spiral Model

The spiral model was defined by Barry Boehm in his 1988 article of Software Development and Enhancement. This model was not the first model to discuss iterative development, but it was the first model to explain why the iteration matters. As originally envisioned, the iterations were typically 6 months to 2 years long. Each phase starts with a design goal and ends with the client (who may be internal) reviewing the progress so far. Analysis and engineering efforts are applied at each phase of the project, with an eye toward the end goal of the project.

The spiral model is evolutionary version of the incremental model, developed by Boehm in 1988, with more emphasis placed on risk analysis. The spiral model has the following phases:

- Customer Communication
- Planning
- Risk Analysis
- Engineering
- Construction and Release
- Evaluation.

The aim of *customer communication* is to establish effective communication between developer and customer. The *planning* objectives are to define resources, project alternatives, time lines and other project related information. The purpose of the *risk analysis* phase is to assess both technical and management risks. The *engineering* task is to build one or more representations of the application. The *construction and release* task is to construct, test, install and provide user support (e.g., documentation and training). The *customer evaluation* task is to obtain customer feedback based on the evaluation of the software representation created during the engineering stage and implemented during the install stage.

A software project repeatedly passes through these phases in iterations (called Spirals in this model). The baseline spiral starting in the planning phase, requirements are gathered and risk is assessed. Each subsequent spiral builds on the baseline spiral. Requirements are gathered during the planning phase. In the risk analysis phase, a process is undertaken to identify risk and alternate solutions. A prototype is produced at the end of the risk analysis phase. Software is produced in the engineering phase,

FIG. 3.5
Spiral Model

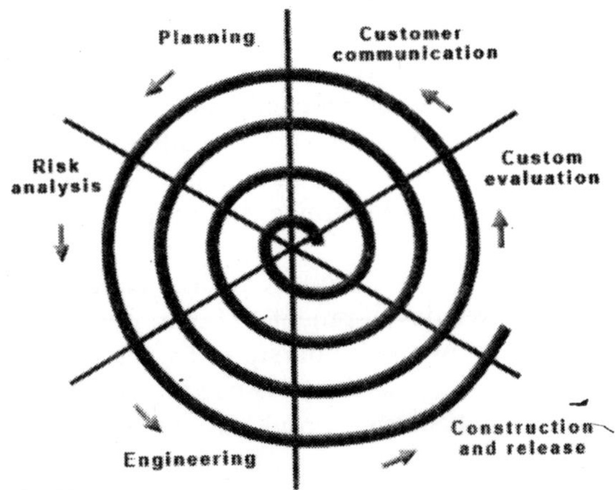

along with testing at the end of the phase. The evaluation phase allows the customer to evaluate the output of the project to date before the project continues to the next spiral.

In the spiral model, the angular component represents progress, and the radius of the spiral represents cost.

The steps in the spiral model can be generalized as follows:

1. The new system requirements are defined in as much detail as possible. This usually involves interviewing a number of users representing all the external or internal users and other aspects of the existing system.
2. A preliminary design is created for the new system.
3. A first prototype of the new system is constructed from the preliminary design. This is usually a scaled-down system, and represents an approximation of the characteristics of the final product.
4. A second prototype is evolved by a four-fold procedure:
   (i) evaluating the first prototype in terms of its strengths, weaknesses, and risks;
   (ii) defining the requirements of the second prototype;
   (iii) planning and designing the second prototype; and
   (iv) constructing and testing the second prototype.
5. At the customer's option, the entire project can be aborted if the risk is deemed too great. Risk factors might involve development cost overruns, operating-cost miscalculation, or any other factor that could, in the customer's judgment, result in a less-than-satisfactory final product.
6. The existing prototype is evaluated in the same manner as was the previous prototype, and, if necessary, another prototype is developed from it according to the four-fold procedure outlined above.
7. The preceding steps are iterated until the customer is satisfied that the refined prototype represents the final product desired.
8. The final system is constructed, based on the refined prototype.
9. The final system is thoroughly evaluated and tested. Routine maintenance is carried out on a continuing basis to prevent large-scale failures and to minimize downtime.

The *advantage* of the Spiral Model over the Waterfall Model is that the iterative approach allows development to begin even when all the system requirements are not known or understood by the development team. As each prototype is tested, user feedback is used to make sure that the project is on track. The risk analysis step provides a formal method to ensure the project stays on track even if requirements do change. If new techniques or business requirements make the project unnecessary, it can be canceled before too many resources are wasted. In today's business environment, the Spiral Model (or its other iterative model cousins) is the most used SDLC model.

An example of application development project that would be a good candidate for the Spiral Model is an online customer support system where it is not well understood which services customers want or can accomplish online. Each iterative prototype helps answer the question, "Can and will customers use this system?". The Spiral Model also lets the development team build application domain experience with iteration. In the home improvement project example, it would be like starting the hardwood flooring project in the upstairs hall to get experience with the flooring process in a low-risk area before moving to living areas where a mistake would be costly.

The spiral model is used most often in large projects. For smaller projects, the concept of agile software development is becoming a viable alternative. The US military has adopted the spiral model for its Future Combat Systems program.

The advantages and disadvantages of this model can be summarized as below:

Advantages

- High amount of risk analysis.
- Estimates (i.e. budget, schedule, etc.) become more realistic as work progresses because important issues are discovered earlier.
- It is able to cope with the (nearly inevitable) changes that software development generally entails.
- Software engineers (who can get restless with protracted design processes) can get their hands in and start working on a project earlier.

Disadvantages

- Can be a costly model to use.
- Risk analysis requires highly specific expertise.
- Project's success is highly dependent on the risk analysis phase.
- Doesn't work well for smaller projects.

2.5 Evolutionary Prototyping Model

Evolutionary prototyping model is a software development lifecycle model in which software prototype created for demonstration and requirements elaboration. Evolutionary prototyping model includes the four main phases:

- Defining the basic requirements.
- Creating the working prototype.
- Verification of the working prototype.

- Changing or elaborating the requirements.

Evolutionary prototyping model allows create working software prototypes fast and may be applicable to projects where:

- System requirements are not known in advance.
- Creating fundamentally new software.
- Developers are not confident in software architecture and algorithms.

Advantages

- The model can be used when the requirements cannot or will not be specified.
- The user can experiment with the system to improve the requirements.

Disadvantages

- Use of the method is exploratory in nature and therefore constitutes a high-risk endeavor. Strong management is required.
- This method is used as an excuse for hacking to avoid documenting the requirements or design, even if they are well understood.

2.6 Rapid Application Development (RAD)

Rapid Application Development was a response to non-agile processes developed in the 1970s, such as the Waterfall model. One problem with previous methodologies was that applications took so long to build that requirements got changed before the system was complete, resulting in inadequate or even unusable systems. Another problem was the assumption that a methodical requirements analysis phase alone would identify all the critical requirements. Ample evidence attests to the fact that this is seldom the case, even for projects with highly experienced professionals at all levels. Starting with the ideas of Brian Gallagher, Barry Boehm and Scott Shultz, James Martin developed the Rapid Application Development approach during the 1980s at IBM and finally formalized it by publishing a book in 1991, Rapid Application Development.

RAD is a incremental software development process model that allows usable systems to be built in as little as 60-90 days, often with some compromises.

With the demand for faster software development, and because of many well-documented failures of traditional SDLC models, Rapid Application Development (RAD) was introduced as a better way to add functionality to an application. The main new tenant of RAD compared to older SDLC models is the use of prototypes. After a quick requirements gathering phase, a prototype application is built and presented to the application users. Feedback from the user provides a loop to improve or add functionality to the application. Early RAD models did not involve the use of real data in the prototype, but new RAD implementations do use real data.

The RAD model is used for information systems development. The Rapid Prototyping Model is used for Graphical User Interface (GUI) applications such as web-based applications.

The *advantage* of Rapid Prototyping Models is that time-to-market is greatly reduced. Rapid prototyping skips many of the steps in traditional SDLC models in favor of fast and low-cost software development. The idea is that application software is a "throw-away." If a new version of the software is needed, it is developed from scratch using the newest RAD techniques and tools.

The big *disadvantage* of the Rapid Prototyping Model is that the process can be too fast, and, therefore, proper testing (especially security testing) may not be done.

Extreme Programming (XP) is a modern incarnation of the Rapid Prototyping Model.

2.7 Rational Unified Process

Rational Unified Process (RUP) is one of the most popular software development methodologies. Rational Software Corporation created RUP in 1988. Based on the iterative Life Cycle Model RUP includes four phases:

- Inception,
- Elaboration,
- Construction, and
- Transition.

RUP is a use case driven development model. Use cases describe interactions between the users and system.

2.8 Object-Oriented Model

Object-Oriented programming became popular in 1990s with the increased use of Smalltalk, C++, and other new object-oriented programming languages. To take full advantage of object-oriented features (i.e. classes, inheritance, methods), the Object-oriented SDLC model was developed.

An important feature of Object-oriented (OO) systems is that software objects represent real-world objects. Objects are derived from Classes, and a class hierarchy allows objects to inherit characteristics from parent classes. This allows software object reuse, less coding, encapsulation of functionality, and many other advantages. A major problem that arose with OO programming is that if the Class hierarchy is not properly designed, all the

OO advantages disappear. The object-oriented model attempts to properly define and document the Class hierarchy from which all the system objects are created and object interactions are defined.

For example, in an accounts payable system for GIAC Bikes, GIAC Bikes is an Object. Space Sprockets is another Object (of class Supplier). Supplier is a Relationship between GIAC Bikes and Space Sprockets. A Supplier Class has attributes such as name, address, and so on. The relationship itself may be considered as an object, having attributes like prime supplier, and so forth. A Supplier Method may be pay, drop, request refund, etc.

Defining all the application classes, methods, relationships, and properties is a complex task. The object-oriented SDLC model provides the development team the tools to accomplish this task.

The object-oriented SDLC model has these phases that roughly correspond to the traditional SDLC phases noted in brackets:

1. Object-Oriented Requirements Analysis (OORA) [Requirement Analysis]: This is where classes of objects and the interaction between them are defined.
2. Object-Oriented Analysis (OOA) [Design Analysis]: In terms of object-oriented concepts, understanding, and modeling a particular problem within a problem domain.
3. Object-Oriented Design (OOD) [System Design]: The object is the basic unit of modularity; objects are instantiations of a class.
4. Object-Oriented Programming (OOP) [Programming and Testing]: Emphasizes the employment of objects and methods rather than types or transformations, as in other programming approaches.

The Object-Oriented SDLC model is characterized by its attempt to model real-world entities (such as company, account, and employee) into abstract computer software objects and all the interactions that can take place between those objects.

2.9 Other Models

Other SDLC models include Model Driven Development, Chaos Model, Agile Programming Model, and many others. One significant trend in the development of new SDLC models is the integration of software design tools into the programming environment (such as Microsoft Visual Studio, IBM Rational Rose). The design team develops a graphical model of the system, and the tool automatically creates a running application.

3. METHODOLOGIES USED IN DIFFERENT MODELS

3.1 Top-Down Model

IBM popularized the Top-down SDLC model in the 1970s, and its concepts are used in other SDLC models such as the Waterfall and Spiral

Models discussed in previous section. In a pure Top-down model, high-level requirements are documented and programs are built to meet these requirements. Then, the next level is designed and built. A good way to picture the Top-down model is to think of a menu-driven application. The top-level menu items would be designed and coded, and then each sub-level would be added after the top-level was finished. Each menu item represents a sub-system of the total application.

The Top-down model is a good fit when the application is a new one and there is no existing functionality that can be incorporated into the new system. A major problem with the Top-down model is that real system functionality is not added and cannot be tested until late in the development process. If problems are not detected early in the project, they can be costly to remedy later.

3.2 Bottom-up Model

In the Bottom-up SDLC model, the lowest level of functionality is designed and programmed first, and finally all the pieces are integrated together into the finished application. This means that, generally, the most complex components are developed and tested first. The idea is that any project showstoppers will surface early in the project. The Bottom-up model also encourages the development and use of reusable software components that can be used multiple times across many software development projects. Again, think of a menu driven system where the development starts with the lowest level menu items.

The disadvantage of the Bottom-up model is that an extreme amount of coordination is required to be sure that the individual software components work together correctly in the finished system. Few systems are developed purely from the Bottom-up model.

3.3 Hybrid Model

The Hybrid SDLC model combines the top-down and bottom-up models. Using the menu driven application example, the design team primarily works top down, but the development team identifies two types of lower level components to work on at the same time as the high-level components. The first type of low-level component would be existing software modules from other projects that can be reused in the new project. The other type of low-level component that would be developed early in the project would be software components with a high risk of failure. This approach allows the development team to make changes to the system early in the project if problems occur with the high-risk components. A new data access technique the team has not used before or a component that might require high amounts of CPU processing time is an example of a high-risk low-level component.

In reality, many of the SDLC models are a variation of the Hybrid Model. The Spiral Model is an example discussed previously.

4. CONCLUSION

SDLC models are tools that allow the development team to correctly follow the SDLC steps to create software that meets a business need. The SDLC models have evolved as new technology and new research have addressed weaknesses of older models. Ideas have been borrowed and adapted between the various models. But it is hard to comment on when to use which model. Developers can generalize the various situations where one SDLC model can be used but there is no hard and fast rule which direct developers to use only a specific model in a specific situation. It is the individual preference and specialization. The developer should also recognize the need and characteristics of top-down and bottom-up development while choosing a specific model.

It is the responsibility of the development teams to follow an SDLC model so that proper confidentiality, integrity and availability controls are designed and built into the software application throughout the software life cycle.

REFERENCES

1. http://en.wikipedia.org/wiki/Software_development_process
2. Roger, S. Pressman, "Software Engineering—A practitioner's approach", McGraw Hill
3. R.E. Fairly, "Software Engineering Concepts", McGraw Hill.
4. Jalota, "An Integrated Approach to Software Engineering", (Narosa Publishing House).
5. Jacobson, I. (1992). "Object-Oriented Software Engineering: A Use Case Driven Approach", Addison Wesley.
6. W. Scachi and J. Noll, "Process-Driven Intranets: Life-Cycle Support for Process Reengineering". IEEE Internet Computing, 1(5), 42-49, September-October 1997.
7. Palvia, P. and Nosek, J. (1993). A Field Examination of System Life Cycle Techniques and Methodologies, *Information and Management*, Vol. 25(2), 73-84.

4

Software Requirements, their Specifications and Standards

MANU SOOD

ABSTRACT

For any software system, the elicitation of requirements, and their specification and representation is one of the most basic but trivial and challenging activity in the software development life cycle. Equally important is to understand the terms 'requirements' and 'specification' as well as the relationship and distinction between the two. A number of approaches including a few published international as well as organization specific standards can be found in literature for this purpose. This paper is an attempt to understand :

(a) the definitions of requirements and specifications for software systems,
(b) the difference between the two,
(c) how the two are related, and
(d) the software requirements specification as a product as well as a process.

1. INTRODUCTION

A mature discipline is the one that is able to identify its dead problems, i.e. the problems that require no further effort. Software engineering has plenty of live problems to solve and will have to go a long way to identify its dead problems. A subset of the most challenging live problems in software engineering includes issues related to composition while engineering a software system; requirements changes, their traceability and management; and modeling and implementation of non-functional properties. The only way to handle these challenges is to use domain specific knowledge (Finkelstein & Kramer, 2000).

As such, 'what to build' and 'how to build' are the two critical dimensions of software development. The hardest part of building a software system is deciding and defining precisely what to build (Aggarwal & Singh, 2005) and more importantly specifying and documenting it for further references. Problems related to requirements engineering are a plenty, and an important subset of the problems pertain to the requirements, their specifications and related documentation. The requirements specification has two major orthogonal dimensions: process (Loucopoulos & Karakostas, 1995) and product (Zeroual, 1989), (IEEE, 1990).

A number of studies have proved that not more than 15% of total cost and duration is spent on the requirements activities in software development projects (Boehm, 1981), (Chatzoglou & Macaulay, 1996) whereas senior software developers and project managers expect the requirements activities to account for about 25% of the total development effort (McPhee & Eberlein, 2002). The probable reasons for this gap include lack of time due to deadline pressures, human psychology, non-compliance to the standard requirements engineering activities due to the lack of commonly acceptable effective and efficient requirements gathering and specification approaches.

About 10% of software errors are due to incorrect requirements specifications (Boehm, 1981) and 44% (UK Health and Safety Executive, 1995) and 80% (Testing Techniques, 1997) of all defects are inserted in the requirements phase. Hence the specification of the software requirements and their representation is one of the most trivial and challenging activity in the Software Development Life Cycle.

FIG. 4.1

Conceptual Model of a Computer-based Information System

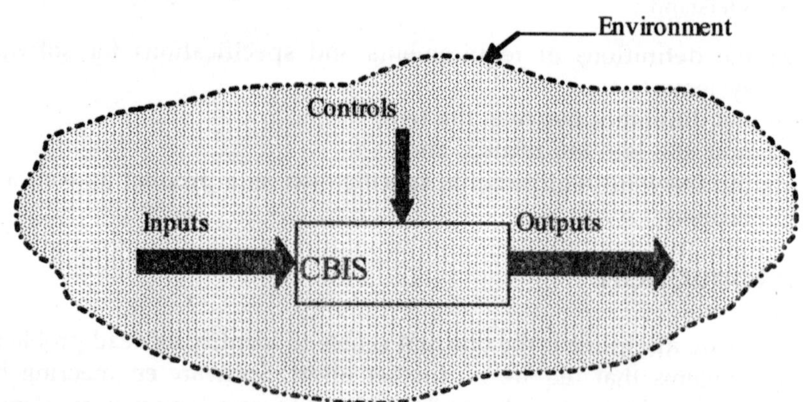

Computer-based Information Systems (CBIS) are the vehicles and the driving force behind the delivery of the most important product of recent times, i.e. Information. Right information at right time, right place and consumed rightly can facilitate right decisions in any environment. We conceptualize a CBIS in its abstract form as shown in Figure 4.1, where predefined inputs are consumed as raw data during processing and the information is produced in the form of expected outputs under certain controls with in an environment.

For any CBIS, the goal of software engineering, like any other branch of engineering, is to produce a well engineered software product from the available predefined inputs, in the form of required outputs. A well engineered product should be maintainable, reliable, and efficient and should offer appropriate user interface(s) (Sommerville, 1995). Since the software engineers cannot build what cannot be properly specified, software requirements and their specifications assume great significance. These are supposed to provide the necessary scope for establishing the scope for the software development for any CBIS in terms of what is to be built and what are the system boundaries.

Requirements analysis as a part of software development process is a sub-process in which 'what is to be done' is elicited, modeled and validated. This process deals with different viewpoints, and uses a combination of methods, tools, and actors. The product of this process is(are) a model(s), from which another product in the form of a document, called software requirements specifications document, is produced (Leite, 1987). During this process, the requirements from the system and its environment are elicited and specified. The requirements may be either for whole of the system or for the software alone resulting in two different kinds of requirements specifications.

From natural languages to formal notations/languages using mathematical expressions have been used for documenting the specifications of software requirements. The structured natural languages used earlier for this purpose were plagued with many problems including the ambiguity in expression, etc. One of the major problems of significance is the paradigm mismatch between analysis and design (Glinz, 1991). Hence, the use of semiformal/formal notations and languages for the representation of various artifacts during analysis phase gained momentum which otherwise have traditionally been considered appropriate only for the design. Semiformal languages have been the powerful means for the description and/or representation of specifications of software requirements for the last thirty years approximately with one of the pioneering works having been presented in (DeMacro, 1978).

The Object-oriented specification languages (Coad & Yourdon, 1991), (Rumbaugh, Blaha, Premerlani, Eddy & Lorensen, 1991), (Jacobson, Christerson, Jonnson & Övergaard, 1992), (Booch, 1994) started appearing in late 80's. In late nineties, three most prevalent Object-oriented approaches were consolidated into Unified Modeling Language (UML) (Rumbaugh,

Jacobson & Booch, 1999). This was done with the goal of unifying the best features of these languages to create a common acceptable industry standard. Incidentally, one of the authors of (Rumbaugh *et al.* 1999), Jacobson had introduced Use Case diagrams in 1992 for the first time in (Jacobson *et al.*, 1992). These were also included in the UML, in order to support the documentation of specifications of dynamic and behavioural properties of the system.

A high quality software requirements specifications (SRS) and equally high quality of its documentation is one of the essential pre-requisites for producing a high quality software product and also for its delivery within estimated time and budget. Problems with the prevalent approaches and lack of common understanding in using various terms involved in requirements engineering makes the process of specification of software requirements as well as their documentation a trivial issue. These factors make the SRS fall short of desirable quality.

Also, there is no single widely accepted and prescribed standard that is being followed by software professionals for the purpose. Therefore, in reference to today's Object-oriented development methodologies, the authors, in a separate study, have tried to bring forward salient features of two convenient and most commonly followed paradigms for the software requirements specifications documentation namely, (a) IEEE Standard 830-1998: Recommended Practice for Software Requirements Specifications, and (b) OMG's UML v1.5/v2.0 Use Case diagrams.

The IEEE Standard 830-1998 uses enumerated specifications using natural languages whereas OMG's UML Use Cases are diagram based scenario models. The study has been done in order to investigate whether and how both of them together can support a good quality Software Requirements specifications product. The objective here was to reduce/ minimize the paradigm mismatch between the analysis and design phases of a software system.

2. ENVIRONMENT, REQUIREMENTS AND SPECIFICATIONS

A system becomes problematic when its current behaviour in an environment starts turning unsatisfactory to its stakeholders. The environment is nothing but a part of the real world related to that system. The software developers identify and specify a new/modified computer-based software system for the CBIS, build it and then connect it to this environment in such a way that its behavior now becomes satisfactory. Although one is accustomed to think of a new system in terms of inputs and outputs, it is also important to realize that these inputs and outputs are phenomena in the environment only (Please refer to figure 1). If they were not part of the environment, they could not possibly connect the new system to the environment or affect the behaviour of the environment.

The idea that a requirements specification should include a model of the environment has been familiar since the early 1980s (Jackson, 1978),

(Balzer & Goldman, 1979), (Lehman, 1980), (Zave, 1982), (Jackson, 1983). But Zave and Jackson in (Jackson & Zave, 1995), (Zave & Jackson, 1997) propose that requirements should contain nothing but information about the environment and all the statements made in the course of requirements engineering are the statements about the environment. Further, the statements in indicative mood (often referred to as assumptions or domain knowledge) describe the environment without the new system in place. The statements in the optative mood describe the environment in the presence of the new system and it is these statements that are commonly called requirements. Haumer, Pohl & Weidenhaupt (1998) also support this perspective by proposing that the requirements specifications define the requirements for the future system but at a conceptual level.

It is very important to distinguish between the indicative and optative statements about the environment. Further, although the focus for describing the environment should be on the 'what' of the system, no statements are made about the 'proposed machine' in describing the environment in the optative mood (i.e. the requirements). Therefore, the problems arising out of the implementation bias into requirements specifications can straightaway be avoided.

The specifications state is not a description of the state of the new system, but rather a description of the state of the environment. Also, as the requirements for a software system exist only in an environment and these state the desired relationships in the environment, the effects and benefits of the computer-based software system will be felt and assessed in that environment only. The computer-based software system is purely a means to the end of achieving the required effect in the environment.

In the same context, specifications describe the behaviour of computer-based software system at its interface with the environment. Like the requirements, these are expressed entirely in terms of environment phenomena. It has two perspectives: software perspective and environment perspective. For the software, it is a starting point for programming; and for the environment, it is a restricted kind of requirement.

The specifications are derived from the requirements (Alagar & Periyasamy, 1998), (Jackson & Zave, 1995). When all the features of a given requirement such as references to environmental phenomena not accessible to the software are purged, it leads to the specifications that would preclude implementation. The derivation is made possible by environment properties that can be relied on regardless of the behaviour of the computer-based software system. These properties are to be explicitly described if they have to be exploited.

Therefore, there is a clear difference between requirements and specifications. A requirement is a condition in an environment needed by a user to solve a problem or achieve an objective. The specifications derived from requirements is a document that specifies in a complete, precise, verifiable manner, the requirements, behaviour, or other characteristics of a system and often the procedures for determining whether these provisions have been satisfied. It may include functional requirements, performance requirements, interface requirements, design requirements, and development standards.

Looking from a user perspective, the requirements are considered to be external, user-visible properties of the system to be built (IEEE, 1990), (Loucopoulos & Karakostas, 1995). These are used to express the proposed system in terms of 'what' to build, with no emphasis on 'how to build it' (Alagar & Periyasamy, 1998). The 'what' part specified by the requirements engineers is developed in 'how' and delivered by the developers.

Several researchers and practitioners have stressed that requirements should only state 'what' a system should do rather than 'how' it should be done (Sommerville & Sawyer, 1997). But interestingly, according to Davis, a 'how' at one level of abstraction may be a 'what' at a lower level of abstraction (Davis, 1993). Hence the level of abstraction plays an interesting and important role in the specifications of requirements. The requirements and their specifications largely describe aspects of the problem to be solved and the constraints on solution; and should be derived from the concepts and relationships in the problem domain (i.e. the environment). These deal with the concepts such as goals, options, agreements, issues and conditions reflecting the interests of all the stakeholders (customers, users, managers, developers) in the system (Boehm, 1988a), (Boehm, 1988b).

Although in literature the requirements have been defined in numerous ways, the standard definition of requirements has been proposed in IEEE Standard 610.12-1990 (IEEE, 1990), which incidentally also matches with definition proposed by Thayer (Thayer & Dorfman, 1990). Another standard definition for the requirements from the point of view of system engineering has been presented in IEEE Standard 1220-1998 (IEEE, 1998b).

In various branches of engineering, the term specifications refer to a statement of particulars describing the structural and behavioural details of the product to be developed. The software specifications denote a precise description of the objects, a set of methods to manipulate them, and a statement on their collective behaviour for the duration of their existence in the system to be developed (Alagar & Periyasamy, 1998).

3. SOFTWARE REQUIREMENTS SPECIFICATION

Loucopoulos and Karakostas (1995) sum up the requirements engineering as a systematic process of developing requirements through an iterative co-operative process of analyzing the problem, documenting the resulting observations in a variety of representational formats, and checking the accuracy gained. The term software requirements specification is used interchangeably to represent the process of specification as well as the product. The product in the form of a document representing specifications of requirements is called the requirements specifications document. If the requirements are about the software, it is known as software requirements specifications document or simply Software Requirements Specifications (SRS).

The aim of requirements engineering is to provide the customer/user with maximum satisfaction by means of meeting their expectations, delivering the software in time and adherence to the estimated budget. Therefore, requirements engineering lays stress on producing quality SRS. Since the SRS is also the main reference document for all subsequent documents generated during the SDLC as well as for the conformance testing, quality of the requirements and their specifications become all the more important.

As per Alagar and Periyasamy (1998), there are three types of specifications produced during the whole software development life cycle: (a) Behavioural specifications, (b) Design specifications, and (c) Program specifications. Behavioural specifications have the distinction of being the only specifications that can be independent of the implementation. According to them, the essential properties of these software specifications are:

1. It must be possible to define the observable behaviour through the software specifications.
2. The interface of a software component should be precise and simple.
3. The behaviour of the whole must be expressible in terms of behaviour of the parts, i.e. it must be possible to compose specifications.
4. The design specifications must contain a description of all behaviours expressed by the behavioural specifications.
5. It must be possible to develop a program from the design specifications.
6. It must be possible to test for conformance, e.g. a program satisfies its program specifications.
7. It must be possible to subject the specifications to rigorous analysis, e.g. given a requirement, specification and a property, it must be possible to determine whether or not the property is a consequence of the specification representing the requirement.

The behavioural specifications are the first kind of specifications that are brought out during the initial phases of SDLC. For this purpose, firstly, the overall requirements are established and from these requirements, these specifications are derived. Establishment of these requirements and their specifications is the central theme to the practices of requirements engineering. Thus one of the most important activities within the realms of requirements engineering is the process of requirements specifications and the outcome of this process is a deliverable called requirements specifications document.

If the specification encompasses requirements about hardware, software, networking, etc., it is named as System Requirements Specifications (SyRS) and if it encompass only the requirements about the software, it is called the Software Requirements Specifications (SRS)

(Aggarwal & Singh, 2005). The Software Requirements Specifications not only cover the behavioural requirements (also known as functional requirements) but also the requirements about the quality of the system/ software and various constraints (also known as non-functional requirements).

Functional requirements each have an origin from which they come, be it a use case, government regulation, industry standard, or a business requirement. In developing an SRS, there is a need to identify these origins and link them to their corresponding requirements. Such a practice not only justifies a requirement but also assures project stakeholders that frivolous or spurious requirements are kept out of the specifications. The Use Cases can be used in system analysis to identify, clarify, and organize system/software requirements, and consist of a set of possible sequences of interactions between system and users in a particular environment and related to particular goals.

To link requirements with their sources, each requirement included in the SRS is labeled with a unique identifier that can remain valid over time as requirements are added, deleted, or/and changed. Such a labeling system helps maintain change-record integrity while also serving as an identification system for gathering metrics and developing requirements traceability matrices.

4. PRODUCT VS. PROCESS PERSPECTIVE

The absence of consensus among the software professionals: practitioners as well as researchers, about the standard definition of the term 'specification' and varying uses of this term to interchangeably represent the process as well as the product are contributing to the difficulties in understanding requirements engineering to some extent. Zeroual (1989) defines the requirements engineering as a process consisting of two steps: eliciting the user's requirements and representing the requirements thus obtained in a suitable form. The process results in a product that represents the specifications of requirements and is referred to as the specifications.

Loucopoulos and Karakostas (1995) used specification more traditionally, suggesting that the requirements engineering consists of three interrelated, overlapping and iterative operations: requirements elicitation, specification, and validation, wherein, the term specification essentially represents a process. The process of requirements specification carries out two sub-activities:

(a) assimilation and analysis of system requirements, and
(b) synthesis and organization of the knowledge into logically coherent requirements.

Here the term 'specifications' has been used to mean the representation of the requirements (the product), and not the requirements definition activity (the process) which is consistent with the definition of requirements specifications as a document that specifies the requirements for a system or component (IEEE, 1990).

5. SRS DOCUMENT

The SRS document is typically developed during the initial product development phase in which information is gathered about what requirements are needed. This information-gathering stage can include onsite visits, questionnaires, surveys, interviews, and perhaps a return-on-investment (ROI) analysis or needs analysis of the customer or client's current business environment.

It represents an organization's understanding (in writing) of a customer or potential client's software requirements and dependencies at a particular point of time in an environment, usually prior to any actual design or development work. It's a two-way insurance policy that assures that both the client and the organization understand each other's requirements from that perspective at a given point of time in an environment.

It also serves the purpose of a reference for all the stakeholders during all the subsequent phases of SDLC. It is this SRS that can form the basis for a legal contract between the developer and the user/customer. This SRS is also used for the purpose of conformance/acceptance testing (Myers, 1976), (Jalote, 2001) so as to ensure whatever features/services (to be developed / provided), that were agreed upon by the developer and the user/customer initially or subsequently, have been satisfactorily incorporated in the final software product.

The SRS also functions as a blueprint for completing a project with as little cost growth as possible. It is often referred to as the parent document because all subsequent project management documents, such as design specifications, statements of work, software architecture specifications, testing and validation plans, and documentation plans, are related to it.

The actual specifications are written after the requirements have been gathered, analyzed and validated. The SRS document states functions and capabilities in precise and explicit language that a software system must provide. It also prescribes any required constraints by which the system must abide. But it does not offer design suggestions, possible solutions to technology or business issues, or any other information other than what the development team understands about the customer's system requirements. An SRS document should also include the ingredients like:

(a) A template,
(b) A method for identifying requirements and linking sources,
(c) Business operation rules, and
(d) A traceability matrix.

Within the framework of these ingredients, several standards organizations (including IEEE) have put in a lot of effort to identify some key areas that need to be taken into consideration for designing and writing a quality SRS. These key areas are: scenarios, goals, sources, interfaces, functional capabilities, performance parameters, safety, reliability, security/privacy, quality, constraints and limitations, portability and maintainability.

A high quality SRS document and adequate support of standards and documentation to the process of requirements engineering is a prerequisite in producing high quality software and also, reduces the development cost (Jalote, 2001). A well-designed, well-written SRS accomplishes four major goals:

1. *User/Customer Feedback*: It is the user/customer's assurance that the developer(s) understands :

   (a) The issues to be addressed,
   (b) The problems to be solved, and
   (c) The software behaviour necessary to address those issues and problems.

   Therefore, an SRS may make use of simple statements in a natural language, charts, tables, data flow diagrams, decision tables, use cases, etc.
2. *Problem Decomposition*: It helps in:

   (a) Breaking down the problem into its component parts in an orderly fashion so that the software requirements are organized in a well-designed format,
   (b) Consolidating ideas, and
   (c) Fixing well defined borders around the problem.

3. *Input to Design Specifications*: Since an SRS serves as the parent document to subsequent documents such as the software design specifications; it must contain sufficient details about the system's functional and non-functional requirements so that an effective design solution can be easily devised.
4. *Product Validation*: It serves as a product validation document and helps in deciding testing and validation strategies for requirements verification.

An ill-written requirements specifications document makes it fairly difficult:

(a) For developers (designers) to decide what to build,
(b) To validate the expected requirements of the system to be built,
(c) For customer/users to know what to expect from the system, and
(d) For testers to decide what to test against.

In contrast, a good SRS offers the following benefits:

1. Establishes the basis for agreement (and legal contract as well) between the users/customers and the supplier/developer on what the functional and non-functional requirements of the software product shall be,
2. Is used as a reference by all the stakeholders in different phases of software engineering,
3. Acts as basis for the estimations of size, costs, effort, etc.,
4. Provides the basis for project management,
5. Acts as input to the Design and Testing phases,
6. Helps in reduction of overall development effort and also in checking its growth during the progress in the SDLC,
7. Provides baseline for verification and validation,
8. Facilitates transfer and installation of a software to the user/customer site(s), and
9. Helps in traceability and easier control of various types of maintenance jobs.

Different application domains may need different notations for documenting the specifications of software requirements using the vocabulary of the domain. Even in the same domain, different notations may have to be used at different stages. From natural languages to semiformal to formal (using mathematical expressions) languages/notations are used for the specifications of requirements in the SRS. There are many alternatives for specification of software requirements in structured natural languages, e.g. native language, pseudo codes, System Definition Language (SDL), form based specifications (input, output, pre-condition, post-condition), Program Description Language (PDL), Use Case description, etc.

The natural languages are easier to understand and provide freedom and expressing power. But these suffer from inherent ambiguities, inconsistencies and multiple interpretations besides providing little support for visualization and/or automated syntactic and semantic checking. Some problems of natural languages like no/little support for automation can be tackled by structuring specifications into enumerated sections with defined contents (Regnell, Andersson & Bergstrand, 1996). According to Glinz (1991), one of the major problems that majority of specification languages suffer from is the paradigm mismatch between analysis and design.

Formal specifications languages (e.g. z-specification language) using the core mathematical expressions are technical and precise, which developers mostly find easier to handle. But these are difficult for other stakeholders to understand and hence act as a deterrent for the users/customers to directly contribute in the requirements engineering activities. Since they are not able to understand or follow these specifications, they start losing their interest in the process and ultimately get isolated. But, since Wiegers (1994) has pointed out that the full customer involvement throughout the SDLC is very essential for the development of a compliant quality software product, this becomes one of the limitations of the formal specifications.

In contrast, use of semiformal languages/notations has become very popular because of the fact that they are easily understood by all the stakeholders and may also provide scope for necessary automation/ formalism, one of the most popular notation being the OMG's UML Use Cases. Using the vocabulary of the domain, the UML Use Cases are specified as graphical notations along with easy-to-understand structured description that may be in:

(a) Natural languages without restrictions
(b) Structured natural languages
(c) Pseudo code
(d) Data Flow diagrams
(e) In the form of state machines (UML, 2003) or
(f) Activity diagrams (Fowler & Scott, 1997).

Here too, the main support for describing Use Cases at requirements level is natural language which is well supported by graphical representation. A graphical representation of Use Cases with well defined syntax and semantics helps visualize functional requirements, and also, gives a more structured, and less ambiguous use case model, compared to natural language representations. It also provides necessary scope of support for the automation.

Textual scenarios supported by the rich capture of reality scenes in multimedia are the other alternatives to facilitate documenting the requirements specifications-related material (Brun-Cottan & Wall, 1995). The combination is also being increasingly proposed for current-state scenarios (Wood Christel & Stevens, 1994), (McGraw & Harbison, 1997), (Haumer *et al.*, 1998).

6. REQUIREMENTS AND SPECIFICATIONS STANDARDS

There are many requirements and specifications standards. They are mostly military standards as opposed to "commercial" standards. In addition, most of the standards are in the systems engineering area. Dorfman & Thayer (1990) is a good reference to many of these standards and is a compilation of international requirements standards and U.S. military standards. Listed below are several relevant standards, but the list is by no means exhaustive:

- IEEE Recommended Practice for Software Requirements Specifications (IEEE standard 830-1998).
- British Standard Guide to Specifying User Requirements for a Computer-based Standard (BS6719-1986).

- Canadian Standard, Basic Guidelines for the Structure of Documentation of System Design Information (Z242.15.4-1979).
- U.S. Military Standards.
- System/Segment Specifications (DI-CMAN-80008A, 2/29/1988).
- Software Requirements Specifications (DI-MCCR-80025A, 2/29/1988).
- Interface Requirements Specifications (DI-MCCR-80026A, 2/29/1998).
- OMG's UML (v1.5/v2.0) Use Cases.

Two general purpose most commonly used international standards that support software requirements specifications are: (a) IEEE Standard 830-1998: IEEE Recommended Practice for Software Requirements Specifications (IEEE, 1998a) that supports software requirements specifications in a structured natural languages; and (b) Object Management Group's (OMG's) Unified Modeling Language (UML) Use Case (UC) paradigm (UML, 2000), (UML, 2003).

7. CONCLUSION

The requirements are considered to be the 'what' part of the environment of the proposed system. The specifications are derived from these requirements and define an interface between the system and the environment. The document containing these specifications is known as the requirements specifications document. The software requirements specifications is called SRS document.

There are various standards for software requirements specifications. In this chapter, we discussed two prominent standards. The IEEE Standard 830-1998 supports enumerated specifications of requirements in structured natural languages and OMG's UML Use Case approach draws its strengths from visual graphical notations and their description.

References

1. Finkelstein, A. and Kramer, J. (2000). Software Engineering: A Roadmap, International Conference on Software Engineering, Proceedings, *Conference on The Future of Software Engineering*, ACM Press, New York, USA, 3-22.
2. Aggarwal, K.K. and Singh, Y. (2005). *Software Engineering: Programs, Documentation & Operating Procedures*, 2nd edition, New Age International Publishers, New Delhi, 144-45.
3. Loucopoulos, P. and Karakostas, V. (1995). *System Requirements Engineering*, McGraw-Hill Book Company, Berkshire, 2-45.
4. Zeroual, K. (1989). An Approach for Automating the Specification-Acquisition Process, Proceedings, *Second International Workshop on Software Engineering and its Applications, (Toulouse '89, EC2)*, Nanterre, France, 349-55.
5. *IEEE Standard 610.12-1990: Standard Glossary of Software Engineering Terminology (ANSI) (revision and re-designation of IEEE Std. 729-1983)*, (1990). Institute of Electrical and Electronics Engineers, New York.

6. Boehm, B.W. (1981). *Software Engineering Economics*, Prentice-Hall, Englewood Cliffs, NJ.
7. Chatzoglou, P.D. and Macaulay, L.A. (1996). Requirements Capture and Analysis: A Survey of Current Practice, *Requirements Engineering*, 1(2), 75-87.
8. McPhee, C. and Eberlein, A. (2002). Requirements Engineering for Time-to-Market Projects, Proceedings, *9th Annual IEEE International Conference on the Engineering of Computer-based Systems (ECBS2002)*, Lund, Sweden.
9. *UK Health and Safety Executive* (1995). Out of Control: Why Control Systems Go Wrong and How to Prevent Failure, Her Majesty's Stationary Office, UK.
10. *Testing Techniques Newsletter* (1997). Software Research, Inc., 625 Third Street, SF, CA, USA, ttn@soft.com, http://www.soft.com.
11. Sommerville, I. (1995). *Software Engineering*, Addison-Wesley.
12. Leite, J. (June, 1987). A Survey on Requirements Analysis, *Advanced Software Engineering Project Technical Report RTP-071*, University of California at Irvine, Department of Information and Computer Science, p. 26.
13. Glinz, M. (1991). Problems and Weaknesses of Structured Analysis, In Timm., M. (ed.), *Requirements Engineering' 91, Informatik-Fachberichte, 273*, Springer, Berlin, 14-39.
14. DeMacro, T. (1978). *Structured Analysis and System Specification*, Yourdon Press, NY.
15. Booch, G. (1994). *Object-Oriented Analysis and Design with Applications*, 2nd Edition, Ca: Benjamin/Cummings, Redwood City.
16. Coad, P. Yourdon, E. (1991). *Object-Oriented Analysis*, Prentice Hall, Englewood Cliffs, N.J..
17. Jacobson, I., Christerson, M., Jonnson, P. & Övergaard, G. (1992). *Object-Oriented Software Engineering—A Use case Driven Approach*. Addison-Wesley, Wokingham, England.
18. Rumbaugh, J., Blaha, M., Premerlani, W., Eddy, F. & Lorensen, W. (1991). *Object-oriented Modeling and Design*, Prentice Hall, Englewood Cliffs, N.J.
19. Rumbaugh, J., Jacobson, I. & Booch G. (1999). *The Unified Modeling Language Reference Manual*, Addison Wesley, Reading, MA.
20. Balzer, R. and Goldman, N. (1979). Principles of Good Software Specification and their Implications for Specification Language, Proceedings, *Specifications of Reliable Software Conference, IEEE Computer Society*, Washington, D.C., 58–67.
21. Jackson, M. (1978). Information Systems: Modeling, sequencing, and transformations, Proceedings, *3rd International Conference on Software Engineering*, IEEE Computer Society Press, Los Alamitos, California, 73–81.
22. Jackson, M. (1983). *System Development*, Prentice-Hall International, Chichester, U.K.
23. Lehman, M.M. (September, 1980). Programs, Life Cycles, and Laws of Software Evolution, Proceedings IEEE 68(9), 1060–76.
24. Zave, P. (May 1982). An Operational Approach to Requirements Specification for Embedded Systems, *IEEE Transactions on Software Engineering*, 8(3), 250-69.
25. Jackson, M. and Zave, P. (1995). Deriving Specifications from Requirements: An Example, Proceedings, *ICSE-17*, ACM Press, NJ.
26. Zave, P. and Jackson, M. (1997). Four Dark Corners of Requirements Engineering, *ACM Transactions on Software Engineering and Methodology*, 6(1), 1-30.
27. Haumer, P., Pohl, K. and Weidenhaupt, K. (December 1998). Requirements Elicitation and Validation with Real World Scenes, *IEEE Transactions on Software Engineering: Special Issue on Scenario Management*, 24(12).
28. Alagar, V.S. and Periyasamy, K. (1998). *Specification of Software Systems*, Springer-Verlag, New York, Inc.
29. Sommerville, I. and Sawyer, P. (1997). *Requirements Engineering—A Good Practice Guide*, Wiley, NJ.
30. Davis, A.M. (1993). *Software Requirements: Objects, Functions and States*, Prentice Hall, Englewood Cliffs, NJ.
31. Boehm, B.W., Egyed, A., Kwan, J., Port, D., Shah, A. and Madachy, R. (1988). Using the WinWin Spiral Model: A Case Study, *IEEE Computer*, 7, 33-44.
32. Boehm, B.W. (May 1988). A Spiral Model of Software Development and Enhancement, *IEEE Computer*, 21(5), 61-72.
33. Thayer, R.H. and Dorfman, M. (1990). *System and Software Requirements Engineering*, IEEE Computer Society Press, Los Alamitos, CA.

34. *IEEE Standard 1220-1994: IEEE Standard for the Application and Management of the Systems Engineering Process* (1998). Institute of Electrical and Electronics Engineers, New York.
35. Jalote, P. (2001). *An Integrated Approach to Software Engineering*, Narosa Publishing House, New Delhi, 2nd Edition, 76-79.
36. Myers, G.J. (1976). *Software Reliability: Principles and Practices*, John Wiley & Sons, NY.
37. Regnell, B., Andersson, M. and Bergstrand, J. (March 1996). A Hierarchical Use Case Model with Graphical Representation, Proceedings, *IEEE International Symposium and Workshop on Engineering of Computer-Based Systems*, IEEE Computer Society Press, NY.
38. Wiegers, K. (July 1994). Creating a Software Requirements Specification, *Software Development*.
39. *OMG Unified Modeling Language Specification (Formal 03-03-01, Version 1.5)* (March 2003) from www.omg.org/uml.
40. Fowler, M. and Scott, K. (1997). *UML Distilled: Applying the Standard Object Modeling Language*, Addison-Wesley, Reading, MA.
41. Brun-Cottan, F. and Wall, P. (1995). Using Video to Represent the Users, *Communications to ACM*, 38(5), 61-71.
42. McGraw K. and Harbison, K. (1997). *User-Centered Requirement: The Scenario-based Engineering Process*, Lawrence Erlbaum Associates Publishers, Mahwah, NJ.
43. Wood, D.P., Christel, M.G. and Stevens, S.M. (April 1994). A Multimedia Approach to Requirements Capture and Modeling, Proceedings, *1st International Conference on Requirements Engineering (ICRE'94)*, IEEE Computer Society Press, Colorado Springs, CO, USA, 53-56.
44. Dorfman, M. and Thayer, R.H. (1990). *Standards, Guidelines and Examples on System and Software Requirements Engineering*, IEEE Computer Society Press, LA, USA.
45. *IEEE Standard 830-1998: Recommended Practice for Software Requirements Specifications* (1998). Institute of Electrical and Electronics Engineers, New York.
46. *OMG Unified Modeling Language Specification*, (March 2000) from www.omg.org/uml.

5

An Approach to Measure Software Maintainability with CK Metrics

PRADEEP KUMAR BHATIA AND RAJBEER MANN

ABSTRACT

Software maintainability is an attribute of software quality. Software quality is low if more effort is required to maintain the software. But software quality cannot be improved unless it can be measured. In this paper, we have derived a new approach to measure the software maintainability of OO code, an attribute of software quality. We have also empirically studied the approach in OO programming language in C++.

1. INTRODUCTION

Every software program needs to be changed to meet the changing requirements of users and customers during its lifetime. It is generally impractical and uneconomical to produce software, which does not need to be changed. Introduction of new hardware also necessitates the change in the software. The process of changing software after it has been delivered and is in use is called software maintenance. This is a task that every development group has to face when the software is delivered to the customer's site, installed and is operational. Some software may be maintained for several decades. Initially, aim of the software development was to write working programs. Then the aim shifted to writing good quality programs, but lastly the aim is to write good maintainable programs. It has been reported that amount of effort spent on maintenance is between 65% and 75% of total software development and support efforts.[4]

1.1 Traditional Metrics

1.1.1 McCabe Cyclomatic Complexity (CC)

Cyclomatic complexity is a measure of a module control flow complexity based on graph theory.[6] Fundamentally, the CC of a module is roughly equivalent to the number of decision points and is a measure of the minimum number of test cases that would be required to cover all execution paths. A high cyclomatic complexity indicates that the code may be of low quality and difficult to test and maintain.

1.1.2 Source Lines Code (SLOC)

The SLOC metric measures the number of physical lines of active code, that is, no blank or commented lines code.[7] In general, the higher the SLOC in a module the less understandable and maintainable the module is.

1.1.3 Comment Percentage (CP)

The CP metric is defined as the number of commented lines of code divided by the number of non-blank lines of code. Usually 20% indicates adequate commenting for C++.[8] A high CP value facilitates in maintaining a system.

1.2 CK Metrics

1.2.1 Weighted Methods Per Class (WMC)

WMC measures the complexity of an individual class. It is equivalent to the number of methods per class as a measure for WMC.[2] The number of methods and complexity of methods involved is a direct predictor of how much time and effort is required to develop and maintain the class.

1.2.2 Depth of Inheritance Tree of a Class (DIT)

DIT is defined as the length of the longest path of inheritance ending at the current module.[2] In cases involving multiple inheritances, the DIT will be the maximum length from the node to the root of the tree.[8] The deeper the inheritance tree for a class, the harder it might be to predict its behaviour due to the interaction between the inherited features and new features. However, the deeper a particular class is in the hierarchy, the greater the potential for reuse of inherited methods.

1.2.3 Number of Children (NOC)

NOC represents the number of immediate sub-classes subordinated to a class in the class hierarchy.[2] A moderate value for NOC indicates scope for reuse and high value may indicate an inappropriate abstraction in the design. Classes with a large number of children have to provide more generic service to all the children in various contexts and must be more flexible, a constraint that can introduce more complexity into the parent class.

1.2.4 Coupling between Objects (CBO)

CBO is defined as the count of the number of other classes to which it is coupled.[2] A class is coupled to another class if it uses the member method and/or instance variables of the other class. Excessive coupling indicates weakness of class encapsulation and may inhibit reuse. High coupling also indicates that more faults may be introduced due to inter-class activities.

1.2.5 Response for a Class (RFC)

RFC gives the number of methods that can potentially be executed in response to a message received by an object of that class.[2] If a large number of methods can be invoked in response to a message, the testing and debugging of the class becomes more complicated since it requires a greater level of understanding required on the part of the tester.

1.2.6 Lack of Cohesion in Methods (LOCM)

LOCM counts the number of method pairs whose similarity is zero minus the count of method pairs whose similarity is not zero. The larger the number of similar methods in a class the more cohesive the class is.[2] Cohesiveness of methods within a class is desirable, since it promotes encapsulation and lack of cohesion implies classes should probably be split into two or more sub-classes.

2. PRIOR LITERATURE

Chidamber and Kemerer proposed a set of six metrics and later on revised their metric suite in 1994 and analytically evaluated against a previously proposed set of measurement principles. They developed an automated data collection tool and then implemented it to collect an empirical sample of these metrics at two field sites in order to demonstrate their feasibility and to suggest ways in which managers may use these metrics for process improvement.[1,2] Wei Li and Sallie Henry, then, proposed set of CK metrics that will predict software maintainability.[5] Dr. Rosenberg, then, suggested that CK metrics can be used to measure quality attributes.[3]

3. PROPOSED APPROACH

Our approach is to derive formula to measure maintainability effort of a code based on following principles:

- The larger the DIT metric, the harder it is to maintain the class because the higher DIT a class has, the more super class properties it may access and may hence violate the encapsulation.[5]
- NOC, the more direct children a class has, the more classes it may potentially effect because of inheritance and hence be harder to maintain.[5]
- RFC, 'the larger the response set for a class, the more complex the class', and hence the higher RFC, the harder to maintain because of it being more difficult to trace with a lot of method calls and responses.[5]
- LCOM, "the more cohesive a class, the easier the class is to maintain", so if LCOM is high, it may be that the class is badly designed and partitioned and hence hard to maintain.[5]
- WMC, the more methods in a class the more complex the class is, and hence harder to maintain.[5]
- The more CBO a class has the more complex the coupling of that class with other classes, hence more effort is required to maintain.[5]

Maintainability Effort of a Class = a*(DIT) + b*(NOC) + c*(CBO) +d(LCOM) + e(RFC) + f(WMC) . . . . . (1)

where a, b, c, d, e, f are empirical constants.

For convenience, we take a = b = c = d = e = f = 1.

Total Maintainability Effort of code = sum (maintainability effort $(\text{class})_i$) . . . . (2)

where i = 1 to n.

4. EMPIRICAL STUDY

To empirically validate the formula we have taken five object-oriented programs and calculated the values of CK metrics for each program.

FIG. 5.1
An Object-oriented Design for Vehicle Classification Program

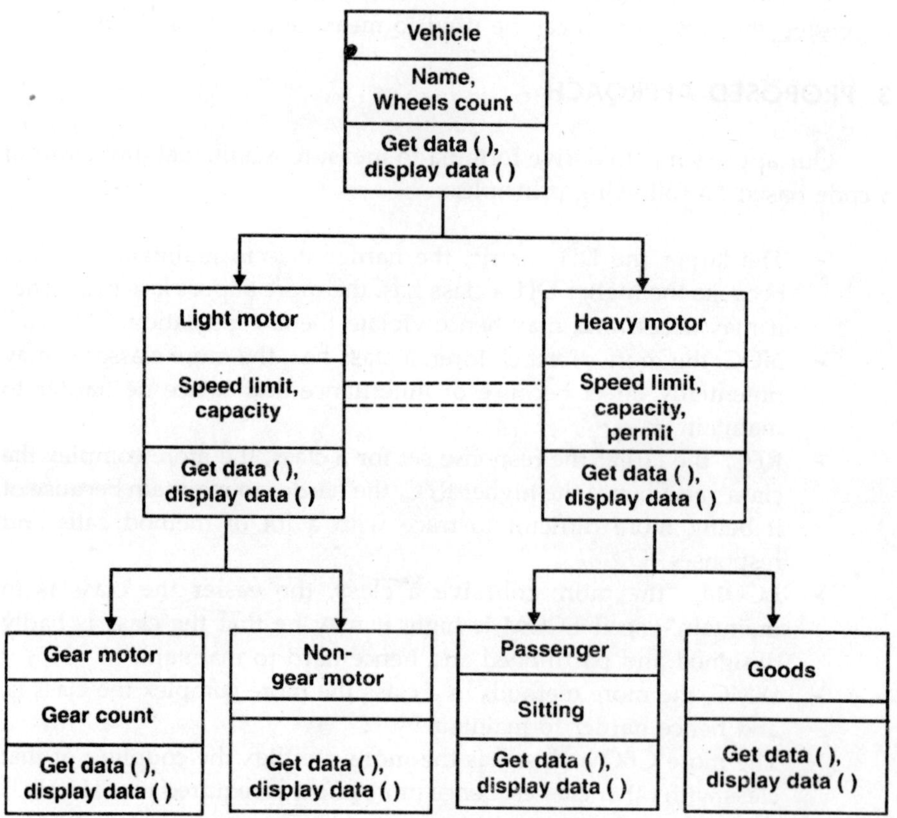

TABLE 5.1
The Values of CK Metrics for Vehicle Classification Obtained fom OO Design

Classes	*WMC*	*DIT*	*NOC*	*CBO*	*RFC*	*LCOM*
Vehicle	2	0	2	0	8	0
Lightmotor	2	1	2	2	6	0
Heavymotor	2	1	2	2	6	0
Gearmotor	2	2	0	0	2	0
Non-gearmotor	2	2	0	0	2	0
Passenger	2	2	0	0	2	0
Goods	2	2	0	0	2	0

TABLE 5.2

The Maintainability Effort of All Classes and Maintainability Effort of Class Diagram Vehicle Classification

Classes	*Maintainability Effort*	*Maintainability Effort of Class Diagram*
Vehicle	12	
Lightmotor	13	
Heavymotor	13	
Gearmotor	6	62
Non-gearmotor	6	
Passenger	6	
Goods	6	

FIG. 5.2

An Object-oriented Design for Student Education Program

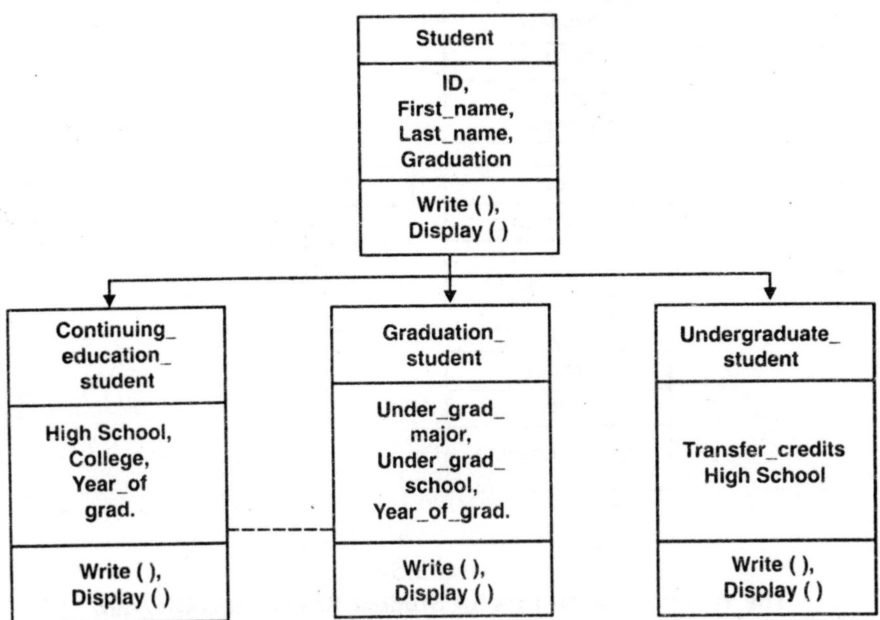

TABLE 5.3

Values of CK Metrics for Student Education

Classes	*WMC*	*DIT*	*NOC*	*CBO*	*RFC*	*LCOM*
Student	2	0	3	0	8	0
Conti. education	2	1	0	1	2	0
Graduation	2	1	0	1	2	0
Undergraduate	2	1	0	0	2	0

TABLE 5.4
The Maintainability Effort of All Classes and Maintainability Effort of Class Diagram Student Education

Classes	*Class reusability*	*Reusability of class diagram*
Student	13	30
Conti. Education	6	
Graduation	6	
Undergraduate	5	

FIG. 5.3
The Object-oriented Design for Student Result Program

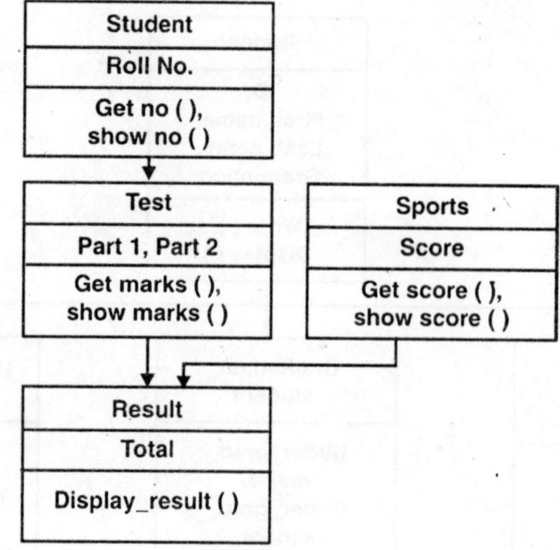

TABLE 5.5
The Values of CK Metrics for Student Result Class Diagram

Classes	*WMC*	*DIT*	*NOC*	*CBO*	*RFC*	*LCOM*
Student	2	0	1	0	3	0
Test	2	1	1	0	3	0
Sports	2	0	1	0	3	0
Result	1	2	0	0	1	0

TABLE 5.6

The Maintainability Effort of All Classes and Maintainability Effort of Class Diagram Student Result

Classes	*Class reusability*	*Reusability of class diagram*
Student	6	
Test	7	
Sports	6	23
Result	4	

FIG. 5.4

Object-oriented Design for Shapes Drawing Program

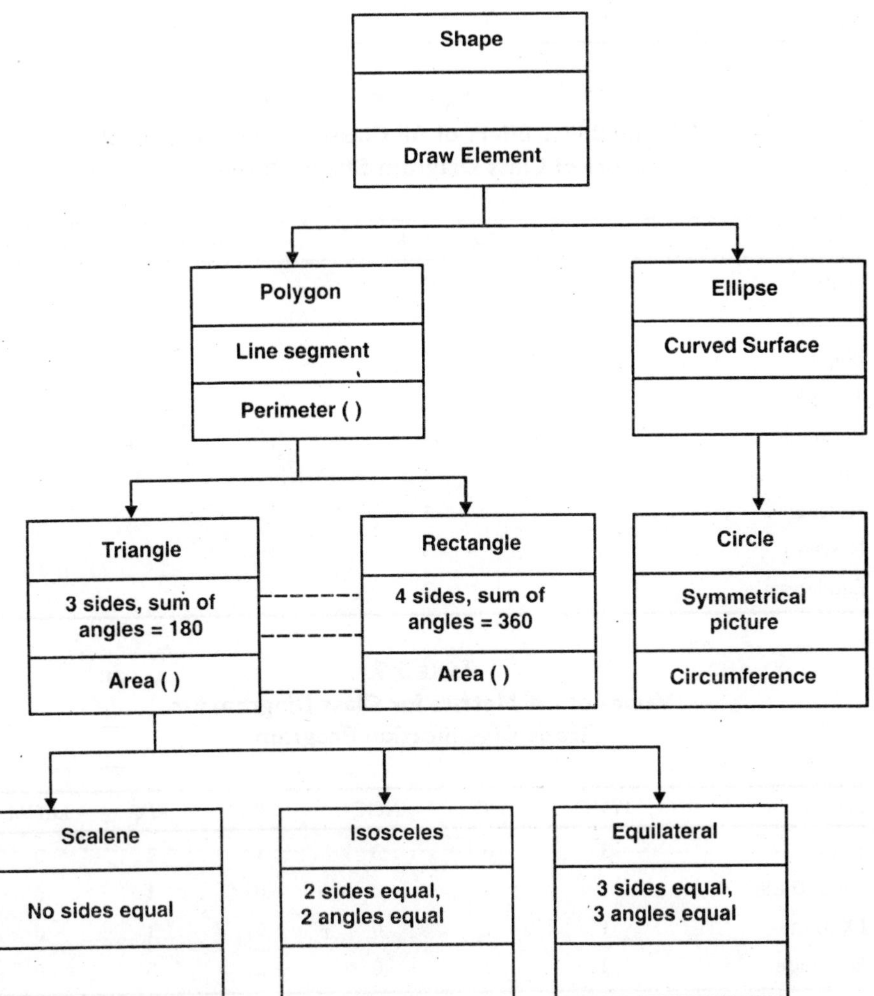

TABLE 5.7
The Values of CK Metrics for Shape Drawing Class Diagram

Classes	*WMC*	*DIT*	*NOC*	*CBO*	*RFC*	*LCOM*
Shape	1	0	2	0	8	0
Polygon	1	1	2	0	9	0
Ellipse	0	1	1	0	0	0
Triangle	1	2	3	3	4	0
Rectangle	1	2	0	3	4	0
Circle	1	2	0	0	1	0
Scalene	0	3	0	0	0	0
Isosceles	0	3	0	0	0	0
Equilateral	0	3	0	0	0	0

TABLE 5.8
The Maintainability Effort of All Classes and Maintainability Effort of Class Diagram Shape Drawing

Classes	*Class reusability*	*Reusability of class diagram*
Shape	11	
Polygon	13	
Ellipse	2	
Triangle	13	
Rectangle	10	62
Circle	4	
Scalene	3	
Isosceles	3	
Equilateral	3	

TABLE 5.9
Values of CK Metrics for Class Diagram for Trade Classification Program

Classes	*WMC*	*DIT*	*NOC*	*CBO*	*RFC*	*LCOM*
Trade	3	0	3	1	4	0
Bond Trade	1	1	0	0	1	0
FX Trade	1	1	0	0	1	0
Eq. Trade	2	1	0	2	3	0

FIG. 5.5
Object-oriented Design for Trade Classification Program

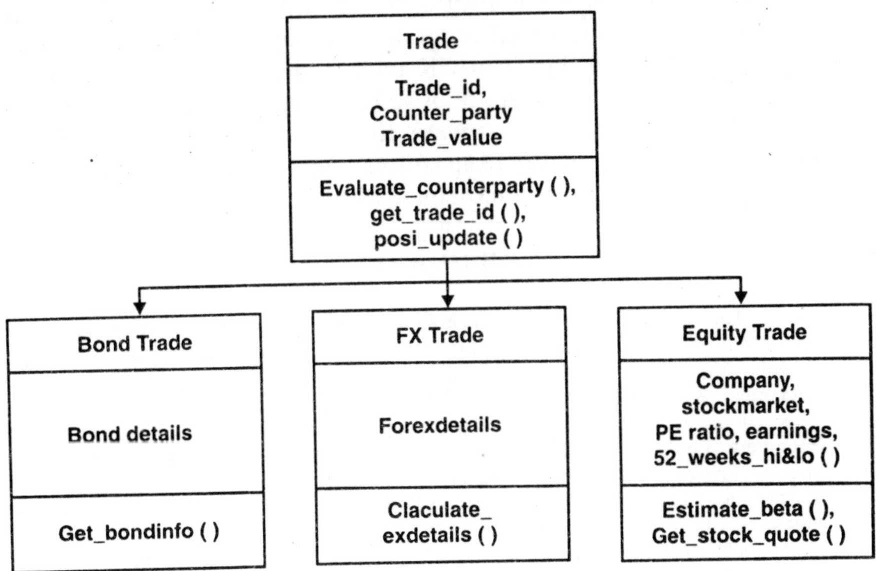

TABLE 10
The Maintainability Effort of All Classes and Maintainability Effort of Class Diagram Vehicle Classification

Classes	*Class reusability*	*Reusability of class diagram*
Trade	11	
Bond Trade	3	
FX Trade	3	25
Equity Trade	8	

The maintainability effort of all Class diagrams is compared in Figure 5.6.

FIG. 5.6
Maintainability Effort of Various Programs

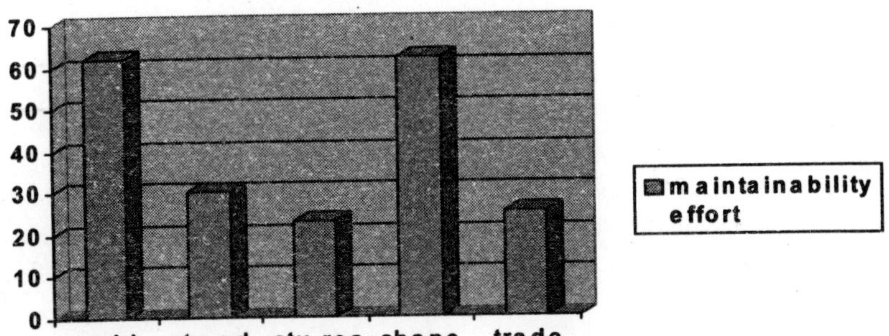

5. CONCLUSION

In this paper, we have proposed an approach to measure the maintainability of object-oriented program based upon CK metrics. We have derived linear equations between CK metrics and maintainability effort. Since maintainability is an attribute of software quality, the more effort we need to apply to maintain the software, the less is the quality of software. We can predict software quality from software maintainability effort. Hence, this approach is important to predict software quality.

REFERENCES

1. S.R. Chidamber and C. Kemerer, "Towards a Metrics Suite for Object-oriented Design", in *Proc. 6th ACM Conf. Object-oriented Programming. Syst., Lung. and Applicat. (OOPSLA)*, Phoenix, AZ, 1991, pp. 197-21, 1.
2. Chidamber, S.R. and Kemerer, C.F., "A Metric Suite for Object-oriented Design", IEEE Transactions on Software Engineering, 20(6):476-93, 1994.
3. Rosenberg, Linda H. and Hyatt, Lawrence E., "Software Quality Metrics for Object-oriented Environment", *Crosstalk Journal*, 1997.
4. Krishan, K. Aggarwal, Yogesh Singh and Jitender Kumar Chhabra, "An Integrated Measure of Software Maintainability", Proceedings Annual Reliability and Maintainability Symposium, 2002.
5. Wei Li and Sallie Henry, "Object-oriented Metrics that Predict Maintainability", *Journal on Systems Software*, 1993; 23:111-22.
6. McCabe and Associates, *Using McCabe QA 7.0*, 1999, 9861 Broken Land Parkway, 4th Floor, Columbia, MD 21046.
7. Lorenz, Mark and Kidd Jeff, *Object-oriented Software Metrics*, Prentice Hall, 1994.
8. Rosenberg, L., and Hyatt, L., "Software Quality Metrics for Object-oriented System Environments", Software Assurance Technology Center, Technical Report SATC-TR-95-1001, NASA Goddard Space Flight Center, Greenbelt, Maryland 20771.

6

Software Reliability as a Software Quality Attribute

DEEPSHIKHA, JASWINDER SINGH AND PARDEEP KUMAR BHATIA

ABSTRACT

Software Reliability is a part of software quality. It relates to many areas where software quality is concerned. The IEEE defines reliability as "The ability of a system or component to perform its required functions under stated conditions for a specified period of time." Reliability is equivalent to correctness to most of the projects, that is, they look to testing and the number of bugs found and fixed. To develop a robust, high quality product through all the stages of the software development lifecycle, it is necessary to assure the software reliability by measuring defects found and defect fixed. Software reliability is different from hardware reliability in that it reflects the design perfection rather than manufacturing perfection. In this paper, we discuss the role of software metrics in improving the quality and reliability of the software product, and also demonstrate that how these quality metrics assist in the evaluation of software reliability.

1. INTRODUCTION

Software Reliability is an important attribute of the software quality, usability, security, portability, cost/benefit, performance, capability, correctness, maintainability, and documentation. Reliability of a software product is an important concern for most users. Users not only want the products they purchase to be highly reliable, but often desire to check the quantitative estimation of the reliability of a product before making buying decisions. This is especially true for safety-critical and embedded software products.

Reliability of the software product, essentially, denotes its trust-worthiness or dependability. According to IEEE, Reliability is defined as "The ability of a system or component to perform its required functions under stated conditions for a specified period of time." IEEE 982.1-1988 defines Software Reliability Management as "The process of optimizing the reliability of software through a program that emphasizes software error prevention, fault detection and removal, and the use of measurements to maximize reliability in light of project constraints such as resources, schedule and performance." Using these definitions, software reliability is comprised of three activities:

1. Error prevention.
2. Fault detection and removal.
3. Measurements to maximize reliability, specifically, measures that support the first two activities.

2. ERRORS, FAULTS AND FAILURES

The terms errors, faults and failures have different meanings, they are often used interchangebly. In software:

An error is usually a programmer action or omission that results in a fault.
A fault is a software defect that causes a failure.
A failure is the unacceptable departure of a program operation from program specifications.

Hardware failure is inherently different from the software failures. Most hardware failure is due to component wear and tear. A logic gate can get stuck at a 1 or 0, or a resistor might have short-circuited. To fix hardware faults, one has to either replace or repair the failed part. On the other hand, a software product would continue to fail until the error is tracked down and either the design or the code is changed. For this reason, when hardware is repaired its reliability is maintained at the level that existed before the failure occurred; whereas when a software failure is repaired, the reliability may either increase or decrease (reliability may decrease if a bug fix introduces new errors).

3. HARDWARE *VS.* SOFTWARE RELIABILITY

Reliability behaviour for hardware and software is very different. To put this fact in a different perspective, hardware reliability study is concerned with stability (for example, the inter-failure duration remain constant). On the other hand, software reliability study aims at reliability growth (i.e. inter-failure duration increases).

FIG. 6.1
Change in Failure Rates of a Product

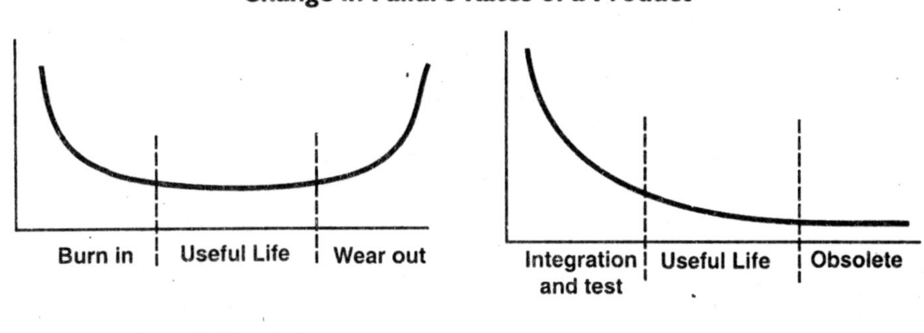

Hardware Failure Rate

Software Failure Rate

The change in failure rate over the product lifetime for a typical hardware product and a software product are sketched in Figure 6.1. Observe that the failure rate is high initially but decreases as the faulty components are identified and removed. The system then enters its useful life. After some time (called the product lifetime) the components wear out, and the failure rate increases. This gives the plot of hardware reliability over time characteristics bath tub shape. On the other hand, for software, the failure rate is at its highest during integration and testing phases. As the system is tested, more and more errors are identified and moved resulting in a reduced failure rate. This error removal continues at a slower pace during the useful life of product. As the software becomes obsolete, no more error correction occurs and the failure rate remains unchanged.

To increase the reliability by preventing software errors, the focus must be on comprehensive requirements and a comprehensive testing plan, ensuring all requirements are tested. Focus, also, must be on the maintainability of the software since there will be a "useful life" phase where sustaining engineering will be needed. Therefore, to prevent software errors, we must:

1. Start with the requirements, ensuring the product developed is the specified one, all requirements clearly and accurately specify the final product functionality.
2. Ensure the code can easily support sustaining engineering without infusing additional errors.
3. A comprehensive test program, that verifies all functionality stated in the requirements, is included.

4. QUALITY FACTORS IMPACTING RELIABILITY

IEEE Std 982.2-1988 includes the diagram in Figure 6.2, indicating the relationship of reliability to the different life cycle phases.

FIG. 6.2

Quality Factors Impacting Reliability

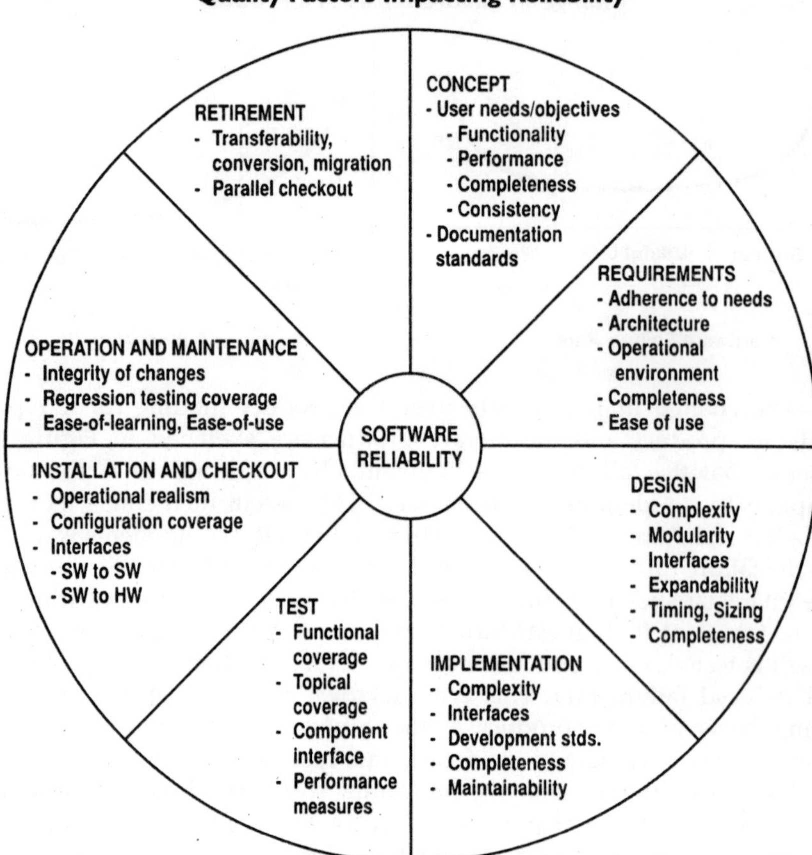

In focusing on error prevention for reliability, we need to identify and measure the quality attributes applicable at different life cycle phases. As discussed previously, we need to specifically focus on requirements, design, implementation, and test phases.

5. RELIABILITY METRICS

The reliability requirements for different categories of software products may be different. For this reason, it is necessary that the level of reliability required for a software product should be specified in the SRS (software requirement specification) document. In order to do this, we need some metrics to quantitatively express the reliability of a software product.

A good reliability measure should be observer-independent, so that different people can agree on the degree of reliability that the system has. For example, there are precise techniques for measuring performance, which would result in obtaining the same performance value irrespective of who is carrying out the performance measurement. However, in practice it is very difficult to formulate a precise reliability measurement technique. The next best case is to have measures that correlate with reliability. We define six reliability metrics which can be used to quantify the reliability of software products.

5.1 Rate of Occurrence of Failure (ROCOF)

ROCOF measure the frequency of occurrence of unexpected behaviors (i.e. failures). The ROCOF measure of a software product can be obtained by observing the behaviour of a software product in operation over a specified time interval and then calculating the total number of failures during this interval.

5.2 Mean Time to Failure (MTTF)

MTTF is the average time between two successive failures, observed over a large number of failures. To measure MTTF, we can record the failure data for n failures. Let the failures occur at the time instants t_1, t_2, ..., t_n. Then, MTTF can be calculated as:

$$\Sigma\ (t_{i+1}-t_i)\ /\ (n-1) \qquad i=1,\ n$$

It is important to note that only run-time is considered in the time measurements, i.e. the time for which the system is down to fix the error. The boot time etc., is not taken into account in the time measurements and the clock is stopped at these times.

5.3 Mean Time to Repair (MTTR)

Once failure occurs, some time is required to fix the error. MTTR measure the average time it takes to track the error causing the failure and then to fix them.

5.4 Mean Time Between Failure (MTBF)

We can combine the MTTF and MTTR metric to get the MTBF metric:

MTBF = MTTF + MTTR

Thus, MTBF of 300 hours indicate that is generally calculated by dividing: t: total test hours by f: once a failure occurs, the next failure is expected to occur only after 300 hours. In this case, the time measurements are real time and not the execution time as in MTTF.

5.5 Probability of Failure on Demand (POFOD)

Unlike the other metrics discussed, this metric does not explicitly involve time measurements. POFOD measures the likelihood of the system failing when a service request is made. For example, a POFOD of 0.001 would mean that 1 out of every 1000 service requests would result in a failure.

5.6 Availability

Availability of a system is a measure of how likely will the system be available for use over a given period of time. This metric not only consider the number of failures occurring during a time interval, but also takes into account the repair time of a system when a failure occurs.

All the above reliability metrics are concerned around the probability of occurrence of system failure but take no account of the consequence of failure.

Measurement is commonplace in other engineering field, but not in software engineering. Though frustrating, the quest of quantifying software reliability has never ceased. Measuring software reliability remains a difficult problem because we don't have a good understanding of the nature of software. We can not find a suitable way to measure software reliability, and most of the aspects related to software reliability. There has been extensive work in measuring reliability using mean time between failure and mean time to failure.[1] Successful modeling has been done to predict error rates and reliability.[1,2,3] These activities address some aspects of reliability, identifying and removing faults so that the software works as expected with the specified reliability. These measurements have been successfully applied to software as well as hardware.

An alternate measure uses calculated MTBF to determine a measurement of reliability

R = e- (t/m)

where R being the probability a device will perform for t is target life-time, m is the MTBF.

Note that:

(a) Usefulness for the software has yet to be determined.
(b) Target life-time for software can not be predicted. Generally, it is always much longer than anyone thought reasonable.

6. CONCLUSION

Software reliability is a key part in software quality. Software reliability measurement is native. Software reliability cannot be directly measured, so other related factors are measured to estimate the software reliability and compare it among products. Metrics to measure software reliability do exist and can be used initially in the requirements phase. At each phase of the development life cycle, potential areas of problems are identified by the metrics, after that they are developed, decrease the cost and prevent potential ripple effects from the changes, later in the development life cycle. Metrics used early can aid in detection and correction of requirement faults that will lead to prevention of errors later in the life cycle. The cost benefits of finding and correcting problems in the requirement phase has been demonstrated to be at least a factor of 14, making a strong argument for pursuing this approach.

References

1. John, D. Musa, Anthony Iannino, and Kazuhira Okumoto, Software Reliability: Measurement, Prediction, Application, McGraw-Hill Book Company, 1987, ISBN 0-07-044093-X.
2. Triantafyllos, G., S. Vassiliadis and W. Kobrosly, "On the Prediction of Computer Implementation Faults via Static Error Prediction Models," *Journal of Systems and Software*, Vol. 28, No. 2, February 1995, pp. 129-42.
3. Waterman, R.E and L.E. Hyatt, "Testing—When Do I Stop?", (Invited) International Testing and Evaluation Conference, Washington, DC, October 1994.
4. IEEE Standard 610.12-1990 Glossary of Software Engineering Terminology.
5. Kitchenham, Barbara, Pfleeger, Shari Lawrence, Software Quality: The Elusive Target, IEEE Software 13, 1 (January 1996) 12-21.
6. Gillies, A.C., Software Quality, Theory and Management, Chapman Hall Computing Series, London, UK, 1992.
7. IEEE Standard 982.2-1987 Guide for the Use of Standard Dictionary of Measures to Produce Reliable Software.
8. Rajib Mall, "Fundamental of Software Engineering", Department of Computer Science and Engineering, India Institute of Technology, Kharagpur.
9. Mordechai Ben-Menachem and Garry S. Marliss, Software Quality: Producing Practical, consistent Software, 1997, ISBN 1-85032-326-7.
10. Wilson, W., Rosenberg, L., Hyatt, L., Automated Quality Analysis of Natural Language Requirement Specifications in Proc., Fourteenth Annual Pacific Northwest Software Quality Conference, Portland OR, 1996.
11. Rosenberg, L., and Hammer, T., Metrics for Quality Assurance and Risk Assessment, Proc. Eleventh International Software Quality Week, San Francisco, CA, 1998.
12. Rosenberg, L., Metrics for Object-oriented Environment, EFAITP/AIE Third Annual Software Metrics Conference, 1997.
13. Hammer, T., Rosenberg, L., Huffman, L., Hyatt, L., Measuring Requirements Testing in Proc. International Conference on Software Engineering (Boston MA, May 1997), IEEE Computer Society Press.
14. Michael R. Lyu, Handbook of Software Reliability Engineering. McGraw-Hill Publishing, 1995, ISBN 0-07-039400-8.
15. Reliability Analysis Center, Introduction to Software Reliability: A state of the Art Review. Reliability Analysis Center (RAC), 1996.
16. Paul Rook, editor, Software Reliability, Handbook, Centre for Software Reliability, City University, London, U.K., 1990.
17. Keene, S.J., Comparing Hardware and Software Reliability, *Reliability Review*, 14(4), December 1994, pp. 5-7, 21.
18. John, D. Musa, Introduction to Software Reliability Engineering and Testing, 8th International Symposium on Software Reliability Engineering (Case Studies), November 2-5, 1997. Albuquerque, New Mexico.

7

A Study of Object-oriented Software Metrics

BALRAJ KUMAR AND PAWAN KUMAR

ABSTRACT

Quality Assurance is one of the most desired characteristic of software which many software products fail to possess. Current software market is driven mostly by urgency and competition. This poses a serious problem to software quality assurance, customer satisfaction and reliability of the software products. One of the methods to ensure software quality is a metrics-based approach. Software metrics have been used to quantitatively evaluate software products.

This paper attempts to discuss different types of traditional metrics as well as metrics used for the measurement of quality of object-oriented design. It also discusses the features like classes, inheritance and polymorphism etc., which differentiate object-oriented approach from conventional approach and why the traditional metrics are inadequate for measuring quality of object-oriented design. It also discusses the various measurable aspects of object-oriented approach and the metrics used for measuring them.

1. INTRODUCTION

Research on software metrics has been an ongoing process for several decades. Initially, in 1970s, they were used for cost estimation only, but now they are also being used for measurement of other various aspects of software development like quality, productivity, etc. Software metrics are used by all people involved in the development processes including customers and managers on one hand, and project leaders, designers and programmers on the other hand.

Object-oriented design and development are popular concepts in today's software development environment. The object-oriented approach centers around modeling the real world in terms of objects; in contrast, the traditional procedural approaches emphasize a function-oriented view which separates data and procedures. In object-oriented design, each kind of data and related operations are collected into a single system entity.

Object-oriented software development requires a different approach from more traditional functional decomposition and data flow-based development methods. This includes the software metrics used to evaluate object-oriented software. Therefore, even though the traditional software metrics are modified to assess object-oriented software system, they are inadequate to cover all the new and unique aspects of object-orientation.

The following questions need consideration:

- Which concepts and structures in object-oriented design affect the quality of the software?
- Can traditional metrics measure the critical object-oriented structures?
- If so, are the threshold values for the metrics the same for object-oriented designs as for functional/data designs?
- Which of the many new metrics found in the literature are useful to measure the critical concepts of object-oriented structures?

The object-oriented metric criteria, therefore, is to be used to evaluate the following attributes:

- *Efficiency*—Are the constructs efficiently designed?
- *Complexity*—Could the constructs be used more effectively to decrease the architectural complexity?
- *Understandability*—Does the design increase the psychological complexity?
- *Reusability*—Does the design quality support possible reuse?
- *Testability/Maintainability*—Does the structure support ease of testing and changes?

2. CHARACTERISTICS OF OBJECT-ORIENTED PROGRAMMING PARADIGM

Object-oriented Programming (OOP) is a programming paradigm that uses objects and their interactions to design applications and computer programs. Programming techniques may include features such as, encapsulation, modularity, polymorphism and inheritance. The term 'object-oriented' means that software is organized as a collection of discrete objects that encapsulate both data structure and behaviour. Generally, the characteristics required by an object-oriented approach include four aspects: identification, classification, polymorphism, and inheritance.

- *Class* is a cohesive package that consists of a particular kind of metadata. It describes the rules by which *objects* behave; these objects are referred to as instances of that class. A class has both an interface and a structure. The interface describes how the class and its instances can be interacted with via methods, while the structure describes how the data is partitioned into fields within an instance.
- *Polymorphism* means the same operation may be implemented differently on different classes. The specific implementation of an operation by a certain class is called a method. An object-oriented operator that is polymorphic, may have more than one method implementing it.
- *Inheritance* is the mechanism that allows sharing of attributes and operations among classes based on a hierarchical relationship. Using inheritance, a class can be refined into sub-classes. Each sub-class inherits all the properties of its superclass and may add its own unique properties. The properties of the superclass need not be repeated in each sub-class.

3. TRADITIONAL METRICS

3.1 Methods-based Metrics

In an object-oriented system, traditional metrics are generally applied to the methods that comprise the operations of a class. A method is a component of an object that operates on data in response to a message and is defined as part of the declaration of a class. Methods reflect how a problem is broken into segments and the capabilities other classes expect from a given class. Two traditional metrics are discussed here: cyclomatic complexity and size (line counts).

3.1.1 Cyclomatic Complexity (CC)

Cyclomatic Complexity is used to evaluate the complexity of an algorithm in a method. A method with a low cyclomatic complexity is generally better, although it may mean that decisions are deferred through message passing, not that the method is not complex. Cyclomatic complexity cannot be used to measure the complexity of a class because of inheritance, but cyclomatic complexity of individual methods can be combined with other measures to evaluate the complexity of the class. In general, the cyclomatic complexity for a method should be below ten, indicating decisions are deferred through message passing. Although this metric is specifically applicable to the evaluation of quality attribute Complexity, it is related to all of the other attributes.

3.1.2 Size (LOC)

Size of a method is used to evaluate the ease of understandability of the code by developers and maintainers. Size can be measured in a variety of ways. These include counting all physical lines of code, the number of statements, and the number of blank lines. Thresholds for evaluating the size measures vary depending on the coding language used and the complexity of the method. However, since size affects ease of understanding, routines of large size will always pose a higher risk in the attributes of Understandability, Reusability, and Maintainability.

3.2 Comment Percentage (CP)

The line counts done to compute the size metric can be expanded to include a count of the number of comments, both on-line (with code) and stand-alone. The comment percentage is calculated by the total number of comments divided by the total lines of code less the number of blank lines. The SATC has found that a comment percentage of about 30% is most effective. Since comments assist developers and maintainers, this metric is used to evaluate the attributes of Understandability, Reusability, and Maintainability.

4. OBJECT-ORIENTED METRICS

Many different metrics have been proposed for object-oriented systems. The object-oriented metrics that were chosen by the SATC measure principle structures that, if improperly designed, negatively affect the design and code quality attributes.

The selected object-oriented metrics are primarily applied to the concepts of classes, coupling, inheritance and polymorphism. For some of the object-oriented metrics discussed here, multiple definitions are given, since researchers and practitioners have not reached a common definition or counting methodology. In some cases, the counting method for a metric is determined by the software analysis package being used to collect the metrics.

4.1 Metrics used in Class

A class is a template from which objects can be created. This set of objects share a common structure and a common behaviour manifested by the set of methods. Three class metrics described here measure the complexity of a class using the class's methods, messages and cohesion.

4.1.1 Method based Metrics

A method is an operation upon an object and is defined in the class declaration.

4.1.1.1 Weighted Methods per Class (WMC)

The WMC is a count of the methods implemented within a class or the sum of the complexities of the methods (method complexity is measured by cyclomatic complexity).

The second measurement is difficult to implement since not all methods are accessible within the class hierarchy due to inheritance. The number of methods and the complexity of the methods involved is a predictor of how much time and effort is required to develop and maintain the class. The larger the number of methods in a class, the greater the potential impact on children, since children inherit all of the methods defined in a class. Classes with large number of methods are likely to be more application specific, limiting the possibility of reuse. This metric measures Understandability, Maintainability, and Reusability.

4.1.2 Message-based Metrics

A message is a request that an object makes of another object to perform an operation. The operation executed as a result of receiving a message is called a method. The next metric looks at methods and messages within a class.

4.1.2.1 Response for a Class (RFC)

The RFC is the carnality of the set of all methods that can be invoked in response to a message to an object of the class or by some method in the class. This includes all methods accessible within the class hierarchy. This metric looks at the combination of the complexity of a class through the number of methods and the amount of communication with other classes. The larger the number of methods that can be invoked from a class through messages, the greater the complexity of the class. If a large number of methods can be invoked in response to a message, the testing and debugging of the class becomes complicated since it requires a greater level of understanding on the part of the tester. A worst case value for possible responses will assist in the appropriate allocation of testing time. This metric evaluates Understandability, Maintainability, and Testability.

4.1.3 Cohesion-based Metrics

Cohesion is the degree to which methods within a class are related to one another and work together to provide well-bounded behaviour. Effective object-oriented designs maximize cohesion since it promotes encapsulation. The third class metrics investigates cohesion.

4.1.3.1 Lack of Cohesion of Methods (LCOM)

LCOM measures the degree of similarity of methods by data input variables or attributes (structural properties) of classes. Any measure of separateness of methods helps identify flaws in the design of classes. There are at least two different ways of measuring cohesion:

1. Calculate for each data field in a class what percentage of the methods use that data field. Average the percentages then subtract from 100 percent. Lower percentages mean greater cohesion of data and methods in the class.
2. Methods are more similar if they operate on the same attributes. Count the number of disjoint sets produced from the intersection of the sets of attributes used by the methods.

High cohesion indicates good class subdivision. Lack of cohesion or low cohesion increases complexity, thereby increasing the likelihood of errors during the development process. Classes with low cohesion could probably be sub-divided into two or more sub-classes with increased cohesion. This metric evaluates Efficiency and Reusability.

4.1.4 Coupling-based Metrics

Coupling is a measure of the strength of association established by a connection from one entity to another. Classes (objects) are coupled three ways:

1. When a message is passed between objects, the objects are said to be coupled.
2. Classes are coupled when methods declared in one class use methods or attributes of the other classes.
3. Inheritance introduces significant tight coupling between super-classes and their sub-classes.

Since good object-oriented design requires a balance between coupling and inheritance, coupling measures focus on non-inheritance coupling.

4.1.4.1 Coupling Between Object Classes (CBO)

CBO is a count of the number of other classes to which a class is coupled. It is measured by counting the number of distinct non-inheritance related class hierarchies on which a class depends. Excessive coupling is detrimental to modular design and prevents reuse. The more independent a class is, the easier its reuse in another application. The larger the number of couples, the higher the sensitivity to changes in other parts of the design and therefore maintenance is more difficult. Strong coupling complicates a system since a module is harder to understand, change or correct by itself if it is interrelated with other modules. Complexity can be reduced by designing systems with the weakest possible coupling between modules. This improves modularity and promotes encapsulation. CBO evaluates Efficiency and Reusability.

4.2 Metrics based on Inheritance

Another design abstraction in object-oriented systems is the use of inheritance. Inheritance is a type of relationship among classes that enables programmers to reuse previously defined classes including variables and operators. Inheritance decreases complexity by reducing the number of operations and operators, but this abstraction of classes can make maintenance and design difficult. The two metrics used to measure the amount of inheritance are the depth and breadth of the inheritance hierarchy.

4.2.1 Depth of Inheritance Tree (DIT)

The depth of a class within the inheritance hierarchy is the maximum length from the class node to the root of the tree and is measured by the number of ancestor classes. The deeper a class is within the hierarchy, the greater the number methods it is likely to inherit making it more complex to predict its behaviour. Deeper trees constitute greater design complexity since more methods and classes are involved, but the greater the potential for reuse of inherited methods. A support metric for DIT is the Number of Methods Inherited (NMI). This metric primarily evaluates efficiency and reuse, but also relates to understandability and testability.

4.2.2 Number of Children (NOC)

The number of children is the number of immediate subclasses subordinate to a class in the hierarchy. It is an indicator of the potential influence a class can have on the design and on the system. The greater the number of children, the greater the likelihood of improper abstraction of the parent and may be a case of misuse of sub-classing. But greater the number of children, greater is the reusability since inheritance is a form of reuse. If a class has a large number of children, it may require more testing of the methods of that class, thus increase the testing time. NOC, therefore, primarily evaluates efficiency, reusability, and testability.

4.3 Metrics-based on Polymorphism

In the context of implementation, polymorphism is defined such that an operation may behave differently in different classes. Metrics of polymorphism will reveal the efforts required to test the super-class caused by polymorphism. At the design stage, the polymorphism can be found out through the object model, since methods with same name but different signatures will appear in different classes in an inheritance hierarchy. When the coding is finished, different size of each polymorphic method will reveal the efficiency of run-time method resolution brought by polymorphism mechanism.

4.3.1 Polymorphism Factor-based on Overriding Methods (PFOM)

The metric PFOM can be used in the early stage of software development life cycle. It represents the efforts needed for testing super class due to methods being overridden in subclasses. PFOM can be defined as:

$$\text{PFOM} = m / n$$

where m is the actual number of overridden methods and n is the maximum possible number of overriding methods.

In C++, polymorphic methods are declared as *virtual* in the superclass, and overridden in the subclasses. There are other multiple defined scenarios in C++, such as operator overloading and multiple constructors. Since multiple constructors have closer relationship with the host class than with sub-class, we will not put multiple constructors in this metric.

In the above formula, the denominator indicates the total number of methods defined for the same functions. The numerator indicates the actual number of overridden methods. Therefore, the final value of PFOM will be between *0 (zero)* and *1 (one)*.

4.3.2 Average Changing Rate of Virtual Methods (ACRV)

This metric compares number of statements in the virtual methods defined in super-class and those in its overridden versions in sub-classes. C++ contains facilities for run-time method resolution. Method resolution and the ability to override a method in a sub-class are only available if the method is declared *virtual* in the super-class. The implementation of run-time method resolution is efficient. At run-time, a virtual method is resolved by retrieving the method structure from the object and selecting a member to find the method address. We can use the metric ACRV to check the efficiency by using run-time method resolution. It is defined as below:

$$\text{ACRV (classname)\_tree} = \frac{\sum_{i=1}^{m}\sum_{j=1}^{k} NSV(subclass\_i, virtual\_method\_j)}{m * \sum_{j=1}^{k} NSV(superclass, virtual\_method\_j)}$$

where

NSV(class, method)	indicates number of statements in *method* defined in *class*. It is zero in the program, we set it to 0.5. The justification for this arrangement is not to leave the denominator as zero. Moreover, a value of 0.5 is reasonably small.
m	number of all the sub-classes in the *superclass-tree*.
k	number of virtual-methods defined in the *super-cluss*.

When subclasses chooses to implement a virtual method, the number of statements for this method in the subclass d increase. The numerator will be greater than or equal to the denominator. The value of *XCRV (super-class-tree)* will be greater than or equal to zero. When ACRV is equal to zero, it means no subclass implement *any* of the virtual methods, which is less possible to happen. The more methods are implemented, the greater the value for ACRV.

5. CONCLUSION

Five criterions for quality code and design are: Efficiency, Complexity, Understandability, Reusability, and Testability/Maintainability. The Software Assurance Technology Center (SATC) has proposed nine metrics for object-oriented systems covering concepts like classes, methods, cohesion, coupling, inheritance and polymorphism. That is, acceptable ranges for each metric will have to be developed, based on the effect of the metric on desirable software qualities.

REFERENCES

1. Chidamber, Shyam and Kemerer, Chris, "A Metrics Suite for Object-oriented Design", IEEE Transactions on Software Engineering, June, 1994, pp. 476-92.
2. Hudli, R., Hoskins, C., Hudli, A., "Software Metrics for Object-oriented Designs", IEEE, 1994.
3. Lee, Y., Liang, B., Wang, F., "Some Complexity Metrics for Object-oriented Programs Based on Information Flow", Proceedings: CompEuro, March, 1993, pp. 302-10.
4. Lorenz, Mark and Kidd, Jeff, Object-oriented Software Metrics, Prentice Hall Publishing, 1994.
5. McCabe and Associates, McCabe Object-oriented Tool User's Instructions, 1994.
6. Rosenberg, Linda and Hyatt, Lawrence, Set Laboratories, UX Metrics, 1994.
7. Rumbaugh, M. Blaha, W. Premerlani, F. Eddy, and W. Lorensen. Object-oriented Modeling and Design. Prentice Hall, Englewood Cliffs, New Jersey, 1991.
8. K.H. MoUer and D.J. Paulish. Software Metncs. Chapman & Hail, London UK, 1993.
9. F.P. Ginac. Software Quality Assurance, Prentice Hall, Upper Saddle River, New Jersy, USA, 1998.
10. S.R. Chidamber and C.F. Kemerer. "A Metncs Suite for Object-oriented Design", IEEE Transactions on Software Engineering, Vol. 20, No. 6, pp. 476-93, June 1994.

8

Overview of Runtime Coupling and Cohesion Metrics for Object-oriented Software Systems

PARAMVIR SINGH, GEETA SIKKA AND HARDEEP SINGH

ABSTRACT

Measuring the performance of an object-oriented software system at runtime is one of the thrilling topics of research in the field of software engineering. This paper collects some latest metrics for measuring the performance of object-oriented software at runtime. These metrics, called the Dynamic or Runtime object-oriented metrics, include some proposed and some empirically evaluated metrics till date.

1. INTRODUCTION

In today's software-oriented world, the key to success for a software application is its regular performance appraisal that further demands certain measurement criteria that can be effectively used to measure the working performance of a software application. Software metrics measure different aspects of software complexity and thus play an important role in analyzing and improving software quality.[11] Previous studies have shown that they provide useful information on external quality aspects of software such as its maintainability, reusability, reliability, fault proneness, etc. by relating them to important characteristics of object-oriented software such as size, polymorphism, inheritance, coupling and cohesion.

In recent years many researchers and practitioners have proposed a number of software metrics for object-oriented software, for example, the CK suite of metrics proposed by Chidamber and Kemerer,[16,17] metric set proposed by Lorenz and Kidd,[12] and MOOD metric set proposed by Harrison *et. al.*[13] Most of these software metrics quantify different aspects of the complexity of the source code, based on a *static analysis* of that code. These static metrics, such as Lines of Code (LOC), Weighted Methods per Class (WMC), Depth of Inheritance Tree (DIT), etc. have been applied to many real world applications in the past[10,14] and have proved to be quite useful in measuring the software performance.

However, these static metrics are not capable of predicting the *dynamic behaviour* of a software application. This is because the behaviour of a software application is not only influenced by the complexity but also by the operational or runtime environment of the source code. A latest research by Sherif M. Yacoub *et. al.*[15] has indicated that useful information may be obtained from a measure of quantifying the dynamic complexity of software in its operational environment. Thus, it is possible to quantify the quality of a software product using a set of dynamic metrics calculated at run-time that evaluate the product's complexity. These metrics by themselves can provide us with useful information, and can also help to calibrate the information obtained from a static analysis.

Working on the same lines, many modern researchers like Aine Mitchell *et. al.*,[1,3] Eric Arisholm[8,9] and Sherif M. Yacoub *et. al.*[15] have come up with some dynamic or runtime object-oriented software metrics in their respective on-going researches. Most of these metrics consist of dynamic cohesion and coupling metrics. This paper defines these dynamic cohesion and coupling object-oriented software metrics in brief.

The remainder of this paper is organized as follows. Section 2 describes some brand new Runtime Cohesion Metrics. Section 3 frames some Runtime Coupling Metrics. Section 4 concludes the paper quoting some future work in Runtime Object-oriented Metrics.

2. RUNTIME COHESION METRICS

Cohesiveness of a class is measured by the degree of similarity in methods of that class. Consider a class A having a method set $\{M_i\}$ and an instance variable set $\{I_i\}$. Then, the degree of similarity in a method pair $\{M_1,M_2\}$ having an instance variable pair $\{I_1, I_2\}$ is given by:

$$\sigma(M_1, M_2) = \{I_1\} \cap \{I_2\}$$

The *degree of similarity* of methods is a major aspect of object class cohesiveness. If an object class has different methods performing different operations on the same set of instance variables, the class is cohesive.

Cohesion of a class in a static code can largely vary from cohesion at runtime. This fact has been strengthened by the introduction of some new object-oriented metrics that are calculated at runtime. This section describes such a few metric sets.

Aine Mitchell and James Power [1] in their currently ongoing work have proposed and empirically validated two Runtime Cohesion Metrics for object-oriented systems. These are:

(i) Runtime or Dynamic Simple Lack of Cohesion in Methods (R_{LCOM}).
(ii) Runtime or Dynamic Call-Weighted Lack of Cohesion in Methods (RW_{LCOM}).

These metrics are briefly explained next.

2.1 Runtime or Dynamic Simple Lack of Cohesion in Methods (R_{LCOM})

R_{LCOM} for a class A is the number of pairs of methods in the class that have no instance variables in common, $|P|$, minus the number of pairs of methods that have common instance variables, $|Q|$ at runtime. However, if $|P| < |Q|$, R_{LCOM} is zero. If none of the methods in a class display any instance behaviour that is they do not use any instance variables, then they have no similarity, and thus the R_{LCOM} will be zero. This metric is an extension of the Chidamber and Kemerer's LCOM metric [16,17].

Consider a class with n methods $m_1, \ldots\ldots m_n$. Let $\{I_i\}$ represent the set of instance variables referenced by method m_i at run-time. Then P and Q are defined as:

$$P = \{(I_i , I_j) | I_i \cap I_j = \phi\}$$
$$Q = \{(I_i , I_j) | I_i \cap I_j \neq \phi\}$$

Then R_{LCOM} can be defined as

$$R_{LCOM} \begin{Bmatrix} |P| - |Q| \\ 0 \end{Bmatrix} \; if \; \begin{Bmatrix} |P| > \} Q | \\ Otherwise \end{Bmatrix}$$

2.1.1 Metric Effect

It is an inverse cohesion measure. A low value of R_{LCOM} for a class indicates that this class is cohesive. As negative values are not permitted, the best possible value obtainable is zero. The higher the value of R_{LCOM}, the less cohesive the class.

If a class A has a high R_{LCOM} than a class B, this may indicate that class A is more complex than class B, as low cohesion increases complexity. Class A may therefore be more difficult to maintain, be susceptible to a greater number of errors and be more difficult to reuse in other applications.

One of the main objectives of object-orientated programming is to design classes that encapsulate their objects. A low R_{LCOM} value indicates the methods of a class are cohesive and this will promote the encapsulation of its objects.

A high value may indicate flaws in the design of a class and may indicate the class may need to be split into a number of smaller sub-classes.

A high R_{LCOM} value for a class indicated that its behaviour would be more difficult to predict, as the class will not be functioning to perform a single function.

2.2 Runtime or Dynamic Call-Weighted Lack of Cohesion in Methods (RW_{LCOM})

RW_{LCOM} is the sum of the number of accesses to instance variables from the number of pairs of methods in the class that have no common instance variables, QP, minus the sum of the number of accesses by the number of pairs of methods that have common instance variables, ΣQ at runtime. If $\Sigma P < \Sigma Q$, RW_{LCOM} is zero. If no methods access any instance variables, P is equated to null.

Consider a class with n methods $m_1, \ldots\ldots m_n$. Let $\{I_i\}$ represent the set of instance variables referenced by method m_i at run-time. Then let N_i be the number of times method M_i dynamically accesses instance variables from the set $\{I_i\}$. There are n such sets $\{I_1\}, \ldots, \{I_n\}$.

$$P = \{(N_i + N_j) | I_i \cap I_j = \phi\}$$
$$Q = \{(N_i + N_j) | I_i \cap I_j \neq \phi\}$$

where $P = \Phi$, if $\{I_l\}, \ldots \{I_n) = \Phi$

Then RW_{LCOM} can be defined as :

$$\begin{Bmatrix} \sum P - \sum Q & \text{if } \sum P > \sum Q \\ 0 & \textit{Otherwise} \end{Bmatrix}$$

This measure is an extension of the RW_{LCOM}, modified to take into account the number of accesses to instance variables by the methods contained within a class.

2.2.1 Metric Effect

The objective of this study was to determine how dynamically cohesive a class was. If two classes A and B achieved an equivalent value for RW_{LCOM}, but the methods of class A accessed their instance variables four times of methods in class B, class A could be deemed to be more cohesive than class B as its methods and instance variables are more closely linked at runtime. This metric attempts to measure cohesion on a call weighted basis.

If a class *A* has a high RW_{LCOM} than a class *B*, this may indicate that class *A* is more complex than class *B*, as low cohesion increases complexity. Class *A* may therefore be more difficult to maintain, be susceptible to a greater number of errors and be more difficult to reuse in other applications.

One of the main objectives of object-orientated programming is to design classes that encapsulate their objects. A low RW_{LCOM} value indicates the methods of a class are cohesive and this will promote the encapsulation of its objects.

A high value may indicate flaws in the design of a class and may indicate the class may need to be split into a number of smaller sub-classes. A high RW_{LCOM} value for a class indicates that its behaviour will be more difficult to predict as the class will not be functioning to perform a single function.

3. RUNTIME COUPLING METRICS

Coupling: Two objects are coupled if and only if at least one of them acts upon the other. Let $X = (x, p(x))$ and $Y = (y, p(y))$ be two objects. Here x, y are the names by which the objects X, Y are represented and $p(x)$, $p(y)$ are their respective set of properties. X is said to act upon Y if the history of Y is affected by X, where *history* is defined as the chronologically ordered states that a thing traverses in time. Also,

$$p(x) = \{M_x\} \cup \{I_x\}$$
$$p(y) = \{M_y\} \cup \{I_y\}$$

where $\{M_i\}$ is the set of methods and $\{I_i\}$ is the set of instance variables of object i. Using the above definition of coupling, any action by $\{M_x\}$ on $\{M_y\}$ or $\{I_y\}$ constitutes coupling, as does any action by $\{M_y\}$ on $\{M_x\}$ or $\{I_x\}$.

3.1 Metrics by Aine Mitchell and James Power

Aine Mitchell and James Power have also proposed and empirically validated three Runtime Coupling Metrics for object-oriented systems. These metrics are:

(i) Runtime or Dynamic Coupling between Objects (CBO) for a class A.
(ii) Degree of Dynamic Coupling between class A and class B at runtime.
(iii) Degree of Dynamic Coupling within a given set of classes.

3.1.1 Runtime or Dynamic Coupling between Objects (CBO) for a Class A

The Runtime or Dynamic CBO for a class A is a count of the number of couples with other classes at runtime. This metric is a direct translation of the CBO metric proposed by Chidamber and Kemerer except, it examines how many classes a class A is coupled to at runtime.

Metric Effect

The greater the value obtained for this metric, the greater the number of classes class A will require to function. This will discourage the reuse of this class, as it will not be self-sufficient. It is desirable that classes be as independent as possible to promote reuse.

This metric may provide an indication of how rigorously an implementation may need to be tested. The greater the level of coupling present, the more rigorous testing needs to be.

Maintenance is made more difficult, the greater the Dynamic CBO is for a class, the class will not change to changes in other classes, the more couples there are.

3.1.2 Degree of Dynamic Coupling between Class A and Class B at Runtime

The Degree of Dynamic Coupling between two classes A and B, is a count of the amount of times a class A accesses methods or instances variables from a class B as a percentage of the total number of methods or instance variables accessed by A.

Degree of Dynamic Coupling from a class A to class B is given by

$$\left(\frac{\begin{array}{c}\text{No. of times } A \text{ accesses} \\ \text{methods of instance variables} \\ \text{from class } B \text{ at runtime}\end{array}}{\begin{array}{c}\text{Total no. of times} \\ \text{class } A \text{ accesses any methods} \\ \text{or instance variables}\end{array}} \times 100\right)$$

In the definition of static CBO, two classes are said to be coupled if one class uses the methods or instance variables contained in the other. Determining the level of coupling between these two classes is a matter of counting the number of times one class uses a method or instance variable from the other, relative to the total number of times it accesses any method or instance variable. This will give a measure of the degree of static coupling between two classes.

This can be translated to the dynamic state, that is, what is happening at runtime. A class A is said to be dynamically coupled to a class B if it accesses methods or instance variables from class B at runtime.

Metric Effect

The degree of coupling between two classes at runtime is useful to know as it reflects how dependent one class is on another. If this percentage is very high for a given class, this means that this class is heavily reliant on the other class to function. In other words it measures how tightly two classes are coupled together.

If a class A has a high value for dynamic degree of coupling to a class B, this will discourage the reuse of the class A, as it will be tightly dependent on class B and frequently request methods or instance variables from that class.

A class that is tightly coupled to another class will also be more difficult to maintain. Errors are more likely to propagate between classes that are tightly coupled together. A class that is tightly coupled to another class is more difficult to understand as its dynamic behaviour will be dependent on the other class.

3.1.3 Degree of Dynamic Coupling within a given Set of Classes

For a given set of classes $c_1, c_2, \ldots, c_n$, degree of dynamic coupling within a given set of classes is given by

$$\left(\frac{\begin{array}{c}\text{Sum of number of accesses}\\ \text{to methods or instance}\\ \text{variables outside each class}\end{array}}{\begin{array}{c}\text{Sum of total no. of}\\ \text{accesses from}\\ \text{these classes}\end{array}} \times 100 \right)$$

This metric is an extension of the metric called 'Degree of Dynamic Coupling between class A and class B at runtime', to indicate the level of dynamic coupling occurring within a given set of classes.

Metric Effect

For a given set of classes this metric will determine to what extent they are as a group accessing methods or instance variables outside of there own classes. This metric could be used, for example to test how reliant a group of classes are on one another. If this value is low, very few classes will be accessing methods or instance variables outside of their own class. This metric is useful if you want to compare groups of classes in an application.

3.2 Metrics by Sherif M. Yacoub *et. al.*

Sherif M. Yacoub *et. al.* [15] have also worked hard on these runtime metrics. They have put on as many as four Runtime Coupling metrics namely

(i) Export Object Coupling (EOC)
(ii) Object Request for Service (*OQFS*)
(iii) Import Object Coupling (IOC)
(iv) Object Response for Service (*OPFS*)

All these metrics are briefly quoted next.

3.2.1 Export Object Coupling (EOC)

$EOC_x(o_i, o_j)$, the export coupling for object o_i with respect to object o_j, is the percentage of the number of messages sent from o_i to o_j with respect to the total number of messages exchanged during the execution of the scenario x, where a scenario x, from a set of scenarios X, is a sequence of interactions between objects stimulated by input data or events. Let $M_x(o_i, o_j)$ be a set of messages sent from object o_i to o_j and MT_x be the total number of messages exchanged among objects during the execution of scenario x. Then

$$EOC_x(o_i, o_j) = \frac{\left|\{M_x(o_i, o_j) \mid o_i, o_j \in O \wedge o_i \neq o_j\}\right|}{MT_x} \times 100$$

Metric Effect

EOC is a measure of mutual coupling between two specific objects. Mutual coupling between objects is important for identifying possible sources for exporting errors, identifying tightly coupled objects, and testing interactions between objects. *EOC* can affect the following design quality attributes:

(i) *Maintainability:* A class whose object has higher *EOC* to another specific object would be more critical to changes due to maintenance and are more likely to export these maintenance changes to that specific object.

(ii) *Understandability*: An object sending many messages to another specific object (higher *EOC* count) is harder to understand because its dynamic behavior tightly depends on that particular object.

(iii) *Reusability*: An object with higher *EOC* to another specific object is less reusable because they tightly depend on another object and frequently request services from that particular object. The two objects are more likely to be used together.

(iv) *Error Propagation:* An object with high *EOC* is a source for error propagation since errors are more likely to propagate from the faulty source to the destination object as a result of the frequent messages sent to the destination.

3.2.2 Object Request for Service (OQFS)

OQFS is percentage of the total number of messages sent by the object o_i to all other objects in the design. It is given by:

$$OQFS_x(o_i) = \frac{\left|\{\sum_{j=1}^{K} M_x(o_i, o_j) \mid o_i, o_j \in O \wedge o_i \neq o_j\}\right|}{MT_x} \times 100 \text{ or } \sum_{j=1}^{K} EOC_x(O_i, O_j)$$

Metric Effect

A higher *OQFS* value could indicate that the calling object is active and hence sends many messages to other objects. *OQFS* also indicates that the object has complex behaviour because it frequently invokes other objects to perform services.

3.2.3 Import Object Coupling (IOC)

$IOC_x(o_i,o_j)$, the import coupling for object o_i with respect to object o_j, is the percentage of the number of messages received by object o_i and was sent by object o_j with respect to the total number of messages exchanged during the execution of the scenario x. $IOC_x(o_i,o_j)$ is given by:

$$IOC_x\,(o_i\,,\,o_j) = \frac{\left|\{M_x\,(o_j\,,o_i)\middle|o_i\,,o_j \in O \wedge o_i \neq o_j\}\right|}{MT_x} \times 100$$

Metric Effect

Similar to *EOC*, *IOC* is a measure of mutual object coupling between two specific objects. They differ in the direction of coupling, which is classified as *Import* and *Export*.[15] The distinction between the directions of coupling is important to distinguish which object has an impact on another, the direction of possible error propagation, and possible impacts of changes due to maintenance. *IOC* can affect the following design quality attributes:

(i) *Maintainability:* A class whose object has higher *IOC* to another specific object is more likely to import changes due to maintenance in the class from which that particular object is instantiated.

(ii) *Understandability*: An object receiving many messages from another specific object (higher *IOC* count) is harder to understand because it provides many services to that specific object. However, it can also provide simple services that are frequently required.

(iii) *Reusability*: An object with higher *IOC* to another specific object is more likely to be reused with the other object using its services.

(iv) *Error Propagation:* Faults in objects with higher *IOC* could easily manifest themselves into failures of the applications because services of these objects are frequently required by other objects.

3.2.4. Object Response For Service (OPFS)

OPFS is percentage of the total number of messages sent to the object o_i by all other objects in the application during the execution of a scenario x. It is given by:

$$OPFS_x\,(o_i) = \frac{\left|\{\bigcup_{j=1}^{K} M_x\,(o_i\,,o_j)\middle|o_i\,,o_j \in O \wedge o_i \neq o_j\}\right|}{MT_x} \times 100 \;\; or \;\; \sum_{j=1}^{K} IOC_x\,(O_i\,,O_j)$$

3.3 Metrics by Erik Arisholm

Eric Arisholm along with Briand and Foyen[8,9] came out with a new set of Runtime Coupling metrics divided along three orthogonal dimensions:

(i) Mapping – object or class.
(ii) Direction – import or export.
(iii) Strength – number of dynamic messages, distinct methods, or distinct classes.

3.3.1 *Import Coupling Metrics*

Dynamic import coupling metrics count the messages sent from an entity (object or class). Here the entity acts as a client. These metrics are defined next at the object-level and the class-level.

Object-level Import Coupling Metrics

Dynamic object-level import coupling metrics quantify the extent to which messages are sent from objects to other objects and classes in the system at runtime.

(i) IC_OD metric counts the number of messages sent from an object A during a given scenario.
(ii) IC_OM metric counts the number of different methods used by an object A to send all the messages in a given scenario x.
(iii) IC_OC metric counts the number of distinct classes to which an object A has sent messages in a given scenario x.

Class-level Import Coupling Metrics

These metrics quantify the extent to which messages are sent from a class to other classes and objects in a system at runtime.

(iv) IC_CD metric counts the number of messages sent from a class A during a given scenario x.
(v) IC_CM metric counts the number of different methods used by a class A to send all the messages in a given scenario x.
(vi) IC_CC metric counts the number of distinct classes to which a class A has sent messages in a given scenario x.

3.3.2 Export Coupling Metrics

Dynamic export coupling metrics count the messages received by an entity (object or class). Here the entity acts as a server. These metrics are defined next at the object-level and the class-level.

Object-level Export Coupling Metrics

Dynamic object-level export coupling metrics quantify the extent to which messages are received by objects from other objects and classes in the system at runtime.

(i) EC_OD metric counts the number of messages received by an object A during a given scenario.
(ii) EC_OM metric counts the number of different methods used by an object A to receive all the messages sent to it in a given scenario x.
(iii) EC_OC metric counts the number of distinct classes from which an object A has received messages in a given scenario x.

Class-level Export Coupling Metrics

Dynamic class-level export coupling metrics quantify the extent to which classes receive messages from other objects and classes in the system at runtime.

(i) *EC_CD:* EC_CD metric counts the number of messages received by a class A during a given scenario x.
(ii) *EC_CM:* EC_CM metric counts the number of different methods used by a class A to receive all the messages sent to it in a given scenario x.
(iii) *EC_CC:* EC_CC metric counts the number of distinct classes from which a class A has received messages in a given scenario x.

3.4 Metrics by Andy Zaidman *et. al.*

Following the metric set given by Sherif M. Yacoub *et. al.*, Andy Zaidman and Serge Demeyer[6] defined a metric called Class Request For Service (CQFS). This metric has been derived from Object Request For Service (OQFS) metric given by Yacoub *et. al.*

3.4.1 Class Request For Service (CQFS)

Class Request For Service (CQFS) metric measures export coupling at class-level. CQFS counts the number of messages sent by a class to the other classes or their objects during the execution of a program.

Let o_i represent an object instantiated by class c_x and o_j represent an object instantiated by class c_y. Let O and C represent the object and the class sets respectively. Then CQFS metric is given by

$$CQFS(cx) = \sum_{j=1}^{k} \left| \{ M_x(o_i, o_j) \middle| o_i \rightarrow c_x \wedge o_j \rightarrow c_y \wedge o_i, o_j \in O \wedge c_x, c_y \in C \wedge c_x \neq c_y \} \right|$$

As the sets are being used, calling the same method more than once will not increment the coupling count, i.e. the duplicate message sends are eliminated. In the context of program understanding, this can be seen as an advantage, as the user gets presented with less information.

On a negative note, some interesting forms of polymorphism are abstracted away. Take for example two instantiations of the same class. Due to a different parameter of one of the methods of these objects, the objects themselves can react differently due to polymorphism. Using CQFS, this behaviour gets abstracted away.

Also the condition $c_x \neq c_y$ eliminates cohesion. Cohesion has been eliminated as the class level coupling deals with inter-class and not intra-class relationships.

4. CONCLUSION AND FUTURE WORK

The evolution of the dynamic or runtime object-oriented software metrics has just begun and many such new dynamic metrics are yet to be found out. The whole of the software engineering community is looking forward to these new dynamic metrics. The research is going on in the direction of tracing a new set of dynamic object-oriented software metrics and measuring the performance of these metrics by applying them on certain open source software applications. Most of the metrics mentioned above have not been empirically validated yet that makes a good future work in software engineering field.

References

1. Aine Mitchell and James, F. Power, "Run-time Cohesion Metrics: An Empirical Investigation", *In Proceedings of International Conference on Software Engineering Research and Practice (SERP'04)*, Las Vegas, Nevada, pp. 532-37, June 21-24, 2004.
2. ———, "Toward a Definition of Run-time Object-oriented Metrics." *In Proceedings of 7th ECOOP Workshop on Quantitative Approaches in Object-Oriented Software Engineering (QAOOSE' 2003)*, Darmstadt, Germany, July 22, 2003.
3. ———, "Runtime Coupling Metrics for the Analysis of Java Programs—Preliminary results from SPEC and Grand Suites", *A Technical Report NUIM-CS-TR2003-07*, Dept. of Computer Science, National University of Ireland, Maynooth, Co. Kildare, Ireland, 2003.
4. ———, "An Empirical Investigation into the Dimensions of Run-time Coupling Metrics in Java Programs", *In Proceedings of the Third International Conference on the Principles and Practice of Programming in Java*, Las Vegas, Nevada, USA, June 16-18, 2004.
5. ———, "Run-time Cohesion Metrics for the Analysis of Java Programs—Preliminary Results from the SPEC and Grande Suites", *A Technical Report NUIM-CS-TR2003-08*, Dept. of Computer Science, National University of Ireland, Maynooth, Ireland, April 2003.
6. Andy Zaidman and Serge Demeyer, "Analyzing Large Event Traces with the Help of Coupling Metrics" *In Proceedings of the 4th International Workshop on OO Reengineering*, Universiteit Antwerpen, June, 2004.
7. Edward V. Berard, "Metrics for Object-Oriented Software Engineering", *A Technical Report*, The Object Agency Inc., 1993.

8. Erik Arisholm, "Dynamic Coupling Measures for Object-oriented Software", In Proceeding of 8th IEEE Symposium on Software Metrics (METRICS'02) pp. 33-42, 2002.
9. Eric Arisholm, Lionel C. Briand and Audum Foyen, "Dynamic Coupling Measurement for Objective-oriented Software", IEEE Transactions on Software Engineering, Vol. 30, n. 8, pp. 491-506 August 2004.
10. G. Denaro, L. Lavazza and M. Pezze, "An Empirical Evaluation of Object-oriented Metrics in Industrial Setting, "The 5th CaberNet Plenary Workshop, Porto Santo, Madeira Archipelago, Portugal, November 2003.
11. Linda, H., Rosenberg and Lawrence, E. Hyatt, "Software Quality Metrics for Object-oriented Environments", A NASA Technical Report, April 1995.
12. M. Lorenz and J. Kidd, Object-oriented Software Metrics, Prentice Hall, Englewood Cliffs, New Jersey, 1994.
13. Rachel Harrison, Steve J. Counsell, Reuben V. Nithi, "An Evaluation of the MOOD Set of Object-oriented Software Metrics", *IEEE Transactions on Software Engineering*, Vol. 24(6), pp. 491-96, June 1998.
14. Radu Marinescu, "Using Object-oriented Metrics for Automatic Design Flaws Detection in Large Scale Systems.", *In Proceedings of ECOOP '98 Workshops*, pp. 252-55, 1998.
15. Sherif, M. Yacoub *et. al.*, "Dynamic Metrics for Object-oriented Designs", *In Proceedings of the 6th International Symposium on Software Metrics*, p. 50, November 04-06, 1999.
16. S.R. Chidamber and C.F. Kemerer, "A Metrics Suite for Object-oriented Design," *IEEE Transactions Software Engg.*, Vol. 20, pp. 476-93, 1994.
17. S.R. Chidamber, and C.F. Kemerer, "Towards a Metrics Suite for Object-oriented Design", *In Proceedings of the Conference on Object-oriented Programming: Systems, Languages and Applications, (OOPSLA '91)*, SIGPLAN Notices, Vol. 26, No. 11, pp. 197-211, 1991.

9

Extension of UML Profile to Model Mobile Information Systems

ACHIN TYAGI AND SANJAY GOEL

ABSTRACT

In this paper, modeling of mobility of devices in mobile information systems is discussed. A new UML profile that extends a previous UML profile is proposed supporting existing real life case studies. A context aware case study, similar to services like R World from Reliance India, Airtel live services—dating on mobile phones at different locations, examination results on mobile devices, Location specific news service on mobile phones has been described and modeled. Important UML diagrams of the case study show the implementation of our proposed extended UML profile; and throw light on importance of inclusion of push and pull activities in UML profile.

1. INTRODUCTION

The introduction of small devices particularly mobile phones, stimulate a constant demand of applications on them. Applications that use data network of the Mobile Services for operator, are categorized in Mobile information systems. Tools are still not available in market to model these applications for mobile phones, whereas there are many desktop modeling tools—IBM Rational Rose, Microsoft Visio, UML Paradigm, etc. The architecture and flow of data in such systems is different due to mobility issues, which were discussed in detail in previous work. This paper is organized as follows. Section 2 gives a comparison of UML stereotypes. The *stereotype* concept provides a way of classifying (marking) elements so that they behave in some respects as if they were instances of new (virtual) metamodel constructs. Instances have the same structure (attributes, associations, operations) as a similar non-stereotyped instance of the same kind; the stereotype may specify additional constraints and required tagged values that apply to instances. In addition, a stereotype may be used to indicate a difference in meaning or usage between two elements with identical structure. Section 2 describes the changes that should be done in stereotypes proposed earlier in [2] to support our case study of mobile information system instead of the famous airplane, passenger example in previous work. We have proposed the extension by including push and pull stereotypes. This is supported by the argument that every mobile information system has push and pull operations. Without knowing their importance, we can't increase the efficiency in modeling by existing UML profile of [2]. Hence in section 3, we describe a case study of a mobile information system. Section 4 describes Sequence, Activity Diagrams according to the stereotypes evolved from our work. Section 5 describes the earlier work in UML profile extension for mobility. Our conclusion and future work are mentioned in Section 6.

2. MOBILE INFORMATION SYSTEMS INVOLVING MOBILITY OF MOBILE DEVICES

The introduction of UML profile in [2] is for mobile information systems. Table 9.1 gives the comparison between the stereotypes created for modeling the mobility of physical objects [1], with those that are proposed for modeling the information systems [2]. Hence the 'clone' stereotype of the first type has been dropped in the second. The authors in [1] described mobility issues of physical objects taking case study involving passenger, aeroplane, and airport objects as mobile objects. The work was taken forward in [2] for mobile information systems. Our research extends the UML profile discussed in latest work of [2].

2.1 Architecture of Mobile Information Systems for Informative Applications

The description of UML profile in [2] does not throw much light on the architecture of mobile information systems that support existing applications. Figure 1 describes the flow of content to be delivered on mobile devices. Every information system has some content to be delivered on mobile devices. Content acquisition is a stage where content is acquired by various sources. In our work, content is mainly text as we did not focus on multimedia applications. Customer interest profile is a database maintained by server applications for all mobile devices. It stores the

TABLE 9.1
Stereotypes Comparison with Earlier Work

Stereotypes suggested by Hubert Baumeister, Nora Koch, Piotr Kosiuczenko, and Martin Wirsing in [1]	*Stereotypes suggested by Vegard Dehlen and Jan Oyvind Aagedal in [2]*	*Our Additional suggested stereotypes from case study in section 3*
Location	Place	Place
Mobile	Mobile element	Mobile element
Move	Move	Move
Clone	None	None
Mobile Location	Mobile element	Mobile element
None	Mobile Software	Mobile Software
None	Network Connection	Network Connection
None	Migrate	Migrate
None	Connect	Connect
None	Node Location	Node Location
None	Software Deployment	Software Deployment
None	Mobility Manager	Mobility Manager
None	None	Push
None	None	Pull

interests of customers for a particular application. Customer device profile stores information about the mobile device of each customer. Handset information, SMS text capacity, supported technologies, Java enabled phone information are all stored here.

Mobile Phone informative applications, to name a few are—context aware Dating, context aware Movie ticket booking, Location specific News software, ring tone listing and download software, Mobile chat/messenger, Railways software. Figure 9.1 shows the architecture for such applications.

Take a brief example of context aware News application on a mobile phone. A person is currently in Chennai with his mobile handset e390 Samsung. He has a application on this device for getting location specific news. He queries the domain 'cricket' through this application, after which, news of cricket matches of Chennai get retrieved and displayed. When he feeds domain as Movies, news of tamil movies appear. News of Chennai is taken from a Chennai website. Next month, when he travels Kolkata and operates the software, Kolkata web location delivers Kolkata specific news to application server in Kolkata through RSS feeds, which is then delivered to him.

- *Content acquisition* is done through RSS feed of a local website. News from RSS feeds for a particular city is then stored in *media storage,* which is the database maintained by News server. Interest for this customer is cricket and movies which was already stored in

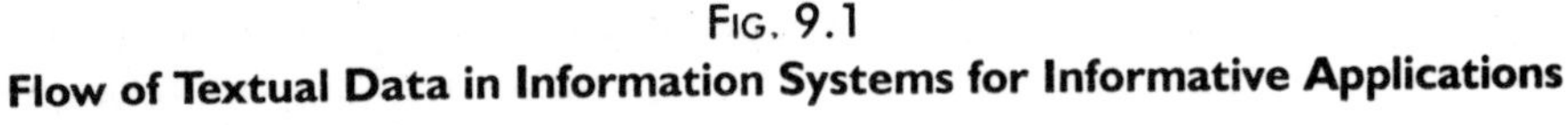

FIG. 9.1

Flow of Textual Data in Information Systems for Informative Applications

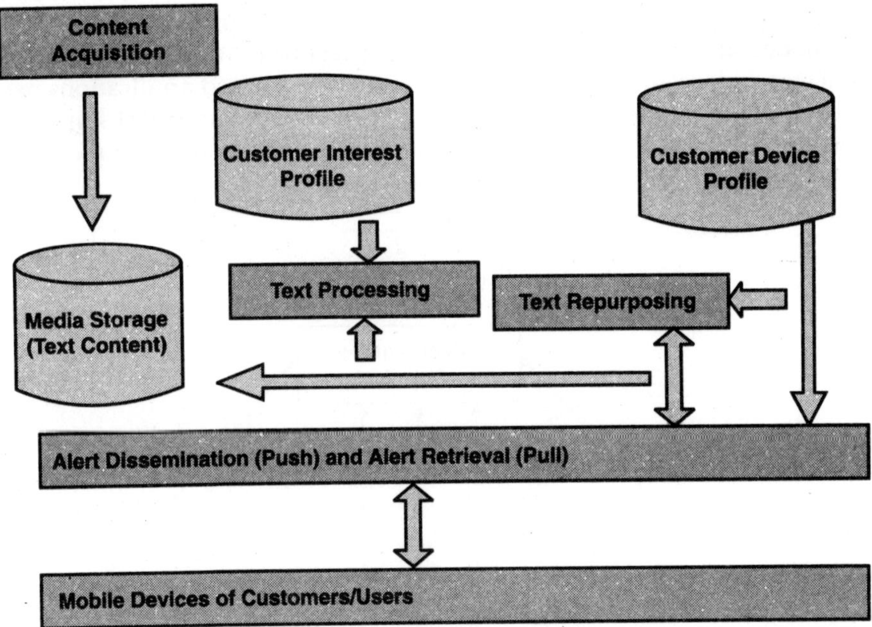

customer interest profile maintained by server. The client side news application software identifies the location, wherever this person goes (Chennai, Kolkata in this example). Based on the customer interest profile, text content from *media storage* is retrieved, processed and stored again for this customer's delivery.

- *Customer device profile* stores details of mobile phone of customer. Based on handset details from it, text content is *repurposed* for sending. Some customers have 150-character limitation in SMS in their phones, some have different configuration of handset. Content is *repurposed* and stored in *media storage*. Immediate delivery and scheduled delivery of forecasts are the tasks that are done by *content dissemination engines* using *push* operation. Push operation is done to multiple mobile phones by the engine. SMSes/ data in a push operation are not initiated by customers [5] whereas in a pull operation, SMSes are initiated by customers, for retrieval of information.

2.2 Push and Pull Stereotypes

It becomes essential to include push and pull activities between two *Mobile Software* stereotypes. Modeling of applications with UML profile described in [2] becomes inefficient from generating code perspective, if these activities are not included. We introduce push and pull activities, which will help in generating code for sending and receiving data between mobile phone application and server end application. It will take into account *text repurposing* and *text processing* of the architecture described in Figure 9.1. The architecture in Figure 9.1 is inspired from media alert [5]. The modeling in our work is specifically for text based applications instead of images, videos and rich multimedia content. Text based applications need to be modeled, due to low bandwidth over GSM networks in most countries. Thus, we propose a push pull extension in activity metaclass, shown in Figure 9.2.

FIG. 9.2

Need for Push, Pull Stereotypes

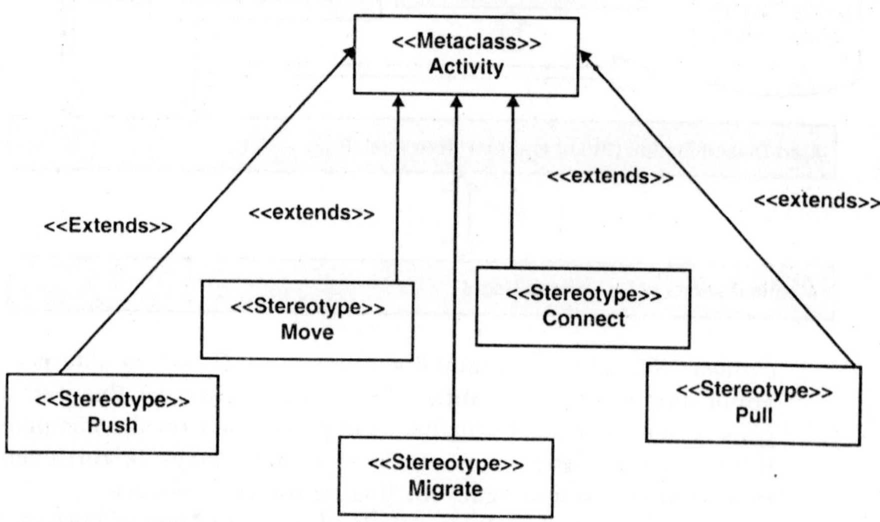

Content delivery in information systems involves huge amount of cost in delivering content to multiple users at same time. Push operation is initiated by server application to all the mobile phone customers. Pull operation is initiated by mobile phones as a query to a server to retrieve information. This operation is not initiated by server side applications. Once a customer initiates this operation, the information flows between server and mobile devices. This is explained with the help of case study.

3. CASE STUDY OF A CELL PHONE APPLICATION INVOLVING MOBILE INFORMATION SYSTEMS

A multiplex in New Delhi, named PVR, has recently launched its chain of multiplexes in Mumbai. Tired of attending incoming customer calls for enquiries of movie tickets and to reduce the company costs, PVR wants a innovative software for mobile phones that can help the customer feeding their queries on their phones and get quick replies from PVR through the software, depending on the customer location—Delhi or Mumbai. PVR Delhi runs this application using mobile operators—Airtel, Hutch, Idea, etc. whereas this application in Mumbai runs on Wi-Fi enabled devices also.

A customer moves to Delhi, checking the availability of tickets of movie 'MOV' in his nearest PVR multiplex 'MUL1', for the timings 'T1'. Show is houseful at 'T1'. Same customer goes to Mumbai the next day with his family. His children ask for another movie in any of the multiplexes of PVR Mumbai at time 'T2'. Customer feeds the following details through a form interface of his PVR software in his phone—movie name, timings, and number of tickets. The application on mobile phone detects the place (Delhi/Mumbai) through data connection objects, starts communicating with PVR server through mobile operator's network. The fed details in client application are, then, passed from mobile phone to PVR server. Information like mobile phone number, current location of mobile phone are automatically captured and passed along with movie ticket details. The availability status of all multiplexes in Mumbai, at time 'T2', appears in front of this customer. After this, booking can be easily done through this application asking bank details.

4. EXTENDING UML DIAGRAMS

4.1 Activity Diagram for Mobility

Activity Diagram for the case study is shown above. Notations are similar to the ones described in [1]. The difference is when 'PvrDServerTicketApplication' acknowledges the client application 'PvrClientApplication'.

Thus, every time a information is initiated, the UML diagrams will have to do repeated usage of Push and Pull in every case study of Mobile Information System. Hence our proposed stereotypes are solving this problem efficiently.

This means that all customers will be notified once by the server, by initiating sending message so that it sends acknowledgements to all its customers of Delhi by using the Push operation. The alert dissemination engine in Figure 9.3, takes care of this activity. Starting Activity is indicated by filled circle. Filled arrows notify the following activities. The dotted arrows represent the object doing the activity.

The first activity is when PVR server located in Delhi connects to Airtel. 'UserCellPhone' now moves to Delhi place and connect to Airtel. The 'PvrClientApplication' in UserCellphone behaves different way after moving Delhi. It becomes context aware. Different program in application executes for Delhi, which is notified by *Migrate* stereotype. Thereafter, starts the information flow by user initiated query that comes in Pull activity hence *Pull* stereotype. If Server (PvrServer) initiates communication to client application, it is called Push operation of information system; hence push activity is shown in Activity and sequence diagrams, Figure 9.3 and Figure 9.4 respectively.

FIG. 9.3
Activity Diagram Concerning Mobility for Case Study

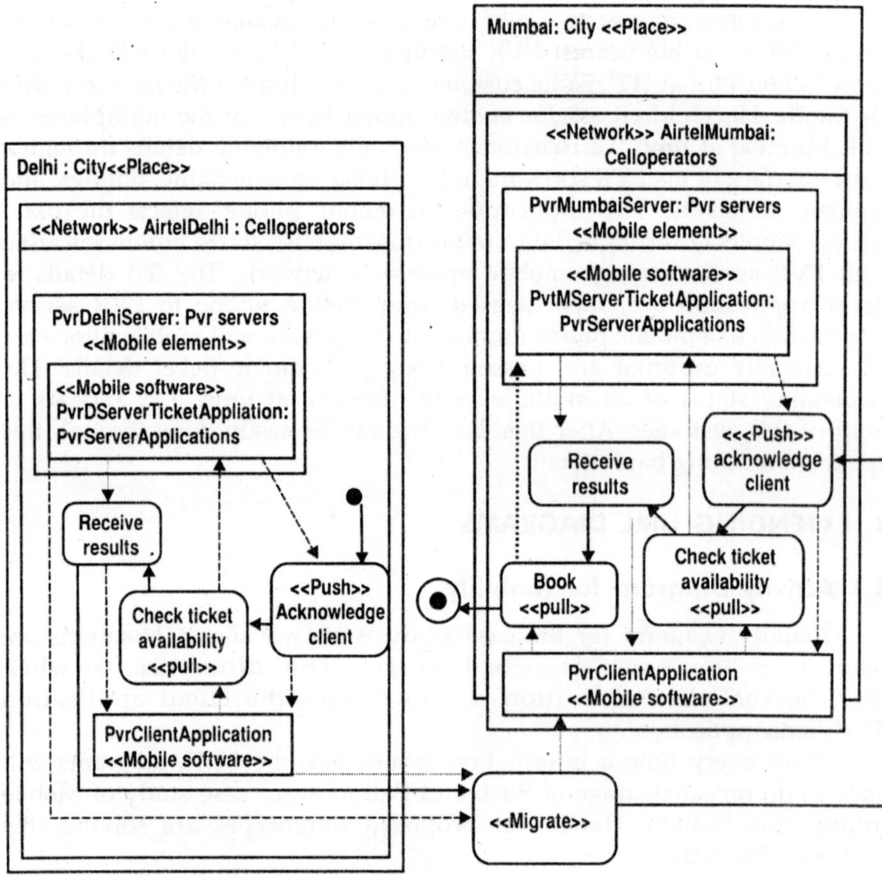

4.2 Sequence Diagram for Mobility

The vertical dotted line represents life of mobile object. Pvrclientapplication of Mobile software in Figure 9.4 is represented 3 times. In Place Mumbai, under Airtel Mumbai network, the 'PvrClientApplication' object performs activities and then its life ends. This is shown by dotted horizontal line intersecting dotted vertical line. Thus new stereotypes push-pull need to be presented in the sequence diagrams also.

5. COMPARISON WITH EARLIER WORK

References [1] and [4] described need for extending activity and sequence diagrams for mobility of Physical Objects in 2003. This work was further extended in [2] to propose new extensions for a UML profile for Mobility in Information systems in 2007. Our approach is inspired by UML

Fig. 9.4
Sequence Diagram Concerning Mobility for Case Study

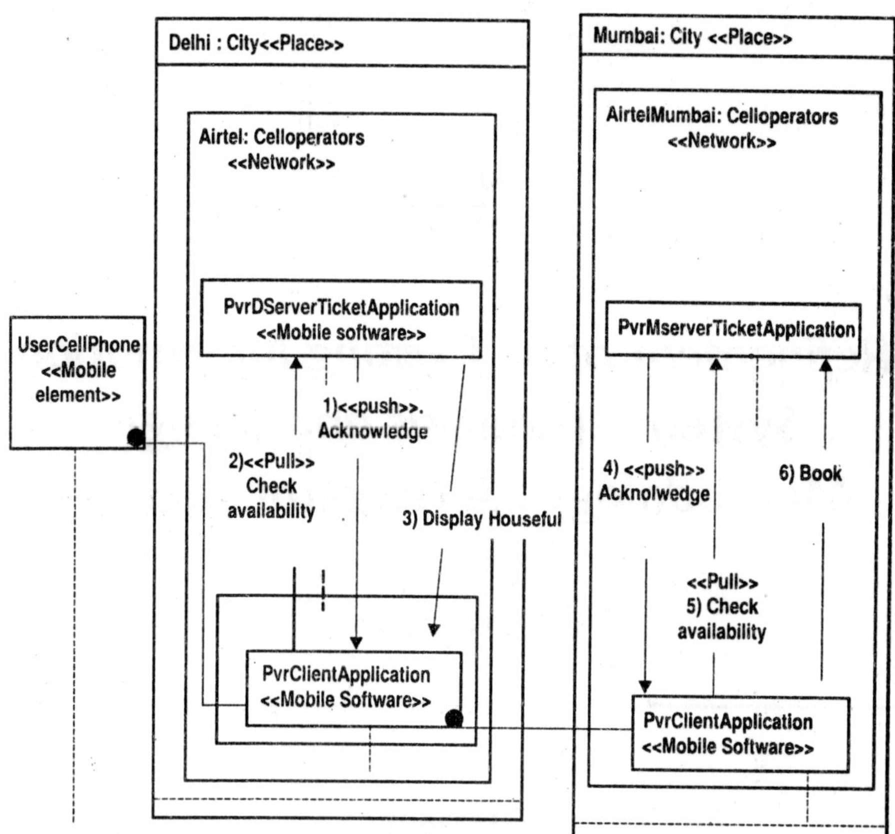

References

1. Hubert Baumeister, Nora Koch, Piotr Kosiuczenko, and Martin Wirsing, Institut f'ur Informatik; Extending Activity Diagrams to Model Mobile Systems, Springer-Verlag Berlin Heidelberg 2003.
2. Vegard Dehlen and Jan Oyvind Aagedal : A UML Profile for Modeling Mobile Information Systems, IFIP International Federation for Information Processing 2007, Springer.
3. Danny Soroker1, Ramón Cáceres1, Danny Dig2, Andreas Schade3, Susan Spraragen1, Alpana Tiwari1 : Pegboard: A Framework for Developing Mobile Applications, *MobiSys'06*, June 19-22, 2006, Uppsala, Sweden, ACM.
4. Piotr Kosiuczenko : Sequence Diagrams for Mobility, IST project Architectures for Mobility funded by the European Commission as a part of the Global Computing Initiative
5. Bin Wei, Bernard Renger, Yih-Farn Chen, Rittwik Jana : Media Alert—A Broadcast Video Monitoring and Alerting System for Mobile Users, AT&T Labs-Research 180, Park Ave Florham Park, NJ 07932.

10

Refinement of an Existing Information System : (Analysis and Design Methodology : A Hospital Setting)

RAJIV KUMAR BHARDWAZ

ABSTRACT

This paper based upon the case study, first, emphasize on the need of computerization of the system and, second, emphasizing on the proper co-ordination of the sub-units of the system to improve overall performance of the system as well as the development of the existing system. The paper advances the long-term project of developing a situated Information Systems analysis and design mechanism already in use. Conventional approaches to information systems design are informed by the widely held view that human purposeful action proceeds by deliberation on a mental model of the world of action. In contrast, situated information systems are informed by the view of situated action theory that routine action is largely non-deliberative and makes crucial use of structures in the action environment for attainment of goals. The expectation is that systems designed using this situated approach will be more effective in supporting routine activity than systems designed using the conventional approach. This paper reports on a case study conducted in the chemotherapy (Treatment of Cancer Using Chemical) unit of a large hospital. The case study was conducted using the pre-existing version of the situated systems methodology with the results of the case study informing further development of the methodology. The detailed study provides further evidence of the ability of information systems informed by a situated model of action to effectively support complex but largely routine activities.

1. INTRODUCTION

This paper reports on completed phases of case study conducted as part of a long-term project to develop a new Information System's analysis and design methodology. This methodology is explicitly informed by situational theories of human action and is for application in work domains where operational activity is large routine. In broad terms, our 'situated systems methodology' involves analyzing routine work practices in terms of action-centered constructs (actions, situations, activities, environmental structures, affordances) in order to identify their core goals, activities and environmental (Internal or External) constraints. This enables reorganization of these work practices in restructured environments so that system goals are achieved more effectively and efficiently using lighter-weight information system support.

Conventional approaches to information systems design are implicitly informed by the widely held view that human purposeful action proceeds by deliberation on a mental model of the world of action. Consequently, these approaches privilege support for the more deliberative aspects of human activity in work systems such as planning, decision-making and simulation. However, activity at the operational level in many work environments is largely routine and poorly supported by such information systems designs. Recent studies in the cognitive sciences under the rubrics of situated action theory and ecological psychology suggests that routine action is largely no deliberative and makes crucial use of structures in the action environment for attainment of goals.

This paper describe different facts referred to above and uses multiple participatory case studies in an iterative process, whereby, the current instantiation of the methodology informs the conduct of the case study as well as the analysis and development of the solution proposed for the case study site. At the same time, reflection on the problems encountered in application of the methodology in each new case study, together with evaluation of the nature of the solutions suggested by it, inform the further development of the methodology. The case study reported here is a medium to notice the progress of methodology development program.

The aim of this paper is to present the learning arising from the case study and apply these in order to formulate another iteration of the methodology. This case study confirmed the usefulness of situated information systems analysis and design methodology in settings where work is complex but largely routine. In such an iterative process, the ability of the methodology to identify the root causes of problems was confirmed through identification of a novel solution to a clearly identified problem. This case is also interesting for its own sake. It describes a class of problems

FIG. 10.1
A Chemotherapy Patient's Journey through the Hospital

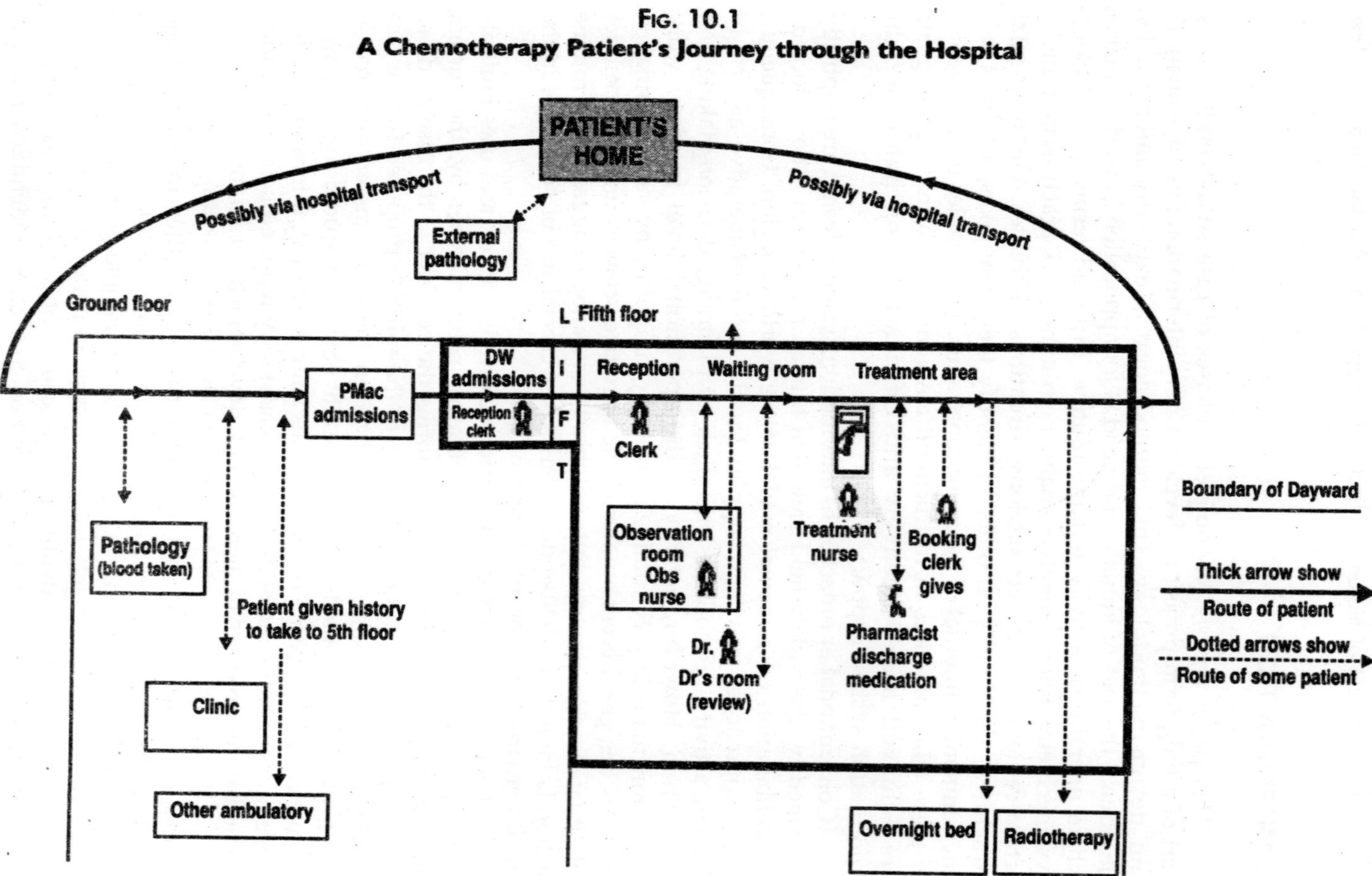

in the health care industry for which there are currently few effective solutions.

2. DETAILS OF CASE STUDY

The system under study was located in the Chemotherapy Unit of a large metropolitan hospital. This ward administered chemotherapy to an average of 40-50 outpatients each day and when the study began, patients were regularly experiencing delays of up to half a day beyond their appointed time to receive chemotherapy treatment.

According to case study for better understanding of existing system in the Chemotherapy Unit, patients were studied in such situations over a period of approximately 20 days during the period of one month. The involved persons used a mixture of participant observation, interviews and direct observation of nurses, clerks, doctors, pharmacists and patients. The extended period of data collection enabled the researcher to obtain a deeper understanding of the system than the traditional systems analyst who relies on a short period of observation and questions. The researcher made detailed notes of field observations and experiences to assist in their organization. Microsoft Vision was used to represent the existing system through the depiction of existing activities.

2.1 Detail of Operations

Administering chemotherapy is a highly complex activity due to the many permutations in how treatment is delivered and the need to coordinate actions with real-time events, the timing of which is uncertain. There were at least 70 different chemotherapy treatments administered in the Chemotherapy Unit. Further, increasing this complexity was the range of requirements associated with the treatment of individual patients. Figure 10.1 shows a schematic outline of a typical chemotherapy patient's journey through the hospital.

The exact route of a chemotherapy patient depends on the particulars of their treatment. In general, a patient needs to have blood taken, either on arrival at the hospital, or at a pathology laboratory the day before their chemotherapy appointment. A patient is often required to be reviewed by a doctor before their chemotherapy treatment, either in a clinic (located downstairs) or in a review room in the Chemotherapy Unit. Patients report at reception before taking a seat in the waiting room. The Observation nurse calls patients out of the waiting room and takes their observations in a small room adjacent. The patient returns to the waiting room until called by a doctor (if scheduled to have a review appointment first) or the Treatment nurse. If the patient is assessed as well enough to receive chemotherapy, the nurse takes the patient into the treatment area and administers the pre-medication and treatment (previously prepared by the cytotoxic suite). The pharmacist dispenses discharge medication to the patient, while the booking clerk gives the patients a card listing future appointments.

2.2 Problem Analysed and Goal was Set

The goal of high quality patient care requires that the patient experience a smooth journey through the unit with no waiting beyond their appointment time. For this to happen several processes need to be coordinated and a range of information communicated to various unit staff. Delays could occur at any stage in the process, often translating to increase waiting times for patients and always translating to increased running around, trying to find where the process is up to and attend to the delays. In the course of observing the unit and talking to staff, it was apparent that the current system was not working efficiently or, in some cases, effectively. Although the information-related aspects of administering chemotherapy should be routine, various unit staff described the current system as 'chaos'. As one staff member put it, 'At the end of the day, everyone has received their chemotherapy treatment, but there has been a lot of distress in the process'.

The other important aspects of a nurses' daily work are to attend to patient needs, for example, talking to the patient and the patient's career and liaising with other health professionals as well as professional development, attending meetings and training. Many of the nurses felt that they did not have the time to do these things: "It's doing patients a disservice. We don't even ask the questions we should because we don't have time." Nurses considered that there was insufficient, if any, time for professional development and fostering links with other parts of the hospital, and that it was even difficult to schedule lunch breaks.

2.3 The Main Problems

Applying the situated systems methodology led to the identification of a number of issues with the current operations. This section describes the core problems.

2.3.1 Lack of timely and ready-to-hand information about when the next patient can be treated

Although administering chemotherapy is a complex activity, when stripped to its essential elements, there are four conditions that need to be met before a nurse can administer treatment. These are that the:

- Patient has to have arrived.
- A bed or couch needs to be available.
- The chemotherapy treatment needs to be prepared.
- The patient needs to be well enough for chemotherapy treatment.

Nurses were required to be by the side of the patients they were currently treating. While it was immediately (visually) obvious to a nurse, when a bed or couch became available, information about whether the other conditions were met could only be obtained by leaving the side of the patient.

A disproportionate amount of time was spent seeking this information, at the expense of attending to patient needs. While treating other patients, each treating nurse had to repeatedly be checking whether other patients had arrived, whether blood results had arrived, and whether the chemotherapy treatment was ready until she/he knew that all conditions for treatment of a patient had been satisfied. This meant that while treating patients, nurses had to regularly walk into the treatment preparation room to check the treatment tables (where the chemotherapy treatments were brought to after being made up in the cytotoxic suite), walk to a computer to check the hospital computer system, visit the waiting room or walk to the reception area to ask about particular patients or to page a doctor.

A further difficulty was that a patient may arrive just after a nurse has looked up the mainframe computer system, the treatment may arrive just after a nurse checks which treatments are in the treatment preparation room, or the blood results may become available just after a nurse has looked up the relevant computer system. Each of these time lags, between the condition being satisfied and the nurse knowing that the condition is satisfied, contributed to an avoidable delay in administering the treatment which compounded to place severe limits on the quality of patient care delivered. So, as well as being spatially remote, the necessary information was not accessed in a timely way.

2.3.2 Missing Chemotherapy Orders

Handwritten chemotherapy orders, essential as an authorization for treatment, were kept in a sleeve inside the patient's paper history file. In theory these histories for chemotherapy patients were meant to be brought up to the Chemotherapy Unit at least a day before the patients' chemotherapy treatment. In practice, some of these histories could not be located. If a patient had a downstairs clinic appointment before their chemotherapy appointment, the patient would be expected to carry their (often bulky) history up to the Chemotherapy Unit afterwards. Finding missing chemotherapy orders was a frustrating task involving much running around by clerks and nurses.

2.3.3 Inappropriate order of Preparation of Chemotherapy Drugs

Chemotherapy drugs were prepared in the cytotoxic suite. Although the pharmacist tried to make up drugs in advance, this was not possible for expensive drugs or those with a short expiry period, and it was fairly common that the treatments for the day's first patients were not ready. Sometimes, they did not arrive until 11 am, by which time all of the day's patients were backed up.

2.3.4 Inefficient Division of Labor

Before the cytotoxic suite could prepare the treatment for a patient, the Liaison nurse needed to have checked the blood results and marked them as OK on the chemotherapy orders. However, the nature of the Liaison's nurse's job (liaising with doctors, nurses, patients, their careers, the pharmacist and other hospital staff) meant that she was constantly interrupted and became a bottleneck in chemotherapy preparation. Thus, the existing division of labour meant that for no good reason, the Liaison nurse became a scarce resource in the system.

2.4 Proposed Solution

To address the problems identified above, four main changes to the existing practices were proposed:

- Nurses carry devices, which alert them in real time about the satisfaction of the prerequisites for patient treatment; that is when their patients arrive, when their patient's blood results arrive and when the chemotherapy treatment is ready. Specifically, it was suggested that each Treatment nurse could carry equipments, which accesses a secure intranet over a wireless network.
- The chemotherapy orders be taken out of the history files and stationed in Day Ward.
- Increased coordination between Day Ward and the Cytotoxic Suite regarding the order of treatment preparation as well as the types of treatment to be booked in early. Because the proposed web interface would allow integration to existing mainframe systems and multiple modalities of access, the pharmacist could see on his desktop computer when patients had arrived and similarly the Liaison nurse could see when treatments were ready. Being provided with the same information allowed them to negotiate the order of preparation as necessary, depending on the current situation.
- Rather than the Liaison nurse checking the blood results and obtaining the chemotherapy orders for all patients, each Treatment nurse was to check blood results and obtain chemotherapy orders for their own patients. This changed division of labor shifted more responsibility for patients to the Treatment nurses and meant that the patient information was in manageable parcels for the Treatment nurses, who were the ones who needed to use the information.

These proposals were arrived at by application of the situated information systems methodology described. Space does not permit full elaboration here but in broad terms, the first steps of the iteration of the methodology involved analyzing existing activities into their constituent situations and responses as well as analyzing the immediate environment of current activities. The next steps involved abstracting to the goals of the activities and the constraints in the environment. Two types of constraints were found:

- Hard Constraints
- Soft Constraints

Hard constraints were those that would necessarily govern aspects of the redesigned system whereas soft constraints were those, which were negotiable with the stakeholders. This led to the design phase where current practice was evaluated in terms of the goals, taking into account the constraints. The final step was to design new ways of doing things and restructure the environment.

The proposals arrived at were situated solutions to the identified problems because, they take explicit account of the constraints of the particular workplace in restructuring various dimensions of the work environment, new divisions of labor, alternative work practices and appropriate (minimal) IT support. The nurses' immediate environment was restructured such that the information, in a sense, came to them, removing the need for them to engage in searches for this information. It also came to them in real-time; in other words the time-grain of information availability now matched the rate at which situations changed. The immediate environments of both the Liaison nurse and the pharmacist were restructured so that they each had easy desktop access to the same information. This gave a better basis for negotiating the order of chemotherapy preparation. The relocation of chemotherapy orders involved a stabilization of the physical environment; the changed division of labor involved a restructuring of the organizational environment.

In summary, solution involved restructuring the environment so that actors had ready-to-hand access to information they need in the course of their daily activities. This information assists them not only to know *what* to do next but also assists them to *do* the next thing.

3. REFINEMENTS TO THE METHODOLOGY

This section shows how the insights from the case study were used to refine the methodology. The previous version of the situated information systems analysis and design methodology is shown in Figure 10.2. The following discussion shows how it was changed to the revised version in Figure 10.3.

The first phase of the case study was about installing telecommunications products in private homes. This second most important phase of the case study, undertaken in the Chemotherapy Unit, presented several theoretically challenging problems in routine work. It was a not-for-profit organization and the success or otherwise of the system had serious

FIG. 10.2

First Version of the Situated Information Systems Analysis and Design Methodology

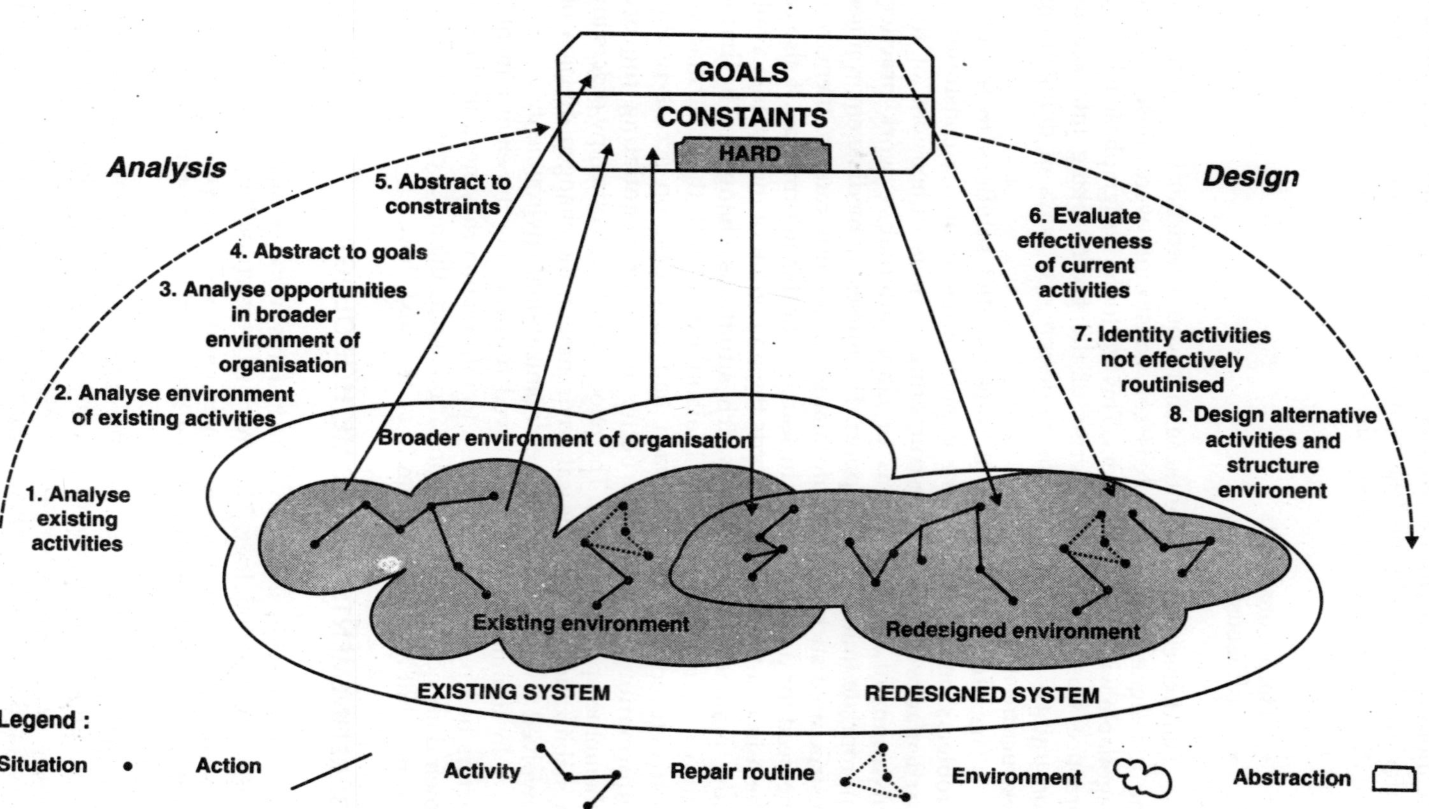

implications for people's health and well-being. It also presented an interesting new constraint—protecting the privacy of information about individual patients. The chemotherapy unit involved more complex coordination among a greater range of actors and there were recognized problems, as effective routines had not been established.

The first step in the previous iteration of the situated information systems analysis and design methodology (Figure 10.2) was "Analyzed existing activities into their constituent situations and responses". In the first phase of the case study the practices involved in the management of installation of telecommunications equipment were linear and ordered enough to know what was going on, who was doing what and why. In second phase, at the Chemotherapy Unit, there were a range of different types of actors (Liaison nurse, Treatment nurses, patients, clerks, doctors, pharmacists) involved in the administration of chemotherapy and there were a number of processes occurring at once. This meant that it required a deal of analytic work to decipher exactly what was going on. Hence, I have made explicit the step of analyzing the information that actors need. In the first phase of case study, this was done after the analysis of existing activities, as the information needed was made explicit by the current activities. In the second phase of case study, this was done in concert with analysis of existing work practices and analysis of existing environmental support. I believe that including the step of analyzing the information that actors need is a better conceptualization of this part of the methodology.

The analysis stage has been clearly separated from the abstraction stage and evaluation has been recognized explicitly as a precursor to design. In addition, the proposed solution in the second phase of the case study involved a new division of labor and new lines of communication. These have been added as discrete aspects of the design phase of the methodology, as they are likely to be reflective of the general case. The numbering of each aspect within the four stages has been removed to emphasize that these are conceptual distinctions and do not imply a rigid temporal order.

4. ANALYSIS STAGE *VS.* ABSTRACTION STAGE

According to me a primary role for mental abstractions as an explanation for routine human action, it is interesting to notify the importance of abstraction in deliberate redesign of routine systems. The analyst, as opposed to the actors in the system must be able to "stand outside the action" in order to appreciate and evaluate the possibilities for change. This is the role of the abstract system in Figure 10.3.

This idea of a design abstraction is somewhat reminiscent of the distinction between the physical and logical system in traditional systems analysis, so I should here point out some crucial differences in the conception of the appropriate abstraction. The differences reflect the

Fig. 10.3
Current Version of the Situated Information Systems Analysis and Design Methodology

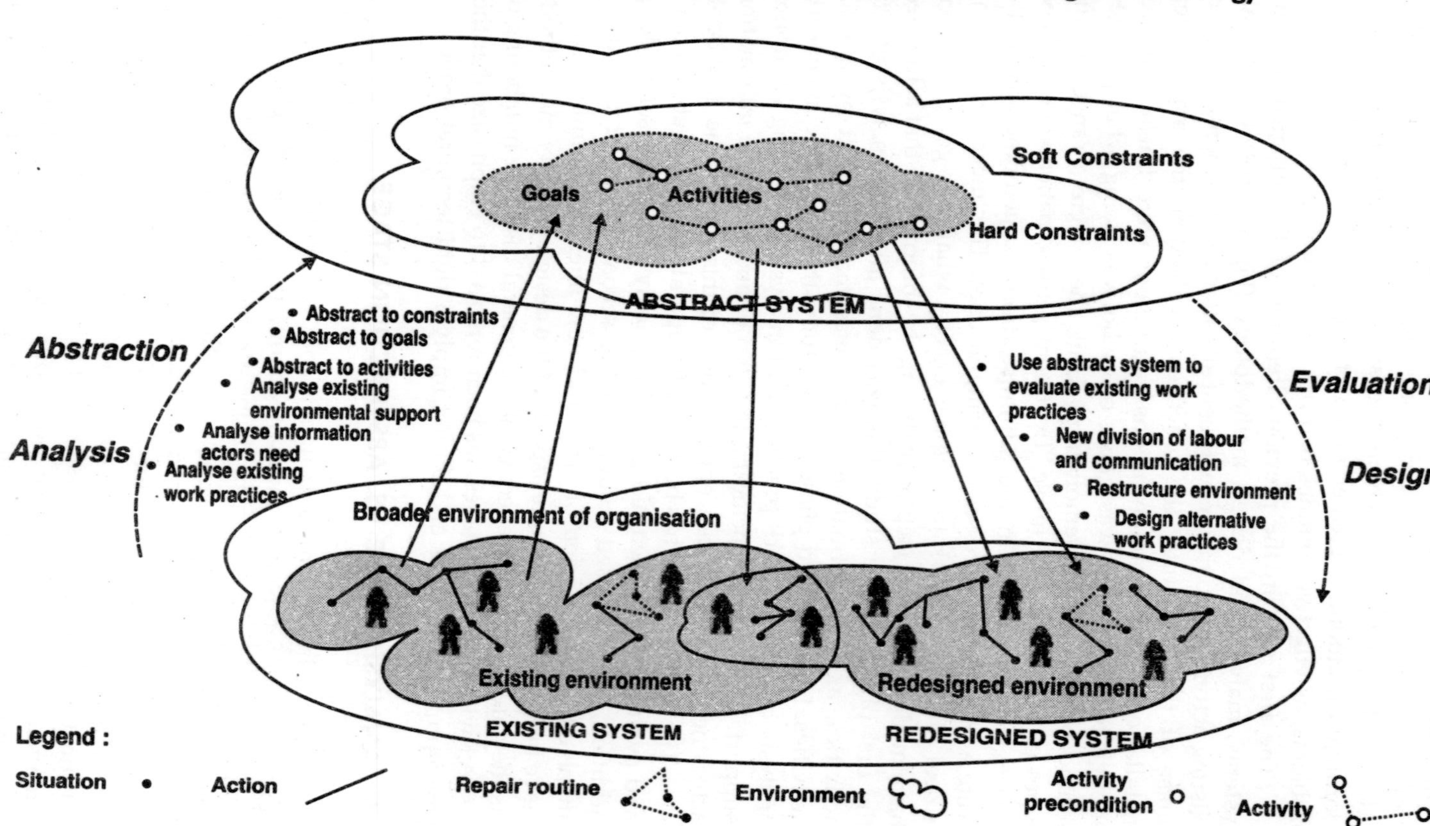

differences in ontologism and theories of action underlie the two approaches.

Firstly, the abstractions are not objective, in either sense of the word. They are expressed using action-centered constructs (activity, goals, and constraints on action) rather than entities, properties, states, events, etc. They express in a generalized form the purposes and key activities of the existing practices as they are made, rather than a model of the world "out there" which actors might refer to and deliberate upon in the course of action. Secondly, such an abstraction is not intended to be a model of an archetype (a very typical example) of which the system in a given organization is an instantiation. The abstractions I envisage are particular to an organizational setting—and are unlikely to apply to any other setting even in the same industry (another chemotherapy ward, for instance). Rather, they are a temporary crutch with which to move from the current practices, which by virtue of their reutilizations are to various degrees opaque, to new more effective revolutionized practices.

Finally, they are not solutions in any sense in the traditional method, arriving at the logical model is in a certain sense the end of the analysts work because the logical System then simply has to be translated into more or less isomorphic computerized information System, a job that can be handed to database designers, programmers, implementers and trainers. In some respect the notion of abstraction is similar to making use of abstraction to goals. My intension is to support routine operational activity rather than cognitive, decision-making activity.

5. CONCLUSION

This paper reports on a case study of the requirements for more effective routine systems in a chemotherapy ward of a major hospital. The case was deliberately selected for its potential to challenge the situated systems analysis and design methodology and, thus, allow it to be tested and refined by a reflective participatory research method. The long-term project of developing a situated information systems analysis and design methodology has theoretical significance as well as practical significance for organizations. While contributing to an understanding of the unique nature of routine action, it also extends our conception of what an information system is. In terms of practical applications, as this paper has shown, the methodology has the potential for providing systems that are both effective and lightweight in areas where activity is complex and routine.

REFERENCES

1. Information System Analysis and Specifications tools at website www.information developmentresearch.com
2. Information Warfare Site, 2001, http://www.iwar.org.uk/psyops/index.htm

3. "Survey report of System Study" by Vivienne Waller, Robert, B. Johnston, Department of Information Systems, The University of Melbourne, Australia.
4. "Understanding of Information Systems Design", *Australian Journal of Information Systems,* 9 (Special Issue): 40-49.
5. "Activity in Organizations". *International Journal of Business Information Systems,* 1: 53-82. Milton, S.
6. Johnston, R.B., Lederman, R. and Waller, V. (2005). "Developing a Methodology for Designing Routine".
7. Information Systems Based on the Situational Theory of Agency. Proceedings of European Conference on Information Systems, Regensburg, Germany.
8. http://www.iseing.org/emcis//Proceedings/Contributions.com

11

Version Control—A Case Study-based Approach

PARMINDER KAUR, KULJIT KAUR AND HARDEEP SINGH

ABSTRACT

As software is developed and deployed, it is extremely common for multiple versions of the same software to be deployed at different sites, and for the software's developers to be working on private updates. Bugs and other issues with software are often only present in certain versions (because of the fixing of some problems and the introduction of others, the program evolves). Therefore, for the purpose of locating and fixing bugs, it is vitally important for the debugger to be able to retrieve and run different versions of the software to determine in which version(s) the problem occurs. All these tasks are related with version control. This paper makes an attempt to show how Subversion, an open source version control tool, is helpful in tracing the changes processed at different times. This paper also shows the comparison between open source and commercial version control tools.

1. INTRODUCTION

Component-based software technology has become an increasingly popular approach to facilitate the development of software systems, as it suggests the solutions to some of the problems of object-oriented development technologies. The aim of component-based software development is to develop new software by widely reusing pre-fabricated software components. One of the basic problems when developing component-based systems is that it is difficult to keep track of components and their interrelationships as component development evolves in small steps or versions. Often, these versions are results of collaborations among different persons. At many times, developer has to move back to a previous version or compare different variants or there is a need to trace the changes to change requests. In order to keep track of software development as well as changes made in a database system, there is a great need of version management.

A developer often needs to revisit and restore the past. It is a hard fact that writing programs is fundamentally a problem-solving process. We often follow a path only to find out that we must retrace our steps, because yesterday's version may be better than today's. Sometimes we have to follow more than one path simultaneously as software development process is teamwork. Version management helps us to retrace and restore our programming past, proceed along two or more development lines in a single project and coordinate our work with the work of others in the same project[1].

2. VERSION CONTROL

Version control or Source control is the management of multiple revisions of the same unit of information. It is most commonly used in engineering and software development to manage ongoing development of digital documents like application source code, art resources such as blueprints or electronic models and other critical information that may be worked on by a team of people. Changes to these documents are identified by incrementing an associated number or letter code, termed the revision number or simply revision and associated historically with the person making the change. So, there is a need of proceedures which can keep history of changes along with suitable comments. Also, if more than one developer handles the project, then there is a need of mechanism which makes sure that no developer can overwrite other's version/revision. To handle these problems, various software tools are increasingly recognized as being necessary for almost all software development projects [2].

2.1 Manual Version Control

The most primitive, but, very common method is hand-hacking. One can snapshot the project periodically by manually copying everything in it to backup. Also, history comments can be included in source files. Verbal or email arrangements can be made with other developers to keep their hands off certain files while hacking them.

The hidden costs of this hand-hacking method are high, especially, when it breaks down. The procedures take time and concentration, they are prone to error, and tend to get slipped under pressure.

As with most hand-hacking, this method does not scale well and also it is very time consuming. It restricts the granularity of change tracking, and tends to lose metadata details such as the order of changes, who did them, and why.

2.2 Automated Version Control

To avoid these problems, one can use a version-control system (VCS), a set of programs that automates away most of the steps involved in keeping an annotated history of project and avoid modification conflicts.

Most VCS's share the same basic logic. To use VCS, one should start by registering a collection of source files—that is, telling VCS to start archive files describing their change histories. Thereafter, to edit one of these files, *check out* the file by creating its working copy. When changes are done, *check in* the file, add changes to the archive, release the lock, and enter the change comment explaining about the change.

VCSs have their problems. The biggest one is that using a VCS involves extra steps every time during edit process of a file. Another problem is that some kinds of natural operations tend to confuse VCSs. For example, renaming files is a notorious trouble spot; it's not easy to automatically ensure that a file's version history will be carried along with it when it is renamed. Renaming problems are particularly difficult to resolve when the VCS support branching.

Despite these difficulties, VCSs are a huge boon to productivity and code quality in many ways, even for small single-developer projects. They help a lot in recovering from mistakes. They make programmers free to experiment by guaranteeing that reversion to a known-good state will always be easy.

3. INSTALLATION OF VERSION CONTROL SYSTEM

Getting a VCS is not very expensive. It depends on the operating system we are using. It might be the case that one is already installed and ready to run—probably CVS (Concurrent Versions System) or RCS (Revision Control System). If not, there is a luxury of wide choices. One can safely pick a free open source system as multimillion-line projects have relied on such systems for more than a decade. If someone can spend some cash, then there are several commercial systems in the market, which offer additional features and a more polished interface. Installing a VCS, typically, involves setting up a repository, the location where the definitive version of source code and its changes will reside [1].

4. VERSION CONTROL SYSTEM—SUBVERSION

Since a significant number of different version control tools are available, it is probably worth mentioning why subversion is preferred. A team of developers who had extensive experience with CVS started the subversion project. The Concurrent Version System (CVS) is free software and its support for networked operation, which allows dozens of geographically dispersed programmers to share their work, fits the collaborative nature of the open-source world very well. CVS and its semi-chaotic development model have become cornerstones of open-source culture.

But like many tools, CVS is starting to show its age. Subversion is a relatively new version control system designed to be the successor to CVS. The designers set out to win the hearts of CVS users in two ways: by creating an open-source system with a design similar to CVS, and by attempting to fix most of CVS's noticeable flaws. While the result isn't necessarily the next great evolution in version control design. Subversion is very powerful, very usable, and very flexible.

5. SUBVERSION'S FEATURES

Subversion is a free/open-source version control system. It manages files and directories over time. A tree of files is placed into a central repository. The repository is much like an ordinary file server, except that it remembers every change ever made to files and directories. This allows us to recover older versions of data, or examine the history of how data changed. In this regard, many people think of a version control system as a sort of "time machine".

Subversion can access its repository across networks, which allows it to be used by people on different computers. Different people can make the modifications and manage the same set of data from their respective locations. Progress can occur more quickly without a single conduit through which all modifications must occur. And because the work is versioned, there is no need to fear that quality is the trade-off for losing that standard—if some incorrect change is made to the data, just undo that change.

Some version control systems are also software configuration management (SCM) systems. These systems are specifically tailored to manage trees of source code, and have many features that are specific to software development—such as natively understanding programming languages, or supplying tools for building software. Subversion, however, is not one of these systems. It is a general system that can be used to manage any collection of files. For you, those files might be source code—for others, anything from grocery shopping lists to digital video mixdowns and beyond[2].

6. BASIC CONCEPTS

The basic Version Control (VC) idea is to separate the files that programmers work on, called working copies, from the master copies of the same files which are stored in a repository. The programmers never work on the repository. They check out their working copies from the repository, make changes, and then check in (commit) their changes. Every time a programmer commits a file, the VC system creates a new version in the repository. In this way, the repository contains all versions of a file.

You might be thinking that with use of version control system, there is wastage of space. But VC systems are cautious storing only the differences between successive versions. Because version also refers to a specific software product release, VC systems often use revision to refer to the successive versions of a VC file.

When two or more programmers want to use the same version, the potential for conflicts may arises. There are two approaches through which these conflicts can be handled:

(a) *Lock-modify-unlock model*, in which, developers can get a lock on any file they wish to change. For, as long as a developer has the file's lock, no one else can change the file, although it's possible to check it out (say, for viewing or compilation). When the developer with the lock finishes working on the file, he or she commits the changes to the repository and unlocks the file.

(b) *Copy-modify-merge model*, in which, developers are always free to modify their working copies. If conflicting modifications appear, the VC system alerts the developers of the conflict, and they must resolve it by merging the modifications.

The lock-modify-unlock model is simple but restrictive. It's especially cumbersome in distributed development, when different people in different geographic locations and possibly different time zones work on the same project. The copy-modify-merge model is more open, but it requires developers to work around conflicts cordially. Subversion employs the copy-modify-merge model [2, 11].

6.1. Working with Subversion

To start work with subversion, first thing to be done is a need to create a repository. Create an empty directory for the repository and then tell subversion to create a new repository in the directory. One can use following commands (for Windows) to create a repository:

```
mkdir c:\svn-repos
svnadmin create c:\svn-repos
```

After creating repository, import project files into the repository using following command:

```
svn import path URL
```

The import keyword tells Subversion that some files are going to import in repository. The parameter URL describes the fact where files are to be imported. Subversion responds by displaying a message that it has added files from a given path and has committed the change into the repository.

To start working with the project files stored in the repository, a working copy of the project files must be prepared. Suppose the project is called *newproject*. One can get a working copy by using the svn checkout command:

svn checkout url...path

For example:

C:\work>svn co file:///c:/svn-repos/project newproject

This command creates a new directory called *newproject* in the current directory and populates it with working copies of all the *project* files in the repository.

All Subversion commands start with svn, followed by the svn operation's name and target, usually a set of files or directories. After making changes, save the latest version in the repository with the command svn commit. For example: you are working on the file named day.txt. The command would be:

svn commit day.txt

A log message can also be added describing the changes here by using the syntax:

svn commit–m "conflict removed" day.txt

With the execution of this command, Subversion adds a new version of the file to the repository. Actually, it stores the current version of the file and the differences between the current version and the previous one. It does this process at each and every commit, thus maintaining a complete history of the file.

Suppose one of our colleagues has committed a newer version in the meantime. Subversion then alerts us that commit is not possible, and we must reconcile the differences between the latest repository version and our working copy. To bring the working copy up to date with respect to the repository, update command can be used:

svn update day.txt

If Subversion can reconcile the differences without conflict, it will do so automatically, and then commit can be done. Otherwise, it will change our working copy, demarcating the changes between it and the repository. It's up to our colleague and us to edit the file, fix the conflicts, and then proceed to commit. One can find the differences between any two versions with the svn diff command. svn diff command shows the changes between the repository version of the file and local file.

At any point in a file's history, one can start a parallel development. Suppose you have shipped your software and are now actively working on the next version. And suppose there is a bug in the shipped version. In this situation, you can go back to that version and create a *branch* on which you can incorporate the bug fix. Figure 11.1 shows the evolution of a file that has two branches and one main line (known as *trunk)*. As the figure shows, changes in the branch can be merged with the trunk.

FIG. 11.1
A Subversion Branching Example

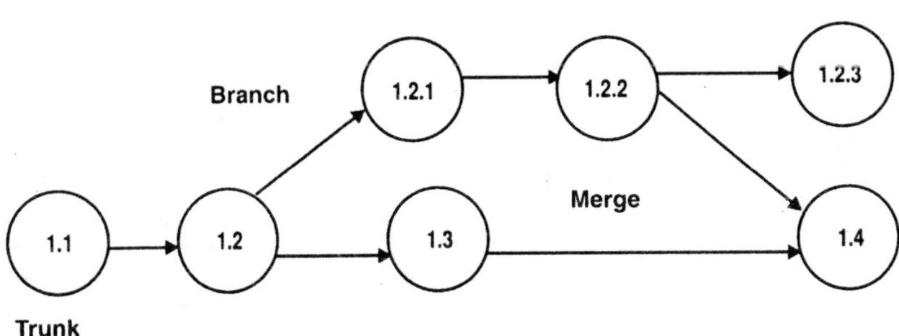

Branches are not used for bug fixes only. These can be used for other purposes like you can put each release of a project onto a separate branch. The release branch can contain one or more releases, i.e. points at which the project is shipped. You can use tags here to define these points. The facility of using tag is of great use. Actually, a tag refers to a symbolic name for a set of files, each with a particular revision number. Tags are helpful when you want to pick and choose a particular version of project components to be packaged together during a release.

Subversion has many more features, including Subversion commands to add new project files and directories (svn add), to remove a file from a project (svn delete), and to import a directory structure into Subversion and start a new project (svn import). For tracking purposes, Subversion keeps a complete log history for each file and offers commands to examine the log of who did what and when at different levels of detail (svn log). To print the status of working copy files and directories, it offers svn status command [2].

7. COMPARISON WITH OTHER VERSION CONTROL SYSTEMS

Subversion [3], as discussed, is an open source project that attempts to remain as similar as possible to CVS while improving its capabilities with

Table 11.1
Comparison of Version Control Systems [12]

Feature	*CVS*	*Subversion*	*Aegis*	*BitKeeper*	*SourceSafe*	*Perforce*	*ClearCase*	*Synergy*
(1)	(2)	(3)	(4)	(5)	(6)	(7)	(8)	(9)
Platforms	MS Windows (clients) UNIX	MS Windows UNIX	UNIX	MS Windows UNIX	MS Windows UNIX	MS Windows UNIX	MS Windows UNIX.	MS Windows UNIX
Atomic Commits	No	Yes	Yes	Yes	No	Yes	Yes	Yes
Tracking Uncommitted Changes	Yes	Yes	Yes	Yes	Yes	Yes	Yes	Yes
File/Directory Moves, Renames	No	Yes	Yes	Yes	Yes	Yes	Yes	Yes
Remote Repository Replication	No	Yes, via tool	Yes	Yes	No	Yes, via tool	Yes, via tool	Yes
Propagating changes to Parent repository	No	Yes, via tool	Yes	Yes	No	No	Yes, via tool	Yes
Repository Permissions	Limited	Yes	Yes	Yes	Limited	Yes	Yes	No
Line-wise History Tracking scripting	Yes	Yes	Yes	Yes	Not directly	Yes	Yes	Via
Ease of Deployment	Good	Good	Medium	Good	Very Good	Very Good	Poor	Medium
Networking Support	Good	Very good	Poor	Good	Good	Good	Poor	Good
Portability	Good	Excellent	Medium	Very good	Good	Excellent	Medium	Very good
License	Open Source	Open Source	Open Source	Proprietary	Proprietary	Proprietary	Proprietary	Proprietary
User License Cost (up to 20 users)	Free	Free	Free	Paid	Paid	Paid	Paid	Paid

additional features. For example, Subversion offers directory versioning. It is also easy to handle file name changes in Subversion than in CVS, which requires a combined copy and deletion to rename a file. Subversion lets you to create and store arbitrary properties (called *metadata*) along with any file or directory; it creates versions of the file properties just as it does for the file contents. It also lets you to treat a collection of file or directory modifications as a single unit.

Subversion is a powerful tool that solves many problems arising in cooperative and distributed development. That does not mean that it has no drawbacks. Subversion is targeted at text files as this allows subversion to merge documents that are edited at the same time by different people. Subversion can even cope with conflicting edits (e.g. two persons changing the same line). Unfortunately, this is not possible for binary files such as Word documents. For Word documents, one can use the internal tracking feature to tell other people about changes, but there is no possibility to merge two Word documents. As such, two persons should never edit Word documents at the same time [4]. Table 11.1 compares Subversion to several other version control systems and try to show how it is better than others.

BitKeeper [5] is a well-known commercial, proprietary alternative. It is supported on most platforms, such as Microsoft Windows, Linux, Unix, and MacOS/X. Users of the Microsoft Visual Studio suite usually take advantage of Microsoft's Visual SourceSafe tool [6]. Perforce[7] is another well-known commercial VC system. It features comprehensive SCM capabilities built around a scalable client/server architecture. Users can access the Perforce Server through a range of Perforce client software. Perforce can be deployed quickly and easily, and requires minimal administration even for large or distributed sites.

IBM Rational offers the comprehensive ClearCase suite [8]. Telelogic Synergy [9] comprises Change Synergy and CMSynergy, which automate change requests and configuration management, respectively. The comparison table helps in selecting an appropriate version control system according to requirements.

8. CONCLUSION

Through this paper, an effort is done to explain the importance of version control. Version control gives us a safety net, helps our team collaborate effectively, allows us to organize our builds and even allows us to do some detective work if things go wrong. Version control is both appropriate and useful to help observe student coding practices as part of a systematic development process [14]. Professional software developers use version control systems to coordinate their work and to provide an unwindable history of their project's evolution.

References

1. Spinellis, D, *"Version Control Systems"*, Software, IEEE, Volume 22, Issue 5, Sept.-Oct. 2005 Page(s): 108-09.
2. Ben Collins-Sussman, Brian W. Fitzpatrick, C. Michael Pilato, *"Version Control with Subversion"*, For Subversion 1.3 (book compiled from Revision 2393).
3. http://subversion.tigris.org
4. http://www.hipeac.net/node/43
5. www.bitkeeper.com
6. http://msdn.microsoft.com/ssafe
7. www.perforce.com
8. http://www-306.ibm.com/software/awdtools/clearcase/
9. www.telelogic.com/corp/Products/synergy
10. Mike Mason, *"Pragmatic Version Control Using Subversion"*, The Pragmatic Starter kit Volume 1.
11. Louridas, P., *"Version Control"* , Software, IEEE, volume 23, Issue 1, Jan.-Feb. 2006, pp. 104-07.
12. http://better-scm.berlios.de/comparison/comparison.html
13. Walter, F. Tichy, *"RCS—A System for Version Control"*, Software: Practice & Experience, Vol. 15, No. 7, 1985, pp. 637-54.
14. Louis Glassy, *"Using Version Control to Observe Student Software Development Processes"*, *Journal of computing Sciences in Colleges*, Volume 21, Issue 3, pp. 99-106, 2006.

SECTION II

Intelligent Systems

12

Artificial Intelligence and Intelligent Systems for Web-based Expert System : A Review

SHILPY SHARMA, MEGHNA SHARMA AND CHANDERKANT VERMA

ABSTRACT

This paper reflects the insight of Artificial Intelligence and their concepts in the real world. As there is vast scope of intelligent systems in every field, the main discussion in this paper is its scope in the field of web engineering. As a case study, the architecture of a web site/application, which includes the Landfill Operation Management Advisor (LOMA) expert system, is presented. Some useful tips have been discussed about the construction of such web sites/applications. Moreover, some explanations are given as the assertion that Web-based expert systems can be considered as a category of Web engineering applications.

1. INTRODUCTION

The paper is organized as follows: Section 2 specifies artificial intelligence and its scope intelligent agents are discussed in Section 3, Section 4 covers intelligent systems. Section 5 covers the web-based expert systems and conclusion is given in Section 6.

2. ARTIFICIAL INTELLIGENCE (AI)

AI is the part of computer science concerned with designing intelligent computer systems, that is, computer systems that exhibit the characteristics we associate with intelligence in human behavior—understanding language, learning, reasoning and solving problems. It is related to the similar task of using computers to understand human intelligence, but AI does not have to confine itself to methods that are biologically observable.

2.1 Theory and Concepts in Artificial Intelligence

2.1.1 Cognitive Robotics

Cognitive Robotics (CR) is concerned with endowing robots with human-like high-level cognitive capabilities to enable the achievement of complex goals in complex environments. Cognitive robotics is focused on using the cognitive behavior of humans as a starting point for the development of robotic computational algorithms. Robotic cognitive capabilities include perception processing, attention allocation, anticipation, planning, reasoning about other agents, and reasoning about their own mental states. Robotic cognition embodies the behavior of intelligent agents in the physical world. A cognitive robot should exhibit: knowledge, beliefs, preferences, goals, informational attitudes and motivational attitudes.

2.1.2 Expert System

An expert system is a computer program that contains the knowledge and analytical skills of one or more human experts, related to a specific subject. It is also known as knowledge-based system. As shown in Figure 12.1 the expert system has two main components:

FIG. 12.1
Expert System

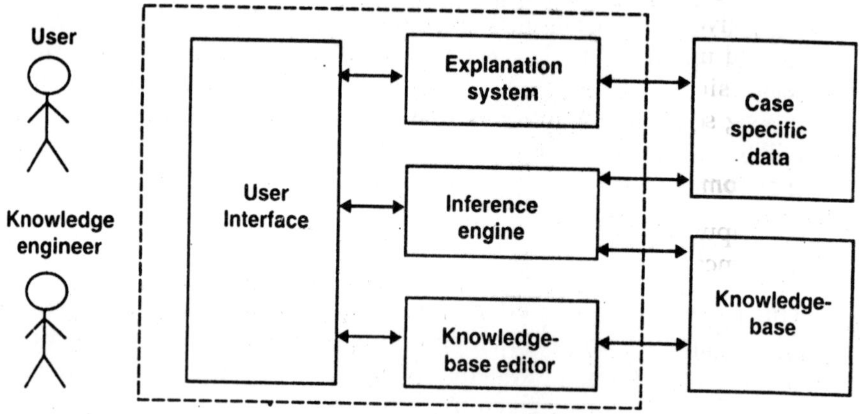

- *Knowledge Representation* is to store knowledge so that programs can process it and achieve the verisimilitude of human intelligence.
- *Knowledge Engineers* are concerned with the representation chosen for the expert's knowledge declarations and with the inference engine used to process that knowledge.

2.1.3 Fuzzy Control System

A fuzzy control system is a control system based on fuzzy logic. It is a mathematical system that analyzes analog input values in terms of logical variables that take on continuous values between 0 and 1, in contrast to classical or digital logic, which operates on discrete values of either 0 and 1 (true and false). Fuzzy logic is used in machine control. Fuzzy logic has the advantage that the solution to the problem can be cast in terms that human operators can understand, so that their experience can be used in the design of the controller.

2.1.4 Genetic Algorithm

A genetic algorithm (GA) is a search technique used in computing to find exact or approximate solutions to optimization and search problems. Genetic algorithms are categorized as global search heuristics. Genetic algorithms are a particular class of evolutionary algorithms that use techniques inspired by evolutionary biology such as inheritance, mutation, selection, and crossover. Genetic algorithms are widely used in bioinformatics, computer science, engineering, economics, chemistry, manufacturing, mathematics, physics and other fields. A typical genetic algorithm requires two things:

- A genetic representation of the solution domain.
- A fitness function to evaluate the solution domain.

2.1.5 Rough Set

A rough set is a formal approximation of a crisp set in terms of a pair of sets which give the lower and the upper approximation of the original set. The lower and upper approximation sets, themselves, are crisp sets in the standard version of rough set theory, but in other variations, the approximating sets may be fuzzy sets as well.

2.1.6 Soft Computing

Soft computing refers to a collection of computational techniques in computer science such as artificial intelligence, machine learning and some engineering disciplines, which attempt to study, model, and analyze very complex phenomena: those for which more conventional methods have not yielded low cost, analytic, and complete solutions. Earlier computational approaches could model and precisely analyze only relatively simple systems. More complex systems arising in biology, medicine, the humanities, management sciences, and similar fields often remained intractable to conventional mathematical and analytical methods. It should be pointed out that simplicity and complexity of systems are relative, and many conventional mathematical models have been both challenging and very productive. Key areas of soft computing are: Neural Networks (NN), Fuzzy Systems (FS), Evolutionary Computation and Swarm Intelligence.

2.1.7 Machine Learning

Machine learning is concerned with the design and development of algorithms and techniques that allow computers to "learn". At a general level, there are two types of learning: inductive, and deductive. Inductive machine learning methods extract rules and patterns out of massive data sets. The major focus of machine learning research is to extract information from data automatically, by computational and statistical methods. Machine learning is widely used in natural language processing, syntactic pattern recognition, search engines, medical diagnosis, bioinformatics and cheminformatics, detecting credit card fraud, stock market analysis, classifying DNA sequences, speech and handwriting recognition, object recognition in computer vision, game playing and robot locomotion.

2.1.8 Hybrid Intelligent System

Hybrid intelligent system denotes a software system which employs, in parallel, a combination of methods and techniques from artificial intelligence subfields as: Neuro-fuzzy systems, Hybrid connectionist—symbolic models, Fuzzy expert systems, Connectionist expert systems, Evolutionary neural networks, Genetic fuzzy systems, Rough fuzzy hybridization, Reinforcement learning with fuzzy, neural, or evolutionary methods as well as symbolic reasoning methods.

3. INTELLIGENT AGENTS

An *intelligent agent (IA)* is a software agent that assists users and will act on their behalf, in performing non-repetitive computer-related task, in the sense of a "representative agent", like an insurance agent or travel agent. Intelligent agents are used for operator assistance or data mining. While they are often based on fixed pre-programmed rules, "Intelligent" in this context is often taken to imply the ability to adapt and learn. In artificial intelligence, an intelligent agent is used for intelligent actors which observe and act upon an environment, in the sense of a rational agent—an entity that is capable of perception, action and goal directed behavior. Such an agent might be a robot or an embedded real time software system—and is intelligent if it interacts with its environment in a manner that would normally be regarded as intelligent if that interaction were carried out by a human being.

FIG. 12.2
Intelligent Agent

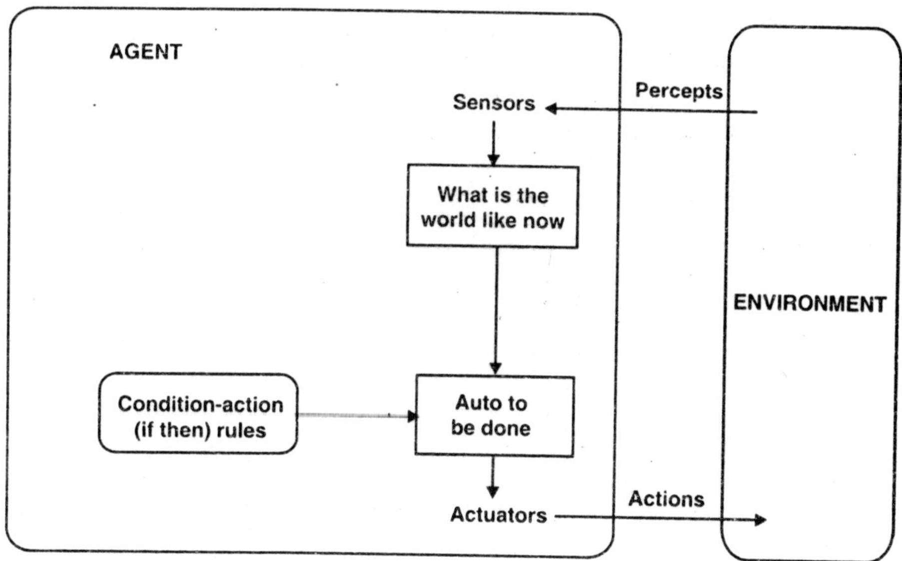

4. INTELLIGENT SYSTEMS

An intelligent system is part of artificial intelligence. It tries to build computer programs that have some function of a human or animal brain, so as to explain the functioning of a brain. Artificial intelligent systems are computer programs that have the majority and eventually all the functions of a brain. Such an intelligent system has senses to gather information from its environment. It can act and has a memory of the results of its actions. It has an objective and by inspecting its memory it can learn from experience, how to better reach its objectives. For complete intelligent systems it should have:

A. *Intelligence* is the system's level of performance in reaching its objectives.
B. *System* is a part of the universe, with a limited extension in space and time. Stronger or more correlations exist between one part of the system and another, than between this part of the system and parts outside of the system.
C. *Sense* is that part of an intelligent system that can receive communications from the environment. Sense organs are needed so that the system can know the environment and act accordingly.
D. *Objective* is a certain situation that some systems try to reach.
E. *Concept* is the basic element of thought. It is a physical,

material storage of information. All the concepts in memory are interrelated; they form a web, a net.

F. *Situation* is a series of concepts that the intelligent system uses to express the information extracted from the environment through its senses.

G. *Action rules* are the results of an experience or the result of observing its memory. It is the physical storage by the intelligent system of a situation and a good corresponding action.

H. *Memory* is the physical storage of concepts and action rules. This includes the situations that the intelligent system has experienced.

I. *Learning* is the most important capacity of an intelligent system. It learns concepts from concurrent sense information. It learns action rules from its experience. Acting, possibly haphazard acting, in a certain situation, is stored with a value. An action rule has a higher value if it helped to reach an objective. Learning includes creating abstract concepts based on concrete examples. It includes learning composite concepts containing the parts of an object. Learning is also the detection of relationships (patterns) between the situation part of an action rule and the resulting future situation.

5. WEB-BASED EXPERT SYSTEMS

To develop a web-based expert system, the developer must know if it will be tempted in to an already developed web site or there is a need to develop a new web site, which will eventually include the developed expert system. In this paper, the focus is on the later case, where a web-based expert system development project can be considered as an attempt to merge two subprojects; an expert system and a probably quite large web site/application.

5.1 Expert System Development Subproject

Following are the activities and challenges within any expert system development project:

1. Domain expert's detection and persuasion for collaboration,
2. Knowledge acquisition,
3. Knowledge representation,
4. Prototype development and programming,
5. Development of the entire expert system and determination of its architecture, and
6. Validation and verification.

5.2 Web Site/Application Development Sub-project

As the web continues to grow exponentially, web sites have been developing with them. Now a day, web site/application developers are using a mix of concepts, tools, methods and best operation practices from several scientific fields like software engineering and information systems to address the specificity of the Web. The essence of Web engineering is to successfully manage the diversity and complexity of Web application development, and hence, to avoid potential failures that can have serious implications. Web engineering principles, must accomplish the following major activities/tasks:

1. Identification of requirements and specifications.
2. Data design process, during which important Web application notions that can/must be displayed to Web users are identified, analyzed and described into implement able data structures.
3. Hypertext design process, during which html code is written and basic objects that constitute the Web pages (e.g. Tables, frames, layers, images, etc.) are identified, taking into consideration criteria like data entities mapping and Web page linking.
4. Architecture design process, during which the main software and hardware components are identified and inter related taking into consideration the efficient Web site/application operation.
5. Implementation.
6. Testing and evaluation.
7. Maintain and evolution.

LOMA's Web site/application developing process is shown in Figure 12.3 explains the workflow process.

5.3 Merging the Sub-projects

Web-based expert systems can be developed by merging the developing processes, and depending on the specifications, by merging the developing processes of other applications like: database management systems, GIS, optimization models, etc. (i.e. which, among with the expert system, can form a Web-based decision support system). These sub-projects can be merged in a manner that activities of the first can be performed in parallel with activities of the second and activities of the second can provide feedback and crucial information for activities of the first and vice versa. Figure 12.4 shows LOMA's Web-based expert system subprojects merging process.

Specifically, during LOMA's Web-based expert system development the following subproject merging points have been identified:

1. During knowledge acquisition process and specifically during the meetings among knowledge engineer and domain experts,

Fig. 12.3
Workflow Process

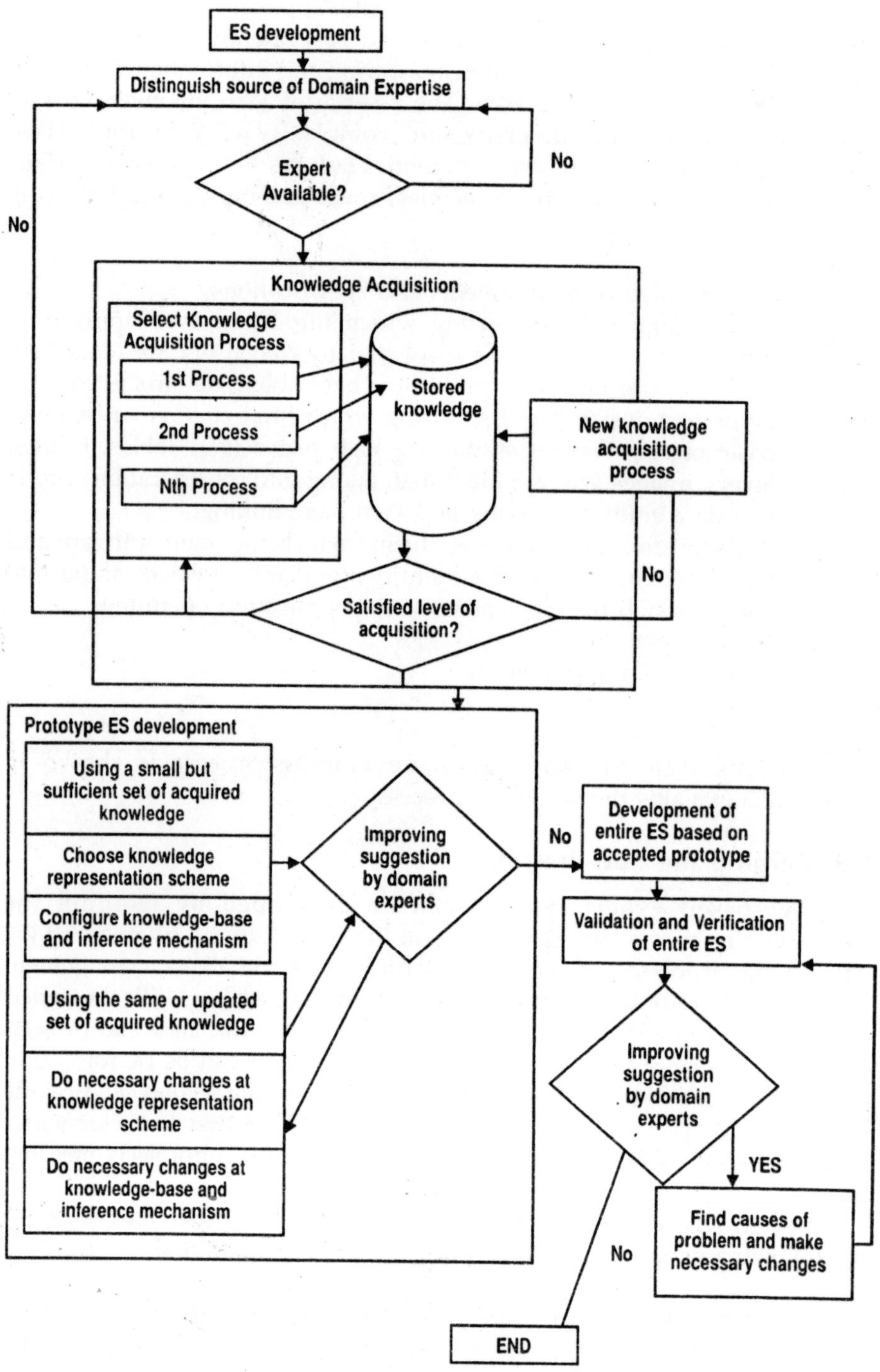

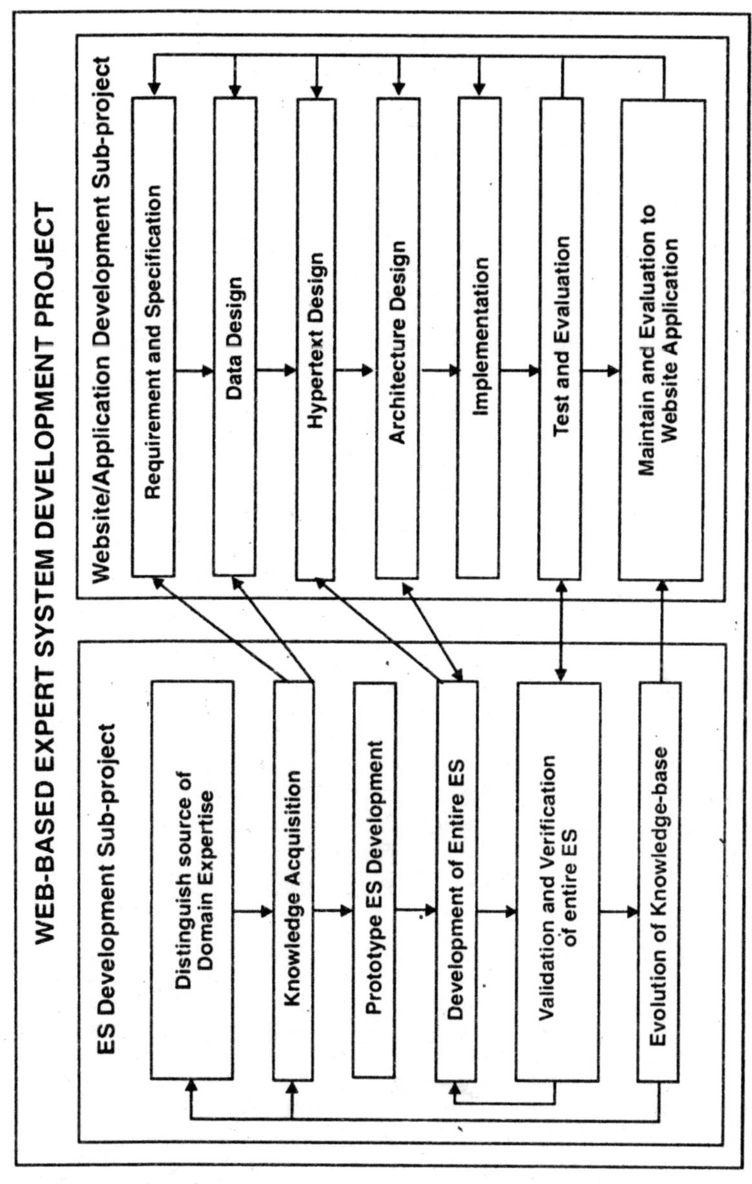

Fig. 12.4
Web-based Expert System Sub-projects Merging Process

questions were asked to domain experts aiming to Web application's requirements apprehension.

2. The knowledge that was acquired during knowledge acquisition process was used also in the data design stage to define implement able data structures.
3. During hypertext design stage, Web page objects were defined and used analogously at the entire expert system development process. Any motivations that were made during the later process to Web page objects were answered back to hypertext design stage.
4. Changes that were made during the entire expert system development process forced changes to architecture design and vice versa.
5. During the validation and verification process of the expert system the identification of some problems by the domain experts forced improving changes not only within the expert system but also within the Web site/application and vice versa.
6. The expert system knowledge-base expanding and evolution process revealed crucial information and inputs that used for the evolution of the Web site/application.

6. CONCLUSION

This paper presents a developing process for web-based expert systems. Based on the process a web based expert system development project can be considered as a merging attempt of two sub-projects; an expert system and a probably quite large web site/application. The process has been followed for LOMA web-based expert system development. Except from the web-based expert system developing process, which can be used as a guide for the development of any web-based system, the main conclusion of this paper is that web-based expert systems can be considered as a web engineering application category.

References

1. Ceri, S. Fraternali, P. Bongio A., Brambilla, M., Comai, S., Matera, M.; Designing Data-Intensive Web Applications. Morgan Kaufman: San Francisco *et al.*, 2003.
2. Developing Web Sites for Web-based Expert Systems: A Web Engineering Approach.
3. Dokas, I.M., Karras, D.A.; Panagiotakopoulos, D.C.: A Fuzzy Expert System Application in the Possibility Estimation of Common Landfill Perational Faults. Civil Engineering and Environmental Systems.
4. Ginige, A., Murugesan, S.; Guest Editors' Introduction: Web Engineering an Introduction. IEEE MultiMedia 8, 2001.

13

Pattern Matching Using Genetic Algorithm

NEELAM AND SAROJ

ABSTRACT

A genetic algorithm begins its search with random solutions of the problem. Every solution is assigned a fitness that is directly related to the objective function of the optimization problem. The initial population is evolved to new population like reproduction, crossover and mutation. A Genetic Algorithm (GA) keeps evolving the successive populations unless some criterion is met or a reasonable acceptable solution is found. Genetic Algorithms are very successful to search the complex spaces due to its global perspective and inherent parallelism. The GA will converge over successive generations towards the global (or near global) optimum. The ability of the algorithm to explore and exploit simultaneously, a growing amount of theoretical justification, and successful application to real-world problems strengthens the conclusion that GAs are a powerful, robust and optimization technique. Main objective is to develop an evolution program for hidden pattern from the user. The program shall access the image and evolve an image matching to the given.

1. INTRODUCTION

Genetic algorithms were formally introduced in the United States in the 1970s by John Holland at University of Michigan. Genetic Algorithms (GA) mimic the evolutionary principals and chromosomal processing of natural genetics. Since then, GAs has been a field of active interest and applied to solve problems almost in all the fields like Computer Science, Electrical Engineering, Mechanical Engineering, Optimization, Biology and Image Processing, etc. One important application of genetic algorithm is to search complex spaces and functional optimization.

A genetic algorithm begins its search with random solutions of the problem. Every solution is assigned a fitness that is directly related to the objective function of the optimization problem. The initial population is evolved to new population like reproduction, crossover and mutation. A genetic algorithm keeps evolving the successive populations unless some criterion is met or a reasonable acceptable solution is found. Genetic Algorithms are very successful to search the complex spaces due to its global perspective and inherent parallelism.

John Holland gave a new technique to search the complex spaces which is known as genetic algorithms. Genetic Algorithms mimic the evolutionary principals of living populations of species and chromosomal processing.

A genetic algorithm starts working on a randomly generated set of solutions, known as initial population. Each solution is represented by a fixed length string of binary numbers (i.e., 1010001). A fitness is associated with each solution. The fitness evaluation is based on objective function.

A genetic algorithm generates new population by selecting the better fit solutions from existing population and applying genetic operators to produce new offsprings of the solutions. The process is repeated successively to generate new populations iteratively. In this way, every successive solution is better fit then the previous population. This process is repeated until some criterion is met or a reasonably acceptable solution is found.

The GA will converge over successive generations towards the global (or near global) optimum. Why these simple operations should produce a fast, useful and robust technique is largely due to the fact that GAs combine direction and chance in the search in an effective and efficient manner.

The ability of the algorithm to explore and exploit simultaneously, a growing amount of theoretical justification, and successful application to real-world problems strengthens the conclusion that GAs are a powerful, robust and optimization technique.

2. COMPONENTS OF A GA

A problem definition as input, and

- Encoding principles (gene, chromosome)
- Initialization procedure (creation)
- Selection of parents (reproduction)
- Genetic operators (mutation, recombination)

- Evaluation function (environment)
- Termination condition

2.1 Representation (encoding)

Possible individual's encoding:

a. Bit strings	0101 ... 1100
b. Real numbers	43.2-33.1 ... 0.0 89.2
c. Permutations of element	E11 E3 E7 ... E1 E15
d. Lists of rules	R1 R2 R3 ... R22 R23
e. Program elements	(genetic programming)
f. Any data structure	

When choosing an encoding method, rely on the following key ideas:

- Use a data structure as close as possible to the natural representation
- Write appropriate genetic operators as needed
- If possible, ensure that all genotypes correspond to feasible solutions
- If possible, ensure that genetic operators preserve feasibility

2.2 Initialization

It starts with a population of randomly generated individuals or use previously saved population or a set of solutions provided by a human expert or a set of solutions provided by another heuristic algorithm.

2.3 Selection

It is used to focus the search in promising regions of the space.

2.4 Recombination (Crossover)

- Enables the evolutionary process to move toward promising regions of the search space.
- Matches good parents' sub-solutions to construct better offspring.

2.5 Mutation

It is a process to simulate the effect of errors that happens with low probability during duplication. It results in movement in the search space and restoration of lost information to the population.

2.6 Evaluation

Each String in initial population or subsequent population is assigned a fitness value which is related to the objective function. For maximizing a function, the fitness can be equal to string's objective function value. To find the optimal minimum the fitness will be equal to 1/(1+f(x)).

Simple Genetic Algorithm

```
Produce an initial population of individuals
Evaluate the fitness of all individuals
While termination condition not met do
        Select fitter individuals for reproduction
        Recombine between individuals
        Mutate individuals
        Evaluate the fitness of the modified individuals
        Generate a new population
End while
```

2.7 Crossover and Mutation

Crossover and Mutation are two basic operators of GA. The performance of a GA depends on them. The ways these operators work depend on the encoding. Here the Crossover and Mutation are shown to work only on binary encoding.

There are number of crossover operators in GA literature (Spears and Dejong, 1991). In the entire crossover operators both strings are cut from an arbitrary place and right portion of the strings are swapped among themselves to create two new strings to represent the two new chromosomes or solutions.

Most often a single point crossover operator is used in GA. The performance of GA depends on the retaining of good building blocks of the strings to successive generations. Crossover operator is responsible to search different areas of the search space. In mutation some bits are inverted. The probability to mutate a bit is kept low. The need for mutation is to keep diversity in the population. After reproduction, crossover and mutation are applied to whole population one generation is completed. The GA operators are applied in the hope that they will produce the better fit solutions. Even if some bad solutions are generated they would not survive over the generations and better solution contributes more to create even better fit solution over successive generations. The success of a GA depends on the right balance of the exploration and refinement of the solutions from the search space.

3. DESIGN OF GENETIC ALGORITHM ENCODING

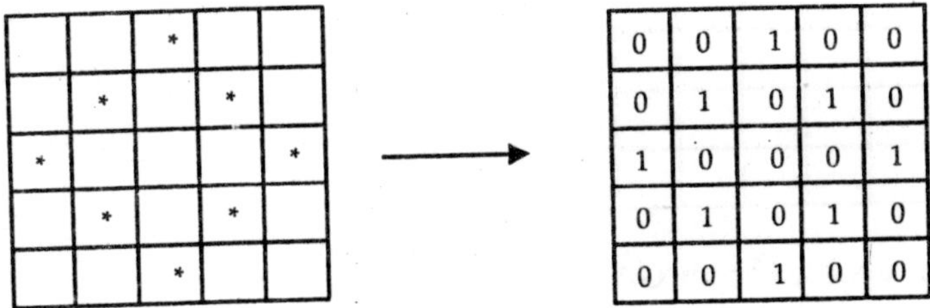

A. Operators

After an initial population is randomly generated, the algorithm evolves the through three operators:

- Selection which equates to survival of the fittest.
- Crossover which represents mating between individuals.
- Mutation which introduces random modification.

B. Crossover

According to GA literature, there are number of crossover operators. In the entire crossover operators both strings are cut an arbitrary place and right portion of the strings are swapped among themselves to create two new strings to represent the two new chromosomes or solutions.

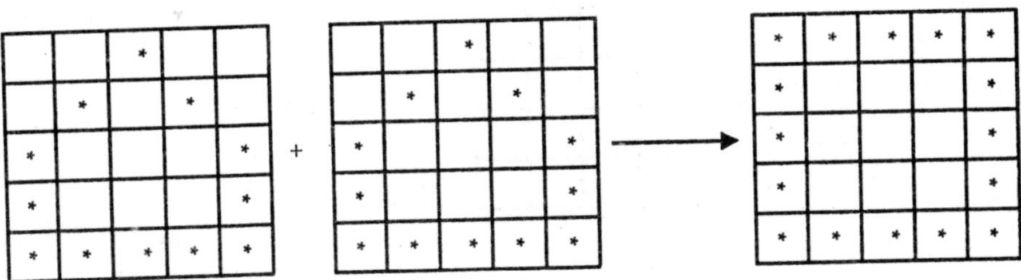

C. Mutation

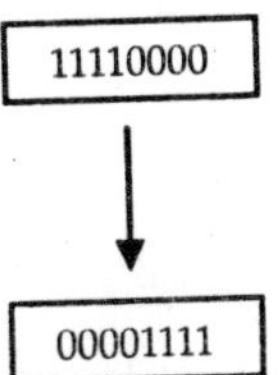

D. Fitness Function

Following are steps for matching of patterns evolution with the given pattern.

	1	1		
		1		
		1		

Pattern evolved from GA

	1	0		
		1		
		1		

Given pattern

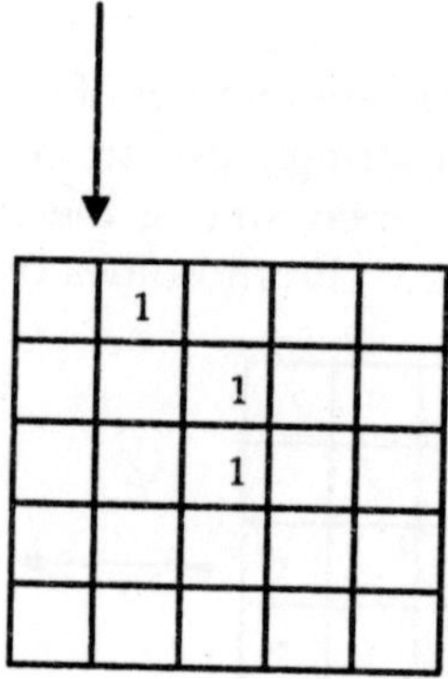

Best fit

Main objective is to develop an evolution program for hidden pattern from the user. The program shall access the image and evolve an image matching to the given.

For this we used different methodology:

- Survey of pattern recognition techniques.
- Survey of evolution algorithms.
- Design of genetic algorithm.
- Selection of pattern/colors can be included.
- Presentation of result.

Scope of methodology is:

- Games
- Pattern Matching
- Image Processing

References

1. C. Darwin, On the Origin of Species by Means of Natural Selection; or, the Preservation of Flavored Races in the Struggle for Life. John Murray, London, 1859.
2. W.D. Hillis, Co-Evolving Parasites Improve Simulated Evolution as an Optimization Procedure. Artificial Life 2, Vol. 10, Addison-Wesley, 1991.
3. J.H. Holland, Adaptation in Natural and Artificial Systems. The University of Michigan Press, Ann Arbor, Michigan, 1975.
4. Z. Michalewicz. Genetic Algorithms + Data Structures = Evolution Programs. Springer-Verlag, Berlin, Third Edition, 1996.
5. M. Sipper, Machine Nature: The Coming Age of Bio-Inspired Computing. McGraw-Hill, New-York, First Edition, 2002.
6. M. Tomassini, Evolutionary Algorithms. In E. Sanchez and M. Tomassini, editors, Towards Evolvable Hardware, Volume 1062 of Lecture Notes in Computer Science, pp. 19-47. Springer-Verlag, Berlin, 1996.
7. Goldberg, D., Genetic Algorithms, Addison Wesley, 1988.

14

Classification and Retrieval of Component using Fuzzy Approach

NAVNEET KAUR

ABSTRACT

Software reuse has become a topic of much interest in the software community due to its potential benefits, which include increased product quality and decreased product cost and schedule, but appropriate classification and retrieval tools have to be provided in order to exploit the pros. A bottleneck in software reuse is the classification schema and retrieval method of components, particularly, when large repositories of components are available. Classification and retrieval for reuse should be flexible to allow the selection of components which, although not perfectly matching requirements, are adaptable with a limited effort. It include Fuzzy classification model for a repository storing descriptors of components. These descriptors include fuzzy-weighted keyword pairs describing components functionalities extracted from code and its design documentation. This approach is used to solve a problem like classification and retrieval of components.

1. INTRODUCTION

Effective software reuse needs classification and retrieval techniques for components to make development by reuse convenient. Fuzzy technique is used for software classification and retrieval based on descriptors constructed from the code and its accompanying documentation. Descriptors are composed by term pairs named features, interpreted as open class keywords describing the component functionalities. Features are assigned a relevance weight between 0 and 1 by means of a weighing function. The list of features in one descriptor has associated weights vectors that interpret as a fuzzy set. This fuzzy set is the basis for components classification and retrieval under uncertainty. [1, 2]

2. REUSE THROUGH FUZZY ACCESS TO A REPOSITORY

The Basic step of classification of components is the extraction of information describing reusable components. Repository consisting of descriptors at three levels: requirement specification, design, and implementation. Reusable components are requirements, design documentation, and code [6, 7]. Here, design level and implementation level is considered.

(i) Design level, and namely on design documents related to Information Systems (IS); the repository contains ER diagrams, describing the IS static part, and transaction design documentation, such as DFDs, or module-level documents, describing the IS dynamic part;

(ii) Implementation level, particularly of object-oriented code; the descriptors characterize (clusters of) classes in terms of attributes and methods;

The repository descriptors are classes of object-oriented type. This choice is done for two reasons;

(iii) Classes merge static and dynamic aspects therefore are a useful paradigm for our descriptors; and

(iv) The reuse system is prototyped using the SIB (Software Information Base) repository implemented in the Telos language. Descriptors are obtained from this IS documentation and from code.

The proposed mechanism is illustrated on unrelated examples of ER schemas and code, to discuss the different issues arising at descriptor construction. This mechanism extracts keywords from the design documentation and code, and assigns them a fuzzy weight. The fuzzy part of the descriptor consists of lists of weighted keyword pairs called features, describing the functionalities provided by the component. The fuzzy weight assigned to features in the list descriptor supports exploration of the repository. In fact, since often the needed component is not available, but rather adaptable components are present, the fuzzy part allows the developer to pose imprecise queries, asking for a set of expected characteristics. Imprecision is bound to fuzzy weights; candidates are returned ranked according to their degree of fitness to the functionalities required in the query, that is, according to their adaptability to the searched component(s). A Thesaurus supports the classification and retrieval, providing unique terms and synonyms. In the following, it specifies the "how well" the features describes the component behavior.

3. CLASSIFICATION AND RETRIEVAL MODEL

This section presents the fuzzy classification and retrieval model based on features, i.e. term pairs describing the functionalities of reusable components. Fuzzy weight assignment to features is presented[3]. The classification is supported by a thesaurus where a fuzzy synonymic relationship is defined. Object-oriented code is considered and, therefore, will employ the terminology of object-orientation. Moreover, component is denoted as a reusable unit of code (either a class or a class cluster) whose granularity has been chosen by the users.

3.1 Fuzzy Behavioral Descriptors

The Component Descriptors (CDs) of the SIB (Software Information Base) have a standard object-oriented part exploiting the characteristics of the Telos SIB description language, and a fuzzy part of the following format:

List-of [feature: fuzzy weight]

Describing the behavior of a software component implies a certain degree of imprecision due to the multiplicity of characteristics usually exhibited even by simple components. A summarization is important for effectiveness in comprehending and possibly reusing code. A multiple descriptor of code components taking into account several behavioral characteristics is a viable approach to deal with this imprecision source.

Software behavior is described by two terms structures called features allowing for a richer semantics than usual single term description, while remaining simple enough to avoid the need for a formal grammar and semantics definition of a component description language, e.g., for object-oriented code, method names are taken as the first term in the feature, and the first argument of the method as the second term. A software descriptor is a list of features describing the characteristics of a software component, that is, of a class, or set of classes, or library, chosen as a unit of reuse by the system maintainers.

In order to handle classification and retrieval by means of descriptors, the features in the list are assigned a relevance measure expressed by a weight, a number between and 1. The role of weights is clarified by the following considerations.

Usually, software components have a basic behavior (e.g., an array will be assigned the basic feature "random access") and a set of additional methods that are common to other components (e.g. "'print-element"). Furthermore, there can be other methods ("sort-self", where "self" is the standard auto-reference) supporting the basic behavior and characterizing only partially the component. For these reasons, the features are weighted in order to enhance the visibility of different behaviors. The mechanism of weights employs a frequency analysis technique of terms used in methods. The technique is taken from text analysis literature: it is an adaptation of the classical term weighting functions to the case of software which has only a skeletal text structure. The weights in a descriptor are viewed as a fuzzy set and fuzzy techniques are used for the retrieval.

3.2 Classification Granularity

Different application domains usually require different granularity in components classification. In some case, the single class is the reusable unit (e.g., in system programming, or in libraries for numerical computation), while in other cases, an entire library is considered as a whole unit (e.g., Computer Graphics applications or Information Systems)[9]. In this approach, descriptors are associated to single classes. Alternatively, one descriptor can be associated to a cluster of *n* classes if the *n* classes are judged as a whole reusable unit, e.g., because they are a set of cooperating classes linked via is-a, part-of, friend of relationships and via message exchange. Often, the repository is updated upon arrival of software libraries, which can be described as a whole (by associating a descriptor to the root class) or can be described at a finer granularity (by associating descriptors to some key classes of the library). These are choices usually left to the system maintainers, although they are an interesting issue for automatic analysis.

3.3 Fuzzy Weights

The assignment of fuzzy weights to features in the descriptors is done automatically in the following way. First, weighting function is chosen in order to associate weights to features [2, 3]. A suitable function is the following Feature Weighting Function (FWF) :

$$W_{ik} = \frac{V_{ik}\ , \log\left(\frac{N}{n_k}\right)}{\sqrt{\sum_{j=1}^{F}(V_{ij})^2\ , \left(\log\left(\frac{N}{n_j}\right)\right)^2}}$$

where w_{ik} is the weight of the *k*-th feature with respect to *i*-th component and v_{ik} is the frequency of the *k*-th feature in that component, N is the repository size and n_k is the number of repository items exhibiting that feature. F is the total number of features in the repository.

A fuzzy weight can be obtained from FWF values by considering that each descriptor is made by contexts. A context is an interpretation domain to which a different behavioral description of the same component is associated. The number C of contexts varies from descriptor to descriptor; the case of context less descriptors can be dealt with simply by introducing a dummy repository-wise context.

Exploiting contexts, a refinement of FWF is computed namely $\{w_{i,k,j}\}$ for j = 1, 2, . . . , C. Each $\{w_{i,k,j}\}$, is the weight of the *k*-th feature with respect to the *i*-th component in the *j*-th context. The fuzzy set W of weights in feature list has characteristic function $\{w_{i,k,j}\}$ and is called the fuzzy weight of the *k*-th feature with respect to the *i*-th component.

Not all the features of a descriptor have the same relevance in describing the properties of the associated component. Moreover, the relevance of features is context-sensitive, that is, it is influenced by the global characteristics of the component base and by the user community. E.g., for a graphical component "graphic-mode" or "draw-line" are highly relevant. Instead, these features are less relevant within a specialized repository for graphical applications. These issues are taken into account by employing a weighting function considering both relevance of features at the component level and repository-wide relevance. This kind of weighting technique is widely used in text-retrieval applications for weighting relevant terms in text documents. An adaptation of such classical weighting functions to our application is described in. Here, the application of the function to some code classes and to ER schemas are shown.

Features Automatically Extracted and Weighted from a Sample Code Base

```
(*class STACK*)
CD [1] =
(store, io: 0.07),
(store, file: 0.13),
(replacefrom, seqcltn: 0.99),
(remove, object: 0.42),
(atallput, object: 0.75),
(indexofsubcollection, seqcltn: 0.75),
(capacity,*: 0.60),
(resize, int: 0.99),
(get,last: 0.95),
(size,*: 0.60),
(hash,*: 0.25),
(isempty,*: 0.60),
(remove, last: 0.75)
```

Features Extracted from ER Schemas

(* class COURSE ORGANIZATION*)
CD [2] = (
(person-name: 0.3),
(student-e-mail: 0.3),
(principal-position: 0.5),
(course-topic: 0.8),
(course-participant: 0.5),
(course-program: 0.4),
(course-teacher: 0.7),
(program-deadline : 0.7),
(program-contents: 0.8))

(*class SEMINAR ORGANIZATION*)
CD [3] = (
(person-name: 0.3),
(secretary-phone: 0.4),
(organizer-position: 0.5),
(seminar-title: 0.8),
(participant-position: 0.5),
(seminar-secretary: 0.3),
(seminar-organizer: 0.7),
(seminar-participant: 0.7))

The maximum relevance degree for Course Organization is equal to 10. Hence, main entities must have degree equal or greater than 5. Moreover, some features have been eliminated by inspection. For Seminar Organization schema the maximum relevance degree is 8, in this case all the entities above 4 are retained. These interpret the set of weights as the characteristic function of a fuzzy set and call the fuzzy weight associated to the descriptor.

4. RETRIEVAL AND QUERY LANGUAGE

Currently, a retrieval mechanism is thoroughly inspired by the classification method. Specifically, a query is composed of a precise part, posed on class attributes such as source language of the component, author, aimed at limiting the search space, and of a fuzzy part that enables to perform imprecise retrieval. The fuzzy query is composed of a list of terms and fuzzy values.

As an example, consider a query searching components with the following feature list:

manage-database, 0.8;
support-transaction, 0.2;
protocols-wide-area, 0.9

Here, components are searched that have distributed database management systems functionalities. The weights express the importance of each feature in the query, that is, ultimately, of the desired functionality in the retrieved components. Queries submitted to the repository are forwarded to the Thesaurus where synonymia values are stored [5]. Synonymia expands the search to increase the recall. In current experimentation, SQLf (Fuzzy extension of SQL) query language is evaluated as an alternative environment to execute fuzzy queries. The fuzzy query is a fuzzy propositional calculus formula with modifiers, such as some, high, and so on. Referring to the example above, it could specify [2] *high* manage-database;

AND *some* support-transaction;
AND *high* protocols-wide-area

This formula can be readily translated in a SQLf form. A prototype is experimenting where SQLf is executing in a traditional relational environment. It is interesting to note that in this a non-standard definition of the fuzzy logic AND connective is chosen. In particular, AND is a weighted mean of the involved characteristic functions, instead of the usual minimum. Informally, it can be said that this choice prevents a component, having a good matching on some of the requested features but not including all of them, to be discarded. An issue that is tackling is the problem of different cardinalities of the query and descriptors.

5. COMPUTATION OF DEGREE OF SATISFACTION

In dKFC (degree of satisfaction of component C related to facet F for each keyword K), the format for the queries is the first step. Since, the keywords stored in the facets do not always represents exactly the component the user is looking for, a degree of fuzziness is introduced [4]. For each of the facets the user can specified one or more keywords and state the degree of evidence with which each of these keywords represents the desired software entity. This is done associating one of the following four specified degrees to the keywords, ordered from the most to the less representative:

VH	Very High
H	High
L	Low
VL	Very Low

This allows the user to deal with incomplete or imprecise specification, and introduces negative statements in the query (the user can impose that a determinate keyword must represent the desired component with a very low degree). Of course, the result of the query on each of the components stored in the library will not be a binary value, but will vary in the range [0, 1] depending on the degrees associated to the keywords in the query and the values asociated to the keywords in the components' descriptors. The pseudo-code describes the search engine.

It simply calculates a degree of satisfaction for the query for each of the component in the library and returns as output all the components with a value for the degree of satisfaction equal to this maximum. The component is done dividing' the query in many sub-queries related to the single facets. The final value of the degree of satisfaction of a component for the query is obtained as the sum of the degree of satisfaction for all of these sub-queries [4, 8].

The sub-query related to a facet can be expressed in the following form: $k_1=d_1$, $k_2=d_2$, ...$k_n=d_n$ where k_i is a keyword in the considered facet, and d_i is the degree of satisfaction wanted for the keyword k_i for the artifacts satisfying the query.

The degree of the satisfaction dFC of a single component for the sub-query can be expressed solving the following fuzzy expression:

```
if k1=d1 AND k2=d2 AND ........AND kn=dn  THEN dFC
Where the fuzzy value of dFC is the minimum of the fuzzy value obtained
evaluating the conditions ki=di
maxdC=0;// maximum degree of satisfaction  for the query for all the
components in the library
IC=empty; // list of all the components with the maximum degree of
satisfaction // for the query
for each component C in the library
{
     dC=0; // degree of satisfaction of C for the query Q
     for each facet F in the vocabulary
     {
          dFC=l; // degree of satisfaction of C for the  part of Q related
          to F
          for each keyword K in Q belonging to F
          {
          using the keyword related to F in the descriptor of C and the tree
          structure of the Facet, calculate the degree dKFC with which K
          represents C; starting from dKFC, obtain dQKFC representing
          the degree of satisfaction of C for the part of Q involving K;
          if dQKFC<dFC then dFC= dQKFC;
          }
     dC=dC+dFC ;
          }
          if maxdC>dC then
          {
               empty IC;
               maxdC=dC;
               }
               add C to IC
}
return IC and maxdC as output;
```

These values are obtained starting from the values representing the degree of representation of k_1 for the component (dKFC), passing it as the argument to an appropriate function. There is such a function for each of the four degree of satisfaction allowed in the query.

In order to complete the computation of the degree of satisfaction of the sub-query, it is required to determinate the value of dKFC, i.e. the degree of representation of the keyword k_i for the considered component. Let k_q be the keyword appearing in the query, k_c the keyword of the descriptor of the component for the facet to which k_q belongs, and d_k the value associated to k_c in the descriptor.

There are four different cases that have to be considered for the computation of dKFC:

- $k_c = k_q$;
- k_q is an ancestor of k_c in the tree representing the facet;
- k_c is an ancestor of k_q in the tree representing the facet;
- k_c and k_q belongs to the same tree (they are keywords of the same facet), so they have a common ancestor, but neither one is a direct ancestor of the other.

(i) The first case is the simplest, since d_c represents, we wanted degree and we can simply write: dKFC= d_c

(ii) If kq is an ancestor of kc, then kc is a specialization of kq, and we can write again: dKFC= dc

(iii) If kc is the father of kq, then we can calculate probability P as the weight of the edge linking kq to kc divided by the sum of the weights of all the edges starting from kc. Then we can compute dKFC as follows: dKFC =dc*P.
If k_c is not the father of k_q, but only one of its ancestors, the computation is very similar and is done in a recursive way. If we denote k_1 the intermediate keywords in the path leading from k_c to k_q for each of the involved edges a probability Pi can be computed in exactly the same way seen above.
The total P will then be the product:
P = π Pi, where i=1 to n
And once again we write:
dKFC = d_c * P = d_c * π Pi, where i=1 to n
Let us consider the sample facet of figure 1: if we are looking for a "black pen" and the considered component is a "pen" with a degree of 0.7, we have P1=0.8/(0.4+0.8)=2/3, and P2=0.6/(0.8+0.6)=0.6/1.4, leading to P=(2/3)*(0.6/1.4)=0.2/0.7.
Finally, we can compute the value of dKFC: dKFC=0.7*(0.2/0.7)=0.2

(iv) Finally, if kc and kq have an ancestor in common, but they are not one a direct ancestor of the other one, a combined version

of the cases 2 and 3 is applied to compute P, and then dKFC is again obtained as the product of dc for P.
At this point we compute the total P as the product: $P=P_c*P_q$
And once again we write: $dKFC = d_c * P$

FIG. 14.1
Sample Facet

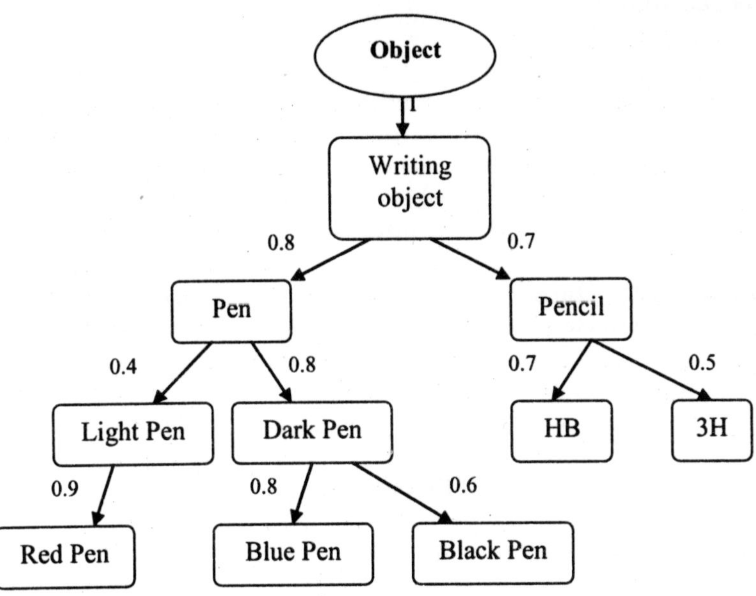

6. AN EXAMPLE APPLICATION

Let us suppose that we are interested in finding a pen which we want to be dark, and we would prefer to be blue. This can be expressed with the following query:

Dark pen=VH (Very High), blue pen=H (High)

FIG. 14.2
Objects Description

If we consider Object 1, first of all we have to determinate the degree of satisfaction of each of the keyword in the query. The keyword in the descriptor is "Black Pen" as shown in Figure 14.2. This means that when we consider the keyword "Dark Pen", we fall in case 2, and dKFC=1. When we consider "Blue Pen", we fall in case 4 and the computation gives dKFC=l*0.8/ (0.8+0.6)=0.8/1.4=0.57.

7. CONCLUSIONS

This paper presents an approach to fuzzy retrieval of components from a repository based on fuzzy-weighted keyword pairs (features) describing the component functionalities. A method for automatic assignment of weights to features has been described. The approach relies on a thesaurus of terms used to describe the reusable components. For Fuzzy Classification retrieval methodology, firstly introduces a parameter in the descriptor describing the degree with which a keyword describes a component. The queries have been refined, too, allowing the user to specify if a keyword represents the characteristics of the searched artifact at a very high, high, low, or very low level. This method allows the user to specify how much a keyword is representative of the searched components, giving the mean to specify the undesired keywords, too, through a set of Fuzzy attributes.

REFERENCES

1. Kimberly Jordan, MJY Team, George Mason University, Software Reuse Term Paper, April 1997.
2. E. Damiani and M.G. Fugini, Design and Code Reuse Based on Fuzzy Classification of Components, ACM, pp. 26-32, 1996.
3. E. Damiani and M.G. Fugini, "Fuzzy Techniques for Software Reuse", Association for Computing Machinery, Inc. (ACM), pp. 552-57, 1996.
4. Francesco Baruchelli and Giancarlo Succi, A Fuzzy Approach to Faceted Classification and Retrieval of Reusable Software Components, pp. 15-20, 1997.
5. E. Damiani, and M.G. Fugini, "Automatic Thesaurus Construction Supporting Fuzzy Retrieval of Reusable Components", Proc. ACM SIG-APP Conf. (SAC'95), Nashville, Feb. 1995.
6. K. Czarnecki, Generative Programming: Principles and Techniques of Software Engineering Based on Automated Configuration and Fragment-based Component Models. Chapter 3, 1998.
7. Larry Smith, STSC, Software Reuse Technologies and Applications, December 1994.
8. Rubén Prieto-Díaz, "Implementing Faceted Classification for Software Reuse", Communications of the ACM, Vol. 34, pp. 88-97, 1991.
9. Rubén Prieto-Díaz, Software Reuse: Issues and Experiences, American Programmer, Vol. 6, No. 8, pp. 10-18, April 1993.

15

A Comprehensiveness to Intrusion Detection System Using Fuzzy Sets and Rough Sets

NANCY MEHTA, ARADHNA MEHTA AND NEERA BAWA

ABSTRACT

Computer intrusion detection is to do with identifying computer activities that may compromise the integrity, confidentiality or the availability of an IT system. Anomaly Intrusion Detection Systems (IDSs) aim at distinguishing an abnormal activity from an ordinary one. In IDS, many intelligent information processing methods, data mining technology and so on have been applied to generating attack signatures automatically, updating signatures easily and improving detection accuracy with ultra data set. This paper presents an improved association rule discovering system under fuzzy set and rough set theory framework of modeling IDSs. The system makes association rule applicable in classifying fields. The system exploits data reductions, rule selection to improve detection accuracy and reduce false alarm and unreal alarm.

1. INTRODUCTION

The name "Intrusion Detection System (IDS)" suggests one to get something that if deployed in a network alarms you in case of an attack.

Systems that also try to block those attacks are known as Intrusion Prevention Systems (IPS). The magic of deciding what is an attack and what is normal is left most of the time to single sensors matching traffic patterns or observing system activity. One who has operated such a system knows what he gets. Sometimes it works quite well; often it fails for several reasons.

Intrusion detection approaches are commonly divided into two categories: misuse detection and anomaly detection [Sundaram, 1996]. The misuse detection approach attempts to recognize attacks that follow intrusion patterns that have been recognized and reported by experts. Misuse detection systems are vulnerable to intruders who use new patterns of behavior or who mask their illegal behavior to deceive the detection system. Anomaly detection methods were developed to counter this problem. With the anomaly detection approach, one represents patterns of normal behavior, with the assumption that an intrusion can be identified based on some deviation from this normal behavior. When such a deviation is observed, an intrusion alarm is produced. Limitations of traditional intrusion detection techniques are as much a function of the ability of a person to process large amounts of information as they are limitations of the techniques themselves. To reduce computational requirements to a realistic level, intrusion detection systems focus on a limited set of system and user attributes. [HDL+90] Dynamic behavior of a hostile user across a networked system is hard to encapsulate and represent with such a limited set. In order to balance the need to examine large quantities of data with the difficulty of comprehending such quantities, we propose a geometric approach to detection. Geometric models lend themselves to combination and prediction. Two things are needed in order to improve the performance of IDS.

- A standard by which to encode and represent complex computer systems.
- A model presenting information in a context which data may be presented as relationships between components.

In this paper we present a discussion of a useful association rules which provides a model comprising of Fuzzy Sets and Rough sets for performing several of the activities used by traditional intrusion detection systems

2. ARTIFICIAL INTELLIGENCE AND INTRUSION DETECTION METHODS

There are two types of intrusion detection methods: misuse detection and anomaly detection. Misuse detection is based on the knowledge of system vulnerabilities and the known attack patterns, while anomaly detection assumes that an intrusion will always reflect some deviations from normal patterns.

Many artificial intelligence techniques have been applied to both misuse detection and anomaly detection as shown in Table 15.1.

TABLE 15.1
Summary of AI Techniques and Intrusion Detection

Intrusion Detection Types	*AI Techniques*	*Pros*	*Cons*
	Rule-based Expert System	Efficiency of pattern matching; Ease of construction	Dependency on audit data
Misuse Intrusion Detection	State Transition Analysis	General rules at higher level Sequential rules	Effort of construction
	Genetic Algorithms	Efficiency of pattern matching	Less general
Anomaly	Inductive Sequential Patterns	Automatic and adaptive learning	A large amount of training time
	Artificial Neural Networks	Tolerance of Noisy data	A large amount of training time
	Data mining Methods	Automatic and adaptive learning; more powerful rules	A large amount of training time

3. DATA MINING AND ASSOCIATION RULES

Data mining techniques have been commonly used to extract patterns from sets of data. Specifically, two data mining approaches have been proposed [Dokas, 2002], [Lee, 1998] and used for anomaly detection: frequency episodes and association rules. Frequency episode techniques [Luo, 2000], [Mannila, 1995], [Mannila, 1996] are effective in detecting sequential patterns of occurrences in a sequence of events. On the other hand, association rule algorithms find correlations between features or attributes used to describe a data set. The most popular algorithm for mining association rules over two-valued attributes is known as the *Apriori* algorithm, which was introduced in 1994 [Agrawal & Srikant, 1994]. It is important to note that this paper explores the use of association rule algorithms to produce rules suitable for anomaly-based and signature-based detection by mining normal (attack-free) and attack network traffic respectively.

Mining of quantitative attributes, as opposed to two-valued attributes, presented a significant challenge: categorizing numerical attributes. One solution to this problem transformed quantitative variables into a set of binary variables by partitioning the domain of the variable into discrete intervals and then applied the *Apriori* algorithm. This approach, however, suffered from a major drawback known as the "sharp boundary problem", i.e., a very small change in value may produce an abrupt change in intervals [Bridges & Vaughn, 2000], [Kuok, 1998], [Luo & Bridges, 2000]. An alternative solution using fuzzy sets [Zadeh, 1996], introduced by Kuok *et al.* [Kuok, 1998] to categorize quantitative variables, offered smooth transitions from one fuzzy set to another. Another solution is using rough sets which is the qualitative generalization of variables applied to Intrusion Detection

4. SOLUTION I—FUZZY LOGIC AND INTRUSION DETECTION

Fuzzy logic techniques have been employed in the computer security field since the early 90's [Hosmer, 1993; Ovchinnikov, 1994]. Its ability to model complex systems made it a valid alternative in the computer security field to analyze continuous sources of data and even unknown or imprecise processes [Hosmer, 1993]. Fuzzy logic has also demonstrated potential in the intrusion detection field when compared to systems using strict signature matching or classic pattern deviation detection. Use of multi-valued logic in pattern-matching tools, such as the remote fingerprinting tool Xprobe, offers a variety of alternatives as opposed to classic binary matching. This tool used four discrete-truth-values when evaluating a match against a signature. Fuzzy logic extends this concept by using membership functions to evaluate the degree of truth of a match.

Artificial Intelligence (AI) techniques have also been explored [Stolfo, 2000] to build intrusion detection systems based on knowledge of past behavior and normal use. They have shown potential for anomaly detection but with limited ability to compete against classic signature-based systems. In any case, most of these approaches do not use fuzzy logic.

The *FIRE* system [Dickerson, 2000] uses a simple data-mining algorithm to identify the features that will be helpful in detecting attacks. Based on analyzed data, the system produces adequate fuzzy sets that are used by a security administrator to develop fuzzy rules. In contrast, our approach proposes mechanisms to automate the rule generation process.

4.1. Architecture

The proposed system architecture (see Figure 15.1) has two modes of operation: rule-generation and detection. When operating in the rule-generation mode, the system processes network data and uses a fuzzy data-mining algorithm to generate rules. A subset of the rules produced by the data-mining algorithm is used as a model for the input data. The detection mode uses this rule subset for intrusion detection.

The following subsections describe the different components of the architecture (including the data mining algorithm and rule selection criteria) as well as their interactions:

FIG. 15.1
System Architecture

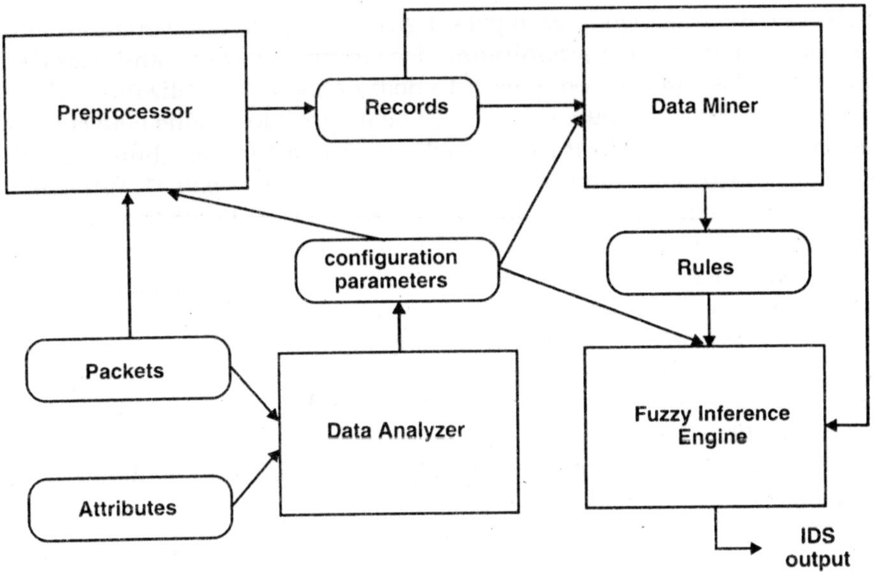

I. Packets

Packets and attributes constitute the initial input for the IDS. The IDS can handle either online or offline operations. During offline operations, the packets are read from a tcp dump file or other similar data repositories. However, in normal operating conditions, the IDS handles real-time traffic as provided by a network packet sniffer.

II. Attributes

Prior to any data analysis, attributes representing relevant features of the input data (packets) must be established. The set of attributes provided to the data analyzer is a subset of all possible attributes pertaining to the information contained in packets headers, packet payloads, as well as aggregate information such as statistics in the number and type of packets or established TCP connections. Attributes are represented by names that will be used as linguistic variables [Zadeh, 1973], [Zadeh, 1975] by the Data Miner and the Fuzzy Inference Engine.

III. Data Analyzer

Once attributes of relevance have been defined and a data source identified, a data analyzer is employed to compute configuration parameters that regulate operation of the IDS. This module analyzes packets and computes aggregate information by grouping packets. Packets can be placed in fixed size groups (*n-group*) or in groups of packets captured in a fixed amount of time (*t-group*). Each *n-group* contains the same number of packets covering a variable time range and each *t-group* contains a variable number of packets captured over a fixed period of time. The module analyzes data contained in each packet group to obtain domain information for each attribute, e.g., minimum, maximum, average and standard deviation. This information is used to help define a normalization scheme for each attribute. Attribute values must be mapped to a value between zero and one when normalization is used. In general, for attribute $attr_i$, the normalized attribute value $attr_i$ is computed as $attr_i = min\ (1, attr_i/attr^N_i)$ where $attr^N_i$ is either a fixed value or a value associated with the maximum value for the attribute. For each attribute a term set is defined to help express rules using fuzzy variables. The term set is the set of linguistic terms used to describe the attribute and is denoted as $TERMS\ (attr_i) = \{term_1, term_2, \ldots, term_n\}$, where $term_j$ is a linguistic term defined by a fuzzy membership function. For instance if *TCP* is an attribute describing the amount of *TCP* packets in a *t-group*, we may define its associated term set as *TERMS (TCP)* = *{Low, Medium, High}*.

The data analyzer can work in any one of three modes to define terms associated with attributes:

- *Fixed:* the value used to normalize the attribute, $attr^N_i$, corresponds to the maximum value the attribute *can* have. For instance, if an attribute is related to an 8-bit field, then the number 255 is used to normalize the attribute.
- *Dynamic:* the value used to normalize the attribute, $attr^N_i$, corresponds to the maximum value the attribute *has* in the data set.
- *User-defined:* the value used to normalize the attribute, $attr^N_i$, is defined by the user.

IV. Configuration Parameters

Upon analyzing data and attributes, the Data Analyzer produces a file where all configuration parameters are stored. Parameter values stored in this file regulate operation of the Preprocessor, Data Mining algorithm and Fuzzy Inference Engine (see Figure 15.1).

The configuration file specifies how attribute values are normalized, associates attributes with a term set, and describes functions corresponding to the fuzzy membership functions associated with each term.

V. Preprocessor

The Preprocessor is responsible for accepting raw packet data and producing records for each *n-group* or *t-group* as specified by the configuration file. This component is used in both rule-generation mode and detection mode and is capable of reading packets from the wire or a tcp dump file. The output produced by this component consists of records, each containing aggregate information for each packet group. Using records and concentrating only on attributes of interest greatly help in reducing the amount of information to be used by more computationally intensive components of the architecture. Specifically, records (and not packets) are used to evaluate fuzzy logic rules used in our system (with the exception of the case where one packet maps to one record).

VI. Data Miner

A variation of Kuok's [Kuok] algorithm is used to implement the Data Miner, which allows for efficient, single-pass, record processing by partitioning data into hierarchical files. The procedure is a deterministic algorithm that produces a set of output rules (or association rules). Candidate rules, are expressed attributes expressed in terms of *itemsets*, a grouping of relevant attributes. In order to minimize the potentially large number of candidate rules, the algorithm uses the concept of *large itemsets* to maximize the expressive power of the rule. Our implementation integrates the *Apriori* and Kuok's algorithm and is capable of discovering association rules for binary, categorical and numerical attributes. The final output of the algorithm is a set of rules that meet the confidence and support constraints given as input. These constraints are quantitative qualifiers used to evaluate the relevance of an association rule. *Support* of a rule is a measure of the fraction of the entire data set for which all predicate terms of the rule hold true. *Confidence* of a rule is a measure of the fraction of the data set for which, if the antecedent holds true, then the consequence holds true. For instance, consider a network where 80% of all the traffic is *TCP* and 40% of all *TCP* traffic is *HTTP*. In that case, the associations rule *TCP. HTTP* has a support of 32% (0.8 * 0.4 * 100) and a confidence of 40%. The main stages of the algorithm are as follows:

- *Initialization*: configuration file and data set is read and internal data structures initialized. A tree is used to represent the data.
- *Partitioning*: data is partitioned according to attribute and category. Informally, partitions represent candidate terms for the rules. The degree of membership for each record is calculated and only those having a positive value are kept. The support for each partition is calculated.
- *Evaluation*: partitions having a support greater than *min Sup* are grouped into a special partition called a large itemset *Li-itemset* where *i* indicates the number of terms per partition. This effectively reduces the number of rules to be considered for discovery.
- *Aggregation*: during this phase combinations of elements in the current large item set are used to create new partitions. The objective is to obtain the *Li+1-itemset* from the *Li-itemset*. The algorithm then proceeds to the previous step, evaluation, and stops when *Li+1-itemset* = Ø and partitions in *Li-itemset* are used to compute the final output.

VII. Rules

Rules are expressed as a logic implication $p \,.\, q$, where p is called the antecedent of the rule and q is called the consequence of the rule. Both p and q are assumed to be in conjunctive normal form (see Figure 15.2), where aa_i, ca_j and cat_{attr} denote an antecedent attribute, a consequent attribute and an attribute category respectively.

The following three conditions hold for each rule: $cat_{aai}.\ TERMS\ (aa_i).\ i.\ 0 = i = m$

$$Catca_j.\ TERMS\ (ca_j).\ j.\ 0 = j = n$$
$$\{aa_0, aa_1, \cdots, aa_m\}\ n\ \{ca_n, ca_1, \cdots, ca_n\} = \varnothing$$

FIG. 15.2
Analysis of Fuzzy Rules

If
aa_o is eat_{aao} A . . . A aa_m is eat_{aam}
then
ea_o is eat_{eao} A . . . ea_a is eat_{ean}

Rule Structure

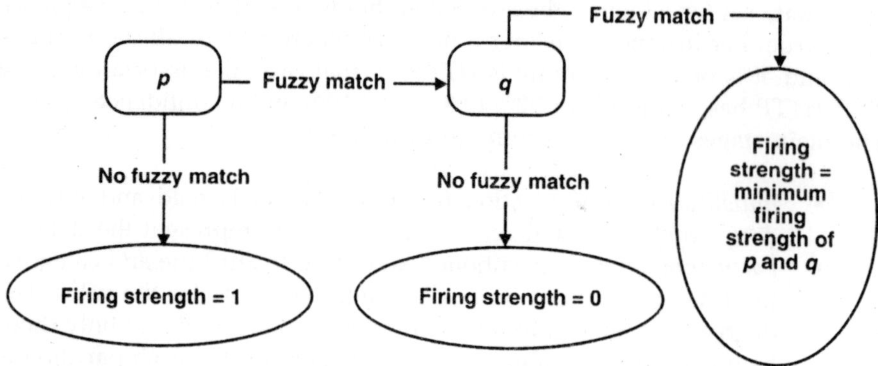

VIII. Fuzzy Inference Engine

The Fuzzy Inference Engine makes use of FuzzyJess [Orchard, 2001], a rule-based expert system shell that integrates the fuzzy logic programs of the FuzzyJ Toolkit with Jess, a Java version of CLIPS [Friedman]. The three inputs to the Fuzzy Inference Engine are : (1) the configuration parameters that FuzzyJess uses to define the linguistic variables as Fuzzy Variables; (2) the rules produced by the Data Miner that must be defined within the FuzzyJess environment; and (3) the records, which are asserted as facts in FuzzyJess. The Fuzzy Inference Engine uses FuzzyJess to determine the firing strength of each rule applied to each fact. FuzzyJess can be configured to use Mamdani or Larsen inference mechanisms to compute output. The evaluation of rules (see Figure 15.2) begins with the analysis of the antecedent, p. The following two cases are considered for the antecedent p:

- p does not have a fuzzy match so the rule does not apply to the record.
- p does have a fuzzy match and the analysis of the consequence q begins.
- Note that a fuzzy match occurs when the truth value of the predicate is greater than zero. Similarly, the following two cases are considered for the consequence q.
- q does not have a fuzzy match and the firing strength of the rule is zero.
- q does have a fuzzy match and the firing strength of the rule is determined to be the minimum of the firing strengths of p and q.

Fuzzy rules, as produced by the data mining algorithm, model a behavior represented by the data set employed to run the algorithm. The output of the Fuzzy Inference Engine is the firing strength of each rule for a given fact. This firing strength determines whether or not the fact satisfies the modeled behavior. Firing strengths that have a value close to one indicate that observed behavior closely follows the modeled behavior, but when several facts register firing strengths at or close to zero for a given rule, then, it is likely that a deviation from the model has been detected (an attack).

5. SOLUTION II—DISCOVERING ASSOCIATION RULE IN ROUGH SET THEORY FRAMEWORK

In the application of association rule mining, sometimes mined rules are not useful, specially in mining classification rules, i.e. Service (Http), Port (80). Even if the confidence of the rule were 100%, the rule is not practical. Such rules are meaningless and lead to the number of detection rules becoming larger, which will lower detection efficiencies and effect detection preciseness. Restricting right-hand-side of association rules to the classification attribute can solve the problem. In this paper association rule mining is redefined under rough set theory frame as following. Given a information system S = (U, A {d}, V, f), as defined in rough set theory, X.Y is called a association rule where X=i <ai,vi>,ai.A,vi=f (ai) and Y.D. The rule measurements of support and Confidence are defined the same as before. In association rule discovering rough set theory are first used to reduct the data horizontally. This is very useful when the quantitative data are large. Then with classical *Apriori* algorithm, all item sets that have support greater than or equal to the user specified minimum support are generated. And all the rules coming from frequent item sets that have minimum confidence are generated. According to the definition of association rule by rough set theory, only the rules whose right-hand-sides belong to classification attribute are finally selected, which can be applied to classifying new connection data, called association classifying rules.

Rule Selection

In this phase, we have got complete set of the association classifying rules that satisfy the user specified minimum support (minsup), minimum confidence (minconf) constraints and classifying constraints. In order to improve the detection efficiency, the system does some rule selection as follows to reduce the number of the rules. If $\beta.\gamma 1$ and $\beta.\gamma 2$ are two rules with the same precedence, but the conclusions are not the same, then the rule with lower *confidence* will be discarded. This can avoid repeated and inconsistent rules. If $\beta 1.\gamma$ and $\beta 2.\gamma$ have the same conclusions but different precedence, and at the same time there exist $\beta 1$, $\beta 2$, $\beta 2.\gamma$ is a redundant rule while $\beta 1.\gamma$ is more general and simple. So the rule $\beta 2.\gamma$ will be deleted from rule sets.

Besides the measurements of the support and confidence of association rules, we need a measure of dependent or correlated events, which is called Interest (correlation, lift) of a association rule defined as: *lift* (β.γ) = P (γ/β) /P/ γ) = P (β.γ)/(P (β) Pγ)β and γ are independent events, If P ($\beta.\gamma$) = P (β P (γ), the rule will be pruned from the rule sets.

If the value of *lift* (â.ã) is less than 1, â and ã are negatively correlated. Even if the support or confidence of the rule were high, = P the rule would mislead the detection. Such rules will be pruned too. Otherwise â and ã are positively correlated; it means the occurrence of â implies the occurrence of ã. The rule should be reserved in the rule sets.

6. CONCLUSION

The main scientific merit of the architecture is its demonstrated ability to work as a hybrid–system using fuzzy logic rules and rough sets produced by a data mining algorithm. Use of fuzzy logic and an improved association rule discovering system under rough set theory framework of modeling IDSs greatly increases the robustness of the end system, and allows for better risk management strategies thanks to a continuous, rather than binary, evaluation of observed network traffic. Contributions of this paper are listed as follows. It proposes a new definition and recognition of association rule mining under the framework of rough set theory. This makes association rule mining techniques applicable to classification tasks. It is important to note that data preprocessing, the use of fuzzy logic and the rough set theory to describe attributes of interest, greatly reduces the amount of data to be analyzed by the inference engine, which is the main bottleneck of most intrusion detection systems in high-bandwidth network segments. We find the detection accuracy of a particular data class is related with some features. This is meaningful when we prepare connection data from hosts or networks for rule mining and detection. With less data the association rule discovering and detecting processes will become more efficient.

REFERENCES

1. Agrawal, R. and R. Srikant; (Sep 1994) "*Fast Algorithms for Mining Association Rules.*" In Proceedings of the 20th International Conference on Very Large Databases, Santiago, Chile, pp. 487-99.
2. Bridges, S.M., and Vaughn, R.B.; (2000) "*Fuzzy Data: Mining and Genetic Algorithms Applied to Intrusion Detection.*" Proceedings of the 23rd National Information Systems Security Conference, Baltimore, MD.
3. Dickerson, J.E. and Dickerson, J.A. (2000) "*Fuzzy Network Profiling for Intrusion Detection.*" Proceedings of NAFIPS 19th International Conference of the North American Fuzzy Information Processing Society, Atlanta, pp. 301-06.
4. Dokas, P., Ertoz, L., Kumar, V., Lazarevic, A., Srivastava, J., and Tan, P. (2002) "*Data Mining for Network Intrusion Detection.*" Proceedings of NSF Workshop on Next Generation Data Mining.
5. Friedman-Hill, E.J.; "Jess, The Java Expert System Shell." Sandia National Laboratories. Available from http://herzberg.ca.sandia.gov/jess.
6. Hosmer, H.A.; (Aug 1993) "*Security is Fuzzy! Applying the Fuzzy Logic Paradigm to the Multipolicy Paradigm.*" Proceedings of the 1992-93 workshop on New Security Paradigms, Little Compton, RI, USA, pp. 175-84.
7. Kuok, C., A. Fu, and M. Wong; (1998), "*Mining Fuzzy Association Rules in Databases,*" The ACM SIGMOD Record, Vol. 27, No. 1, pp. 41-46.
8. Lee, W., Mok, K.W., and Stolfo, S. J.; (1998) "*Mining Audit Data to Build Intrusion Detection Models.*" Proceedings of the Fourth International Conference on Knowledge Discovery and Data Mining, New York City, August, pp. 66-72.
9. Luo, J. and S. Bridges; (2000) "*Mining Fuzzy Association Rules and Fuzzy Frequency Episodes for Intrusion Detection.*" *International Journal of Intelligent Systems*, John Wiley & Sons, pp. 687-703.
10. Mannila, H., H. Toivonen and I. Verkamo; (1995) "*Discovering Frequent Episodes in Sequences.*" In First International Conference on KDD.
11. Mannila, H. and H. Toivonen (Aug 1996) "*Discovering Generalized Episodes Using Minimal Occurrences.*" Proceedings of the Second International Conference on Knowledge Discovery and Data Mining, Portland, Oregon, by AAAI Press, pp. 146-51.
12. Orchard, R.; (2001) "*Fuzzy Reasoning in Jess: The FuzzyJ Toolkit and Fuzzy-Jess*". Proceedings of the ICEIS 2001, 3rd International Conference on Enterprise Information Systems, Setubal, Portugal, pp. 533-42.
13. Ovchinnikov, S.; (1994) "*Fuzzy Sets and Secure Computer Systems*" Proceedings of the workshop on new security paradigms, pp. 54-62, Little Compton, Rhode Island, United States.
14. Stolfo, S.J. Lee, W., Chan, P.K., Fan, W., and Eskin, E.; (2000) "*Data Mining-based Intrusion Detectors: An Overview of the Columbia IDS Project.*" SIGMOD Record, Vol. 30, No. 4, pp. 5-14.
15. Sundaram, A. (1996), *An Introduction to Intrusion Detection*. http://www.cs.purdue.edu/cost/archive/data/categ24.html (Accessed 10 November 1999).
16. Zadeh, L.A.; (1965) "Fuzzy Sets." Information and Control, Vol. 8, Num. 3, pp. 338-53.
17. Zadeh, L.A.; (1973)."Outline of A New Approach to the Analysis of Complex Systems and Decision Processes," IEEE Transactions on Systems, Man, and Cybernetics, Vol. SMC-3, No. 1.
18. Zadeh, L.A. (1975); "*The Concept of a Linguistic Variable and its Application to Approximate Reasoning*", Parts 1, 2, and 3, Information Sciences, 1975, 8:199-249, 8:301-357, 9:43-80.

16

Crisp Interpretations of Fuzzy and Possibilistic Clustering Algorithms

RAKESH SHARMA

ABSTRACT

Today, almost every company is dealing with different kinds of databases. But the state of databases is so high that it is very difficult for companies to focus on the important information content. Data mining is a technique of extracting meaningful information from those large databases. It uses a variety of analysis tools. Clustering is one of the analysis tools, which partitions the database in various groups. Its use in data mining is growing very fast. There are different clustering methods but the major focus here is on partitioning-based clustering which requires prior information from the outside world of the number of clusters into which the database is to be divided. In this paper, we examine methods of analyzing data using fuzzy clustering techniques.

1. INTRODUCTION

The Hard C Means Algorithm (HCM) and the Fuzzy C Means Algorithm (FCM) are commonly used in many pattern recognition and computer vision applications. When noise is present in the data set, both algorithms can give distorted results or even fail completely. Krishnapuram and Keller presented the possibilistic family of clustering algorithms which differ from the previous algorithms in that the membership of a point in a cluster is independent of all other clusters. Hence, the difference between these three families of algorithms lies in the way that a point can belong to the clusters in the data set: hard memberships force a given point to belong exclusively to one cluster, fuzzy memberships allow a point to belong to all clusters with varying degrees, but the memberships in all clusters must sum to one, and possibilistic memberships are rather degrees of typicality of feature points in different clusters, where each cluster is considered to be independent of all other clusters.

In this paper, we derive equivalent crisp objective functions for each of the three families of algorithms. We show that the concept of memberships can be totally bypassed using these crisp reformulations. We also show that the objective functions of the hard and fuzzy C Means can infact be derived from the same crisp objective function. We, then, show that the possibilistic C Means is equivalent to C simultaneous, and independent W or M estimators of the clusters' prototypes. To conclude, we propose a more general objective function which includes many common clustering algorithms as a special case.

2. EQUIVALENT CRISP OBJECTIVE FUNCTIONS FOR HARD AND FUZZY CLUSTERING ALGORITHMS

Let X = {xj I j = 1...N} be a set of feature vectors in an n-dimensional feature space with coordinate-axis labels [x1, x2, . . ., xn], where xj = [xj1, xj2, . . ., xjn]T. Let B = (β1,...,βC) represent a C-tuple of prototypes each of which characterizes one of the C clusters. Each βi consists of a set of parameters. In the following, we use βi to denote both cluster i and its prototype. In the Hard C Means, only the distance from each feature vector to the cluster to which it is assigned (the closest one in the minimum distance classifier sense) is summed in the objective function, i.e., the objective function is defined to be

$$J_H (B;X)=\sum_{i=1}^{C}{}_{x_j} \sum^{N}{}_{\beta i} d^2 (x_j \cdot \beta_i) \tag{1}$$

where d2(xj,βi) represents the distance from a feature point xj to cluster β_i. The above objective function can be written as

$$J_H = \sum_{j=1}^{N} \min_i d^2 (x_f \cdot \beta_i) \tag{2}$$

It is well known that the min operator can be written as a limit of the following expression when p ϕ.

$$\min_i d^2 (x_j , \beta_i) = \lim_{p\phi-} \left\{ \sum_{i=1}^{C} d^2 (x_f , \beta_i) p \right\}^{1/p} \tag{3}$$

Hence, we can rewrite JH as

$$J_H = \lim_{p\phi-} J_{(p)}$$

Where

$$J_{(p)} = \sum_{j=1}^{N} \left\{ \sum_{i=1}^{C} d^2 (x_f, \beta_i) p \right\}^{(1-p)p} (x_j - c_i) \quad (4)$$

We assume that the prototypes are represented by cluster centers ci and d2(xj, βi) = | | xj-ci | | 2. Differentiating J(p) with respect to the centers gives

$$\frac{\partial J(p)}{\partial C_i} = -2 \sum_{j=1}^{N} d^2 (x_j, \beta_i)^{p-1} \left\{ \sum_{i=1}^{C} d^2 (x_j, \beta_i) p \right\}^{(1-p)/p} (x_j - c_i) \quad (5)$$

Setting the above equation to 0 yields the following implicit equation which can be solved iteratively

$$c_i (p) = \frac{\sum_{j=1}^{N} \left(\frac{d^2 (x_j, \beta_i)^p}{\sum_{k=1}^{C} d^2 (x_j, \beta_k)^p} \right)^{(p-1)/p} x_j}{\sum_{j=1}^{N} \left(\frac{d^2 (x_j, \beta_i)^p}{\sum_{k=1}^{C} d^2 (x_j, \beta_k)^p} \right)^{(p-1)/p}} \quad (6)$$

Note that ci(p) occurs on both sides of the above equation since d2(xj,βi) involves ci(p). Therefore, one way to solve for ci is to use the following equations in an alternating fashion.

$$c_i (p) = \frac{1}{N_i} \sum_{j=1}^{N} w_{ij} x_j \text{, where } N_i = \sum_{j=1}^{N} w_{ij} \text{ and} \quad (7)$$

$$w_{ij} = \left(\frac{d^2 (x_p, \beta_i)^p}{\sum_{k=1}^{C} d^2 (x_j, \beta_k)} \right)^{(p-1)/p} \quad (8)$$

In FCM, the centers are updated using the following equation [1]

$$c_{iF} = \frac{\sum_{j=1}^{N} u_{ij} m x_j}{\sum_{j=1}^{N} u_{ij} m} \quad (9)$$

The expression of ci(p) is identical to the center update equation in (9) with the weights wij = uijm , and m = (p–1)p (1,). Hence, the objective function of the FCM can be reformulated as the sum of generalized harmonic means

$$J_F = \sum_{j=1}^{N} \left\{ \sum_{i=1}^{C} d^2 (x_j, \beta_i)^p \right\}^{1/p} \tag{10}$$

where p (–,0) controls the amount of crispness or equivalently fuzziness in the resulting partition. At the lower end of the spectrum as p "– or equivalently m."1, minimizing the objective function becomes stricter, requiring prototypes that are reasonably close to every point. This results in a hard partition with hard centers, i.e.,

$$J_H = \lim_{p\phi-} J_F$$

and the centers that minimize JH are given by

$$c_i H = \lim_{p\phi-} c_i (p) \tag{11}$$

It can be seen from the expression for the weights or memberships in the centers update equations in (8) that as p " –, the values of memberships become 1 if the point belongs to the given cluster (total commitment), or 0 otherwise (no commitment). As p or m increases, the objective function is minimized by choosing prototypes such that the generalized harmonic mean of the distances of every point to all prototypes is minimized, thus the partition 3 becomes fuzzier. For instance, when p = –1 (corresponding to m = 2 in the FCM), the objective function in (10) becomes

$$J_F = \sum_{j=1}^{N} \left(\frac{1}{\sum_{i=1}^{C} \frac{1}{d^2 (x_j, \beta_i)}} \right) \tag{12}$$

This objective function is minimized by choosing prototypes such that the harmonic mean distance of every point to all prototypes is minimized. At the higher end of the spectrum, as p " 0, it is easy to show that all cluster centers converge to a unique point, i.e.,

$$\lim_{p\phi 0} c_i (p) = \frac{1}{N} \sum_{i=1}^{N} x_j$$

Therefore all centers become identical, that is the partition is extremely fuzzy, yielding absolutely no information about the structure of the feature space.

From the above discussion, we see that the HCM and FCM are derived from the same objective function, and p (–, 0) or equivalently m = (p–1)p (1,) controls the amount of fuzziness present in the resulting partition. The partition gets less fuzzy for lower values of m and p, eventually reaching a hard partition when m.1 or equivalently p.–. It can be seen that the objective function in (10) does not really involve any fuzzy memberships, and the memberships (or weights) occur as temporary variables if we choose to minimize the objective function using the alternating optimization technique.

3. EQUIVALENT CRISP OBJECTIVE FUNCTIONS FOR THE POSSIBILISTIC C MEANS

The Possibilistic C Means family of clustering algorithms is designed to alleviate the noise problem by relaxing the constraint on memberships used in the FCM [5, 6]. It uses the following objective function

$$J_p(B,U,X) = \sum_{i=1}^{C}\sum_{j=1}^{N}(u_{ij})^m\, d^2(x_j,\beta_i) + \sum_{i=1}^{c}\eta_i \sum_{j=1}^{N}(1-u_{ij})^m \tag{13}$$

where ·i are suitable positive numbers. It is easy to show (6) that U may be a global minimum of Jm(B, U, X) only if the memberships are updated by

$$u_{ij} = \frac{1}{1+\left(\dfrac{d^2(x_j,\beta_i)}{\eta_i}\right)^{\frac{1}{m-1}}} \tag{14}$$

We now derive the connection between the PCM and the W estimator (2) of robust statistics. Suppose we are interested in estimating the prototypes of C clusters simultaneously using the W estimator. We can consider minimizing the sum of C independent W estimator merit functions as follows :

$$J_w = \sum_{i=1}^{C}\sum_{j=1}^{N} W(d^2(x_j,\beta_i),a_i)\,d^2(x_j,\beta_i) \tag{15}$$

where W is a function of the distances and a parameter vector ai. Treating the weights as constants, the centers that minimize Jw are given by

$$c_i w = \frac{\sum_{j=1}^{N} w(d^2(x_j,\beta_i),a_i)\,d^2(x_j,\beta_i)}{\sum_{j=1}^{N} w(d^2(x_j,\beta_i),a_i)} \tag{16}$$

Hence, the centers and the weights are iteratively updated in an alternative manner. If the Cauchy estimator (3) is used, then the weights become 4.

$$W(d^2(x_j,\beta_i);\eta_t) = \left[\frac{1}{1+\left(\dfrac{d^2(x_j,\beta_i)}{\eta_i}\right)}\right]^{-1}$$

where ·i are scale parameters that relate to the variance of each cluster. We see that the center update equation is identical to that of the PCM for the special case of m = 2, where each weight is seen to be a possibilistic membership or typicality of a feature point in a given cluster. The more general possibilistic weight function uses a fuzzifier m that affects its shape as will be discussed below,

$$W(d^2(x_j,\beta_i);\eta_t,m)=\left[\frac{1}{1+\left(\frac{d^2(x_j,\beta_i)}{\eta_i}\right)^{1/(m-1)}}\right]^{m-1} \tag{17}$$

Given the equivalent weights between the possibilistic C Means and the W-estimator, the possibilistic objective function can now be rewritten in its equivalent form as

$$J_p=\sum_{i=1}^{C}\sum_{j=1}^{N}\left[\frac{1}{1+\left(\frac{d^2(x_j,\beta_i)}{\eta_i}\right)^{1/(m-1)}}\right]^{m-1} d^2(x_j,\beta_i) \tag{18}$$

It is also interesting to note that JP is of the form

$$J_p=\sum_{i=1}^{C}\sum_{j=1}^{N}\rho(d^2(x_j,\beta_i);\eta_t,m) \tag{19}$$

where the loss function

$$\rho(d^2(x_j,\beta_i);\eta_t,m)=\left[\frac{1}{1+\left(\frac{d^2(x_j,\beta_i)}{\eta_i}\right)^{1/(m-1)}}\right]^{m-1} d^2(x_j,\beta_i)$$

$$=\left[\frac{d^2(x_j,\beta_i)^{1/(m-1)}}{1+\left(\frac{d^2(x_j,\beta_i)}{\eta_i}\right)^{1/m-1)}}\right]^{m-1}$$

Hence, the PCM can also be considered as a robust estimator representing C independent simultaneous M-estimators (4), with ·i being the scale parameter related to the spread of the corresponding cluster, and m being a parameter that determines the shape of the figure of merit function.

4. GENERALIZED OBJECTIVE FUNCTION FOR CLUSTERING

The crisp version of the objective function of the FCM can be generalized to the following functional form :

$$J_f=\sum_{j=1}^{N}f^{-1}\left[\sum_{i=1}^{C}f(d^2(x_j,\beta_i),a_i)\right] \tag{20}$$

where f is a monotonically non-increasing function and ai is a vector of parameters. For the case of the FCM f is a power function

$$f(d^2(x_j, \beta_i), p) = \{d^2(x_j, \beta_i)\}^p$$

In their deterministic annealing approach to clustering, Rose et. al. used the following objective function

$$J_f = \frac{-1}{\beta}\sum_{j=1}^{N}\log\left[\sum_{i=1}^{C}\exp(-\beta d^2(x_f, \beta_i))\right]$$

In this case,

$$f(d^2(x_j, \beta_i), \beta) = \exp(-\beta d^2(x_j, \beta_i))$$

It can easily be shown that the centers that minimize the generalized objective function Jf are given by the implicit equation.

$$c_{if} = \frac{\sum_{j=1}^{N}\left(\frac{f(d^2(x_j, \beta_i))}{\sum_{k=1}^{C} f(d^2(x_j, \beta_k))}\right)x_j}{\sum_{j=1}^{N}\left(\frac{f(d^2(x_j, \beta_i))}{\sum_{j=1}^{N} f(d^2(x_j, \beta_k))}\right)} \tag{21}$$

5. CONCLUSION

We have showed that the objective functions of the HCM and FCM can be derived from the same non-fuzzy objective function. The only difference between them is that the surface of the objective function for FCM is smoother, since the summation in the FCM involves the distances from a given feature point to all clusters inducing an averaging effect, whereas, the summation in the HCM involves the distances from feature points assigned to a given cluster. This increases the HCM's chances to get stuck in local minima. From the centres update equations, we can also conclude that for a noiseless data set, when both the HCM and FCM converge to the global minima of their respective objective functions, the centers' estimates found using HCM should be more accurate than those resulting from FCM, since in the latter, the center's calculation for a given cluster is affected by points belonging to other clusters. This tends to bring the centers closer to each other, i.e., if the clusters are well separated and noise-free, the HCM solution is better provided the algorithm converges to the global minimum. When the clusters are too close, the HCM centers estimates can be more distorted than those of the FCM due to arbitrary assignments of points that lie between 2 clusters, whereas FCM assigns 0.5 memberships in each cluster to these points, hence not drastically distorting the results. However, for a noisy data set, the FCM estimates tend to be always more accurate than those of the HCM, since a noise point contributes only partially to the centers of all clusters in the FCM resulting in a less drastic effect on the centers estimates.

We have also established a connection between the PCM and robust W- and M-estimators. The PCM is more robust in the presence of noise because its objective function and center update equations involve unconstrained weights that decrease with the distance from the cluster centers. This results in low weights for outliers and decreases their influence. Another feature of the PCM is that it tries to find the C best clusters independently of each other, so it is possible that C identical clusters minimize the PCM objective function. However, this only happens when the algorithm is badly initialized. The PCM's strength does not lie in "partitionning", but rather in finding valid clusters and giving a robust estimate of the centers after a suitable preliminary initialization.

Finally, we have shown that the objective functions for the HCM and FCM are part of a more general family of objective functionals, which opens the gate to considering new objective functions that fall into this category.

References

1. J.C. Bezdek, Pattern Recognition with Fuzzy Objective Function Algorithms, Plenum Press, New York, 1981.
2. C. Goodall, "M-estimator of Location: An Outline of the Theory", in Understanding Robust and Exploratory Data Analysis, D.C. Hoaglin, F. Mosteller, and J.W. Tukey, Eds. New York: 1983, pp. 339-403.
3. P.W. Holland, and R.E. Welsch, "Robust Regression Using Iteratively Reweighted Least-Squares", *Commun. Statist.—Theor. Meth.*, Vol. A6, No. 9, pp. 813-27, 1977.
4. P.J. Huber, Robust Statistics, John Wiley & Sons, New York, 1981.
5. R. Krishnapuram and J.M. Keller, "A possibilistic approach to clustering", *IEEE Transactions on Fuzzy Systems*, Vol. 1, No. 2, May 1993, pp. 98-110.

17

Role of Java in Object-oriented Petri Nets

DALJEET SINGH MATHARU

ABSTRACT

Petri net is widely used to analyze and model various systems formally. Recently, many Petri nets mania devoted their efforts to enhancing and extending the expressive power of Petri nets. One such effort is to extend Petri nets with object-oriented concepts. An object-oriented paradigm provides excellent concepts to model real-world problems. Object-oriented concepts allow us to build software systems easily, intuitively and naturally. Although several high-level Petri nets with the concept of objects are suggested, these nets do not fully support the object-oriented concepts. Object-oriented Methodology lacks the rigor to verify and validate the designed system. Petri nets provide formal graphical representation, incorporate concurrency and parallelism. This paper proposes a modeling language for developing concurrent software, Object-oriented Petri Nets (OOPN), which combines the maintainability and reusability of Object orientation (OO) and the advantages of Petri nets a graphical interface and a sound theoretical background. By doing so, each benefit from the other and their negative aspects are effectively diminished. It also discusses about different types of Petri nets and application areas. The implementation of the OOPN-Integrated Development Environment (OOPN-IDE) and a unique strategy for using OOPN are then explored. Potential applications for this modeling language and possibilities for future work are also considered.

1. INTRODUCTION

A *Petri net* (also known as a *place/transition net* or *P/T net*) is one of several mathematical representations of discrete distributed systems. A Petri net is a formal and graphical appealing language which is appropriate for modeling systems with concurrency and resource sharing. Petri nets has been under development since their invention in 1962 by Carl Adam Petri. It was the first time a general theory for discrete parallel systems was formulated. The language is a generalization of automata theory such that the concept of concurrently occurring events can be expressed.

A Petri net consists of places, transitions, and directed arcs. Arcs run between places and transitions—not between places and places or transitions and transitions. The places from which an arc runs to a transition are called the input places of the transition; the places to which arcs run from a transition are called the output places of the transition.

Places may contain any number of tokens. A distribution of tokens over the places of a net is called a *marking*. Transitions act on input tokens by a process known as *firing*. A transition is *enabled* if it can fire, i.e. there are tokens in every input place. When a transition fires, it consumes the tokens from its input places, performs some processing task, and places a specified number of tokens into each of its output places. It does this atomically, i.e. in one non-interruptible step. Execution of Petri nets is non-deterministic. This means two things:

(a) Multiple transitions can be enabled at the same time, any one of which can fire.
(b) None are *required* to fire—they fire at will, between time 0 and infinity, or not at all (i.e. it is totally possible that nothing fires at all).

Since firing is non-deterministic, Petri nets are well suited for modeling the concurrent behavior of distributed systems.

A *Petri net* is a 5-tuple, (S, T, F, M_0, W), where:

- S is a set of *places*.
- T is a set of *transitions*.
- S and T are disjoint, i.e. no object can be both a place and a transition
- F is a set of arcs known as a *flow relation*. The set F is subject to the constraint that no arc may connect two places or two transitions, or more formally: $F \subseteq (S \times T) \cup (T \times S)$
- $M_0 : S \rightarrow \mathbb{N}$ is an *initial marking*, where for each place, $s \in S$, there are $n_s \in \mathbb{N}$ tokens.

- $W : F \to \mathbb{N}^+$ is a set of *arc weights*, which assigns to each arc $f \in F$ some $n \in \mathbb{N}^+$ denoting how many tokens are consumed from a place by a transition, or alternatively, how many tokens are produced by a transition and put into each place.

A variety of other formal definitions exist. Some definitions do not have arc weights, but they allow multiple arcs between the same place and transition, which is conceptually equal to one arc with a weight of more than one.

2. PETRI NETS AND OBJECT ORIENTED PROGRAMMING

Petri nets are a graphical and mathematical modeling tool which is useful for modeling systems with concurrent, asynchronous, distributed or parallel properties. They have been observed to have broad application in modeling finite state machines, parallel activities, data flow computations, communication protocols, synchronization control, discrete event systems, and asynchronous circuits [1]. They were introduced by Carl Adam Petri in 1962 [3]. In early 1970's, MIT was very active in the research of Petri nets. Since the late 1970's, European researchers have organized workshops and published conference proceedings on Petri nets [1].

With the popularization of Object Oriented (OO) theory over the 1980s, the Petri net community also appealed to OO concepts in that object orientation features abstraction, encapsulation, and inheritance, which may help to build layered Petri Net models instead of "flat" ones [6]. Until recently, a tremendous number of Petri Net modeling languages have emerged embodying more or less OO concepts, such as G-Net, COOPN [4], LOOPN [5], PROT, OOCPN. The efforts indeed helped to avoid state explosion to some extent; however, problems still remain. Some languages claim to be object oriented simply by regarding token as objects, and some otherwise require profound mathematical knowledge.

2.1 Some Aspects of OO

Developing concurrent software by using object oriented languages is not one for all solutions [2]. Some aspects need to be considered such as:

- Software has become the dominant technology in many, if not most, technical systems, which makes software more and more complex. Scaling-up of a software system is not merely a repetition of the same elements in larger sizes, but an increase in the number of different elements. In most cases, the elements interact with each other in some nonlinear fashion and the complexity of the whole increases much more than linearly. What makes the situation worse is that objects in the internet era are more likely to run concurrently or in parallel. It is extremely difficult to accurately represent the communication and synchronization amongst them.

- Encapsulation is a major feature of OO, and only the public methods or attributes of an object are accessible to others; however, OO does not impose constraints upon the access, such as the order of several method invocations, which thus complicates the relationships amongst objects.
- According to OO theory, the state of an object is made up of the values of all its attributes. State transformations occur when any of such values changes; OO however does not provide facilities for representing the state transformations according to the inherent application logic.
- OO brings hierarchy and modularization, which increases the possibility for formal verification by using a divide-and-conquer strategy, but no popular OO methodology, provides such a mechanism.

Fortunately, the integration of Petri Nets and OO can diminish or totally avoid the above negative aspects of Object Oriented languages.

2.2 Object Oriented Petri Nets (OOPN)

OOPN, originated from OPNets [7], features all major concepts of OO while remaining in a standard format. It does not introduce any new facilities so that all analysis methods or theorems regarding Petri Nets are still applicable.

An *Object Oriented Petri net* is defined on a collection of elements comprising constants, variables, net elements (i.e. places and transitions), class elements (i.e. object nets, method nets, synchronous ports, and message selectors), classes, object identifiers, and method net instance identifiers. An OOPN has its initial class and initial object identifier, as well. The so-called universe of an OOPN contains (nested) tuples of constants, classes, and object identifiers.

Object nets consist of places and transitions. Each place has some (possibly empty) initial marking. Each transition has conditions and preconditions (i.e. inscribed testing and input arcs), a guard, an action, and post-conditions (i.e. inscribed output arcs).

Method nets are similar to object nets but, additionally, each of them has a set of parameter places and a return place. Method nets can access places of the appropriate object nets, which allow running methods to modify the states of the objects which they are running in. *Constructors* are method nets intended for initializing objects.

Synchronous ports are special transitions which cannot fire alone but only dynamically fused to some regular transitions. These transitions activate the ports from their guards via message sending. Every synchronous port embodies a set of conditions, preconditions, and post-conditions over places of the appropriate object net, and furthers a guard and a set of parameters. Parameters of an activated port can be bound to constants or unified with variables defined on the level of the transition or port that activated.

A *class* is given by its object net, its sets of method nets and synchronous ports, and a set of message selectors corresponding to its methods and ports. Object nets describe what data particular objects encapsulate and what activity they exhibit on their own. Method nets specify how objects asynchronously respond to received messages. Synchronous ports allow remotely testing and changing states of objects in an atomic way.

2.3 The Dynamic Behaviour of OOPNs

A state of an OOPN can be encoded as a *marking*, which can be structured into a system of objects. Thus, the dynamic behaviour of OOPNs corresponds to an evolution of a system of objects. An *object* of a certain class c is a system of net instances that contains exactly one instance of the object net of and a set of currently running instances of method nets from c. Every *net instance* entails its identifier and a marking of its places and transitions. A *marking of a place* is a multiset of elements of the universe. A *transition marking* is a set of records about method net instances invoked from the appropriate transition.

For a given OOPN, its *initial marking* corresponds to a single, initially marked object net instance from the initial class. A change of a marking of an OOPN is a result of an occurrence of some *event*. Such an OOPN event is given by :

(i) Its type,
(ii) The identifier of the net instance it takes place in,
(iii) The transition it is statically represented by, and
(iv) The binding tree containing the bindings of the variables used on the level of the involved transition as well as within all the synchronous ports (possibly indirectly) activated from that transition.

There are four kinds of events according to the way of evaluating the action of the appropriate transition:

A – An atomic action involving trivial computations only,
N – A new object instantiation via the message new,
F – An instantiation of a Petri-net described method, and
J – Terminating a method net instance.

An invocation of a constructor over a class leads to a sequence built of an N, F, and J event.[8]

2.4 OPNets

Here we will only introduce the modeling language briefly by giving an example. Figure 17.1 shows the model of the producer/consumer system.

FIG. 17.1
A Producer/Consumer Model

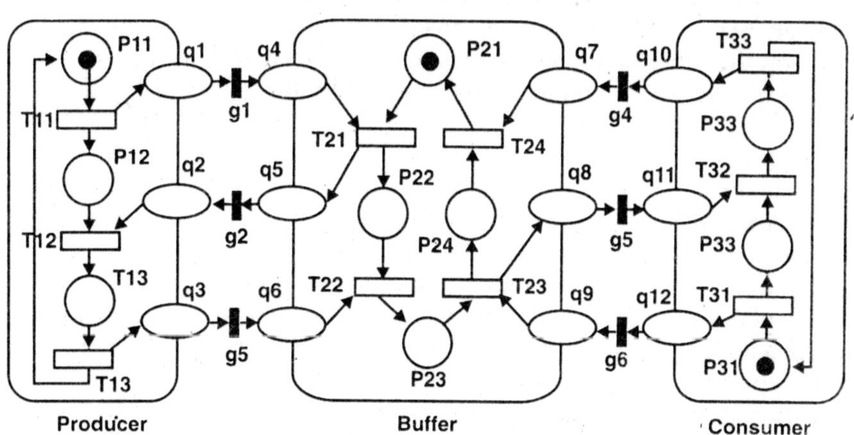

Producer

P11 : Idle
P12 : Waiting for production permission
P13 : Producing
T11 : Makes production request
T12 : Obtains production permission
T13 : Finishes production

Consumer

P31 : Idle
P32 : Waiting for consumption permission
P33 : Consuming
T31 : Makes consumption request
T32 : Obtains consumption permission
T33 : Finishes consumption

Buffer

P21 : Empty
P22 : Waiting for production
P23 : Full
P24 : Waiting for Consumption

T21 : Responds to production request
T22 : Receives product
T23 : Responds to consumption request
T24 : Sends product

Following OPNets, OOPN represents *classes* by predicate subnets wrapped in rounded rectangles embodying abstraction and encapsulation. A class may have multiple instances or objects, denoted as *tokens,* and the places where they stay show their current states. The external interface of a class is defined by elliptic *message queues* across the class boundary, which is similar to circular places inside the class. Message passing between objects is represented by connecting message queues with solid black rectangular *gates*.

The internal behavior of a class described by the predicate subnet is similar to that of classic Petri Nets except that at most one state can exist among the predecessors or successors of a transition which, thus, prohibits the internal direct interaction between instances of one class.

Message transmission is the only way for objects to communicate. Every transition is associated with preconditions and actions that are supposed to execute when it is fired. A transition is enabled to fire whenever there is a token in each of its predecessors and the pre-condition is satisfied.

Values may be read by a transition in the pre-condition and written in the action. Messages transmitted between objects, denoted also as tokens, are structured data and can only reside in message queues. The messages which enable a transition to fire are destroyed after the firing actually occurs; on the other hand, a new message will be created in each successor message queue, whose content is determined by the action of the involved transition.

A class could be *simple* or *composite*. A simple class is defined by a subnet, whereas a composite one is in turn made up of several smaller classes. An OOPN system consists of multiple OOPN classes with instances specified that may pass messages to one another.

Figure 17.1 defines a producer, a consumer, and a buffer with the capacity of 1. At the beginning, the producer (consumer) makes a request by sending a message to the buffer through *g1* (*g6*). If the buffer is empty (full), it will respond by returning a permission message through *g2* (*g5*). Once the permission is available, the producer (consumer) may proceed to produce (consume). When the action finishes, it again notifies the buffer through *g3* (*g4*). The process may go in the same way periodically.

A class may have attributes and each object of this type is associated with its own corresponding values. These OPNets were originally designed for modeling Flexible Manufacturing Systems (FMS). To meet the need for developing complex concurrent software, more mechanisms have yet to be supported. We obtained OOPN by extending OPNets as described in the following sections.

3. THE WHOLE LIFE CYCLE OF OBJECTS

OPNets disallow dynamic construction or destruction of objects during runtime so as to reduce the analysis complexity of FMS models which, however, is not sound for generic software systems. OOPN supports the following two special transitions: *source* and *sink*. The former, as depicted in Figure 17.2a, has no predecessor and only one successor state; the latter, in Figure 17.2b, alternatively, has only one predecessor and no successor state.

FIG. 17.2(a) and (b)
Source Transition and Sink Transition

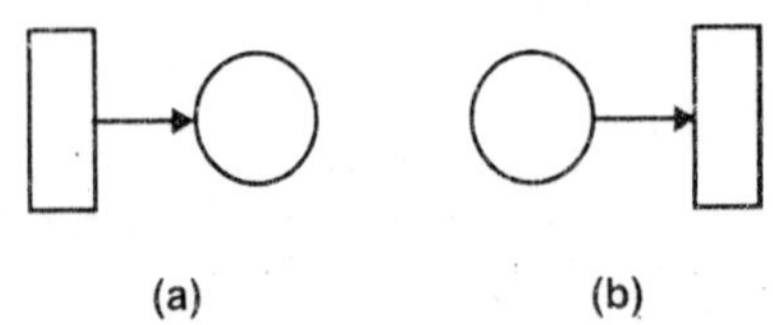

When the generator fires, a new object will be generated and put in the following state, whereas when the tomb fires, the involved object in the preceding state will be destroyed. In this way, objects could be dynamically generated or destroyed.

3.1 Inheritance

Inheritance is usually regarded as the unique characteristic that distinguishes OO [10], but OPNets provide no support for this mechanism. Based on the common practices in programming languages and the graphical structure of Petri Nets, we introduced single inheritance in OOPN.

FIG. 17.3
Inheritance in OOPN

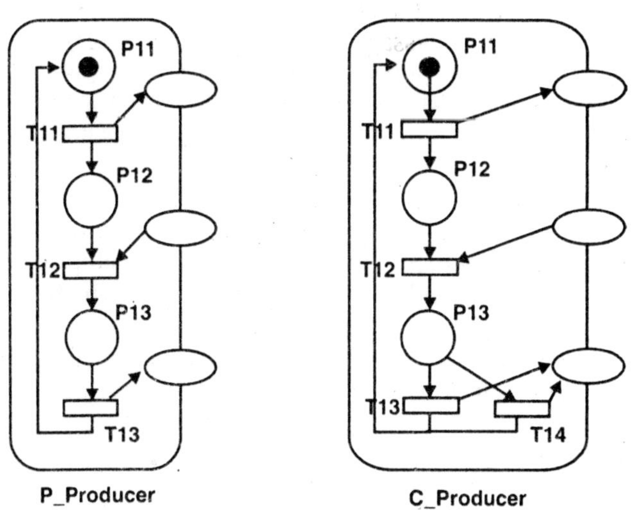

Like various programming languages, where inherited methods are automatically available in a sub-class, every OOPN subclass receives the Petri Nets structure of its superclass, and hence the internal behavior and external interface. Since every OOPN object is also regulated by meaningful sequential behavior, more detailed specification is necessary to define the semantics of inheritance rather than merely specifying a superclass. As shown in Figure 17.3, sub-class *C_Producer* extends superclass *P_Producer* by introducing a new transition *T14* so that at state *P13*, *C_Producer* instances could randomly choose to do either of two kinds of production. In this case, besides the parent-child relationship, the connections amongst the involved states, transitions, and message queues should also be redefined.

3.2 Inhibitory Arcs

Inhibitory arcs are introduced to obtain the capability of a so called *zero test* so that the firing of a given transition can be forbidden when its preceding place is not empty. What's more, inhibitory arcs could only lead from a message queue to a transition in the OOPN rather than from a state, otherwise a transition may fire when no object is involved, which is against the object-centric view of object orientation.

3.3 Use Java for Semantics Definition

Java provides an object-oriented, portable, powerful way to simulate a Petri net while reducing implementation errors and modeling system behavior simulation accurately and efficiently. Although the OOPN graphical structure could model the skeleton of a real application very well, a scripting language is necessary to describe the detailed semantics. OOPN utilizes Java to define:

- Pre-conditions and actions of transitions and gates,
- Class types for message tokens in message queues, and
- OOPN class attributes, which could be variables of simple Java data types, e.g. *int*, or class objects, e.g. *java.util.Vector.*

4. OOPN-IDE

To support OOPN modeling, an integrated development environment, OOPN-IDE, has been implemented in Java, in which the specification of concurrent software can be designed, verified, and implemented. The three phases in terms of OOPN, respectively refer to building up an OOPN model, dynamic and static verification upon the model, and generating java code automatically from it.[9]

Java Library OOPN Extension Package

The core of OOPN-IDE is the class architecture for implementing OOPN, which turns out to be the *Java library OOPN extension package*. The classes for OOPN components and their inheritance relations are depicted in Figure 17.4.

The *OOPNComponent* is the root class in the Petri Nets structure family and *Token* in the instance family. An *OOPNClass*object stands for an occurrence of an OOPN class, since a class may appear more than once in a system. *OOPNClass* uses hash tables to store the internal structure and external interface of an OOPN class.

OOPNNode presents a node in classical Petri nets, which could be connected by *Arc*. *OOPNClassInstance* and *Message* are designed respectively for OOPN class instances and message instances. All these classes feature both graphical characteristics and Petri Nets semantics so that they can be used not only for editing models interactively but also for the execution of the real application system.

There are two different but related concepts of class:

- *OOPN model class*: or simply OOPN class, such as *producer* in Figure 17.1.
- *OOPN Java class*: the Java implementation of OOPN model class.

In OOPN-IDE, every OOPN class can be compiled into its corresponding OOPN Java class, which extends the OOPNClass.

FIG. 17.4
Java classes for OOPN model

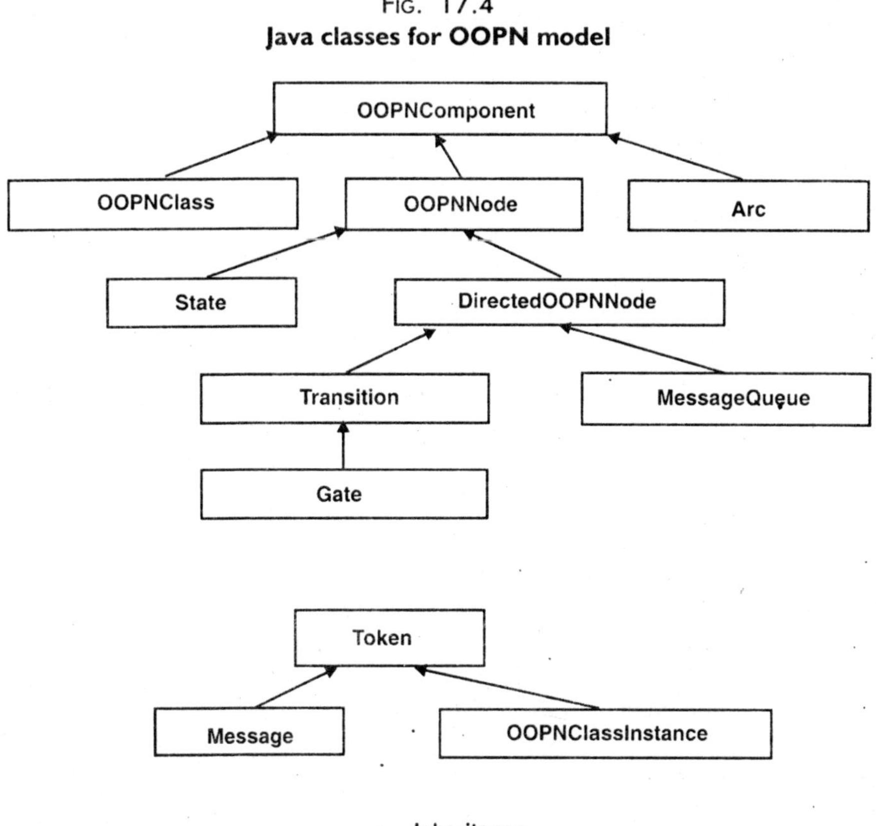

For example, the following is part of source code generated automatically by OOPN-IDE for the producer class in Figure.

```
package opn.opnclass;
...
public class prod extends OOPNClass{
public Message q3;
...
void setupGraphStructure(){
setClassName("producer");
```

```
setShape(50,50,359,424,20,20);
setColor(new Color(255,200,0));
...
State s = null;
addComponent(s = new State("P13"));
s.setRadius(30);
s.setColor(255,0,0);
s.setLabelLocation("N");
...
Transition t = null;
addComponent(t=new Transition("T13"));
t.setColor(0,0,255);
...
addComponent(new MesQueue("q2"));
...
Arc a = null;
OPNNode b = null, e = null;
addComponent(a = new Arc("T13—q3");
b = getNode("T13");
a.setPre(b);
e = getNode("q3");
a.setPost(e);
b.addPostCom(a);
e.addPreCom(a);
}
}
public class prod_in extends OOPNClassInst{
...
public boolean T13_preCond(){
// NB: your code follows.
return true;
}
public void T13_action(Message q3){
// NB: your code follows.
}
}
```

5. SYSTEM TOPOLOGY

As shown in Figure 17.5, OOPN-IDE adopts the client/server architecture, where the front end provides a graphical interface for interactive development, and the back end synchronizes multiple users' working on the same project.

The distributed architecture is adopted based on the observation that concurrent and distributed systems are also likely to be developed concurrently by team members at different locations.

At the back end, access control and consistency control are imposed so that no invalid actions are requested for execution, e.g. a user is trying to add an arc to a node whereas the latter is just deleted by another user.

OOPN model classes and their corresponding Java classes, once verified and compiled, will be exported respectively to the *OOPN Class Library* and *OOPN Java Class Library*. Users may import existing model classes for inheritance or simply build up a composite class, and thus achieve reusability.

At the front end, two ways are available for users to build up OOPN models: graphical mode and text mode. Under text mode, a XML scripting language is used and the input should be checked for syntactical errors; under graphical mode, different graph components could be easily put together by drag-and-drop. The network communication module wraps up the low level communication details over the Internet and provides a concise API for both the front end and back end.[9]

FIG. 17.5
System Topology

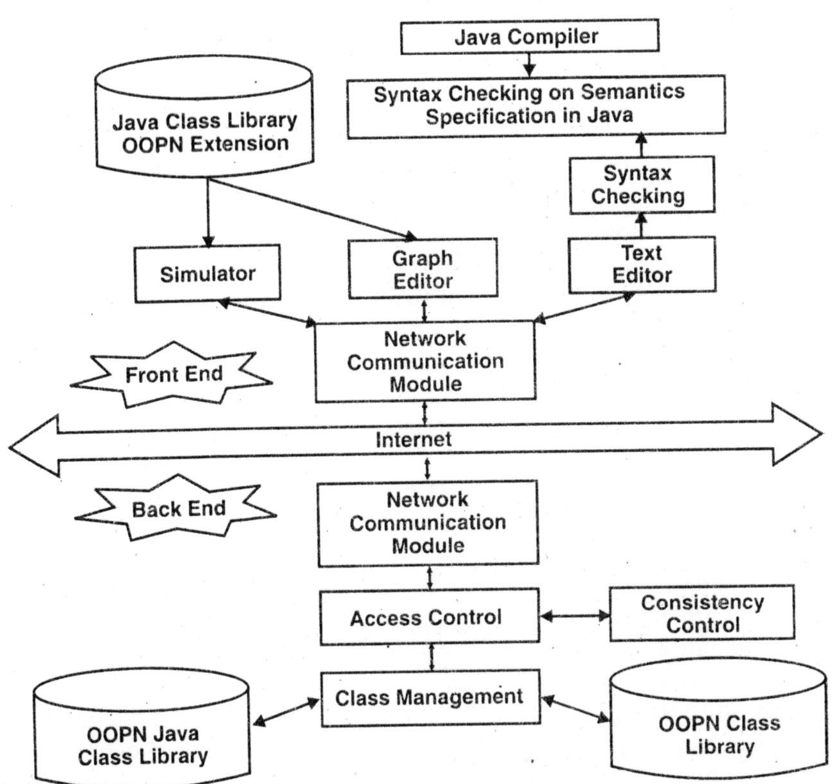

6. HOW NEAR TO THE REAL APPLICATION

A major difficulty in the traditional application of Petri Nets to concurrent software development is that there is a huge gap between the model and the target real system. In other words, even though a perfect model is built and thoroughly verified, errors could probably be introduced during the translation from the Petri Net language to a regular programming language. A unique strategy is hence used in OOPN-IDE.

Similar to the cases in which programmers use arrays, queues, or stacks in their programs, the net structure of OOPN model and the associated logic are explicitly kept in the real system generated by the OOPN-IDE. In such a way, an OOPN model is actually the prototype of the real application, which could be enriched incrementally until a full-fledged system is obtained.

The advantages of this method are obvious:

- No more brutal translation is needed and a run-able ongoing development version of the target system could always be available.
- The graphical interface of OOPN may present a vivid overview of the running system, thus debugging becomes much easier.

7. CONCLUSIONS

The OOPN modeling language and role of java presented in this paper concisely and intuitively conveys all major OO features while it still possesses the classical Petri net structure. Petri nets can do a good job in representing certain tasks, operations, or certain services, but not some others, e.g. data storage. To achieve applicability to a variety of systems, Petri nets facilities and non-Petri nets components should be interoperable. A user-friendly layer could be utilized to veil the underlying Petri net model.

The advantages of OOPN in more detail are as follows:

- The representation power is increased while the advantages of Petri nets, e.g. graphical structure and operability, still hold.
- The concept of OOPN class brings abstraction, encapsulation, and inheritance, which together enhance the reusability of OOPN models dramatically.
- Composite classes make it possible to build up a hierarchical OOPN system and thus a divide and conquer analysis method can be employed more or less avoiding state explosion.

The supporting tool of OOPN, OOPN-IDE, has been developed to model, simulate, and implement concurrent software systems in an integrated environment. Since OOPN models may be seamlessly embedded in the target system, simulation is actually equivalent to debugging or execution of the real system.

Future work about OOPN and OOPN-IDE could be done at interoperability, scalability and friendliness. Until now, OOPN and OOPN-IDE in java have been applied to the development of real-time operating systems, agent systems, grid computations, and cluster computations; and promising progress has already been made.

References

1. T. Murata, *"Petri Nets: Properties, Analysis and Applications"*, *Proc. of the IEEE, 77*(4), 1989, 541-80.
2. Jinzhong Niu, *Research and Implementation of an OO Petri Nets Based Integrated Development Environment for Concurrent Software*, Master Thesis, Beijing University of Aeronautics and Astronautics, 1999.
3. Carl Adam Petri, *"Kommunikation mit Automaten"*, Ph.D. thesis, Bonn: Institut fuer Instrumentelle Mathematik, 1962.
4. Olivier Biberstein, Didier Buchs, *"An Object-oriented Specification Language based on Hierarchical Algebraic Petri Nets"*, *Proc. of ISCORE-1994*, Amsterdam, Holland, 1994, 47-62.
5. C.D. Keen, C.A. Lakos, *"A Methodology for the Construction of Simulation Models Using Object-oriented Petri Nets"*, *Proc. of the European Simulation Multi-conference*, 1993, 267-71.
6. Michael Zapf, Armin Heinzl, *"Techniques for Integrating Petri-Nets and Object-oriented Concepts"*, *Working Papers in Information Systems*, University of Bayreuth, 1999.
7. Yang Kyu Lee, Sung Joo Park, *"OPNets: An Object-oriented High-Level Petri Net Model for Real-Time System Modeling"*, *Journal of Systems and Software, 20*(1), Jan. 1993, 69-86.
8. Milan Ceska, Vladimir Janousek, Tomas Vojnar, *"Modelling, Prototyping, and* Verifying Concurrent and Distributed Applications Using Object-oriented Petri Nets".
9. Jinzhong Niu, Jing Zou, "OOPN: An Object-oriented Petri Nets and Its Integrated Development Environment".

18

Intrusion Detection System

AMIT SHARMA AND S.N. PANDA

ABSTRACT

An Intrusion Detection System (IDS), generally, detects unwanted manipulations of computer systems, mainly through the Internet. The manipulations may take the form of attacks by crackers. An intrusion detection system is used to detect several types of malicious behaviors that can compromise the security and trust of a computer system. This includes network attacks against vulnerable services, data driven attacks on applications, host-based attacks such as privilege escalation, unauthorized logins and access to sensitive files, and malware (viruses, trojan horses, and worms). An IDS is composed of several components: sensors which generate security events, a console to monitor events and alerts and control the sensors, and a central engine that records events logged by the sensors in a database and uses a system of rules to generate alerts from security events received. There are several ways to categorize an IDS depending on the type and location of the sensors and the methodology used by the engine to generate alerts. In many simple IDS implementations, all three components are combined in a single device or appliance.

1. INTRODUCTION

An Intrusion Detection System (abbreviated as IDS) is a defense system which detects hostile activities in a network. The key is, then, to detect and possibly prevent activities that may compromise system security, or a hacking attempt in progress including reconnaissance/data collection phases that involve, for example, port scans. One key feature of intrusion detection systems is their ability to provide a view of unusual activity and issue alerts notifying administrators and/or block a suspected connection. According to E. Amoroso [1], Intrusion Detection is "a process of identifying and responding to malicious activity targeted at computing and networking resources". In addition, IDS tools are capable of distinguishing between insider attacks originating from inside the organization (coming from own employees or customers) and external ones (attacks and the threads posed by hackers).

According to Mukherjee and Heberlein [2], intrusion detection does not mean the detection of persons is a problem, but the very problem is associated with their criminal activities, for instance intrusions and/or security breaches and, therefore, "detection of intruder activity" would explain such things better.

At SRI, Dr. Denning revealed the necessary information for commercial intrusion detection system development.

2. TYPES OF INTRUSION-DETECTION SYSTEMS

In a Network based Intrusion Detection System (NIDS), the sensors are located at choke points in the network to be monitored, often in the Demilitarized Zone (DMZ) or at network borders. The sensor captures all network traffic and analyzes the content of individual packets for malicious traffic. In systems, PIDS and APIDS are used to monitor the transport and protocols illegal or inappropriate traffic or constructs of language (say SQL). In a host-based system, the sensor usually consists of a software agent, which monitors all activities of the host on which it is installed. Hybrids of these two systems also exist.

A network intrusion detection system is an independent platform which identifies intrusions by examining network traffic and monitors multiple hosts. Network intrusion detection systems gain access to network traffic by connecting to a hub, network switch configured for port mirroring, or network tap. An example of a NIDS is Snort.

A protocol-based intrusion detection system consists of a system or agent that would typically sit at the front end of a server, monitoring and analyzing the communication protocol between a connected device (a user/PC or system). For a web server, this would typically monitor the HTTPS protocol stream and understand the HTTP protocol relative to the web server/system it is trying to protect. Where HTTPS is in use, then, this system would need to reside in the "shim" or interface between where HTTPS is un-encrypted and immediately prior to it entering the Web presentation layer.

An application protocol-based intrusion detection system consists of a system or agent that would typically sit within a group of servers, monitoring and analyzing the communication on application specific protocols. For example, in a web server with database this would monitor the SQL protocol specific to the middleware/business-login as it transacts with the database.

A host-based intrusion detection system consists of an agent on a host which identifies intrusions by analyzing system calls, application logs, file-system modifications (binaries, password files, capability/acl databases) and other host activities and state. An example of a HIDS is OSSEC.

A hybrid intrusion detection system combines two or more approaches. Host agent data is combined with network information to form a comprehensive view of the network. An example of a hybrid IDS is Prelude. Intrusion Detection (ID) functions include:

- Monitoring and analyzing both user and system activities,
- Analyzing system configurations and vulnerabilities,
- Assessing system and file integrity,
- Ability to recognize patterns typical of attacks,
- Analysis of abnormal activity patterns, and
- Tracking user policy violations.

ID systems are being developed in response to the increasing number of attacks on major sites and networks, including those of the Pentagon, the White House, NATO, and the U.S. Defense Department. The safeguarding of security is becoming increasingly difficult, because the possible technologies of attack are becoming ever more sophisticated; at the same time, less technical ability is required for the novice attacker, because proven past methods are easily accessed through the Web.

Typically, an ID system follows a two-step process. The first procedures are host-based and are considered the passive component, these include: inspection of the system's configuration files to detect inadvisable settings; inspection of the password files to detect inadvisable passwords; and inspection of other system areas to detect policy violations. The second procedures are network-based and are considered the active component: mechanisms are set in place to reenact known methods of attack and to record system responses.

In 1998, ICSA.net, a leading security assurance organization, formed the Intrusion Detection Systems Consortium (IDSC) as an open forum for ID product developers with the aim of disseminating information to the end-user and developing industry standards.

3. PROCESS MODEL FOR INTRUSION DETECTION SYSTEM

Many IDSs (Bace and Mell (1989)) can be described in terms of three fundamental functional components:

Information Sources

The different sources of event information used to determine whether an intrusion has taken place. These sources can be drawn from different levels of the system, with network, host, and application monitoring most common.

Analysis

The part of intrusion detection systems that actually organizes and makes sense of the events derived from the information sources, deciding when those events indicate that intrusions are occurring or have already taken place. The most common analysis approaches are misuse detection and anomaly detection.

Response

The set of actions that the system takes once it detects intrusions. These are typically grouped into active and passive measures, with active measures involving some automated intervention on the part of the system, and passive measures involving reporting IDS findings to humans, who are then expected to take action based on those reports.

3.1 IDS Analysis

There are two primary approaches to analyzing events to detect attacks: misuse detection and anomaly detection. Misuse detection, in which the analysis targets something known to be "bad", is the technique used by most commercial systems. Anomaly detection, in which the analysis looks for abnormal patterns of activity, has been and continues to be, the subject of a great deal of research. Anomaly detection is used in limited form by a number of IDSs. There are strengths and weaknesses associated with each approach, and it appears that the most effective IDSs use mostly misuse detection methods with a smattering of anomaly detection components.

3.2 Misuse Detection

Misuse detectors analyze system activity, looking for events or sets of events that match a predefined pattern of events that describe a known attack. As the patterns corresponding to known attacks are called signatures, misuse detection is sometimes called "signature-based detection". The most common form of misuse detection used in commercial products specifies each pattern of events corresponding to an attack as a separate signature. However, there are more sophisticated approaches to doing misuse detection (called "state-based" analysis techniques) that can leverage a single signature to detect groups of attacks. Various advantages are:

- Misuse detectors are very effective at detecting attacks without generating an overwhelming number of false alarms.
- Misuse detectors can quickly and reliably diagnose the use of a specific attack tool or technique. This can help security managers prioritize corrective measures.
- Misuse detectors can allow system managers, regardless of their level of security expertise, to track security problems on their systems, initiating incident handling procedures.

Its disadvantages are:

- Misuse detectors can only detect those attacks they know about therefore they must be constantly updated with signatures of new attacks.
- Many misuse detectors are designed to use tightly defined signatures that prevent them from detecting variants of common attacks. State-based misuse detectors can overcome this limitation, but are not commonly used in commercial IDSs.

3.3 Anomaly Detection

Anomaly detectors identify abnormal unusual behavior (anomalies) on a host or network. They function on the assumption that attacks are different from "normal" (legitimate) activity and can therefore be detected by systems that identify these differences. Anomaly detectors construct profiles representing normal behavior of users, hosts, or network connections. These profiles are constructed from historical data collected over a period of normal operation. The detectors then collect event data and use a variety of measures to determine when monitored activity deviates from the norm. The measures and techniques used in anomaly detection include:

- Threshold detection, in which certain attributes of user and system behavior are expressed in terms of counts, with some level established as permissible. Such behavior attributes can include the number of files accessed by a user in a given period of time, the number of failed attempts to login to the system, the amount of CPU utilized by a process, etc. This level can be static or heuristic (i.e., designed to change with actual values observed over time).
- Statistical measures, both parametric, where the distribution of the profiled attributes is assumed to fit a particular pattern, and non-parametric, where the distribution of the profiled attributes is "learned" from a set of historical values, observed over time.
- Rule-based measures, which are similar to non-parametric statistical measures in that observed data defines acceptable usage patterns, but differs in that those patterns are specified as rules, not numeric quantities.

- Other measures, including neural networks, genetic algorithms, and immune system models. Only the first two measures are used in current commercial IDSs.

Unfortunately, anomaly detectors and the IDSs based on them often produce a large number of false alarms, as normal patterns of user and system behavior can vary wildly. Despite this shortcoming, researchers assert that anomaly-based IDSs are able to detect new attack forms, unlike signature-based IDSs that rely on matching patterns of past attacks. Furthermore, some forms of anomaly detection produce output that can in turn be used as information sources for misuse detectors. For example, a threshold-based anomaly detector can generate a figure representing the "normal" number of files accessed by a particular user; the misuse detector can use this figure as part of a detection signature that says, "if the number of files accessed by this user exceeds this normal figure by ten percent, trigger an alarm". Although some commercial IDSs include limited forms of anomaly detection, few, if any, rely solely on this technology. The anomaly detection that exists in commercial systems usually revolves around detecting network or port scanning. However, anomaly detection remains an active intrusion detection research area and may play a greater part in future IDSs.

Advantages are:

- IDSs based on anomaly detection detect unusual behavior and, thus, have the ability to detect symptoms of attacks without specific knowledge of details.
- Anomaly detectors can produce information that can in turn be used to define signatures for misuse detectors.

Disadvantages are:

- Anomaly detection approaches usually produce a large number of false alarms due to the unpredictable behaviors of users and networks.
- Anomaly detection approaches often require extensive training sets of system event records in order to characterize normal behavior patterns.

4. TYPES OF ATTACKS

There are a large variety of attack types (Fyodor, 2000). An attacker may attempt to guess a user's password. An attacker may also monitor the network to obtain the information they require to launch an attack. Sometimes, attackers try to put unauthorized programs onto computers that they have access to. Sometimes, they may steal information or corrupt information. They may also try to perform a denial of service attack.

FIG. 18.1
Overlapping Packets

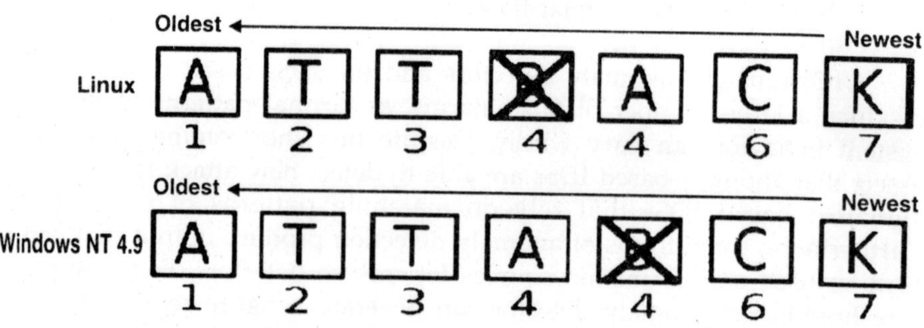

In the section below, various attacks are explained. These attacks may be referred to in other parts of this document to describe the behavior of an IDS to some variants of the attack (Fyodor, 2000).

A. Buffer Overflow

A Buffer overflow attack exploits code that does not check the bounds of a buffer. The attacker may overwrite sensitive data on the stack of an executing process. For example, the instruction pointer on the stack may be overwritten to point to an instruction that the attacker wishes to execute. A detailed description of this problem, as well as possible remedies, can be found in (M.E. Donaldson, 2002).

B. Teardrop

A teardrop attack is an attack that exploits incorrect handling of overlapping packets. Teardrop is a type of Denial of Service (DoS) attack because it crashes any machine that is vulnerable to this attack (Fyodor, 2000). Some older Windows and Linux systems have been reported to be vulnerable to this attack.

C. Ping of Death (PoD)

The ping of death is a Denial of Service (DoS) attack that uses improperly formatted pings. These ping packets have a length greater than the 65535 octets that are allowed. Some Windows, Linux, and Macintosh systems are vulnerable to this attack (Fyodor, 2000).

5. ATTACK VARIATIONS ACROSS OPERATING SYSTEMS

Attacks will vary across operating systems. Some operating systems that are discussed here includes Windows, Linux, and FreeBSD (T.H. Ptacek and T.N. Newsham, 1998). There are several factors that cause the variance in attacks across these operating systems. Each operating system has different default behavior for handling incoming packets on a network. Packets do not always arrive in order. To prevent miscommunication, packets in the same connection are numbered by the sender and then reconstructed by the receiving computer. The problem is that different receivers construct packets differently. For example, consider the problem of overlapping packets. If two packets have the same sequence number in a connection, they are overlapping packets. In this case, the system must decide how to handle the overlapping packets. The default behavior in Linux is to favor new packets, while the default behavior in Windows is to favor old packets. In (T.H. Ptacek and T.N. Newsham, 1998), they state that the overlap behavior and response to incorrect options are two factors that can differ between OSes. In (S. Siddharth, 2005), the concept of reassembly timeout and how it differs between operating systems is explained in detail. All of the factors listed in these two papers determine how the operating system handles packets. The defaults themselves do not cause the attacks, but rather allow an attacker to slip by an IDS that doesn't behave like the operating system it guards. Overlap behavior is the behavior an operating system exhibits when responding to overlapping packets. Overlapping packets are packets that are assigned the same TCP reassembly number and have other identical fields but may have different payloads. Windows always favors older overlapping packets and discards the newer packet, a policy called 'First'. Packet sniffers gather information about packets but do not determine whether those packets are part of an attack or not. The packet information can help the user decide whether an attack is taking place, however. Wireshark/Ethereal (G. Combs, 2006) is one open source packet sniffer.

5.1 Intrusion Detection

Intrusion Detection is the art of identifying attacks on a computer. While there are a large variety of attacks, most of them fit into one of four categories:

- Probe
- Denial of Service (DoS)
- User to Root
- Remote to User

A. A probe attack is an attempt to learn specific setup information about a network or individual computer. This is not exactly an attack in itself, but rather an attempt to learn information that could facilitate an attack. A probe may be an indication of an impending attack. Many attacks are likely preceded by probes of some sort.

B. A DoS is an attack that overloads the resources of a system and prevents legitimate users from accessing the system. Such an attack is a concern for commercial applications or mission-critical network components.

C. A 'user to root' attack is an attack where someone with user permissions attempts to gain root permissions.

D. A 'remote to user' attack is an attempt to go from an unauthenticated state with a system to a state where the attacker has user permissions. This type of attack can then escalate into a 'user to root' attack.

IDS systems can be described by several characteristics. One of these characteristics is the location they watch for attacks. Thus, IDS's can generally be divided into two categories (B. Laing and J. Alderson, 2000).:

- Network-based IDS use raw packets as the data source
- Host-based IDS, which are of three types:

  (a) Examines logs of host looking for attack patterns,
  (b) Examines patterns in network traffic (but not in promiscuous mode, which would allow it to view network traffic that is not addressed to the particular host the IDS resides on, and
  (c) Executes both log-based and stack-based IDS.

The types of detection techniques are pattern, frequency, and anomaly (B. Laing and J. Alderson, 2000). Pattern detection, also known as signature detection, uses known information about attacks to detect them. Anomaly detection requires the collection of normal activity, and flags any deviation from normal activity as abnormal (although not necessarily an attack). Frequency detection checks for behavior that crosses a certain threshold (M. Wood, 2000).

5.2 Strengths and Limitations of IDSs

Although intrusion detection systems are a valuable addition to an organization's security infrastructure, there are things they do well, and other things they do not do well. As you plan the security strategy for your organization's systems, it is important for you to understand what IDSs should be trusted to do and what goals might be better served by other types of security mechanisms.

Intrusion detection systems perform the following functions well:

- Monitoring and analysis of system events and user behaviors.
- Alerting appropriate clients by appropriate means when attacks are detected.
- Measuring enforcement of security policies encoded in the analysis engine.

- Allowing non-security experts to perform important security monitoring functions.
- Clients can also communicate with each other and also with the server.
- Messages can be unicasted as well as broadcasted.

Intrusion detection systems cannot perform the following functions:

- Compensating for weak or missing security mechanisms in the protection infrastructure. Such mechanisms include firewalls, identification and authentication, link encryption, access control mechanisms, and virus detection and eradication.
- Instantaneously detecting, reporting, and responding to an attack, when there is a heavy network or processing load.
- Detecting newly published attacks or variants of existing attacks.
- Effectively responding to attacks launched by sophisticated attackers.
- Automatically investigating attacks without human intervention.
- Testing the security states of system configurations.
- Base lining the security state of a system, then tracking any changes to that baseline.
- Recognizing patterns of system events that correspond to known attacks.
- Recognizing patterns of activity that statistically vary from normal activity.
- Managing operating system audit and logging mechanisms and the data they generate.

5.3 Determining Attacker Location from IDS Output

In notifications of a detected attack, IDSs will often report the location of a attacker. This location is most commonly expressed as an source IP address. The reported address is simply the source address that appears in the attack packets. The whole record of successful users and unsuccessful users is being maintained at the server from where it can be determined which unauthorized users have tried to access the server and which users are authorized. The server keeps a record of all the users who have previously accessed the server.

6. CHALLENGES

The challenges mainly lie in detecting attacks like system scanning and, also, in the implementation of firewall. A scanning attack occurs when an attacker probes a target network or system by sending different kinds of packets. Scanning attacks may yield:

- The topology of a target network,
- The types of network traffic allowed through a firewall,
- The active hosts on the network,
- The operating systems those hosts are running,
- The server software they are running, and
- The software version numbers for all detected software.

With the implementation of firewall, the IDS becomes very strong, safe and secure.

References

1. E. Amoroso, Wykrywanie intruzów, Wydawnictwo, RM, Warszawa, 1999 (in Polish).
2. B. Mukherjee, T.L. Heberlein, K.N. Levitt, Network intrusion detection, IEEE Network 8 (3), 1994, pp. 26-41.
3. Bace, R. and Mell, P. 1989. Intrusion Detection Systems. NIST Special Publication on Intrusion Detection Systems, 12: 1-51.
4. Fyodor, "Insecure.org: Exploit world. http://insecure.org/sploits.html." Website, 2000.
5. M.E. Donaldson, "Inside the bu_er overflow attack: Mechanism, method, and prevention".http://www.sans.org/reading_room/whitepapers/securecode/386.php. Website, 2002.
6. T.H. Ptacek and T.N. Newsham, "Insertion, evasion, and denial of service: Eluding network intrusion detection," tech. rep., Secure Networks, Inc., Suite 330, 1201 5th Street S.W, Calgary, Alberta, Canada,T2R-0Y6, 1998.
7. S. Siddharth, "Evading nids, revisited. http://www.securityfocus.com/ infocus/1852." Website, 2005.
8. G. Combs, "Wireshark." Website, 2006.
9. B. Laing and J. Alderson, "How to guide: Intrusion detection systems". http://www.snort.org/docs/issplacement. pdf. Website, 2000.
10. "Promiscuous mode". http://www.linktionary.com/p/promiscuous.html.
11. M. Wood, "Selecting a site for the software sentry". http://www.securitymanagement.com/library/000763.html.

19

Change Detection in Satellite Imageries Using ANN

ABHILASHA SINGH

ABSTRACT

Remotely sensed images are major source of data and information that are used in various fields such as environmental studies, forest management, and urban change detection. So far, many efforts have been made to extract information from remotely sensed images and various methods have been developed in this field. One of the main approaches is quantitative analysis (digital interpretation). Among digital techniques, classification is a common and powerful information extraction method, which is used in remote sensing. Classification of satellite images is the process in which different areas (like water, soil, vegetation, etc.) are separated. The classified image helps the analyst to study the area, to gain more information about the areas and to analyze the area. Artificial Neural Network (ANN) techniques have recently been used to have better classification. To classify the given satellite image using ANN technique i.e., Unsupervised Learning. From these images, we take the classified image as an input and the output is the image in which we show the change between the images. We compare two images of different month or different year and detect changes. We have to find the trend of change of the images after certain period of time of any classified images. By how much amount it is increase or decrease after that certain period of time. If there is any crop season, then, the vegetation area is more prominent. But, when this season is off, vegetation area is decreased. So, there is a change in the image during or after the crop season.

During flood, water bodies' area is more than other area. When these areas recover the problem of flood, the area of civilian, water, vegetation all is available. So, we have to detect the changes among the area of different type. We detect changes mainly in two areas, i.e. vegetation and water area. The output is the change detected between the satellite images. These changes are detected by various ways—

1. To detect the change by comparing two images of same place (that is pixel by pixel).
2. To detect the changes among the images by observing image differences.
3. To extract the features of the image and by comparing the extracted features we detect the change.

We represent these changes in different ways, i.e. to represent the changes by a single image, to represent the changes with the help of pixel values, or to represent the changes by a graph.

1. NEURAL NETWORKS

A neural network is a powerful data-modeling tool that is able to capture and represent complex input/output relationships. The motivation for the development of neural network technology stemmed from the desire to develop an artificial system that could perform intelligent tasks similar to those performed by the human brain. Neural networks resemble the human brain in the following two ways:

- A neural network acquires knowledge through learning.
- A neural network's knowledge is stored within inter-neuron connection strengths known as synaptic weights.

Neural networks are learning devices inspired by the workings of the brain. A neural network is a massively parallel-distributed processor made up of simple processing units, which has a natural propensity for storing experimental knowledge and making it available for use. Neural networks are composed of multiple units connected by links, where each link has an associated numeric weight. At each processing step, every unit does some local computation to determine its activation level, given the input links and weights and its previous activation level. Some units serve as input units and others as output units. A network learns from a set of training examples, which specify the values for the input and output units, by adjusting the weights on the links accordingly.

FIG. 19.1
Neural Network Structure

- Artificial Neuron

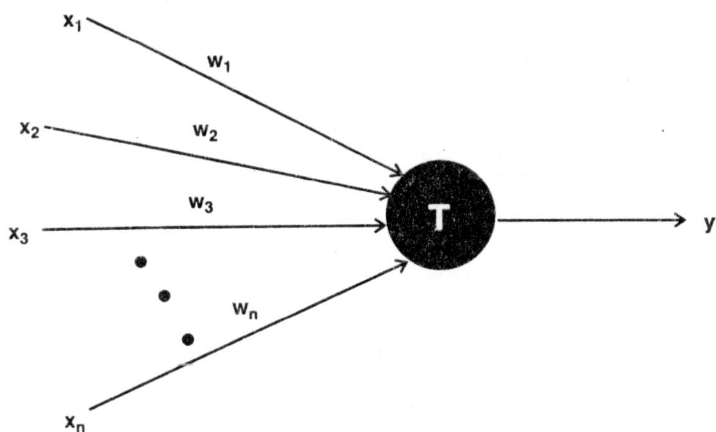

- An ANN is a set of processing elements (PEs) and connections with adjustable strengths (weights)

Schematic Diagram of a Neural Network

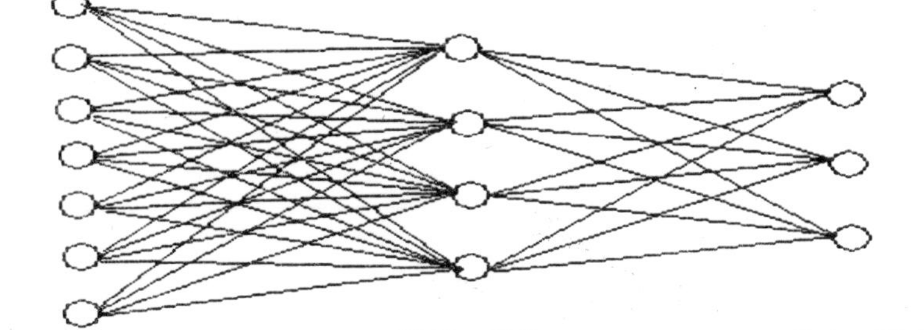

The procedure used to perform the learning process is called a learning algorithm, the function of which is to modify the synaptic weights of the network in an orderly fashion to attain a desired design objective. All learning methods used for adaptive neural networks can be classified into two major categories:

(a) *Supervised Learning*
Supervised Learning which is referred to as Learning with a teacher. The most common neural network model is the

multiplayer perceptron (MLP). This type of neural network is also known as a supervised network because it requires a desired output in order to learn. The goal of this type of network is to create a model that correctly maps the input to the output using historical data so that the model can then be used to produce the output when the desired output is unknown.

(b) *Unsupervised Learning*

There is no external teacher or critic to oversee the learning process. There is a provision is made for a task independent measure of the quality of representation that the network is required to learn, and the free parameters of the network are optimized with respect to that measure. Once the network has become tuned to the statistical regularities of the input data, it develops the ability to form internal representations for encoding features of the input and thereby to create new class automatically.

FIG. 19.2
Learning Process

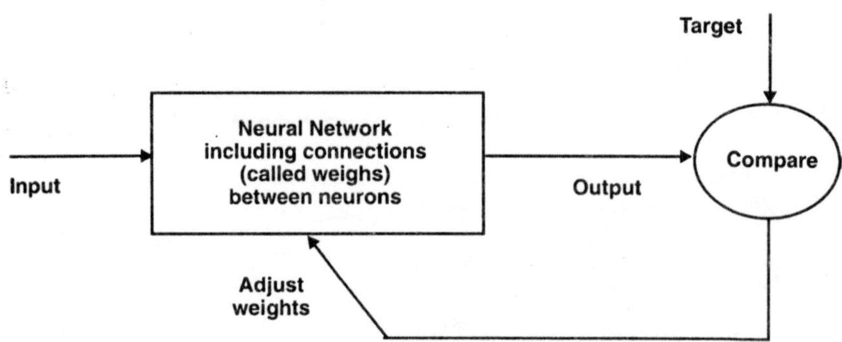

2. APPLICATIONS OF NEURAL NETWORKS

Neural networks have broad applicability to real world business problems. Since neural networks are best at identifying patterns or trends in data, they are well suited for prediction or forecasting needs including:

- Sales forecasting
- Industrial process control
- Customer research
- Data validation
- Risk management
- Target marketing
- Future land cover

We have covered the *"future land cover"* application of neural network. Neural network is used to classify the given image by unsupervised learning method and, then, extract the feature and on the basis of that feature we compare the image and detect the changes. Among digital techniques, classification is a common and powerful information extraction method, which is used in remote sensing. ANN techniques have been used with the features of the satellite image to have better classification. Features are the characteristics of the land cover type that identifies it uniquely. Features can be of the types—statistical features, band ratio, and difference between two images of same area (i.e. taken at different of time interval). The statistical features are the mean, maximum, minimum, variance, covariance, correlation, standard deviation etc. Feature selection depends upon the various conditions and necessity classification network required. If we require classifying the land cover basically for the vegetation, then, the feature must be selected that identify those cover types. Area like vegetation have a unique identifying feature (Infrared band)/(Red band). Likely, various other cover areas have different feature that would identify that area separately.

3. LEARNING PROCESS

FIG. 19.3
Class Samples for Training

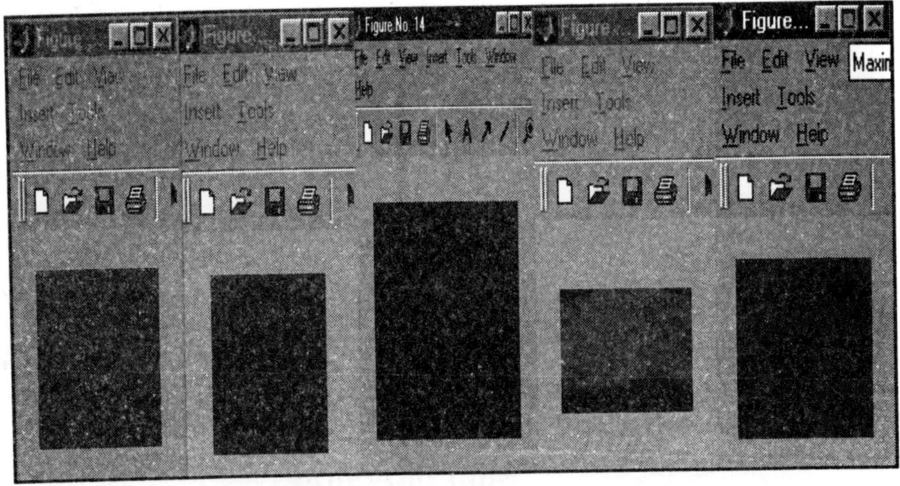

Class :: 1 Class :: 2 Class :: 3 Class :: 4 Class :: 5

Class 1:: Light Vegetation
Class 2:: Heavy Vegetation
Class 3:: Water bodies
Class 4:: Dry Land Area
Class 5:: Hilly Area

In this work, we are classifying the whole area into different classes. So, to classify all the different cover area, the "mean" feature acts appropriately. For this, the network is trained with the mean of the sample. As the network operates on the mean feature, then, the network is highlighted to some characteristics for particular feature value then that is considered as the input factor for classification.

The above five sample of image is used to train the network as in Figure 19.3. The ability to learn is a fundamental trait of intelligence. From this learning process, the network knows which area comes under which class. Now, the network is ready to classify the given image. For classification the input is the satellite image of any place and the output is the classified image of that given image. On the basis of this classified image we detect the changes. For detecting changes in the given image of different months we compare their pixel values. Mainly we work on the vegetation and water area for change detection.

One application of change detection is the use of a Markov model to predict future land-cover/land-use change based on rates of past change. Markov models have been used in many other research studies to generate probabilities of transition from one cover type to another across landscapes. Markov models are based on the probability that a given piece of land (or pixel) will change from one mutually exclusive state to another. These probabilities are generated from past land-use changes and, then, applied to predict future changes.

FIG. 19.4

Example of Changing the Path of the River

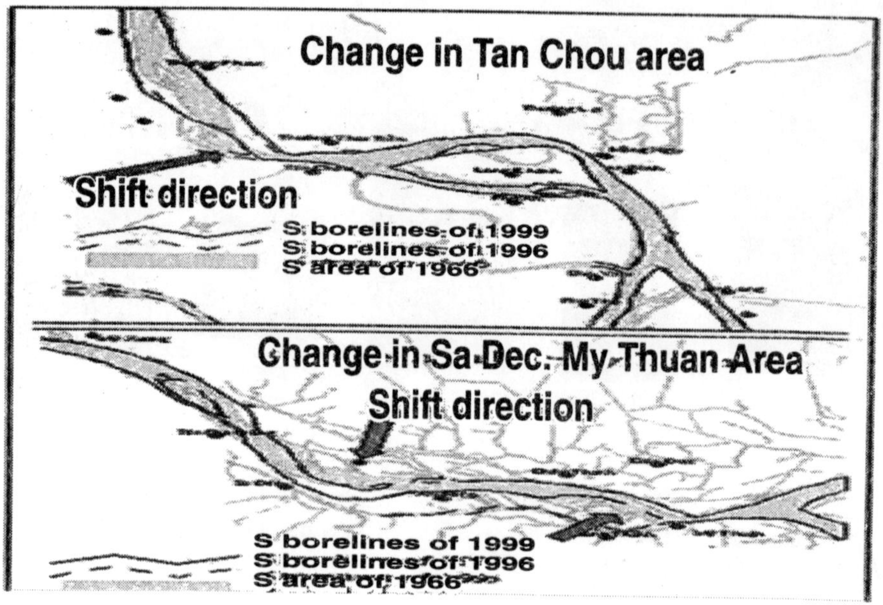

From the Fig. 4, it is clear that the path of the river is changed. The arrow sign shows that path of the river that has been changed.

4. VARIOUS WAYS TO REPRESENT CHANGE DETECTED

4.1 Changes Detected in the Images

We represent the change detected in the images by single image. In this, we represent the change between the areas. The Single image shows the change between all the images on those we perform comparisons.

FIG. 19.5
Change Detected of the Images by Single Image

Land sat TM 1984

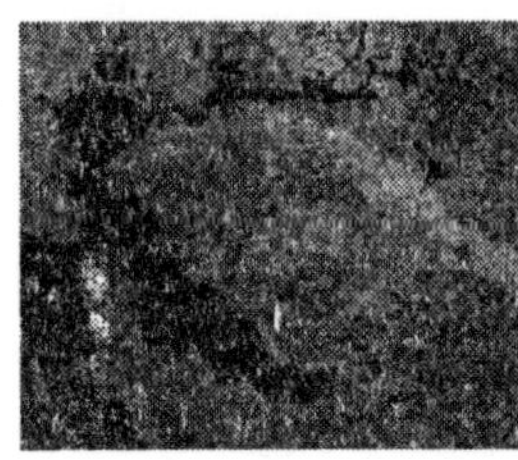

Land sat TM 1993

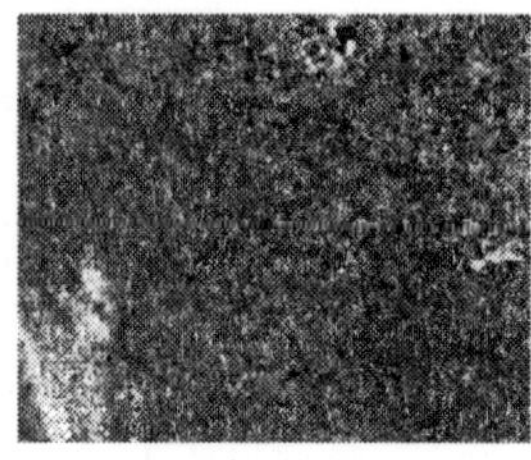

1984 *v.* 1993
(Changed Image)

- *Magenta*—These pixels/locations were more vegetated in 1984 than in 1993. Examples of this are the loss of wetlands along the Bay or where there is less natural vegetation/grass in the foothills in 1993 due to differences in the amount of rainfall. Also, the vegetation type can be the same on both dates but either the density or level of maturity of the vegetation on the two dates is different (i.e., more dense/mature in 1984 than 1993).
- *Green*—Green is the opposite of magenta (i.e., more vegetated in 1993 than in 1984). This mostly occurs in agricultural areas and is related to crop rotation, crop type changes, or crop density/maturity differences between the two dates.
- *Blue*—Most areas that are blue represent urban growth between 1984 and 1993. These are areas where either new residential or industrial development occurred between 1984 and 1993. Examples include the blues seen on the east side of extreme South Bay which represents mostly new industrial buildings, while the blues north and elsewhere are areas with new residential development between the two dates.
- *White*—White areas show where dramatic changes in surface brightness/reflectance occurred; these areas were much brighter in 1993 than in 1984. Examples of this are the clouds in the lower left

portion of the image, and areas that were burned in 1984 and have recovered by 1993. Other examples are seen north of Mallard Island and an area due east from the image center/east side of the foothills.

- *Black*—The black areas also had a dramatic change in surface brightness/reflectance, but were darker rather than brighter in 1993 *versus* 1984. Examples of this are areas burned in 1993 or were natural landscape areas in 1984 that were converted to agricultural lands and recently tilled.

4.2 Changes Detected of the Images by Numeric Values

We represent the change detected of the images by numeric values.

FIG. 19.6
Change Detected of the Images by Numeric Values

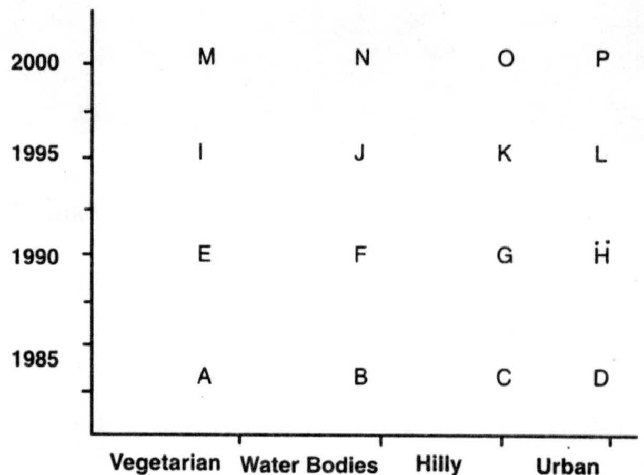

In the Figure 19.6, A, B, C.............alphabets represents the numeric value of different changes between the areas after each 5 years.

4.3 Changes Detected of the Images by Graph

The change detected between the images by the graph. The graph shows the changes between the areas of the satellite images of different time period.

The Figure 19.7 shows how pixel value of vegetation area is varying with time to time.

In 1983, the area of vegetation is maximum and between 1985 and 1990 the vegetation area is decreased. From this graph it is very clear that after 1990 the area also increases and from 1995 to 2000 area of vegetation is constant. There is no variation in the pixel value of vegetation from 1995.In

FIG. 19.7
Value of Vegetation Area is Varying with Time to Time

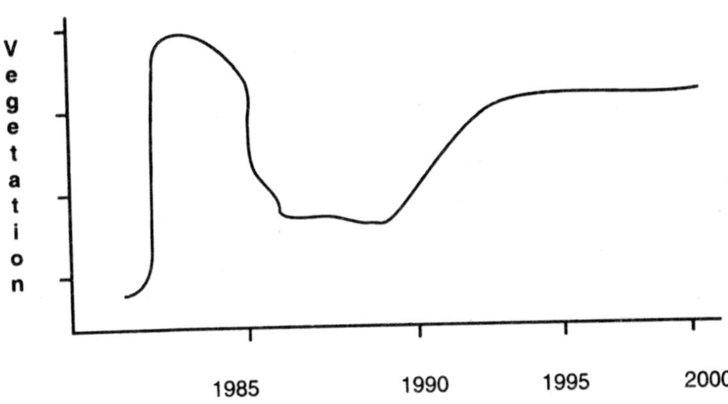

1981 the vegetation area is minimum. We can also represent more than one type of area in the same graph and show its pixel variation in different time period.

The Table 19.1 shows the pixel value of vegetation and water area in different months of same year as shown in Figure 19.8.

TABLE 19.1
Pixel Value of Vegetation and Water Area in Different Months of Same Year

Months	*January 2002*	*February 2002*	*March 2002*
Vegetation	11,825	10,025	2,570
Water	1,300	1,275	700

From the above table, we can say that vegetation and water area both are decreased.

5. CONCLUSION

There are two cropping seasons in a year, one from October to last of February and second season from May to August. From our classified images and land study, we see that in January and February vegetation is maximum because this time is the peak growth time of crop. After February crop season is finished so vegetation area decreased. For water body, we have taken Masi-dam area and some other water areas for classification. We have covered dry-land area and from March to June temperature is very high. For these two reasons water body area decreases from last February.

Fig. 19.8

Classification Results of Images of IRS 1d L3 Multispectral FCC Image Unsupervised Classification

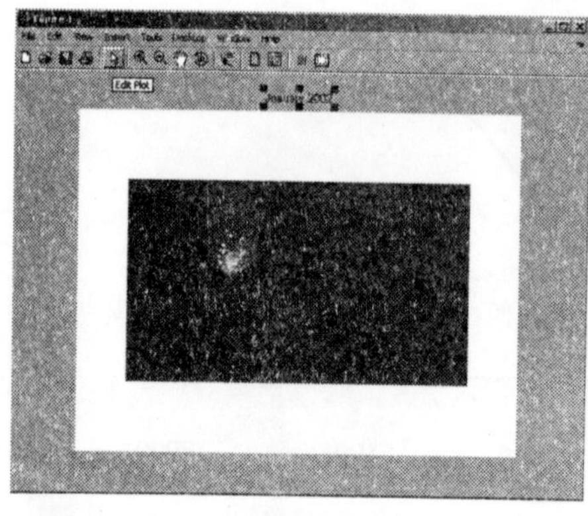

A: FCC image of January 2002

B: Classified image of January 2002

C: FCC image of February 2002

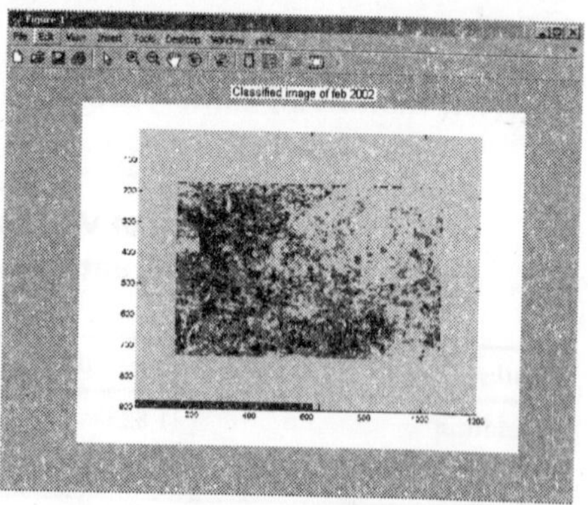

D: Classified image of February 2002

E: FCC image of March. 2002

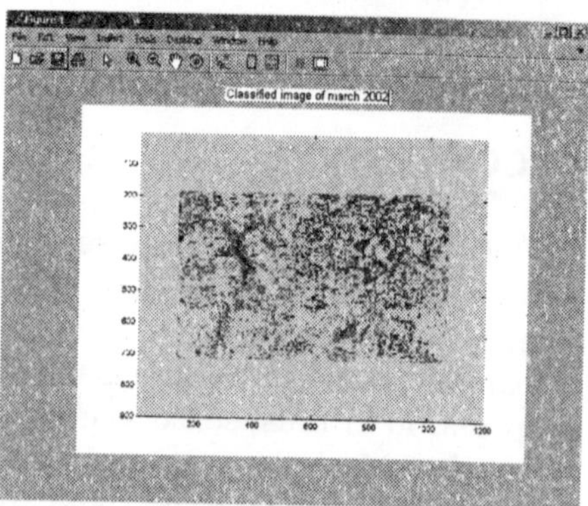

F: Classified image of March 2002

In the process of change detection if a Time series images of the same area are taken then, the calculation of the changes of the subsequent images can result in the series of the changes of the particular area. So, this series of changes could be analyzed to predict the changes that would occur in the future. In time series prediction the goal is to construct a model that can predict the future of the measured process under interest.

References

1. http://www.ip-atlas.com/pub/nap/index.html
2. http://www.benbest.com/computer/nn.html
3. http://citeseer.ist.psu.edu/551841.html
4. http://www.cormactech.com/neunet/whatis.html
5. Sangeeta Pal, "Classification of Satellite Images Using Unsupervised Learning Method of Neural Network".
6. "Self-Organizing maps: Optimization approaches", in Proc. Int. Conf. Artif. Neural Networks, Espoo, Finland, June 1991, pp. 981-90.
7. D.L. Kerry, D. Weng *et. al.*, IEEE On Signal Processing magazine, Jan. 2002, Vol. 19, No. 2.
8. Haykin Simon, Neural Network: A Comprehensive Foundation, Prentice Hall, 1994.
9. Hepner, Artificial Neural Network Classification Using a Minimal Training Set: Comparison to Conventional Supervised Classification, Phogrammetric Eng. & Remote Sensing, April, 1990.
10. Jain, A.K., Fundamental of Digital Image Processing.
11. http://www.gsd.harvard.edu/gis/manual/image_class/
12. http://www.yale.edu/ceo/Documentation/ChangeDetectionPrep.pdf
13. http://www.infosar.co.uk/docs/node42.html
14. http://www.personal.psu.edu/users/j/b/jbs191/example_change_detection.html
15. http://terraweb.wr.usgs.gov/projects/eolian/chngdetc.html
16. http://cbcl.mit.edu/projects/cbcl/publications/ps/mohan-ieee.pdf

20

Virtual Reality and Augmented Reality

Roopali Sood, Pallavi Mehta and Deepika Thakur

ABSTRACT

Virtual Environment is a computer generated three-dimensional scene which requires high performance computer graphics to provide an adequate level of realism. Augmented Reality is new innovative technology that combines the concepts of virtual reality and the real world. This paper presents the advantages, disadvantages of virtual reality, and challenges faced in implementing augmenting reality.

1. INTRODUCTION

Virtual Reality is an upcoming technology that encompasses a broad spectrum of ideas. Virtual reality is the simulation of a real or imagined environment that can be experienced visually in the three dimensions of width, height, and depth. Virtual Reality (VR) is a technology that allows you to enter and interact with a world that is generated by a computer. This virtual environment is interactive computer-generated three-dimensional scene which requires high performance computer graphics to provide an adequate level of realism. Special graphics, video images and stereo sound make this pretend world seem real. The user is immersed in this virtual environment.

Virtual reality can be divided into:

- The simulation of real environments such as the interior of a building or a spaceship often with the purpose of training or education.
- The development of an imagined environment, typically for a game or educational adventure.

The uses for virtual reality are infinite. It can be used for air traffic control, medicine, entertainment, office work and industrial design. Virtual reality has very important uses in all types of architecture and industrial design. Virtual reality has been a huge boost in the aviation business. By using VR, designers can design, build and test their aircraft in a virtual environment without having to build a real aircraft. Virtual reality is also being used in drug research. Scientists are able to create the molecules and, then, visualize and feel how they react with each other. So, it is likely that virtual reality will have a strong impact on the speed with which new drugs and remedies are developed and become available in the future. Using virtual reality, doctors have already been inside a body. At the University of North Carolina, USA, virtual reality allowed doctors to enter a cancer patient's thorax (part of the chest) to make sure that radiation beams needed to treat the cancer were in the right place. Doctors will soon be able to look at and study tumours at first hand and in 3-D rather than from scans and x-rays.

The possibilities for virtual reality are enormous. It can visualize the unknown or the unpredictable. This might lead to virtual reality operators carrying out repairs in space, with the help of a robot. In a technique called virtual puppetry, a robot is controlled by a skilled operator and mimics all the operator's movements. Future residents of new towns will be able to walk around virtual streets, shops, houses and parks before a single brick has beer laid. There are already plans to redesign the whole of the city of Berlin, the capital of Germany, using virtual reality.

2. AUGMENTED REALITY

Augmented Reality (AR) is a growing area in virtual reality research. *Augmented Reality (AR)* is a field of computer research which deals with the combination of real-world and computer-generated data. Augmented reality is an environment that includes both virtual reality and real-world elements. An augmented reality system generates a composite view for the user. It is a combination of the real scene viewed by the user and a virtual scene generated by the computer that augments the scene with additional information. The augmented reality presented to the user enhances that person's performance and perception of the world. The ultimate goal is to create a system such that the user can not tell the difference between the real world and the virtual augmentation of it. To the user of this ultimate system it would appear that he is looking at a single real scene. Augmented reality system is defined as a system which:

- combines real and virtual, and
- is interactive in real-time.

The augmented reality has the potential to be used in almost ever industry such as maintenance and construction, military, instant information, entertainment, etc. The biggest challenge facing developers of augmented reality is accurately register the computer generated virtual objects with the real world in all dimensions. Errors in this registration will prevent the user from seeing the real and virtual images as fused. The correct registration must also be maintained while the user moves about within the real environment. Discrepancies or changes in the apparent registration will range from distracting which makes working with the augmented view more difficult, to physically disturbing for the user making the system completely unusable.

3. TYPICAL AUGMENTED REALITY SYSTEM

A standard virtual reality system seeks to completely immerse the user in a computer-generated environment. This environment is maintained by the system in a frame of reference registered with the computer graphic system that creates the rendering of the virtual world. For this immersion to be effective the ego centered frame of reference maintained by the user's body and brain must be registered with the virtual world reference. This requires that motions or changes made by the user will result in the appropriate changes in the perceived virtual world. Because the user is looking at a virtual world, there is no natural connection between these two reference frames and a connection must be created. The task is to register the virtual frame of reference with what the user is seeing. This registration is more critical in an augmented reality system because users are more sensitive to visual misalignments than to the type of vision-kinesthetic errors that might result in a standard virtual reality system. Figure 20.1 shows the multiple reference frames that must be related in an augmented reality system.

The scene is viewed by an imaging device, which in this case is depicted as a video camera. The camera performs a perspective projection of the 3D world onto a 2D image plane. The intrinsic (focal length and lens distortion) and extrinsic (position and pose) parameters of the device determine exactly what is projected onto its image plane. The generation of the virtual image is done with a standard computer graphics system. The virtual objects are modeled in an object reference frame. The graphics system requires information about the imaging of the real scene so that it can correctly render these objects. This data will control the synthetic camera that is used to generate the image of the virtual objects. This image is, then,

FIG. 20.1
Reference Frames that must be Related in an Augmented Reality System

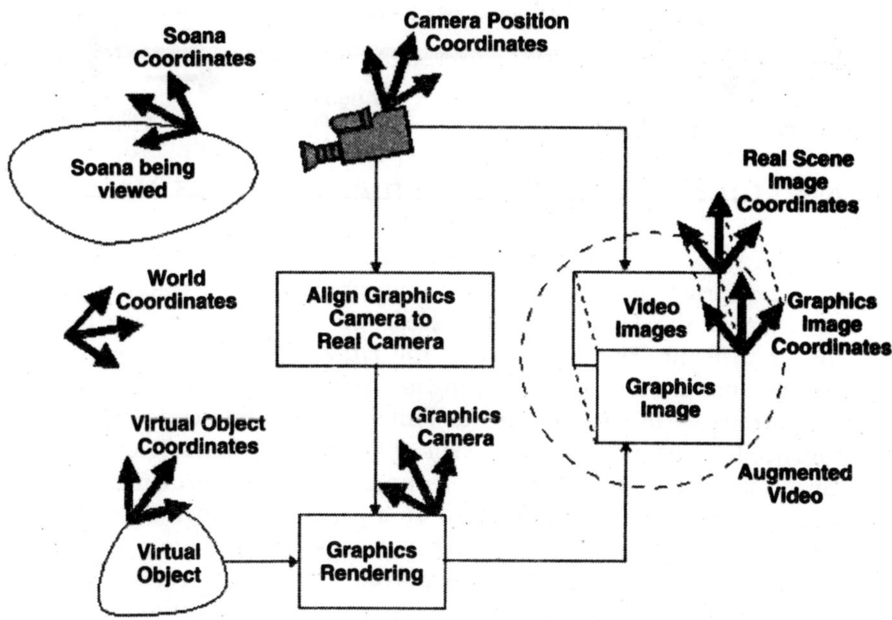

merged with the image of the real scene to form the augmented reality image.

4. PERFORMANCE ISSUES IN AN AUGMENTED REALITY SYSTEM

Augmented reality systems are expected to run in real-time so that a user will be able to move about freely within the scene and see a properly rendered augmented image. This places two performance criteria on the system. They are:

- Update rate for generating the augmenting image, and
- Accuracy of the registration of the real and virtual image.

5. AUGMENTED REALITY V. VIRTUAL REALITY

Augmented reality and virtual reality work are related.

The real world and a totally virtual environment are at the two ends of this continuum with the middle region called Mixed Reality. Augmented reality lies near the real world end of the line with the predominate perception being the real world augmented by computer generated data. Virtual reality, creates immersible, computer-generated environments, and the real world, augmented reality is closer to the real world.

FIG. 20.2
Milgram's Reality—Virtuality Continuum

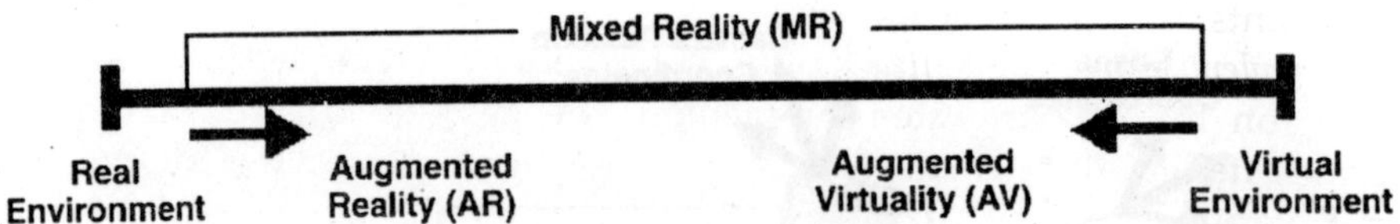

6. CASE STUDY: IMPLEMENTING VIRTUAL REALITY AT NASA

The Software Technology Branch of NASA's Lyndon B. Johnson Space Center is exploring the use of virtual environments as a training aid as Maintenance of the Hubble Space Telescope as well as Space Station Freedom is difficult. The objectives of the Hubble Space Telescope repair and maintenance are to help developing an virtual environment suitable for training astronauts in preparation for Hubble Space Telescope repair and maintenance missions. Graphical models of the Hubble Space Telescope and a large number of digitized close-out photographs of the instrument are available. A virtual environment based on a graphical model of the HST is under development in which high fidelity, detailed images are needed, and appropriate digitized images will be displayed. The system will be designed to address specific elements of future missions that will require location of objects and interaction with handholds, panels, fasteners, and orbital replacement units.

Another project, Training for EVA (Extra Vehicular Activity) Payload Interaction has started. The main objective of this demonstration is to allow users to experience a training session in an interactive virtual environment by exchanging a faulty battery in the Hubble Space Telescope (HST) with a new replacement battery. The user moves to the HST, opens the door to the battery bay, takes it back to the space shuttle orbiter, and places it on top of the hardware pallet in the payload bay. The user than takes the new battery from the cargo bay hardware pallet to the HST and installs it behind the battery bay door. A narrator will introduce a few details to the user in the beginning of the session, and correct the user when he/she makes a wrong move. The user can grab the bay door or the battery by reaching out and clinching the yellow handle with the gloved hand. Movement about the environment is accomplished with the two hand-controllers of the chair. This chair emulates the functionality of a Manned Maneuvering Unit and uses a translational control (left side) to move in any straight line by pulling or pushing in the desired direction of motion. Also, a rotational control (right side) adjusts the user's orientation about his/her center point. Changes are initiated in yaw by twisting the control left or right, in pitch by pulling it back or pushing forward, and in roll by tilting it left or right. In addition to the direct anticipated benefits of using a virtual environment for training. the Software Technology Branch is also collaborating with the

Marshall Space Flight Center to enable personnel at the two centers to simultaneously share the same virtual environment. Using these techniques joint training exercises could be conducted without the usual collocation constraints.

Implementing Augmented Reality: Three year project under EuroPARC is based on human-computer interaction. The goal of this research is to investigate and implement new methods for human-computer interaction, and to apply and evaluate their use in the specific discipline of electronic publishing. The work builds in Cambridge (EuroPARC) on the DigitalDesk—an ordinary desk augmented with a computer display using projection television and a video camera to monitor inputs. A number of prototype systems have been implemented to demonstrate its feasibility. This research will investigate the technology further, address issues of performance and explore and evaluate its application to electronic publishing. In particular, it will be used to develop a strategy for combining electronic and printed documents to give a richer presentation than that afforded by either separate medium. This also relates to work in the Department of Applied Mathematics at Cambridge on educational computing materials, especially interactive courseware and Computer Illustrated Texts.

6. CONCLUSIONS

Augmented Reality (AR) is a growing area in virtual reality research. Augmented reality is still in an early stage of research and development. Once researchers overcome the challenges that face them, augmented reality will truly change the way we view the world and pervade every corner of our lives. It has the potential to be used in almost every industry.

References

1. Virtual Reality—Wikipedia, the free encyclopedia
2. Virtual Reality Laboratory virtualrealityhair.com
3. howstuffworks.com/augmented-reality
4. augmented-reality.org
5. technologyreview.com/Infotech/18291
6. www.cs.unc.edu/~azuma/azuma_

SECTION III

E-Learning in Education

21

Role of E-Learning in Education in a New Millennium

SATBIR RUPAL

ABSTRACT

Learning is the acquisition of values, beliefs, skills and knowledge, and E-learning is commonly referred to the intentional use of networked information and communications technology in learning. The term e-learning comprises a lot more than online learning, virtual learning, distributed learning, networked or web-based learning. Growing number of teachers are increasingly using information and communications technology to support their teaching. A key attribute of information and communication technology is its ability to enable flexible access to information and resources, especially in distance education. E-learning can manifest itself in four different ways, i.e. Individualized self-paced e-learning online, Individualized self-paced e-learning offline, Group-based e-learning synchronously and Group-based e-learning asynchronously. Different pedagogical designs are suggested for optimizing e-learning. It is widely acknowledged that the role and influence of media (i.e. information and communications technology) on learning and teaching is optimized especially when it is skillfully integrated into the educational experience. In short, we can say that the factors that influence learning include learner readiness, their interest and motivation in the study of the subject matter, the nature and quality of the learning experience including the nature of the assessment activities, and the nature and quality of feedback and support that is available to students influences the learning.

1. INTRODUCTION

Cutting edge information and communication technologies have brought about a tremendous change in every sphere of education, especially, in the ways of learning. e-Learning environments have a tremendous potential in enhancing training programmes beyond the walls of the classroom or a campus. e-Learning environments give students the flexibility and control over time, space and pace of their learning, by liberating the learners from the classroom paradigm. e-Learning is a combination of learning service and technology that provides high value integrated learning; any time, any place. High level of interaction for the learner with the interaction of teacher and peer group which can be introduced through e-mails, discussion groups, chat sessions, web conferencing, etc. learners can pursue these courses along with their normal jobs.

2. DEFINITION AND SCOPE

Learning is the acquisition of values, beliefs, skills and knowledge and E-learning is commonly referred to the intentional use of networked information and communications technology in teaching and learning. A number of other terms are also used to describe this mode of teaching and learning. They include online learning, virtual learning, distributed learning, network and web-based learning. Fundamentally, they all refer to educational processes that utilize information and communications technology to mediate asynchronous as well as synchronous learning and teaching activities. On closer scrutiny, however, it will be clear that these labels refer to slightly different educational processes and as such they cannot be used synonymously with the term e-learning.

The term e-learning comprises a lot more than online learning, virtual learning, distributed learning, networked or web-based learning. As the letter "e" in e-learning stands for the word "electronic", e-learning would incorporate all educational activities that are carried out by individuals or groups working online or offline, and synchronously or asynchronously via networked or standalone computers and other electronic devices high quality resources made available in multimedia formats. These various types or modalities of e-learning activity are represented in Table 21.1.

TABLE 21.1
E-Learning Modalities

Individualized E-Learning		*Group-based E-Learning*	
Self-paced E-Learning Offline	Self-paced E-Learning Offline	e-learning synchronously	e-learning asynchronously

(Romiszowski, 2004)

1. *Individualized self-paced e-learning online* refers to situations where an individual learner is accessing learning resources such as a database or course content online via Intranet or Internet. A typical example of this is a learner studying alone or conducting some research on the Internet or a local network.
2. *Individualized self-paced e-learning offline* refers to situations where an individual learner is using learning resources such as a database or a computer-assisted learning package offline (i.e. while not connected to an Intranet or the Internet). An example of this is a learner working alone off a hard drive, a CD or DVD.
3. *Group-based e-learning synchronously* refers to situations where groups of learners are working together in real time via an Intranet or the Internet. It may include text-based conferencing, and one or two-way audio and videoconferencing. Examples of this include learners engaged in a real-time chat or an audio-video conference.
4. *Group-based e-learning asynchronously* refers to situations where groups of learners are working over an Intranet or the Internet where exchanges among participants occur with a time delay (i.e., not in real time). Typical examples of this kind of activity include on-line discussions via electronic mailing lists and text-based conferencing within learning managements systems.

3. ISSUES AND TRENDS IN E-LEARNING

The growing interest in e-learning seems to be coming from several directions. These include organizations that have traditionally offered distance education programs either in a single, dual or mixed mode setting. They see the incorporation of online learning in their repertoire as a logical extension of their distance education activities. The corporate sector, on the other hand, is interested in e-learning as a way of rationalizing the costs of their in-house staff training activities. E-learning is of interest to residential campus-based educational organizations as well. They see e-learning as a way of improving access to their programs, and also, as a way of tapping into growing niche markets.

The growth of e-learning is directly related to the increasing access to information and communications technology, as well it's decreasing cost. The capacity of information and communications technology to support multimedia resource-based learning and teaching is also relevant to the growing interest in e-learning.

Growing number of teachers are increasingly using information and communications technology to support their teaching. The contemporary student populations (often called the "Net Generation", or "Millennials") who have grown up using information and communications technology also expect to see it being used in their educational experiences. Educational organizations, too, see advantages in making their programs accessible via a range of distributed locations, including on campus, home and other community learning or resource centers.

Despite this level of interest in e-learning, it is not without constraints and limitations. The fundamental obstacle to the growth of e-learning is lack of access to the necessary technology infrastructure, for without it there can be no e-learning. Poor or insufficient technology infrastructure is just as bad as it can lead to unsavory experiences that can cause more damage than good to teachers, students and the learning experience.

While the costs of the hardware and software are falling, often there are other costs that have often not been factored into the deployment of e-learning ventures. The most important of these includes the costs of infrastructure support and its maintenance, and appropriate training of staff to enable them to make the most of the technology (Naidu, 2003). Educators should articulate the learning and teaching needs of the organisation along with the estimation of how the e-learning technology can be used in an optimized way. Teachers should take care of the changing needs of the society in relation to expanding information.

4. THE FLEXIBILITY THAT E-LEARNING TECHNOLOGY AFFORDS

A key attribute of information and communications technology is its ability to enable flexible access to information and resources. Flexible access refers to access and use of information and resources at a time, place and pace that is suitable and convenient to individual learners rather than the teacher and/or the educational organization.

The concept of distance education was founded on the principles of flexible access (Willems, 2005). It aimed to allow distance learners, who were generally adult learners in full or part-time employment to be able to study at a time, place, and pace that suited their convenience. The goal of distance education was to free these learners from the constraints of conventional residential educational settings. They would not be required to live or attend lectures in locations away from where they may be living and working. The printed distance study materials, which each distance learner received, would carry the core subject matter content they would need including all their learning activities and assessment tasks. Students would be required to complete these tasks, submit their assignments and take their examinations within a set time frame. While these printed study materials allowed distance learners a great deal of freedom from time, place and pace of study, it had its limitations. For one thing, non-printed subject matter content and simulations, etc. could not be easily represented in print form.

Access to information and communications technology changed all that as it offered a range of possibilities for capturing and delivering all types of subject matter content to learners and teachers in distributed educational settings. This meant access to subject matter content and learning resources via networked information and communications technologies across a range of settings such as conventional classrooms, workplaces, homes, and various forms of community centers.

Contemporary educational institutions, including conventional distance education providers, often pride themselves in being able to meet the learning needs of their students and staff at a time, place and pace that is most convenient to them. They have been able to do this with the help of information and communications technologies which afford learners access to up-to-date information as and when they need them, and also the opportunity to discuss this information with their peers and teachers at their convenience. This is becoming increasingly affordable and palatable with a wide range of software applications and computer conferencing technologies for collaborative inquiry among students and asynchronous discussion. These applications enable learners and teachers to engage in synchronous as well as asynchronous interaction across space, time, and pace.

5. APPROACHES TO E-LEARNING

A growing body of literature on learning and teaching is suggesting that learning is greatly enhanced when it is anchored or situated in meaningful and authentic problem-solving activities (Barron, Schwartz, Vye, Moore, Petrosino, Zech, Bransford & The Cognition and Technology Group at Vanderbuilt, 1998; Evensen & Hmelo, 2000; Naidu, 2004; Schank & Cleary, 1995; McLellan, 1996; The Cognition and Technology Group at Vanderbilt, 1990). This approach to learning and teaching is founded on the principles of learning by doing and experiencing. It places or confronts learners with authentic situations and scenarios which are motivating and which require learners to carry out tasks or solve problems and reflect upon their actions (Naidu, 2004).

While such learning designs are suited for any learning and teaching context or media, their effectiveness and efficiency can be somewhat constrained by the fixed time, space and pace limitations of learning and teaching in conventional campus-based classroom settings. Similarly, printed study materials, while they afford transportability, are limited by their inability to capture and carry much else other than text, pictures, and illustrations.

Information and communications technologies, on the other hand, afford us a wide range of opportunities to capture, store and distribute information and resources of all types and formats.

Along with text, pictures and illustrations, these include multimedia-based simulations of complex processes from all sorts of domains such as the biological and medical sciences, agriculture, engineering and educational practice which are not easily or cheaply accessible in real time settings.

6. OPTIMIZING THE INFLUENCE OF MEDIA IN LEARNING

Skillful integration of media and instructional method (i.e. learning and teaching strategies) is critical for the optimization of the influence of media in learning. This has to do with careful selection and matching of media attributes with learning and teaching strategies.

It is important to consider the elements that are to be added. Four types of elements—Text, Graphics, Sound and Video clippings are generally added. Text and graphics are still media which takes less bandwidth as compared to moving media like sounds and video clippings. When dynamic media like sound and video files are added, the users must be made aware of file size, file format, software and hardware requirements. For designing the content, Factors like accessibility, bandwidth and browser compatibility are crusial. (Uma Kanjilal).

Contemporary information and communications technologies afford a wide range and variety of opportunities to re-think and re-engineer the nature of our teaching and learning practices. A major part of this re-engineering process includes shift in the roles of teachers from being providers and deliverers of subject matter content to becoming moderators and facilitators of learning within the context of a learner and learning-centered approach to education.

Learner and learning-centeredness is regarded as a desirable trait in education and training generally. Learner and learning-centered educational environments are those, where the learner and the learning process is the focus of program design, development and delivery. In such educational settings, the learner, not the teacher, organization, or technology, is in charge of the learning experience.

Learner and learning-centered educational processes are defining characteristics of situated learning environments. The concept of situated learning is grounded in the principles of constructivist learning theory (Wilson, 1996). It is based on the belief that learning is most efficient and effective when it takes place within the context of realistic educational settings which are either real or contrived. The roots of situated approaches to education and training are traceable to the concepts of experiential learning (see Dewey, 1938), and problem-based learning (see Barrows, 1994; Kohler, 1925, Koffka, 1935; Orrill, 2000). Exemplar situated learning environments use "authentic learning tasks" to immerse learners in the total ecology and culture of the subject matter that is being taught and learned, much like an apprentice carpenter is immersed in a building site with architects and experienced builders. These are so called authentic learning tasks serve to "anchor" learning and teaching activities in order to scaffold learning and cognition (The Cognition and Technology Group at Vanderbuilt, 1990).

The notions of situated learning and the use of authentic learning tasks that serve to anchor and scaffold learning and teaching are heavily dependent on the use of real-world or contrived educational activities that adequately reflect real-world settings. These sorts of educational activities are inherently complex and as such time-consuming to manage. They are harder to integrate into conventional classroom settings which are limited by the opportunities they afford to engage students in authentic real world problem-solving. While field trips and excursions offer occasional and limited opportunities, they are not enough. Therefore, many teachers and organizations refrain from engaging in situated learning activities in their classes and instead, depend on approaches that are a lot more expedient and teacher and subject matter centered.

Since e-learning realize the learners initiative, providing content in an appropriate form must be the highest priority. For online courses, following basic design criteria should be taken into consideration:

(i) *Accessibility*—Content must be information rich without overstretching the bandwidth. Since access to the web costs money users would like to use their time effectively.

(ii) *Clarity*—Clarity of language, information structure and visual representation are most important for an effective learning environment.

(iii) *Efficiency*—Presentation of the content must be precise and to the point.

(iv) *Focus*—The aim should be to achieve depth of information without distracting the learners' focus or attention.

(v) *Consistency*—Design of the online course must follow a consistent format for the user.

(vi) *Flexibility*—The structure of the presentation must be flexible to encourage novices.

(vii) The layout and structuring needs to be adaptable to changes.

Nelson has suggested the following parameters for designing on line courses. They are:

- Easy to learn
- Efficient to use
- Easy to remember
- Few errors
- Pleasant to use

7. PEDAGOGICAL DESIGNS FOR OPTIMIZING E-LEARNING

It is widely acknowledged that the role and influence of media (i.e. information and communications technology) on learning and teaching is optimized, especially, when it is skillfully integrated into the educational experience. For this to happen, we need to focus our attention foremost on the careful design of the learning experience rather than the presentation of the subject matter content or the technology. This means careful orchestration of what the learners are going to do in the learning environment.

This concept of "learning by doing" has been popularized, among others, by Roger Schank and his collaborators, and it is at the heart of pedagogical designs that stand to optimize e-learning. These pedagogical designs include "scenario-based learning", "goal-based learning", "problem- based learning", "case-based learning".

These pedagogical designs are grounded in the principles of constructivism and situated cognition, and in the belief that learning is most efficient and effective when it is contextualized and when it is based on real world or similarly authentic settings.

7.1 Scenario-based Learning

A very good example of learning by doing is scenario-based learning. Scenario-based learning is a pedagogical design where one or more learning scenarios serve to anchor and contextualize all learning and teaching activities (see Naidu, Menon, Gunawardena, Lekamge & Karunanayaka, 2005). The scenarios in these educational settings are usually drawn from real life situations. They may be contrived but they aim to be as authentic as possible and reflect the variety and complexity that is part of real life situations. For the teacher and the tutor, this scenario provides a meaningful context which can be used to explain abstract concepts, principles and procedures a lot more easily. For the learner, it serves to make learning relevant, meaningful and useful.

Typically, a good learning scenario will reflect a common occurrence from the relevant field (see Naidu, Menon, Gunawardena, Lekamge & Karunanayaka, 2005). It may be a case, problem or incident that is commonly encountered in the workplace. Using such cases, problems or incidences from the workplace in the education of learners serves to more adequately prepare them for the workforce as opposed to focusing their attention on the mastery of the subject matter content. The use of such scenarios is particularly relevant and meaningful in professional education.

A typically, good learning scenario will sound like a story or a narrative of a common occurrence. It will have a context, a plot, characters and other related parameters. It usually involves a precipitating event which places the learner or a group of learners in a role, or roles that will require them to deal with the situation or problems caused by the event. The roles that learners might be asked to assume are those that they are likely to play in real life as they enter the workforce. Attached to these roles, will be goals that learners will be required to achieve. In order to achieve these goals they will be assigned numerous tasks and activities, some of which may require them to collaborate with their peers and other relevant groups, if these are part of the intended learning outcomes of their subject. While these activities essentially serve as learning enhancement exercises, a selection of them could be made assessable and given a mark which would contribute to the student's final grade in the subject.

In order to attain the goals that learners are assigned in the scenario, and complete all the required activities, learners will have to access a wide range of relevant resources. These resources could include textbooks and other relevant reading material, multimedia content, and also experiences from the field of how expert practitioners have gone about solving or dealing with similar cases, situations, problems or incidences.

The learning scenario, it's accompanying learning activities, and the assessment tasks serve as essential scaffolds for promoting and engendering meaningful learning activity. They, also, serve to contextualize learning and motivate learners who are turned off by too much focus on the mastery of the subject matter content and not enough on practical and generalizable skills. The assessment tasks and learning activities, which the students are assigned, are critical to the achievement of the intended learning outcomes. It is therefore essential that they are congruent with the intended learning outcomes for the subject. While they are embedded within the learning scenario they must be carefully designed and skillfully applied to direct students to the core subject matter content. By successfully completing these assessment tasks and learning activities, it is expected that learners will have accomplished the intended learning outcomes of the subject.

7.2 Related Pedagogical Designs

Other pedagogical designs that are also grounded in the concept of learning by doing include "problem-based and goal-based learning", "case-based learning", "role-play-based learning", and "learning by designing". They are different from scenario-based learning in the nature of the "precipitating event" or "trigger" in the situation. A brief discussion of each follows.

7.3 Problem-based and Goal-based Learning

Of all learning by doing type pedagogical designs, these two designs are in fact most similar in orientation to scenario-based learning. In problem-based learning, a problem situation serves as the context and anchor for all learning and teaching activities (see Barrows, 1994). Problem-based learning begins with the presentation of a problem to students, which can be in the form of short video clip, a picture with text, or just text. Upon encountering this problem situation, students are expected to analyze it and decide what needs to be done next.

A critical feature of problem-based learning is small group problem-solving and inquiry. Students work in small groups to analyze the presenting problem, make decisions on what needs to be done next, and act upon them to resolve the problem situation satisfactorily. In so doing they will have been expected to achieve the intended learning outcomes.

While problem-solving is implicit in problem-based learning, learners are not told explicitly what their role in the problem is or what they are supposed to do as they seek to analyze the presenting problem. In goal-based learning, on the other hand, they are told very specifically what their role in the scenario is and what they are supposed to do in order to resolve the problem satisfactorily. How they go about analyzing the problem to achieve a satisfactory solution to the problem is left to their imagination and creativity. Both, problem-based and goal-based learning designs have been widely used in the study of medical, education and environmental sciences.

7.4 Case-based Learning

In case-based learning, a case serves to provide the context and anchor for all learning and teaching activities. Cases have been very widely used in the study and teaching of law, business, accounting and economics. In these instances, students are required to use the case to explore issues, concepts and problems that they are likely to encounter.

Cases that stand to optimize learning and teaching opportunities are those that have the richness, complexity and variety that is embedded in real life situations and encounters. It is therefore most important that the cases that are selected for study and teaching are carefully selected to match the intended learning outcomes for the subject.

7.5 Learning by Designing

In learning by designing, the design task affords the essential anchor and scaffold for all learning and teaching activities (Newstetter, 2000). In this learning design students are required to engage in a learning activity which comprises conceptualizing and building something. This is a common learning and teaching activity in the study of architecture, and engineering sciences. As in goal-based learning, in the case of learning by designing, the goal is made very clear to the students. How the students chose to pursue that goal and achieve the targeted learning outcomes is left to their imagination and creativity (see Naidu, Anderson & Riddle, 2000).

7.6 Role-play-based Learning

In role-play-based learning, the role-play provides the anchor and scaffold for all learning and teaching activities. Role-play is widely used as a valuable learning and teaching strategy in social sciences and humanities subjects where very complex processes are prevalent. This learning design comprises the playing out of identified roles by learners which is followed with reflection upon the activity and its analysis in order to focus attention on the expected learning outcomes for the study.

8. LEARNING OBJECT

A "learning object" is any item that has the potential to promote learning. As such, a printed book, a journal article, or a newspaper report is a learning object. The term "learning object" is derived from object-oriented programming where items of potential educational use are seen as "objects". An object in this context is generally understood as an amalgamation of related variables and methods. Therefore, an object that can promote learning and teaching is seen as a "learning object").

A key attribute of learning objects is their discrete nature. Their discreteness enables learning objects to be categorized and stored independently, and reused in a range of educational settings. Developers of learning objects have used a range of descriptors to capture their discrete character. Describing and labeling learning objects accordingly will enable them to be easily and accurately identified for reuse by multiple users and in a range of educational settings.

8.1 Digital Learning Object

A "digital learning object" is any electronic resource that has the potential to promote learning. Typically, these include scripts, images, and multimedia modules, etc. in digital format. They are often developed as discrete entities so that they can be reused by multiple users and in a range of educational settings.

Since the development of digital learning materials is an extremely time-consuming and expensive undertaking, the assumption is that once developed, they ought to be able to be used, reused and shared by a large number of people and in a wide range of settings.

8.2 Characteristics of Learning Objects

Apart from being discrete entities, learning objects are identifiable by several other notable features. For instance, learning objects must necessarily be able to be easily transported, and reused in a variety of educational settings, otherwise there isn't much point in developing these as discrete entities. They must also be interoperable in a range of educational environments otherwise their potential for reuse is compromised, which will clearly impact their value and use.

Moreover, as interest in learning objects grows, there is likely to be a wide variety of learning objects that are developed, just as there are a wide variety of other types of learning resources that can be found in bookshops and libraries. Some of these learning objects will comprise just the content item. However, others will comprise much more than the content including expected learning outcomes, assessment items to ascertain if these learning outcomes have been achieved as well as metadata on the object.

9. PURPOSE AND MISCONCEPTIONS

It is widely acknowledged that digital learning objects (and indeed all types of learning objects) are developed to promote learning and teaching. It has also been suggested that "the future of learning is inextricably linked to the development of quality learning objects" (McGreal, 2004, p. 14).

While there is no doubt that learning can benefit from good quality learning resource materials, high quality learning is the result of many more factors than learning objects or resources. The factors that influence learning include learner readiness, their interest and motivation in the study of the subject matter, the nature and quality of the learning experience including the nature of the assessment activities, and the nature and quality of feedback and support that is available to students. Hence, it seems unwise to suggest that learning objects (digital or other) are going to determine the future of learning. Just as best selling books have not necessarily improved the quality of learning, there is no reason to assume that learning objects are going to significantly impact the quality of learning. So, in e-learning content must be information rich which is easy to learn. The content must be clear to facilitate learning, then in true sense we will be able to achieve the aims of e-learning

References

1. Barron, B.L., Schwartz, D.L., Vye, N.J., Moore, A., Petrosino, A., Zech, L., Bransford, J.D., and The Cognition and Technology Group at Vanderbuilt (1998). Doing with understanding: Lessons from Research on Problem and Project-based Learning. *Journal of the Learning Sciences*, 3/4, 271-312.
2. Barrows, H.S. (1994), Problem-Based Learning Applied to Medical Education. School of Medicine. Springfield, IL: Southern Illinois University.
3. McGreal, R. (2004), Introduction. In R. McGreal (Ed.), Online Education Using Learning Objects (p. 14), London: Routledge Falmer.
4. Naidu, S. (Ed.). (2003), Preface. Learning and Teaching with Technology : Principles and Practices. London, UK & Sterling, VA, USA: Kogan Page.
5. Romiszowski, A. (2004), How's the e-learning baby? Factors Leading to Success or Failure of an Educational Technology Innovation, *Educational Technology*, 55 44(1), January-February, 5-27.
6. Uma Kanjilal (2005),"Proceedings of the National Convention on Library and Information Networking (NACLIN 2005)".
7. Willems, J. (2005). Flexible Learning: Implications of "when-ever", "where- and what-ever". *Distance Education*, 26(3), 429-35.

22

Learning in the Age of Global Information and Communication Technology : E-learning in India, Its Prospect and Future

GANESH CHANDRA DEKA AND MALAYA DUTTA BORAH

ABSTRACT

Advancement in Information and Communication Technology (ICT) have made it possible today a whole range of high quality and cost effective services relating to video, voice and data content through a single communication channel. E-learning is such area where the use of ICT provides innovative ways to complement the traditional student-teacher interaction world-wide to optimize resource usage, sharing and collaboration. In the Indian context, adult and youth literary rate is 61.3 and 73.3 accordingly, whereas, the rural population of India is around 12.2% of the world's population and among whom 207,000,000 are adult illiterates. Literacy in India is an indispensable means for effective social and economic participation, contributing to human development and poverty reduction. The benefits of newer technologies have to reach the rural masses of India also; otherwise, it will be the root cause of digital divide. If this digital divide is not removed, it will be not be possible to achieve the vision of India to become a developed nation by the year 2020. In this paper our approach is based on:

- E-Learning—Applicability and Usefulness in tomorrow's Indian Education System.
- To promote Innovation, Increase Productivity, and Enrich the quality of lives of people living in India.

Keywords: Information and Communication Technology (ICT), Digital Divide, EDUSAT, Tele-Education, Web-based Training (WBT), Virtual Universities, CBT (Computer Based Training).

1. INTRODUCTION

Building technological capability is a vital strategy for economic growth of the country. There are three important components to the technological capability:

- Human beings with knowledge and skills.
- Organization which bring together such individuals and make it possible to attempt the development of an utilization technologies.
- Creating common purpose without which no tangible results can be produced.

Therefore, investment in science and technology in education is an investment in the growth of the country. We can place the education sector as an economic sector where investments bring tangible economic returns. So, to implement a new ICT like e-learning is nothing but the economic growth of India.

E-learning (Electronic learning) is a general term used to refer to a form of learning in which the instructor and student are separated by space or time, where the gap between the two is bridged through the use of online technologies. The main advantage of e-learning is that a student or executive can gain knowledge and skills without any time-barriers or geographical-boundaries. This creates immense possibilities of learning and development.

2. APPLICATION OF E-LEARNING IN INDIAN EDUCATION SYSTEM

Access to academic resources is at a level that was two decades ago. But use of E-learning is subject to wide variation in practice, which has become a common mode of education delivery worldwide. Hence, World Wide Web (www) opened a new dimension to computer-based training where learners can learn anywhere, anytime with possibilities for huge cost savings in corporate training.

E-learning has potential in India but adoption has been slow and will need a major marketing and awareness effort. According to IDC, the revenue earned worldwide from e-learning was $6 billion in 2003. This is expected to rise to $21 billion by 2008. As is apparent from the above figures, the Indian e-learning market is still at a nascent stage. But emphasis on honing individual skills, e-learning is slowly becoming popular in India.

3. UNIVERSAL TELE-EDUCATION

Now with the successful launch of Educational Satellite (EDUSAT) on 20th September 2004, it is possible to work on a viable distance education programme for many parts of the nation. A three-pronged approach is essential to make distance education programme viable and a successful proposition through the universal tele-education system to all remote parts of the country. The three components may be the:

- Connectivity,
- Tele-Education System, and
- The Quality Content Generation and Deployment.

3.1 Connectivity

EDUSAT is expected to provide 1,50,000 ground terminals in its full capacity. The other parts of the country have to be covered by providing broadband and wireless communication network in an integrated fashion. Terrestrial optical communication is becoming cost effective and can complement the space communication with its low cost, high bandwidth and networking capability. An integrated networked system comprising EDUSAT, broadband and wireless networks should provide a highway for reaching quality education to all parts of the country.

3.2 Initiative Towards Providing Satellite-based Tele-Education

A major initiative towards providing satellite-based tele-education facilities to engineering colleges in the country was launched January 1, 2008 jointly by Indian Space Research Organization (ISRO) in association with Indian Institute of Technology, Bombay. This EDUSAT network provides satellite-based tele-education facilities to students and teachers of the engineering colleges across the country. The teaching end is set-up at IIT, Bombay by ISRO which will provide satellite bandwidth and install ground equipment at various recipient institutes across the country, while IIT, Bombay will arrange for delivering full-fledged courses on various engineering topics through its faculty on this network. A Memorandum of Understanding (MOU) in this regard was signed between ISRO and IIT, Bombay during November 2007. To begin with, IIT, Bombay has scheduled 13 full-fledged courses on this channel. About 50 colleges including IITs, several National Institutes of Technology (NIT), VJTI, Mumbai, Samrat Ashok Technological Institute, Vidisha, Sona College of Engineering and Technology, Salem and Delhi College of Engineering which already have the compatible ground terminal equipments are interconnected with the engineering colleges, polytechnics and Indian Institute of Technology, Delhi having compatible infrastructure. New institutes who wish to join this programme will be provided ground equipments soon. In the EDUSAT Network ISRO has set-up more than 45 broadcast and interactive networks covering 20 states including north-eastern states and islands states/UT of the country. More than 30,000 classrooms have been provided connectivity through EDUSAT and the number is still growing steadily.

3.3 National and Regional Beam

The national beam is planned to be used for:

1.	Indira Gandhi National Open University	100 terminals across the country and another 20 terminals in the North-East for teachers' training
2.	National Council for Educational Research and Training	100 terminals for Secondary and Higher Secondary Education and Teachers' Training
3.	Indian Institutes of Technology at Kharagpur and Chennai	70 and 5 Terminals respectively
4.	Institute of Electronics and Tele-communication Engineers	18 for DST/National Council of Science Museums — 25
5.	Centre for Environmental Education	5 Terminals

Regional beams of EDUSAT are planned to be as follows:

- *Southern beam:* Anna University, Chennai (260 nodes), Annamalai University, Chennai (57 nodes), Gandhigram Rural Institute, Dindigal (90 nodes), Bharathidasan University, Tiruchirapalli (22 nodes), Sarva Shiksha Abhiyan, Tamilnadu (442 nodes).
- *Western beam:* Gujarat Government, Department of Education (148 nodes), Maharashtra Knowledge Corporation Ltd., (50 nodes), Department of Higher Education, MP (50 nodes), Tribal Development, MP (50 nodes), BITS, Pilani (20 nodes), Technical Education Board, Rajasthan (91 nodes) and Blind People's Association, Ahmedabad (25 nodes).
- *Northern beam:* State Institute of Educational Technology (67 nodes), Guru Nanak Dev University, Amritsar (40 nodes), Tapar Institute of Engineering and Technology, Patiala. (10 nodes), Department of Training and Technical Education, New Delhi (40 nodes), UP Rajashri Tandon Open University, Allahabad (55 nodes).
- *Eastern beam:* West Bengal University of Technology, Kolkata (40 nodes), Vidyasagar University, Midnapore, West Bengal (10 nodes), Netaji Subhas Open University, Kolkata (90 nodes), Jarkhand Education Project Council, Ranchi (192 nodes).

- *North-Eastern beam:* Assam Agricultural University, Jorhat (18 nodes), Arunachal University, Itanagar (13 nodes), Manipur University, Imphal (200 nodes), Nagaland University, Kohima (10 nodes), Sikkim Government Law College, Gangtok (20 nodes).

Thus, EDUSAT is expected to herald a new era in the educational sector by bridging the distances and allowing effective optimum sharing of scarce resources for teaching.

4. TELE-EDUCATION SYSTEM

Once we have the connectivity, then there should be a universal tele-education system in place for making full utilization of the connectivity to bring virtual classrooms in a multi class environment with seamless two-way interaction between the teachers and students in a collaborative environment. This system should not only enable the lecture delivered from the studio at the university to reach any remote corner but also enable a good teacher in the remote area to provide multicast information to other participants of the programme.

4.1 Virtual Universities

Countries without university education can access universities in other countries via the Web, a solution much cheaper than building university infrastructure. In underdeveloped countries, e-learning can raise the level of education, literacy and economic development. This is especially true for countries where technical education is expensive, opportunities are limited, and economic disparities exist. However, one of the problems with e-learning in India is the lack of course content, especially outside the mainstream focus areas of IT education, English language content, and tutorial-like courses. There will be high demand for people who can develop multi-lingual courseware that addresses various topics.

4.2 Web-based Training (WBT)

E-learning services have evolved since computers were first used in education. There is a trend to move toward blended learning services, where computer-based activities are integrated with practical or classroom-based situations known as *Computer Based Training (CBT).* Web-based training (WBT) is a type of training that is similar to CBT; however, it is delivered over the internet using a web browser. Web-based training frequently includes interactive methods such as bulletin boards, chat rooms, instant messaging, videoconferencing, and discussion threads. Web-based training is usually a self-paced learning medium though some systems allow for online testing and evaluation at specific times e.g. Classontheweb.com, the portal of Everonn Systems India Limited caters to all academic and scholastic needs of a student. It focuses on developing digital educational content that will help the teaching and learning community through its concept of e-learning through digitised animated textbooks and teachers and learners use technology to enhance their teaching and learning experience. The digitized educational content imparts highly focused curriculum-based learning in English Grammar, Mathematics, Physics, Chemistry, Social Sciences, Business studies, Economics and Accountancy for students of standards VI to XII.

4.3 Government Initiatives

Recently completed E-Learning R&D projects under Department of Information Technology:

Project Title	*Executive Agency*	*Project Objectives*	*Duration (in months)*
Multimodal Digital Distance Education for IT and other Critical Technologies	Jadavpur University	To evolve appropriate Courseware Engineering methodologies for making available quality courseware at reasonable cost. Field experiments with different modes of Digital Distances Education modes	51
Training of Trainers in E-learning	DOEACC (Aurangabad and Kolkata)	To introduce fundamentals of E-learning, H/w and S/w and train teachers for implementing e-learning for the better educational methodologies.	24
Enhancing Competency of IT teachers and Industry Professionals	K. Re. SIT, IIT, Mumbai	To enhance quality of services in the remote/VSAT reception to enhance competency of IT Teachers and Industry Professionals	27
Development of content delivery tools to enhance the existing experimental education technology services	IIT, Kanpur	To augment an existing IT-based education support system based on existing web tech to a much better and manageable system	36
Data Compression Techniques and its Application to E-Learning/Education	IIT, Kanpur	To develop a group of data compression techniques that can be applied to images, scanned documents and videos; and hence creating a system that adapts itself to the quality of services (QoS) offered by the Internet (Network) connection instead of expecting a specific QoS on the Network	12

4.3 Quality Content Generation

There are three components education: lectures, laboratory and library. The content includes all the three. Content can be generated in many ways.

The first one is the assimilation of the subject by an expert teacher through research study of many books and articles leading to the generation of quality and creative content in a presentable format. The teacher presents it in a unique and innovative way to make the content appealing and easily understandable to the students. The second form of content could be on a self-learning method by breaking down the content into a series of question-answer models. Third may be from various books, which can be extracted through a digital library and presented just-in-time to all the remote students.

5. APPLICATION OF UP-COMING TECHNOLOGY: A SOLUTION FOR THE INDIAN EDUCATIONAL AND ALLIED INSTITUTIONS

Technology has helped to expand the scope and depth of education across borders. Educational technology has enabled students to access more information and connect with more people than ever before. Learning can now be more individualized and students can access resources that will enable them to drive their own learning.

5.1 Grid Computing

The term *Grid computing* originated in the early 1990s as a metaphor for making computer power as easy to access as an electric power grid in Ian Foster and Carl Kesselmans seminal work, *"The Grid: Blueprint for a new computing infrastructure"*. While the web is a service for sharing information over the internet, the new system, Grid computing is a phrase in distributed computing which is a service for sharing computer power and data storage capacity over the internet. The internet could soon be made obsolete by "the grid" at the speed about 10,000 times faster than a typical broadband connection. The grid will be able to send the entire Rolling Stones back catalogue from Britain to Japan in less than two seconds. It will lead to :

- Offering online computation or storage as a metered commercial service, known as utility computing, *computing on demand*, or *"cloud computing"* where people keep all their data online and access them from anywhere.
- The creation of a *"virtual supercomputer"* by using a network of geographically dispersed computers. Voluntier computing, which generally focuses on scientific, mathematical, and academic problems, is the most common application of this technology.
- The grid is being made available to dozens of other academic researchers, including astronomers and molecular biologists. It has already been used to help design new drugs against malaria which kills one million people worldwide each year. Researchers used the grid to analyze 140 m compounds—a task that would have taken

standard internet-linked PC 420 years. So, grid technologies could revolutionize society.

5.2 Wi Max(Worldwide Interoperability for Microwave Access)

It is a new technology aimed at providing wireless data over long distances in a variety of ways, from point-to-point links to full mobile cellular type access. It is based on the IEEE 802.16 standard, which is also called *WirelessMAN*. The name *WiMAX* was created by the *WiMAX* forum, which was formed in June 2001 to promote conformance and interoperability of the standards. The forum describes WiMAX as "a standards-based technology enabling the delivery of wireless broadband access as an alternative to cable and DSL."

There has to be a long-term strategy in order to reap benefits from the advantages of WiMax. Approval from TRAI and other Government nodal agencies will play an important role in the allocation of WiMax spectrum and its use. ISP's like Bharati TeleVentures, Reliance, SIFY, BSNL and VSNL (Tata group) have licenses in 3.3 GHz ranges and have already started with the trails. So, WiMax will help bring a major reorganization in the education sector services such as virtual classrooms which are only talked about today, can become a reality in educational institutions. It will help the delivery of educational resources to off-classrooms and off-campus locations. It can be a very effective tool for higher education in rural areas where the network cost can be reduced. The use of Orthogonal Frequency Division Multiple Access (OFDMA) ensures super performance of WiMAX.

5.3 POD Casting

Pod casting, a fusion of two words: *iPod*, Apple's popular digital music player, and *broadcasting* is the latest in web technology, and is creating waves in the e-learning world. It has already been adopted as teaching tool in many well known universities like—Drexel University, Allegheny College, the University of Chicago, University of Michigan, Purdue University, Duke University and Stanford University.

Podcasts are basically digital audio programs that can be subscribed to and downloaded by listeners by RSS (Really Simple Syndication). It can be accessed on an array of digital audio devices, like Mp3 players, desktop computer, laptops, mobiles, etc. They can be easily produced with any computer having a soundcard; microphone, recording software and an internet connection. Podcasting is a godsend for people who have learning disabilities like dyslexia or for the blind. It has made online learning straightforward and available for them. Pod casting has revolutionized education and particularly higher education by enabling up-to-date content. E-learning through pod casting not only makes learning easy, but also helps students with retention issues.

5.4 Natural Language Interfaces

Natural language is one of many 'interface styles' (or 'interaction modalities') that can be used in the dialog between a human user and a computer. There is a significant appeal in being able to address a machine and direct it's operations by using the same language we use in everyday human to human interaction, which could be of great use in e-learning. The MIT is already involved in several projects such as Bharat Bhasha Kosh, web- based learning system in Indian languages, Speech Synthesis system at CEERI Pilani and Multilingual dictionaries. IIT Madras have developed an Indian Language word processor which has been tested at an NGO in Madras. So, developments can be made by which our villagers will be able to access the Net in their own language and hence dependency on an English translator will be reduced and hence villager will be freed from his lack of literacy and therefore inability to communicate.

6. CONCLUSION

In the 21st century right application of science and technology is the most effective route to societal transformation. E-learning has potential in India but adoption has been slow and will need a major marketing and awareness effort. According to IDC, the revenue earned worldwide from e-learning was $6 billion in 2003. That's expected to rise to $21 billion by 2008. As discussed above, the indian e-learning is still at a nascent stage. But emphasis on honing individual skills, e-learning is slowly becoming popular in India. E-learning has created a new dimension in education, both within and beyond the curriculum and is still looking at further opportunities of becoming more useful via new emerging technologies. We are really on the threshold of new opportunities and this is just the beginning of a new horizon of education.

References

1. http://www.hindu.com/yw/2008/04/04/stories/2008040450610500.htm
2. www.everonn.com
3. http://en.wikipedia.org/wiki/EDUSAT_(Satellite)
4. http://mlsondhi.org/kalam.htm
5. http://www.isro.org/newsletters/spaceindia/oct2004jun2005/Chapter8.htm.
6. DCE Convocation address of Smt Sheila Dikshit Hon'ble Chief Minister, Government of NCT, Delhi on 30th April, 2008.
7. E-Learning Technologies for Rural India : Nilay M. Yajnik, Narsee Monjee Institute of Management Studies, Vile Parle (W), Mumbai.
8. Home Page of Ministry of Information Technology, Government of India.

23

E-Learning Platform for Teaching Large Classrooms

HARPRIT KAUR AND SHIV KUMAR MODGIL

ABSTRACT

There are many difficulties in teaching large sized classrooms. This paper presents an E-Learning platform, E-learning hub, to promote learning by practice in large classes. The proposed E-learning hub is based on experiential learning theory and integrates practice into every step of learning process. It combines various teaching and learning strategies in a single platform to suit the needs of students with different learning styles in a large class. The combined strategy allows E-Learning Hub to achieve the following educational objectives:

1. To improve student comprehension abilities on the concepts so that their thinking ability is enhanced.
2. To stimulate deep thinking and enhance student's capabilities of transferring what they have learnt to new situations so that transfer of learning takes place.
3. To develop and foster independence of learning in which student develops the ability to discover and reconstruct knowledge for themselves.

The E-learning hub creates a learner-centered environment and makes learning more effective, efficient, meaningful, and joyful in a large class.

1. INTRODUCTION

E-learning is learning which takes place as a result of experience and interaction in an Internet environment. It is not restricted to a regular school day and can take place in a variety of locations including home, school and community locations, e.g. libraries, cafes, etc. With the increased enrolment and shrunk budget in colleges and universities, teaching large classes in higher education becomes unavoidable. It is a very different experience in teaching a large class compared to a small one. The difficulties encountered in large classes include [1] engaging students in active learning, personalizing the environment, working with diverse student needs and backgrounds, managing classroom disruptions, adapting one's teaching style to the large lecture situation, etc. How do we overcome these difficulties and enhance the learning experience in a large class? One possible solution is to leverage on the vast experience accumulated in teaching small classes. In order to do so, we need to identify the differences between large and small classes and try to create a small-class environment in a large one so as to achieve the same quality as in a small class. It is generally accepted that learning outcomes are inversely proportional to class size, i.e. the smaller the class is, the better the student learns. The size of a class is not the most important factor affecting the learning outcomes; rather the teaching quality plays an important role in the learning process. The key to the success is the student's participation in the learning process. The main advantage small classes has over large ones is that they provide students with more opportunities for interaction, feedback and more personalized environment, which leads to higher teaching quality and greater student satisfaction.

2. LEARNING-BY-DOING IN A LARGE CLASS

A large class usually consists of a wide spectrum of students. With the increased diversity in the student population, not only in race and culture, but also in age and knowledge background, it is important to address the different learning styles and comprehension abilities. The needs of all learners are best met through the use of a variety of activities that best match their preferred learning styles. According to Kolb's theory, learning is enhanced as more of the learning stages are used. It is better to provide all the four learning styles, active, reflective, abstract and concrete, so that all students in the class can use their preferred styles to study. The learning-by-doing provides various learning activities to cater to different learning styles by spending time to teach each of the different learning styles through the learning cycles and encourage students to adopt to different learning styles. By providing preferred learning styles for each student learning-by-doing realizes personalized environment in larger classes as in smaller classes. Such an approach provides a learner-centered environment for students and promotes active learning in a large class.

3. TUTORIAL TOOLS

3.1 SMS Tutorial System with Instant Feedback

One advantage of smaller classes have over the larger ones is that it provides more opportunities to get feedback from students. *E-learning hub* addresses this problem by reinforcing the interaction between students and the lecturers, and provides instant feedback by using SMS-based instant feedback system. It is most cost effective way to gather instant feedback and is easy to integrate with a web-based system. It is an effective method to grasp students' interest and attention and engage them in the learning process. Students are very familiar with SMS service. They are very excited when such a service is applied to learning. The SMS instant feedback system is designed for all students. To implement it in a large class, many small discussion groups of 2-4 students are formed at the beginning of the course with each group having at least one mobile phone. A think-pair-share approach is adopted when an in-class quiz is conducted. The students work on the quiz individually and then pair up to compare and improve their answers before they submit a final one to SMS system. In such a way, the system does not leave out the students without a mobile phone. Such think-pair-share approach not only allows students to share hand phone, but also promotes the cooperative learning.

3.2 Simulation

Simulation offers a fun and effective way to enable students to learn by doing and provide opportunities for active experimentation in solving practical problems, which requires the application of knowledge learnt. Simulation models a real or theoretical system through which students are allowed to manipulate input variables and observe the consequences, to formulate and test hypotheses, to interpret principles or properties displayed by models. The most important is that simulations provide a controlled environment which offers the individual an opportunity to learn by making mistakes, correcting errors and receive additional information in the form of instructive feedback. In the course of DSP, a single sentence and mathematical answers are always possible for a specific tutorial question. It is highly appreciated if student can carry out a reasoned simulation before answering the question. MATLAB is such a tool that is capable of such a simulation, but the learning curve involved in understanding the tools can distract a student from trying to adopt it. *E-Learning hub* provides many simulations to help students to assimilate abstract ideas, concepts and principles, such as to illustrate the relationship between continuous-time and digital signals, to show the effects of sampling an analog signal, to design a frequency response masking filter, and to examine the effect of interpolation.

4. E-LEARNING AND ITS IMPACT ON TEACHERS

The networked environment of this new internet-connected world has expanded the opportunities for teaching and learning, in ways that we are only beginning to understand. What makes the implementation of e-teaching so challenging is that we are asking teachers of the dot.com age to teach in a way in which they have never been taught when they were at school. They will work in an environment in which they have never been learners and may have had few first-hand experiences.

5. VIEWS ABOUT E-LEARNING

5.1 Instructional Developers

(i) Developers can develop training, demonstrations with in very specific details, how to perform a task such as repairing equipment.
(ii) E-Learning sets a framework for standardized course delivery.
(iii) Facilitates modifying training and education materials, by using HTML.
(iv) Allows developers to design once and use the same module in several programs, by using 'template-like' learning objects.
(v) Promotes the orderly layout of course materials, assignments and general administration through a web site.

5.2 Learners

(i) E-Learning fosters interaction among students and instructors. Interaction stimulates understanding and the recall of information.
(ii) Accommodates different learning styles and fosters learning through a variety of activities that apply to different learning styles.
(iii) Fosters self-paced learning, whereby, students can learn at the rate they prefer.
(iv) Convenient for students to access any time, any place.
(v) Reduces travel time and travel costs for students.
(vi) Encourages students to browse information through hyperlinks to sites on the worldwide web and thereby find information relevant to their personal situations.
(vii) Allows students to select learning materials, or to be directed to content that meets their level of knowledge, interest and what they need to know to perform more effectively in their particular activity.
(viii) Provides context sensitive help (electronic performance support systems) to computer users and helps them complete tasks on-the-fly.

(ix) Develops knowledge of the internet that will help learners throughout their careers.

(x) Encouraging students to take responsibility for their learning and succeeding by self-knowledge and self-confidence

5.3 Instructors

(i) E-Learning permits instructors to develop materials using the world-wide resources of the Web.

(ii) Retains records of discussion and allows for later reference through the use of threaded discussion on bulletin boards.

(iii) Allows instructors to communicate information in a more engaging fashion than in text-based distance education programs. E-Learning offers a wide-range of text, diagrams and images with video and sound, including virtual reality technology that in the future will improve the effectiveness of the approach even further.

(iv) Convenient for instructors to access any time, any place. Allows instructors to package essential information for all students to access. Instructors can then concentrate on high level activities.

(v) Generates more personal gratification for instructors through quality student participation.

(vi) Reduces travel and accommodation costs associated with training programs.

5.4 Training and Education Administrators

(i) E-Learning accommodates automated, continuous assessment of student progress.

(ii) Reduces capital costs associated with traditional bricks and mortar schools and training facilities.

(iii) Can be accessed by a variety of platforms such as Windows, UNIX and Mac because they all read html files.

(iv) Template approach to developing online learning engenders consistency.

(v) Allows institutions to build the eLearning modules from courses of leading instructors

6. COMPARISON OF E-LEARNING AND CONVENTIONAL LEARNING

	Conventional learning	*E-learning*
1.	Students attend a school in their local community or attend a boarding or correspondence school.	Students participate from a variety of locations and may attend multiple learning institutions and/or their local school.
2.	Classes are scheduled according to school hours and timetables.	Students may determine the times when they access e-learning opportunities.

3.	Students are directed to work individually or in groups.	Students can choose to work individually or collaboratively with people who may or may not be in their *regular* class.
4.	Classes are synchronous and teachers and students interact in real time.	Students may take classes from more than one school.
5.	Students are generally enrolled with one school. Learning objectives are set by the teacher and institution.	Students may set their own objectives and explore their own learning needs and agendas.
6.	Students follow a linear pattern influenced by the needs of other class members and the teacher's planning.	Students can follow a non-linear path at a pace that meets their individual needs at that time, i.e. just-in-time learning.
7.	Teachers work in one school.	The teacher is facilitating the activity. E-teachers can work in more than one school.

7. CONCLUSION

The success of *e-learning hub* is the integration of learning by doing in every step of learning process. It guides students through four stages in the learning cycles, provides different tools to suit students preferred learning styles, encourages them to participate in different learning activities, and provides personalized learning environment in a large class. *E-learning hub* facilitates learning by doing in a learner-centered environment and makes learning more effective, efficient, meaningful, and joyful in a large class.

REFERENCES

1. Large Classes: A Teaching Guide Large Class Introduction, http://www.cte.umd.edu/library/large/intro.html.
2. Teaching Large Classes at UCSB, http://www.oic.id.ucsb.edu/Resources/Teaching/Large.ucsb.html.

24

The Use of IT to Enhance Management School Education

RAMANPREET KAUR AND HARDEEP SINGH

ABSTRACT

To use information technology to improve learning processes, the pedagogical assumptions underlying the design of information technology for educational purposes must be understood. This paper reviews different models of learning, surfaces assumptions of electronic teaching technology, and relates those assumptions to the differed models of learning. Our analysis suggests that initial attempts to bring information technology to management education follow a classic story of automating rather than transforming. IT is primarily used to automate the information delivery functions in classrooms. In the absence of fundamental changes to the teaching and learning process, such classrooms may do little but speed up ineffective processes and methods of teaching. Our mapping of technologies to learning models identifies sets of technologies in which management schools should invest in order to inform, ate up and down and ultimately transform the educational environment and processes. For researchers interested in the use of information technology to improve learning processes, the paper provides a theoretical foundation for future work.

1. INTRODUCTION

"An outsourcing agreement is a bit like getting married; the most important thing is to show understanding on both sides. I'm highly satisfied with the level of service provided to us and very happy with the attention that we receive."

The management of Information Technology (IT) and Information Systems (IS) is considered a complex exercise by academics and practitioners alike. The reason for this is that there are ubiquitous portfolios of tangible and intangible benefits that are offered to an organization following the adoption of IT/IS that, in turn, all needed managing to ensure realization. Organizations also have to take into account the direct and often larger indirect costs that are typically associated with IT deployments. The organization's experiences in solving the problems associated with the implementation of their IS offers a learning opportunity for those companies that are seeking a competitive advantage through technology management.

The adoption of Information Technology (IT) in organizations has been growing at a rapid pace. The use of technology has evolved from the automation of structured processes to systems that are truly revolutionary in that they introduce change into fundamental business procedures. Indeed, it is believed that "More than being helped by computers, companies will live by them, shaping strategy and structure to fit new information technology". While the importance of the relationship between information technology and organizational change is evidenced by the considerable literature on the subject, there is a lack of comprehensive analysis of these issues from the economic perspective. The aim of this article is to develop an economic understanding of how information systems affect some key measures of organization structure. The concept of IT as a powerful competitive weapon has been strongly emphasized in the literature, yet the sustainability of the competitive advantage provided by IT applications is not well-explained. This work discusses the resource-based theory as a means of analyzing sustainability, and develops a model founded on this resource-based view of the firm. This model is, then, applied to four attributes of IT-capital requirements, proprietary technology, IT skills, and managerial IT skills—which might be sources of sustained competitive advantage. From this resource-based analysis, we conclude that a managerial IT skill is the only one of these attributes that can provide sustainability.

2. INFORMATION TECHNOLOGY AS COMPETITIVE ADVANTAGE: THE ROLE OF HUMAN, BUSINESS, AND TECHNOLOGY RESOURCES

This paper investigates linkages between information technology (IT) and firm performance. Although showing recent signs of advance, the existing IT literature still relies heavily on case studies, anecdotes, and consultants' frameworks, with little solid empirical work or synthesis of findings. This paper examines the IT literature, develops an integrated, resource-based theoretical framework, and presents results from a new empirical study in the retail industry. The findings show that IT alone has not produced sustainable performance advantages in the retail industry, but some firms have gained advantages by using IT to leverage intangible, complementary human and business resources such as flexible culture, strategic planning-IT integration, and supplier relationships. The results support the resource-based approach, and help to explain why some firms outperform others using the same IT, and why successful IT users often fail to sustain IT-based competitive advantages.

2.1 Creating Competitive Advantage with Interorganizational Information Systems

Many well-known examples of the use of information technology for competitive advantage involve systems that link an organization to suppliers, distribution channels, or customers. In general, these systems use information or processing capabilities in one organization to improve the performance of another or to improve relationships among organizations. Declining costs of capturing and using information have joined with increasing competitive pressures to spur numerous innovations in use of information to create value. This article draws on concepts of competitive advantage and on experience gained from successful innovations to generate classifications, and a framework to guide the search for opportunities. The ideas do not constitute a procedure leading inexorably to competitive advantage. However, they have been of value when combined with an appreciation of the competitive dynamics of specific industries and a grasp of the power of information.

2.2 Information Literacy

- Tool literacy, or the ability to understand and use the practical and conceptual tools of current information technology relevant to education, and the areas of work and professional life that the individual expects to inhabit.
- Resource literacy, or the ability to understand the form, format, location and access methods of information resources, especially, daily expanding networked information resources.
- Research literacy, or the ability to understand and use the IT-based tools relevant to the work of today's researcher and scholar.

2.3 Information Literacy and Information Technology

Information literacy is related to information technology skills, but has broader implications for the individual, the educational system, and for society. Information technology skills enable an individual to use computers, software applications, databases, and other technologies to achieve wide variety of academic, work-related, and personal goals.

Information literacy, while showing significant overlap with information, technology skills, is a distinct and broader area of competence. Increasingly, information technology skills are interwoven with, and support of the information literacy. A 1999 report from the National Research Council promotes the concept of "fluency" with information technology and delineates several distinctions useful in understanding relationships among information literacy, computer literacy, and broader technological competence. The report notes that "computer literacy" is concerned with learning of specific hardware and software applications, while "fluency with technology" focuses on understanding the underlying concepts of technology and applying problem-solving and critical thinking to use of technology. The report also discusses differences between information technology fluency and information literacy as it is understood in K-12 and higher education. Among these are information literacy's focus on content, communication, analysis, information searching, and evaluation; whereas information technology "fluency" focuses on a deep understanding of technology and graduated, increasingly skilled use of it.

"Fluency" with information technology may require more intellectual abilities than the learning of software and hardware associated with "computer literacy", but the focus is still on the technology itself. Information literacy, on the other hand, is an intellectual framework for understanding, finding, evaluating, and using information-activities which may be accomplished in part by fluency with information technology, in part by sound investigative methods, but most importantly, through critical discernment and reasoning. Information literacy initiates, sustains, and extends lifelong learning through abilities which may use technologies but are ultimately independent of them.

2.4 Effect on Education

Because information literacy skills are vital to future success:

- Information literacy skills must be taught in the context of the overall process.
- Instruction in information literacy skills must be integrated into the curriculum and reinforced both within and outside of the educational setting.

2.5 Technology

Information technology is a great enabler. It provides, for those who have access to it, an extension to their powers of perception, comprehension, analysis, thought, concentration, and articulation through a range of activities that include: writing, visual images, mathematics, music, physical movement, sensing the environment, simulation, and communication (Carpenter, 1989, p. 2).

Technology, in all of its various forms, offers users the tools to access, manipulate, transform, evaluate, use, and present information. Technology in schools includes computers, televisions, video cameras, video editing equipment, and TV studios. Two approaches to technology in K-12 schools are, technology as the object of instruction approach, and technology as the tool of instruction approach.

Schools are starting to incorporate technology skills instruction in the context of information literacy skills. This is called technology information literacy. Technology is changing the way higher education institutions are offering instructions. The use of the internet is being taught in the contexts of subject area curricula and the overall information literacy process. There is some empirical indication that students who use technology as a tool may become better at management

3. OBJECTIVES OF THE STUDY

- To study impact of placements and quality in management schools with upcoming of IT boom.
- To study upto what extent information technology improves learning and teaching processes.
- To study use of IT in management schools in decresing cost of education.
- To study information technology improves communication skills, efficiency and decision-making in organisation.
- To study whether IT acts as catalystic agent for transforming educational processes.
- To study whether IT is an efficacious means of enabling intentional changes in teaching and learning processes.
- To integrate new information into an existing body of knowledge.
- To develop successful search strategies.
- To study the impact of IT in shrinking of time and buisness.

4. RESEARCH METHODOLOGY

4.1 Research Design

The research carried out in this project was descriptive in nature. The study was aimed at describing the existing phenomenon. For that matter researcher consulted various magazines, newspapers, books and reference materials. Then, researcher conducted pilot survey based on the schedule. On the basis of the results of pilot survey, researcher formulated final schedule for the study with the help of his guide.

Collection of Data

Primary Data	Survey through questionnaire
Secondary Data	Various Publications of organized retailing in form of annual reports, various papers and journals published time to time.
Research Approach	The method adopted for research is field survey.

4.2 Contact Method

The data is collected through interviews carried out in person.

Sampling unit	The target population must be defined that will be sampled. It is necessary to develop a sampling frame, so that everyone in the target population has an equal chance of being sampled.
Sample Size	120 Respondents
Sample Method	Non-probability convenience sampling method is used.

4.3 Limitations of Study

1. Scantiness of information
2. Existence of biasness
3. Limited scope

5. RESULTS AND FINDINGS

- On comparison it has been found that before dotcom boom the quality of education was poor, as 90% according to survey, have opinon that education literacy has increased.
- 95 percent of respondents say that there shrinking of time and business is there in with upcoming use of information technology in management schools.
- 85 percent of respondents have opinion that with upcoming of IT in management, the cost of education is increasing.
- 85 percent of respondents opinon is information technology improves communication skills, efficiency and decision making in organisation
- 70 percent of respondents experince the increased competive pressure, becouse information technology is one area which is used as catalystic agent for transforming educational processes.
- 80 percent of respondents have opinon that IT is an efficacious means of enabling intentional changes in teaching and learning processes.
- 90 percent of respondents have opinon that Information technology improves learning and teaching processes.

6. CONCLUSION

Our nation is at a turning point. We know that the world in which our education system was created—the industrial world of the 19th and early 20th centuries—no longer exists. Today we live in a technology-driven global marketplace where ideas and innovation outperform muscle and machine. In an age of digital content and global communications, we must build an education system that meets the new demands of our time. Information technologies can be used to support the effective application of these learning models in engineering higher education. The effectiveness of an information technology is analyzed through the appropriateness of the technology in supporting a particular learning model. Rapid development in IT have generated potential changes to teaching and learning. So, technology has mediated learning. So, technology meditated leaning is becoming increasingly important to business curricula. Report notes that "computer literacy" is concerned with role learning of specific hardware and software applications, while "fluency with technology" focuses on understanding the underlying concepts of technology and applying problem-solving and critical thinking to use of technology. The report also discusses differences between information technology fluency and information literacy as it is understood in K-12 and higher education. Among these are information literacy's focus on content, communication, analysis, information searching, and evaluation; whereas information technology "fluency" focuses on a deep understanding of technology and graduated increasingly skilled use of it.

The mapping of information technologies to learning models identifies technologies in which engineering schools should invest in order to improve their educational environment and quality. Technology can help us create schools where every child has the opportunity to succeed, while, we work to close the achievement gap, and address the economic and workforce needs of the future.

References

1. Brian L. Dos Santos, Information Technology Investments: Characteristics, Choices, Market Risk and Value, *Information Systems Frontiers*, Vol. 5, No. 3, pp. 289-301, September 2003.
2. Mu Yen Chen, An-Pin Chen, Integrating Option Model and Knowledge Management Performance Measures: An Empirical Study, *Journal of Information Science.*
3. Ram L. Kumar, Managing Risks in IT Projects: An Options Perspective, *Information and Management*, Vol. 40, No. 1, pp. 63-74, October 2002.
4. Nivedita Mukherji , Balaji Rajagopalan , Mohan Tanniru, A Decision Support Model for Optimal Timing of Investments in Information Technology Upgrades, *Decision Support Systems*, Vol. 42, No. 3, pp. 1684-96, December 2006.
5. John C. Henderson , Christine M.A. Lentz, Learning, Working, and Innovation: A Case Study in the Insurance Industry, *Journal of Management Information Systems*, Vol. 12, No. 3, pp. 43-64, December 1995.
6. Qizhi Dai, Robert J. Kauffman, Salvatore T. March, Valuing Information Technology Infrastructures: A Growth Options Approach, *Information Technology and Management*, Vol. 8, No. 1, pp. 1-17, March 2007.
7. Mu-Yen Chen, An-Pin Chen, Knowledge Management Performance Evaluation: A Decade Review from 1995 to 2004, *Journal of Information Science*, Vol. 32, No. 1, pp. 17-38, February 2006.
8. American Association of School Librarians and Association for Educational Communications and Technology, (1988). *Information Power: Guidelines for School Library Media Programs*. Chicago: Author. (Ed. 315 028)

9. American Library Association and Association for Educational Communications and Technology (1998). *Information Power: Building Partnerships for Learning.*
10. American Library Association Presidential Committee on Information Literacy (1989). *Final Report*. Chicago: Author. (Ed. 315 028).
11. Association of College Research Libraries (2000). *Information Literacy Competency Standards for Higher Education.* Retrieved November 3, 2007, from Association of College Research Libraries (2007). *The First-Year Experience and Academic Libraries: A Select, Annotated Bibliography.* Retrieved April 20, 2008.
12. Barner, R. (1996, March/April). Seven Changes that will Challenge Managers and Workers. *The Futurist,* 30(2), 14-18.

25

Information of Academic Enterprise Establishment

ACHINTYA DAS, BISWARUP NEOGI AND JESMIN ZAKARIA

ABSTRACT

This paper emphasizes the information regarding development of the manpower in industry. Academic institute is interrelated with the industry. To enrich product quality, technical support and supportive processed management is required but for the development and, to enrich quality academics interaction is require to develop industry institute interaction is discussed in this paper. The substance of technology is produced here which are related among them. The steps of technological dispersal are emphasized here for our society by development of academic institution.

1. INTRODUCTION

In the enterprise learning area, students apply knowledge, skills, experience and resources to the development of technological solutions that are designed to meet the changing needs of individuals, societies and environments. Students become innovative, adaptable and reflective as they select and use appropriate materials, information systems and processes to create solutions that consider the short- and long-term impact on societies and environments.

2. DEFINITION AND RATIONALE

The enterprise learning area relates to the processes of applying knowledge, skills and resources to satisfy human needs and wants, extending capabilities and realising opportunities. Enterprise involves the development and application of skills and attitudes that enable people to actively respond to and be involved in social and economic change.

Enterprise is not new. It is as old as human civilization and developed from the fundamental needs of humans for food, shelter and clothing. Its explicit inclusion in the school curriculum provides exciting opportunities for students to become involved in a range of learning experiences, set in relevant contexts with outcomes that have meaning in students' lives.

3. MEETING THE DEMANDS OF CHANGING WORLD

The enterprise learning area provides opportunities for students to become actively involved in dealing with change and meeting the needs of individuals, families and societies. It can develop confidence and competence in its use of equipment and processes and evaluate the appropriateness of technological innovations. Enterprise influences all aspects of people's daily lives and transforms societies, for example, a growing population and increased need for food resulted in human societies changing from hunting and gathering to fixed-site agriculture; and information technology and telecommunications have transformed the ways in which societies function, changing how and where people work, learn and run their lives. Students acquire the knowledge, skills, understandings and values to actively deal with and contribute to such change and to operate in the world now and in the future.

4. DEVELOPING SKILLS AND EXPERIENCING SYSTEMS AND PROCESS

Students are able to experience the reality of technological systems and processes by bringing ideas from conception to tuition. By responding to a range of challenges students try out their ideas for adapting or creating technology and operate in environments influenced by technology. They work individually and collaboratively, carry out investigations into the issues related to a challenge, draw on understandings from other disciplines to support hypotheses, and critically examine what others have achieved before them. They ascertain what contributed to decisions made during processes of technological innovation. They evaluate the success of technology in contributing to individual, family and community well-being. This research leads to a deeper understanding of the implications of challenges that informs the quality and repertoire of their ideas for innovation. Students develop the practical skills needed to work with materials, systems and information. The major focus of this learning area is students' understanding and effective use of information technologies and associated communication technologies. Through continual use and adaptation of these technologies, students are able to refine their skills, transfer these to a variety of contexts and to respond critically, reflectively and effectively to the challenges of a rapidly-changing world.

5. BEING ENTERPRISING

Students are encouraged to develop and practice enterprising behaviors such as initiative, resourcefulness, responsibility, adaptability and entrepreneurship. Through these behaviors, they enhance their critical and creative thinking, and organizing, collaborative and team-building skills. They identify needs, wants and opportunities and use, adapt, manage or develop a range of equipment, resources, processes, systems, services and environments to meet them. These behaviors and skills are transferable across the curriculum and are valuable acquisitions for career and life experiences. Students, also, have the opportunity to develop an enterprising ethos in which the ethical and responsible realization of opportunities is valued. By practicing enterprising skills and behaviors in a range of different contexts students become flexible and creative, both in their application of technologies and in the development of solutions to meet changing societal needs.

6. CONSIDERING THE SOCIAL AND ENVIRONMENTAL IMPACT OF SOLUTIONS

In seeking solutions students select, adapt and develop enterprises that make efficient use of resources, and are effective in managing social and environmental impacts. They understand the social, economic, political, cultural and environmental issues surrounding the use, development and disposal of technology. They are aware that the development of solutions will have consequences other than those intended. Students understand that the creation, adaptation and application of enterprise is dependent on achieving a balance between the responsibilities of the designer and the developer, and the needs of the user. Students consider their own attitudes, cultural beliefs and values, and those of others, as well as long- and short-term consequences of innovations for individuals, families, communities and environments. They come to understand that making decisions about enterprise often involves a complex mixture of consensus, conflict and compromise, as humans seek to meet needs and realize opportunities in a sustainable way.

7. TECHNOLOGY IN SOCIETY

Figure 25.1 describes the technology flow in the society. In the first layer, the technology skill, technology process and the enterprise are inter-related.

FIG. 25.1

The Representation of Steps to Develop Techno Society

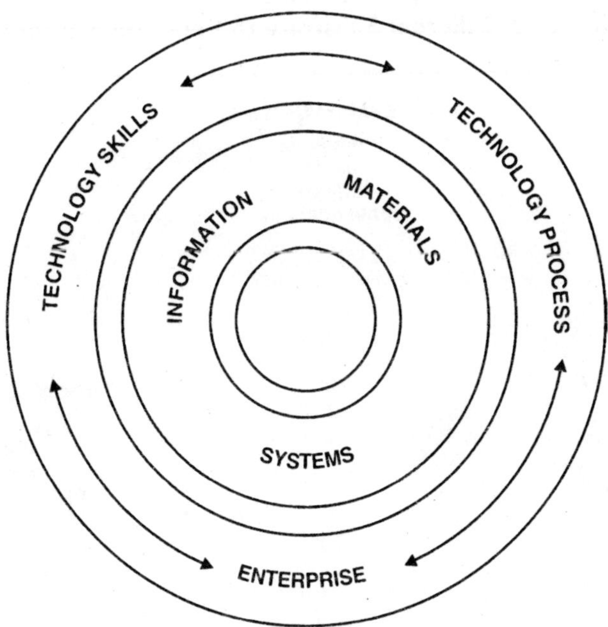

From these three consecutive and interconnected related tuples generates information, material and organized system. Using all of these sequential procedures the technology skill in society are developed.

8. SUBSTANCE TO GENERATE TECHNO PROCESS

How students apply a technology process to create and modify products, process, systems, services or environments to meet human needs and realize opportunities, i.e. the elements of a technological process is shown in Figure 25.2. The elements are—evaluating, investigating, devising and producing. Figure 25.2 shows that these four elements are interconnected to each other. Through these versions of the technology process, students find out more through investigation and research, develop ideas to devise a range of solutions, select and produce a solution and evaluate both the results of their endeavors and the process they adopted. When meeting human needs and realizing opportunities, students select how they use the elements of the technology process. They understand that the process can be both 'cyclic' and 'iterative', and those they may choose to revisit a particular element a number of times before they complete their solution: for example, as they develop a design, they may need to further investigate the properties of the materials they are using. In achieving this outcome, students demonstrate competence in the use of each element of the technology process, and select and use all of them when developing a

FIG. 25.2

Representation of Different Substrate to Generation Techno-society

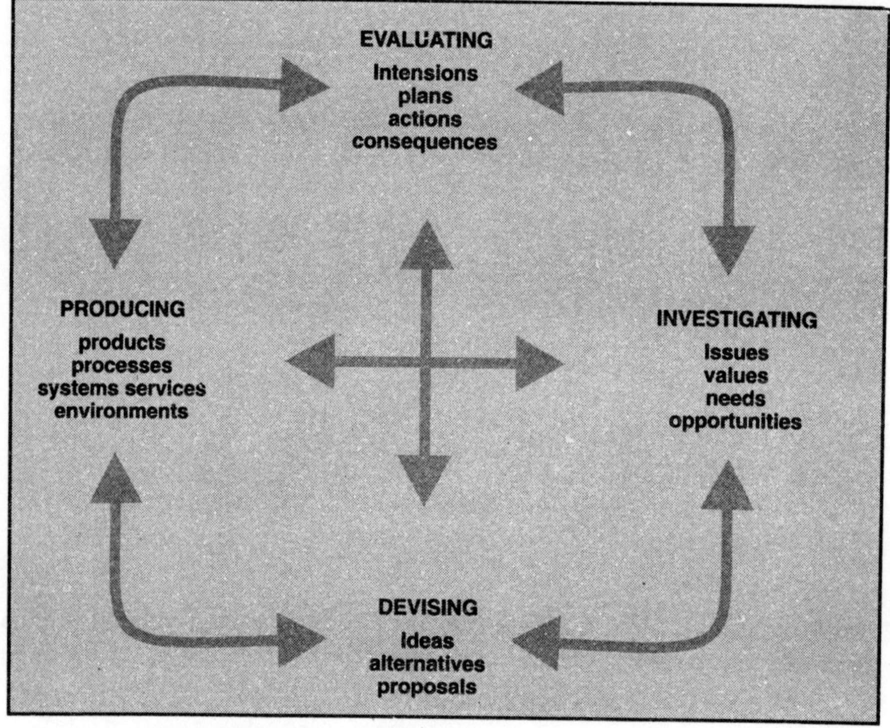

new or modified solution.

Students investigate by reflecting on what they already know about the problem or issue they are trying to solve or address. They locate and select data about materials, systems and information products and processes by, for example, surveying people, searching databases, observing or testing in real situations. They also consider the short- and long-term implications of the impact of technologies on societies and environments. As part of the process of investigation, students clarify what they are trying to achieve.

Students devise ways of creating or modifying existing technology based on their understanding and experience with the materials, information products, processes and systems they use. They devise solutions by developing a range of ideas that can take into account information they have gathered. They visualize consequences, think laterally, test ideas and represent or communicate to others a range of options.

When producing or modifying products or processes students select and use skills and techniques appropriate to their understanding of the nature of materials, information and systems. They organize and manage production, adapting and adjusting procedures to develop models, prototypes, processes or products.

Students review and evaluate information, processes, products, ideas, skills and techniques, considering their potential for refinement. They assess the implications of these and their impacts on societies and environments. They reflect on individual and/or group decisions, ways they have preceded and what they have accomplished.

As students create or modify a range of technological solutions, they enhance their ability to be enterprising, such as, flexibility, adaptability and innovation when seeking and realizing opportunities. Students may, for example, design and make products such as a nutritious snack for a pre-school child, a container to transport fragile items, a mask for a class celebration of an historical event or a piece of everyday jewel; adapt a community-based waste recycling system for use at school that incorporates the process of collecting and recycling materials from classrooms; identify a need, design and implement modifications to the classroom environment to reduce the effect of heat from the afternoon sun; evaluate accessibility and implement improved access to all areas of a school for a wheelchair-bound student; or devise and deliver a service to enhance the quality of social contact for the residents of a retirement village.

9. CONCLUSION

The human ethics is important phenomenon for the technical person by which the society has been developing. The technical academic institution is generated based on not only technology but also human ethics. The paper is describing the different class to develop our society by spreading technology through the humans.

References

1. An Assessment of Engineering colleges/Institutions in West Bengal, C.T. Bhunia, P. Purkait, D. Ghosh and T.K. Jana, National Conference on Emerging Technology and Technical Education (ET & TE, 2007), pp. 30-34.
2. www.curriculum.wa.edu.au-Technology & Enterprise.
3. Emerging Learning Trends Industry Institute Interaction, Mr. S.N. Dharwadkar., National Conference on Emerging Technology & Technical Education (ET & TE, 2007), pp. 35-38.
4. Jhon, D. Bransford, Annl. Brown Rodney R. Cocking, "Behavioral and Social Sciences and Education National Research Council".

5. Bob, Jensen, "Asynchronous Learning Network".
6. www.infy.com-campus connects section.
7. M.P. Dale, S.N. Dharwadkar, M.I. Agnani, "Vision for Education--The New Era"—ISTE 06.
8. M.P. Dale, K.H. Munde, "Potential Role of ICT in Supporting Technical Education"—ISTE 06.
9. N.R. Sexena, B.K. Mishra, R.K. Mohenty, "Teacher Education".
10. Total Quality Management: An Introduction, Mustakim Ansari, National Conference on Emerging Technology and Technical Education (ET and TE, 2007). pp. 72-74.

SECTION IV

Databases Integration

26

An Empirical Study to Identify Testing Issues during Extraction, Transformation and Loading Phase of Data Warehouse Development

JAITEG SINGH AND KAWALJEET SINGH

ABSTRACT

Like any development project, a data warehouse needs testing. The heterogeneity and multi-source data, and massive size of the data warehouse are the two major challenges that add to the complexity of testing it. The method to populate data warehouse is still in developing phase. Accordingly, there are no well defined rules and procedures to test a data warehouse effectively. Presuming the hypothesis that the quality of data in a data warehouse depends upon the extraction, transformation and loading procedures, this empirical study has tried to identify certain factors for testing the extraction, transformation and loading procedures of a data warehouse.

1. INTRODUCTION

Most product development methodologies contain well established metrics for testing. From literature survey, it has been experienced that these metrics fall well short of the requirements for testing a data warehouse application. Testing of a data warehouse is not just similar to traditional testing procedure. The main reason for this is the absence of well established procedures for data warehouse testing. According to a recent market review conducted by Gartner Research (Gartner, 2005) a variety of commercial ETL tools exist in the market which are associated with the big brand names like IBM, Informatica, Microsoft, Oracle since 2005 which is a very small time epoch. In the absence of well defined and established procedures, the second major concern for testing a data warehouse is the ever growing size of the data warehouse. This makes it extremely difficult to define the size of the system one should test. Many operations within a data warehouse do not scale linearly, which signifies the fact that the results derived from small systems may not be legitimate live systems. Inability to test the whole data warehouse may validate a design that simply does not work when the system grows. Generally, data warehouse systems start off unfilled because the viability to purchase complete system in the beginning is suspicious. Hence, it is unlikely that full scale testing can even be performed on the data warehouse hardware.

The only solution seems is to test a small-scale full system that can be carried out on the initial configuration, and scalability tests can be performed on larger systems afterwards. The normal metrics for testing are generally not efficient enough to predict the testing effort required appropriately. According to Sam Anahory and David Murray, if normal metrics throw up the figure of 50 person days of testing, then experience says to add 50% contingency, bringing the total to 75 person days. But, in reality, the total effort required for testing comes out to be double, i.e 150 person days. If insufficient time is allowed to testing before going live, then one may end up performing system tests on the live system itself which will lead to irate users and rapidly disillusioned management breathing down your neck [7].

Another major problem that a tester may confront during testing is that where the test data is going to come from? Test data should be real data, if it is not available in plenty then to generate "synthetic data" or "test data" is justified. But one should ensure priory that the data generated should have perfect balance and skew. Here, it is also essential that the ratio of facts and dimensions should be correct and so on. Historical data is considered good for testing purposes because it, generally, has the same data skews and biases as the data that a data warehouse will take care of, but, here the only difficulty is how to capture the real data in first place? Performing the system test offshore is not always viable. Even if one can arrange real data, the problem is how to load that data? For example, in a one terabyte system, at least 10 to 20 percent of system data is required which comes out to be 100 to 200 gigabytes of data. This means to accomplish this non-diminutive task one may require huge storage and processing capabilities. The generation of synthetic data may also inflict some questions like:

- How to generate data?
- From where to generate data and how to load it?

- Will the data represent a correct balance and skew?

The source data requires modifications on the source systems before being transferred into data warehouse. If the changes have not been made on the source system in time than the data warehouse may get data in a different form from the data it usually stores. Moreover, some organizations like banks don't allow real data off site for legal and competitive reasons. Keeping in view this situation, we collected some old student's data which was not having much importance in legal and competitive point of view. To generate appropriate amount of data we used DTM data generator developed by DTM Soft. DTM data generator is a very handy tool for generating accurate and meaningful data. The data was produced in the following manner:

Step 1 : Open the application and select the new DB data generator project radio button. (Refer Figure 26.1(a)).

Step 2 : Specify the database connection if any or browse the database file if saved locally. (Refer Figure 26.1(b)).

Step 3 : After specifying the type of database this interface will show all the attributes of the selected relational table of the selected database. On the upper right corner of the interface (Refer Figure 26.1(c)) the user can specify norms to generate meaningful and trustworthy data.

Step 4 : After specifying the constraints for data generation the user may select generate data button, if every rule specified is semantically correct than a log file will display the records which were successfully generated else it will show an error log (Refer Figure 26.1(d)).

After availing the data, now it is the turn of an application which should imitate the environment of a data warehouse. The data warehouse is a big architecture and it requires terabytes or even pentabytes of storage capacity with extremely fast processors along with efficient backup and recovery routines. Because of the unavailability of such environment, this study is concentrating itself on elementary level of data warehouse testing using automated methods. The hypothesis followed is that the quality of data in a data warehouse depends upon the extraction, transformation and loading procedures followed.

The Extract, Transform and Load (ETL) are trio distinct functions that are integrated into a common programming tool. The extract utility deciphers data from a particular resource and pulls out a preferred section of data which after conversion is handed over to the load utility to write the consequential data to a target database, which may or may not previously exist [3]. To retain the diagnostic capability of business processes, data warehouse should be loaded on regular basis. To achieve this, data from one

FIG. 26.1
DTM Data Generator Developed by DTM Soft

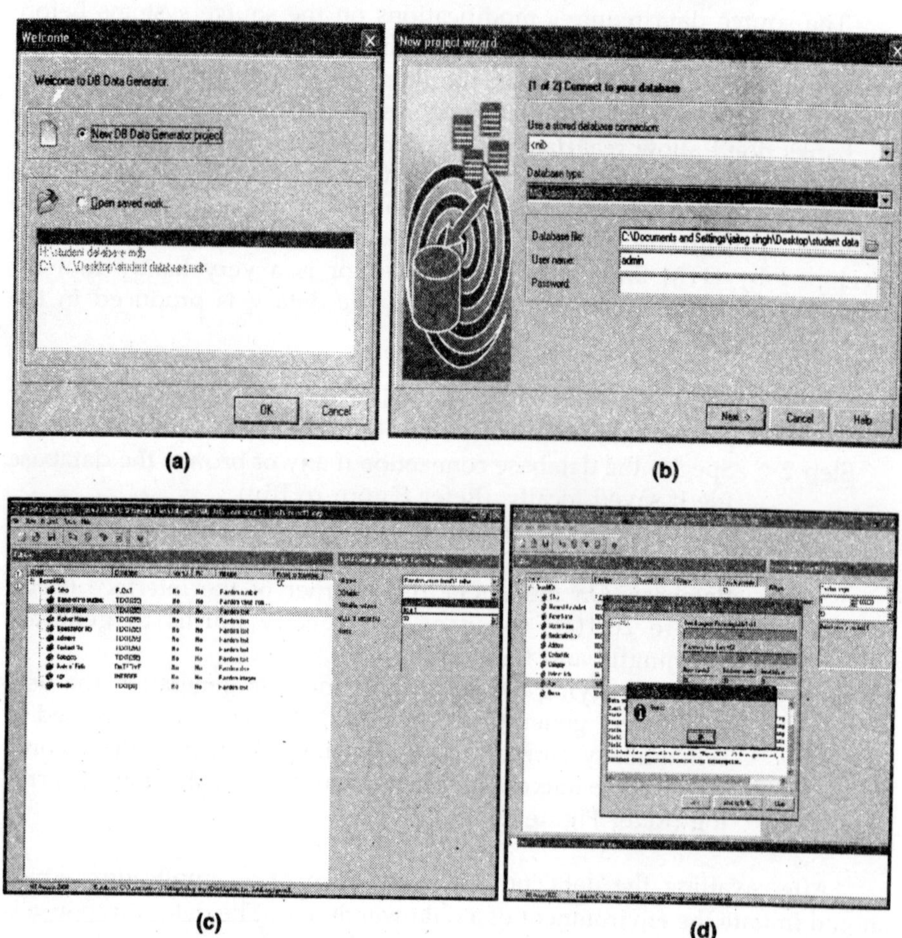

(a) (b)

(c) (d)

or more outfitted systems ought to be pulled out and pasted into the warehouse. Extraction, Transformation and Loading (ETL) are, basically, the process by which data is pulled out from the source systems and brought into the data warehouse. The acronym ETL is rather too simplistic, in the sense that it excludes the transportation phase and implies that each of the other phases of the process are discrete. ETL, therefore, refers to a wide-ranging process, and not necessarily three illustrated steps. The issues of integrating, rearranging and consolidating data over many systems are some of the anathemas facing the data warehouse atmosphere [4]. Hence, one can say that ETL is an indispensable part of data warehouse and is, chiefly, responsible for the quality of data within a data warehouse. The development of ETL is a stepwise procedure given in Figure 26.2.

Fig. 26.2
ETL Procedure

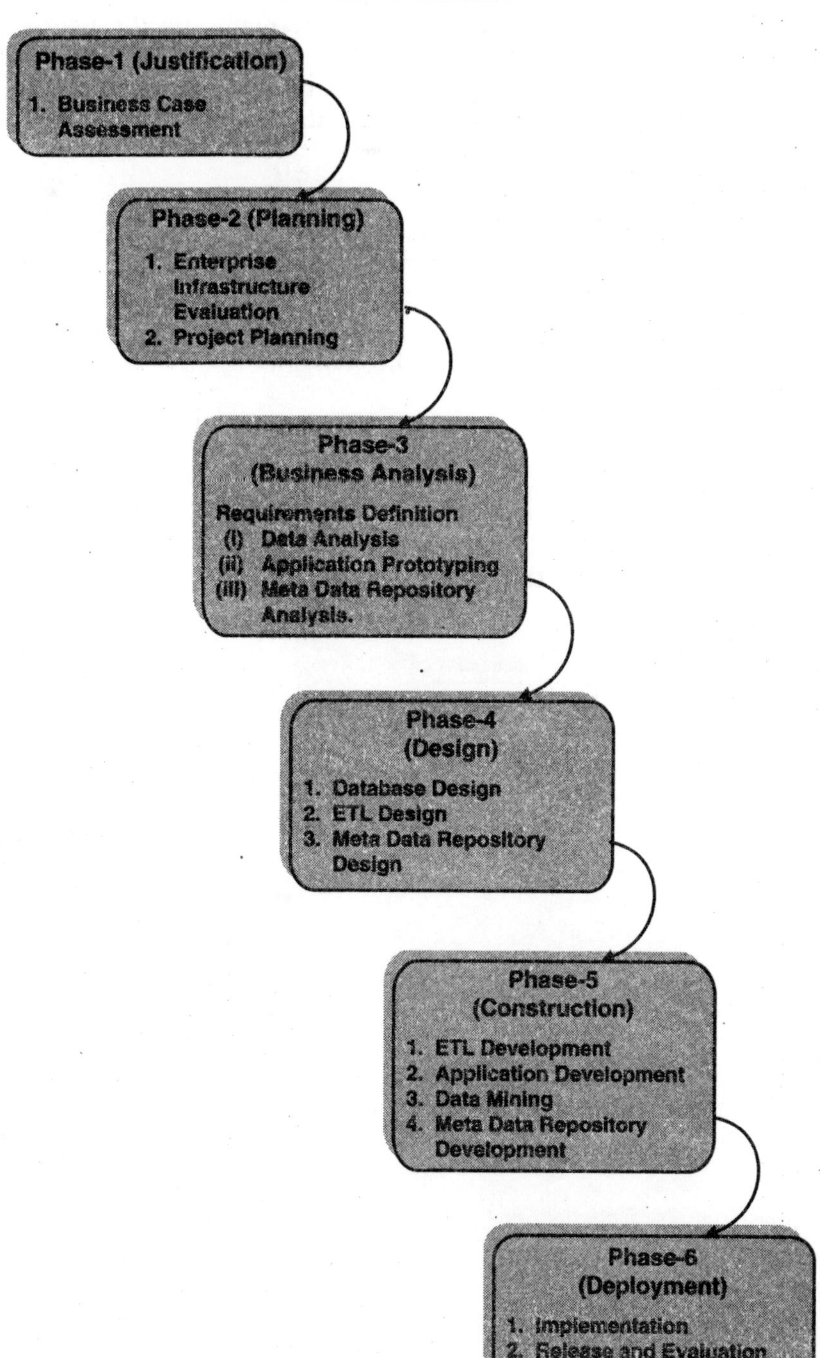

2. EXTRACT/TRANSFORM AND LOAD DESIGN

As the data warehouse architecture is domain specific hence the definition of data quality and the preferences during the ETL phase will vary from time to time. In this study the data quality and ETL preferences have been defined on the basis of generated student data.

2.1 Experimental Setup

It has been observed at our end that the quality of source data determines the scope of transformation and consistency of data within a data warehouse. To thoroughly study the issues during ETL, a data extraction tool was developed, which is capable of fetching data from a number of sources. Hence, the test data generated earlier was extracted with the help of the developed tool.

The data extraction tool started with the specification of source and target databases. Refer to Figure 26.3. The facility to view data instance was also provided for convenience.

FIG. 26.3
Data Extraction Tool

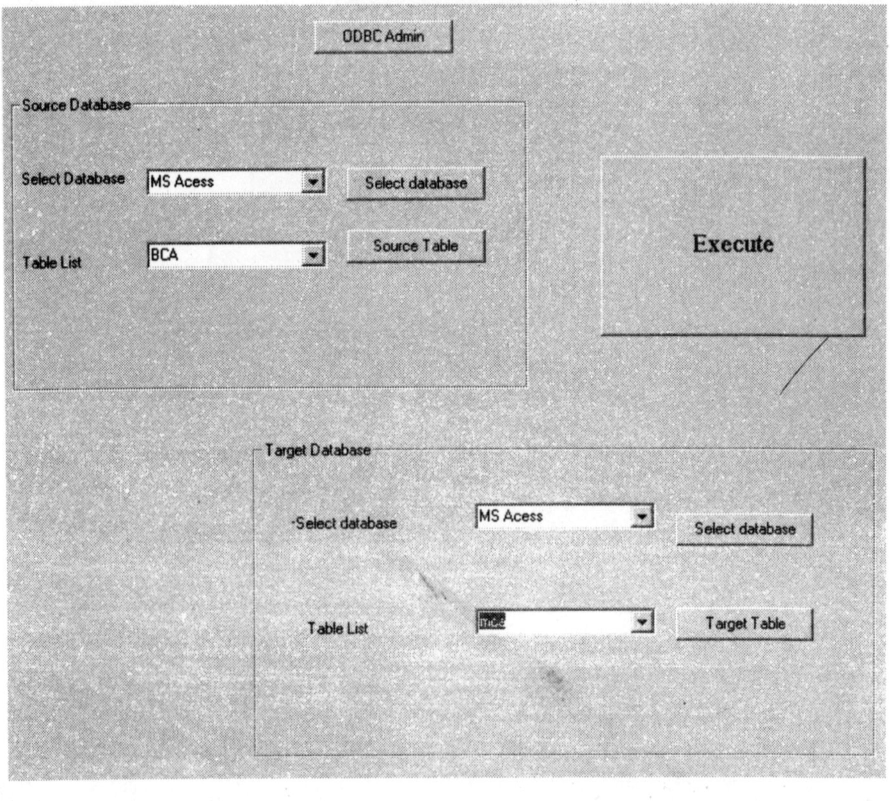

Initially, the user specifies the source database from where the data has to be extracted. The target database comprised almost all the fields available in the source data base and most of the fields were declared as text. The populated data in the target database is detailed in Figure 26.4. As shown in the Figure 26.4, the serial no. field is having values in absurd manner. This further lightens the violation of primary key, i.e the serial no. field. As there were no integrity checks enforced during the extraction of data and the inappropriate choice of primary key are responsible for such capricious results.

With the help of simulated ETL tool, the following anomalies have been identified in the target database:

FIG. 26.4

Populated Data in the Target Database

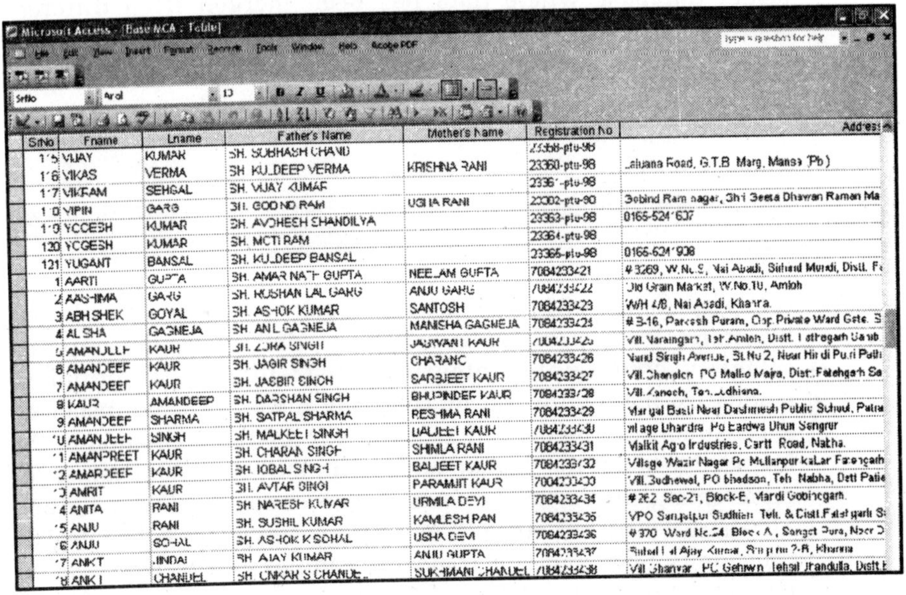

SrNo	Fname	Lname	Father's Name	Mother's Name	Registration No	Address
115	VIJAY	KUMAR	SH. SUBHASH CHAND		23358-ptu-98	
116	VIKAS	VERMA	SH. KULDEEP VERMA	KRISHNA RANI	23360-ptu-98	Laluana Road, G.T.B Marg, Mansa (Pb)
117	VIKRAM	SEHGAL	SH. VIJAY KUMAR		23361-ptu-98	
118	VIPIN	GARG	SH. GOBIND RAM	USHA RANI	23302-ptu-90	Gobind Ram nagar, Shri Geeta Bhawan Raman Ma
119	YOGESH	KUMAR	SH. AVDHESH SHANDILYA		23363-ptu-98	0165-5241637
120	YOGESH	KUMAR	SH. MOTI RAM		23364-ptu-98	
121	YUGANT	BANSAL	SH. KULDEEP BANSAL		23365-ptu-98	0166-5241938
1	AARTI	GUPTA	SH. AMAR NATH GUPTA	NEELAM GUPTA	7084233421	# 3269, W.No.5, Nai Abadi, Sirhind Mandi, Distt. Fa
2	AASHIMA	GARG	SH. ROSHAN LAL GARG	ANJU GARG	7084233422	Old Grain Market, W.No.10, Amloh
3	ABHISHEK	GOYAL	SH. ASHOK KUMAR	SANTOSH	7084233423	WH 4/8, Nai Abadi, Khanna.
4	ALISHA	GAGNEJA	SH. ANIL GAGNEJA	MANISHA GAGNEJA	7084233424	# 3-16, Parkash Puram, Opp. Private Ward Gate. S
5	AMANDEEP	KAUR	SH. ZORA SINGH	JASWANT KAUR	7084233425	Vill. Narainagarh, Teh.Amloh, Distt. Fatehgarh Sahib
6	AMANDEEP	KAUR	SH. JAGIR SINGH	CHARANO	7084233426	Nand Singh Avenue, St.No 2, Near Hindi Puri Path
7	AMANDEEP	KAUR	SH. JASBIR SINGH	SARBJEET KAUR	7084233427	Vill.Chanalon, PO Malko Majra, Distt.Fatehgarh Sa
8	KAUR	AMANDEEP	SH. DARSHAN SINGH	BHUPINDER KAUR	7084233428	Vill.Kanech, Teh.Ludhiana.
9	AMANDEEP	SHARMA	SH. SATPAL SHARMA	RESHMA RANI	7084233429	Mangal Basti Near Dashmesh Public School, Patra
10	AMANDEEP	SINGH	SH. MALKEET SINGH	BALJEET KAUR	7084233430	Village Bhardra Po Bardwa Dhuri Sangrur
11	AMANPREET	KAUR	SH. CHARAN SINGH	SHIMLA RANI	7084233431	Malkit Agro Industries, Cantt Road, Nabha.
12	AMARDEEP	KAUR	SH. IQBAL SINGH	BALJEET KAUR	7084233432	Village Wazir Nagar Po Mullanpur kaLar Fatehgarh
13	AMRIT	KAUR	SH. AVTAR SINGH	PARAMJIT KAUR	7084233433	Vill.Budhewal, PO bhadson, Teh Nabha, Distt Patia
14	ANITA	RANI	SH. NARESH KUMAR	URMILA DEVI	7084233434	# 262 Sec-21, Block-E, Mandi Gobindgarh.
15	ANJU	RANI	SH. SUSHIL KUMAR	KAMLESH RAN	7084233435	VPO Sanghol Sudhian Teh. & Distt.Fatehgarh S
16	ANJU	SOHAL	SH. ASHOK K SOHAL	USHA DEVI	7084233436	# 370 Ward No.24 Block A, Sangat Pura, Near D
17	ANKIT	JINDAL	SH. AJAY KUMAR	ANJU GUPTA	7084233437	Suhel Lal Ajay Kumar, Shop no 2-B, Khanna
18	ANKIT	CHANDEL	SH. ONKAR S CHANDE..	SUKHMANI CHANDEL	7084233438	Vill Ghanvar, PO Gehwn, Tehsil Jhandulla, Distt.E

1. *Lexical Anomalies:* Syntactical errors are, generally, lexical errors which would name discrepancies between the structure of the data items and the specified format. In a relational data base, the data is stored in the table form with each row representing a tuple and each column representing an attribute. If there are five attributes of a relation or table, then, each tuple will also have five attributes. But, if some or all of the rows contain only four columns then the actual structure of the data will not confirm to the specified format. This will result in lexical errors. For example, record no. 125 is lexically erroneous because the name column is representing a numeric value and the roll number column is representing a character string.

123	SAHIL	MAHAWAR	SH. RAKESH GUPTA	ASHA GUPTA	7084233546	#60, Sec-24A, St.No.7, Dilip Nagar, New
124	SANDEEP	KAUR	SH. SARABJIT SINGH	HARJIT KAUR	7084233547	Gobind Nagar, Near I.T.I., Sangrin Road, N
125	SANJEEV	KUMAR	SH. VED PARKASH	7084233548	Gulmohar Nagar,	9888153518
126	Santosh	Pun	Dam Bahadur Pun	MAN MAYA PUN	7084233549	# & Bihar Ncc BN Sub.Maj.D.B.Pun Sadh:

2. *Format Errors*: These errors specify errors where the value of a given attribute does not conform to the anticipated domain. For example record no. 56 is representing a correct name but in a wrong way. As the last name is specified first and the first name is specified as the last name, hence, it is violating the domain format.

55	GURPREET	SINGH	SH. KRISHAN SINGH		7084233477	#42, Sec. - 10, Block - A, Guru Ki Nagri, N
56	KAUR	GURVEER	SH. SHINGARA SINGH	CHARANJEET KAUR	7084233478	Vill.Sahapur, Distt.Sangrur.
57	HARINDER	KAUR	SH. HARBANS SINGH	JASWANT KAUR	7084233479	#335, W.No.10, Sardar Colony, Bassi Roac

3. *Irregularities:* Irregularities are apprehensive with non-consistent use of values, units and abbreviations, etc. For example, in the target database where data has been merged from different sources, the sex attribute has been represented as M/F and Male/ Female. Such anomalies will create a bottleneck for developing a generalized formula or query for data processing.

0165-5241607			5/29/1984	23	m
	GEN		5/28/1982	25	m
0165-5241908			8/27/1985	22	m
#3269, W.No.9, Nai Abadi, Sirhind Mondi, Distt. Fathegarh Sahib.	988841859	Gen	8/29/1984	23	female
Old Grain Market, W.No.10, Amloh	9417197114	Gen	12/11/1985	22	female
W/H 4/8, Nai Abadi, Khanna.	01628-229284	Gen.	11/4/1986	21	male

4. *Integrity Constraint Violations:* Integrity constraint violation illustrates that set of tuples which do not satisfy the imposed integrity constraints. Integrity constraints are essential to emphasize the mini world by confining the set of valid instances. A constraint can be defined as a rule for the representation of the knowledge about the domain along with the set of valid values for representing the concerned facts. For example, the Dates 30th and 31st February are not possible and, hence, are violating the integrity constraints. Such values become apparent, especially, when data is imported from text/flat files where there is no provision to declare any integrity constraint. In the same way age cannot be zero if there is an entry for the date of birth column.

Vill & P.O. Mangoo Teh.Arki, Distt. Sihan, H.P.	01796-247059	GEN	22-Dec-85	22	m
			28-Feb-85	22	m
			15-Nov-85	22	m
			15-Dec-87	0	m
			01-Mar-85	22	m
			02-Apr-82	25	m

5. *Contradictions:* Contradictions refers to the values within a tuple of a relational database that contravene some kind of dependency between values. For example, the formula for calculating age is (current date (date on which transaction was recorded)—date of birth). If this constraint is not followed correctly it may result in

contradictions. For example, in the snapshot given below the second record has date of birth value equal to 05 April 1986 and the age is 24.

			05-Apr-85	22	m
			05-Apr-86	24	m
# 1625A, Old Gadda Khana, Near Arya Samaj Park, Patiala	0175-5004278	GEN	07-Jun-87	20	m
			14-Sep-84	23	m

6. *Duplicates:* Duplicates can be stated as tuples representing the same world entity from the concerned mini-world. The values of these tuples do not need to be completely similar. These records may also result contradictions as they represent the same entity but with different values for all or some of its properties. Like in snapshot 9 the record no. 8 and 9 are representing the same entity from the mini world because the name and registration no. fields are same in both cases but information provided here is bewildering.

7	GUPTA	ANKUR	SH. NARESH KUMAR GUPTA	KUSUM LATA GUPTA	23250-ptu-98	# 1625A, Old Gadda Khana, Near Arya Sa
8	ANKUSH	KHURANA	SH. SHIV K. KHURANA		23251-ptu-98	
9	ANKUSH	KUMAR	SH. SHIV K. KHURANA	USHA DEVI	23251-ptu-98	Sandeep Cloth House Kamal Road, Rama
10	ANTARPREET	KAUR	SH. CHANCHAL MEHBOOB S		23253-ptu-98	S.C.H Kamal Road, Raman Mandi, Distt. I

7. *Data Type Mismatch:* The data type mismatch can impose a serious problem while merging data from various sources. For example, it is possible to store an integer value in text data type, but it is not possible to store a text value in an integer data type.

28	GAGANDEEP	KAUR	SH. GAMDUR SINGH	SHAMSHER KAUR	23271-ptu-98	# 2567, Sector-70, Mohali
29	KAUR	GAGANDEEP	SH. MOHAN SINGH	MANJEET KAUR	23272-ptu-98	Plot No. 126, Ranjit Nagar, Sirhind R
30	GAURAV	SHARMA	SH. BRIJMOHAN SHARMA		23273-ptu-98	
31	GURMEET	SINGH	SH. AVTAR SINGH		23274-ptu-98	
32	GURPREET	KAUR	SH. DEVINDER SINGH		23275-ptu-98	
33	SINGH	GURPREET	SH. SWARN SINGH		23276-ptu-98	
34	GYPSY	ANEJA	SH. BAKSHI LAL ANEJA		23277-ptu-98	

8. *Missing Values:* These values are the result of omissions during data collection. The major reason for missing values is constraint violations like we have null values for attributes where there exists a non-null constraint for them. If missing values are present this means there is no such constraint imposed during data extraction. These values impose a major problem when one wants to substitute values for such records for example one cannot insert null values into an integer field because by default its value is set to zero. This insinuates that, if we try to consolidate data by filling dummy values in null fields then numeric data types may require special attention because their default value is set to zero.
9. *Typographical Errors:* Typographical errors are those errors which grounds due to typing mistakes. These errors are almost impossible to identify with automatic checks. For example, due to typing mistake male can be written as amle. The possible solution is to rearrange the data in ascending or descending order and analyze it manually afterwards.

10. *Transformation and Preservation of Meaning:* The transformation challenge is expressed in terms of successfully matching data fields. But this is not the best way to think about it. The real challenge is preserving the meaning held in records throughout the transformation process. To eliminate data inconsistency and integrity problems (as stated above), one tries to purify data through data transformations. It is again not an easy job.
11. *Normalization Break-up:* Illogically or inconsistently stored data can cause a number of problems. A poorly designed database may provide erroneous information, may be difficult to use, or may even fail to work properly. Most of these problems are the result of two bad design features called: redundant data and anomalies. Redundant data is unnecessary reoccurring. Anomalies can be defined as any occurrence that weakens the integrity of your data due to irregular or inconsistent storage, for example, delete, insert and update irregularity that generates the inconsistent data. Basically, normalization is the process of efficiently organizing data in a database to reduce redundancy. Hence, the two main objectives of the normalization process can be stated as to eliminate redundant data, which means storing the same data in more than one table, and to ensure that the data dependencies should make sense. Both of these are valuable goals as they reduce the amount of space a database consumes and ensure that data is logically stored. Generally, it is considered as impossible to normalize a database but it can be possible with the help of a smart ETL routine, which should be competent enough to normalize the target database before populating data into it.

2.2 Statistical Analysis

After merging data from different sources into a common database, a manual analysis was done which was further investigated with the help of statistical methods. The analysis unveiled following observations:

- Total Records in Target Database 254
- Correct Records 121
- Percentage of correct items (121/254) * 100 = 47.64%

The study observed that out of the total records inserted, less than 50% were correct. The count of different types of errors identified is:

- Missing Values 177 (E_1)
- Format Errors 169 (E_2)
- Duplicates 18 (E_3)
- Contradictions 37 (E_4)
- Other Syntax and Semantic errors 12 (E_5)

If all these categories of errors are abbreviated as E_1, E_2, E_3, E_4 and E_5 then total no. of errors can be defined as $\Sigma E_{i=1\text{-}5}$. Hence, $\Sigma E_{i=1\text{-}5} = 413$ (177+169+18+37+12).

The calculated percentage of these errors is:

- Missing Value (177/413)*100 = 42.85%
- Format Error (169/413)*100 = 40.92%
- Duplicate (18/413)*100 = 4.35%
- Contradiction (37/413)*100 = 8.95%
- Other Syntax and Semantic Errors (12/413)*100 = 2.91%

FIG. 26.5
Analysis of Percentage of Errors

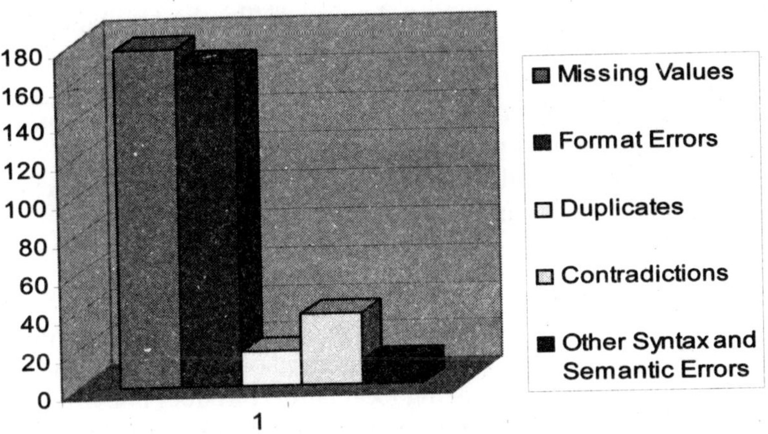

ETL processes can be quite intricate, and imperative operational anomalies might result with poorly designed ETL systems. The assortment of data values or data quality in an operational system could be beyond the expectations of designers at the time validation and transformation rules. Data silhouetting of the source during data analysis is recommended to illustrate the data conditions that will need to be administered by transform regulations. This leads to an amendment of validation rules explicitly and implicitly implemented in the ETL process. From this analytical study, the importance of testing is clearly perceptible.

3. TESTING "THE PROCESS"

As per the definition, testing is a process of locating errors within a system. Hence, testing is a stepwise process which includes Unit Testing, Integration Testing, System Testing and Acceptance Testing Phases. After all these phases, data warehouse is tested as a whole.

3.1 Unit Testing

Unit testing for data warehouses should test out the extraction, transformation and loading events which includes mappings and jobs along with the developed front-end reports. The processes by which data from transaction systems or from other sources are loaded in the database schema with the help of customized routines are called ETL procedures. In case of a data warehouse, the unit testing is performed on ETL (extraction, transformation and loading) Unit. The following tests are conducted in this phase:

1. Whether extraction methods are having approach to the required source data.
2. To check that all the business rules are properly followed and the data is entered in warehouse tables by transformation methods.
3. Testing for slowly changing dimension like the marital status of a customer.
4. Checking of format specifications.
5. Checking of graphs for categories, colors and tags associated with every color representing a different category, etc.
6. To check whether the data from data warehouse tables/schema is reflected correctly in reports.

3.2 Integration Testing

Integration testing is the second phase of testing, in other words, we can say that it is performed after the completion of unit testing. The testing of individual units helps in removing local faults, but does not work out the communications among different units. Integration testing is the activity of exercising such interactions by hauling together the different modules composing a system. It is characterized by involving different interacting units which have been, in general, developed by different programmers. In case of ETL—individual jobs are made to run as a batch. This is usually done by using a shell script or by using batch facilities in the ETL tool. Finally, a series of batches are prepared as modules and run in a single shot. Integration testing is performed to test the following conditions:

1. The sequence of batches during the single shot runs.
2. Generation of error logs.
3. Impact of failure of a job on the subsequent batch jobs.
4. Processing of altered records which are updated at a later stage after being initially processed.
5. Automatic or manual restarting in case of any failure.
6. Processing of rejected records.
7. Generation of logs created at the end of every process.

3.3 System and Acceptance Testing

System and acceptance testing are basically different from each other. But, it is advantageous to combine the two phases in case of tight time lines and budget constraints. The system is tested with full functionality and is expected to function as in production. At the end of this phase, the system should be acceptable to the client for use in terms of ETL process integrity and business functionality. To implement this phase, it is necessary for the testing team to understand the working of the business process and to validate that the correct amount of data is transferred from the source systems to the target data warehouse. System testing takes the final phase of integration testing to the next level by requiring that the testing team push the limits on the volume to be loaded into the test environment [1]. Large data sets extracted directly from the operational systems can be utilized if possible for the system testing. Final DASD size can be determined, load times can be calculated or validated and proper procedures to put jobs into production can be reviewed. Due to limitations in most test environments of limited direct access storage devices (DASD) and CPU cycles during operational hours, these tests are very useful, but may not be able to identify all of the potential errors during the actual load if the warehouse is being developed on a shared platform. As far as the scope of this study is concerned because of the involvement of highly expensive platforms and appropriate system environment it is restricting itself to the first two phases of testing, but one can still try to project the impact of these techniques on the full system testing.

3.4 Test Automation in Data Warehouses

The automation approach would be a blend of Errands automation and Tests automation. Under Errands automation there is a need to do the pre-requisite steps before starting the ETL, for example, if one has to load data from flat file than one has to bring flat files to landing pad platform by using copy operation. Another check which is desired is to remodel all the present files in the format which is needed by ETL. The test automation process can be considered as a three phase procedure. After initial processing launch the ETL through your automation code, which will read the data from flat files and load it to Phase 1 database where you will do the cleanup of data. Here you need to write a good automation logic which will keep check on the data loading process because data loading might vary from 5 minutes to several weeks time. You can't run next task until this process is completed.

Once Phase 1 is completed, ETL might create a Job to load data to Phase 2. Trigger the job from your automation tool. Once Phase 2 is loaded completely, the test automation will come into picture. You need to keep track of row count loaded into each table. In some cases, you might want to check the data values which are very difficult in case of data warehouses, so we went by row count basis. Once Phase 2 is loaded and data transformation is done, trigger the next Job of ETL which will load the data to Phase 3. Now is the place where your test case should define what should be the expected outcome after transformation of data from Phase 2 to Phase 3. Now, automate your test case which will verify row count as expected from Phase 2 to Phase 3 in expected tables. Analyze the whole process to record the pass/fail result of the checks imposed by the automated routines in the form of a bug database. Logging should be done for each and every step along with the time taken for each step to complete with data time stamp. Your automation code should be able to take parameter from files, command line, etc. It would help to run the same ETL for various scenarios.

4. CONCLUSION

Testing of a data warehouse is not just similar to the traditional testing of developed code. The main thing to verify here is that all the parts of data warehouse should work correctly, and ensure that the end to end load, aggregate and query procedures work as expected. At the outset a smaller-scale full system test can be carried out on initial configuration, and then the scalability tests can be performed on larger benchmark systems.

REFERENCES

1. Adam Wolszczak, Marcin Dabrowski , "Automation in Data Warehouse Testing— Where is it Applicable?," 12th Software and Systems Quality Conferences, 25th-27th April 2007, Germany.
2. Beate List 1, Robert M. Bruckner 1, "A Comparison of Data Warehouse Development Methodologies Case Study of the Process Warehouse", IBM Press Brochure Issue, 2003.
3. Connolly, Begg, "A Practical Approach to design, Implement and Management of Databsae Systems". Pearson Education, third edition, 2007.
4. Dorothy, M. Blakeslee and John Rumble, "The Essentials of a Data Warehouse Quality Process", *Data Science Journal,* 12 February 2003.
5. Eckerson, W., "Smart Companies in the 21st century: The Secrets of Creating Successful BI Solutions." A Report of the Data Warehouse Institute, August 2003.
6. Jason Gartner, Scott Maberry and Bill O'Connell, "Data Warehouse Maintenance Strategy", IBM Corporation Guide, June 2005.
7. Sam Anahory and Dennis Murray, "Data Warehousing in the Real World: A Practical Guide for Building Decision Support Systems", Addison-Wesley Publications 2000.

27

Implementation Issues of Data Warehousing

Harjot Singh

ABSTRACT

Data warehousing has become the buzz word of database industry and simultaneously coined the terms Data Integration, Data Scrubbing and Temporal Database, etc. Warehousing is the process which fetches the data from heterogeneous data sources and render a view into a single repository. The process includes integrators, wrapper and translators. Data warehousing supports direct and parallel processing of queries. This paper proposes general purpose architecture of Data warehouse starting from the integration process and finally various technical aspects as well as problems arising in implementation of the architecture.

1. INTRODUCTION

The backbone of data warehousing is data integration; and providing integrated access from multiple, distributed heterogeneous sources to a common view is the burning issue in today's database research. Data integration allows organizations to access all their fragmented data, create an accurate and consistent view of their information assets, and leverage those assets to drive business decisions and operations.

The two main components of data integration:

- Application Integration
- Data Integration

While application integration focuses on transaction management and process integration, data integration resolves the complex issues that arise from data fragmentation—including poor data quality, inconsistencies in the structure and meaning of data and inadequate data governance.

Hypothetically, Integration is a very simple two step approach:

(i) *Recognize a Query:* Determine the appropriate information sources, scanning, parsing, validating and generation of appropriate sub-queries.

(ii) *Obtain Results:* It comprises query optimization, execution plan, code generation and fetching of result.

This is traditional approach and known as on-demand approach to data integration, i.e. whenever a query is posed it is first evaluated locally into the data warehouse without accessing the original source. Also, some time referred as lazy approach.

The Modern approach is in-advance access to data (also known as eager approach), i.e to collect data related to the query to a view before the query is posed. However, it is still a issue of on-going research up to what extent a data warehouse view should fetch data from the original sources.[1]

Which approach we should adopt? The answer is purely dependent upon the need of client since the repository serves as a warehouse storing the data of interest. A lazy approach to integration is appropriate for information that changes rapidly, for clients with unpredictable needs, and for queries that operate over vast amount of data from very large numbers of information sources. However, the lazy approach may show inefficiency and delay in query processing, especially, when queries are issued multiple times, when information sources are slow, expensive or periodically unavailable, and when significant processing is required for the translation and merging steps.

In cases, where information sources do not permit *ad-hoc* queries, the lazy approach is simply not feasible. In in-advance (eager) approach, the integrated information is available for immediate querying and analysis, and suitable for clients require summarized information from large data sources with high performance, but, not necessarily require the most recent updated states of information.

After analyzing the above mentioned facts, there are three important steps of data warehousing process. These are going to serve as guidelines on the basis of which later, we will drive the warehousing architecture:

1. Warehouse design
2. Data-mining design
3. Metadata design

All three aspects of the design process rest on an inter-related set of computing platforms. The software and the skill-sets necessary to work on these different machines are not shown in the model but are fundamental to the success of the process. Each of the three design processes is based on a slightly different understanding of the word "data". A comparatively simple representation of warehouse architecture with it's various components is shown in Figures 27.1 and 27.2.

Fig. 27.1

Basic Architecture of Data Warehousing Process

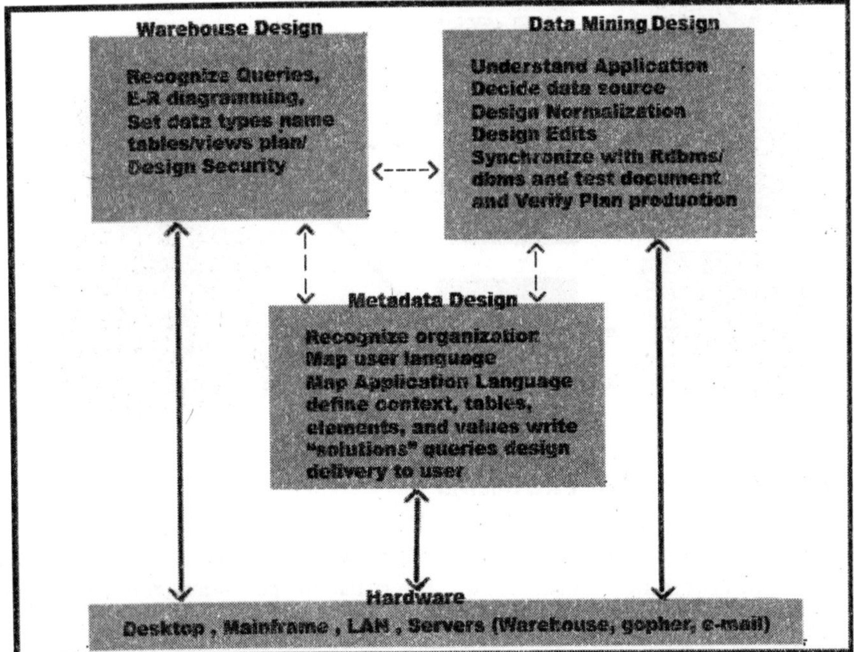

In this integrated environment each and every component has well defined responsibilities. Let's explore them one by one, the job assigned to *wrapper* component of this module is translating information from the local format of the source into the format and data model used by the warehousing system, while the *monitor* module is responsible for automatically detecting alterations of interest in the source data and converging them to the integrator.

When a new information source is attached to the warehousing system or when relevant information at a source changes, the new or modified data is propagated to the integrator.

The *integrator* is responsible for providing unified information to the warehouse, which may include altering the information, summarizing it, or merging it with information from other sources. In order to properly combine new information into the warehouse, it may be necessary for the integrator to obtain further information from the same or different information sources.

FIG. 27.2
Data Warehousing Environment and Related Components

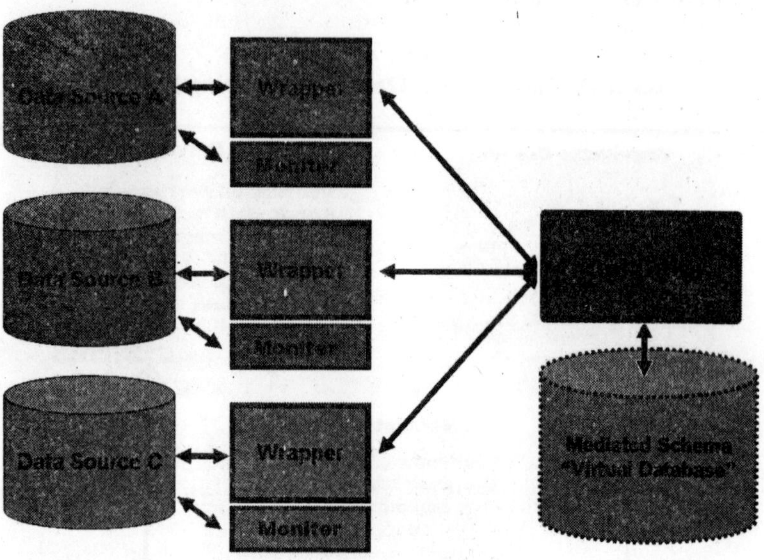

2. IMPLEMENTATION PROBLEMS

Based upon the above general architecture, let's have a deep analysis of different components and outline the different problems related to them while implementing the warehousing approach.

2.1 Wrapper/Monitors

The wrapper/monitor components illustrated in Figure 27.2 have two interrelated responsibilities:

1. *Translation:* Making the underlying information source appear as if it subscribes to the data model used by the warehousing system. For example, if the information source consists of a set of non-relational fields but the warehouse model is relational, then the wrapper/monitor must maintain an interface that presents the data from the information source as if it were relational. The translation problem is intrinsic in almost all approaches to data integration both on-demand and in-advance, and is not specific to data warehousing. Typically, a component that translates an information

source into a common integrating model is called a translator or wrapper [3, 5].

2. *Change Detection:* Monitoring the information source for changes to the data that are relevant to the warehouse and propagating those changes to the integrator. Note that this functionality relies on translation.

   Changes to the data must be translated from the format and model of the information source into the format and model used by the warehousing system. One approach is to overlook the change detection issue altogether and simply propagate entire copies of relevant data from the information source to the warehouse periodically. An example is Stripe and Mirror Everywhere (SAME) technique used in Oracle data warehouse support systems.

2.3 Integration

The integrator can combine this data with existing warehouse data from other sources or it can request complete information from all sources and re-compute the warehouse data from scratch. Ignoring change detection may be acceptable in certain scenarios, for example, when it is not important for the warehouse data to be current and it is acceptable for the warehouse to be on-line occasionally. However, if concurrency, efficiency, and continuous access are required, then, we believe that detecting and propagating changes and incrementally folding the changes into the warehouse will be the preferred solution. In these situations Active/Dynamic data warehousing feature offered by some vendors enhance the system efficiency to provide online instantaneous information in the data warehouse view.

In considering the change detection problem first of all, we have identified several relevant types of information sources:

- *Cooperative sources*: Sources that provide triggers or other active database capabilities[6], although with the help Active/Dynamic data warehousing features that notifications of changes of interest can be programmed to occur automatically. In replacement of historic information the performance of overall data warehouse environment deteriorate. Mostly, in commercial data warehousing systems, it is assumed that both the source database and the warehouse are relational. So translation problem occur rarely. However to provide reusable Wrapper/Monitor component is an issue that still need attention. Mostly warehouse use separate Wrapper/Monitor component for each and every database, thus, there is decrease in efficiency level of the warehouse. However, for common tasks special purpose Wrappers are usually provided by the vendor like Query able sources; sources that allow the wrapper/monitor to query the information at the source so that

Table 27.1
Comparison of Different Data Warehousing Supportable DBMS's

	Name of the Product	*Unique Data Warehousing Features*			*Query Optimization*
(1)	*(2)*	*(3)*	*(4)*	*(5)*	*(6)*
Oracle	Oracle 11g (Coherence Data Grid)	SAME (Stripe and Mirror Everywhere) For Input/ Output Load balancing	Enhanced OLAP (EOLAP), STAR query optimization make it easy to make complex DSS queries run at super-fast speeds.	Oracle Data Integration Suite	Row-based
IBM	DB2 UDB Version 8	Cross platform data integration		DB2-information integrator	Row-based
Microsoft	SQLSERVER2008 WMS(Warehouse Management System)	SQL Server Management Studio (SSMS) for Custom Reporting	SQL managed data extraction	SSIS (sql server integration service)—ETL tool	Row-based
Sybase	Sybase IQ	**Parallel computing (PC):** Speed, flexibility in querying, but significant hardware expense. Complex query from one impacts all. *Examples: Teradata, Netezza*	**OLAP (OL)**: Speed in querying, but low flexibility. *Examples: Hyperion*, Microsoft, Cognos, Business Objects*	Data integration Suite—ETL (extract, transform and load)	Column-based
NCR Teradata	Teradata 12.0	Teradata parallel Transporter: unified load facility for continuous multitable loads from a variety of source.	Tera-miner can be used with OLAP extensions	Active Data Warehousing: Integrating multi-subject, cross-channel information to optimize business opportunities	Row-based

* Hyperion is business intelligent tool used to analyze database schema.

periodic polling can be used to detect changes of interest. Useful to reduce the network load because only results are to be transmitted to the warehouse view simultaneously reduce the Query execution time.

- *Snapshot sources*: Snapshot is periodic dump of information; sources that do not provide triggers, logs, or queries. Instead, periodic dumps or snapshots of the data are provided on-line, and changes are detected by comparing successive snapshots.

The other unique features offered by different vendors are summarized in the table given below:

Thus an important problem in all of these scenarios discussed above is to develop appropriate representations for the changes to the data, especially, if a non-relational model is used. [4] Finally, we note that a different wrapper/monitor component is needed for each information source, since the functionality of the wrapper/monitor is dependent on the type of the source (database system, legacy system, news wire, etc.) as well as on the data provided by that source. Clearly, it is undesirable to hard-code a wrapper/monitor for each information source participating in a warehousing system, especially, if new information sources become available frequently. Hence, a significant research issue is to develop techniques and tools that automate or semi-automate the process of implementing wrapper/monitors, through a toolkit or specification-based approach [7].

3. CONCLUSION

Today's businesses organizations are adopting a new approach to integrate heterogeneous, multiple distributive information sources. Data warehousing is practical and superior alternative to traditional approaches. Data warehouse overcomes the drawbacks of on-demand traditional approach by following in-advance approach which continuously request, processes the queries so that the information is readily available for direct as well as parallel query analysis. However, the quality of the analysis is directly linked with the design of the database. If invalid or corrupt data is allowed to get into the data warehouse, the analysis done with this data is likely to be invalid. So, special attention should be given to the issues like slowly changing dimensions, rapidly changing dimensions, multivalued dimensions of information sources in the data warehouse environment. After the rapid acceptance of data warehousing systems during past years, there will be many more enhancements and adjustments to the data warehousing system model. Further evolution of the hardware and software technology will also continue to greatly influence the capabilities that are built into data warehouses.

References

1. Jennifer wisdom, Proc. of 4th Int'l Conference on Information and Knowledge Management, Stanford CA, Nov. 1995.
2. Available at
   A. www.or acle.com/solutions/business_intelligence/dw_home.html
   B. www.ibm.com/software/data/db2/dwe
   C. www.microsoft.com/sql/techinfo/whitepapers/sql-for-datawarehousing_2008.mspx
   D. www.sybase.com/products/datawarehousing/sybaseiq
   E. www.teradata.com/enterprise-data-warehouse
3. S. Chawathe, H. Garcia-Molina, J. Hammer, K. Ireland, Y. Papakonstantinou, J. Ullman, and J. Widom. Integration of heterogeneous information sources. In Proceedings of 100th Anniversary Meeting of the Information Processing Society of Japan, pages 7, 18, Tokyo, Japan, October 1994.
4. S. Chawathe, A. Rajaraman, H. Garcia-Molina, and J. Widom. Change detection in hierarchically structured information, technical report, Dept. of Computer Science, Stanford University, 1995.
   Available by anonymous ftp to db.stanford.edu in le pub/chawathe/1995/tdiff2-0.ps.
5. G. Wiederhold. Mediators in the architecture of future information systems. IEEE Computer.
6. J. Widom and S. Ceri. Active Database Systems: Triggers and Rules for Advanced Database Processing. Morgan Kaufmann, San Francisco, California, 1995.
7. Y. Papakonstantinou, A. Gupta, H. Garcia-Molina, and J. Ullman. A query translation scheme for rapid implementation of wrappers. In Proceedings of the Fourth International Conference on Deductive and Object-Oriented Databases, Singapore, December 1995.
8. Sugandhi Abishek, M.Tech Course Seminar report, Dept. Comp. Sc. and Engg. IIT Bombay available by www.cse.iitb.ac.in/~abhisheks/seminar/seminarreport/rep6.pdf

28

Analysis of Decision Tree—A Technique of Data Mining

SHWETA MONGIA, PRIYANKA ARORA AND ALIZA TANWIR

ABSTRACT

Advances in technology have enabled us to collect data from observations, simulations and experiments at an ever-increasing pace. For the scientist to benefit from these enhanced data collecting capabilities, it is becoming clear that semi-automated techniques, such as the ones in data mining, must be applied to find the useful information in the data. Data mining involves the use of sophisticated data analysis tools to discover previously unknown, valid patterns and relationships in large data sets. Decision tree is one common technique used in data mining to extract predicted information. Due to its inherent parallelism, it has been widely adopted in high performance applications and developed into various parallel decision tree algorithms in order to deal with huge datasets and complex computations.

1. INTRODUCTION

Generally, data mining (sometimes called data or knowledge discovery) is the process of analyzing data from different perspectives and summarizing it into useful information—information that can be used to increase revenue, cut costs or both. Consequently, data mining consists of more than collecting and managing data; it also includes analysis and prediction.

It allows users to analyze data from many different dimensions or angles, categorize it and summarize the relationships identified. Data mining can be performed on data represented in quantitative, textual, or multimedia forms. Technically, data mining is the process of finding correlations or patterns among dozens of fields in large relational databases. Data mining is a relatively unique process. Data mining involves the use of sophisticated data analysis tools to discover previously unknown, valid patterns and relationships in large data sets. These tools can include statistical models, mathematical algorithms, and machine learning methods (algorithms that improve their performance automatically through experience, such as neural networks or decision trees).

In most standard database operations, nearly all of the results presented to the user are something that they knew existed in the database already. A report showing the breakdown of sales by product line and region is straightforward for the user to understand because they intuitively know that this kind of information already exists in the database. If the company sells different products in different regions of the country, there is no problem translating a display of this information into a relevant understanding of the business process.

Data mining, on the other hand, extracts information from a database that the user did not know existed. Relationships between variables and customer behaviors, that are non-intuitive, are the jewels that data mining hopes to figure out. And because the user does not know beforehand what the data mining process has discovered, it is a much bigger leap to take the output of the system and translate it into a solution to a business problem.

Data mining is used for a variety of purposes in both the private and public sectors such as financial sectors, health centers, and oil and gas industries. Industries such as banking, insurance, medicine, and retailing commonly use data mining to reduce costs, enhance research, and increase sales.

2. DATA MINING TECHNIQUES

Data mining techniques are broadly divided into two sections, each with a specific theme:

- Classical Techniques : Statistics, Neighborhoods and Clustering.
- Next Generation Techniques : Decision Trees, Neural Networks and Rules.

These two sections have been broken up based on when the data mining technique was developed and when it became technically mature enough to be used for business, especially to aid in the optimization of customer relationship management systems.

Description of the techniques is given as follows:

- *Statistics*—Statistical techniques are driven by the data and are used to discover patterns and build predictive models.
- *Neighborhood*—Nearest neighbor is a prediction technique that is quite similar to clustering.
- *Clustering*—Clustering is the method by which like records are grouped together. Clustering and the Nearest Neighbor prediction technique are among the oldest techniques used in data mining.
- *Decision Trees*—A decision tree (or diagram) is a decision support tool that uses a graph or model of decisions and their possible consequences, including chance event outcomes, resource costs, and utility.
- *Neural Networks*—Neural networks are biological systems that detect patterns, make predictions and learn. The artificial ones are computer programs implementing sophisticated pattern detection and machine learning algorithms on a computer to build predictive models from large historical databases.
- *Rules Induction*—The rules that are pulled from the database are extracted and ordered to be presented to the user based on the percentage of times that they are correct and how often they are applied.

In this paper we are focusing on the latest technique for data mining that is Decision tree.

3. DECISION TREE

A Decision Tree is a predictive model that, as its name implies, can be viewed as a tree. Specifically, each branch of the tree is a classification question and the leaves of the tree are partitions of the dataset with their classification. The Decision Tree is one of the most popular classification algorithms which is, currently, in use in Data Mining and Machine Learning.

Following are some of the features of Decision Trees:

- It divides up the data on each branch point without losing any of the data.
- The data conserved as you move up or down the tree.
- It is pretty easy to understand how the model is being built (in contrast to the models from neural networks or from standard statistics).

From a business perspective decision trees can be viewed as creating a segmentation of the original dataset (each segment would be one of the leaves of the tree). In the past this segmentation has been performed in order to get a high level view of a large amount of data—with no particular reason for creating the segmentation except that the records within every segmentation were somewhat similar to each other.

In this case, the segmentation is done for a particular reason—namely for the prediction of some important piece of information. The records that fall within each segment fall there because they have similarity with respect to the information being predicted—not just that they are similar—without similarity being well defined. Thus, the decision trees and algorithms that create them may be complex; the results can be presented in an easy to understand way that can be quite useful to the business user.

3.1 Method of Decision Tree

Step 1.	Data Exploration	The decision tree technology can be used for exploration of the dataset and business problem. This is often done by looking at the predictors and values that are chosen for each split of the tree. Often, these predictors provide usable insights or propose questions that need to be answered.
Step 2.	Data Preprocessing	Once the data has been explored then it is processed for other prediction algorithms. Because the algorithm is fairly robust with respect to a variety of predictor types (e.g. number, categorical, etc.) and because it can be run relatively quickly, decision trees can be used on the first pass of a data mining run to create a subset of possibly useful predictors that can then be fed into neural networks, nearest neighbor and normal statistical routines—which can take a considerable amount of time to run, if, there are large number of possible predictors to be used in the model.
Step 3.	Data Prediction	Although some forms of decision trees were initially developed as exploratory tools to refine and preprocess data for more standard statistical techniques like logistic regression. They have also been used and more increasingly often being used for prediction. This is interesting because many statisticians will still use decision trees for exploratory analysis effectively building a predictive model as a by-product but then

ignore the predictive model in favor of techniques that they are most comfortable with. Sometimes veteran analysts will do this even excluding the predictive model when it is superior to that produced by other techniques. With a host of new products and skilled users now appearing this tendency to use decision trees only for exploration now seems to be changing.

3.2 Performances of Decision Trees

Decision trees are powerful and popular tools for classification and prediction. The attractiveness of decision trees is due to the fact that, in contrast to neural networks, decision trees represent rules. Rules can readily be expressed so that humans can understand them or even directly use in a database access language like SQL so that records falling into a particular category may be retrieved. In some applications, the accuracy of a classification or prediction is the only thing that matters. In such situations we do not necessarily care how or why the model works. In other situations, the ability to explain the reason for a decision is crucial. In marketing one has describe the customer segments to marketing professionals, so that they can utilize this knowledge in launching a successful marketing campaign. This domain expert must recognize and approve this discovered knowledge, and for this we need good descriptions. There are a variety of algorithms for building decision trees that share the desirable quality of interpretability. A decision tree can be used to classify an example by starting at the root of the tree and moving through it until a leaf node, which provides the classification of the instance.

Decision tree induction is a typical inductive approach to learn knowledge on classification. The key requirements to do mining with decision trees are:

- *Attribute-value description*: Object or case must be expressible in terms of a fixed collection of properties or attributes. This means that we need discrete continuous attributes, or this must have been provided in the algorithm.
- *Predefined classes (target attribute values)*: Categories to which examples are to be assigned must have been established beforehand (supervised data).
- *Discrete classes*: A case does or does not belong to a particular class, and there must be more cases than classes.
- *Sufficient data*: Usually hundreds or even thousands of training cases.

3.3 Strengths and Weakness of Decision Tree Technique

The strengths of decision tree methods are:

- Decision trees are able to generate understandable rules.
- Decision trees are able to handle both continuous and categorical variables.
- Decision trees perform classification without requiring much computation.

The weaknesses of decision tree methods are:

1. Decision trees are less appropriate for estimation tasks where the goal is to predict the value of a continuous attribute.
2. Decision trees can be computationally expensive train. The process of growing a decision tree is computationally expensive. At each node, each candidate splitting field must be sorted before its best split can be found. In some algorithms, combinations of fields are used and a search must be made for optimal combining weights. Pruning algorithms can also be expensive since many candidate sub-trees must be formed and compared.
3. Decision trees are prone to errors in classification problems with many classes and relatively small number of training examples.

References

1. CRS Report RL31798, Data Mining: An Overview, by Jeffrey W. Seifert.
2. David B. Skillicorn, Parallel Data Mining.
3. Chao-Tung Yang Shu-Tzu Tsai, Kuan-Ching Li, "Decision Tree Construction for Data Mining on Grid Computing Environments", Proceedings of the 19th International Conference on Advanced Information Networking and Applications (AINA'05).
4. M. Berry and G. Linoff, Data Mining Techniques, John Wiley, 1997.
5. Technology Report, Two Crows Corporation: "Introduction to Data Mining and Knowledge Discovery", Third Edition.

29

Evaluating Metrics for Privacy Preserving Data Mining

ARADHNA MEHTA, NANCY MEHTA AND GOPAL SINGH

ABSTRACT

Privacy preserving data mining algorithms work on security and knowledge discovery. The aim of algorithms is the extraction of relevant knowledge from large amount of data, while protecting at the same time sensitive information. Privacy preserving classification methods, instead, prevent a miner from building a classifier which is able to predict sensitive data. A crucial issue is to determine which ones among these privacy-preserving techniques better protect sensitive information. However, this is not the only criteria with respect to which these algorithms can be evaluated. It is also important to assess the quality of the data resulting from the modifications applied by each algorithm, as well as the performance of the algorithms. There is thus the need of identifying a comprehensive set of criteria with respect to which to assess the existing PPDM algorithms and determine which algorithm meets specific requirements. We propose a classification hierarchy that sets the basis for analyzing the work which has been performed in this context. A detailed review of the work accomplished in this area is also given, along with the coordinates of each work to the classification hierarchy. A brief evaluation is performed, and some initial conclusions are made.

1. INTRODUCTION

Data mining and knowledge discovery in databases are two new research areas that investigate the automatic extraction of previously unknown patterns from large amounts of data. Recent advances in data collection, data dissemination and related technologies have inaugurated a new era of research where existing data mining algorithms should be reconsidered from a different point of view, this of privacy preservation. It is well documented that this new area without limits explosion of new information through the Internet and other media, has reached to a point where threats against the privacy are very common on a daily basis and they deserve serious thinking.

Privacy preserving data mining [Chris Clifton, 1991]; [Donald Marks,1996], is a novel research direction in data mining and statistical databases [Nabil Adam and John C. Wortmann, 1989] where data mining algorithms are analyzed for the side-effects they incur in data privacy.

The main consideration in privacy preserving data mining [Rakesh Agrawal and Ramakrishnan Srikant, 2000] is two-fold. First, sensitive raw data like identifiers, names, addresses and the like should be modified or trimmed out from the original database so that the recipient of the data would not to be able to compromise another person's privacy. Second, sensitive knowledge which can be mined from a database by using data mining algorithms should also be excluded because such knowledge can equally well compromise data privacy as we will indicate. The main objective in privacy preserving data mining is to develop algorithms for modifying the original data in some way so that the private data and private knowledge remain private even after the mining process.

The problem that arises when confidential information can be derived from released data by unauthorized users is also commonly called the "database inference" problem. [LiWu Chang and Ira S. Moskowitz ,1998]. In this report, we provide a classification and an extended description of the various techniques and methodologies that have been developed in the area of privacy preserving data mining.

2. CLASSIFICATION OF PRIVACY PRESERVING TECHNIQUES

There are many approaches which have been adopted for privacy preserving data mining [LiWu Chang and Ira S. Moskowitz, 2000]. We can classify them based on the following dimensions:

- Data Distribution
- Data Modification
- Data Mining Algorithm
- Data or Rule Hiding
- Privacy Preservation

The first dimension refers to the distribution of data. Some of the approaches have been developed for centralized data, while others refer to a distributed data scenario. Distributed data scenarios can also be classified as horizontal data distribution and vertical data distribution. Horizontal distribution refers to those cases where different database records reside in different places, while vertical data distribution refers to the cases where all the values for different attributes reside in different places.

The second dimension refers to the data modification scheme. In general, data modification is used in order to modify the original values of a database that needs to be released to the public and in this way to ensure high privacy protection. It is important that a data modification technique should be in concert with the privacy policy adopted by an organization. Methods of modification include:

- Perturbation, which is accomplished by the alteration of an attribute value by a new value (i.e., changing a 1-value to a 0-value, or adding noise).
- Blocking, which is the replacement of an existing attribute value with a "?"
- Aggregation or merging which is the combination of several values into a coarser category.
- Swapping that refers to interchanging values of individual records.
- Sampling that refers to releasing data for only a sample of a population.

The third dimension refers to the data mining algorithm, for which the data modification is taking place. This is actually something that is not known beforehand, but it facilitates the analysis and design of the data hiding algorithm. We have included the problem of hiding data for a combination of data mining algorithms, into our future research agenda. For the time being, various data mining algorithms have been considered in isolation of each other. Among them, the most important ideas have been developed for classification data mining algorithms, like decision tree inducers, association rule mining algorithms, clustering algorithms, rough sets and Bayesian networks.

The fourth dimension refers to whether raw data or aggregated data should be hidden. The complexity for hiding aggregated data in the form of rules is of course higher, and for this reason, mostly heuristics have been developed. The lessening of the amount of public information causes the data miner to produce weaker inference rules that will not allow the inference of confidential values. This process is also known as "rule confusion".

The last dimension which is the most important refers to the privacy preservation technique used for the selective modification of the data. Selective modification is required in order to achieve higher utility for the modified data, given that the privacy is not jeopardized. The techniques that have been applied for this reason are:

- Heuristic-based techniques like adaptive modification that modifies only selected values that minimize the utility loss rather than all available values.

- Cryptography-based techniques like secure multiparty computation where a computation is secure if at the end of the computation, no party knows anything except its own input and the results.
- Reconstruction-based techniques where the original distribution of the data is reconstructed from the randomized data.

It is important to realize that data modification results in degradation of the database performance. In order to quantify the degradation of the data, we mainly use two metrics. The first one, measures the confidential data protection, while the second measures the loss of functionality.

3. REVIEW OF PRIVACY PRESERVING ALGORITHMS

3.1. Randomization-based Techniques

The randomization algorithm is chosen so that aggregate properties of the data can be recovered with sufficient precision, while individual entries are significantly distorted.

Suppose that some company needs to construct an aggregate model of its customer's personal data. For example, a retail store wants to know the age and income of its customers who are more likely to buy DVD players or mountain ski equipment; a movie recommendation system would like to learn users' movie preferences in order to make advertisements more targeted; or an on-line business arranges its web pages according to an aggregate model of its website visitors. In all these cases, there is one central server (the company), and many clients (the customers), each having a piece of information. The server collects this information and builds its aggregate model using, for example, a classification algorithm or an algorithm for mining association rules. Often the resulting model no longer contains personally identifiable information, but contains only averages over large groups of clients.

The usual solution to the above problem consists of having all clients send their personal information to the server. However, many people are becoming increasingly concerned about the privacy of their personal data. They would like to avoid giving out much more about themselves than is required to run their business with the company. If all the company needs aggregate model, a solution is preferred that reduces the disclosure of private data while still allowing the server to build the model. One possibility is as follows: before sending its piece of data, each client perturbs it so that some true information is taken away and some false information is introduced. This approach is called randomization.

Another possibility is to decrease precision of the transmitted data by rounding, suppressing certain values, replacing values with intervals, or replacing categorical values by more general categories up the taxonomical hierarchy [G.T. Duncan, R. Krishnan, R. Padman, P. Reuther, and S. Roehrig, 1997].

The usage of randomization for preserving privacy has been studied extensively in the framework of statistical databases [G.T. Duncan and S. Mukherjee, 2000]. In that case, the server has a complete and precise database with the information from its clients, and it has to make a version of this database public, for others to work with. One important example is census data: the government of a country collects private information about its inhabitants, and then, has to turn this data into a tool for research and economic planning. However, it is not assumed that private records of any given person should not be released nor be recoverable from what is released. In particular, a company should not be able to match up records in the publicly released database with the corresponding records in the company's own database of its customers.

In the case of statistical databases, however, the database is randomized when it is already fully known. This is different from our problem where the randomization procedure is run on the client's side, and must be decided upon before the data is collected. A randomization for a statistical database is, usually, chosen so that it preserves certain aggregate characteristics (averages and covariance matrices for numerical data, or marginal totals in contingency tables for categorical data), or changes them in a predetermined way. Besides randomization, other privacy preserving transformations are used such as sampling and swapping values among records. Our choice is more limited due to the nature of our problem.

3.2. Cryptography-based Techniques

A number of cryptography-based approaches [Yehuda Lindell and Benny Pinkas, 2000] have been developed in the context of privacy preserving data mining algorithms to solve problems of the following nature. Two or more parties want to conduct a computation based on their private inputs, but neither party is willing to disclose its own output to anybody else. The issue here is how to conduct such a computation while preserving the privacy of the inputs.

This problem is referred to as the Secure Multiparty Computation (SMC) problem [Wenliang Du and Mikhail J. Attalah, 2001]. In particular, an SMS problem deals with computing a probabilistic function on any input, in a distributed network where each participant holds one of the inputs, ensuring independence of the inputs, correctness of the computation, and that no more information is revealed to a participant in the computation than that's participant's input and output.

Two of the papers falling into this area, are rather general in nature and we describe them first. The first one proposes a transformation framework that allows to systematically transform normal computations to secure multiparty computation [Wenliang Du and Mikhail J. Attalah, 2001]. Among other information items, a discussion on transformation of various data mining problems to a secure multiparty computation [Wenliang Du and Mikhail J. Attalah, 2001] is demonstrated. The data mining applications which are described in this domain include data classification, data clustering, association rule mining, data generalization, data summarization and data characterization. The second paper [Yehuda Lindell and Benny Pinkas, 2000] presents four secure multiparty computation-based methods that can support privacy preserving data mining. The methods described include, the secure sum, the secure set union, the secure size of set intersection, and the scalar product. Secure sum is, often, given as a simple example of secure multiparty computation, and we present it here as well, as a representative for the techniques used. Assume that the value u=$\sum_{l=1}^{8} u_l$ *to* be computed is known to lie in the range [0, n]. One site is designated as the master site and is given the identity 1. The remaining sites are numbered 2. . , s. Site 1 generates a random number R, uniformly chosen from [0, n]. Site 1 adds this number to its local value $u1$ and sends the sum $R + u1 \bmod n$ to site 2. Since the value of R is chosen uniformly from [0, n] the number $R + u1 \bmod n$ is also distributed uniformly across this region, so site 2 learns nothing about the actual value of u1. For the remaining sites l = 2. . .s –1, the algorithm is as follows. Site l receives mod n.

Since this value is uniformly distributed across v=R+$\sum_{j=1}^{l-1} u_j$ [0, n], i learns nothing. Site i then computes $R + \sum_{j=1}^{l} u_j \bmod n = (u_j + V) \bmod n$ and passes it to site $l + 1$. Site s performs the above step, and sends the result to site 1. Site 1, by knowing R, can subtract R to get the actual result. Below we present the approaches which have been developed by using the solution framework of secure multiparty computation. It should be made clear that because of the nature of this solution methodology, the data in all of the cases that this solution is adopted is distributed among two or more sites.

4. EVALUATION OF PRIVACY PRESERVING ALGORITHMS

An important aspect in the development and assessment of algorithms and tools, for privacy preserving data mining is the identification of suitable evaluation criteria and the development of related benchmarks.

It is often the case that no privacy preserving algorithm exists [Dakshi Agrawal and Charu C. Aggarwal, 2001] that outperforms all the others on all possible criteria. Rather, an algorithm may perform better than another one on specific criteria, such as performance and/or data utility. It is, thus, important to provide users with a set of metrics which will enable them to select the most appropriate privacy preserving technique for the data at hand; with respect to some specific parameters they are interested in optimizing.

A preliminary list of evaluation parameters to be used for assessing the quality of privacy preserving data mining algorithms is given below:

- The *performance* of the proposed algorithms in terms of time requirements, that is the time needed by each algorithm to hide a specified set of sensitive information.
- The *data utility* after the application of the privacy preserving technique, which is equivalent with the minimization of the information loss or else the loss in the functionality of the data.
- The *level of uncertainty* with which the sensitive information that have been hidden can still be predicted.
- The *resistance* accomplished by the privacy algorithms, to different data mining techniques.

Below, we refer to each one of these evaluation parameters and we analyze them.

4.1 Performance of the proposed algorithms

A first approach in the assessment of the time requirements of a privacy preserving algorithm is to evaluate the computational cost. In this case, it is straightforward that an algorithm having an $O(n^2)$ polynomial complexity is more efficient than another one with $O(en)$ exponential complexity.

An alternative approach would be to evaluate the time requirements in terms of the average number of operations needed to reduce the frequency of appearance of specific sensitive information below a specified threshold. This value, perhaps, does not provide an absolute measure, but it can be considered in order to perform a fast comparison among different algorithms.

The communication cost incurred during the exchange of information among a number of collaborating sites should also be considered. It is imperative that this cost must be kept to a minimum for a distributed privacy preserving data mining algorithm.

4.2 Data Utility

The utility of the data, at the end of the privacy preserving process, is an important issue because in order to hide sensitive information, the database is essentially modified through the insertion of false information (swapping of values is a side effect in this case) or through the blocking of data values.

We should notice here that some of privacy preserving techniques, like the use of sampling, do not modify the information stored in the database, but still, the utility of the data falls since the information is not complete in this case. It is obvious that the more the changes are made to the database, the less the database reflects the domain of interest. Therefore, an evaluation parameter for the data utility should be the amount of information that is lost after the application of privacy preserving process. Of course, the measure used to evaluate the information loss depends on the specific data mining technique with respect to which a privacy algorithm is performed.

For example, information loss in the context of association rule mining will be measured either in terms of the number of rules that were both remaining and lost in the database after sanitization, or even, in terms on the reduction/increase in the support and confidence of all the rules. For the case of classification, we can use metrics similar to those used for association rules. Finally, for clustering, the variance of the distances among the clustered items in the original database and the sanitized database can be the basis for evaluating information loss in this case.

4.3 Uncertainty Level

The privacy preservation strategies operate by downgrading the information that we want to protect below certain thresholds. The hidden information, however, can still be inferred even though with some uncertainty level. A sanitization algorithm, then, can be evaluated on the basis of the uncertainty that it introduces during the reconstruction of the hidden information. From an operational point of view, a scenario would be to set a maximum to the perturbation of information, and then consider the degree of uncertainty achieved by each sanitization algorithm under this constraint. We expect that the algorithm that will attain the maximum uncertainty level will be the one which will be preferred over all the rest.

4.4 Endurance of Resistance to Different Data Mining Techniques

The ultimate aim of hiding algorithms is the protection of sensitive information against unauthorized disclosure. In this case, it is important not to forget, that intruders and data terrorists will try to compromise information by using various data mining algorithms. Consequently, a sanitization algorithm developed against a particular data mining technique that assures privacy of information may not attain similar protection [LiWu Chang and Ira S. Moskowitz, 2000] against all possible data mining algorithms.

In order to provide for a complete evaluation of sanitization algorithms, we need to measure its endurance against data mining techniques which are different from the technique that a sanitization algorithm has been developed for. We call such a parameter the transversal endurance. The evaluation of this parameter needs the consideration of a class of data mining algorithms which are significant for our test. Alternatively, we may need to develop a formal framework that upon testing of a sanitization algorithm against pre-selected data sets, we can transitively prove privacy assurance for the whole class of sanitization algorithms.

5. CONCLUSION

We have presented a classification and an extended description of various privacy preserving data mining algorithms. The work presented here, indicates the ever increasing interest of researchers in the area of securing sensitive data and knowledge from malicious users. The conclusions that we have reached from reviewing this area manifest that privacy issues can be effectively considered only within the limits of certain data mining algorithms. The inability to generalize the results for classes of categories of data mining algorithms might be a tentative threat for disclosing information.

REFERENCES

1. Chris Clifton and Donald Marks (1996), Security and privacy implications of data mining, in proceedings of the ACM SIGMOD Workshop on Research Issues on Data Mining and Knowledge Discovery, 15-19.
2. Dakshi Agrawal and Charu, C. Aggarwal (2001), on the Design and Quantification of Privacy Preserving data Mining Algorithms, In Proceedings of the 20th ACM Symposium on Principles of Database Systems, 247-55.
3. Daniel, E. O'Leary (1991), Knowledge Discovery as a Threat to Database Security, In Proceedings of the 1st International Conference on Knowledge Discovery and Databases, 107-516.
4. G.T. Duncan, R. Krishnan, R. Padman, P. Reuther, and S. Roehrig (1997), Cell suppression to limit content-based disclosure. In Proceedings of the 30th Hawaii International Conference on System Sciences, Vol. 3. IEEE Computer Society Press.
5. G.T. Duncan and S. Mukherjee (2000), Optimal disclosure limitation strategy in statistical Databases: Deterring tracker attacks through additive noise. *Journal of the American Statistical Association*, 95(451), 720-29.
6. LiWu Chang and Ira S. Moskowitz (1998), Parsimonious downgrading and decision trees applied to the inference problem, In Proceedings of the 1998 New Security Paradigms Workshop, 82-89.
7. LiWu Chang and Ira S. Moskowitz (2000), an integrated framework for database inference and privacy protection, Data and Applications Security, 161-72, Kluwer, IFIP WG 11.3, The Netherlands.
8. Nabil Adam and John, C. Wortmann (1989), Security-Control Methods for Statistical Databases: A Comparison Study, *ACM Computing Surveys* 21, No. 4, 515-56.
9. Rakesh Agrawal and Ramakrishnan Srikant (2000), Privacy-preserving Data Mining, In Proceedings of the ACM SIGMOD Conference on Management of Data, 439-50.
10. Wenliang Du and Mikhail, J. Attalah (2001). Secure multi-problem computation problems and their applications: A review and open problems, Tech. SIGMOD Record, Vol. 33, No. 1, March 2004, 56, Report CERIAS Tech Report 2001-51, Center for Education and Research in Information Assurance and Security and Department of Computer Sciences, Purdue University, West Lafayette, IN 47906.
11. Yehuda Lindell and Benny Pinkas (2000), Privacy preserving data mining, In Advances in Cryptology-CRYPTO, 36-54.

30

Comparative Analysis of OODB Architectures

AMANDEEP KAUR

ABSTRACT

The Object Oriented Database Management System (OODBMS) have now been in existence for nearly two decades. The major vendors conceived and began implementing them in the late 80's accommodating OO languages like Smalltalk, C++ and Java, with commercial products shipping in the mid-90's. In the beginning, there was a great expectation that the OODBMS would replace the RDBMS as the database of choice for future applications.

The "great expectation" has not come to fruition and it is an assertion in this paper that one of the major reasons for this comes down to OODBMS architecture. That is, the OODBMS architecture and it's impact on the expectations of early adopters. Many successfully deployed applications have demonstrated that choosing the right OODBMS architecture allows the building of high performance, highly concurrent and scalable solutions. This paper seeks to examine the issue of expectation along with examining the differences between the three most common commercial OODB architectures.

1. INTRODUCTION

At the time the OODB started commercial deployments, relational technology was already well rooted and while still a hearty battle ground, the major relational vendors had all staked out a portion of the database market. At the time, businesses were actually transitioning away from making application database infrastructure technology decisions to making application business capability decisions. The database comparisons had all, but been made and heavily publicized. Application suites with the highly desired business capabilities either came from an incumbent relational database vendor or were designed to support any relational database by adhering to the SQL standards. The characteristics of the databases were close enough that there was no particular advantage to be held by supporting one vendor over others. The general perception was that relational databases were very similar in capabilities and these similarities were well documented. So, the decision of which database to use was often more political than technical, facilitating business alliances rather than necessitating a choice for "best" solution left up to the purchaser of the application. The general perception was indeed true, there are little differences from one relational vendor to the next, and performance and scalability numbers showed variations by percentage points rather than orders of magnitude.

This is where OODB architecture and user expectations get into the mix. While RDB architectures are very similar (server centric, index-based, relational algebra execution engines) exhibiting performance and scalability characteristics differentiated by small percentages, OODB architectures vary considerably and exhibit wildly different characteristics. After so many years of conditioning that RDB's behave essentially the same, it was rather natural to apply the same reasoning to the ODB and proclaim, they are basically the same. In making that assumption, if by chance an early adopter choose an ODB whose architecture was ill-suited for their application needs, the reasoning lead immediately to the conclusion that no ODB was suited to solve their needs. From this illogical thinking came the permeation of misconceptions regarding the OODB: they are too slow, they don't handle high concurrency, they don't scale with large data, etc. These are all misconceptions and the reality is that you need to carefully consider your application characteristics and understand which OODB architecture is best suited to fulfil them. Choosing the right OODB architecture can mean orders of magnitude difference in performance and scalability characteristics rather than a few percentage points as found in relational implementations. Armed with this understanding, lets now explore the differences so that one can make an informed decision which will assist in leading to the successful adoption of the technology.

There are several key distinguishing implementation differences that lead to the vastly different runtime characteristics. The primary areas include: the core architecture, the concurrency model, the query implementation, the network model and identity management.

2. CORE ARCHITECTURE

The following presents three well known OODB architectural implementations. Each OODB implementation provides degrees of distribution, parallel processing and remoting that are used to create elaborate system level designs, but these are the core architectural types underpinning those systems. In this paper they are termed as: container-based, page-based and object-based which reflects both their unit of transfer-across network calls and lowest level granularity of locking. Each in turn provides caching, query processing, transactions and object lifecycle management. Let's take a look at each more closely.

2.1 Container Based Architecture

The "container-based" architecture is a client centric design. It uses standard to ship segments of disk around the network, called containers, to the clients which implement the majority of the database functionality. The user application code is linked with the database client libraries which provide caching of containers, query processing, transactions and object life cycle management. All objects must reside inside a container and a container can hold many objects, multiple containers can be used if the limit per container is reached. In this architecture, application developers must ensure container models are layered over application domain models to facilitate access to objects within database.

FIG. 30.1

Container Based Architecture Based Archetecture

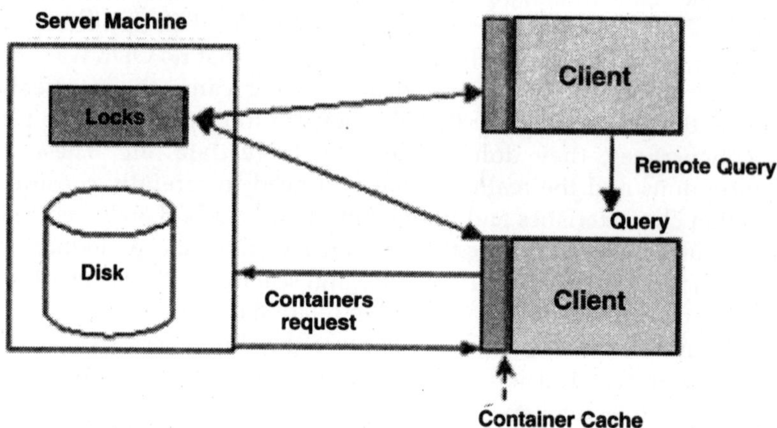

2.2 Page Based Architecture

The "page-based" architecture is a client centric design which runs a server process to fulfil page requests in a distributed virtual memory mapping model. It uses a server process to ship pages of disk around the network which get address translated into the virtual memory space of the application, where the majority of the database functionality is implemented. The user application code is linked with the database client

FIG. 30.2
Page Based Architecture

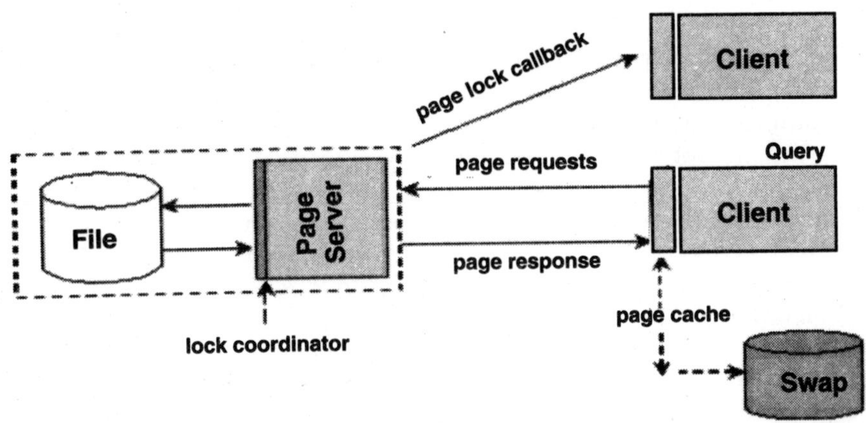

libraries which provide caching of pages, query processing, transactions, and object life cycle management. Special object placement strategies have to be implemented.

2.3 Object Based Architecture

The "object-based" architecture is a balanced design with caching and behavior in both the application and database server processes. The server process caches pages of disk and manages indexes, locks, queries and transactions. The user application code is linked with the database client libraries which provide object caching, local locking and object lifecycle management. No special object placement strategies need to be implemented.

FIG. 30.3
Object Based Architecture

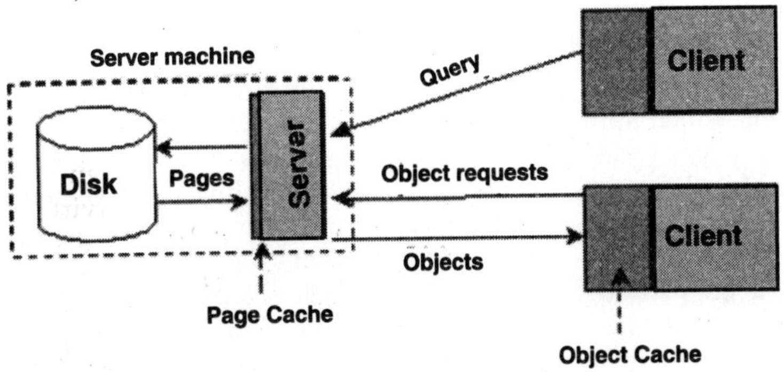

3. CONCURRENCY MODEL

The three core architectures have differing concurrency control models as described below. The concurrency models solve the issue of transaction isolation and are closely tied with the network behavioral characteristics. Each architecture has it's ways of relaxing locking for certain types of applications where full ACID (Atomic, Consistent, Isolated, Durable) properties are not required. The following is focused on behavior required for the consistency and isolation of proper database transactions that are not relaxing the ACID properties. All implementations can cache locks locally at the client across transaction boundaries to minimize unnecessary lock requests. However, updates will always cause lock coordination and cache consistency operations. With container and page-based systems, object placement and locking are tightly coupled while in the object-based systems these issues are orthogonal. Let's take a look at how each one of architecture deals with these issues.

3.1 Container-Concurrency

In this design, a separate lock server process coordinates concurrent access to information in the same container. Clients coordinate with a centralized lock process to request locks on containers in each database on a server machine before being allowed to cache a container at the client through the NFS page server. A request for update will establish a lock request queue on a container if there are existing readers of that container.

The requests will either time-out or go through when existing clients release their locks on the container. Locks are generally released at transaction boundaries. When a queue is established by an update request, all other subsequent requests fall in queue behind the update request. Once the update request has been filled, all queued read requests rush in and get their read lock, return the container pages, and if there are no other updates, the queue disappears. Clients who had cached an updated container must refresh the container on subsequent read. Containers can hold many objects, so it is possible to get false waits and false dead locks.

3.2 Page-Concurrency

In this design, the page server coordinates concurrent access by tracking which applications are accessing each page, granting permissions to lock pages locally, and using lock callbacks. A request for update will cause the page server to use callbacks, requesting other clients to release their locks on that page and give up permissions to lock the page locally. All clients either release their lock and permissions to lock locally and the request goes through or it blocks on each objecting client for a specified duration. Each client that released its permissions will refresh the page and acquire new permissions and locks on the next access of information on the page, going through the process just described. Locks and permissions are taken out at the page level and pages may contain many objects, so false waits and false deadlocks can occur.

3.3 Object-Concurrency

In this design, the database server process maintains lock request queues at the object level to control concurrency of access to the same object. A request for update will establish a queue if there are any existing readers of an object. The request either goes through when all current readers release their locks or times-out. Locks are generally released at transaction boundaries. When a queue is established by an update request, all other subsequent requests fall in queue behind the update request. Once the update request has been filled, all read requests in the queue rush in and get their read lock, return the object, and if there are no other updates, the queue disappears. Clients who had cached an updated object must refresh the object on subsequent read. In this architecture, locks are done at the object level so false waits and false deadlocks do not occur.

3.4 Concurrency Model Implications

The different concurrency models can impact application performance in multi-user environments which have many updates. Applications which have conflicting updates are potentially hampered by all concurrency models, but that is why there are concurrency models. Applications which have heavy updates, but not necessarily conflicting updates, are potentially hampered further by both container and page-based architectures due to the fact that locking occurs in a way that can block other objects not involved in the transaction introducing false waits and deadlocks.

In addition to potential pitfalls on false waits and deadlocks, the granularity of the objects involved in the application transactions can have greater impact on architecture over the other. In the page-based architecture, due to locking callbacks, a lot more network calls are required to coordinate lock release in a highly granular update system.

Applications which have relatively fixed models, well segmented into an independent cluster with mostly non-conflicting updates, will generally do best in page and container-based architectures. This is true because only high level locking is required and mostly non-conflicting updates will minimize lock coordination. One example which fits well with these characteristics is a CAD (Computer Aided Design) type application. For applications of this type, using an OODB can provide orders of magnitude improvement in performance over traditional relational databases. Applications which have increasing levels of conflicting updates and increasing granularity of models, will generally do best in the object-based architecture.

The implications of performance under concurrency are, generally, tied to the number of concurrent users or processes. The issues above are exaggerated in their effect as the user-base or number of processes accessing the database system is increased. In general, the object-based architecture is best suited for the largest numbers of concurrent users and processes, especially, in systems that are not well segmented for isolation.

The other issues surrounding the concurrency models involve long-term expected use of the data. including evolution and maintenance of the applications. In many systems, fixed, well segmented data, can be achieved for a given application and its access patterns. An important question arises regarding the introduction of newer applications or increased capabilities of existing applications over the original data. New applications and capabilities often require different access patterns. As the number of access patterns increase, designs that remain fixed and well segmented become much more difficult to achieve and changing the object placement strategy has a major effort and impact. In effect, an adopter of the technology should consider future use of the data carefully during the selection process.

As discussed below, note that lock coordination also has tremendous implications on the network model, because an update will require network activity to refresh client caches.

4. NETWORK IMPLEMENTATION

The three core architectures have differing network models affecting the bandwidth utilization and performance in a distributed system design. Each network model is closely tied to the locking model whereupon obtaining a lock, the subsequent transfer of information occurs unless already cached locally. The lowest level granularity of the transfer across the network is tied to the lowest granularity of the lock.

4.1 Container-Network

For this architecture, the unit of transfer on object request is the container. All objects must reside in a container and a client request for an object is resolved by the NFS server sending the container's pages across the network to the client where the container is cached and the object subsequently accessed. When transferring the container, all objects contained will also be transferred, regardless, if they are accessed or not. When transferring the container, a lock is placed on the container regardless which specific objects in the container are actually accessed by the clients requesting transaction.

4.2 Page-Network

For this architecture, the unit of transfer on object request is the page. All objects must reside in a page and a client request for an object is resolved by the page server paging across the network to the client where it is address translated and cached and the object subsequently accessed. When transferring the page, all objects residing on the page will also be transferred, regardless, if they are accessed or not. When transferring the page, a lock is placed on the page regardless which specific objects on the page are actually accessed by the clients requesting transaction.

4.3 Object-Network

For this architecture, the unit of transfer on object request is an object or group of objects depending on specified depth as illustrated below. An object may be a collection in which case many objects are transferred in a single network call. An object or collection request may include a depth request which will retrieve related objects at each depth in a single network call. When transferring an object, a lock is placed on the object. In the case of a collection and/or depth request, a lock is placed on each object sent to the client. For example, if all objects in the following illustration were to be loaded to the client, it would take 3 network requests. If only the employees themselves or one particular employee were requested, then only a single network call would be required. Customized depth requests are possible, allowing use case specific loading patterns which eliminate excess object loading while minimizing network calls.

4.4 Network Model Implications

The different network models can impact application performance by impacting the number of network calls and simultaneously bandwidth utilization impacted by the amount of relevant data that is sent across the network. The behavior in a networked environment is closely tied to the application models and access characteristics.

An application whose characteristics are to access a mostly fixed model, well segmented into an independent cluster, in a non-conflicting update and/or without lots of small transactional updates, will generally perform well with a container or page-based architecture. This is because network calls are limited, grabbing a fixed container of related objects and moving them to the client cache in a single network call. Fixed models, tied to a specific use case where other logically related objects will be accessed at the same time in the same transaction, work well in these architectures because all logically related objects will already be located in the client cache after first object access and network calls will be minimized with efficient bandwidth utilization. The object-based architecture will generally require more network calls, a call for each level of depth in the model. For example, this could lead to 1-to-3 ratio in network calls for a model like that shown in the figure above. However, this is assuming all objects in the figure are in the same page or container. If they were segmented (physically clustered) differently, then it is possible to have even more network calls in the page or container-based architecture than in the object-based architecture. For this reason, the networked performance and for that matter, the performance under concurrency is critically tied to the physical layout of objects on disk for both the page and container-based architectures. In an application with these characteristics, bandwidth utilization will be nearly as efficient in all architectures because groups of logically-related objects will be transferred and excess objects will not be moved across the network.

As conflicting updates increase, performance with page and container-based architectures will decrease and the object-based architecture will provide an advantage. This is because conflicting updates will necessitate cache refresh in conflicted clients. For page and container-based architectures, this can mean that pages or containers are need to be shipped around the network for cache consistency. The biggest penalty here is network bandwidth, because if only a single object of a few bytes is updated, several thousand bytes, the page or container, will need to be refreshed across potentially many client processes. The full page or container refresh is required because this is the smallest unit of granularity in the network model.

To clarify what is meant here by conflicting updates, "conflicting" is not necessarily the update of the same object, but updates of objects that are in the same page or container. This is why for container and page-based architectures, the model needs to be well segmented in a physical cluster, because if not well segmented, then even updates to non-related objects can cause conflicts at the page or container level which leads to lock waiting and network utilization to ensure cache consistency. The reason small transactional updates need to be avoided with container and page-based architectures, is because an update must write the smallest unit of data transfer, the page or container, across the network for long-term storage. If updates can be well batched together in a single transaction impacting a single page or container, then performance will not suffer as a result of the architecture and in fact application performance will excel tremendously as compared to the traditional relational system.

As conflicting updates increase, the object-based network model shows advantage because the granularity of transfer is much smaller. If an object only a few bytes in size is updated and requires a refresh from clients for cache consistency, only that few bytes is transferred across the network. Further, the notion of conflicting updates changes a bit. In all architectures, any update requires cache consistency work. So, if models are fixed and well segmented, then the object, page and container-based architectures behave nearly the same except the size of data transfer across the network is different. However, if the models are not well segmented and/or object relationships span pages or containers with only a few objects in the page or container getting impacted, then many pages or containers with lots of excess objects potentially need to be refreshed and that means a lot more network bandwidth will get utilized transferring the excess objects around the network in addition to the objects that truly need refreshing.

Another implication of the concurrency and network model for architecture is in how they behave in multi-tiered architectures, embedded inside an application server middleware. All of the issues above apply, because caching is done locally in the application servers and so the issues and behavior described above are required to keep the cache consistency across the cluster of application servers which are in essence a cluster of OODB database clients.

Of course, all of the above is again impacted by increasing numbers of users or processes accessing the database. The issues above are exaggerated in their affect as the user base or numbers of processes accessing the database system are increased. In general, the object-based architecture is best suited for the largest number of concurrent users and or processes, especially in systems that are not well segmented for isolation or require flexibility in future proofing more access patterns.

Hopefully from the above discussion it is clear that each architecture's network model has it's advantages and disadvantages. The page and container architectures require careful physical layout of application models to achieve optimal performance. In a fixed model that is well segmented, this results in efficient network utilization. This benefit comes at the cost of rigidity in access patterns which can impact long-term data use and performance under high concurrency. The object-based architecture requires a logical use case understanding for optimal performance. Unlike with page and container-based architectures which need that understanding for physical modeling, the object-based architecture needs the understanding so each application can use special coding or meta data to define use case based model loading. The effort is rewarded by facilitating high concurrency and scalability for extremely large number of transactions while improving flexibility in allowing overlapping access patterns for future data use.

5. QUERY IMPLEMENTATION

Object database implementations focus on their ability to navigate seamlessly between related objects using the language constructs. The native support of a navigational access pattern is a key advantage of OODBMS over the RDBMS complex join concept. Essentially, relationships are a static part of the system rather than runtime calculated, which makes them inherently faster to use. For each implementation, it is theoretically possible to define one master object which once retrieved would provide navigational access to everything else in the database. However, as a matter of practicality, application implementations are typically use case driven. It does not make sense to needlessly bring in objects that are not relevant to the use case. Further, the scalability requirements of large databases mandate efficient use of disk, network and memory. So, object databases provide a means of querying to retrieve the first level objects of a use case and then allow subsequent navigation from those starting objects. Again, it is not meant here to explain the detailed behavior of each query engine, but instead the fundamentals of the implementation. Specific details like the ability to return id's, for lazy loading, instead of actual objects, etc. are left out.

5.1 Container-Query

The container-based implementation uses query processing at the client. The "client" may be another remoted instance of a client, but it is a process separate from the NFS page server process. You can contrast this with the typical relational database which is the opposite in architecture. In the RDB, everything is contained within the database server process: query, indexing, locking, and page management making it a server centric implementation *versus* a client centric implementation. In the container-based implementation, all objects from the database server involved in the query must be identified by database/container which includes any potential indexes, and loaded into the client process for query execution. Once all potential objects or indexes are loaded and the query is executed, the results returned are containers holding the resulting objects that satisfied the query. The result as seen from the network and locking perspective may therefore contain many objects that did not actually satisfy the query predicate. If the client was remoted, then results are returned through several tiers to the original requesting client process. Through a combination of system wide identifiers, multi-threading, remoting and aggregation, parallel distributed queries are possible.

5.2 Page-Query

The page-based implementation uses query processing at the client. In the page-based implementation, all objects from the database server involved in the query must be contained within collections that are loaded into the client process for query execution. Queries and indexing can only operate on these collections. Once the collection of objects is loaded and the query is executed, the results are references to the objects that satisfied the query predicate and implicitly the pages containing those objects have already been loaded across the network and address translated into the client memory space. The result as seen from the network and locking perspective may therefore contain many objects that did not actually satisfy the query predicate.

5.3 Object-Query

The object-based implementation uses a query execution engine that runs within the database server process. Any object in the database is reachable via query even if it has no relationship to other objects. Object attributes can be indexed with maintenance done by the database server. The query is done as a statement sent to the server, executed using an optimizer and indexing on the server, and a result set of objects returned to the client. The only thing transferred across the network is the statement for execution to the server and the collection of objects satisfying the predicate back to the client. Through the use of system wide identifiers, multi-threading and aggregation, parallel distributed queries are possible.

5.4 Query Model Implications

The different query models can impact application performance significantly. The primary factors in achieving optimal performance are:

(1) where does the query execution take place,
(2) flexibility on what can be queried, and
(3) indexing capabilities.

The object database implementations have always focused on navigational access as the primary means of retrieving information from the database. Again, it is not the intent here to dissect all query capabilities, like projection, aggregation, views, mathematical evaluation, cursors, composite indexing, etc. The intent here is to provide an understanding of the core implementation. As a general rule, none of the implementations were as complete as people have come to expect in the relational world where all access to data is via query. Fortunately, this has been changing, as all the vendors gain a new understanding of the complementary role of query and navigational access. It is reasonably safe to say, that after nearly 2 decades, all of the implementations have matured capabilities that make them useful; the real question now is one of scalability and performance.

The single biggest killer of performance in query operations is when the potential objects that satisfy the query need to be moved to another process space for predicate evaluation. This can have tremendous performance implications, especially, when there is large data involved. The page and container-based query implementations suffer from this problem.

The page-based architecture, in particular, is most vulnerable to this problem as only objects which exist in special collections can be the subject of a query and indexes apply only to those collections. All pages containing the objects in those collections or, if indexed, the indexes for those collections must be loaded across the network for query execution. Those pages will undoubtedly contain many unnecessary objects wasting network bandwidth and performance as more time can be spent transferring the pages than actually evaluating the query. Think of the case where there are a million objects, but you are only looking for one of them. Plus, any insertion, then, requires that potential indexes are maintained and since they, are potentially distributed across many client processes, there are potentially many page invalidation's and refreshes across the network for the collection and indexes adding to the network bandwidth consumption.

The container-based architecture behaves in the same way as the page based architecture. However, queries are remotable, can be split and indexes are maintained in a centralized process. So, even though containers of objects and/or indexes must be loaded into another process for evaluation, execution can be done in parallel and only the containers satisfying the results of the predicate need to be moved across the network to the originating tier of the calling client. While not ideal, this is more scalable than the query design in the page-based architectural implementation.

The object-based design, which offers server side indexing and query execution similar to relational databases, offers the optimal query capabilities among these architectures. There are no excess objects that need to get moved across processes; indexes are managed locally, and execution optimization is performed in the database server process returning only the object or set of objects that satisfy the predicate. Further, multi-threading in the client process allows the query execution to be performed in parallel across multiple physical databases. With page and container-based systems, the index management is, typically, integrated into the application code. This has an impact on the maintenance of the applications. With object-based systems, the index is managed by the server. New indices can be defined without changing the application.

6. CONCLUSION

Understanding the core architectural implementation of an OODB and matching it with the characteristics of your application use can make the difference between success or failure in the adoption of OODB technology. Unlike relational technology, a given OODB's architecture can exhibit orders of magnitude difference in performance and scalability under a given set of application characteristics. Page and container-based architectures provide a good solution for applications with relatively fixed models, low or medium concurrency and well segmented data. With object-based architectures, the concepts of object locking, object placement and object shipment are independent and provide the best solution for high concurrency, growing and evolving applications and data.

An adopter should consider carefully such issues as data growth over time, number of concurrent users or processes, expected future requirements on changing domain models, and the anticipated demand on the network. It has been proven time and again that the object database can be a superior solution to relational technology for applications with complex domain models that don't fit well in the relational storage paradigm. Choosing an OODBMS with the right architecture for your application is the key to harnessing the power of the technology and ensuring success.

REFERENCES

1. Versant Object Database Fundamental Manual http://www.versant.com/developer/resources/objectdatabase/documentation/database_fund_man.pdf
2. Objectivity Inc. Technical Overview http://www.objectivity.com/Misc/docs/oodb_techOverview.pdf
3. Locking and Concurrency, Objectivity Inc, http://wwwasd.web.cern.ch/wwwasd/lhc++/Objectivity/V5.2/Java/guide/jgdLocking.fm.html
4. Object Store Architecture Introductory http://www.techsmiths.com/wapug/exch03/white_papers/objectstore/OStoreVMAA2_redux.doc

31

MIS—Evolution, Stages and Selected Applications of Data Mining Techniques

JAGJIT SINGH AND LAKWINDER KAUR

ABSTRACT

While MIS is very broad and has all encompassing aspects the authors in this paper try to trace the development of MIS concepts and usage ending with the latest concept of Data Mining. For most management professionals, MIS means something of a 'computer' technology, which someone with a background or education in computers can tackle. Here, the authors have tried to relate (by taking few applications) that Data Mining is a technique which can be used by management practitioners, albeit, with a little help from computer professionals. The article introduces the evolution of MIS and the stages in which MIS can be implemented in the field of education and goes on to discuss the basics of data mining techniques with selected examples in various fields like education, retailing, crime, etc. The article aims at assisting the executives in varied fields to vision out the prospective implementation of data mining.

1. INTRODUCTION

Management professionals and more so marketing professionals are normally wary of the use of computers and quantitative techniques in their day-to-day applications. Though with increasing number of professionals finding their way into their fields, apart from the mundane percentage analysis, pie charts, and bar charts, etc. a basic understanding and use of elementary techniques like regression and time series analysis are finding increasing acceptability. These are the stepping stones to data mining which are attempted in the following sections.

There are various ways of looking at the development of a Management Information System (MIS), and, consequently different ways of looking at it. On the basis of physical components MIS is described in terms of its components viz. hardware, software, database, procedures, operating personnel, input and output, etc. On the basis of information system processing functions MIS could be in terms of Transaction Processing System and Decision Support System. Transaction Processing System is the system used for routine transactions and is a store house of information which could be used by various applications. Using Decision Support System, decisions can be structured or unstructured or lie anywhere in the continuum between the two. Structured decisions can be programmed and can be fairly easily automated. On the basis of levels of management activities, management hierarchy can be classified into three levels viz. strategic planning level, management control level, operational control level. The design and requirement of information system is different for each of these levels. According to organizational functions, management information system can also be organized around various functional areas of the organization viz. Production, sales and marketing, finance and accounts, materials, personnel and information system, etc. Other areas for which management information system can be applied could be general support systems, i.e. Business expert systems, knowledge management systems and strategic information systems. These systems could be of interest to management practitioners who are looking for meaningful patterns that could be of commercial value.

2. FROM MIS TO DATA MINING

The term Data Mining describes the process of discovering knowledge from databases stored in data marts or data warehouses. The purpose of data mining is to identify valid, novel, useful and ultimately understandable patterns in data. Data mining is a useful tool, an approach that combines exploration and discovery with confirmatory analysis.

With the widespread use of computers in organizations, they collect and store huge amount of operational or transactional data on day-to-day basis, whether that be in the form of past patient records or inventory shipping manifests or record of students' performance. But, generally there is no integrated approach for using this data. They generally store data as in old files, gathering it till some specific information is required. Traditional database queries are one-dimensional and historical, for example, what was the sale in the month of March or what were the highest marks scored by the student or measures of central tendency or dispersion, but, data mining attempts to discover patterns and trends in the data to infer rules from these patterns. Data mining techniques can, thus, help utilize historical data to analyze patterns and predict the future.

The literature on data mining often uses terms like data warehouse and data marts. A data warehouse is an electronic repository for databases that organizes large volumes of data into categories to facilitate retrieval, interpretation and sorting by end users. The data warehouse provides an accessible archive to support dynamic organizational intelligence applications. The key words here are dynamically accessible. Data warehouses that offer archaic methods for data retrieval are seldom used. Data in a data warehouse must be continually updated to ensure that managers have access to data appropriate for real-time decisions. In a data warehouse, the contents of departmental computers are duplicated in a central repository where standard architecture and consistent data definitions are used. These data are, thus, made available to departments or cross functional teams for direct analysis or through intermediate storage facilities or data marts that compile locally required information. Care must be taken to ensure that the entire system is closely integrated and compatibility exists among different data marts.

The algorithms used in data mining have existed for more than two decades. The U.S. government has employed customized data-mining software using neural networks, fuzzy logic, and pattern recognition to spot tax frauds, eavesdrop on foreign communication and process satellite imagery. Until recently, these tools had been available only to large corporations or government agencies due to their higher cost. However, this

TABLE 31.1
Evolution of Data Mining

Evolutionary Step	*Investigative Questions*	*Enabling Technologies*	*Characteristics*
Data Collection (1960s)	What were average annual sales over last five years?	Computers, Tapes, Discs, Other storage media	Retrospective, Static data delivery
Data Access (1980s)	What were the sales in North India last year?	Relational Databases (RDBMS), Structured Query Language (SQL), ODBC	Retrospective, Dynamic data delivery at record level
Data Navigation (1990s)	What were the sales in North India last year? Break it down to each month territory-wise.	Online Analytic Procession (OLAP), Multidimensional Databases, Data warehouses	Retrospective, Dynamic data delivery at multiple levels
Data Mining (2000)	What is likely to happen to North India sales next quarter? Why?	Advance algorithms, Multiprocessor Computers, Massive Databases	Prospective, Proactive information delivery

is changing rapidly with the increasing availability of hardware and software at affordable prices.

In the evolution from business data to information (Table 31.1), each new step is built on the previous one.

Functional areas of management and select industries are currently driving data-mining projects: marketing, customer service, administrative or financial analysis, sales, manual distribution, insurance, fraud detection, and network management (Figure 31.1).

FIG. 31.1
Data Mining in Business

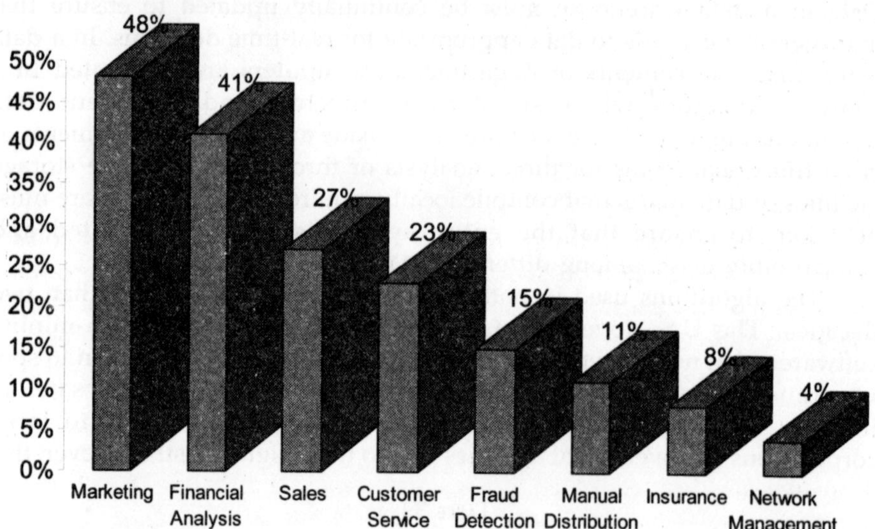

2.1. Data Mining

Data mining technology provides two unique capabilities to the researchers: pattern discovery and prediction, both providing a valuable insight into hitherto innate data.

2.1.1 Pattern Discovery

Data mining tools can be programmed to sweep regularly through databases and identify previously hidden patterns. An example of the same can be the detection of stolen credit cards based on the analysis of credit card transactions. Mastercard processes 12 million transactions daily and uses data mining to detect fraud. Other uses include finding retail purchase patterns (used for inventory management, store layout design), identifying call center volume fluctuations (used for staffing), and locating anomalous data that could represent data entry errors (used to evaluate the need for training, employee evaluation or security).

2.1.2 Predicting Trends and Behaviour

A typical example of a predictive problem is targeted marketing. Using data from past promotional mailings to identify the target most likely to subscribe to a particular offering is a sure shot way to maximize the effectiveness of the campaign. For example, both Bank of America and Mellon Bank use data-mining software to pinpoint marketing programmes that attract high margin, low risk customers. Bank of America focuses on credit lines and retail lending; Mellon bank has used data mining to optimize its home equity line of credit marketing to existing customers. Other predictive problems include forecasting bankruptcy, loan default and finding population segments with similar responses to a given stimulus. Data mining tools, also, can be used to build risk models for a specific market such as discovering the top 10 most significant buying trends each week.

3. DATA MINING TOOLS

Before we come to the applications, a selection of data mining tools is presented. For each tool, there is a simple definition of the model, a discussion of some appropriate uses of the model, a brief explanation of the algorithm, and a discussion of the model's strengths and weaknesses.

3.1. Expert Systems

An expert system (ES) consists of a knowledge-base of rules (extracted from experts), facts (or data), and a logic-based inference engine (or control) which creates new rules and facts based on previously accumulated knowledge and facts. Expert systems can mimic, to some extent, the reasoning of experts whose knowledge of a narrow domain is deep, thus permitting human experts and expert systems to arrive at similar conclusions.

Expert systems are highly supervised (i.e. the original configuration (or training) of the system is not automatic but must have significant user supervision). The knowledge engineer elicits expert knowledge from either human experts through interviews or from textbook procedures. This procedure is the most difficult and time-consuming aspect of developing good expert systems.

Expert systems can perform as well as human experts can on problem domains consisting of cognitive-based, very specific expertise. Ideal knowledge domains are very narrow in scope and allow experts to resolve problems in a relatively short period of time. The knowledge should be easy to capture, self-consistent, simple to explain, straightforward to represent (and/or code, typically as if/then rules), and should avoid dependency on common sense.

If then rules are, usually, used in expert systems to represent knowledge. A sample knowledge-base might consist of rules like the following :

1. if A then D
2. if (B or D) then C
3. if C then E

Each rule consists of an "if"-part (antecedent) and a "then"-part (consequent). Each of the symbols A, B, C, D, and E represents a statement. For example, assume A represents "economic growth indicators are up", B represents "the stock market is up", C represents "buy", D represents "interest rates are down", and E represents "redistribute assets", then rule two would state "if the stock market is up or interest rates are down then buy".

During the implementation phase, if the ES is informed that D is true then the system will fire rule two since its antecedent (B or D) is true, thereby creating a new piece of information, namely, C is true (i.e. D and rule two imply C). This new fact, in turn, fires rule three, and this chain of discovery leads to the fact that E is also true. A large ES might use a similar but longer, more complicated forward chaining sequence either to present the user with expertly generated knowledge or to solve a user problem or query. Using a similar back chaining process, it can also be deduced that C will be true if A is true.

ESs are not well suited for use on broad domains of knowledge. Although the most difficult and time-consuming aspect of developing good expert systems is attaining knowledge from the experts, ESs are only as good as the knowledge captured. Expert systems are not very robust since they are notoriously brittle and cannot easily support illogical complexities, poor clarity (in the facts and/or the rules), or internal inconsistencies. ESs are not easy to scale, that is, if more rules are added to the knowledge base (or even if the rules were rearranged) unforeseen results may occur. Expert systems do, however (unlike the other data mining tools), possess a high degree of explanatory power.

3.2. Fuzzy Expert Systems

To help solve the brittleness problem inherent in expert systems, fuzzy expert systems (FESs), which employ fuzzy logic concepts, were developed. The truth or falsity of a fact can be measured in a fuzzy way using values from the real number interval zero to one inclusive. In expert systems (ESs), information is crisp, that is, it is either totally false (i.e. zero) or totally true (i.e. one), but in fuzzy expert systems (FESs), truth values can lie anywhere on the 0.0 to 1.0 (zero to one) interval of real numbers. Some facts are close to being true or close to being false (these have low entropy), while other facts lie close to the middle ground between true or false (these have high entropy). Using fuzzy operators, such as AND, OR, NOT, VERY, and SOMEWHAT, the system can make fuzzy implications. Expert systems can mimic, to some extent, the reasoning of experts whose knowledge of a narrow domain is deep. In this way, human experts and expert systems can arrive at similar conclusions. Since an FES is not as brittle as an expert system, it can easily handle illogical complexities, poor clarity (in the facts and/or rules), or internal inconsistencies. Fuzzy expert systems are highly supervised since like expert systems, the knowledge engineer elicits fuzzy expert knowledge from either human experts through interviews or from textbook procedures. Knowledge elicitation is the most difficult and time-consuming aspect of developing fuzzy expert systems.

Fuzzy expert systems can perform as well as, or sometimes better than human experts on problem domains consisting of cognitive-based, very specific expertise. Ideal knowledge domains are very narrow in scope and allow experts to resolve problems in a relatively short period of time. The knowledge should be easy to capture, simple to explain, straightforward to represent (and/or code, typically as fuzzy if/then rules), and should avoid too much dependency on common sense. FESs afford the knowledge user more flexibility in generating solutions since consistency and exactness (i.e. crispness) restrictions are loosened.

Earlier, Rule II of the miniature expert system stated if (B or D) then C. A similar FES rule might state if (SOMEWHAT B OR VERY D) then C, that is, if the market is somewhat up or interest rates are extremely down then buy.

FESs obviate the need for exact mathematical representations and are easier to debug. They better simulate reality and provide the user with a wider range of possible solutions. Although, like ESs, the most difficult and time-consuming aspect of developing good fuzzy expert systems is attaining knowledge from the experts, FESs make knowledge elicitation simple. Fuzzy expert systems are robust (i.e. not as brittle as ESs) and can easily support illogical complexities, internal inconsistencies, and poor clarity or contradiction in the facts and/or the rules. In addition, FESs are easy to scale and they have a high degree of explanatory power.

3.3. Decision Tree

Decision trees are based on simple tree models where at each branch during tree growth, the data set is strategically partitioned into different classes and sub-classes. At each split, the most effective way of partitioning and classifying the data set is accomplished by using the most distinguishing feature encountered at that step of the algorithm. Decision tree systems are highly unsupervised (i.e. the training of the system is automatic and little or no user supervision is required).

Decision trees are used to predict and/or classify. They can also be effective when the knowledge seeker desires a quick and dirty exploratory partitioning of the data set in order to get a gut feel for the data.

During the training phase, the data set is partitioned iteratively. During each pass (i.e. iteration), the data set is split on that feature (or attribute) that produces the most effective classification. Only those most significant factors to the effective partitioning are used.

The implementation phase, then, produces decision rules which are equivalent to the partitions (or branchings) created during the training phase. These rules are used to generate new information when presented with novel situations.

Decision trees are easy to understand, straightforward to build, and simple to explain. They give the knowledge user intuitive, high level, and very explainable overviews of the structure of their data set. Decision tree construction usually requires little or no data preprocessing. Since training times are quick, scalability is usually accomplished by simply retraining and creating a new partition.

3.4. Rule Induction

Rule induction uses statistical discovery methods to develop rules which depend on the frequency of correlation, the rate of accuracy, and the accuracy of prediction. Typically, if/then type rules are created by focusing on either a particular antecedent (i.e. the variables forming the "if" part of a rule) or a particular consequent (i.e. the variables forming the "then" part of a rule). Sometimes, however, the novelty, significance, value, or exceptionality of a rule is deemed to be most interesting. Rule induction methods are highly unsupervised. However, they do require the evaluation of generated rules by experts. First, simple rules are generated based on data set statistics, then more complex rules are created, and combined with old rules using standard rule combining techniques.

This technique is most often used when new rules need to be generated. Owing to the combinatorially explosive nature of generating rules in this manner such models usually run in the background or at times when computing demand is low.

On the negative side, rule induction produces too many patterns, thus too many trivial, contradictory, counter-intuitive, and/or worthless rules are generated. However, sometimes golden nuggets of information are planned. Since rule induction considers all possibilities, it requires constant expert evaluation of the rules generated by the system which can be a very time-consuming and expensive exercise. This technique only shows correlations (i.e. no cause and effect relationships are produced). On the positive side, rule induction is an easy to explain an intuitive modeling method. Rule induction also produces rules which are directly based on actual data set statistics.

3.5. Genetic Algorithms and Genetic Programming

Genetic Algorithms (GAs) and Genetic Programs (GPs) are based on the biological mechanisms of natural selection and survival of the fittest.

Through the use of simulation, solutions evolve using a broad-based parallel (or pseudo parallel) search. While genetic algorithms evolve complex data structures, genetic programming evolves complex algorithmic structures, i.e. computer programs. These genetic systems are highly unsupervised, i.e. the original configuration (or training) of the system needs no user intervention.

GAs are useful for finding solutions to hard optimization problems, that is, they generate optimal or near optimal solutions to such problems. They are excellent at initially locating potentially good regions so that other local optimizers, like a backprop neural network, can continue with a more rigorous local search. GAs can be used to fine tune the parameters of other DM models (e.g. ANNs) and they are also good at classification. First, a population of potential solutions is randomly initialized. The generic genetic algorithm consists of the following steps :

- Each population member is evaluated for fitness.
- The population is increased through a process of mating and mutation of certain members of the population thus creating new population members.
- Poorly performing members are then eliminated reducing the population.
- Finally, before reiterating the process with this new generation a check for a terminal condition is made (sample terminal conditions might include finding a satisfying solution, no significant change in the population has occurred for a long period of time, or a prespecified number of iterations has been reached).

In this way, better solutions evolve in the population from one generation to the next. One advantage of using the genetic algorithm model is that many possibilities can be suggested as solutions (i.e. any number of the top performing members of the population are candidate solutions). Some strengths of the GA model are that it is an easy to explain, robust, and intuitively appealing model which examines the search space with a broad brush and can easily handle multidimensional problems. The weaknesses of the GA paradigm include the non-explanatory aspects of the model and the not always so obvious choice of data representation, fitness function selection, and methods of mating and mutating.

3.6. Backpropagation

Neural networks such as for example, backprop (BP), are based on the biological concept of learning and memory creation using a highly interconnected group of neurons (or nerves). Such models attempt to mimic brain activity by adapting the weights of the interconnections among the neurons in the network allowing learning and memory creation to take place. Backprop systems are highly supervised. The backprop neural network model is ideal for prediction and classification in situations where there are a good deal of historic data available for training.

The training phase consists of initially assigning random weights to the connections of an interconnected layered network of neurons. One layer (distinguished as an input layer) is iteratively presented with random historical records picked from the data set. Each piece of data activates the network producing a result on another layer called the output layer. If the result in the output layer agrees with historical fact, nothing happens and the iteration process continues. But if the result in the output layer disagrees with historical fact, weight adjustment reflecting this difference is propagated back through the network from the output layer toward the input layer. The iteration process then resumes.

The training phase adjusts the weights in the network so that its outputs agree with historical fact. During the implementation phase, novel data are presented to the input layer, thereby activating the network which produces the resulting output.

The strengths of the BP model are that it can handle multidimensional data, it is robust (e.g. even if there is a loss or error in some of the connections, the model still produces), and it can handle noisy data. Some of the weaknesses of this model include a very low degree of explanatory power, data preprocessing is needed, and long training times are required.

3.7. Associative Memories (AMs)

Pairs (or larger groups) of associated data items are memorized (or forgotten) using a long-term memory (LTM) network model. Data pair retrieval occurs when a partial stimulation of the long-term memory network generates network activity which gradually dissipates resulting in a retrieved data pair. This retrieved pair may have been either a previously memorized pair or the best attempts of the network in trying to compromise the initial stimulus with a reasonable output pair response. AM systems are highly unsupervised. AMs are best suited for memorizing data associations, data association retrieval given noisy input, and creative data association retrieval given novel input.

Training is based on the Hebbian learning rule which states that similarities between data pairs strengthen the neural connections in the LTM network, while dissimilarities between data pairs weaken the LTM connections. This rule permits immediate memorization (or equivalently, immediate forgetting) by simply adding (or subtracting) the Hebbian matrix reflecting a data pair's similarities and dissimilarities to (or from) the LTM matrix of neural connection weights. Initially, the LTM weights are all set to zero. Therefore, the LTM memorizes the set of data pairs by simply calculating the sum of their respective Hebbian matrices.

During the implementation phase, a stimulus presented to the LTM resonates bidirectional, searching back and forth through the LTM, until a data pair finally stabilizes, that is, further bidirectional search produces the same data pair. This stable pair is the result that the AM finds in response to the initial stimulus.

The main strengths of the AM model are its ability to immediately memorize or forget, always return a data pair response to any stimulus in a relatively short number of iterations, generate creative solutions in response to novel stimuli, handle somewhat noisy data and retrieve the appropriate memorized data pair and finally, learn using very short training times.

3.8. Clustering

Clustering methods group together closely related data records in the database, thereby classifying them based on their similarities. Clustering usually involves data preprocessing (e.g. normalization) that ensures every reduced data record (i.e. containing only those attributes to be analyzed) has an unbiased influence in the classification process. Clustering systems are highly unsupervised.

Clustering techniques are ideal for classification and category prediction problems. Training begins by initially creating a set of random, normalized representatives. There, then, follows an iterative process consisting of the following steps: randomly choose a record from the preprocessed normalized database, order the representatives by their proximity (i.e. similarity) to the random record, slightly adjust the closest representative in the direction of the data record, then similarly adjust each of the other representatives, in order, away from that record (the closer representatives getting larger adjustments), this process continues until a satisfy classification is made, or no significant movement in the representatives occurs for a long period of time (i.e. they stabilize their positions), or a prespecified number of iterations have occurred. The implementation phase simply finds the closest representative when presented with novel data.

Clustering methods are intuitive, scalable models which are easy to explain and can handle noisy, multidimensional data sets. Though they have long training times, they always return a solution quickly during the implementation phase.

3.9. Hybrid Systems

There are many hybrid systems that can be created by cross-pollinating key ideas taken from different models in the broad gamut of data mining paradigms. Among these are Artificial Neural Networks (ANNs), (e.g. backprop) which optimize their weights using a genetic algorithm (Whitley and Shaffer, 1992) fuzzy Associative Maps (FAMs) (Kosko, 1992) are radial basis function networks which borrow concepts from both nearest neighbor clustering and neural networks (Haykin, 1994), and hybrid rule induction systems which evolve fuzzy rules using an innovative combination of genetic algorithmic, local search, and rule induction methods.

3.10 Visualization

Visualization is a method of clearly presenting the results found using data mining tools. This is the best way to display complex interdependencies among many attributes in order to get an intuitive feel of the data and the knowledge resulting from their analysis. Visualization allows users to quickly assess and make sense of vast amounts of data. Users can easily compare, rescale, get an overview, and confirm or validate an intuition using visualization techniques. They can also employ the explanatory power of visualization to best interpret results. Colors, shapes, sounds, and virtual reality are some of the primary tools available for visualization. These techniques can be used standalone or in various combinations, for example, to display two and three dimensional images, visualize multidimensional records, show the weight strengths in a neural net, display statistical scatter plots, construct decision trees, demonstrate the results of curve fitting, present geographical maps, examine the fractalness of a database, or display a development dashboard which tracks and controls the evolution of a DM modeling tool.

4. SOME APPLICATIONS OF DATA MINING

Although data mining is still in its infancy, companies in a wide range of industries—including retail, finance, heath care, manufacturing, transportation, and aerospace—are already using data mining tools and techniques to take advantage of historical data. By using pattern recognition technologies and statistical and mathematical techniques to shift through warehoused information, data mining helps analysts recognize significant facts, relationships, trends, patterns, exceptions and anomalies that might, otherwise, go unnoticed.

For businesses, data mining is used to discover patterns and relationships in the data in order to help make better business decisions. Data mining can help spot sales trends, develop smarter marketing campaigns, and accurately predict customer loyalty. Specific uses of data mining include:

- *Market segmentation*—Identify the common characteristics of customers who buy the same products from your company.
- *Customer churn*—Predict which customers are likely to leave your company and go to a competitor.
- *Fraud detection*—Identify which transactions are most likely to be fraudulent.
- *Direct marketing*—Identify which prospects should be included in a mailing list to obtain the highest response rate.
- *Interactive marketing*—Predict what each individual accessing a web site is most likely interested in seeing.

- *Market basket analysis*—Understand which products or services are commonly purchased together; e.g., beer and diapers.
- *Trend analysis*—Reveal the difference between a typical customer this month and last

Data mining is primarily used today by companies with a strong consumer focus—retail, financial, communication, and marketing organizations. It enables these companies to determine relationships among "internal" factors such as price, product positioning, or staff skills, and external factors such as economic indicators, competition, and customer demographics. And, it enables them to determine the impact on sales, customer satisfaction, and corporate profits. Finally, it enables them to "drill down" into summary information to view detail transactional data.

With data mining, a retailer could use point-of-sale records of customer purchases to send targeted promotions based on an individual's purchase history. By mining demographic data from comment or warranty cards, the retailer could develop products and promotions to appeal to specific customer segments. For example, Blockbuster Entertainment mines its video rental history database to recommend rentals to individual customers. *American Express* can suggest products to its cardholders based on analysis of their monthly expenditures.

WalMart is pioneering massive data mining to transform its supplier relationships. WalMart captures point-of-sale transactions from over 2,900 stores in 6 countries and continuously transmits this data to its massive 7.5 terabyte Teradata data warehouse. WalMart allows more than 3,500 suppliers, to access data on their products and perform data analysis. These suppliers use this data to identify customer buying patterns at the store display level. They use this information to manage local store inventory and identify new merchandising opportunities. In 1995, WalMart computers processed over 1 million complex data queries.

The National Basketball Association (NBA) is exploring a data mining application that can be used in conjunction with image recordings of basketball games. The Advanced Scout software analyzes the movements of players to help coaches orchestrate plays and strategies. For example, an analysis of the play-by-play sheet of the game played between the New York Knicks and the Cleveland Cavaliers on January 6, 1995 reveals that when Mark Price played the Guard position, John Williams attempted four jump shots and made each one! Advanced Scout not only finds this pattern, but explains that it is interesting because it differs considerably from the average shooting percentage of 49.30% for the Cavaliers during that game.

By using the NBA universal clock, a coach can automatically bring up the video clips showing each of the jump shots attempted by Williams with Price on the floor, without needing to comb through hours of video footage. Those clips show a very successful pick-and-roll play in which Price draws the Knick's defense and then finds Williams for an open jump shot.

Data mining techniques can be applied in various areas. For example, Vararuk, Petrounias and Kodogiannis have discussed the application of data mining techniques for HIV/AIDS data management in Thailand to investigate the patterns in patient data for better management of the disease and more appropriately targeting of resources. They used data comprising of 2,50,000 records and manipulated using database techniques and applying clustering and association rule discovery. Their work helped cluster highlighted groups of patients with common characteristics and also errors in data. Association rules identified associations that were not expected in the data and were different from traditional reporting mechanisms utilised by medical practitioners. It, also, allowed the identification of symptoms that co-exist or are precursors of other symptoms. Identification of symptoms that are precursors of other symptoms can allow the targeting of the former so that the later symptoms can be avoided. This study shows that providing a pragmatic and targeted approach to the management of resources available for HIV/AIDS treatment can provide a much better service, while at the same time reducing the expense of that service. This study can also be used as a means of implementing a quality monitoring system to target available resources.

Similarily, in their paper Solomon, Nguyen, Liebowitz and Agresti have used data mining to demonstrate how well there techniques can help to evaluate how well cameras that monitor red-light-signal controlled intersections improve traffic safety by reducing fatalities. The paper demonstrates several different data modeling techniques—decision trees, neural networks, market-basket analysis and K-means models. This paper builds upon prior research in DM and also extends the body of research that examines the effectiveness of red camera programs as they mature. This paper can act as a guide to follow for red light camera program managers or local municipalities to conduct their own analysis.

5. CONCLUSION

Of the models discussed in this article, the expertise of the marketing manager to choose the appropriate one will come with usage and experience, and the examples illustrated in the last section are intended to help him in the same. The return on investment for each of these data mining models is high. That is, there is usually a good payoff on a relatively small investment. Each model can be individually evaluated on the following criteria:

- Robustness
- Degree of automation
- Speed
- Explanatory power
- Accuracy
- Amount of preprocessing needed

- Scalability
- Ease of integration
- The ability to handle many attributes

All of the DM models discussed have a good accuracy rate, can be easily integrated into the decision support process, can handle multiple attributes, and run quickly after training. Rule induction, the genetic paradigms, backprop, and clustering, however, usually require some training time. With the notable exception of expert systems, all are scalable, robust, and easy to automate. Many of the models (except backprop and often the genetic paradigms) have good explanatory power. Finally, most of the models, except for the decision tree and rule induction models, usually require the data to be preprocessed.

References

1. Cooper, Donald R., and Schindler, Pamela, S., Business Research Methods, 9th Edition, Tata McGraw-Hill Publishing Company Limited, New Delhi.
2. Anthony, R.N., Planning and Control Systems: A Framework for Analysis, Divison of Research, Graduate School of Business Administration, Harvard University, Cambridge MA, 1965.
3. Vararuk, A., Petrounias, I. and Kodogiannis, V. , Data mining techniques for HIV/AIDS data management in Thailand, *Journal of Enterprise Information Management*, Vol. 21, Number 1, 2008.
4. Solomon Scott, Nguyen Hang, Liebowitz Jay, and, Agresti William, Using data mining to improve traffic safety programs, Industrial Management and Data Systems, Vol. 106, No. 5, 2006.
5. http://www.anderson.ucla.edu/faculty/jason.frand/teacher/technologies/palace/datamining.htm
6. R. Srikant and R. Agrawal, "Mining Sequential Patterns: Generalizations and Performance Improvements." Proceedings, 5th International Conference on Extending Data-base Technology, Paris, France, March 1996.
7. DePompe, B., "There's Gold in Databases", CMP Publications, January 8, 1996 http://techweb.cmp.com/iwk.

32

The Uniqueness of Data Grid Over Other Data-Intensive Paradigms

JASWINDER SINGH, NAVDEEP KAUR AND RAJWINDER SINGH

ABSTRACT

A Data Grid provides a platform through which users can access aggregated computational, storage and networking resources to execute their data-intensive applications on remote data. It promotes a rich environment for users to analyze data, share the results with their collaborators, and maintain state information about the data seamlessly across institutional and geographical boundaries. This paper discusses about Data Grid terminology, their characteristics and compares it with other similar data-intensive paradigm in order to bring out the uniqueness of Data Grid.

1. INTRODUCTION

With the development of scientific applications, huge amounts of datasets have been produced which are located over wide geographic areas. To share, access, process, transport and manage these large datasets, there is need of new integrated architecture that concentrates on issues like multi-domain applications, cooperation and coordination of resources and blurring of system boundaries. Grid computing [1] is one such integrated architecture that proposes aggregating geographically distributed heterogeneous computing, storage, and network resources to provide unified, secure and pervasive access to their combined capabilities. That is, grid computing is applying the resources of many computers in a network to a single problem at the same time-usually to scientific or technical problem that requires a great number of computer cycles or access to large amount of data. Such aggregations are also called Grids.

Data Grids have been adopted as the next generation platform by many scientific communities that need to share, access, transport, process and manage large data collections distributed worldwide. Data Grids [2], [3] primarily deal with providing services and infrastructure for distributed data-intensive applications that need to access, transfer, and modify massive datasets stored in distributed storage resources. For users to derive maximum benefits out of the infrastructure, following capabilities are needed:

(a) Ability to search through numerous available datasets for the required dataset and to discover suitable data resources for accessing the data.
(b) Ability to transfer large-sized datasets between resources least possible time.
(c) Ability for users to manage multiple copies of their data.
(d) Ability to select suitable computational resources and process data on them.
(e) Ability to manage access permissions for the data.

Some other paradigms with similar requirements for supporting a distributed data-intensive infrastructure are content delivery networks, peer-to-peer file-sharing networks and distributed databases. In section 2, we provide a general overview and systematic characterization of Data Grids, and section 3 contains a general overview of other data intensive networks like CDN, P2P and DDB. A thorough examination of their differences from the distributed data-intensive mechanisms is mentioned in section 4, and at last we summarize the paper. Our goal in this paper, therefore, is to enlighten very clearly the uniqueness of Data Grids from other similar paradigms and provide a basis for categorizing present and future developments in this area.

2. GENERAL OVERVIEW

2.1 Terms and Definitions

Data Sets and Repositories : Data produced, analyzed and manipulated by the applications in data-intensive computing environments are in the range of hundreds of Megabytes (MB) to PetaBytes (PB) and beyond [Moore *et al.* 1998]. This data is organized as collections or datasets and are, typically, stored on mass storage systems, also known as repositories such as tape libraries or disk arrays.

Replica, Replica Management System and Replica Catalog : To reduce latencies involved in wide-area data transfers and to improve application performance, user can create local copies or replica of datasets accessed from different locations. A replica may be a complete or a partial copy of the original dataset. Replica management system or data replication mechanisms allow users to create, register and manage replicas and may also allow them to update the replicas if the original datasets are modified. The system may also create replicas on its own guided by replication strategies that take into account current and future demand for the datasets, locality of requests, and strong capacity of the repositories. A *replica catalog* contains information about locations of datasets and associated replicas and the metadata associated with these datasets. Users query the catalog using metadata attributes to conduct operations such as locating the nearest replica of a particular dataset.

Metadata: *Metadata*, or data about data, is information that describes the datasets and could consist of attributes such as name, time of creation, size on disk and time of last modification. Metadata may also contain specific information such as details of the process that produced the data.

Resources : Any hardware or software entity such as printer, storage systems or applications that are shared between users of a Grid is called a *resource*. Resources are also known as *nodes* in the network.

Services : The network enabled capabilities of the resources that can be invoked by users, applications, or other resources are called *services*.

2.2 Data Grid

The basic functions of data grid are providing:

(a) High performance and reliable data transfer mechanism.
(b) A scalable and management mechanism.

Data grid provide different types of services like consistency management for replicas, metadata management, and data filtering and reduction mechanism during the transfer and manipulation of the data from distributed repositories; and creation and management copies of these data sets in heterogeneous environment. Along with above given two aspects, data grid performs one more aspect of maintenance of shared collections of data distributed across administrations domains. More prominently, it is required that the data and information associated with data such as metadata, access controls, and version changes be preserved even in the face of platform changes. These requirements lead to the establishment of persistent archival storage [4].

Figure 32.1 shows a high-level view of a worldwide Data Grid consisting of computational and storage resources in different countries that are connected by high-speed networks. The thick lines show high bandwidth networks linking the major centers, and the thinner lines are lower capacity networks that connect the latter to their subsidiary centers. The data generated from an instrument, experiment or a network of sensors

Fig. 32.1
A high-level View of a Data Grid

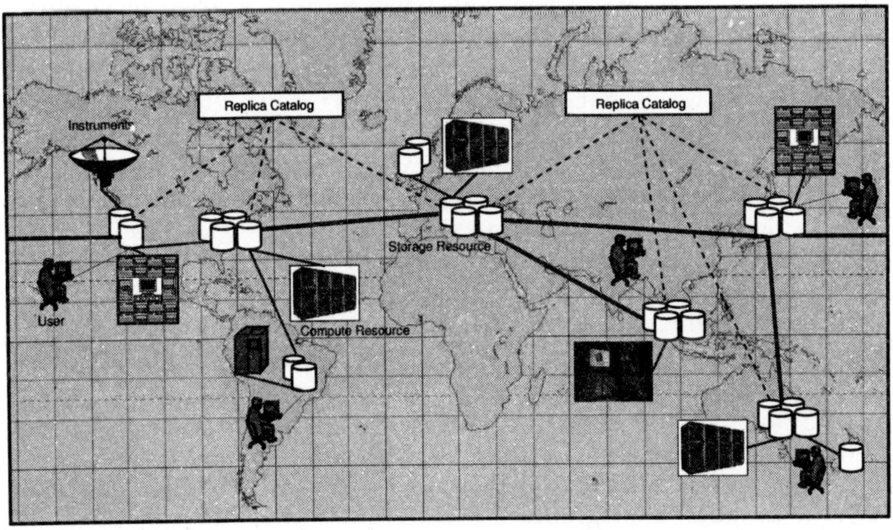

is stored in its principal storage site and is transferred to the other storage sites around the world on request through the data replication mechanism. Users query their local replica catalog to locate datasets that they require. If they have been granted the requisite rights and permissions, the data is fetched from the repository local to their area if it is present there; otherwise it is fetched from a remote repository. The data may be transmitted to computational sites such as a cluster or a supercomputer facility for processing. After processing, the results may be sent to a visualization facility, a shared repository or to the desktops of the individual users.

Hence, we have seen that data grid provides a platform through which users can access aggregated computational, storage and networking resources to execute their data-intensive applications on remote data. It promotes a rich environment for users to analyze data, share the results with their collaborators and maintain state information about the data seamlessly across institutional and geographical boundaries. An example for data grid is CERN (These Data Grids will involve thousands of physicists spread over hundreds of institutions worldwide and will be replicating and analyzing terabytes of data daily), where a huge amount of data is being analyzed which is produced by the CMS (Compact Muon Solenoid), ATLAS (A Toroidal LHC Appratus), ALICE (A Large Ion Collider Experiment), and LHCb (LHC beauty) experiments at the Large Hadron Collider (LHC) [5].

2.3 Data Grid Characteristics

Resources in a Grid are heterogeneous in terms of operating environments, capability and availability and are under the control of their own local administrative domains. These domains are autonomous and retain the rights to grant users access to the resources under their control. Therefore, Grids are concerned with issues such as sharing of resources, authentication and authorization of entities, and resource management and scheduling for efficient and effective use of available resources. Under the clouds of these issues, data grid has their own unique set of characteristics listed here.

- *Massive Datasets*. Data-intensive applications are characterized by the presence of large datasets of the size of gigabytes (GB) and beyond. For example, the CMS experiment at the LHC is expected to produce 1 PB (1015 bytes) of RAW data and 2 PB of event summary data (ESD) annually when it begins production [6]. Resource management within Data Grids, therefore, extends to minimizing latencies of bulk data transfers, creating replicas through appropriate replication strategies, and managing storage resources.
- *Shared Data Collections*. Resource sharing within Data Grids also includes, among others, sharing distributed data collections. For example, participants within a scientific collaboration would want to use the same repositories as sources for data and for storing the outputs of their analyses.
- *Unified Namespace*. The data in a Data Grid share the same logical namespace in which every data element has a unique logical filename. The logical filename is mapped to one or more physical filenames on various storage resources across a Data Grid.
- *Access Restrictions*. Users might wish to ensure confidentiality of their data or restrict distribution to close collaborators. Authentication and authorization in Data Grids involves coarse to fine-grained access controls over shared data collections.

2.4 Data Grid Services

Data access and metadata access are the two fundamental services provided by the data grid. The data access service provides mechanisms for accessing, managing and initiating third-party transfers of data stored in storage systems. The metadata access service provides mechanisms for accessing and managing information about data stored in storage systems. Along with these two basic services, there is existence of a number of other basic services, including the following:

1. An authorization and authentication infrastructure that supports multi-institutional operation. The public key-based Grid Security Infrastructure (GSI) [7] meets our requirements.
2. Resource reservation and co-allocation mechanisms for both storage systems and other resources such as networks, to support end-to-end performance guarantees required for predictable transfers (e.g., [8]).
3. Performance measurements and estimation techniques for key resources involved in data grid operation, includes storage systems, network and computers (e.g., the Network Weather Service [9]).
4. Instrumentation services that enable the end-to-end instrumentation of storage transfers and other operations (e.g., [10], [11], [12]).

3. OTHER RELATED DATA-INTENSIVE PARADIGMS

Following are the related distributed data-intensive areas that have similar properties and share similar requirements, functions and characteristics with data grid.

3.1 Peer to Peer Network (P2P)

A peer-to-peer network allows computer hardware and software to function without the need for special server devices. P2P is an alternative to client-server network design. It is a popular technology for file sharing software applications like Kazaa, WinMX and Overnet. Thus, Peer-to-peer (P2P) networks [13] are formed by *ad hoc* aggregation of resources to form a decentralized system within which each peer is autonomous and depends on other peers for resources, information, and forwarding requests.

Objective : The primary objective of a P2P network is to ensure scalability and reliability by removing the centralized authority to ensure redundancy, share resources and ensure anonymity.

Characteristics : P2P systems have two main key characteristics:

- *Scalability*: There is no algorithmic or technical limitation of the size of the system, e.g. the complexity of the system should be somewhat constant regardless of number of nodes in the system.

- *Reliability*: The malfunction on any given node will not affect the whole system (or may be even any other nodes).

By keeping in mind the volatility and requirements for scalability and reliability, algorithms and strategies are designed such that any entity can join or leave the P2P network anytime.

Focus: In content and file-sharing P2P networks such as those involve data distribution, networks have mainly focused on creating efficient strategies to locate particular files within a group of peers, to provide reliable transfers of such files in the face of high volatility, and to manage high load caused by demand for highly popular files. But, currently, major P2P content sharing networks do not provide an integrated computation and data distribution environment [14].

3.2 Contents Delivery Networks (CDN)

Content Delivery Networks (CDNs) [15][16][17] provide services that improve network performance by maximizing bandwidth, improving accessibility and maintaining correctness through content replication. They offer fast and reliable applications and services by distributing content to cache or edge servers located close to users [15]. A CDN has some combination of content-delivery, request-routing, distribution and accounting infrastructure. The content-delivery infrastructure consists of a set of edge servers (also called surrogates) that deliver copies of content to end-users. The request-routing infrastructure is responsible for directing client request to appropriate edge servers. It also interacts with the

FIG. 32.2
Abstract Architecture of a Content Delivery Network (CDN)

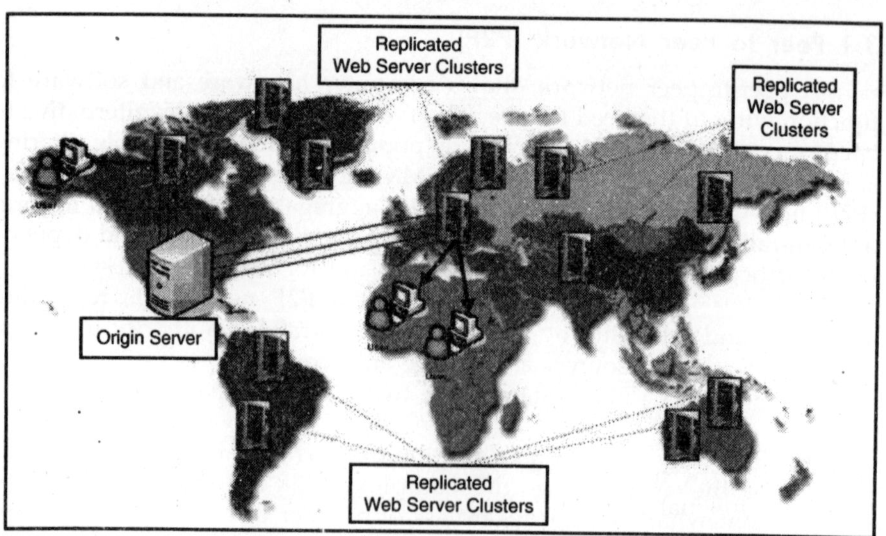

distribution infrastructure to keep an up-to-date view of the content stored in the CDN caches.

The distribution infrastructure moves content from the origin server to the CDN edge servers and ensures consistency of content in the caches. The accounting infrastructure maintains logs of client accesses and records the usage of the CDN servers. This information is used for traffic reporting and usage-based billing. In practice, CDNs typically host static content including images, video, media clips, advertisements, and other embedded objects for dynamic Web content. Typical customers of a CDN are media and internet advertisement companies, data centers, Internet Service Providers (ISPs), online music retailers, mobile operators, consumer electronics manufacturers, and other carrier companies. Figure 32.2 gives overlook of abstract architecture of a Content Delivery Network (CDN) and Figure 32.3 describes about content/services provided by a CDN.

FIG. 32.3
Content/Services Provided by a CDN

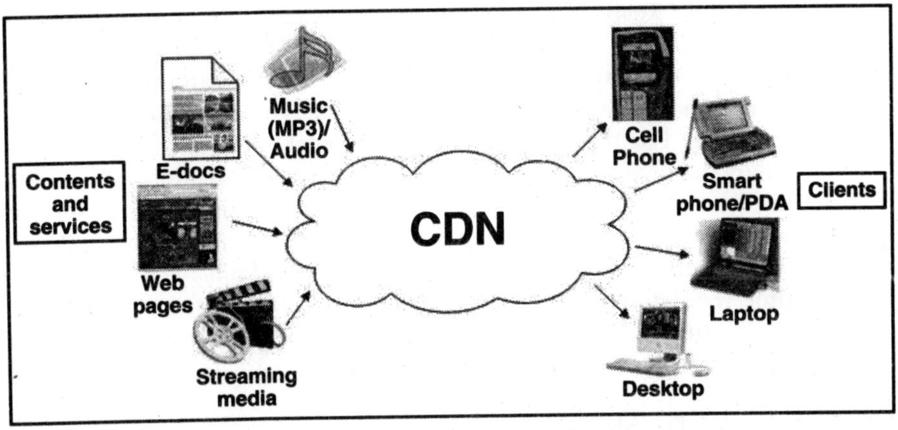

3.2.1 Functionality

The typical functionality of a CDN includes:

- Request redirection and content delivery services to direct a request to the closest suitable surrogate server using mechanisms to bypass congestion, thus overcoming flash crowds or Slash Dot effects.
- Content outsourcing and distribution services to replicate and/or cache content to distributed surrogate servers on behalf of the origin server.
- Content negotiation services to meet specific needs of each individual user (or group of users).
- Management services to manage the network components, to handle accounting, and to monitor and report on content usage

3.2.2 Focus

A CDN focuses on the following business goals: scalability, security, reliability, responsiveness and performance :

1. *Scalability*: The main business goal of a CDN is to achieve scalability. Scalability refers to the ability of the system to expand in order to handle new and large amounts of data, users and transactions without any significant decline in performance.
2. *Security:* One of the major concerns of a CDN is to provide potential security solutions for confidential and high-value content [18]. Security is the protection of content against unauthorized access and modification. Without proper security control, a CDN platform is subject to cyber fraud, distributed denial-of-service (DDoS) attacks, viruses, and other unwanted intrusions that can cripple business [19]. A CDN aims at meeting the stringent requirements of physical, network, software, data and procedural security.
3. *Reliability*: Responsiveness and Performance: Reliability refers to when a service is available and what are the bounds on service outages that may be expected. A CDN provider can improve client access to specialize content through delivering it from multiple locations. For this a fault-tolerant network with appropriate load balancing mechanism is to be implemented [20]. Responsiveness implies, while in the face of possible outages, how soon a service would start performing the normal course of operation. Performance of a CDN is typically characterized by the response time (i.e. latency) perceived by the end-users. Slow response time is the single greatest contributor to customers' abandoning Web sites and processes [19].

3.3 Distributed Databases

A distributed database (DDB) [21], [22] is a logically organized collection of data stored at different sites of a computer network. Each site, has a degree of autonomy, is capable of executing a local application, and also participates in the execution of a global application. A distributed database can be formed either by taking an existing single site database and splitting it over different sites (top-down approach) or by federating existing database management systems so that they can be accessed through a uniform interface (bottom up approach) [23]. Distributed databases [14] have evolved to serve the needs of large organizations which need to remove the need for a centralized computer center, to interconnect existing databases, to replicate databases to increase reliability, and to add new databases as new organizational units are added. This technology is very robust. It provides distributed transaction processing, distributed query optimization, and efficient management of resources. However, these systems cannot be employed in their current form at the scale envisioned for Data Grids as they have strong requirements for ACID (Atomicity, Consistency, Isolation, and Durability) properties [24] to ensure that the state of the database remains consistent and deterministic.

4. COMPARISON OF DATA GRID WITH OTHER DATA INTENSIVE PARADIGMS

In this section, we compare newly developed integrated architecture (Data Grid) with other data intensive paradigms (P2P, CDN and Distributed database) in order to bring out the uniqueness of Data Grid. The reasons by which data grid become unique over other paradigms are listed (see on the next page).

The explanation of above summarized properties is the main purpose of peer-to-peer network of vertically integrated solutions for a single goal, for example file-sharing. CDNs provide services that improve network performance by maximizing bandwidth, improving accessibility and maintaining correctness through content replication and dedicated to caching web content so that clients are able to access it faster. DDBs are used for integrating existing diverse databases to provide a uniform, consistent interface for querying and/or for replicating existing databases for increasing reliability or throughput while data grid are primarily created for enabling collaboration through sharing of distributed resources in order to obtain the benefits of aggregation. Nodes in the formation of network can be aggregated either in *ad hoc* process mode or in specific process mode. Former is used when nodes are subscribed without any prior arrangement and in latter case nodes are summarized for a particular purpose. As in P2P, any node can join or leave the network any time so aggregation is *ad hoc* and dynamic in nature. In case CDNs infrastructure is dedicated to caching content from origin server and in DDBs network is tightly coupled. Both CDN and DDB are managed by single entity with full authorization of adding or removing nodes. So they are specific and stable in nature. But due to the concept of virtual organization (VO), data grid is specific but dynamic in nature. (A VO defines the resources available for the participants and the rules for accessing and using the resources, and the conditions under which the resources can be used)

In the organization of networks, CDN is hierarchical in nature as data are transformed from original server to surrogate server and then to client machine but there are different topologies used in P2P, like Gnutella use two level hierarchy and in Napster, peer is connected to centralized server while Freenet [25] use content-based hashing. So P2P is centralized, two-level hierarchy and flat in nature. In DDBs Global relations are split into fragments that are allocated to either one or many physical sites. Thus, centralized and federated in nature. In data grid there are four different types of models like monadic, hierarchical, federated, and hybrid, so data grid are Hierarchical, Federation, bottom up or hybrid in nature. There are

TABLE 32.1
Comparison of Data Grid with Other Data-intensive Paradigm

Property	*P2P*	*CDN*	*DDB*	*Data Grids*
(1)	*(2)*	*(3)*	*(4)*	*(5)*
Purpose	File sharing	To reduce network impact on the response time of user requests	Integrating existing Databases, Replicating Database for Increasing reliability and throughput	Analysis, Collaboration
Aggregation	*Ad hoc*, Dynamic	Specific, Stable	Specific, Stable	Specific, Dynamic
Organization	Centralized, Two-level Hierarchy, flat	Hierarchical	Centralized, Federation	Hierarchical, Federation, bottom up Or hybrid
Data Access Type	Read with Frequent writes	Read-only	Equally Read and Write	Read with Rare Writes
Data Discovery	Central directory, Flooded requests or document routing	HTTP Request	Relational Schemas	Catalogues
Latency Management and Performance	Replication, Caching, Streaming	Caching, Streaming	Replication, Caching	Replication, Caching, Streaming, Pre-staging, High-speed data Movement, Optimal Selection of data Source and sink
Consistency Requirements	Weak	Strong	Strong	Weak
Transaction Support	None	None currently	Yes	None currently
Computational Requirements	None currently	None (Client-side)	Transaction Processing	Data Production and Analysis
Autonomy	Operational, Participation	None (Dedicated) Participation	Operational (Federated)	Access, operational
Management Entity	Individual	Single Organization	Single Organization	Virtual Organization
Security Requirements	Anonymity	Data Integrity	Authentication, Authorization, Data Integrity	Authentication, Authorization, Data Integrity

two basic operations on data: Read and Write. On the basis of these operations we can distinguishes among the networks that what type of data are accessed? In CDNs, it is read only for end users while updating are performed at central server. It is mostly read only in P2P except when node enter new data. In DDBs, data is read as well as write frequently. Data access in data grid is same as P2P with a difference that it supports updating of replicas.

With different organizations in P2P, discovery of data is also different. Central directory, flooded requests or document routing methods are used to discover the data. HTTP (Hyper Text Transfer Protocol) is used in CDN for discovering the data. As DDBs are organized using relational schema so data can be searched for and retrieved using SQL (Structured Query Language). Discovery of data in data grid is performed through catalogs that map the logical description of data to the actual physical representation. Along with these searching mechanisms, data can search through metadata. Metadata has to be created properly; otherwise it would affect the efficiency and accuracy of data discovery. Replicating data close to the point of consumption, caching of data, streaming data, and prestaging the data are some techniques used to reduce the latency of data transmission. Replication and caching both are different to each other in the sense that former need both creation as well as maintenance while later case just creation of new copy at consumption side. CDN deploy Caching and streaming to reduce the latency. It also supports replication in the absence of consistency and availability guaranteed. P2P networks also employ replication, caching, and streaming of data in various degrees. Replication and caching are used in distributed database systems for optimizing distributed query processing [26]. In Data Grids, all of the techniques mentioned are implemented in one form or another.

Consistency is an important property, which determines how fresh the data is. Data grids and P2P networks, generally, do not provide strong consistency guarantee because of the overhead of maintaining locks on huge volumes of data and the *ad hoc* nature of the network, respectively. In P2P networks, Oceanstore [28] is a distributed file system that provides strong consistency guarantees through expensive locking protocols. CDNs, while the data in a cache may go stale; the system always presents the latest version of the data when the user requests it. Therefore, the consistency provided by a CDN is strong. Due to strong requirements for satisfying ACID properties, updates are more frequent and can happen from within any site in the network. These updates have to be migrated to other sites in the network so that all the copies of the data are synchronized. Transaction support implies the existence of check-pointing and rollback mechanisms so that a database or data repository can return to its previous consistent state in case of failure. It is essential and important condition for DDBs. Whereas there is no need for transaction support in CDNs, as data access is read only. But P2P Networks and Data Grids currently do not have support for recovery and rollback. However, efforts are on to provide transaction support within Data Grids to provide fault tolerance for distributed transactions [28].

As CDN, P2P, DDBs and Data grids is the networks of different nodes so it is necessary to know where the data to be processed. CDNs are exclusively data-oriented environments with a client accessing data from remote nodes and processing it at its own site. While current P2P content sharing networks have no processing of the data but Computation within DDBs involves transaction processing which can be conducted in two ways: the requested data is transmitted to the originating site of the transaction and the transaction is processed at that site, or the transaction is distributed among the different nodes which have the data. High performance computing sites that generally constitute existing Data Grids are shared facilities and are oversubscribed most of the time. Therefore, application execution within Data Grids has to take into account the time spent in queues at these sites as well. In the network of nodes in heterogeneous environment each node has its own autonomy to decide whether to grant access to a user or another node within the network which is called access autonomy the ability of a node to conduct its own operations without being overridden by external operations of the network is called Operational autonomy, a node has the ability to decide the proportion of resources it donates to the network and the time it wants to associate or disassociate from the network is called Participation autonomy. Data Grid nodes have all the three kinds of autonomy to the full extent. While nodes in a P2P network do not have fine-grained access controls against users, they have maximum independence in deciding what share they will contribute to the network. CDNs are dedicated networks, and individual nodes have no autonomy at all. Tightly coupled databases retain all control over the individual sites, whereas multidatabase systems retain control over local operations.

The management entity administers the tasks for maintaining the aggregation. For the Data Grid, the concept of VO (Virtual Organization) is in use. Though entities in a P2P network are independent, a central entity may provide directory service as in the case of Napster. CDNs are owned and maintained by a corporation or a single organization. Likewise, DDBs are also maintained by single organizations even though the constituent databases may be independent. In a data distribution network, *security* may have to be ensured against corruption of content (data integrity), for safeguarding users' privacy (anonymity), and for resources to verify users' identities (authentication). P2P Networks such as Freenet are more concerned with preserving the anonymity of the users as they may be breaking local censorship laws. A CDN primarily has to verify data integrity as access for manipulating data is granted only to the content provider. Users have to authenticate against a DDB for carrying out queries and transactions, and data integrity has to be maintained for deterministic operations. Since Data Grids are multi-user environments with shared resources, the main security concerns are authentication of both users and resources and granting of permissions for specific types of services to a user (authorization). Also, more complicated access controls than those required in Grids are needed for safeguarding confidential data in Data Grids.

5. SUMMERY AND CONCLUSION

In this paper, we have studied, characterized several aspects of Data Grid systems. Data Grids have several unique features such as presence of applications with heavy computing requirements, geographically distributed and heterogeneous resources under different administrative domains, and a large number of users sharing these resources and wanting to collaborate with each other. We have enumerated several characteristics where Data Grids share similarities with, and are different from other distributed data-intensive paradigms such as content delivery networks, peer-to-peer networks, and distributed databases. Resources in a Grid are heterogeneous in terms of operating environments, capability and availability, and are under the control of their own local administrative domains. These domains are autonomous and retain the rights to grant users access to the resources under their control. Therefore, Grids are concerned with issues such as sharing of resources, authentication and authorization of entities, and resource management and scheduling for efficient and effective use of available resources.

References

1. Foster, I. and Kesselman, C. 1999. *The Grid: Blueprint for a Future Computing Infrastructure.* Morgan Kaufmann Publishers, San Francisco, CA.
2. Chervenak, A., Foster, I., Kesselman, C., Salisbury, C., and Tuecke, S. 2000. The Data Grid: Towards an Architecture for the Distributed Management and Analysis of Large Scientific Datasets. *J. Net. Comput. Appl.* 23, 3, 187–200.
3. Hoschek, W., Jaen-Martinez, F. J., Samar, A., Stockinger, H., and Stockinger, K. 2000. Data management in an international data Grid project. In Proceedings *of the 1st IEEE/ACM International Workshop on Grid Computing (GRID'00).* Bangalore, India. Springer-Verlag, Berlin, Germany.
4. Moore, R., Rajasekar, A., and Wan, M. 2005. Data Grids, digital libraries and persistent archives: An integrated approach to publishing, sharing and archiving datas. *Proceedings of the IEEE (Special Issue on Grid Computing) 93,* 3.
5. Lebrun, P. 1999. The large hadron collider, a megascience project. In *Proceedings of the 38th INFN Eloisatron Project Workshop on Superconducting Materials for High Energy Colliders,* Erice, Italy.
6. Holtman, K. and Colleagues. 2001. CMS requirements for the Grid. In *Proceedings of Conference on Computing in High Energy Physics (CHEP'01).* Beijing, China. Science Press.
7. Foster, C. Kesselman, G. Tsudik, and S. Tuecke. A security architecture for computational grids. In ACM Conference on Computers and Security, pages 83{91}. ACM Press, 1998.
8. Foster, C. Kesselman, C. Lee, R. Lindell, K. Nahrstedt, and A. Roy. A distributed resource management architecture that supports advance reservations and co-allocation. In Proceedings of the International Workshop on Quality of Service, pages 27-36, 1999.
9. R. Wolski. Forecasting network performance to support dynamic scheduling using the network weather service. In Proc. 6th IEEE Symp. on High Performance Distributed Computing, Portland, Oregon, 1997. IEEE Press.

10. B. Tierney, W. Johnston, B. Crowley, G. Hoo, C. Brooks, and D. Gunter. The NetLogger methodology for high performance distributed systems performance analysis. In Proc. 7th IEEE Symp. on High Performance Distributed Computing. IEEE Computer Society Press, 1998.
11. Daniel Reed and Randy Ribler. Performance analysis and visualization. In [10], pages 367-93.
12. Jerey Hollingsworth and Bart Miller. Instrumentation and measurement. In [10], pages 339-65.
13. Oram, A. 2001. *Peer-to-Peer: Harnessing the Power of Disruptive Technologies*. O'Reilly and Associates, Inc., Sebastopol, CA.
14. Srikumar Venugopal, Rajkumar Buyya, and Kotagiri Ramamohanarao. A Taxonomy of Data Grids for Distributed Data Sharing, Management, and Processing. In ACM Computing Surveys, Vol. 38, March 2006.
15. G. Pallis, and A. Vakali, "Insight and Perspectives for Content Delivery Networks," Communications of the ACM, Vol. 49, No. 1, ACM Press, NY, USA, pp. 101-06, January 2006.
16. Vakali, and G. Pallis, "Content Delivery Networks: Status and Trends," *IEEE Internet Computing*, IEEE Computer Society, pp. 68-74, November-December 2003.
17. G. Peng, "CDN: Content Distribution Network," Technical Report TR-125, Experimental Computer Systems Lab, Department of Computer Science, State University of New York, Stony Brook, NY, 2003. http://citeseer.ist.psu.edu/peng03cdn.html
18. R. Brussee, H. Eertink, W. Huijsen, B. Hulsebosch, M. Rougoor, W. Teeuw, M. Wibbels, and H. Zandbelt, "Content Distribution Network State of the Art," Telematica Institute, June 2001.
19. Akamai Technologies Inc., "Akamai-The Business Internet—A Predictable Platform for Profitable E-Business," 2004.
20. B. Molina, C. E. Palau, and M. Esteve, "Modeling Content Delivery Networks and their Performance," *Computer Communications*, Vol. 27, Issue 15, pp. 1401-11, September 2004.
21. Ceri, S. and Pelagatti, G. 1984. *Distributed Databases: Principles and Systems*. McGraw-Hill, New York, NY.
22. Ozsu, M.T. and Valduriez, P. 1999. *Principles of Distributed Database Systems*, 2nd Ed. Prentice-Hall, Inc., Upper Saddle River, NJ.
23. Sheth, A.P. and Larson, J. A. 1990. Federated database systems for managing distributed, heterogeneous, and autonomous databases. *ACM Comput. Surv.* 22, 3, 183–236.
24. Gray, J. and Reuter, A. 1993. *Transaction Processing: Concepts and Techniques*. Morgan Kaufmann Publishers, San Mateo, CA.
25. Clarke, I., Sandberg, O., Wiley, B., and Hong, T.W. 2001. Freenet: A distributed anonymous information storage and retrieval system. In *International Workshop on Designing Privacy Enhancing Technologies*. Berkeley, CA. Springer-Verlag, Berlin, Germany, 46-66.
26. Kossmann, D. 2000. The State of the art in Distributed Query Processing. *ACMComput. Surv.* 32, 4, 422-69.
27. Kubiatowicz, J., Bindel, D., Chen, Y., Czerwinski, S., Eaton, P., Geels, D., Gummadi, R., Rhea, S., Weatherspoon, H., Wells, C., and Zhao, B. 2000. Oceanstore: An Architecture for Global-scale Persistent Storage. In *Proceedings of the 9th International Conference on Architectural Support for Programming Languages and Operating Systems (ASPLOS IX)*. Cambridge, MA. ACM Press, New York, NY, 190-201.
28. Transaction Management Research Group (GGF). 2005. http://www.data-grid.org/tm-rg-charter.html.

33

Data Mining Tools and Techniques in Context to its Application for Life Insurance Sector in India

KANWAL GARG, DHARMINDER KUMAR AND M.C. GARG

ABSTRACT

Because of the rapid progress of information technology, the amount of information stored in databases is rapidly increasing. These huge databases contain a wealth of data and constitute a potential goldmine of valuable business information. We found that data mining is one of the method for the efficient discovery of previously unknown patterns out of large database. It is an interactive information discovery process that includes data acquisition, data integration, data exploration, model building and data validation.

There are many traditional techniques for analyzing data including statistics, management reporting and data display. Data mining offers a new approach to data analysis using techniques based on machine learning alongside the conventional methods. These techniques work with "Learning" patterns in data. They find patterns and make predictions by generating predictive models.

Michael A. King *et. al.* (1998) has discussed fourteen data mining desktop tools which may be implemented in Windows 95/NT operating system environment. In this paper, we will give a brief view on his study and try to find out its scope for implementation in life insurance sector in India.

In this research paper we will study data mining tools and techniques for its implementation in the life insurance sector in India. In the last section of this paper, we will conclude that how data mining techniques may be useful on the data so collected for the prediction on customer trend of investment, customer acquisition, new product launching and product pricing for life insurance sector in India.

1. INTRODUCTION

The past two decades has seen a dramatic increase in the amount of information or data being stored in electronic format. This accumulation of data has taken place at an explosive rate. It has been estimated that the amount of information in the world doubles every 20 months and the size and number of databases are increasing even faster.

Therefore, the objective of Data Mining is to extract valuable information from your data, to discover the "hidden gold". The gold is the valuable information in that data.

FIG. 33.1
The Growing Base of Data

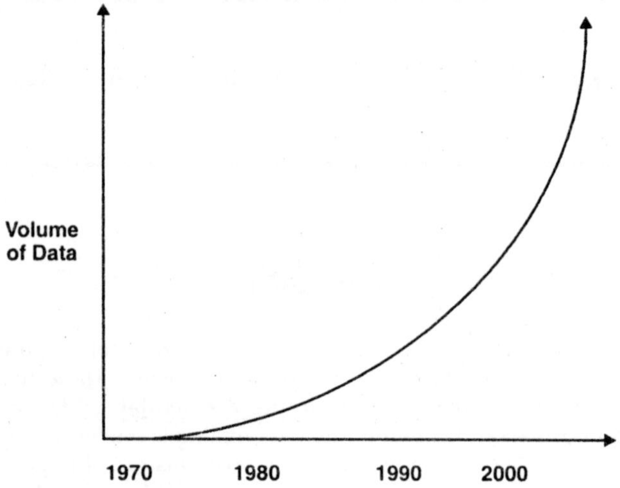

Volume of Data

1970 1980 1990 2000

Data mining out of the data is the search for relationships and global patterns that exist in large databases but are hidden among the vast amount of data, such as a relationship between customers of life insurance companies and the type of life insurance policy they buy. These relationships represent valuable knowledge about the database and the objects in the database.

The most critical step in any data mining project is obtaining good data. Good data means that data should be clean, accurate, predictive, timely, accessible and/or actionable. Analyst says that data extraction and preparation are often the most time consuming part. A research shows that almost 50% of the time, the analyst spent only for the preparation of data.

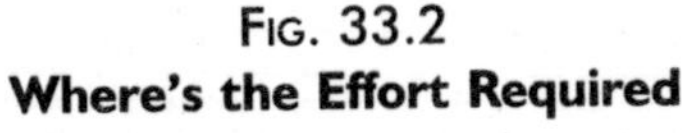
Fig. 33.2
Where's the Effort Required

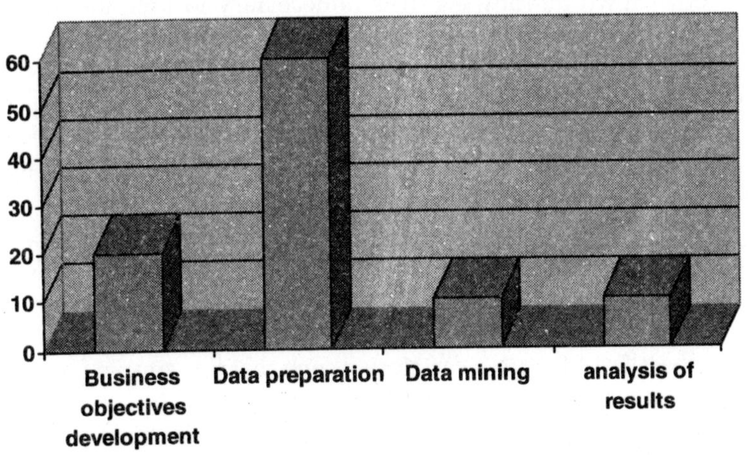

2. DATA MINING STAGES/PROCESSES

The phases depicted start with the raw data and finish with the extracted knowledge which was acquired as a result of the following stages:

- *Selection*—Selecting or segmenting the data according to some criteria e.g. all those people who has a life insurance policy, in this way subsets of the data can be determined.

Fig. 33.3
Data Mining Life Cycle

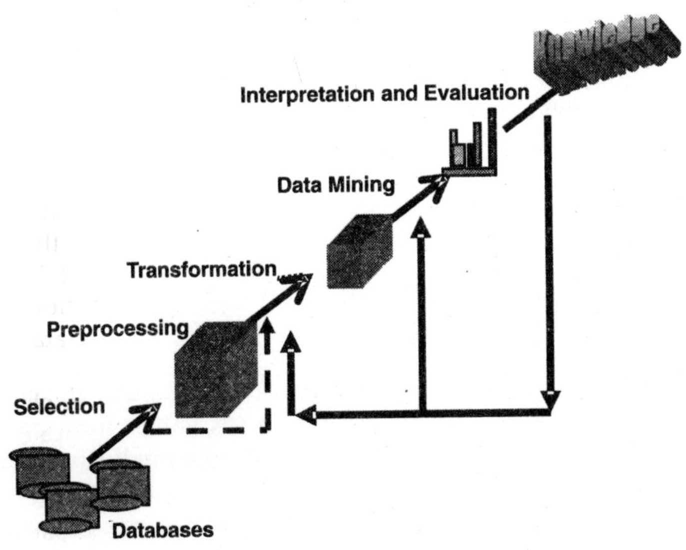

- *Preprocessing*—This is the data cleansing stage where certain information is removed which is deemed unnecessary and may slow down queries, e.g. it is unnecessary to note the name of the person when studying the behavioral trend of investment in life insurance companies in India.
- *Transformation*—The data is not merely transferred across but transformed in that overlays may be added such as the demographic overlays commonly used in market research. The data is made useable and navigable.
- *Data Mining*—This stage is concerned with the extraction of patterns from the data. A pattern can be defined as given a set of facts(data) F, a language L, and some measure of certainty C a pattern is a statement S in L that describes relationships among a subset Fs of F with a certainty c such that S is simple in some sense than the enumeration of all the facts in Fs.
- *Interpretation and Evaluation*—The patterns identified by the system are interpreted into knowledge which can, then, be used to support human decision-making e.g. prediction and classification tasks, summarizing the contents of a database or explaining observed phenomena.

3. DATA MINING TECHNIQUES

This section provides the most common data mining techniques, which are in use today for prediction or trend evaluation. The discussion has been broken into two sections, each with a specific theme:

- *Classical Techniques:* Statistics, Neighborhoods and Clustering.
- *Next Generation Techniques*: Trees, Networks and Rules.

Although there may be some other technique or the same techniques with some variation but out of these six techniques at least one will always be used in real world deployments of data mining systems.

3.1 Statistics

The term "prediction" is used for a variety of types of analysis that may elsewhere be more precisely called regression. Regression simplifies the concepts and emphasize on the common and most important aspects of predictive modeling.

There are a variety of different types of regression in statistics but the basic idea is that a model is created that maps values from predictors in such a way that the lowest error occurs in making a prediction. The simplest form of regression is simple linear regression that just contains one predictor and a prediction. The relationship between the two can be mapped on a two-dimensional space and the records plotted for the prediction values along the Y-axis and the predictor values along the X-axis.

Fig. 33.4

Linear Regression is Similar to the Task of Finding the Line

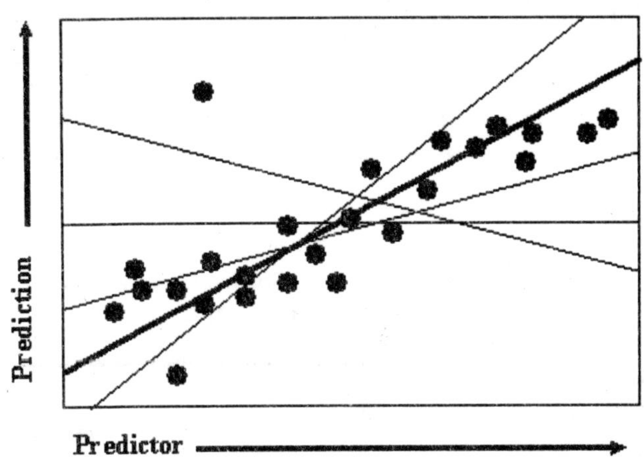

The predictive model is the line shown above. The line will take a given value for a predictor and map it into a given value for a prediction. The actual equation would look something like:

Prediction = a + b * Predictor which is just the equation for a line Y = a + bX.

This technique may be useful to analyze the trend of investment of a customer in India that how much he invest in life insurance policy and how much in other sectors like mutual funds, shares/securities, PPF and in other postal schemes. For this purpose, we may apply multiple linear regressions where the equation of line will be:

$$Y = a + b1(X1) + b2(X2) + b3(X3) + b4(X4) + b5(X5)$$

3.2 Nearest Neighbor

The nearest neighbor prediction algorithm simply stated is:

> Objects that are near to each other will have similar prediction values as well. Thus if you know the prediction value of one of the objects you can predict it for it's nearest neighbors.

Nearest Neighbor techniques are among the easiest to use and understand because they work in a way similar to the way that people think—by detecting closely matching examples. They also perform quite well in terms of automation, as many of the algorithms are robust with respect to dirty data and missing data.

One of the essential elements underlying the concept of nearest neighbor is that one particular object can be closer to another object than the third object. Most people would agree that an apple is closer to an orange than it is to a tomato, and that a Toyota Corolla is closer to a Honda Civic than to a Tavera. This sense of ordering on many different objects helps us place them in time and space and to make sense of the world.

One of the improvements that is, usually, made to the basic nearest neighbor algorithm is to take a vote from the "K" nearest neighbors rather than just relying on the sole nearest neighbor to the unclassified record. In the Figure 33.5, we can see that C has a nearest neighbor that is a defaulter and yet is surrounded almost exclusively by records that have good paying capacity.

FIG. 33.5
The Nearest Neighbors are Shown Graphically for Three Records: A, B, C

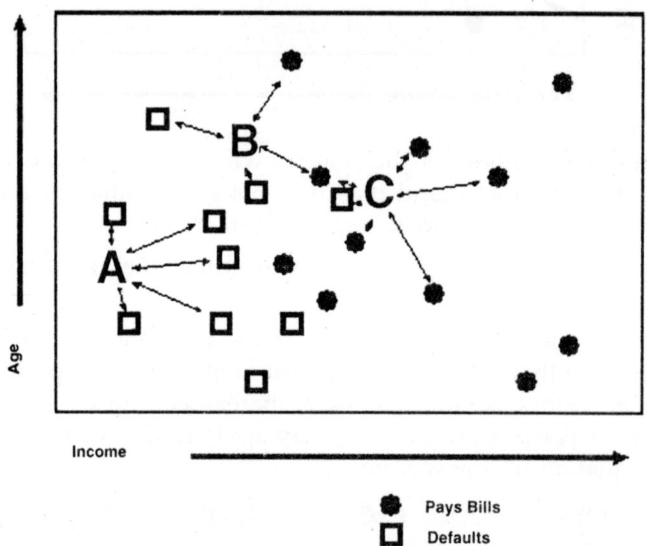

This technique may be useful to predict the intention of the customer for investment in life insurance companies in India as per their geographical location, age group, income group and other socio-economic factor. We may, also, view a tree for a specific type of life insurance policy.

3.3 Cluster Analysis

In an unsupervised learning environment, the system has to discover its own classes and one way in which it does this is to cluster the data in the database as shown in the following diagram. The first step is to discover subsets of related objects and then find descriptions e.g. D1, D2, D3, etc. which describe each of these subsets.

Clustering and segmentation, basically, partition the database so that each partition or group is similar according to some criteria or metric. Clustering according to similarity is a concept which appears in many disciplines. If a measure of similarity is available there are a number of techniques for forming clusters. Membership of groups can be based on the level of similarity between members and from this the rules of membership can be defined. Another approach is to build set functions that measure some property of partitions, i.e. groups or subsets as functions of some parameter of the partition. This latter approach achieves what is known as optimal partitioning.

Many data mining applications make use of clustering according to similarity, for example, to segment a client/customer base. Clustering according to optimization of set functions is used in data analysis e.g. when setting insurance tariffs the customers can be segmented according to a number of parameters and the optimal tariff segmentation achieved.

FIG. 33.6
Discovering Clusters and Descriptions in a Database

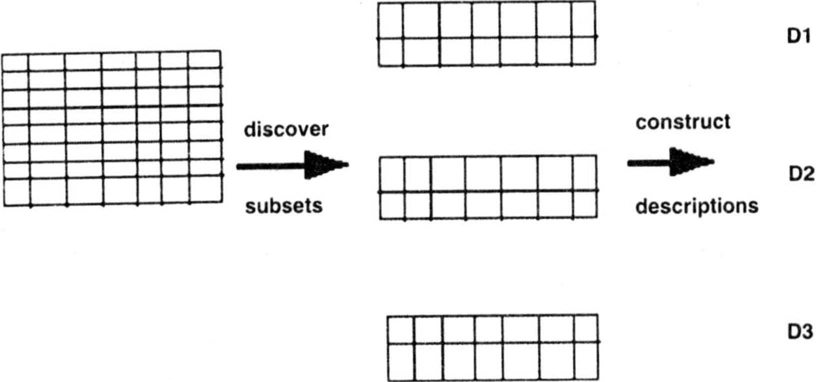

Clustering/segmentation in databases are the processes of separating a data set into components that reflect a consistent pattern of behaviour. Once the patterns have been established they can then be used to "deconstruct" data into more understandable subsets and also they provide sub-groups of a population for further analysis or action which is important when dealing with very large databases. For example, a database could be used for profile generation for target marketing of life insurance companies in India where previous response to mailing campaigns can be used to generate a profile of people who responded and this can be used to predict response and filter mailing lists to achieve the best response.

3.4 Decision Trees

A decision tree is a predictive model that, as its name implies, can be viewed as a tree.

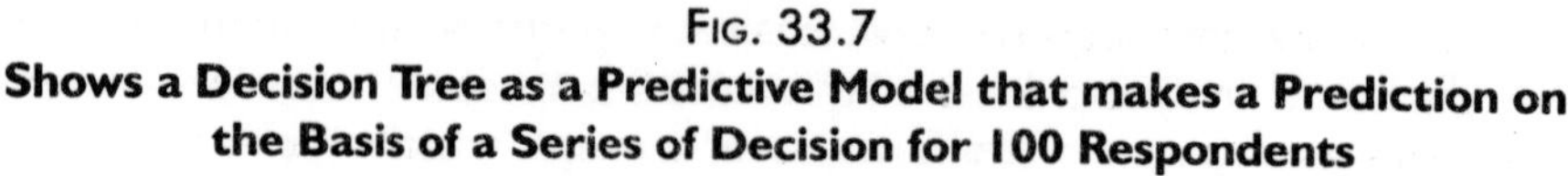

FIG. 33.7
Shows a Decision Tree as a Predictive Model that makes a Prediction on the Basis of a Series of Decision for 100 Respondents

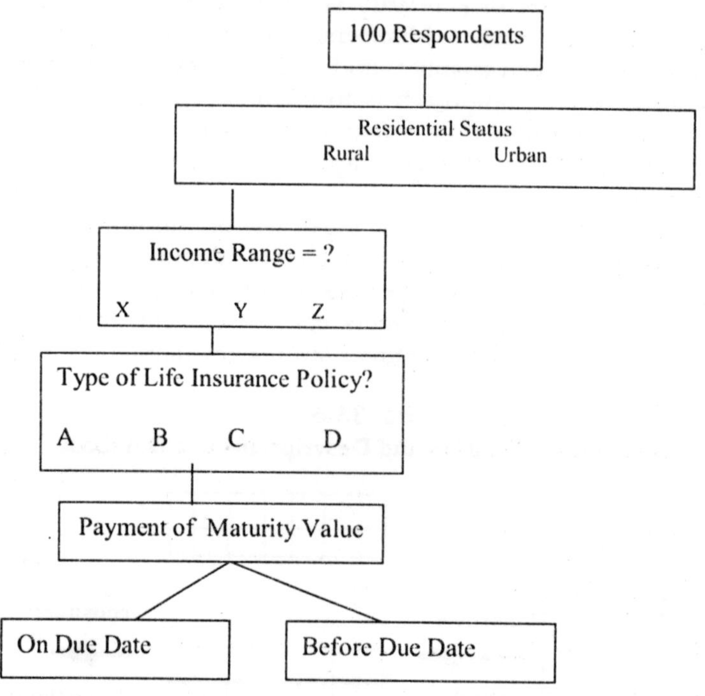

Specifically, each branch of the tree is a classification question and the leaves of the tree are partitions of the dataset with their classification. For instance, if we were going to classify customers who on the basis of their nature, job profile, their income level opt for a specific life insurance policy in India. This decision tree may provide a prediction for a kid of policy the customer generally buy, the maturity value they generally get either on due date or before due date.

This prediction may help the life insurance service provider to make a target to specific income group customer to buy their newly launched policies. Another way that the decision tree technology has been used is for preprocessing data for other prediction algorithms. Because the algorithm is fairly robust with respect to a variety of predictor types, and because it can be run relatively quickly, decision trees can be used on the first pass of a data mining run to create a subset of possibly useful predictors that can, then, be fed into neural networks, nearest neighbor and normal statistical routines—which can take a considerable amount of time to run if there are large number of possible predictors to be used in the model. Some forms of decision trees were initially developed as exploratory tools to refine and preprocess data for more standard statistical techniques like linear regression. They have also been used for prediction.

3.5 Neural Networks

When data mining algorithms are talked about, these days most of the time people are talking about either decision trees or neural networks. Neural networks do have disadvantages that can be limiting in their ease of use and ease of deployment, but they also have some significant advantages. Foremost among these advantages is their highly accurate predictive models that can be applied across a large number of different types of problems.

Neural networks are used in a wide variety of applications. They have been used in all facets of business from detecting the exercise such as forfeiture/surrender/switchover of life insurance policies in India. They have a long history of application in other areas such as the military for the automated driving of an unmanned vehicle at 30 miles per hour on smooth roads.

In order to make a prediction, the neural network accepts the values for the predictors on what are called the input nodes. These become the values for those nodes, those values are then multiplied by values that are stored in the links (sometimes called links and in some ways similar to the weights that were applied to predictors in the nearest neighbor method). These values are then added together at the output node. A special function is applied and the resulting number is the prediction.

A simplified version of the calculations made in the Figure 33.8. Here the value age of 47 is normalized to fall between 0.0 and 1.0 and has the value 0.47 and the income is normalized to the value 0.65. This simplified neural network makes the prediction of no default for a 47 year old earning

Fig. 33.8
Neural Network

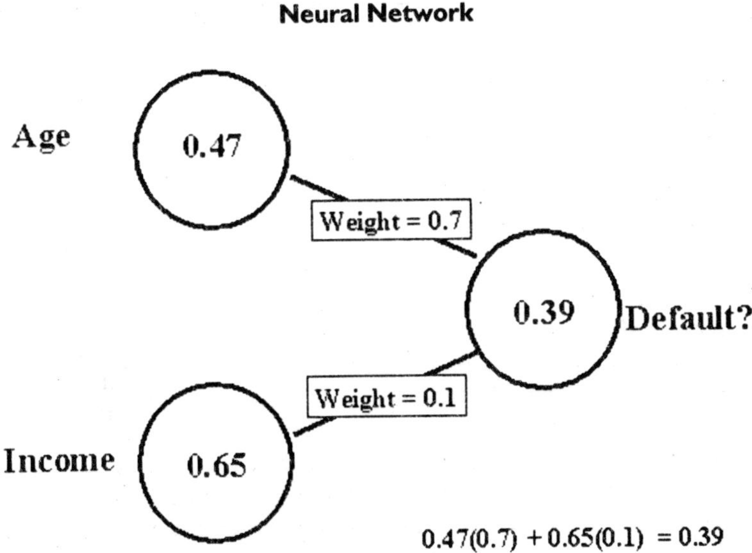

Rs. 65,000. The links are weighted at 0.7 and 0.1 and the resulting value after multiplying the node values by the link weights is 0.39. The network has been trained to learn that an output value of 1.0 indicates default and that 0.0 indicate non-default. The output value calculated here (0.39) is closer to 0.0 than to 1.0 so the record is assigned a non-default prediction.

3.6 Rule Induction

In rule induction systems, the rule itself is of a simple form of "if this and this and this then this". For example, a rule that a supermarket might find in their data collected from scanners would be: If paper plates are purchased then plastic forks are purchased. In order for the rules to be useful, there are two pieces of information that must be supplied as well as the actual rule:

- *Accuracy*—How often is the rule correct?
- *Coverage*—How often does the rule apply?

Rule induction systems are highly automated and are probably the best of data mining techniques for exposing all possible predictive patterns in a database. They can be modified for use in prediction problems but the algorithms for combining evidence from a variety of rules comes more from rules of thumbs and practical experience.

In general, these rules are relatively simple such as for a market basket database of items scanned in a consumer market basket you might find interesting correlations in your database shown in the table given below:

Rule	*Accuracy*	*Coverage*
If breakfast cereal purchased then milk purchased.	85%	90%
If bread purchased then cheese purchased.	82%	75%

This technique may be used to predict the combination of the interest of customer for buying various life insurance policies along with riders.

4. DATA MINING TOOLS

Michel A. King *et. al.* (1998) in his research says that there are many desktop data mining tools currently available using a variety of technologies to solve classification/estimation problems and to build a predictive model out of Data mining. The 14 desktop tools were evaluated from leading vendors which were available to his research team and which uses one of the four technologies: Decision Tree, Rule Induction, Neural Network and Network Neighborhood. The rating of these tools as per his research in solving the real life problems such as business problems, medical problems and problems related to customer interaction is given below:

TABLE 33.1
Data Mining Tool Evaluation Summary

Technology	*Tool*	*Capability*	*Learnability/ Usability*	*Inter-operability*	*Flexibility*	*Accuracy*
Tree	CART	+	√	-	√+	+
	Scenario	√-	+	+	-	—
	See 5	√	√-	√	√-	+
	S-Plus	+	√-	++	+	+
Rule Induction	WizWhy	√	√+	√	√-	-
	DataMind	√+	++	+	√-	√
	DMSK	-	—	√-	-	+
Neural Network	NeuroShell2	-	√	-	-	++
	PcOIPARS	√-	-	-	√-	√
	PRW	√+	+	++	√	++
Network Neighbor	MQ Expert	+	√	√	√+	+
	NeuroShell2	√-	√	√	√-	+
	Gnosis	√-	√	—	√-	++
	Knowledge Miner	-	-	-	√-	+

++ = Excellent; += Good; √ = Average; - = Needs Improvement; — = Poor.

5. CONCLUSION

Application of data mining tools & techniques in context of life insurance sector in India: the success of knowledge discovery depends on several aspects, among them the quality and completeness of the data, the clarity of task and the availability of efficient tool and techniques. In this study, life insurance sector in India has been selected as the potential application for data mining. Therefore, to develop a predictive model or to evaluate the trend of some of the objectives like investment trend (ratio of investment) of the customer in life insurance product, type of the policies in which the customer generally prefer to invest, to select a geographical location for launch of new insurance policies, pricing of life insurance product and to analyze the claims of forfeiture/surrender/switchover for life insurance companies in India, we may opt any of the data mining technique mentioned earlier.

Statistics as a DM technique may be useful to analyze the trend of investment of a customer in India that how much he invest in life insurance policy and how much in the other sector like mutual funds, shares/ securities, PPF and in other postal schemes. To analyze the trend of investment, we may apply multiple linear regressions.

As we are aware that in India the customer does not invest regularly throughout the year, therefore, nearest neighbor technique may be useful to predict the intention of the customer for investment in life insurance companies in India as per their geographical location, age group, income group and other socio-economic factor. We may also view a trend of investment for a specific type of life insurance policy. We may analyze that at what time a serviceman, businessman, farmer, students, housewives, etc. invest in life insurance sector and from which geography do they belong.

Similarly, in Clustering we can develop certain segments of customers as per their income group, age group, marital status and their object for investment in life insurance sector in India. Decision tree can help us to predict that when a customer buys a policy, what are the possibilities that a particular segment of customer will buy the new launched life insurance polices. Rule induction may help us to predict the possibilities of surrender/ switchover/surrender the life insurance policies of a customer. This is also helpful to analyze that what type of riders along with the policy may attract the customer to buy new launched life insurance policies.

Neural Network is also an important technique of data mining, which is based on the scheme of input, hidden, output layer. In it, on the basis of certain hypothesis, we may draw certain predictive rule at the hidden layer. Through input layer we will enter certain parameter in the system and the output layer will provide us the prediction for the exercise, e.g. a customer of 65 year and the income group of Rs. 75,000 p.a. will make the default or not with the life insurance companies.

After analyzing all of the techniques and their possibility of implementation for meeting the objective drawn in this study insist us to implement any of the two data mining techniques which suitably meet the purpose. The result of these techniques may be further filtered using the data mining tools given earlier for the development of a predictive model for life insurance sector in India.

References

1. Adya, M. 1998. "How Effective Are Neural Networks at Forecasting and Prediction? A Review and Evaluation." *Journal of Forecasting* 17(5-6, Sep-Nov): 481-95.
2. Berry, M.A., and G.S. Linoff. 2000. *Mastering Dam Mining*. New York, N.Y.: Wiley.
3. Bishop, C.M. 1995. *Neural Networks for Pattern Recognition*. New York: Oxford University Press.
4. Breiman, L., J.H. Friedman, R.A. Olsben, and C.J. Stone. 1984. *Classification and Regression Trees*. New York, N.Y.: Chapman & Hall.
5. Borok, L.S. 1997. "Data mining: Sophisticated Forms of Managed Care Modeling through Artificial Intelligence." *Journal of Health Care Finance*. 23(3), 20-36.
6. Carpenter, G., and S. Grossberg. 1988. "The ART of Adaptive Pattern Recognition by a Self-Organizing Neural Network." *IEEE Computer*, 21(3): 77-88.
7. Cheesman, P. 1996. "Bayesian Classification (AutoClass): Theory and Results," in *Advances in Knowledge Discovery and Data Mining*, ed. by Fayyad, U., G. Piatetsky-Shapiro, P. Smyth, and R. Uthurusamy. Menlo Park, CA: AAAI Press/The MIT Press: 153-80.
8. Chessman, P., J. Kelly, M. Self, J. Stutz, W. Taylor, and D. Freeman. 1988. "Auto Class: A Bayesian classification system." *5th Int'l Conf. on Machine Learning*, Morgan Kaufmann.24.

9. Goldberg, D.E. 1989. *Genetic Algorithms in Search, Optimization and Machine Learning.* Morgan Kaufmann.
10. Guha, S., R. Rastogi, and K. Shim K. 1998. "CURE: An Efficient Clustering Algorithm for Large Databases." *Proceedings of the ACM SIGMOD Conference.*
11. Ester, M., H. Kriegel, J. Sander, and X. Xu. 1998. "Cluttering for Mining in Large Spatial Databases." *Special Issue on Data mining, KI-Journal,* 1. Scien Tec Publishing.
12. Fayyad, U.M., G. Piatetsky-Shapiro, P. Smyth, and R. Uthumsamy (Eds.). 1996. *Advancesin Knowledge Discovery and Data Mining.* Cambridge, MA: The MIT Press.
13. Fisher, D., M. Pazzani, and P. Langley. 1991. *Concept Formation: Knowledge and Experience in Unsupervised Learning.* San Mateo, CA: Kanfmann.
14. Quinlin, J.R. 1983. "Induction of Decision Trees." *Machine Learning* 1: 81-106.
15. D.E. Rumelhart, G.E. Hinton, and R.J. Williams. 1986. "Learning Internal Representation by Error Propagation." *Parallel Distributed Processing,* ed. by Rumelhart, D.E., J.L.
16. McClelland, and the PDP Research Group. Cambridge, MA: The MIT Press: 318-62.
17. SAS Institute. 2000. *Enterprise Miner,* Cary, N.C.: SAS Institute.
18. Tufte, E.R. 1983. *The Visual Display of Quantitative Information,* Graphics Press, Cheshire, CN.

SECTION V

Software Agents and Internet Computing

34

Design and Other Issues in Software Agents

VIKRAM SINGH

ABSTRACT

The discipline of software agents is rapidly evolving, developing and spans over human engineering, artificial intelligence and software engineering. However, to many people in the software arena, it is still unclear what agents are and what they can do. Agents are naturally useful as a tool to analyze systems. The underlying concept of agents often relates well to the way we naturally think about complex tasks and thus, agents can be useful to model such tasks.

1. INTRODUCTION

A software agent is a concept, similar to methods and objects in object orientation. The concept of an agent provides a convenient and powerful way to describe a complex software entity that is capable of acting with a certain degree of autonomy in order to accomplish tasks on behalf of its user or another software. A software agent behaves like a human agent, i.e., acts on behalf of a user or other software. Actions carried out on behalf of user/ program implies the delegation of power or authority to decide which action is appropriate. Moreover, the agents are delegated the power to make decisions as to when an action need to be carried out. The basic concept behind agents is that they are not explicitly invoked for a task, rather they invoke/activate themselves.

Historically, the concept of software agent can be traced back to Hewitt's Actor Model (Hewitt, 1977), wherein, an agent is defined as *"A self-contained, interactive and concurrently-executing object, possessing internal state and communication capability."* As independent research links, software agents are also directly evolved from Multi-Agent Systems, which in turn evolved from Distributed Artificial Intelligence, Distributed Problem Solving and Parallel Artificial Intelligence, thus, inheriting all characteristics of its underlying disciplines.

A 1987 video "Knowledge Navigator" by John Sculley (Apple, 1997) depicted the relationship between end-users and agents. Initially, this field experienced a series of unsuccessful top-down implementation, instead of piece-to-piece, bottom-up approach. 1990 onwards, a wide range of agent systems is available, e.g. WWW, search engines, search agents, etc.

FIG. 34.1
Classification of Software Agents

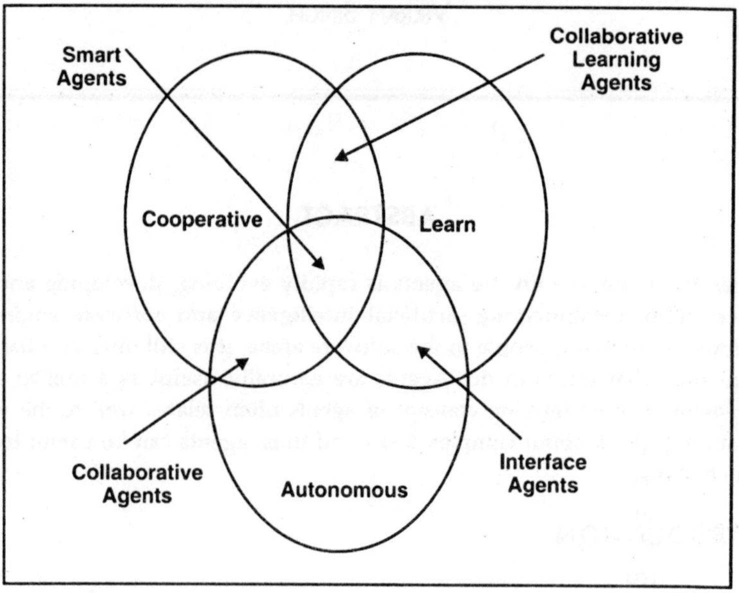

Source : Nwana, 2001.

2. CLASSIFICATION

Nwana (Nwana, 2001) has classified agents on the basis of their primary attributes, namely, cooperation, learning capability:

- *persistence* (code is not executed on demand but runs continuously and decides for itself when it should perform some activity),
- *autonomy* (agents have capabilities of task selection, prioritization, goal-directed behaviour, decision-making without human intervention),
- *social ability* (agents are able to engage other components through some sort of communication and coordination, they may collaborate on a task), and
- *reactivity* (agents perceive the context in which they operate and react to it appropriately).

Depending upon features and capabilities, software agents might be categorised as *intelligent* agents (those agents which exhibit some aspect of Artificial Intelligence, e.g. learning and inferencing capability), *autonomous* agents (those agents which are capable of modifying their *modus operandi*), *distributed* agents (those agents which execute in distributed environment), *multi-agent systems* (stributed agents which cooperate and communicate with other agents to achieve an objective), and *mobile* agents (agents which can relocate themselves onto different processors alongwith their state of execution).

A. Intelligent Agents

Design and development of intelligent software agents is an area of artificial intelligence research. Such agents should have following capabilities:

(i) *Adaptability*—Adaptation means capability of sensing the environment and reconfiguring itself in response to the environmental variables. This can be achieved through the choice of alternative algorithms. Adaptation may also include other aspects of an agent's internal construction, such as recruiting processor or storage resources.

(ii) *Learning*—Learning implies that the agents should be capable of learning new procedures and modify their behaviour accordingly. Learning may be achieved through trial-and-error or by example and generalization. Trial and error method implies a capability of introspection and analysis of behaviour and success, whereas learning by example proceeds by abstraction and generalisation.

B. Autonomous Agents

Such agents are are self-contained and capable of making independent decisions, and taking actions to satisfy internal goals based upon their perceived environment. Autonomy on one hand, the software agents controlling important real-time applications are closely supervised by people who start them up, monitor and continually modify their behaviour, and shut them down as and when necessary. Popek and Goldberg (1974) describe a virtualization requirements technique—a hardware solution to the supervision problem. The underlying concept is to prevent the execution of critical instructions without entering a supervision system mode, e.g. super-user mode.

C. Distributed Agents

As the software agents are self-contained and include their required resources in their description, they can be designed to be very loosely coupled and it becomes particularly easy to have them executed as independent threads and on distributed processors. Such agents are called distributed agents and there upon apply the considerations of distributed computing. The code of such agents should be particularly easy to implement in a distributed fashion and should be scaleable as well.

D. Software Agents

Several agents may be interacting with each other and act in coordination and collaboration to achieve a common goal. Such a group of multiple software agents is popularly called known as a multi-agent system or alternatively a *software agency*. Individual agent in such systems does not have all data or all methods available to achieve an objective and thus will have to collaborate with other agents. Moreover, there is usually little or no global control, and thus, such systems are sometimes referred to as swarm systems. On the pattern of distributed agents, here also data are decentralised and methods are executed asynchronously.

E. Mobile Agents

Such agents code is capable of moving itself alongwith its execution state on to another processor to continue execution there. Such agents are particularly suitable to gather system information remotely, taking back-up of the files by copying them in client-server environment, monitoring network throughput or to check resource availability and moderating the resource utilisation of system by monitoring the services running on system.

F. Fuzzy Agents

These are software agents that work on the principle of fuzzy logic. Such code interacts with its environment through an adaptive database of rules. These agents can, therefore, be considered as a type of intelligent agent.

Fanklin & Graesser (1997) discuss four key notions that distinguish agents from arbitrary programs: reaction to the environment, autonomy, goal-orientation and persistence. Agents might be distinguished from objects on following accounts:

- agents are more autonomous than objects;
- agents have flexible behaviour: reactive, proactive, social; and
- agents have at least one thread of control but may have more (Wooldridge, 2002).

(Wooldridge, 2002) distinguishes software agents from expert systems based on following three point:

- Expert Systems do not intercact with their environment;
- Expert Systems are not designed as self-invoking code; and
- Expert Systems do not consider exhibit social behaviour.

3. DESIGN ISSUES

There are two main levels at which software agent systems are designed:

- The domain level, and
- The individual agent level.

At the domain level, there are few unique challenges to mixed-initiative system design. However, at the individual agent level, the agent itself must be designed to interact with the human and the agent system, integrating the two into a single system. A third kind of design approach, namely, mixed-initiative system is one in which humans interact directly with software agents in a collaborative approach to problem-solving.

Interesting issues to be considered in the development of agent-based systems include:

- The way the agents recruit resources. Event content might be combined with the rule-base or knowledge content provided by the user to train the agent and recruit the resources.
- The way the agents are re-instantiated in different environments.
- The way the internal states of agents are stored.
- The way the agent behaviour changes due to a change of environment.
- The way the agents prioritise the tasks. The agent may employ its learning mechanism to increase its weight for a particular kind of event.
- The way the agents communicate with each other and the user. The agent may make use of a user-access method to deliver that message to the user.
- The way the tasks are scheduled.
- The way the tasks are synchronised.

- The way the agents coordinate and collaborate with each other. For software agents to work together efficiently, they must share semantics of their data elements. This can be done by having computer systems publish their metadata. The agent uses its access methods to go out into local and remote databases to forage for content. These access methods may include setting up news stream delivery to the agent, or retrieval from bulletin boards, or using a spider to walk the web.
- Which hierarchies of agents are useful. In software agencies, individual agents could be arranged in alternative hierarchies. This arrangement should portray the natural hierarchy of agents in real systems.

Complex and embedded software agents are best designed using a multi-layer architecture. These systems demonstrate the complex behaviour that the aggregates of relatively simple interacting agents exhibit in real systems. Another approach to the design of software agents is bottom-up approach.

References

1. Nwana, H.S. (2001), "*Software Agents: An Overview,*" *Knowledge Engineering Review*, Cambridge University Press, Vol. 11, No. 3, pp. 1-40.
2. Popek, G.J. and Goldberg, R.P. (1974), "*Formal requirements for virtualisable third generation architectures*", *ACM Communications*, Volume 17, No. 7, pp. 412-21.
3. Wooldridge, M. (2002), "*An Introduction to Multi-agent Systems*", John Wiley & Sons, Chichester, England.
4. Franklin, S. and Graesser, A. (1996), "*Is it an agent of just a program? A Taxonomy for Autonomous Agents*", in Proceedings of third International Workshop on Agent Theories, Architectures, and Languages, New York, Springer-Verlag.
5. Hewitt, C. and Atkinson, R. (1977), "*Synchronization in Actor Systems*", Proceedings of the 4th ACM SIGACT-SIGPLAN symposium on Principles of Programming Languages.
6. Apple (1987), "*Knowledge Navigator*", Apple Computer's concept video for a hypothetical product.

35

Towards Defining Semi-Markov Dynamic Conditional Random Fields (Semi-DCRFs)

PARAMVIR SINGH

ABSTRACT

Probabilistic modeling frameworks are used for labeling and segmentation tasks in various text and speech processing applications like Part-of-Speech (POS) tagging, information extraction, etc. The latest probabilistic models that are being used for these tasks are called Dynamic Conditional Random Fields (DCRFs). These models have improved the accuracy of these tasks to a great proportion in comparison to the previous models but the inference method of these models is still intractable. This paper proposes a tractable extension to the inference method of DCRFs leading to the introduction of a new probabilistic model called Semi-Markov Dynamic Conditional Random Fields (Semi-DCRFs).

1. INTRODUCTION

Probabilistic models are quite frequently applied to a wide variety of problems in text and speech processing. These problems include Part-Of-Speech (POS) tagging, information extraction, text segmentation and syntactic disambiguation. All these problems need to segment and label data, which are performed by the various probabilistic models.

Hidden Markov Models (HMMs) [1] were the first and the most widely used probabilistic models for segmentation and labeling tasks. HMMs are generative models that work by assigning a joint probability to paired observation and label sequences. A generative model needs to evaluate all the observation sequences to define a joint probability over observation and label sequences. But, it had a couple of serious problems. First, it was not practical to represent multiple interacting features or long-range dependencies of the observations. Second, the inference problem for such models is intractable. This second problem was resolved by K.P. Murphy's *Hidden Semi-Markov Models* [5] that are a tractable extension to HMMs.

A conditional model specifies the probabilities of possible label sequences given an observation sequence. It is better than a generative model as it does not waste any effort on modeling the observations that are already known at test time. *Maximum Entropy Hidden Markov Models (MEMMs)* [3] are conditional models in which each source state has an exponential model that takes the observation features as input and then outputs a distribution over possible next state. The major problem in MEMM is the Label Bias problem [4].

A modern probabilistic framework called Conditional Random Fields (CRFs) [4,12] is an enhancement of MEMMs. It not only carries all the advantages of MEMM but also solves the label bias problem in a decent way. It uses a single exponential model for the joint probability of entire sequence of labels given an observation sequence. It suffers from two problems. First, the inference algorithm used in CRF fails while representing complex interactions between labels. Second problem is again the intractability problem.

Andrew McCallum and Bell Welner [16] gave latest frameworks, called Semi-Markov Conditional Random Fields (Semi-CRFs), which are the tractable extension to CRFs. Semi-CRF models improve the inference method accuracy of CRFs by using a tractable extension. Semi-CRFs are a conditionally trained version of semi-Markov models. They are used in Named Entity Recognition (NER), gene-finding and NP-chunking.

Dynamic Conditional Random Fields (DCRFs) [13] are a generalization of linear chain CRFs. DCRFs are undirected graphical models whose structure and parameters are repeated over a given sequence. They can deal with the multiple label sequences simultaneously given an observation sequence during labeling and segmentation tasks. They can handle complex interactions among labels that CRFs fail to handle. The key problem is the intractable nature of DCRFs in segmentation and labeling tasks.

This paper proposes a tractable extension to the inference method of DCRFs to improve its inference method accuracy for Segmentation and Labeling tasks. We believe that tractable extension to CRFs used in building Semi-CRFs can also be used in DCRFs to make their inference method tractable.

2. DYNAMIC CONDITIONAL RANDOM FIELDS

Charles Sutton, Khashayar Rohanimanesh, Andrew McCallum [13] introduced Dynamic CRFs (DCRFs), which are a generalization of linear-chain CRFs that repeat structure and parameters over a sequence of state vectors— allowing us to represent distributed hidden state and complex interaction among labels, as in Dynamic Bayesian Networks (DBNs) [6], and to use rich, overlapping feature sets, as in conditional models. For example, a typical factorial structure can include links between co-temporal labels, explicitly modeling limited probabilistic dependencies between two different label sequences. Other types of DCRFs can model higher-order Markov dependence between labels, or incorporate a fixed-size memory. For example, a DCRF for part-of-speech tagging could include for each word a hidden state that is true if any previous word has been tagged as a verb.

A Dynamic CRF is a conditionally trained undirected graphical model whose structure and parameters are repeated over a sequence. As with a DBN, a DCRF can be specified by a template that gives the graphical structure, features, and weights for two time steps, which can then be unrolled given an instance x. The same set of features and weights is used at each sequence position so that the parameters are tied across the network.

The exact inference method in DCRF consists of:

- Viterbi Algorithm, used to label a new sequence, and
- Marginal Computation, used for parameter estimation.

Due to inefficiency and heavy cost of exact inference method, an approximate inference method called loopy belief propagation algorithm was devised. Loopy belief propagation algorithms provide a more accurate inference method to DCRFs.

The inference methods in both CRFs and DCRFs are not tractable, i.e. we end up making several approximations in the inference algorithms which gives better results but is by no means an appropriate method. We need least number of approximations in the inference method of these models.

3. SEMI-MARKOV DYNAMIC CONDITIONAL RANDOM FIELDS (SEMI-DCRFS)

DCRFs having an approximate inference technique can be used in combination with Semi-CRFs to give a new probabilistic model called Semi-Dynamic Conditional Random Fields (Semi-DCRFs). This new model will have all the productive features of DCRFs along with a tractable inference method.

We are here looking into the tractable extension used in Semi-CRFs so that the same can be applied to DCRFs. Let us have a brief make up of how this can be done. The *tractable extension* that can be applied to DCRFs includes following two major steps:

- Segmentation $S_i(m,n,Y_i)$ of the observation sequence $X_m, \ldots, X_n$, where each segment consists of:
  - start positio m,
  - end position n, and
  - a label Y_i.
- Defining a *segment feature function 'g'* which maps the observation sequences to label sequences.

Figure 35.1 shows an intractable DCRF with X_i as observation elements, Y_i as labeling elements and w_i as weights. The observation elements X_i have been shown as grouped in segments S_i in Figure 35.2, with segments now taking the original positions of individual observation elements.

FIG. 35.1
A DCRF Model with X_i as Observation Elements, Y_i as Labeling Elements and w_i as Weights

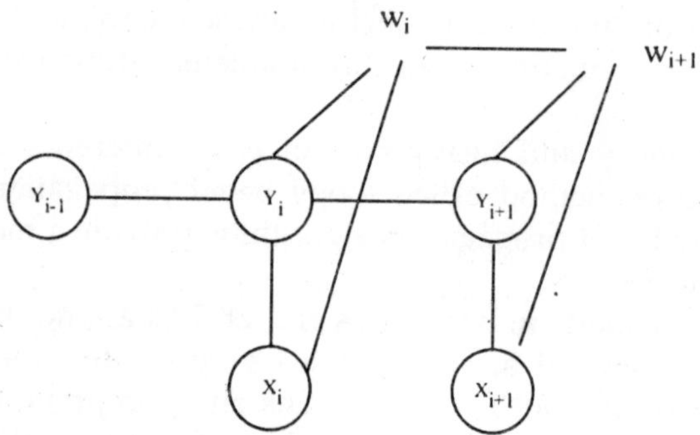

4. CONCLUSIONS AND FUTURE WORK

The intractable nature of the inference methods in CRFs was eliminated with the introduction of semi-CRFs. This tractable methodology has not yet applied to the latest frameworks called DCRFs. DCRFs have eliminated all the major problems in the previous probabilistic models including multiple interactions among labels, simultaneous cascaded labeling problem, and have resolved a lot of other ambiguities. The stage is set to empirically prove whether the tractable extension used in CRF can be applied to DCRF to improve its inference method accuracy to give a concept called Semi-Markov Dynamic Conditional Random Fields (Semi-DCRFs).

Fig. 35.2
A Potential Tractable DCRF Model

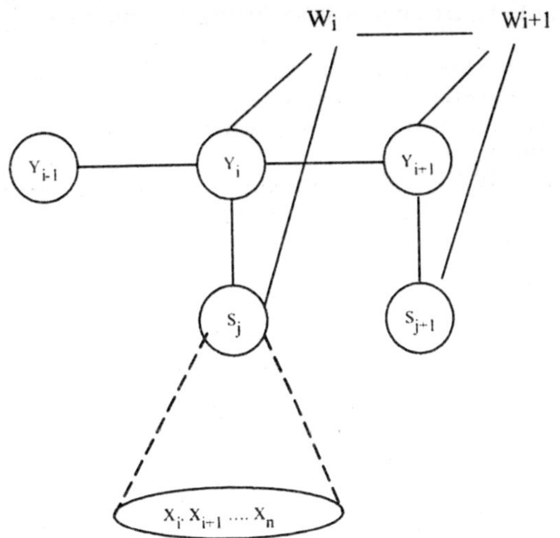

References

1. Rabiner, L.R., Juang, B.H. (1986). An Introduction to Hidden Markov Models. In Proceedings of the IEEE ASSP (Acoustic Speech Sign Process) Mag., pp. 4-16.
2. Rabiner, L.R. (1989). A tutorial on hidden Markov models and selected applications in speech recognition. In Proceedings of IEEE ASSP Mag., pp. 257–85.
3. McCallum, A., Freitag, D. and F. Pereira (2000). Maximum entropy Markov models for information extraction and segmentation. In Proceedings of ICML 2000. International Conference on Machine Learning, pp. 591-98.
4. Lafferty, J., McCallum, A. and Pereira F. (2001). Conditional random fields: Probabilistic models for segmenting and labeling sequence data. In Proceedings of ICML-2001. International Conference on Machine Learning, pp. 282-89.
5. Murphy, K.P. (2002). Hidden Semi-Markov Models (HSMMs).
6. Murphy, K.P. (2002). Dynamic Bayesian Networks: Representation, Inference and Learning. In Ph.D. Thesis, Dept. Computer Science, UC Berkeley.
7. Skounakis, M., Craven M.and Ray S. (2003). Hierarchical hidden Markov Models for Information Extraction. In *Proceedings of the 18th (IJCAI-2003)*. International Joint Conference on Artificial Intelligence, pp. 427-33.
8. Sha, F. and Pereira, F. (2003). Shallow Parsing with Conditional Random Fields. In *Proceedings of HLT-NAACL*, pp. 124-32.
9. McCallum, A. and Li W. (2003). Early Results for Named Entity Recognition with Conditional Random Fields, Feature Induction and web-enhanced lexicons. In Proceedings of The Seventh Conference on Natural Language Learning (CoNLL-2003), pp. 188-91.
10. McCallum, A. and Welner, B. (2003). Toward Conditional Models of Identity Uncertainty with application to proper noun coreferences. In Proceedings of IJCAI-2003 Workshop on Information Integration on the web, pp. 79-86.
11. Pinto, D., McCallum, A., Wei, X. and Croft, W.B. (2003). Table Extraction using Conditional Random Fields. In Proceedings of the ACM SIGIR-2003, pp. 235-42.
12. Wallach Hanna, M. (2004). Conditional Random Fields: An Introduction.

13. Sutton, C., Rohnimanesh, K. and McCallum, A. (2004). Dynamic Conditional Random Fields: Factorized probabilistic models for labeling and segmenting sequence data. In Proceedings of ICML-2004, pp. 245-53.
14. Bunescu, R. and Mooney, R.J. (2004). Relational Markov networks for collective information extraction. In Proceedings of Workshop on Statistical Relational Learning (SRL-2004).
15. Cohen, W.W., Sarawagi, S. (2004). Exploiting dictionaries in named entity extraction: Combining semi-Markov Extraction processes and data integration methods. In Proceedings of the Tenth ACM SIGKDD International Conference on Knowledge Discovery and Data Mining.
16. Sarawagi, S. and Cohen, W.W. (2004). Semi-Markov Conditional random fields for Information Extraction. In Proceedings of NIPS Conference.

36

Stream Control Transmission Protocol : An Innovative Next Generation Protocol

Dinesh Kumar and Deepak Kaushik

ABSTRACT

Stream Control Transmission Protocol (SCTP) is an end-to-end, connection-oriented protocol that transports data in independent sequenced streams. SCTP is a unicast transport protocol for IP network that is standardized in RFC2960 by the IETF. SCTP endpoints support multi-homing; therefore, interface redundancy is built into the protocol. Through selective transmission mechanisms, SCTP resolves errors and buffers the data transmission process. These days most applications that need a reliable in-order delivery of the bytes use the Transmission Control Protocol (TCP). Since TCP is a byte stream-oriented protocol, TCP is not always well suited for applications that need reliable message-based transport. Therefore, Stream Control Transfer Protocol (SCTP) was designed to provide this feature. SCTP itself works very much like TCP, providing reliable transport and keeping the channel alive through the whole process until completion.

SCTP provides applications with enhanced performance, reliability, and control functions. This protocol is essential where detection of connection failure and associated monitoring is mandatory. Furthermore, SCTP could be implemented in network systems and applications that deliver voice/data and support quality real-time services (e.g., streaming video and multimedia). This paper begins by discussing the evolution of SCTP and continues with an explanation of the fundamental concepts of the protocol. Following the explanation, the discussion elaborates the unique features that distinguish SCTP from other transport protocols.

1. INTRODUCTION

Over the past few decades, packet-switched networks have merged with new technologies to facilitate more efficient communication channels within network systems. The popularity of Internet Protocol (IP)-based networks is attributed to the emergence of the Internet and a host of highly popular network applications. IP networks and telephony-based networks are converging to support the inter-working of applications and services. In addition, Integrated Services Digital Networks (ISDN), Asynchronous Transfer Mode (ATM) networks, and mobile networks are increasingly routing their signaling traffic via IP networks. SCTP provides flexible delivery and reliable transfer within IP networks.

SCTP provides numerous advantages over User Datagram Protocol (UDP) and Transmission Control Protocol (TCP). For instance, SCTP combines the datagram orientation of UDP with the sequencing and reliability of TCP. Additionally, SCTP uses multi-stream, message-oriented routing in multi-homed environments.

The SCTP datagram has been derived from the MDTP. Its feature has been highly improved and many mistakes have been solved, but the basic idea remained and the final design of SCTP is internally much closer to MDTP than it could be thought at a first sight [5]

The SCTP transport service layer is positioned between the SCTP user application and the network service being used. Since SCTP is based on interfacing two SCTP endpoints, there are certain Application Programming Interfaces (APIs) that run in between the transport service layer and SCTP user layer. In addition, each endpoint hosts multiple IP addresses.

SCTP deploys multiple paths and streams to transport messages across two endpoints. In SCTP, data is transmitted between endpoints through a connection referred to as an "association". An association begins with an "initiation" and is maintained until all data has been successfully transmitted and received. Once all data is successfully received, the association is gracefully terminated through a "shutdown".

Within SCTP, user data and control information are assembled in chunks. Multiple chunks and a common header comprise a Protocol Data Unit (PDU), also referred to as an "SCTP packet". SCTP packets contain data chunks and control chunks. SCTP provides ordered message delivery within "SCTP streams" and supports network fault tolerance in multi-homing environments.

The fundamental SCTP properties include the following:

- *Validation and Acknowledgement Mechanisms*—During initiation, the validation mechanism bundles the data into a "cookie" that

FIG. 36.1
Stream Control Transmission Protocol

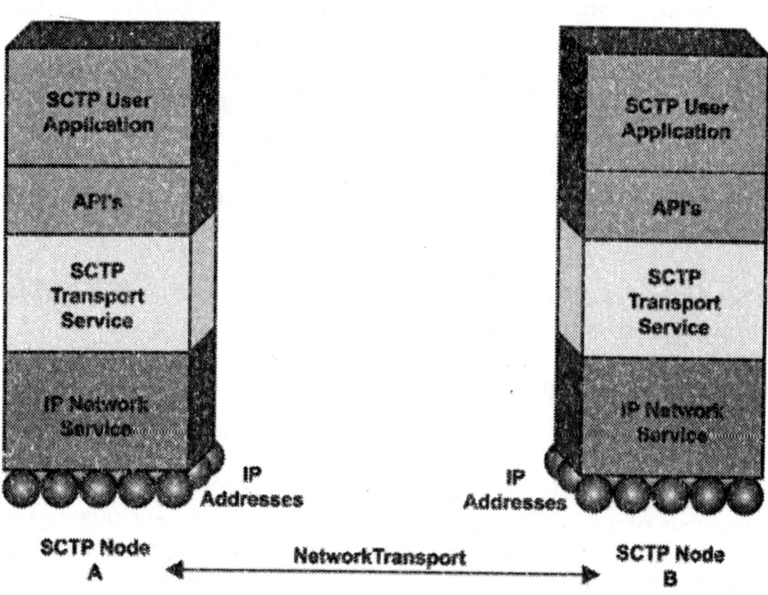

includes a secure hash of values and a secret key. Cookies are digitally signed with Message Authentication Codes (MAC), which are used to prevent denial-of-service attacks. Within an association, Selective Acknowledgement (SACK) chunks acknowledge the receipt of data chunks. SACK chunks are also used to inform the endpoint of duplicated or missing chunks. The pay load (DATA) and the Selective Acknowledgement (SACK) chunk are used for the data transfer[5].

- *Path Selection and Monitoring*—SCTP packets are routed to the destination IP address of a peer endpoint through a "primary path". The primary path allows the user to determine the primary route for data flow [2]. In addition, alternate paths exist for each IP address that the peer endpoint supports. SCTP closely monitors the transmission paths to the peer endpoint using HEARTBEAT chunks that test the connectivity of a path. In SCTP, a path is considered "active" when it has been acknowledged by the peer endpoint or has been used previously for SCTP packet transfer. A path is considered "inactive" if previous path transmissions have failed. The heartbeat request (Heartbeat) and heartbeat acknowledgement (Heartbeat ACK) chunks are used to track the state of the different network interfaces used in he association [5].
- *Flow and Congestion Control*—While SCTP flow control is based on each association, congestion control is established within each transmission path. The peer endpoint assigns a receiver-window

variable for flow control. The receiver-window variable alerts the endpoint of the amount of space available in the peer endpoint's inbound buffer. SCTP deploys congestion control within each stream using a congestion-window variable. This variable limits the number of bytes that may be sent before an acknowledgement is received. A set of flow and congestion control parameters is subtly retained within the association and each transmission path[2]. The Explicit Congestion Notification Echo (ECNE) and the Congestion Window Reduced (CWR) are used for flow and congestion control[5].

These features give SCTP numerous advantages over TCP and UDP, as the following section elaborates.

2. SCTP MULTI-HOMING

A Host which has more than one interface is said to be multihomed[3]. Host on the internet have typically been single homed due to the relatively high expense of network interface compared to any serious need to be connected to more than a single network at a time. The traditional Internet Protocol (IP), TCP and UDP have no concept of multihoming[6]. The multi-homing feature enables SCTP endpoints to support multiple IP addresses. Multi-homing protects an association from potential network failures by steering traffic to alternate IP addresses. During the initiation of an association, SCTP endpoints exchange lists of IP addresses. Therefore, each endpoint can send and receive messages from any of the IP addresses listed at the remote endpoint. For example, one of the listed IP addresses will be designated as the primary address during the initiation. If the primary address repeatedly drops chunks, however, all chunks will be transmitted to

FIG. 36.2
Multihoming in SCTP[6]

an alternate address until a connection to the primary address can be re-established.

An SCTP Association between host A and host B consists of the entire set of addresses available at each point in this case ({A1, A2}, {B1, B2}). SCTP can use any feasible combination of these available addresses [6]. The multihoming gives SCTP a certain network level fault tolerance[4].

FIG. 36.3
SCTP Multi-Streaming [7]

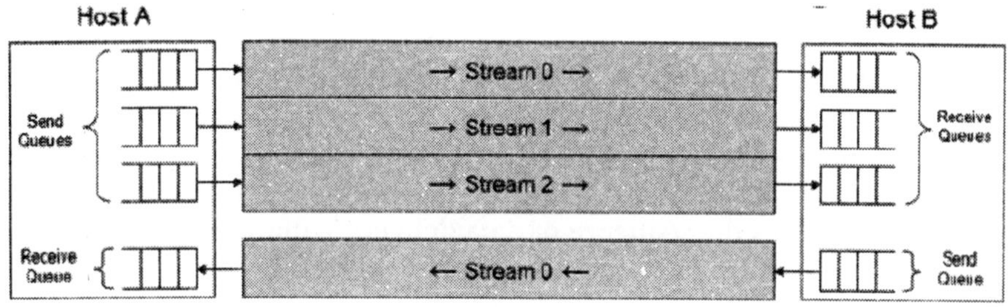

3. SCTP MULTI-STREAMING

The multi-streaming feature separates and transmits user data on multiple SCTP streams. These streams are capable of independent, sequenced delivery. Message loss in a particular stream will only hinder delivery within that stream. Therefore, other streams within an association are not affected.

Through multi-streaming, SCTP eliminates unnecessary blocking that often occurs in TCP transmissions. In TCP, a stream is defined as a sequence of bytes that conform to strict in-sequence delivery. In-sequence delivery, results in a major drawback known as "head-of-the-queue blocking" where messages within a stream are not allowed to bypass each other. Since SCTP streams are independent, retransmitted and high-priority messages can bypass less significant messages. Figure 36.3 illustrates a multistreamed association between hosts A and B. In this example, host A uses three output streams to host B (numbered 0 to 2), and has only one input stream from host B (numbered 0). The number of input and output streams is an SCTP association negotiated during association setup.[8]

4. SCTP FEATURES

In the three stages of association, SCTP applies mechanisms that set it apart from TCP and UDP.

- *Initiation Features*—In contrast to the three-way handshake that occurs in TCP, SCTP uses a four-way handshake to initiate an association. This four-way handshake defends against denial-of-service attempts caused by attackers bombarding the SCTP nodes with counterfeit PDUs. In addition, SCTP packets that contain invalid verification tags are identified during initiation and removed from the transmission path. The verification tag values and the cookie mechanism shield the initiation procedure from SYN-type attacks (commonly known as blind attacks) that are commonplace in TCP[2].

- *Data Transmission Features*—During data transmission, the chunk-bundling feature allows DATA chunks to be multiplexed with control chunks. The peer endpoint acknowledges the receipt of a data chunk by sending a SACK chunk. SACK chunks contain Transmission Sequence Numbers (TSN) that reveal any gaps in the sequence of data chunks. Within each stream, SCTP packets are also assigned Stream Sequence Numbers (SSN). The SSN determines the sequence of data delivery within each independent stream. If the peer endpoint indicates gaps in the SSN, then, the message will not be delivered until the gap is filled.
- *Shutdown Features*—SCTP shutdown procedure has some significant advantages over TCP. For instance, a TCP connection is considered "half-open" when one endpoint continues to send data though the peer endpoint is no longer transmitting data. In contrast, SCTP implements a graceful close of an association by exchanging three messages. These messages acknowledge that both endpoints will cease in their transmissions of data.

5. SCTP: A STRUCTURAL OVERVIEW

This section discusses the structure of the SCTP packets. A detailed illustration of the SCTP packet is illustrated in the Figure 36.4. The common header includes the following:

- The source port address
- The destination port address
- The verification tag
- The checksum of the entire packet

The source port number is used by the receiving endpoint to identify the association to which the SCTP packet belongs. The destination port number is the SCTP receiver's address for which the packet is destined. Each endpoint assigns a verification tag (32-bit value) that identifies the association. The checksum acts as a data integrity tool for each SCTP packet.

The chunk fields within a chunk can be described as follows:

- *The chunk-type field*: identifies the type of chunk being transmitted,
- *The chunk flag*: specifies whether bits will be used in the association,
- *The chunk length*: determines the size of the entire chunk in bytes, and
- *The chunk data*: includes the actual data payload of the chunk.

As indicated in Figure 36.4, there are N chunks (number of chunks) indicated in a single SCTP packet. The number N is determined by the Maximum Transmission Unit (MTU) size of the transmission path. SCTP allows chunks to be multiplexed in one packet to full MTU capacity, with the exception of initiation (INIT) and initiation-acknowledgement (INIT

FIG. 36.4
SCTP Packet Format

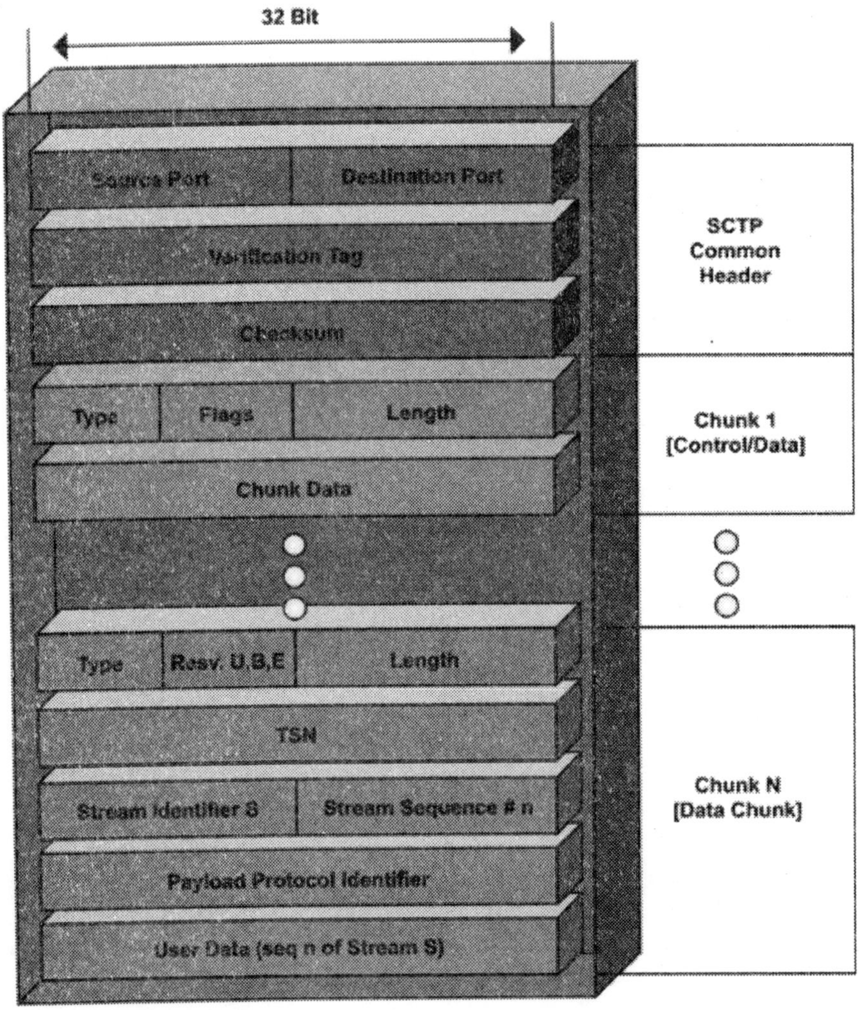

ACK) chunks. There are 14 types of chunks in all, including one DATA chunk and 13 types of control chunks. The DATA chunk contains the actual data payload. The definition and parameters of the control chunks are summarized in Table 36.1.

TABLE 36.1
Control Chunk Types and Their Definitions by Function

Chunk	*Definition*
Initiation INIT	The INIT chunk is sent in order to initiate a SCTP association between two endpoints.
Initiation Acknowledgement INIT ACK	INIT ACK chunk acknowledges the receipt of an INIT chunk. The receipt of the INIT ACK chunk establishes an association.
Selective Acknowledgement SACK	SACK chunks acknowledge the receipt of DATA chunks.
Cookie Echo •COOKIE ECHO	The COOKIE ECHO chunk is used exclusively during the initiation process and is sent to the peer endpoint.
Cookie Acknowledgement COOKIE ACK	The COOKIE ACK chunk acknowledges receipt of the COOKIE ECHO chunk. The COOKIE ACK chunk must take precedence over any DATA chunk or SACK chunk sent in the association. The COOKIE ACK chunk may be bundled with DATA chunks or SACK chunks
Heartbeat Request HEARTBEAT	HEARTBEAT chunks are sent from one SCTP endpoint to its peer in order to test the connectivity of a specific destination address in the association.
Heartbeat Acknowledgement HEARTBEAT ACK	Every time a HEARTBEAT chunk is received by an endpoint, a HEARTBEAT ACK chunk is sent to the source IP address in order to acknowledge receipt of the HEARTBEAT chunk.
Abort Association ABORT	The ABORT chunk is an indication to the peer endpoint to close the association. In addition, the ABORT chunk informs the receiver of the reason for aborting the association in the cause parameters.
Operation Error ERROR	The ERROR chunk is sent to the peer endpoint to report certain error conditions that may exist. The ERROR chunk may contain parameters that determine the type of error that has taken place.
Shutdown Association SHUTDOWN	The SHUTDOWN chunk triggers a graceful close of an association with a peer endpoint.
Shutdown Acknowledgement SHUTDOWN ACK	A SHUTDOWN ACK is used to acknowledge the receipt of the SHUTDOWN chunk at the end of the shutdown process.
Shutdown Complete SHUTDOWN COMPLETE	The SHUTDOWN COMPLETE concludes the shutdown procedure.

6. SCTP FUNCTIONS: TRACKING THE TRANSMISSION PROCESS

This section describes the data transport process within the three main phases of an SCTP association: initiation, data transmission and shutdown. The endpoint that initiates the association will be referred to as "Node A"; the peer endpoint that receives the association establishment requests will be referred to as "Node B". Note: ABORT chunks and ERROR chunks can be generated by either endpoint or can be sent at any time during the association. In these two cases, the endpoints undergo immediate shutdown.

6.1. Association Initiation

(i) Node A generates an INIT chunk and sends it to Node B. Node A starts the INIT timer.

(ii) If Node B wishes to accept the association, it generates an INIT ACK chunk that includes a cookie. It then sends the INIT ACK chunk along with a cookie, back to Node A.

(iii) Node A receives the INIT ACK chunk and stops INIT timer. Node A generates a COOKIE ECHO chunk, which is then sent to Node B. Node A starts the cookie timer. DATA chunks may also be bundled in this packet.

(iv) Node B checks the validity of the cookie. Following validation it sends a COOKIE ACK back to Node A.

(v) Node A receives the COOKIE ACK and enters into the next phase of data transmission.

FIG. 36.5

The Four-Way Handshake in the Initiation of SCTP Association

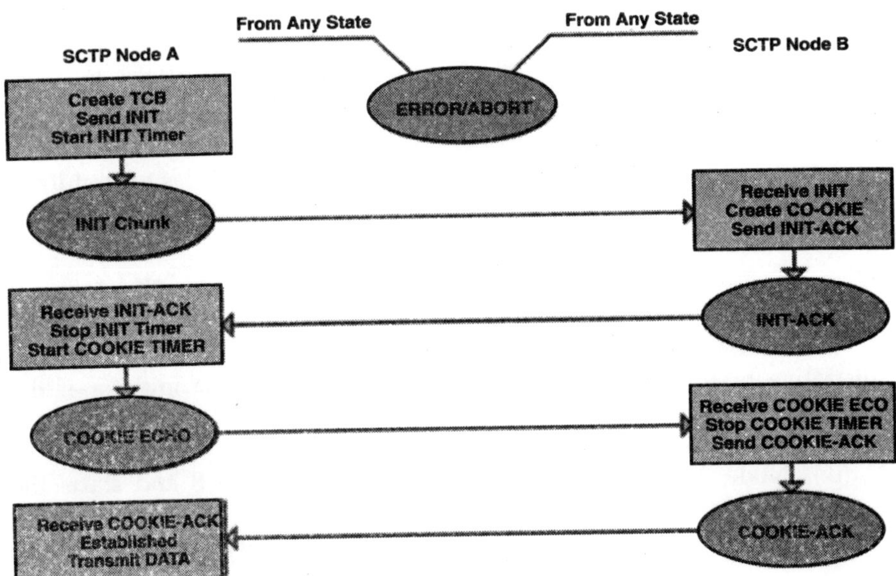

6.2 Association Data Transmission

Node A and Node B seamlessly transmit data. Throughout the data transmission process, HEARTBEAT and HEARTBEAT ACK chunks are exchanged between the nodes at regular-time intervals regulated by the heartbeat timer. These chunks test the connectivity of the endpoints, thereby, preserving the validity of the data transmission.

FIG. 36.6
Tracking The Data Transmission Process in SCTP[2]

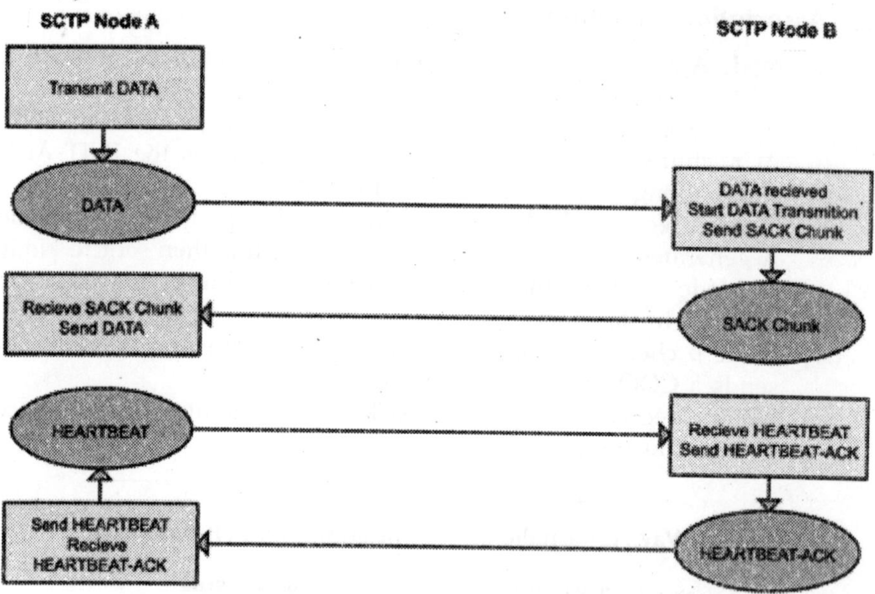

(vi) Node A and Node B exchange DATA chunks.

(vii) After each DATA chunk is received, the receiving endpoint returns a SACK chunk to acknowledge the receipt.

(viii) Data is transmitted until one of the endpoints decides to shutdown the association by sending a SHUTDOWN chunk bundled in one of the packets.

6.3 Association Shutdown

The SHUTDOWN chunk can be sent by any one of the two nodes. For illustrative reasons, Node A is considered here to be the initiator if the Shutdown process.

(ix) Node A sends a SHUTDOWN chunk to Node B and starts the shutdown timer.

(x) Node B acknowledges the receipt of the SHUTDOWN chunk

FIG. 36.7
Graceful Termination of an SCTP Association [2]

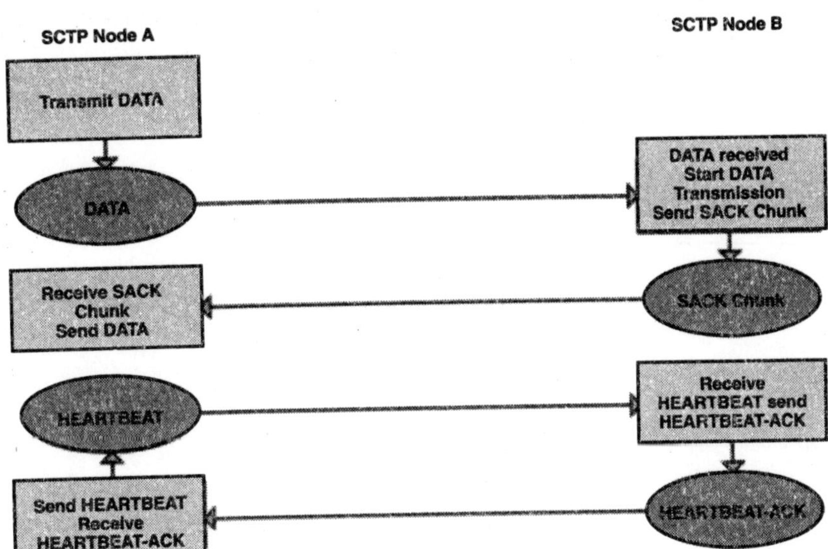

through generation of SHUTDOWN ACK chunk, which is sent to Node A.

(xi) Node A receives the SHUTDOWN ACK and responds by stopping the SHUTDOWN timer. Then, Node A generates a SHUTDOWN COMPLETE chunk and sends the chunk to Node B.

7. CONCLUSION

The TCP protocol is widely used in almost all the data transmission applications with some limitations. The new Stream Control Transmission Protocol (SCTP) is introduced to overcome the limitation of TCP and UDP. This paper discusses the structure and the new feature which are helpful to overcome the limitations of the TCP and UDP protocol.

REFERENCES

1. Sukwoo, Kang and Matthew Fields "Experimental study of the SCTP compared to TCP", http://www.iec.org
2. B. Braden. Requirements for Internet Hosts—Communication Layers. RFC 1122, Internet Engineering Task Force, October 1989.
3. Thomson Ravier, Rob Brennan Teltec DCU, Dublin, Ireland, "Experimental Studies of SCTP multi-homing".
4. Ivan, Arias Rodrigguez, "Stream Control Transmission Protocol the Design of a New Reliable Transport Protocol For IP Network" Master's Thesis, 2002.
5. Ryan, W. Bickhart, "Transparent TCP-SCTP Translation SHIM Layer", Master's Thesis, 2005.

6. Preethi Natrajan, Janardhan, R., Paul, D. Amer and Randall Stewart, "SCTP: An innovative layer protocol for the web", ACM 1-59593-323-9/06/0005.
7. Stream Control Transmission Protocol, www.sctp.org
8. Stewart, R.; Xie, Q.; Morneault, K.: RFC 2960—"Stream Control Transmission Protocol", IETF, Network Working Group, October 2000.

37

Soft-Computing for Biometric-Applications

SUKHDEV SINGH, ARUN JAIN AND CHANDER KANT

ABSTRACT

Biometrics, the computer-based validation of a person's identity, is becoming more and more essential due to the increasing demand for high-security systems. A biometric system testifies the authenticity of a specific physiological or behavioral characteristic possessed by a user. New requirements over actual biometric systems such as robustness, higher recognition rates, tolerance for imprecision, and uncertainty and flexibility call for the use of new computing technologies. In this context, soft computing is increasingly being used in the development of biometric applications. Soft-Biometrics corresponds to a new emerging paradigm that consists the use of soft-computing technologies for the development of biometric applications. The aim of this paper is to motivate discussions on the application of soft-computing approaches in specific biometric measurements. The feasibility of soft-computing as a tool-set for biometric applications should be investigated. Finally, an application example on static signature verification is presented, providing evidence of soft-computing's impact in biometrics.

1. INTRODUCTION

Biometrics is automated methods of recognizing a person based on a physiological or behavioral characteristic. Among the features measured are; face prints, fingerprints, hand geometry, handwriting, iris, retinal, vein, and voice. Biometric technologies are becoming the foundation of an extensive array of highly secure identification and personal verification solutions. As the level of security breaches and transaction fraud increases, the need for highly secure identification and personal verification technologies is becoming apparent.

Biometric-based solutions are able to provide confidential financial transactions and personal data privacy. The need for biometrics can be found in federal, state and local governments, in the military, and in commercial applications. Enterprise-wide network security infrastructures, government IDs, secure electronic banking, investment and other financial transactions, retail sales, law enforcement, and health and social services are already benefiting from these technologies.

Biometric-based authentication applications include workstation, network and domain access, single sign-on, application logon, data protection, remote access to resources, transaction security and web security. Trust in these electronic transactions is essential to the healthy growth of the global economy. Utilized alone or integrated with other technologies such as smart cards, encryption keys and digital signatures, biometrics are set to pervade nearly all aspects of the economy and our daily lives. Utilizing biometrics for personal authentication is becoming convenient and considerably more accurate than current methods (such as the utilization of passwords or PINs). This is because biometrics links the event to a particular individual (a password or token may be used by someone other than the authorized user), is convenient (nothing to carry or remember), accurate (it provides for positive authentication), can provide an audit trail and is becoming socially acceptable and cost effective.

Biometrics offers new perspectives in high-security applications while supporting natural, user-friendly and fast authentication. Biometric identification considers individual physiological characteristics and/or typical behavioral patterns of a person to validate their authenticity. Compared to establish methods of person identification, employing PIN-codes, passwords, management or smart cards, biometric characteristics offer the following advantages:

- They are significant for each individual.
- They are always available.
- They cannot be transferred to another person.
- They cannot be forgotten or stolen.
- They always vary (The presentation of two 100% identical feature sets indicates fraud).

2. BIOMETRICS

Biometrics (ancient Greek: bios = "life", metron = "measure") refers to two very different fields of study and application. The first, which is older and used in biological studies including forestry, is the collection, synthesis, analysis and management of quantitative data on biological communities such as forests. Biometrics in reference to biological sciences has been studied and applied for several generations, and is somewhat simply viewed as "biological statistics."

More recently and incongruently, the term's meaning has been broadened to include the study of methods for uniquely recognizing humans based upon one or more intrinsic physical or behavioral traits.

Some researchers have coined the term behavior metrics for behavioral biometrics such as typing rhythm or mouse gestures where the analysis can be done continuously without interrupting or interfering with user activities.

Biometrics is used to identify the identity of an input sample when compared to a template, used in cases to identify specific people by certain characteristics.

- *Possession-based*: using one specific "token" such as a security tag or a card
- *Knowledge-based*: the use of a code or password.

Standard validation systems often use multiple inputs of samples for sufficient validation, such as particular characteristics of the sample. This intends to enhance security as multiple different samples are required such as security tags, codes and sample dimensions.

3. SOFT-COMPUTING

Since the early days of Artificial Intelligence, scientists and engineers have been searching for new computational paradigms capable of solving real-world problems efficiently. Soft-Computing (SC) is one of such paradigms that have emerged in the recent past as a collection of several models of computation, which work synergistically and provide the capability of flexible information processing. The principal constituents of SC are fuzzy logic, neural networks, evolutionary computing, probabilistic reasoning, chaotic theory and parts of machine learning theory. SC is more than a melange of these disciplines; it is a partnership, in which each of the partners contributes a distinct methodology for addressing problems in its domain. In this perspective, these disciplines are complementary more than competitive. SC technologies are currently attracting a great deal of attention, and have already found a number of practical applications ranging from industrial process control, fault diagnosis and smart appliances to speech recognition, image processing and pattern recognition. We are going to concentrate ourselves in the description of fuzzy logic, neural networks and evolutionary computing because these are the SC technologies which are mostly used in biometric applications. In this perspective, the principal contribution of fuzzy logic is to provide algorithms for dealing with imprecision and approximate reasoning and computing with words, while neural network theory provides an effective methodology for learning from examples, and evolutionary computing a way to solve search and optimization problems. Fuzzy Logic (FL) corresponds to a mathematical approach for translating the fuzziness of linguistic concepts into a representation that computers can understand and manipulate. Because FL can transform linguistic variables into numerical ones without jettisoning partial truth along the way, it allows the construction of improved models of human reasoning and expert knowledge. FL and, in general, the fuzzy sets theory provides an approximate, effective and flexible means of describing the behavior of systems which are too complex or too ill-defined to admit precise mathematical analysis by classical methods and tools. Since the theory of fuzzy sets is a generalization of classical set theory, it has greater flexibility to capture faithfully the various aspects of incompleteness or ambiguity in information of a situation. In this way, more than to operate just with linguistic variables, modern fuzzy set systems are designed to deal with any kind of information uncertainty. Artificial Neural Network (ANN) research takes its inspiration from biological neuronal systems.

ANNs have some attributes as universal approximation, the ability to learn from and adapt to their environment, and the ability to invoke weak assumptions about the underlying physical phenomena responsible for the generation of the input data. ANNs are suitable to solve problems where no analytical model exists or where the analytical model is too complex to be applied. Basic units called artificial neurons that somehow model the working principles of their biological counterparts compose an ANN. Moreover, ANNs try not only to model the biological neurons but also their interconnection mechanisms and global functional properties. The mechanisms that drive natural evolution are reproduction, mutation and survival of the fittest. They allow the adaptation of life forms to particular changing environments over successive generation. From a computational point of view, this can be seen as an optimization process. The application of evolution mechanisms by artificial/computational systems is called Evolutionary Computing (EC). From that we can say EC takes the power of natural selection to turn computers into automatic optimization tools. EC algorithms are efficient, adaptive and robust search processes, producing near optimal solutions and have a large amount of implicit parallelism.

4. SOFT-BIOMETRICS: SOFT-COMPUTING AND BIOMETRICS

SC is increasingly being used in biometric systems whereas biometrics employing SC approaches are referred as soft-biometrics. SC, by its ability to consider variations and uncertainty is data, is suitable for biometric measurements due to the following reasons:

- Biometric features do not have an absolute "ground truth" and they will hardly reach this. Biometric features always vary!
- Derivations from the "ideal" biometric characteristic are difficult or even unable to describe analytically.
- High accuracy within the measurement may cause inflexibility and loss of generalization ability.

No Biometric is truly universal; the National Institute of Standards and Technology (NIST) report that fingerprints cannot be obtained from 2% of the American population [NIST], whilst [Golfarelli] show that hand geometry and Facial biometrics have a limited number of distinguishable patterns 105 and 103 respectively, indicating that they have a limited 'uniqueness' factor. Whilst Multi-Modal biometrics systems overcome these problems, there are two overall limiting factors that affect them:

(a) The higher the dimensionality of the data vectors produced during fusion, the longer the computation time required to analyses them.
(b) The more biometrics used, the more expensive the infrastructure, to set-up and run, becomes.

To overcome these issues, the concept of 'soft biometrics' has been introduced. Soft biometric traits are those characteristics that provide some information about the individual, but lack the distinctiveness and permanence to sufficiently differentiate any two individuals [JDN]. Examples of Soft Biometrics include: height, gender, ethnicity and eye colour, whilst these traits are easily identified by a human operator. Work has also been carried out to enable automated capture. When such automated systems become available, the integration of soft biometrics into a fusion system will diversify the differentiating traits that we all exhibit, increasing the uniqueness factor that a biometric system so heavily relies upon.

5. CONCLUSION

Soft-Biometrics, the application of soft-computing in biometrics is motivated. Taking the example of signature verification, it is shown that SC approaches can be employed within all components of the biometric system, e.g. for data pre-processing itself or for designing of adapted pre-processing filters. Also, it can be applied for extracting significant features for reference determination, as classifiers or as decision of sub-module-results by using fuzzy fusion.

REFERENCES

1. Arun Ross and Anil Jain, "*Information Fusion in Biometrics*", Department of Computer Science, Michigan State University, 2002.

2. *Definition of Biometrics* from Wikipedia, the free encyclopedia.
3. Golfarelli, Maio and Maltoni, *"On the Error-Reject Trade-Off in Biometric Verification Systems"*, IEEE Transactions on Pattern Analysis and Machine Intelligence, Vol. 19, No. 7, July 1997.
4. K. Franke and M. Koppen, *"A computer-based system to support forensic studies on handwritten documents", International Journal on Document Analysis and Recognition*, 3(4):218{231, 2001.
5. K. Franke, M. Koppen, and B. Nickolay, *Fuzzy image processing by using Dubois and Prade,* Fuzzy norm. In Proc. 15th International Conference on Pattern Recognition (ICPR), pages 518-21, Barcelona, Spain, 2000.
6. John Daugman, *Combining Multiple Biometrics,* The Computer Laboratory, Cambridge University, Daugman, 2004.

38

A Study of B2C and G2C Applications in India

MAHESH PARAMJIT KUMAR AND MINAKSHI SETH

ABSTRACT

At the brink of new millennium, role of Information Technology (IT) in commerce and business has considerably increased. More and more enterprises are integrating IT with commercial operations. This has led to emergence of phenomenon called Electronic Commerce, better abbreviated as e-Commerce. Today e-commerce has become a topic of discussion not just among business managers and CEOs but also among aware consumers, learned citizens and students. In fact, the winners will be those, who shall seize and exploit the technology as a strategic weapon to achieve personal and organizational success. Since Indian business environment is rapidly changing, multiple technological breakthroughs are taking, product life cycles are getting shortened and markets rapidly are changing. These developments are forcing Indian businesses to adopt e-commerce technology. Today Indian businesses are using e-commerce technology, not only for online trading but also for rendering services online like travel and tourism, stock trading, career consultancy, etc. Government of India as well as various state governments have also started taking initiatives of using IT to raise quality of services delivered to citizens and businesses. The present paper analyses key strengths, identifies limitations of major initiatives taken for e-commerce, e-services and e-governance applications in India, and forwards suggestions to ensure successful implementation of such application.

1. INTRODUCTION

Commerce is basic economic activity that is concerned with movement of goods and services from producer to consumer. In present day electronic era, commercial transactions are performed by using the electronic means like computer networks, Internet and World Wide Web. Electronic commerce, therefore, is concerned with application of information technology for carrying out commercial transactions.

E-commerce can be defined from four perspectives:

- Communication perspective,
- Business process perspective,
- Service perspective, and
- Online perspective.

From a communication perspective, electronic commerce is the delivery of information, products/services or payments via telephone lines, computer networks or any other means. From business process perspective, electronic commerce is application of technology towards automation of business transactions and workflows. From service perspective, electronic commerce is a tool that addresses the desire of firms consumers and management to cut service cost while improving quality of goods and increasing the speed of service delivery. From online perspective, electronic commerce provides the capability of buying and selling of products and information on the internet and other online services (Kalakota and Whinston, 2000:3)

E-commerce is a broad term and must not be restricted to buying and selling of goods over the internet. E-commerce also serves as a channel of communication, a tool for business process automation and a means of delivery of services electronically. Traditional commerce is taking place since times immemorial, but E-commerce is outcome of integration of digital technology with commercial transactions and business processes. Internet, WWW and protocols that govern the internet provide technological foundation for e-commerce. The technology behind e-commerce ensures two-way communications between buyer and seller. On one hand, firms can communicate with consumers through e-commerce enabled website. On the other hand, consumers can also fill order form, feed back forms, etc. and can communicate with business. E-commerce is inter-disciplinary in nature in the sense that its implementation requires knowledge of managerial, technological, social and legal issues (Kumar, 2007:5). Understanding of consumer behavior, marketing tools and financial aspects is as important as designing interactive website. Broadly speaking E-commerce transactions are classified into Business-To-Business (B2B), Business-To-Consumer (B2C), Consumer-To-Consumer (C2C), Business-To-Government (B2G), Government-To-Business (G2B) and Government-To-Citizen (G2C). B2B refers to all e-commerce transactions that occur between business organizations like retailers, manufacturers, suppliers, distributors and electronic fund transfer providers. So, when companies and institutions buy from each other or sell to one another online, B2B E-commerce transaction takes place. B2B has become a vital instrument of supply chain management as more and more companies are outsourcing parts of their supply chain to their trading partners. B2C covers those e-commerce websites and transactions, through which business organizations sell goods to consumers over the internet. B2C is also known as Internet Retailing or just e-tailing. C2C refers to those E-commerce transactions which take place between and among consumers. Now many websites offer C2C dealing where a consumer can visit the site, upload the pictures of clothes, personal artwork or handicraft he has to sell and mentions the demanded price. B2G refers to those E-commerce transactions through which business enterprises sell to government. G2B refers to service delivery by government to business organizations. With G2C, government has started providing traditional government services to citizens over the Internet. G2C, B2G and G2B are collectively known as e-governance.

2. VOLUME OF E-COMMERCE TRANSACTIONS AND RECENT INFORMATION TECHNOLOGY RELATED TRENDS IN INDIA

A well endorsed feature of e-commerce is its global flavor. Today Indian businesses are embedding technology in trading. Volume of E-commerce transactions is an evidence of rising levels of usage of E-commerce technology by Indian corporate houses. So far, no centralized body has been set-up to deal with E-commerce statistics in India. Certain estimates are made by NASSCOM (National Association of Software and Service Companies) from time to time. Volume of electronic commerce transactions as per certain surveys available on internet shows that E-commerce transactions have grown considerably in the past. In 1998-99, the volume amounted to 28 million US dollars which increased to 98 million US dollars in 1999-2000 and further to 580 million US dollars in 2000-01. In 2003-04, it sharply rose to 10.6 billion US dollars from 2.32 billion dollars in 2002-03. B2B constitutes a major portion of EC transactions and ranges between 80 to 90 percent of the total volume. The dollar values, however, must not lead us to conclude that E-commerce is a western concept. In fact, available trend indicates that E-commerce has started to show good potential in India. Total Internet users in India rose from 1.5 million in 1999 to about 20 million in 2004. This is largely because government monopoly over telecom sector was abolished in 1994 and private players were allowed. Now internet access is available not just through traditional phone and cable network but also through data cards that ensure wireless access to Internet. So wider access choices, and lowering telecom tariffs are acting as drivers of internet growth in India. Total software and services employment was around 1,287,000 by the end of the 2006 and is forecasted at 1,550,000 for the year 2008. More than 68% of Indian software houses have informed of strong expertise in supply chain and distribution management solutions. Out of all internet users in India, 20% own credit cards. This enhances the possibility of converting visitor into an online buyer. One of four Non-Resident Indian (NRIs) make some sort of buying from India based EC venture. Shaadi.com, naukri.com, yatra.com, indiabull.com, 5paisa.com, 99acres.com, ebizel.com and other similar Indian websites and businesses fared quite well. Inter-bank electronic settlements are allowed through Real Time Gross Settlement (RTGS) system. The required changes have been made in Reserve Bank of India (RBI) Act. Branded and packaged software is a taxable commodity in India. This has been held in the case of Tata Consultancy Services (TCS) *vs.* State of Andhra Pradesh. Controller of Certifying Authorities (CCA) appointed under Information Technology Act, 2000 acts as regulator of growth of e-commerce and e-governance in India (Sharma, 2006).

3. ORGANIZATIONAL SUPPORT FOR GOVERNMENT

National Informatics Centre (NIC) is the main information technology organization set-up for developing websites and doing networking of government and government-related organizations. NIC headquarter is based at New Delhi but its units exist in all the 28 states and union Territories and 600 district centers. NIC Computer Cells are located in all the Ministry Bhawans of the Central Government and apex officers including Prime Minister's Office, the Rashtrapati Bhawan and the Parliament. NIC has many divisions including Computer Aided Design (CAD) division, Computer Aided Paperless Examination System (CAPES) division, Cyber Security Group, Electronic Data Interchange (EDI) Application Division, e-Governance division, Industry Information systems division, Infrastructure Group, Intellectual property and know-how, satellite communications divisions, science and technology division, video conferencing division, wireless communication division, web services and multimedia applications division, etc. The web services and multimedia application division provides a wide range of World Wide Web related services. It does feasibility study for government related web sites, does complete design, development and hosting of government websites in India. It publishes large government-related documents on websites, develops government websites in English, Hindi and other regional languages and adds audio and video content to websites. Government of India (GOI) directory, http://goidirectory.nic.in, is a one of its kind comprehensive collection of links to websites of various Government of India entities. A large number of government-related websites have been categorized under headings such as executive, legislative and judiciary. Moreover, it has links named cultural, educational science, financial, medical, sports, tourism, Indian missions abroad, etc. It serves as a single window for all e-information of Indian Government. All state and central government websites are hosted on 'nic.in' and 'gov.in' domains. The domain name nic.in is owned by National Informatics Center and the same can be allotted to Indian Government entities only. Moreover, NIC is authorized registrar of 'gov.in' domains and it advises all government departments to host the site under 'gov.in' domains. NIC has conceptualized, developed and implemented a very large number of projects for various central and state government ministries, departments and organizations. E-governance projects of NIC are touching lives of millions of citizens of India. Some of the projects like examination result portal, land record information system, public grievance redress and monitoring system, video conferencing, etc. have proved quite beneficial in providing e-governance services to the citizens of India. In fact, NIC is providing state-of-art infrastructure and services to central and state government ministries, departments and organizations.

4. ELECTRONIC PAYMENT INSTRUMENTS

In a contract of sale, the merchants sell the goods to customers and customers pay the price. In offline world the payments are made with cash or through cheque. However, in online sales accepting payment is a crucial aspect of the transaction. Many different electronic payment systems are in use. The important among them are credit cards, smart cards, debit cards, etc. Delhi Metro Smart Card issued by Delhi Metro Rail Corporation, driving license smart card of Government of India, Vehicle Registration smart card of Government of India, bus pass smart card of BEST (Brihan Mumbai Electricity Supply & Transport Undertaking) and Kolkata metro smart card are some of the applications of chip-based smart cards in India. All the ATM Cards, debit cards and credit cards of banks are magnetic stripe cards issued in collaboration with credit card companies like VISA and Master card.

5. E-COMMERCE SUPPORT FOR INDIAN SERVICE INDUSTRY

Delivery of services to consumers over the internet is being referred as E-services. Presently, many services are offered online. These include online travel, online real estate, online banking, online stock trading, online financial services, online education, online recruitment, online publishing, online consultancy, online entertainment, online computer games, etc.

Service sector is largely a knowledge and information intensive industry. Service sector is most rapidly expanding sector of Indian economy. Online career consultancy, online banking, online stock trading and online travel are rapidly expanding e-services in India. But to be successful an e-service must ensure that website does not crash. Customers are recognized when they log onto the site, and there must be effective response system. It implies that customer e-mails are responded quickly within hours and preferably within minutes. Everyone in the organization, including technical staff, is trained to deal with customers effectively. All this helps an E-service provider to serve the customer by providing high value information and speedy services. In fact, be it e-service or e-commerce, one cannot exist without the other.

5.1 Online Travel and Tourism

Travel industry is characterized by multi-channel presence. It means physical presence of travel agency is combined with online travel and tourism website. By nature, travel services are well suited for online market place. That is why more and more websites are coming up to meet the travel needs of individual customers and corporate clients. These include makemytrip.com and yatra.com

Today there is no need to physically rush to travel agent's office to book air ticket, train ticket, book hotel room, etc. Rather travel website meets this requirement. The customer specifies his travel requirements like proposed date of departure etc. and web-site searches database or uses software agents to explore other websites and respond to the consumer. So, the website response tries to meet customer requirements by providing information about travel schedule, prices and make suggestions for making changes in travel plans that could result in cheaper tickets. Such sites offer one-stop shop to serve global travelers and offer far more information than physically present travel agent. The main services they provide include reservation of tickets for your trip, booking of hotel rooms, making arrangement for auto rentals like hiring of car, booking of cruises, providing electronic travel magazines, providing comparative analysis of travel fares, assist in currency conversion.

One such site 'MakeMyTrip.com' was launched in the year 2000 and started operations in India in 2005. It provides services like search, comparison and booking of tickets on any airline, real time booking of over 1500 hotels, taxi booking for airport transfers and other trips. Moreover, it offers holiday packages within India and international destinations. For instance, in the summer of 2007, it offered holiday package to Thailand (starting at Rs. 8,100), Indonesia (Rs. 16,299), Maldives (Rs. 27,550), Switzerland (Rs. 44,900) etc. Similarly, it offers dozens of holiday packages in India to destinations like Goa, Tirupati, Mata Vaishnodevi, Gangtok, Kerala, etc. It also offers weekend breaks from Mumbai, Bangalore, Chennai, Delhi, Ahmedabad, Cochin, Kolkata etc. Deep Kalra, Founder and CEO, started the company in April 2000 to capture booming travel market. Total travel market is estimated at Rs. 4500 crores, of which makemytrip.com holds 4% share. In 2006, makemytrip.com was having 350,000 customers. The year end target for 2007 is set at one million customers. In 2006, it had a huge turnover of Rs. 200 crores, which is estimated at Rs. 600 crores in 2007. makemytrip.com has been ranked as number one travel website by Juxt Consult. In a recent development, Red Herring adjudged, 'makemytrip.com' among the top 100 online companies in Asia.

5.2 Online Real Estate Applications

Online real estate services are provided by web sites that show listing of houses, shops and flats put up for sale or rent. In Indian context, they cannot replace real estate dealers and offline agents. Online real estates sites, however, play supporting role for property dealers. For instance, builders now can use virtual reality technology on their website to demonstrate three dimensional floor plans to buyers. This helps real estate companies to attract buyers. So, transaction normally can be initiated online but materialize offline in a face-to-face contact of parties. Many websites are providing online real estate services. 99acres.com is the most popular website in this field. At 99acres.com, owners can advertise their property put up for sale. Buyers can search for properties and browse for such properties. By filling a registration form a person can register himself as owner, broker or a builder. It claims to be a forum, where buyers, sellers and brokers can exchange information quickly, effectively and inexpensively. 99acres.com is a part of Info Edge (India) Ltd. It was, initially, founded in 1989 and renamed in 1995. This parent company has 99 acres.com, naukri.com as job search portal, and jeevansathi.com for matrimonial services, etc. as its group of companies.

5.3 Online Banking

Online banking is also known as electronic banking, virtual banking and Internet banking. Online banking is defined as automated delivery of new and traditional banking products and services through electronic and interactive communication channels. Customers access online banking services by using electronic devices like personal computer, laptop, palmtop, ATM, Kiosks, etc. To start with electronic services, ATM were installed for cash extractions and deposits. It is interesting to note that initially ATMs were designed for customers with low bank balance. The idea was that customers with high banks balance will use live tellers at bank branch and customers with low balance shall go to ATM to avoid rush at bank branch. But customers soon, discovered that ATMs are more convenient and now ATMs are equally popular among customers of all segments. Initially ATMs were installed at sensitive places like airports, super markets, etc. But with passage of time and expansion of electronic banking, ATMs are now present in every nook-and-corner of all cities in India. In fact, network of ATMs has created an interface between customer and bank that has changed the way banks provide service for day-to-day needs of customers. On one hand, banks have network of ATMs to provide basic services like withdrawals and deposits of cash. On the other hand, banks target educated clients to take up internet banking. This net banking facility allows clients having PC, modem, internet browser and internet connection to avail intermediate services like paying bills, transferring funds and opening of new account while sitting at home. This phenomenon is also known as *home banking*. As computers and Internet access is getting cheaper day-by-day, internet banking is likely to pick-up considerably in near future. Banking also offer cash management package to large corporate clients. This allows information import/export between client PC and banking application. More sophisticated applications are also being developed and deployed by banks that enable to pay bills online automatically on a specified day of each month. The software keeps track of instructions and never forgets to transaction payment. Scenario at Indian bank building has changed considerably. Bank offices in India are now equipped with network of computers running core banking software to transact business online.

The banks through internet banking allows customer to know account balance at any time, make available credit card statement, pay bill electronically through instructions given to a bank to transfer funds to a business account on some specified date, enable customer to download account transaction and embed them in money management software and allow customer to transfer money between accounts without personally going to bank. Indian banks now deal with new financial instruments like debit cards, credit cards, electronic checks, etc. So, online banking has to deal with e-money rather than just hard currency. HDFC Bank and ICICI bank are among pioneer institutions providing such internet banking services. For instance, with HDFC clients can not only view account balance but also open a fixed deposit, transfer fund, pay electricity, telephone and cell phone bills. With a service called 'one view', customer can view not only balance of HDFC account but also transactions of ICICI bank, Citibank, HSBC, Standard chartered bank, City Bank credit card and HDFC Bank demat account. So client can view his accounts in six different banks. Moreover, through a service called 'InstaAlert', a customer keeps on getting information about debit card transactions like salary credits, withdrawals, etc. via SMS on his cell phone. In fact, internet is changing the face of financial services. Today size and network are treated as two significant parameters of the strength of commercial banks. For instance, State Bank of India is considered as strongest bank because of its massive size and network of branches that exist even in rural areas. But Internet banking has its impact on network of branches. More internet banking implies fewer branches. Banks with strong internet banking support but with fewer braches can still emerge stronger. Moreover, certain staffing issues need to be resolved. Banks have strong unions. Computerization is rendering staff surplus. That is why banks are trying to tackle human resource issue through ban on recruitment, exit policy and VRS (Voluntary Retirement Schemes). In India, with amendments in law, RBI has allowed Real Time Gross settlement between banks whereby payment settlement is done throughout the day in real time rather than netted against each other once at the end of day. India lags behind many countries with regard to infrastructure. There exist low awareness levels; particularly in rural areas people do not have access to Internet. Pace of obsolescence of technology is a matter of concern for all policy planners and implementers.

In spite of all these limitations, banking scenario has considerably changed in the recent past. Now, you go to bank to deposit some money in your saving or current account, reach your office, connect to internet and pay utility bills online, move in retail store and make purchases using your debit card, stop at some road side and use ATM to withdraw some cash. You keep on getting information about your debit transactions, salary credits, weekly account balance and utility bill alerts from time to time via SMS on cell phone. In fact, Indian banks have started offering world class multi-channel services through online banking.

5.4 Online Stock Trading

Across the globe, developments in information, communication and network technologies have created paradigm shifts in security market operations. Stock exchanges all over the world have realized the potential of IT and have moved to online trading systems. In India, only registered stock exchanges can operate the stock market activities and the recognition is governed under the provisions of securities and Contract (Regulation) Act, 1956. There as 24 regional stock exchanges in India including Bombay Stock Exchange (BSE) and National Stock Exchange (NSE). Daily turnover of all stock exchanges is more than Rs. 100,000 crores.

Trading in stock exchange is done through the authorized members who are duly registered with concerned stock exchange through Securities and Exchange Board of India (SEBI). They have to pay certain sum of money as security and some margin money in advance for dealing in securities. In 1994, NSE started screen-based trading system where a member can key in the quantity of a security and the price at which he likes to transact. The transaction is executed as soon as it finds a matching sale or purchase order from a counter party. In 1995, BSE also started screen-based trading system. VSAT (Very small Aperture Terminals) technology is used by computerized stock exchanges for satellite communications. One of the software products launched by NSE, NEAT-XS is an order routing software for broker members with multiple locations. The software has two editions named workgroup edition (used by small brokers) and enterprise edition (used by large brokers). NEAT-IXS, software enables broker members of NSE to offer internet trading to their clients.

Internet-based trading enables online buying and selling of shares from your home or office. Earlier shares were held by individuals in physical form, that is, share certificates. The shares were traded by the physical transfer of the certificates and later name of buyer was changed as owner. But, with the advent of online trading, the process of stock trading has taken a new turn. In online trading, you will access to stock brokers website through your internet enabled PC and place orders through the brokers internet-based trading engine. These orders are electronically routed to stock exchange without manual intervention and executed in a matter of seconds. In Internet trading the net is used as medium to communicate orders to stock exchange through broker's website or specially provided software. These e-broking software and websites (like ICICIdirect.com, IndiaBulls.com, sharekhan.com, etc.) enable investors to track the fluctuations in various stocks and market as a whole, while deciding to execute the order and also while the order is being executed. The confirmation of the order is also shown on the real time basis. The order routing system on which internet-based trading is done is compatible with screen-based terminals.

To start internet trading, an investor has to register himself with a broker offering online services. He provides information like permanent account number issued by income tax authority, ID proof, etc. The registered member opens a bank account, say in HDFC Bank, as well as a Demat account with the broker and puts up some capital into it. The client is given a user ID; log in password and transaction password. The broker assigns the investor a limit up to which he can do the trading (say Rs. 5 lakhs). Investor, then uses, web page link and start bidding. The bids get logged on to the trading platforms. If client orders exceed the assigned trading limit, the transactions get rerouted to the broker's server for authorization or rejection. Once the investors bid are accepted, the investor's account is accordingly settled. Normally, investor trade through margin account or cash account. In margin, investor is interested in price difference of purchase and sale. He is not interested in share delivery. But an investor using cash account, purchases the stock for investment purposes and purchased shares become a part of this portfolio. Such Internet-based trading provides unparalleled liquidity and enhances market efficiency.

National Stock Exchange of India better known as NSE was promoted by certain financial institutions in November 1992. In April, 1993, NSE was recognized as stock exchange under securities Contract (Regulation) Act, 1956. In April, 1996, its index called nifty was launched. In December, 1996, it commenced trading and settlement in dematerialized securities. It is top information technology user among all stock exchanges in India. In November, 1997, it got best information technology usage award from computer society of India. In 1999, it launched automated lending and borrowing mechanism. In February, 2000, it commenced internet trading and in December 2000, it commenced online trading. NSE's information technology setup is largest among all the stock exchanges in India. It uses satellite communication technology to allow participation from around 320 cities in India. The trading system used by NSE is known as NEAT system. This online trading system is based on client-server application. The server system runs on a fault tolerant STRATUS mainframe and clients run on windows PCs. Each NSE trading member trades with other members through a PC located in trading member's office anywhere in India. NSE is one of the largest interactive VSAT based stock exchanges in the world. It supports more than 3000 VSATs. NSE-network is largest private wide area network in the country. NSE-network can handle 60 lakh trades per day in capital market segment. NSE has more than 1000 companies listed from various industries in India. Listing improves company's profile among investors as high listing standards foster investor confidence. NSE displays live stock quotes on its website www.nseindia.com.

Bombay Stock Exchange Limited is the oldest stock exchange in Asia and is popularly known as BSE. It was established as 'The Native Share and Stock Brokers' Association' in 1875. It was first stock exchange in the country to obtain permanent recognition in 1956 from Government of India under securities contracts (Regulation) Act, 1956. Its index sensex is tracked world wide. The exchange is professionally managed under the overall direction of board of directors. The board comprises eminent professionals, representatives from trading members, and managing director of the Exchange. The day-to-day operations are managed by MD and CEO of the exchange. The exchange provides an efficient and transparent market for trading in equity, debt instruments and derivatives. BSE's online trading system abbreviated as BOLT system. The system is 9001:2000 ISO certified.

5.5 Online Recruitment Services

Online recruitment and career services provided by websites like timesjobs.com, naukri.com and monster.com are rapidly becoming popular among Indian Jobseekers. Naukri.com is widely used online recruitment platform. Naukri.com was setup with a vision to create a platform where every Indian who is looking for a job can find some suitable job. At naukri.com employers, placement agencies and job seekers can exchange information quickly, effectively and inexpensively. Till today, more than 25,000 companies have advertised jobs through naukri.com. Naukri.com offers resume services to job seekers. Searching and applying for jobs online is free. Naukri.com charges Rs. 700 for uploading and displaying résume for a period of 6 months and Rs. 800 for one year. Moreover, job seekers can send resume copies to 800/1000 domestic placement agencies for a fee of Rs. 800/Rs. 900. Moreover job seekers can use services of experts to get their resume developed. Naukri.com charges fee of this service as well. An interesting feature of this website is its job search window on the home page. Jobseeker inputs keywords for job search and location preference and click on the word 'go'. The results of search are displayed as index of jobs. To get full details, the job seeker clicks on the job from this list. Later job seeker can e-mail to the company or send hard copy of resume at postal address, if specified in the vacancy details. Naukri.com provides job posting services and application handling software to recruiters. Moreover, it also provides recruiters with resume database product through which companies can access database of job seekers. In 2007, resume database had over a million searchable resumes and over 2,00,000 Job postings. In a nutshell, large number of companies in the fields of automobiles, call centers, information technology, telecom, pharmacy, biotech, retail, marketing, etc. advertises their jobs on naukri.com. Job seekers search for jobs and apply online.

6. E-GOVERNANCE IN INDIA

The main motivation behind e-governance initiatives in India is to provide SMART—Simple, Moral, Accountable, Responsive and Transparent Government. These principles are guiding forces and all government agencies agree that ICT can be used to provide speedy and quality services to citizens and businesses.

E-Governance is defined as application of electronic means in interaction between government and citizens, government and businesses, as well as, in internal government operations, to simplify and improve democratic and business aspects of governance. So, E-governance is about the use of information technology to raise quality of services governments deliver to citizens and businesses. It is also concerned with performing government's administrative activities in an efficient and speedy manner. E-Governance is supposed to reinforce the connection between public officials and ordinary citizen and thereby leading to more accountable and inclusive democracy.

E-Governance in India has broadly two objectives; Internal and External. Internal strategic objective is of providing a speedy, transparent, accountable and effective process of performing government's internal administrative activities. So, internal strategic objectives result in G2G (Government-to-Government) and G2E (Government-to-Employee) type of transactions. External strategic objectives of e-governance are to satisfactorily fulfil the public needs and expectations on the front-office side. In this sense, e-governance aims at providing citizens and businesses government services without making personal visits or going through bureaucratic procedures. Interaction with government can be one way, that is, from government to citizen or two-way, which allows citizen and businesses to communicate with government. These external strategic objectives result in G2C (Government-to-Citizen), G2B (government-to-Business), C2G (Citizen-to-Government) and B2G (Business-to-Government) type of transactions.

All e-governance initiatives require strong infrastructure. Some of these concepts have already been implemented in India. For instance, smart card based driving license with biometric identification was introduced by Gujarat Government in 1999. The whole process of issue of driving license has been computerized. When an applicant reaches issue center, his data is fed into PC and photograph of the person is taken on camera. After this, fingerprints are captured through a fingerprint scanner and stored in a database and memory of the chip on smart card. Signature of license holder is also captured electronically. Once the software capture all the details, the card is printed on smart card printer. The details are stored electronically on the chip. The whole process although seems quite technical, takes only a few minutes and the person just walks out with a license. Smart card based driving license is unique and hence cannot be duplicated. Such card can easily be accepted as ID proof with highest authenticity. This license is of the same size as credit card and can easily be carried by the holder. The plastic is weather proof and long lasting than paper-based license. Hand held terminals for checking and challans serve as smart card reader. More than 5 million smart card licenses have been issued by Government of Gujarat. Other significant E-Governance initiatives in India include Bhoomi (Karnataka), CARD (Andhra Pradesh), Sarita: Maharashtra, Akshaya (Kerala) and E-Seva (Andhra Pradesh).

Bhoomi is one of the well implemented e-governance projects. Bhoomi is concerned with computerization of land records. The project was implemented by Revenue Department, Government of Karnataka. The project computerized more than 17 million land records, documents in Karnataka. With online application, farmers of the state can apply for mutation of land records (that is change of title) in an hour at land Record Kiosks (booths with multimedia computers and printers). This is big scale project that covered computerization of 29,000 villages in the State. Bhoomi was implemented with technical support from NIC. It greatly helped land administration as revenue department collected revenue from respective owners according to extent of land owned by them. Farmers have easy access to land records. Today, its variations are implemented in other states also.

CARD stands for Computer Aided Administration of the Registration Department. The main functions performed are registration of legal deeds relating to immovable properties like sale deeds, mortgage deeds and gift deeds. The registration involves collection of stamp duty between 11 to 14 percent of the value of property. This project is implemented at 387 sub-registrar offices in the state of Andhra Pradesh. The CARD has capacity to complete the registration of land deed at Sub-registrars office within 60 minutes and issuance of encumbrance certificate within 15 minutes of the request. The project was implemented with support from NIC and about 1.2 million sale deeds are registered through CARD. The biggest limitation of CARD project is that it could not bring down the corruption involved in sale deed transaction. The service is not available on internet; rather person has to physically present himself at sub-registrars office.

State Government in Maharashtra started stamp duty registration with IT application (SARITA) in August 2000. The state government implemented this project to reduce delays and corruption in the system. It helped in improving the efficiency of Registration and Stamps department that contributes about 15% to the state government revenues.

Project Akshaya is implemented to enhance electronic literacy. Under this scheme at least one member of the family shall be trained to use computer and search information on internet. This e-governance project aims at further improving the level of literacy in the state that has already achieved 100% rate of literacy.

The state government of Andhra Pradesh has emerged as a pioneering state in application of computers, Internet and intranet for effective implementation of its services to citizens and businesses. The Government of Andhra Pradesh in moving with a vision to create society by using information technology in all aspects development and governance. E-Seva centres provide many citizen-friendly services at one-stop shop called E-Seva Center. So, E-Seva provides citizen service through E-Governance. The main services provided at E-seva centers to citizens include electricity bills payment, water and sewerage bills payment, telephone bills (BSNL and TATA tele services) payment, property tax payment, sales tax payments, registration of births and deaths, issue of birth and death certificates, license renewal issue and renewal of trade licenses, issue of driving licenses, renewal of driving licenses, issue of learner licenses, registration of new vehicles, change in address of vehicle owner, transfer of ownership of vehicle, reservation of state roadways bus tickets, reservation of water tanker, sale of passport application forms, receipt of complaints regarding citizen services, etc.

There are 46 e-seva centres with 400 service counters fully computerized and working for providing services to citizens in an effective manner. All e-seva centres operate from 8.00 am to 8.00 pm on working days and 9.00 to 3.00 pm on holidays (second saturdays and sundays). These e-seva centres are one-stop shop for over 66, G2C and B2C services. The state government has set-up AP online to serve as e-governance gateway for the Government of Andhra Pradesh. This portal, www.aponline.gov.in, was launched by AP government in partnership with Tata Consultancy Services (TCS).

In rural areas, the government of AP has started Rajiv Internet village programme. The programme aims at providing broadband connectivity in rural areas providing computer literacy to at least one member in the family and delivering needed information and services to people in rural areas. The planned target was to reach 22,000 villages by December 2006 in a phased manner. In fact, AP government has successfully integrated ICT to provide services to citizens and businesses. Pioneering efforts are made to take the benefits of ICT to the citizens in urban and rural areas.

7. CONCLUSION AND SUGGESTIONS

The Web-based commerce experienced initial boom in 1998 Christmas shopping season when US consumers spent $ 3 billion over the internet going beyond all predictions. These developments forced the businesses and retailers of all kinds to consider e-commerce seriously. Attracted by the phenomenal growth, not only the IT companies but all business houses around the world made plans to invest in IT infrastructure and electronic way of doing business. Not only multinationals but also Indian entrepreneurs made huge spending for the installation of IT-related infrastructure. In 1998-99, banking and finance sector took a lead and banks like Indian Overseas Bank, Union Bank of India, ICICI Banking Corporation Ltd. and ANZ Grindlays Bank invested heavily for installing information technology-related infrastructure with spending of Rs. 30 crore, Rs. 20 crore,

Rs. 15 crore and Rs. 5 crore, respectively. Eight years later Indian enterprises have invested Rs. 8,974 crore in information technology (IT) in 2006-07 that was 26% more as compared to Rs. 7,123 crores the 2005-06 (http://www.bpowatchindia.com/2007/05/it-spend-by-india-inc-to-near-rs-9000cr-in-fy08).

The annual survey by Dataquest and IT research and advisory firm IDC India reported that overall, about 42% of the total spending was on hardware, while expenditure on packaged software and services software stood at 26% each, respectively. PCs, laptops and servers accounted for 50% of the hardware expenditure. On the software front, system and application software accounted for more than half of the amount spent. The IT investment of Rs. 2646 crore by 35 banks, financial institutions and insurance companies was the highest among the IT buyers. Incidentally, Public Sector Undertakings (PSUs) constituted more than half of the top 50 IT spenders in 2006-07, exploding the myth that modernization processes can take place only in private sector companies in India. The average IT investment by an IT mega-spender Indian company was Rs. 34 crore in 2006-07, and is expected to grow 26% to Rs. 43 crore in the current fiscal. However, according to AMI-Partners' latest report on Small and Medium Enterprises (SMEs) in India's, usage of IT is quite low.

The Small Scale companies that employ between one and 99 employees, fewer than one-third of those surveyed owned a PC. Medium-sized businesses, defined as companies with between 100 and 999 employees, implemented advanced security and storage technologies (Chan, 2007). The SMEs in India are 15-20 years behind their counterparts in developed countries. So, a good deal of spending for Web-based technologies, e-commerce projects and infrastructure development needs to be ensured by SMEs. It requires participation of banking industry that is to provide finance facilities to SMEs and credit facilities to the online buyers.

Enactment of Information Technology Act, 2000, is regarded as a significant development in E-commerce landscape. The IT bill was introduced in Parliament in 1998. But because of government changes and other political problems, it took two years for the bill to become law. India's IT Act, blesses electronic signatures and e-transactions that is changing the way Indians do business and thereby advancing the country's position in the global high-tech industry. In addition to giving legal sanctity to digital signatures and Internet transactions, the law adopted in June, 2000 also allows people to file taxes electronically and imposes prison terms and fines for hackers and other cyber criminals. The Law, however, has its own shortcomings. For instance, it is unclear how the Indian law will apply if cyber crimes or e-transactions are initiated overseas. Moreover, the law does not address taxation issues or credit card fraud. In fact, elaborate e-commerce and cyber laws are required to deal with taxation issues and weed out the bad elements that have entered the web with desire of making quick bucks by deceiving, as faith cannot be installed so long as there exists something called 'The top 10 Web Scams'.

Infrastructural development for e-commerce and e-governance in India is the need of the hour. The country with more than 1 billion people has around 20 million Internet users. Power supply and telephone connections are erratic, particularly, in rural India. The digital divide is a hard reality as for over 700 million people across 600,000 villages in India; technology is a distant, non-existent dream. This rural population, at the bottom of the pyramid subsists on less than Rs. 100 (around USD 2) a day. People understand the value of education and information, but cannot afford to buy Rs. 30,000 (around USD 700) computer. That is why transforming rural India is a challenge that should focus the best of Indian minds. It is perhaps the single biggest barrier to making India a developed country. Development of IT infrastructure can play a vital role in rural transformation. Of course, one can argue that what the poor need is food, water and electricity, more than technology. It is an argument we have been making since our Independence in 1947. But, with enhanced connectivity farmers can ascertain commodity prices faster and get information on new agricultural techniques. The rural youth would get details on job opportunities across the state and country. The district administration can gather details of problems in real-time.

The eligible could search for matrimonial matches across adjacent villages. The village officials could share governance best practices faster among their counterparts elsewhere. This is a must as no nation can progress leaving behind more than two-thirds of its populace, and computing as a utility in every village can bring wonders in transforming rural India. Efforts have already been initiated. For instance, Gyandoot Project was launched in 2000 as an intranet in Dhar district in central India that has a population of 1.7 million of which 60% live below the poverty line. Later, it was extended to other districts of Madhya Pradesh. The goal of the Gyandoot project has been to establish community-owned, technologically innovative and sustainable information kiosks in a poverty-stricken, tribal dominated rural area of Madhya Pradesh. During the design phase of the project, meetings were held with villagers to gather their input. Among the concerns highlighted by villagers was the absence of information about prevailing agriculture produce auction centre rates. Consequently, farmers were unable to get the best price for their agricultural produce. Copies of land records were also difficult to obtain. A villager had to go out in search of the patwari (village functionary who maintains all land records), who often was difficult to get hold of as his duties include extensive travel. To file complaints or submit applications, people had to go to district headquarters (which could be 100 miles away), resulting in a loss of wages/earnings. Later, it came up to actually provide all these facilities to rural masses. The project was awarded the Stockholm Challenge IT Award 2000 in the 'Public Service and Democracy' category.

The citation mentioned: "Project Gyandoot is a unique government to citizen Intranet project implemented in a tribal district (Dhar) in Central India, with numerous benefits to the region, including a people-based self-reliant sustainable strategy. Gyandoot is recognized as a breakthrough in e-government, demonstrating a paradigm shift which gives marginalized tribal citizens their first ever chance to access knowledge, with minimum investment". However, it is very clear that the power supply, connectivity, and human support (with new value propositions) are the essential pre-requisites to benefit from such technological advancements. So, the issue of infrastructural development must stand high on government agenda. Further, it is to be ensured that e-commerce is not treated as a fad. It is an innovative way of selling and buying that enjoys confidence of the masses. All these measures can go a long way to ensure successful transformation of India as a nation of IT savvy people.

References

1. Chan, I. *Indian SMB IT spend to grow 24 percent.* http://www.zdnetindia.com/index.php?action=pro_how_to&prodid=2487&Ref=developerHome
2. Kalakota, R. and Whinston, A. 2000. *Electronic Commerce: A Manager's Guide.* Singapore: Addison Wesley Longman.
3. Kumar, M.P. 2007. *Electronic Commerce with Indian Application.* Chandigarh : Unistar.
4. Sharma, V. 2006. *Information Technology Law and Practice: Cyber Laws and e-commerce.* Delhi: Universal.

39

Risk Management with Online Banking and E-Commerce

KANIKA LAKHANI

ABSTRACT

E-Commerce is a modern business methodology which helps banks, companies and customers to have better business facilities with less cost while improving the quality of services and increasing speed of transactions. E-Commerce covers online transactions, electronic data and funds transfer, e-banking, interactive marketing etc. Online Banking is the feature of e-commerce for performing transactions, payments etc. over the internet through secure websites. It allows customers to do banking outside of banking hours. While the e-payment, associated with online banking, is replacing traditional currency and paper cheques; it also involves risks associated with these payments. The notion of security of payments is insufficient to provide appropriate conceptual framework for the design of internet payment systems. E-Commerce systems are based on internet use, which provides open and easy communication on a global basis. Because the internet is unregulated, unmanaged and uncontrolled, it increases a wide range of risks and threats to the systems operating on it. Risk management is an approach that recognizes that e-payment entails a series of interrelated risks: financial risks, technological risks, operational risks and legal risks. Some of these risks are generic to banking business, others are specific to e-payments such as interception of messages, break into security infrastructure. It is essential that banks have a comprehensive risk management process in place that is subject to appropriate oversight by the management.

1. INTRODUCTION

In an increasingly competitive global marketplace, it is extremely important for businesses to embrace the latest methods and trends to conduct their businesses. A large percentage of electronic commerce is conducted entirely electronically for virtual items such as access to premium content on a website. But privacy issues present a different set of challenges here. The same technology that facilitates business activities and provides wonderful services is also a major threat to individual freedom. Large databases linking information about economic activity from different sources (purchases, banking activity, and medical records) provide great economic advantages by making marketing more efficient, loans more targeted, and medical information ubiquitous.

2. E-COMMERCE

Electronic commerce consists of the buying and selling of products or services over electronic systems such as the Internet and other computer networks. The amount of trade conducted electronically has grown extraordinarily since the spread of the Internet. A wide variety of commerce is conducted in this way, spurring and drawing on innovations in electronic funds transfer, supply chain management, internet marketing, online transaction processing, Electronic Data Interchange (EDI), inventory management systems, and automated data collection systems. Modern electronic commerce typically uses the World Wide Web at least at some point in the transaction's lifecycle, although it can encompass a wider range of technologies such as e-mail. Electronic commerce is, generally, considered to be the sales aspect of e-business..It also consists of the exchange of data to facilitate the financing and payment aspects of the business transactions.

3. BUSINESS APPLICATIONS OF E-COMMERCE

Some common applications related to electronic commerce are:

- E-mail and messaging
- Documents, spreadsheets, database
- Accounting and finance systems
- Orders and shipment information
- Enterprise and client information reporting
- Domestic and international payment systems
- Newsgroup and Conferencing
- On-line Banking
- Messaging

FIG. 39.1
Business Applications of E-Commerce

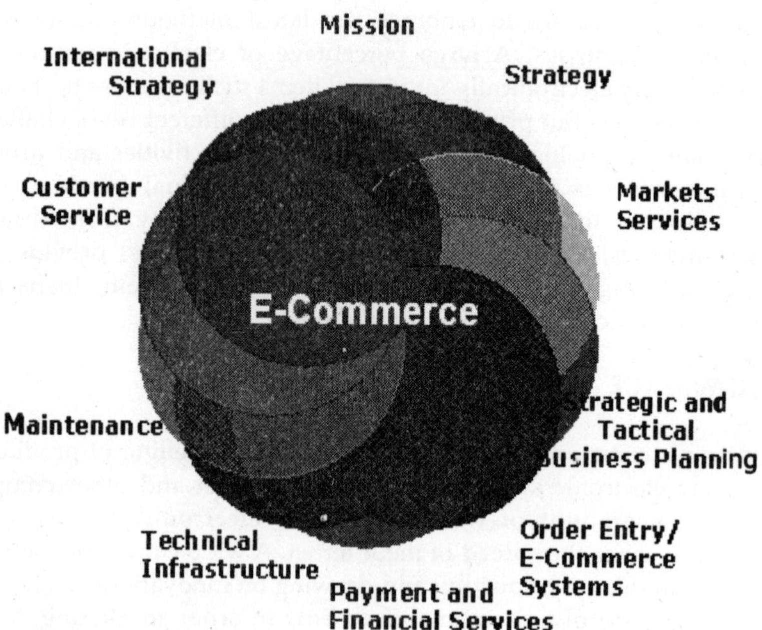

3.1 Online Banking

Online Banking offers following features:

- Bank statements with the possibility to import data in a personal finance program.
- Electronic bill payment.
- Funds transfer between a customer's own checking and saving accounts, or to other customer's accounts.
- Investment purchase or sale.
- Loan applications and transactions, such as repayments.
- Accounts aggregation to allow the customers to monitors all of their accounts in one place.

3.2 Core Banking Solution (CBS)

CBS is networking of branches, which enables customers to operate their accounts, and avail banking services from any branch of the bank on CBS network, regardless of where he maintains his accounts. CBS is a step towards enhancing customer convenience through "Anywhere and Anytime Banking". All CBS branches are inter-connected with each other. The various services provided by CBS are:

- To make inquiries about the balance, debit and credit entries in accounts.
- To obtain cash payment out of the account by tendering a cheque.
- To deposit a cheque for credit into the account.
- To deposit cash in the account.
- To get statement of account.
- To transfer funds in-between accounts.

CBS improves the quality and efficiency of services by providing a convenient and delightful banking.

3.3 Electronic Payment System (EPS)

EPS are online payment systems. The goal of their development is to create analogs of checks and cash on the internet. Its features are:

- Protecting customers from merchant's fraud by keeping credit card numbers unknown to merchants.
- Allowing people without credit cards to engage in online transactions.
- Protecting confidentiality of customers.
- Provides anonymity of customers.

EPS provides following advantages:

- Decreased technology cost.
- Reduced operational and processing cost.
- Increasing online commerce.

FIG. 39.2
Online Banking Security Components

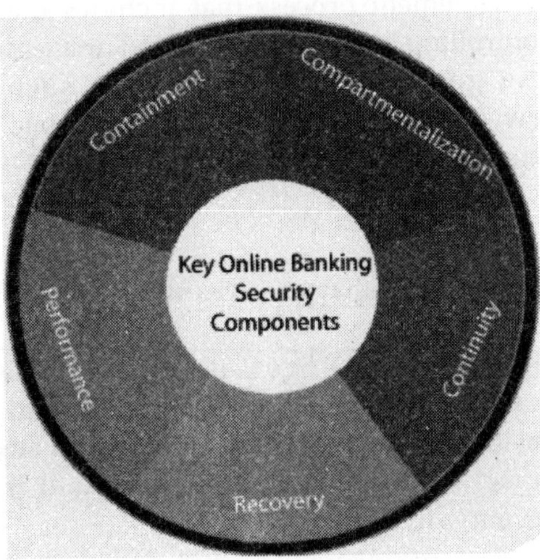

4. RISKS ASSOCIATED WITH ONLINE BANKING AND EPS

Electronic money schemes may be attractive to money launderers if the system offers liberal balance and transaction limits, and provide for limited audibility of transactions. Application of money laundering rules may be in appropriate for some forms of electronic payments. The risks involved are:

(i) *Operational Risks:* They arise from the potential for loss due to deficiencies in system reliability or integrity. This may also arise due to customer misuse, and from inadequately designed or implemented electronic banking and electronic money systems.

(ii) *Credit Risks:* It is the risk that a counter party will not settle an obligation for full value, either when due or at any time. Banks engaging in e-banking activities may extend credit via non-traditional channels, and expand their market beyond traditional geographic boundaries. Inadequate procedures to determine the creditworthiness of borrowers applying for credit via remote banking procedures could heighten credit risks for banks.

(iii) *Legal Risks:* They arise from violation of laws, rules, regulations or prescribed activities, or when the legal rights and obligations of parties to a transaction are not well established.

(iv) *Risks from Viruses, Trojans and Worms:* Viruses, Trojan horses and Worms are all computer programs that can infect computers. These programs gain access to sensitive data such as account information and passwords with a view to perpetrating fraud.

4.1 Risk Management for Online Banking and EPS

The rapid pace of technological innovation is likely to change the nature and scope of the risks, banks face in electronic money and electronic banking. A risk management process that includes the basic elements of assessing risks, controlling risk exposures, and managing risks will help banks attain these goals. Banks may employ such a process when committing to new electronic banking and electronic money activities. Various risk management techniques are:

4.1.1 Assessing Risks

It is an ongoing process that involves three steps.

(i) A bank may engage in a rigorous analytic process to identify risks and to quantify them. Bank management should form a reasonable and defensible judgment of the magnitude of any risk with respect to the impact it could have on the bank and the probability that such an event will occur.

(ii) Second step in assessing risk is for the board of directors to determine the bank's risk tolerance, based on an assessment of the losses the bank can afford to sustain in the event a given problem materializes.

(iii) Finally, management can compare its risk tolerance with its assessment of the magnitude of a risk to ascertain if the risk exposure fits within the tolerance limits.

4.1.2 Managing and Controlling Risks

This phase of risk management process includes activities such as implementing security policies and measures, co-coordinating internal communication, evaluating and upgrading products and services, implementing measures to ensure that outsourcing risks are controlled and managed, providing disclosures and customer education, and developing consistency plans. Banks increase their ability to control and manage the various risks inherent in any activity when policies and procedures are set out in written documentation and made available to all relevant staff.

4.1.3 Monitoring Risks

For electronic banking and electronic money activities, monitoring is important because the nature of activities are likely to change as rapidly as innovation occurs, and because of the reliance of some products on the use of open networks such as internet. The important elements of monitoring are:

(i) *System Testing and Surveillance*: Testing of system operations help detect unusual activity patterns and avert major system problems, disruptions and attacks. Penetration testing focuses upon the identification, isolation and confirmation of flaws in the design and implementation of security mechanism through controlled attempts to penetrate a system outside normal procedure. Surveillance is a form of monitoring in which software and audit applications are used to track activity.

(ii) *Auditing*: Internal and external auditing provides an independent control mechanism for detecting deficiencies and minimizing risks in the provision of e-banking and EPS. Audit personnel must have sufficient specialized expertise to perform an accurate review. An internal auditor should be separate and independent from employees making risk management decisions.

5. CONCLUSION

As the use of internet continues to grow, websites are assuming greater importance as the public face of business. Further, the revenues generated by e-commerce systems mean that organizations are becoming more reliant upon them as core elements of their business. With this high level of dependency upon the services provided by e-commerce systems, it is essential that they are protected from the threats posed by hackers, viruses, frauds and Denial-of-Service (DoS) attacks. It is important to understand the risk being faced by the e-commerce system in Online Banking and the potential impact of any security incident. A risk assessment can be carried out to provide an organization with a clear understanding of the risks being faced by its e-commerce system and associated business processes.

References

1. American Institute of Certified Public Accountants and Canadian Institute of Chartered Accountants. (1999). *SysTrust (TM/SM) Principles and Criteria for Systems Reliability.*
2. American Institute of Certified Public Accountants. (updated annually). *CPA WebTrust: Practitioner's Guide for Business to Consumer Electronic Commerce.*
3. Kilmer, William E. (1999). *Getting Your Business Wired: Using Computer Networking and the Internet to Grow your Business.* New York: AMACOM.
4. Rosen, Anita. (2000). *The e-Commerce Question and Answer Book: A Survival Guide for Business Managers.* New York: American Management Association.
5. U.S. Government's Framework for Electronic Commerce, (1997, July 1). The White House, http://www.ecommerce.gov
6. Frank, Stephen E. *NetWorth: Successful Investing in the Companies that Will Prevail through Internet Booms and Busts.* New York: Simon and Schuster, 2001.
7. Lessig, Lawrence. *Code and Other Laws of Cyberspace.* New York: Basic, 1999.
8. Schiller, Dan. *Digital Capitalism: Networking the Global Market System.* Cambridge, Mass.: MIT Press, 1999.

40

Banking on the Internet : Feeling the Pulse

REKHA HANDA

ABSTRACT

Internet is such a powerful and compelling technology that it has revolutionized the way we live, work, act, interact, buy, sell and the way we invest and save. For businesses, the Internet breaks down logistical barriers, offering greater flexibility and power in the way they do business. In this revolutionary sweep, the banking sector was also taken into folds. Internet banking (also referred as e-banking) is the latest of technological wonders in the recent past involving use of internet for delivery of banking products and services. Internet banking is changing the banking industry and is having the major effects on banking relationships. This paper attempts to gauge the extent and nature of internet banking services being offered by banks in India. The sample of the banks chosen for study were analysed for the various services and options made available to the net banking customers through their websites, against the backdrop of an exhaustive list of service options that can be provided. The paper also attempts to touch on the extended version of the internet banking: the Mobile banking, which seems to be the latest buzzword in the banking scenario.

1. INTRODUCTION

During his evolution journey from Neanderthals to Homo erectus and then to Homo sapiens, man has come long way. Because of his continuous quest for more and more amenities and facilities, the nineties have seen a

Fig. 40.1
Growth of Internet Users in the World between 2000-08

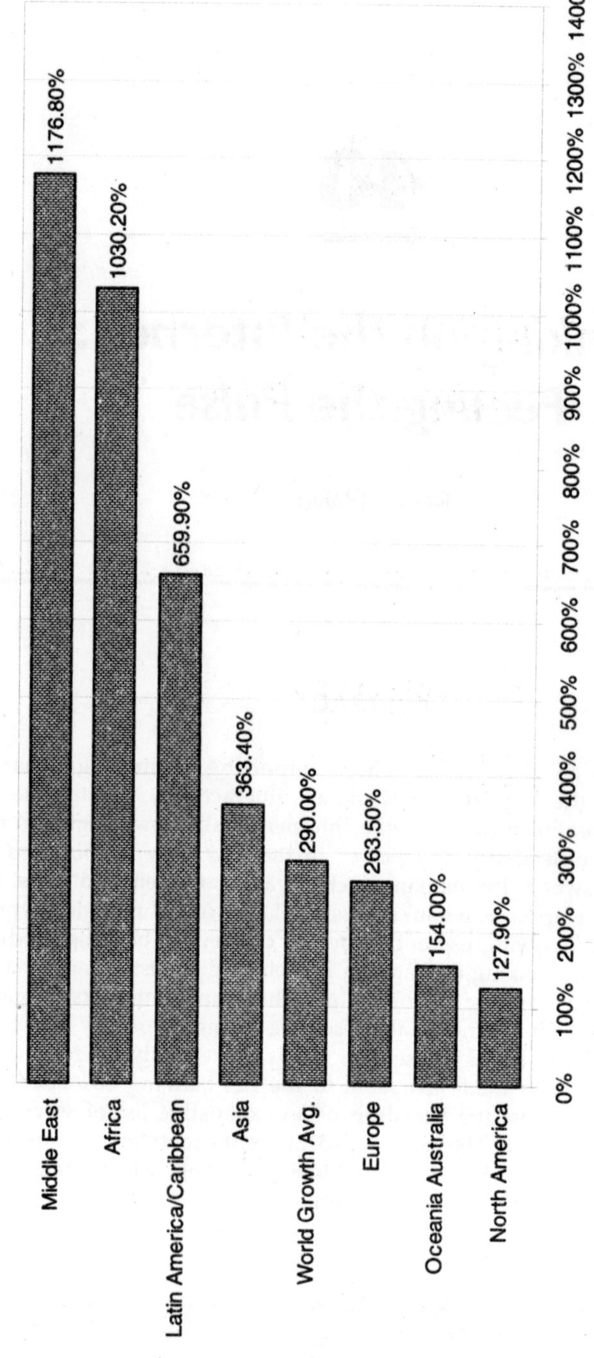

Growth in Percentage (2000-08)

Source : www.internetworldstats.com/stats.htm

major turn around with the invention of computers followed closely on heels with the internet. Internet is such a powerful and compelling technology that it has revolutionized the way we live, work, act, interact, buy, sell and the way we invest and save. For businesses, the Internet breaks down logistical barriers, offering greater flexibility and power in the way they do business. Then how could the banking sector be left behind? In today's times, after the coronation of the consumer as the emperor, and in the face of the proliferating competition, the service and product providers kow tow to the whims and fancies of consumers and serve them with the latest technology driven convenience products. Internet banking (also referred as e-banking) is the latest of technological wonders in the recent past involving use of internet for delivery of banking products and services.

Internet banking is changing the banking industry and is having the major effects on banking relationships. The massively burgeoning internet usage base all around the world and more specifically in Asia and India promises a strong growth potential for internet banking. The Figure 40.1 highlights the growth of Internet users worldwide in the time period 2000-08.

India boasts of an ever-increasing user base whose understanding of the Internet is at par with any advanced nation worldwide. This rapid expansion has spurred businesses and banking businesses more specifically, to devote larger portions of their efforts and focus on the internet banking-based products and services. According to comScore Networks, India, China and Russia experienced the highest year-on-year growth rates in terms of internet users. The Indian internet population grew at 33 percent, making it one of the fastest-growing countries of internet users. The following comparative display of the top ten Asian countries and their internet user base of December 2007 support this fact.

Banks and financial institutions in India are in the process of web-enabling their services in order to offer internet banking to its customers. It's the new generation of banking in India which promises many benefits like: greater reach to customers, quicker time to market, ability to introduce new products and services quickly and successfully, ability to understand its customers' needs, increase customer loyalty, reduce customer attrition to name a few. Indian banks are going for the retail banking in a big way. However, much is still to be achieved. Unfortunately, nationalized banks have been unable to evolve as fast as most private sector and MNC banks. Thus, the present paper intends to gauge the extent and nature of Internet banking services being offered by the public sector banks in India. Seeing and realizing that these nationalized banks have been late starters and still struggling to catch up with their better-off and stronger rivals, the study is focused at these less mighty forces in the Indian banking arena.

Mobile usage has seen an explosive growth in most of the Asian economies like India, China and Korea. As mobile phones have spread, a new economic benefit is coming into view: using them for banking, and so improving access to financial services, not just telecoms networks.

Fig. 40.2
Top 10 Asian Internet Countries as in December 2007

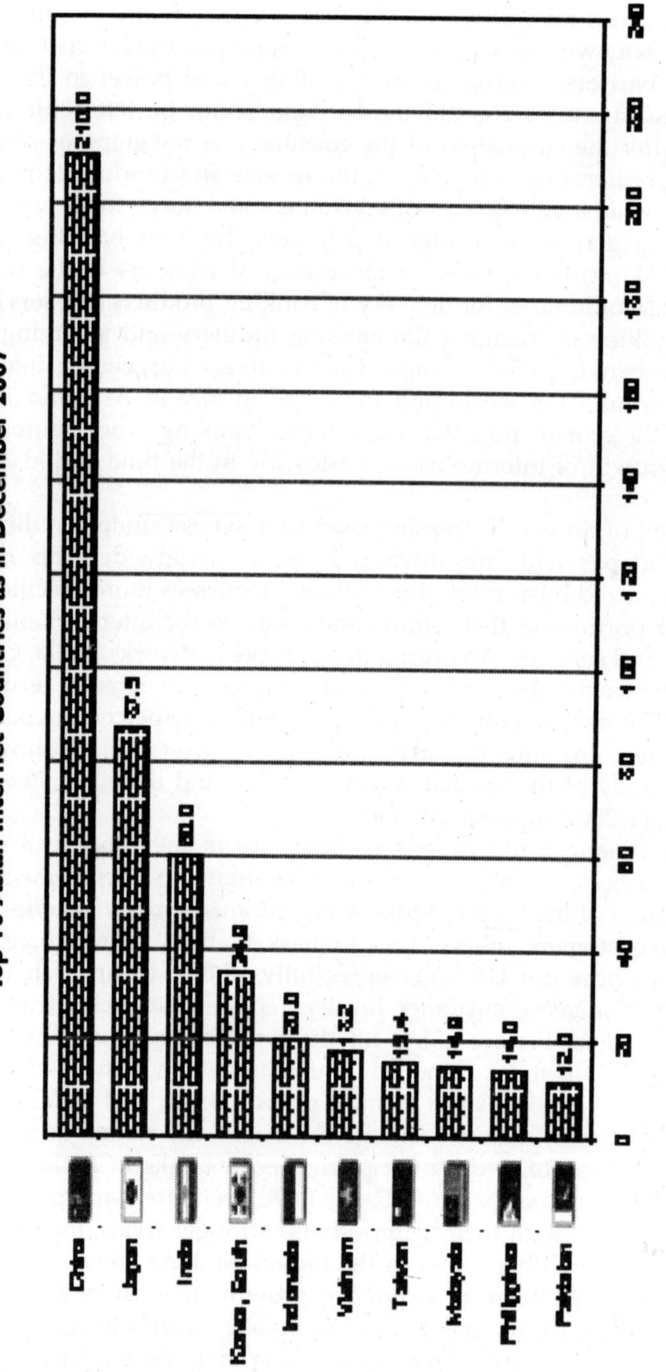

Source :www.internetworldstats.com/stats.htm

M-banking (regarded in the banking community as the extension of internet banking) is being viewed by major banks the world over as a necessity rather than a business proposition. According to a survey conducted by Sybase 365, the world's leading mobile messaging company, Mobile Banking is the hottest area of development in the banking sector and is expected to replace the credit/debit card system in future. In view of this mobile fever catching up, this paper also devotes a part of analysis to mobile banking services being offered, if at all by the public sector banks in India.

2. METHODOLOGY

The present paper is an attempt to study the scope and extent of internet banking services being provided by the public sector banks in India.

2.1 Objectives of the Study

The present study is aimed at understanding the Indian internet banking scenario from the perspective of the public sector banks. The study is focussed on comparative analysis of the myriad forms of services and products offered by these banks to their internet banking customers. It also evaluates the various offerings of internet banking and their provision by these banks. Hence, the objectives of the study are bank-wise analysis and service/product-wise analysis of internet banking in India in the context of public sector banks.

2.2 Data Collection

For the purpose of above objective, primary data has been collected through the survey of websites of the various public sector banks. The site address for these websites were discovered through the use of search tools, primarily www.google.com. For fulfilling the objective, an exhaustive master list was designed of the various internet banking services that are or can be offered by the players in the banking industry. Using this as a check list, the various banks were studied (through their websites) for the disclosure of internet banking products and services being offered by them.

2.3 Period of the Study

The survey of the banks' websites was conducted during the week May 12-17, 2008. All disclosures made by the public sector banks on their websites during this period were included and analysed.

2.4 Scope of the Study

The scope of the present study is limited to the public sector banks operating in India and the various internet banking products and services being offered by them, including the banking services provided through mobiles.

2.5 Data Anlysis

The data gathered from the survey of the various bank websites was checked with the checklist as the base. The cumulative score of each of the banks (derived from the offering of these internet products and services), was analysed using the simple percentages.

3. ANALYSIS OF INTERNET BANKING DISCLOSURES BY PUBLIC SECTOR BANKS

The data was gathered after accessing the websites of individual public sector banks to check the extent and scope of internet banking services being offered by the various banks operating in India. The data collected was then checked against the master list of internet banking and services. For the analysis, bank-wise score, percentages and ranking are calculated.

3.1 Extent of Internet Banking Provided by the Banks

The bank-wise comparative ranking of the banks with regards to the extent of interbanking offerings by them have been tabulated in the Table 40.1.

TABLE 40.1
Ranking of Banks on the Basis of Extent of Internet Banking Services

Public sector Internet banks	Extent (in percentage)	Rank
1. Allahabad Bank	48.8	11
2. Andhra Bank	53.7	9
3. Bank of India	41.5	20
4. Bank of Baroda	65.9	5
5. Bank of Maharashtra	39.0	22
6. Central Bank of India	43.9	16
7. Canara Bank	73.2	1
8. Corporation Bank	68.3	3
9. Dena Bank	58.5	6
10. Indian Bank	58.5	7
11. Indian Overseas Bank	34.1	25
12. Oriental Bank of Commerce	51.2	10
13. Punjab National Bank	58.5	8
14. Punjab & Sind Bank	36.6	23
15. Syndicate Bank	48.8	12
16. UCO Bank	43.9	17
17. Union Bank of India	68.3	4
18. United Bank of India	36.6	24

19.	Vijaya Bank	22.0	27
20.	State Bank of India	70.7	2
21.	State Bank of Hyderabad	48.8	13
22.	State Bank of Indore	41.5	21
23.	State Bank of Bikaner & Jaipur	34.1	26
24.	State Bank of Mysore	43.9	18
25.	State Bank of Patiala	46.3	14
26.	State Bank of Saurashtra	46.3	15
27.	State Bank of Travancore	43.9	19

The above table highlights the overall picture of Internet banking among the public sector banks. It clearly indicates that Canara Bank offers maximum services through its Internet banking with an extent of 73.2%. The second place is bagged by the State Bank of India whose extent of services provided is almost 72%. On the third and fourth position lie the Corporation Bank and the Union Bank of India. The laggards in this Internet banking zone are the Vijaya Bank and the State Bank of Bikaner and Jaipur where this extent of services is as low as 22% and 34% respectively.

The overall picture of the public sector banks as pointed out by the above figures clearly indicates the low level of adoption of Internet banking facilities and variants by these banks. The banks being of long standing and experience are still not imbibing the emergent need of Internet focused services to have a firm foothold in the competitive arena. The highest extent being just limited to a lowly 73% calls for technology driven focus towards the customers' requirements to achieve and sustain a competitive edge.

3.2 Internet Banking Services and Their Provision by Banks

Next, in the analysis an attempt was made to analyse the various Internet banking offerings and rank them in order of their provision by the various banks.

The above table highlights the individual Internet banking services and their ranking on the basis of them being offered by each of the banks. The results show that the basic service where customers can know their bank balances online, 'Balance Enquiry', is offered by all of the banks and thus, it occupies the first rank. Online tax payment is the next commonly provided service by the Internet banking providers, which is covered by 96% of the banks. The Inter-branch funds transfer service is provided by almost 89% of the banks and thus occupies third place. The premium of the internet banking services like brokerage facilities, one view account, financial planning and foreign exchange trading provisions are not very common a product being served by these public sector banks and thus lie in the lowest of the ranks as exhibited by the Table 40.2.

A close look at the internet banking trends above gets us to the conclusion that the basic of the services like balance enquiry, funds transfer

TABLE 40.2
Ranking of Internet Services on the Basis of Provision by PSBs

	Internet Banking Service/Product	*Provision (in percentage)*	*Rank*
1.	Balance Enquiry	100.0	1
2.	Funds Transfer (Inter-branch)	88.9	3
3.	Third Party Funds Transfer	63.0	16
4.	Inter-bank Funds Transfer	85.2	4
5.	Bills Payment	81.5	9
6.	Account Opening Application	25.9	27
7.	Insurance	77.8	11
8.	Demat holdings	74.1	12
9.	Brokerage	7.4	38
10.	Investments	22.2	30
11.	Loan applications	70.4	14
12.	Receive Alerts	33.3	25
13.	Requests/Standing Orders/Instructions	63.0	17
14.	Deposit Applications	11.1	35
15.	Credit card operations/payments	25.9	28
16.	Interest rates Updates	85.2	5
17.	Foreign exchange rates Updates	25.9	29
18.	Trading online	44.4	23
19.	Foreign exch. trading	3.7	41
20.	Online shopping	14.8	34
21.	Market Watch	11.1	36
22.	Cheque status	48.1	20
23.	TDS Enquiry	18.5	33
24.	One view account	7.4	39
25.	Financial planning	7.4	40
26.	Charity online	11.1	37
27.	Online tax payment	96.3	2
28.	Online Ticket Booking	55.6	19
29.	Customer correspondence	48.1	21
30.	Change password and User Profile	59.3	18
31.	Demonstration of I-Banking	40.7	24
32.	Corporate Internet Banking	85.2	6
33.	Security procedures	85.2	7
34.	Transaction details	85.2	8
35.	Loan/Deposit/EMI calculation	48.1	22
36.	Term deposit details	22.2	31
37.	Account statement	81.5	10
38.	Remittance services	70.4	15
39.	Mobile/SMS Banking	33.3	26
40.	Mobile recharge/mobile bills	22.2	32
41.	Grievance settlement	74.1	13

and online tax payments are most common of the services being provided through internets. But, the edge comes through the premium of the services that are provided by relatively less number of banks.

4. MOBILE BANKING SERVICES OFFERED BY BANKS

The sorry state of affairs is all the more aggravated when we turn towards mobile banking, which is of late being referred to as the 'Future of Banking'. For analysis, eight of the commonly provided basic SMS services were studied and amongst these limited service offerings, too, the scenario was not very encouraging.

TABLE 40.3
Extent of Mobile Banking Among PSBs

Mobile Banking Services	*No. of Banks Offering*	*Extent (percentage)*
Balance in Account	6	22.2
Issued cheque status	5	18.5
Term deposits details	2	7.4
SMS Alerts	5	18.5
Cheque book request	2	7.4
Transaction details	6	22.2
Change of primary a/c	2	7.4
Pay by mobile service	1	3.7

The above table depicts the very low extent of mobile banking as among the public sector banks of India. Of the 27 public sector banks covered in the study a measly 9 of them offered SMS/Mobile banking to their customers (as advertised through their websites) lot needs to be done in respect of mobile banking services, especially, so in the light of the mobile usage increasing by leaps and bounds.

5. FINDINGS AND CONCLUSION

The present study indicates the Internet banking scenario in the public sector banks as regards to the various public sector banks. The study brings forth significant disclosures with regards to the extent of net-based banking services offered by the nationalized banks of India. The major findings of the study can be summarized as below:

- The maximum extent of Internet banking services among the public sector banks is limited to 73%, Canara Bank taking the lead amongst these banks.

- The provision of internet banking products by the public sector banks is limited to the basic services and thus, these banks have a long road to travel.
- Online tax payment service is a common feature being offered by banks that is provided by almost 96% of the banks.
- Basic services like balance enquiry, inter-branch transfer of funds and inter-bank transfer of funds are very common and a high majority of banks offer these to their net banking customers.
- Mobile banking as a service is still to pick up with the public sector banks where it is still in its nascent stage.
- Security safeguards, transaction details, corporate net banking, provision of account statement are the few of the services which are, commonly, offered through the internet banking bouquet by these public sector banking players.

Hence the extent and disclosure of internet banking services by the age old public sector banks pinpoints many chinks in there banking armory. The need is to stand up to the demands of the incessantly changing technology and demands of the banking sector to keep pace with the stronger and better armed private and foreign players in the banking sector. The net banking now is more of a norm rather than an exception due to the fact that it is the cheapest way of providing banking services. In the developing countries like India, banks should have a long foresighted vision on developments of banking operations and internet banking operations to be precise.

References

1. Arunachalam, L., Sivasubramanian, M., (2007) "The future of Internet Banking in India", *Academic Open Internet Journal*, Volume 20.
2. Das Gupta, S., (2003,) "Towards Online Banking", Retrieved May 17, 2008 from http://www.networkmagazineindia.com/200302/feature.shtml
3. Infogile Technologies, "Mobile Banking: The Future" August 2007.
4. Mishra, A.K., "Internet Banking in India", Retrieved on May 11, 2008 from http://www.banknetindia.com/banking/ibkg.htm
5. Pakhare, J., "Advantages and Disadvantages of Internet" available at http://www.buzzle.com/articles/advantages-disadvantages-internet.html
6. Patrick, A.R., "The New Face of Banking: Technology in Banking" Retrieved on May 16, 2008 from http://www.networkmagazineindia.com/200305/tech1.shtml
7. Reserve Bank of India (2001), Report on Internet Banking available at www.rbi.org.in, June 22 February.
8. Singh, B. and Malhotra, P., (2004), "Adoption of Internet Banking: An Empirical Investigation of Indian Banking Sector", *Journal of Internet Banking and Commerce*, Vol. 9(2).
9. Sybase 365, Press Release: Research Reveals Global Appetite for Mobile Banking Services, October 15, 2007.

41

A Conceptual Pervasive Grid Framework with Context Computing for Medical Science

NEERA BAWA AND NANCY MEHTA

ABSTRACT

This paper presents context-aware pervasive grid framework for medical science and its design challenges. Use of pervasive networks in the domain of medical science was introduced earlier and now they are taken in view pervasively. However, due to the unavailability of any common framework, solutions that are developed in this domain are location, environment and problem dependent. Keeping in view the need of common framework for medical science, Context-Aware Pervasive Grid Framework is proposed. It will be helpful in developing solutions for majority of the problems related to consumer monitoring devices such as blood pressure, cuffs and glucose meters that can upload data to a personal computer for collection and dissemination to professional caregivers to detect patterns of concern that could require immediate action and regular monitoring of patients, etc. due to the capability of adjusting according to location and environment. The proposed framework is composed of three-layer architecture including Context-aware application layer, Grid middleware layer and Pervasive Grid layer.

I. INTRODUCTION

Medical science is one of the most important areas on which human life is very much dependent. There is a need of use of different technologies to support this domain to have low cost and appropriate solutions to many different problems. The proposed framework is combining three well known technological domains namely Context-aware computing, Grid computing and Pervasive computing.

The field of context-aware computing has been closely related to the development of intelligent and ubiquitous systems. According to Dey *et al.* [Dey and Abowd, April 2000] "A system is context-aware if it uses context to provide relevant information and/or services to the users, where relevancy depends on the user's task". The context-aware computing term was first coined by Schilit and Theimer in 1994. Author describes context-aware applications that "adapt according to its location of use, the collection of nearby people and objects, as well as the changes to those objects over time".

Grid computing is an area that has been evolved rapidly and effectively in the discipline of distributed computing. The term Grid computing was introduced in 1996 and formalized in 1999 [Foster, 2003]. In the last 10 years, definition of Grid undergone through several amendments. Gregor von Laszewski used the term 'Production Grid' to define the Grid concept.

The Grid is defined [Laszewski, 2005] as follows: "A production Grid is a shared computing infrastructure of hardware, software, and knowledge resources that allows the coordinated resource sharing and problem solving in dynamic, multiinstitutional virtual organizations to enable sophisticated international scientific and business oriented collaborations". The Grid provides the platform to share resources attached to it, i.e. applications, computing power, memory, data storage facilities etc. across multiple organizations and administrative domains. After the introduction of Open Grid Service Architecture (OGSA) [Kesselman, Foster, Nick, and Tuecke, 2002], concept of service oriented grid evolved that is to provide a shared pool of resources in such a way that any node can get the resource as service on demand as the resource is directly attached to it.

Pervasive computing is another evolving area. Pervasive Computing creates a ubiquitous environment that combines processors and sensors with network technologies (wireless and otherwise) and intelligent software to create an immerse environment to improve life.

In the scenario, the responder is very active, interacting with the local sensors and the global infrastructure. One should understand that much of the tasks should be automated, delegated and performed transparently by his device. The pervasive grid ecosystem, which integrates computers, networks, data archives, instruments, observatories, experiments, and embedded sensors and actuators, is also enabling new paradigms in science and engineering—ones that are information/data-driven and that

FIG. 41.1
Flow of Data in Computing to Global Smart Space

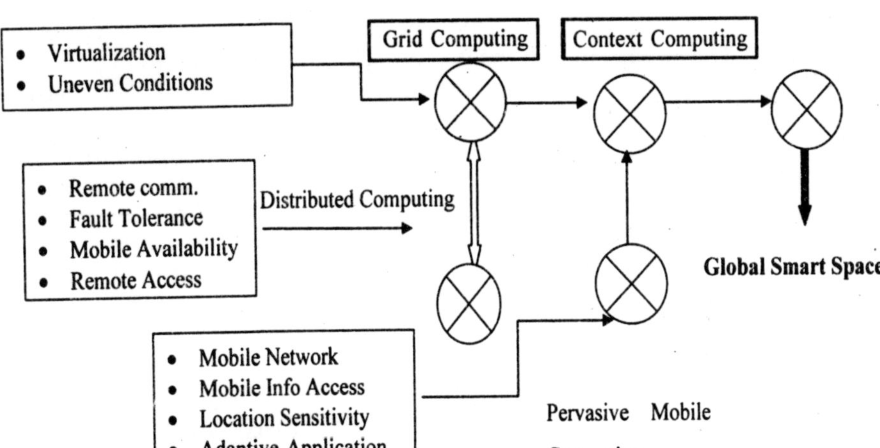

symbiotically and opportunistically combines computations, experiments, observations, and real-time information to understand and manage natural and engineering systems. For example, an Instrumented Oil-Field can (theoretically) achieve efficient and robust control and management of diverse subsurface and near subsurface geo-systems by completing the symbiotic feedback loop between measured data and a set of computational models, and can provide efficient, cost-effective and environmentally safe production of oil reservoirs. Similar strategies can be applied to medical science, management, military, health, agriculture, home, etc. which are the major application areas of Pervasive Grids.

In the *Grid-based Medical Devices for Everyday Health*, the physiological signals and context information are relayed back to a grid-based system, which performs the appropriate signal processing and makes the data available to medical, identifying episodes, which need priority attention. The information is fed back to medical via portable devices. Designing of Context-Aware Pervasive Grid framework for medical science is an effort in this regard. The rest of this paper is organized as follows. Section 2 provides framework details and its design challenges. Section 3 discusses about related work in the area of medical science. Finally, we offer our conclusions in section 6.

2. CONTEXT-AWARE GRID FRAMEWORK FOR MEDICAL SCIENCE

Context-Aware Pervasive Grid is a combination of three promising technological domains that are context-aware computing, grid computing and Pervasive computing. In very simple words Context-Aware Pervasive Grid can be defined as follows:

"The Context-aware pervasive Grid is a distributed computing environment that has shareable resources having the power to sense the physical world with the capability of high computing power on low price. It is adjustable to the environment autonomously on the basis of collected information." The architecture of the pervasive grid can be seen in Figure 41.2.

Our proposed context-aware pervasive grid framework for medical science is adaptable to different conditions of patient, i.e. his blood pressure, heart rate, diabetic control. In addition, it also has the provision to deal with different muscular problems. A special technology feature can be taken into consideration a new enabling technology for physiological monitoring, "conductive-fabric garment for a cable-free body area network," which describes a promising approach to making a wearable garment that can interconnect a wide range of sensors around a person's body. Such technologies will enrich the toolset that physicians and patients can count on for continuous telemetry.

The framework comprises of three layers namely Context-aware application layer, Grid middleware layer and Pervasive Grid layer.

FIG. 41.2

Context-Aware Pervasive Grid Architecture

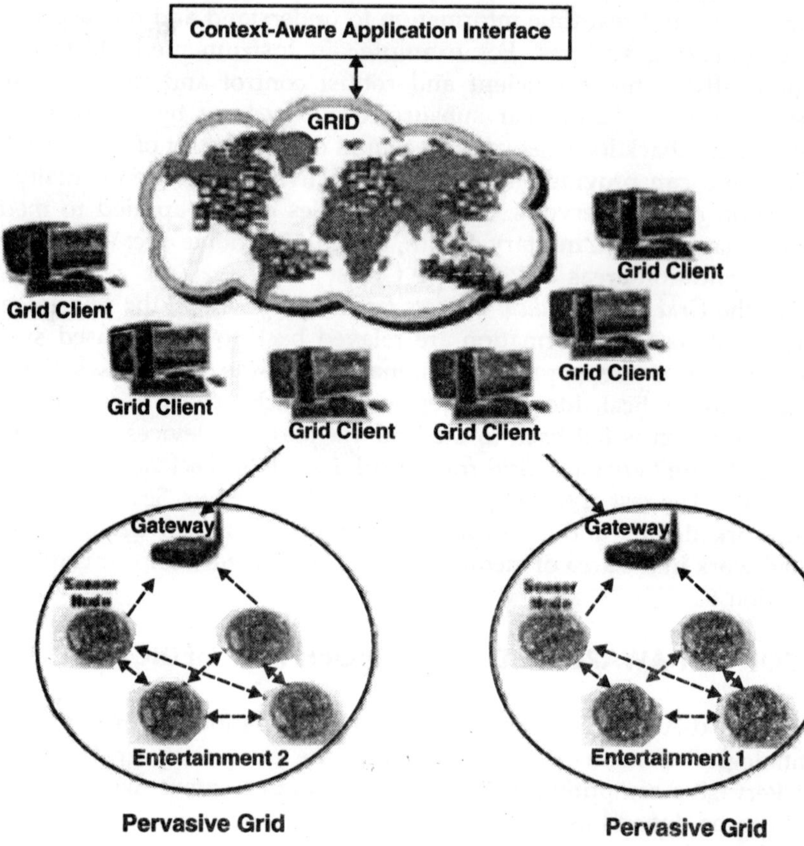

3. BUILDING BLOCKS OF THE FRAMEWORK

FIG. 41.3
Context-Aware Pervasive Grid Framework

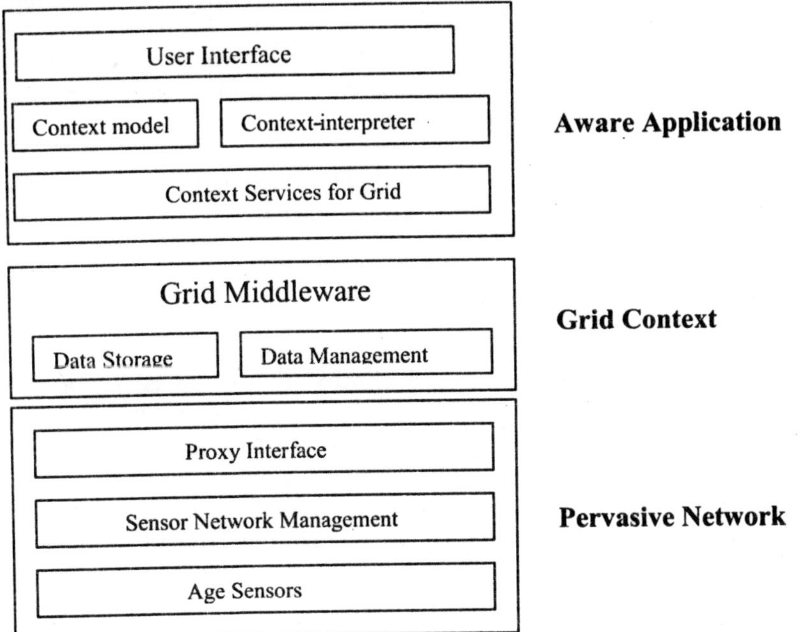

Major building blocks of the framework are:

A. *Context Model* — Context model block is to deal with the context acquisition, definition and storage.

B. *Context Interpreter* — This block is to provide service to the administrator in interpreting context values as primitive input.

C. *Context Services to Grid* — To make the grid context enabled, there is a need of grid services that are not available in OGSA. This block is to cater such services.

D. *Data Storage and Management* — This block is to deal with data services for storage and management. Due to the heterogeneous and quantity of sensors, variety of data in bulk will be collected. There will be need of data classification, clustering, aggregation and fusion. This block will help for such issues.

E. *Proxy Interface* — Connectivity of sensor network with grid requires an interface that can provide facility to convert data format in grid compatible form. Proxy interface block is to provide such facility.

F. *Sensor Network Management*	Sensor network management is an important task as sensor network is highly dynamic in nature. This block is to deal with sensor communication, topology, power management, etc
G. *Medical-Sensors*	Medical domain requires monitoring of patient conditions and locations, etc. for that purpose different sensor are needed. Medical-Sensors block is to deal Medical-science related sensors and their requirements.

4. CHALLENGES IN DESIGNING CONTEXT-AWARE PERVASIVE GRID FRAMEWORK FOR MEDICAL SCIENCE

There are several challenges in the design of context-aware pervasive grid framework that require special consideration.

A. *Context Model:* Ontology-based context modeling is a popular approach. The important rationales in designing context ontology include simplicity, flexibility, extensibility, generality and expressiveness. In case of medical science, context can be seen from two points of view. One is the sensed data values that can be used with location and time values to extract the current context or situation of the patient, while second is the context as implicit inputs that can be defined for different sources available for treatment, etc. In the proposed framework, there is a need of combining both types of context values. Main challenge in this regard is to develop a flexible and extensible ontology that can define several different location conditions and medical requirements.

B. *Grid Services for Context-Awareness:* Applications that are developed for grid uses grid services. Open Grid Service Architecture (OGSA) that is defined by Global Grid Forum (GGF) presents several services to use grid as service-oriented grid. But unfortunately OGSA does not provide the support for context-aware services till now. In 1994, Kerry Jean *et. al.* [Jean, Tan and Galis, 2004] presented some extensions for context-aware OGSA-based grid services. The challenge of defining such services is partially solved but more work is needed in this regard.

C. *Data Management and Storage:* Data clustering, classification, aggregation, fusion are very important and critical functions of sensors data management. In medical scenario, variety of sensors with different connectivity approaches are used. In Context-aware scenario, there is a need of a technique that can address context-sensing challenges. Huadong Wu work in this regard is a good contribution. Such solutions are needed that can be implemented in grid environment.

D. *Sensor Network Connectivity with Grid:* Different approaches have already been provided to connect pervasive network with grid that include middleware approach [Coulson, 2006], [Gaynor, Moulton, 2004], proxy-based approach [Lim, Teo, 2005], agent-oriented runtime approach [Hingne, Joshi, Finin, 2003], overlay network approach [Coulson, 2006], [Grace, Nov. 2005], etc. The problems with majority of available solutions are either they are proprietary or they support fixed kind of sensor topology. There is a need of open source solution that can handle variety sense of pervasive grid architecture.

5. RELATED WORK

Pervasive computing is often mentioned in the context of improving healthcare. Usually, these examples involve consumer-monitoring devices such as blood pressure cuffs and glucose meters that can upload data to a personal computer for collection and dissemination to professional caregivers. By collecting patient data in settings more varied than doctors' offices, healthcare providers hope to better understand the many facets of patients' daily lives and then modify therapies to the individual. Another important context is emergency care to accelerate access to medical records at the emergency site or to bring experts to the scene virtually. By giving medical professionals appropriate, complete information, we expect to deliver better care that's tuned not only to the situation but also to the patient's history.

The surgical field also receives much attention, as surgeons and nurses must monitor and control various vital functions under intensely stressful conditions. Technologists are developing systems to collect and process an ever-increasing range of telemetry from instruments used in an operating room and to augment human ability to detect patterns of concern that could require immediate action.

Proponents tout pervasive computing as benefiting healthcare in at least three ways:

- Lowering costs by getting appropriate care to the people who need it much faster than previously possible;
- Making expert care accessible to more people, thereby, increasing the scale at which first-rate healthcare is applied; and
- Making healthcare more personalized, prompting individuals to take more responsibility for maintaining their health.

6. CONCLUSION

Need of common framework for medical scenario instigated us to develop context-aware pervasive grid framework for medical science. This framework has the capability to deal with different problems related to

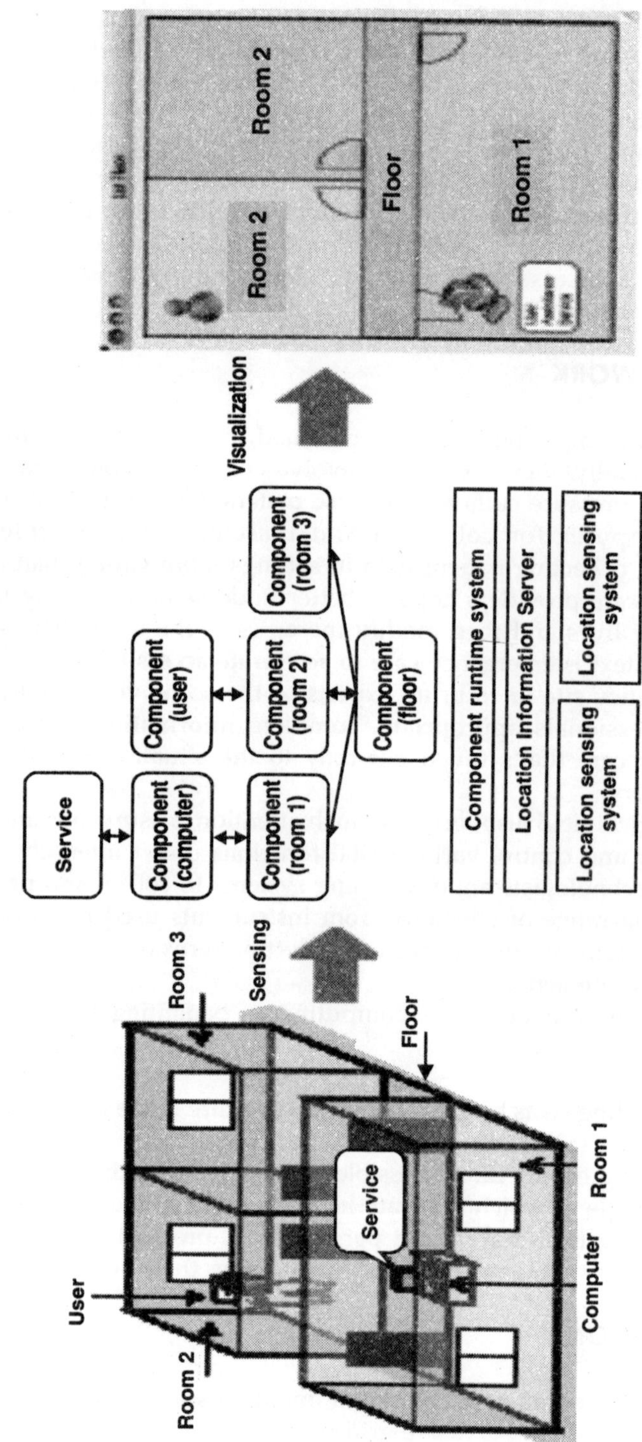

Fig. 41.4
Rooms on Floor in Physical World and Components in Location Model

consumer monitoring devices such as blood pressure, cuffs and glucose meters and his physiological monitoring etc. Context-awareness capability along with the grid computing facility makes it highly dynamic and low cost solution that can be used for diverse conditions and locations. Several challenges are pointed out that need profound consideration to make this proposed framework a reality.

References

1. Coulson, G. (2006.) *"Pervasive Grids: Integrating Sensor Networks into the Fixed Grid,"* invited Paper, in Proc. Euro-American Workshop on Middleware for Sensor Networks, International Conference on Distributed Computing in Sensor Systems (DCOSS '06), San Francisco, USA, June 18–20.
2. Dey, A.K., and Abowd, G. (April, 2000), *"Towards a Better Understanding of Context and Context-Awareness,"* presented at the Workshop on The What, Who, Where, When, and How of Context-Awareness, as part of the 2000 Conference on Human Factors in Computing Systems (CHI, 2000), The Hague, The Netherlands.
3. Foster, Ian (July 2002), *"What is the GRID? A three point checklist,"* GRID Today, Foster I. and C. Kesselman, (2003), *The Grid: Blueprint for a New Computing Infrastructure*, Morgan Kaufmann Publishers, 2nd Edition.
4. Gaynor Mark, Moulton Steven L., Welsh Matt, La Combe, Rowan Ed Austin, Wynne John, (2004). *"Integrating Wireless Sensor Networks with the Grid,"* IEEE Internet Computing, Vol. 08, No. 4, pp. 32–39, Jul./Aug.
5. Grace, P. Coulson G., G. Blair's, B. Porter, (Nov. 2005), *"Deep Middleware for the Divergent Grid,"* in Proc. IFIP/ACM/USENIX Middleware, France.
6. Hingne, Vipul, Joshi Anupam, Finin Tim, Kargupta Hillol, Houstis Elias, (2003)*"Towards a Pervasive Grid,"* ipdps, p. 207b, International Parallel and Distributed Processing Symposium (IPDPS'03).
7. Huadong, Wu (December 2003), *"Sensor Data Fusion for Context-Aware Computing Using Dempster-Shafer Theory,"* Ph.D. dissertation, Carnegie Mellon University, Pittsburgh, Pennsylvania.
8. Jean Kerry Tan Alvin and Galis Alex (2004), *"Context-Aware GRID Services: Issues and Approaches"*, University College London, Electrical Engineering Department, Torrington Place, London.
9. Kesselman, Foster I., Nick C.J., and Tuecke, S. (2002), *The Physiology of the Grid: An Open.*
10. *Grid Services Architecture for Distributed Systems Integration"*, Globus Project, Available: www.globus.org/research/papers/ogsa.pdf.
11. Korpipää Panu and Mäntyjärv Jani (2003), *"An Ontology for Mobile Device Sensor-Based Context Awareness"*, in Proc. Context '03, LNAI No. 2680.
12. Laszewski, Gregor von 2005, *"The Grid-Idea and Its Evolution"*, Information Technology, Volume: 47, Issue: 6, pp. 319-29, Oldenbourg Wissenschaftsverlag Gmb, Germany.
13. Lim Hock Beng, Teo Yong Meng, (2005), *"Sensor Grid: Integration of Wireless Sensor Networks and the Grid,"* in Proc. the IEEE Conference on Local Computer Networks 30th Anniversary (LCN'05), pp. 91-99.
14. Schilit, B.N., and Theimer, (1994), *"Disseminating Active Map Informatin to Mobile Hosts"*, IEEE Networks, 8(5), pp. 22-32.

SECTION VI

Security and Privacy

42

Study and Analysis of SRAM Cells

POONAM AND VIJAY NEHRA

ABSTRACT

Static Random Access Memory (SRAM) is a type of semiconductor memory. The word "static" indicate that the memory retains its contents as long as the power is tuned on and refresh operation is not required. SRAM consists of a latch that is why cell data is kept as long as the power is tuned on. In this paper, we have studied the architecture of SRAM and various types of SRAM cells which are used to store the bit information. We also studied the comparison of 4-transistor Polysilicon Register Load, conventional 6T SRAM cells and Loadless 4T SRAM cell and their analysis.

1. INTRODUCTION

The main components of SRAM are memory cells which are used to store the binary information. Typical SRAM cell consists of two cross-coupled inverters forming latch and access transistors. To access the read and write operation, it is necessary to enable access transistor; and when the cell is not addressed two access transistors are closed and data is kept to stable state. SRAM cell has to provide non-destructive read access, write capability and infinite storage (data retention) time provided the power is supplied to the cell. Hierarchically, memory cells are arranged in cores, which can be further divided into blocks and arrays depending upon the system speed and power requirement.

Different types of SRAM cells are based on the type of load used in the elementary inverter of the flip-flop cell. There are currently three types of SRAM memory cells:

- The 4T cell (four NMOS transistors plus two poly load resistors).
- The 6T cell (six transistors—four NMOS transistors plus two PMOS transistors).
- Loadless 4T cell (two NMOS transistors plus two PMOS transistors).

In this paper, we look into SRAM and specially 4T and 6T SRAM cells. The rest of the paper is organized as follows. In section 2, we discuss the organization of SRAM. In section 3, 4 and 5, we present an overview of 4T Polysilicon Register Load, 6T and Loadless 4T SRAMs with their layout. Next section discusses comparisons between them. We conclude in Section 7.

2. ARCHITECTURE OF SRAM

In its simplest form the SRAM has a monolithic architecture as shown in Figure 42.1. It has only one memory array which is accessed byte row and column decoders. This architecture has major disadvantages as the size of the array grows. The word line RC delay grows as the square of the number of cells in the row, and bit line power grows linearly with the number of columns. Thus, for larger SRAM designs, the memory array is partitioned into sub-arrays, commonly, referred to as macros. The size of each macro can vary anywhere from 16kB to 256kB. Any macro greater than 256kB is further divided into smaller sub-macros. Each macro stores a part of the accessed word called the sub-word, and all of these sub-words are accessed simultaneously to access the complete word. Each macro can be treated as a separate SRAM, as each has its own set of local word line drivers and sense amplifiers. They, however, share some parts of the decoder.

A typical SRAM block consists of memory core (cell arrays), address decoders, column multiplexers, sense amplifiers, I/O, precharge cell and a control circuitry. The functionality of the control circuit is to generate internal signals of the SRAM. In the following, the functionality and design of other components are briefly discussed.

2.1 Memory Core

Usually there is more than one memory core (cell array) in an SRAM circuit. Figure 42.1 shows only one of them. Memory core structure can access any cell by accessing a particular row and column. A row can be activated by global line spanning all the cells of row and is termed as the word line. This line enables cells to be written into or read out. Every column can be accessed individually through vertical bit lines. The size of the cell array depends on both performance and density requirements. Generally speaking, as technology shrinks, cell arrays are moving from tall to wide structures [2, 3]. However, using wider arrays needs more circuitry for column multiplexers and sense amplifiers.

2.2 Precharge Cells

Precharge differential read/write schemes are used for memory cells. This requires bit lines to be set-up in well-defined state before an access. Precharge cells accomplish this. Dynamic schemes use a clocked precharge cell to charge bit lines. Static schemes leave the precharge continuously on, in which case, they resemble a load cell on the bit lines.

2.3 Address Decoder

The address decoder is often broken into two pieces. The first piece, called *predecoder*, is placed before the long decoder wires and the second part, *row decoder*, which usually consists of a single NAND gate and buffers. The set of cells that generate word line signal form the row decoder. This structure takes the set of n address lines and generates 2^n word lines. At most one of the word lines is activated at a time.

2.4 Column Multiplexers and Sense Amplifiers

Column multiplexing is inevitable in most SRAM designs because it reduces the number of rows in the cell array and as a result increases the speed. Since bit or bit-bar line is discharged during a read operation, sense amplifiers accomplish the conversion of bit line differential to logic levels. It is used to sense a small voltage difference and generate a digital value [1].

3. 4T SRAM CELLS WITH POLYSILICON REGISTER LOAD

4T cell use poly resistor load (PRL) [10] as shown in Figure 42.2 which is typically using poly layer. The value of registers must be as high as possible to reduce the current consumption and leads to lower stand by power consumption that helps retain a reasonable noise margin. 4T SRAM cell is concerned with getting an appropriate ratio of the pass transistors M1/M2 with respect to the pull-down transistor M3/M4. We shall refer to this as the aspect ratio of the cell. It is clear that the aspect ratio should ensure that at no time interval cell voltages rise to a value large enough to upset the cell state. It is important to note that energy dissipation due to discharge of bit line capacitance is considerably larger than energy required to switch the cell.

4. 6T SRAM CELL

The CMOS implementation of the 4T SRAM cell replaces the inverters

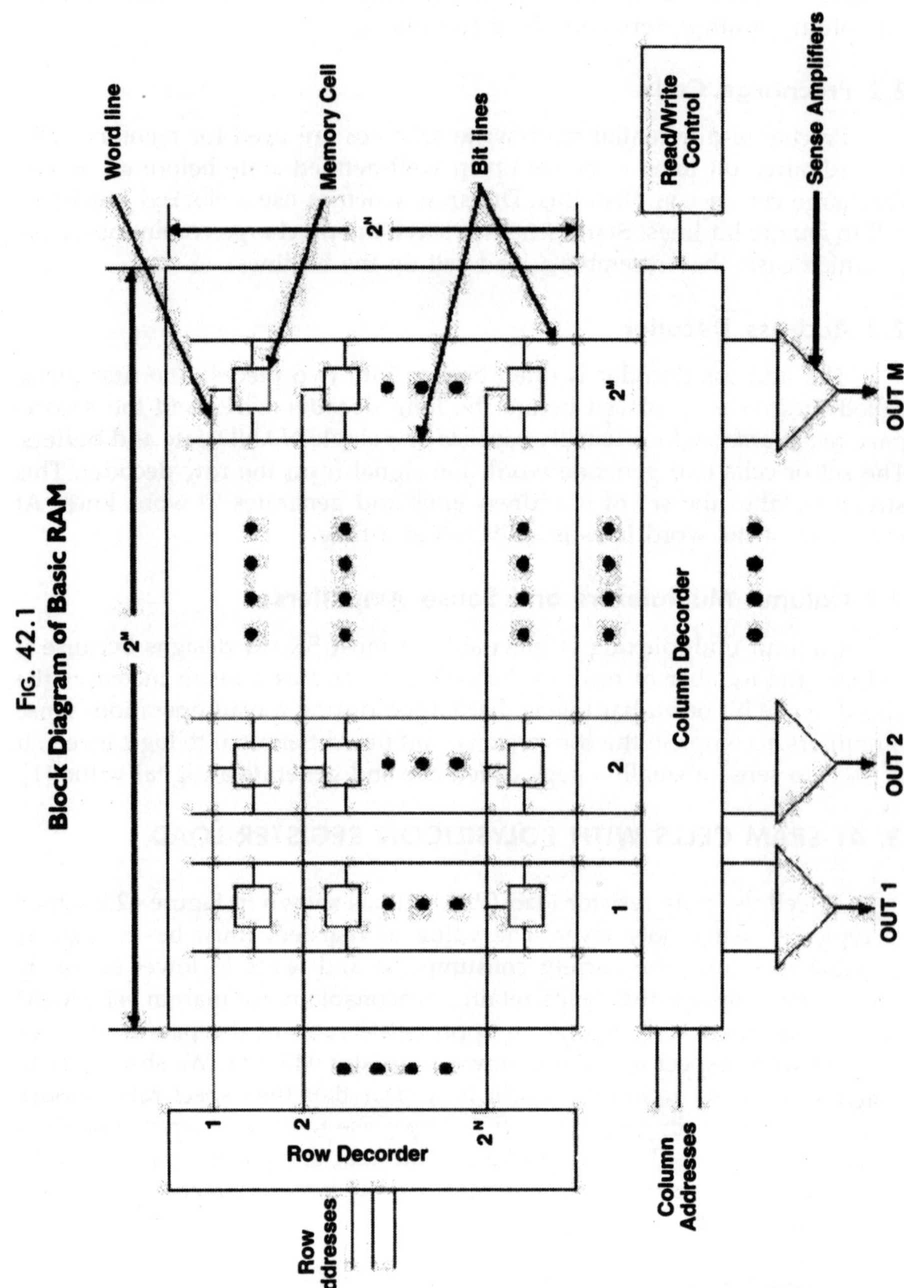

Fig. 42.1
Block Diagram of Basic RAM

Fig. 42.2
6 T SRAM Cell

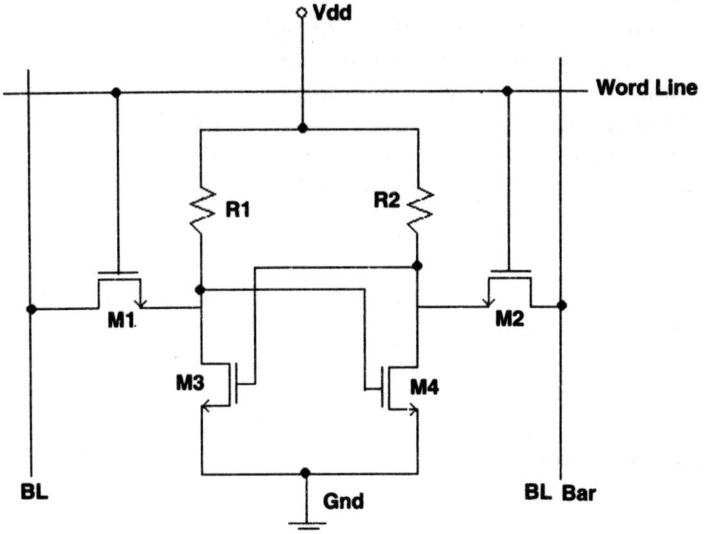

Vdd
Word Line
R1
R2
M1
M2
M3
M4
BL
Gnd
BL Bar

by fully complemented CMOS inverters. PMOS device play the role of register and often minimize geometry. Each bit in an SRAM stored on four transistors that form two cross-coupled inverters. This storage cell has two stable states which are used to denote 0 and 1. Two additional access transistors serve to control the access to a storage cell during read and write operations. It, thus, typically takes six MOSFETs to store one memory bit.

Fig. 42.3
6 T SRAM Cell

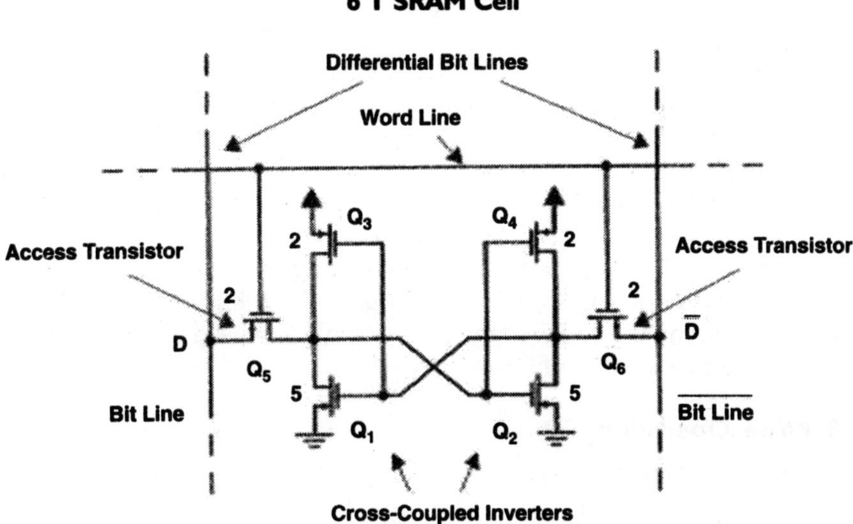

Access to the cell [11] is enabled by the word line (in fig. 3) which controls the two *access* transistors Q_5 and Q_6 which, in turn, control whether the cell should be connected to the bit lines: BL and BL Bar. They are used to transfer data for both read and write operations. While it's not strictly necessary to have two bit lines, both the signal and its inverse are typically provided since it improves noise margins.

A SRAM cell has three different states. It can be in *standby* where the circuit is idle, *reading* when the data has been requested and *writing* when updating the contents. The three different states work as follows:

4.1 Standby

If the word line is not asserted, the *access* transistors Q_5 and Q_6 disconnect the cell from the bit lines. The two cross coupled inverters formed by $Q_1 - Q_4$ will continue to reinforce each other as long as they are disconnected from the outside world.

4.2 Read Operation

To read a "D=0"

- W/L at 0V, both access transistors are off
- Pre-charge both bit lines high (either VDD or VDD/2)
- Correct W/L will go high
- If a "D=0 D=1" is stored, then W/L=H causes Q5 to pass 0V to Q2/Q4, VDD to Q1/Q3
- Charge flows Q4->Q6, thus charging the B bit line voltage
- Charge flows Q5->Q1, thus discharging the B bit line voltage
- Differential B to B voltage of 50-100mV is sensed at the sense amp; must be small so FF doesn't flip

To read a "D=1"

- W/L at 0V, both access transistors are off
- Pre-charge both bit lines high (either VDD or VDD/2)
- Correct W/L will go high
- If a "D=1 D=0" is stored, then W/L=H causes Q5 to pass VDD to Q2/Q4, 0V to Q1/Q3
- Charge flows Q6->Q2, thus discharging the B bit line voltage
- Charge flows Q3->Q5, thus charging the B bit line voltage
- Differential B to B voltage of 50-100mV is sensed at the sense amp; must be small so FF doesn't flop

4.3 Write Operation

To write a "1", initially at a "0"

- W/L at 0V, both access transistors are off

- Pre-charge one bit line high (D=B=VDD), the other low (D=B=0V)
- Correct W/L will go high
- Source (B) of Q5 goes to 0->(VDD-Vt), and drain (B) of Q6 goes to VDD->0V
- Positive feedback takes over, and cell stores a "1" on D

To write a "0", initially at a "1"

- W/L at 0V, both access transistors are off
- Pre-charge one bit line high (B=VDD), the other to ground (B=0V)
- Correct W/L will go high
- Source (B) of Q5 goes to VDD->0V, and drain (B) of Q6 goes to 0->(VDD-Vt)
- Positive feedback takes over, and cell stores a "0" on D

5. LOADLESS 4T SRAM CELL

This section presents a new design concept of loadless 4T-SRAM cell without any additional circuits. This 4T-SRAM fabricated in a CMOS logic process, but it described mainly a specialized circuit to hold the cell data. The loadless 4T-SRAM is to achieve a smaller cell size than conventional 4T-cell, with the same stability and the same compatibility with CMOS logic processes as 6T-SRAM cells. Figure 42.4 shows a circuit equivalent to a developed Loadless 4T-SRAM cell. The single cell comprises two nMOSFETs for drive transistors and two pMOSFETs for transfer transistors. Compared

FIG. 42.4
Load Less 4T SRAM Cell

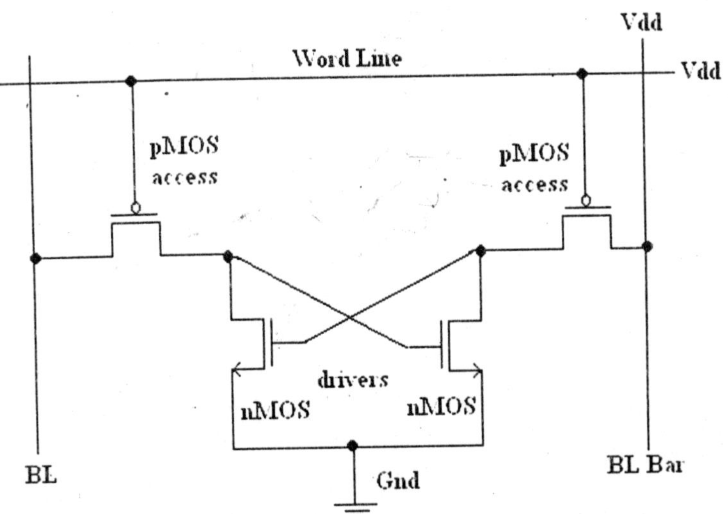

with the conventional 4T-SRAM having nMOSFETs and load elements, the pMOSFETs is that a high-node level rises to V_{DD} right after a READ or WRITE operation. During a stand-by cycle, bit lines are precharged at the V_{DD}. At this time, the pMOS transfer transistors, which are turned off, work as load elements.

6. COMPARISON BETWEEN 4T, 6T AND LOADLESS 4T SRAM CELL BASED ON 0.18μM TECHNOLOGY

6.1 Comparison between 4T and 6T SRAM cell

4T memory cell has a smaller area. It also has lower stability as compared to the 6T cell [9]. The 6T cells have a much better Static Noise Margin (SNM) over the 4T cells. This is especially true for lower voltage levels. In order to maintain stability the 4T cells have to maintain higher cell ratios compared to the 6T cells. 4T SRAM cells are more expensive to fabricate as compared to 6T SRAM cells. Also, as pointed out by [9] the 6T cells have historically been more robust to Soft Error Rates (SER) as compared to the 4T cells. However, with the 6T cells also being scaled down to smaller sizes and with the reducing voltages, SER will become a significant issue in 6T cells as well. The working of a 6T cell has been described in many publications [8, 4]. MP1, MP2, MN1 and MN2 form the cross-coupled inverter pair that stores the data. Ma1 and Ma2 are the access transistors, which allow data to be written or read from the cell. The gates of Ma1 and Ma2 are controlled by the word line and their drains are connected to the two bitlines. For the 4T cells, the pMOS transistors MP1 and MP2 are replaced by resistors R0 and R1.

6.2 Comparison between Loadless 4T and 6T SRAM cell

For the same access speed and comparable SNM, the 4T SRAM cell area is smaller as compared to area of conventional 6T SRAM cells [5]. Loadless 4T SRAM cell is having higher static noise margin and lower sensitivity [7] to V_{TH} fluctuation than 6T cell. Loadless 4T cell has a stronger read current degradation at reduced $V_{DD.}$ Impact of technology parameter variations, such as threshold voltage (V_{TH}), effective channel length (L_{eff}), gate oxide thickness (T_{ox}) as well as V_{DD} scaling and operating temperature increase on stability of Loadless 4T SRAM cells in comparison with conventional 6T SRAM cells. Static noise margin of Loadless 4T SRAM cell is more sensitive to increase of operating temperature than the SNM of 6T cell. Loadless 4T SRAM cell is less SNM sensitive to V_{TH} fluctuation and stronger dependence on L_{eff} than conventional 6T SRAM cells.

6.3 Comparison between 4T and Loadless 4T SRAM Cell

4T-SRAMs (PRL) need a complex process to form a load element and have poor stability at low voltage. The Loadless CMOS 4T-cell is promising for high-speed [6] and high-density SRAMs embedded in any logic devices, as well as for stand-alone SRAM applications. SNM will not limit the scaling of the Loadless 4T-SRAMs until 0.1μm generation. The single cell comprises two nMOSFETs for drive transistors and two pMOSFETs for transfer transistors. Compared with the conventional 4T-SRAM having nMOSFETs and load elements.

TABLE 42.1
Parameters of .18μm Technology

	nMOSFET	*pMOSFET*
Tox (nm)	3.8	3.2
L_{Poly} (μm)	0.18	0.18
V_{TH} (V)	0.7	-0.4
W/L (μm)	0.24/0.18	0.24/0.18

FIG. 42.5
Noise Margin of 6T SRAM Cell

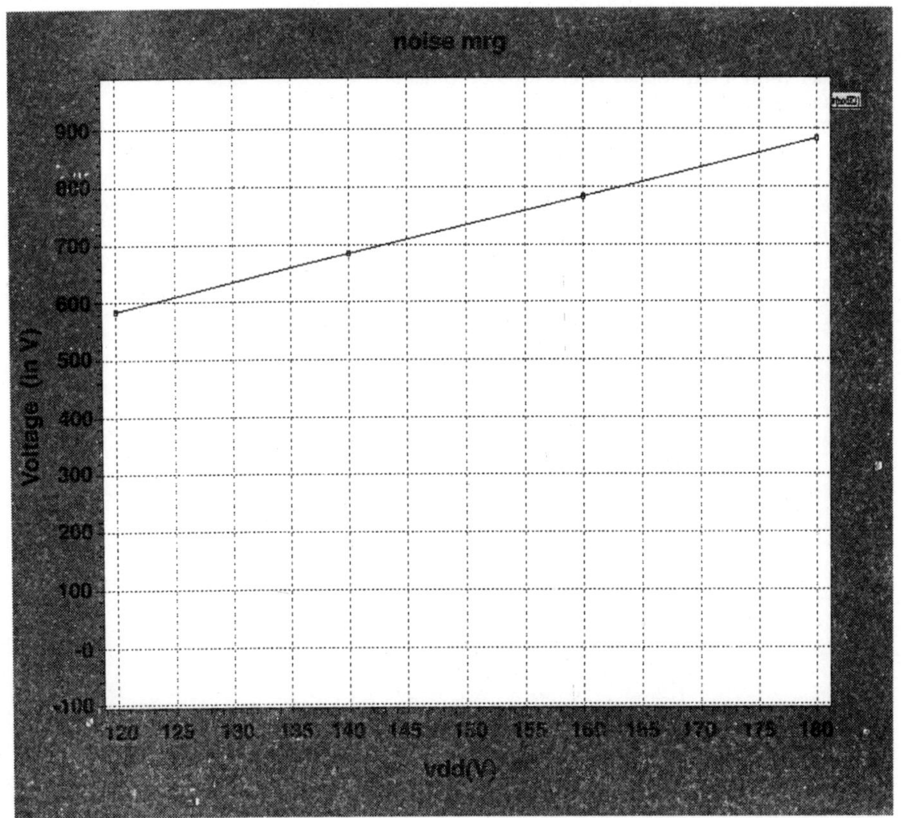

7. CONCLUSION

In this paper, we studied the conventional 4T, 6T and recently proposed CMOS SRAM CELLS based on 0.18µm technology. We compared stability as well as noise margin and area of these cells. We found loadless 4T SRAM cell has a higher static noise margin and lower sensitivity than 6T SRAM cells. Loadless 4T SRAM cell has lower cell area than 6T SRAM cells. 6T cells have been more robust to Soft Error Rates (SER) as compared to the 4T cells. In this paper, we discussed the architecture of SRAM and an overview of 4T Polysilicon Register Load, 6T and Loadless 4T SRAMs. We have also reviewed comparisons between these cells.

REFERENCES

1. B. Wicht, "Current sense amplifier for embedded sram in high-performance so Designs," Advanced Microelectronics, 2003.
2. K. Zhang *et al.*, "SRAM design on 65-nm CMOS technology with dynamic sleep transistor for leakage reduction," IEEE J. Solid-State Circuits, Vol. 40, No. 4, April 2005, pp. 895-901.
3. F. Hamzaoglu *et al.*, "Dual Vt-SRAM cells with fullswing single-ended bit line sensing for high-performance on chip cache in 0.13ìm technology generation," in Proc. of ISLPED, 2000, pp. 15-19.
4. J.B. Kuo, B. Wang., "A novel two-port 6t cmos sram cell structure for low-voltage vlsi sram with single-bit-line simultaneous read-and-write access (sblsrwa) capability", The 2000 IEEE International Symposium on Circuits and Systems, 2000. Proceedings. ISCAS 2000 Geneva., 5, 2000.
5. Y. Nakagome *et. al.*, "Review and future prospects of low-voltage RAM circuits," IBM J. RES and DEV., Vol. 47, No. 5/6, September/November 2003.
6. Kenji Noda, Member, IEEE, Koujirou Matsui, Koichi Takeda, and Noritsugu Nakamura, "A Loadless CMOS Four-Transistor SRAM Cell in a 0.18-µm Logic Technology," IEEE Transactions on Electron Devices, Vol. 48, No. 12, December 2001.
7. Anderi Pavlov *et. al.*, "Sub-quarter micron SRAM cells stability in low-voltage operations: a comparative analysis," IEEE IRW Final Report, 2002.
8. M. Ishida *et. al.*, "A novel 6t-sram cell technology designed with rectangular patterns scalable beyond 0.18 µm generation and desirable for ultra high speed operation", International Electron Devices Meeting, 1998.
9. Craig Lage *et. al.*, "Advanced sram Technology—The race between 4t and 6t cells", International Electron Devices Meeting, 1996.
10. Gary, K. Yeap, "Practical low power digital vlsi design", Kluwer Academic Publishers Group, Printed in the United States of America, 1998.
11. Kaushik Roy and Sharat Prasad, "Low-power cmos vlsi circuit design", A Wiley-Interscience Publication, Printed in the United States of America, 2000.

43

Distributed Denial of Service : Taxonomies of Attack and Countermeasures

PREETI, YOGESH CHABA AND YUDHVIR SINGH

ABSTRACT

Distributed Denial of Service (DDoS) attacks have become a large problem for users of computer systems connected to the Internet. DDoS attackers hijack secondary victim systems using them to wage a coordinated large-scale attack against primary victim systems or DDoS attack is a distributed, large-scale attempt by malicious users to flood the victim network with an enormous number of packets. This exhausts the victim network of resources such as bandwidth, computing power, etc. The victim is unable to provide services to its legitimate clients and network performance is greatly deteriorated. As new countermeasures are developed to prevent or mitigate DDoS attacks, attackers are constantly developing new methods to circumvent these new countermeasures.

In this paper, we describe DDoS attack and propose taxonomies to characterize the scope of DDoS attacks and countermeasures available.

1. INTRODUCTION

A Distributed Denial of Service (DDoS) attack [4, 5, 6] is a coordinated attack on the availability of services of a given target system or network that is launched indirectly through many compromised computing systems. The services under attack are those of the "primary victim", while the compromised systems used to launch the attack are often called the "secondary victims". The use of secondary victims in a DDoS attack provides the attacker with the ability to wage a much larger and more disruptive attack while remaining anonymous since the secondary victims actually perform the attack making it more difficult for network forensics to track down the real attacker.

Even though denial of service attacks has existed for some time, their recent distributed formats have made these attacks more difficult to prevent. In this paper, we look into various methods for detection and prevention of DDoS attacks. The rest of the paper is organized as follows. The next section discusses the characteristics of DDoS attacks. In section 3, we describe various taxonomies for DDoS attacks. Next section shows the effects of DDoS on network. In section 5, we present various defense mechanisms against DDoS attacks. We conclude in Section 6.

2. CHARACTERISTICS OF DISTRIBUTED DENIAL OF SERVICE ATTACKS

A denial of service (DoS) attack is characterized by an explicit attempt by an attacker to prevent legitimate users of a service from using the desired resources. Examples of denial of service attacks include [15]:

- attempts to "flood" a network, thereby preventing legitimate network traffic,
- attempts to disrupt connections between two machines, thereby preventing access to a service,
- attempts to prevent a particular individual from accessing a service, and
- attempts to disrupt service to a specific system or person.

A DDoS (Distributed Denial-Of-Service) attack is a distributed, large-scale attempt by malicious users to flood the victim network with an enormous number of packets. This exhausts the victim network of resources such as bandwidth, computing power, etc. The victim is unable to provide services to its legitimate clients and network performance is greatly deteriorated. The distributed format adds the "many to one" dimension that makes these attacks more difficult to prevent. A distributed denial of service attack is composed of four elements, as shown in Figure 43.1. First, it involves a victim, i.e., the target host that has been chosen to receive the brunt of the attack. Second, it involves the presence of the attack daemon agents. These are agent programs that actually conduct the attack on the target victim. Attack daemons are usually deployed in host computers. These daemons affect both the target and the host computers.

FIG. 43.1

The Four Components of a Distributed Denial of Service Attack: a Real Attacker, a Control Master Program, Attack Daemons and the Victim

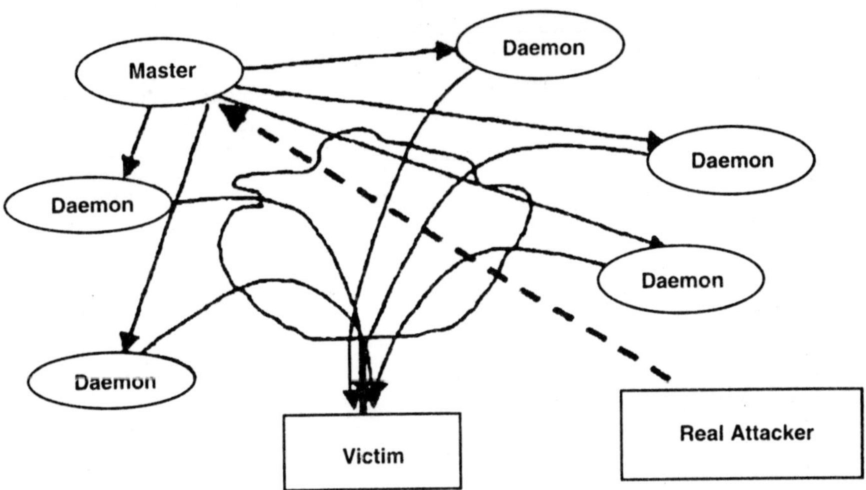

The task of deploying these attack daemons requires the attacker to gain access and infiltrate the host computers. The third component of a distributed denial of service attack is the control master program. Its task is to coordinate the attack. Finally, there is the real attacker, the mastermind behind the attack. By using a control master program, the real attacker can stay behind the scenes of the attack. The following steps take place during a distributed attack:

- The real attacker sends an "execute" message to the control master program.
- The control master program receives the "execute" message and propagates the command to the attack daemons under its control.
- Upon receiving the attack command, the attack daemons begin the attack on the victim.

3. DDOS ATTACK TAXONOMY

There are a wide variety of DDoS attacks. There are two main classes of DDoS attacks: bandwidth depletion and resource depletion attacks shown in Figure 43.2. A *bandwidth depletion attack* is designed to flood the victim network with unwanted traffic that prevents legitimate traffic from reaching the primary victim. A *resource depletion attack* is an attack that is designed to tie up the resources of a victim system making the victim unable to process legitimate requests for service.

FIG. 43.2
DDoS Attack Taxonomy

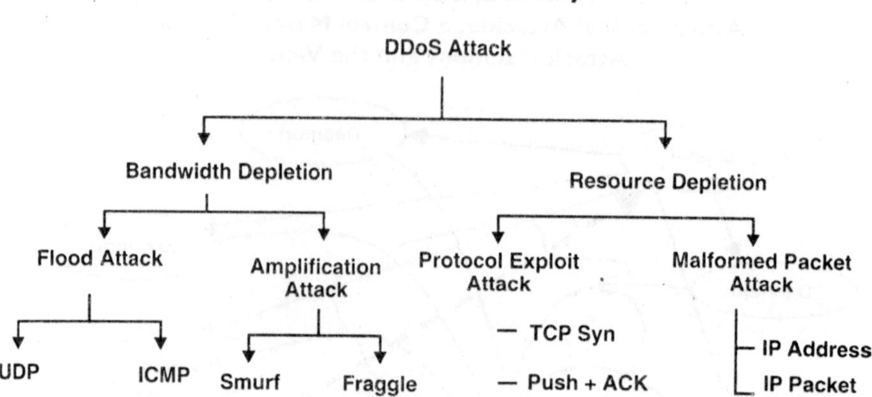

3.1 Bandwidth Depletion Attacks

Bandwidth depletion attacks can be characterized as flood attacks and amplification attacks.

3.1.1 Flood Attacks

A *flood attack* involves zombies sending large volumes of traffic to a victim system, to congest the victim system's network bandwidth with IP traffic. The victim system slows down, crashes, or suffers from saturated network bandwidth, preventing access by legitimate users. Flood attacks have been launched using both UDP (User Datagram Protocol) and ICMP (Internet Control Message Protocol) packets.

In a *UDP Flood attack*, a large number of UDP packets are sent to either random or specified ports on the victim system. The victim system tries to process the incoming data to determine which applications have requested data. If the victim system is not running any applications on the targeted port, it will send out an ICMP packet to the sending system indicating a "destination port unreachable" message.

Often, the attacking DDoS tool will also spoof the source IP address of the attacking packets. This helps hide the identity of the secondary victims since return packets from the victim system are not sent back to the zombies, but to the spoofed addresses. UDP flood attacks may also fill the bandwidth of connections located around the victim system. This often impacts systems located near the victim.

An *ICMP flood attack* occurs when the zombies send large volumes of ICMP_ECHO_REPLY packets ("ping") to the victim system. These packets signal the victim system to reply and the combination of traffic saturates the bandwidth of the victim's network connection. During this attack, the source IP address of the ICMP packet may also be spoofed.

3.1.2 Amplification Attacks

An amplification attack involves the attacker or the zombies sending messages to a broadcast IP address, using this to cause all systems in the subnet reached by the broadcast address to send a reply to the victim system. The broadcast IP address feature is found on most routers; when a sending system specifies a broadcast IP address as the destination address, the routers replicate the packet and send it to all the IP addresses within the broadcast address range. In this attack, the broadcast IP address is used to amplify and reflect the attack traffic, and thus reduce the victim system's bandwidth.

The attacker can send the broadcast message directly, or use the agents to send the broadcast message to increase the volume of attacking traffic. If the attacker decides to send the broadcast message directly, this attack provides the attacker with the ability to use the systems within the broadcast network as zombies without requiring to infiltrate them or install any agent software.

A DDoS *Smurf attack* is an example of an amplification attack where the attacker sends packets to a network amplifier (a system supporting broadcast addressing), with the return address spoofed to the victim's IP address. The attacking packets are typically ICMP ECHO REQUESTs, which are packets (similar to a "ping") that request the receiver to generate an ICMP ECHO REPLY packet [1]. The amplifier sends the ICMP ECHO REQUEST packets to all of the systems within the broadcast address range, and each of these systems will return an ICMP ECHO REPLY to the target victim's IP address [2]. This type of attack amplifies the original packet tens or hundreds of times.

Another example is the DDoS *Fraggle attack*, where the attacker sends packets to a network amplifier, using UDP ECHO packets [3]. There is a variation of the Fraggle attack where the UDP ECHO packets are sent to the port that supports character generation (chargen, port 19 in Unix systems), with the return address spoofed to the victim's echo service (echo, port 7 in Unix systems) creating an infinite loop. The UDP Fraggle packet will target the character generator in the systems reached by the broadcast address. These systems each generate a character to send to the echo service in the victim system, which will send an echo packet back to the character generator, and the process repeats. This attack can generate more bad traffic and cause more damage than a Smurf attack.

3.2 Resource Depletion Attacks

DDoS resource depletion attacks involve the attacker sending packets that misuse network protocol communications or are malformed. Network resources are tied up so that none are left for legitimate users.

3.2.1 Protocol Exploit Attacks

We give two examples, one misusing the TCP SYN (Transfer Control Protocol Synchronize) protocol, and the other misusing the PUSH+ACK protocol.

In a DDoS *TCP SYN attack*, the attacker instructs the zombies to send bogus TCP SYN requests to a victim server in order to tie up the server's processor resources, and hence prevent the server from responding to legitimate requests. The TCP SYN attack exploits the three-way handshake between the sending system and the receiving system by sending large volumes of TCP SYN packets to the victim system with spoofed source IP addresses, so the victim system responds to a non-requesting system with the ACK+SYN. When a large volume of SYN requests are being processed by a server and none of the ACK+SYN responses are returned, the server eventually runs out of processor and memory resources, and is unable to respond to legitimate users.

In a *PUSH + ACK attack*, the attacking agents send TCP packets with the PUSH and ACK bits set to one. These triggers in the TCP packet header instruct the victim system to unload all data in the TCP buffer (regardless of whether or not the buffer is full) and send an acknowledgement when complete. If this process is repeated with multiple agents, the receiving system cannot process the large volume of incoming packets and the victim system will crash.

3.2.2 Malformed Packet Attacks

A *malformed packet attack* is an attack where the attacker instructs the zombies to send incorrectly formed IP packets to the victim system in order to crash it. There are at least two types of malformed packet attacks.

In an *IP address attack*, the packet contains the same source and destination IP addresses. This can confuse the operating system of the victim system and can cause the victim system to crash.

In an *IP packet options* attack, a malformed packet may randomize the optional fields within an IP packet and set all quality of service bits to one so that the victim system must use additional processing time to analyze the traffic. If this attack is multiplied, it can exhaust the processing ability of the victim system.

4. DDoS ATTACKS IN NETWORK

As DDoS attacks are both distributed and denial-of service attacks [11], they are often large-scale in nature and can greatly deteriorate the performance of the victim network. In a typical DDoS attack, the malicious users first build a network of vulnerable hosts which are used to launch the attack. The vulnerable nodes, known as zombies, are then installed with attack tools, which allow them to carry out attacks under the control of the attacker.

J. Mirkovic and P. Reiher in [12] provide a comprehensive overview of the DDoS problem and design space by proposing taxonomies of DDoS attack and defense mechanisms. There are many proposed methods in the literature which aim to handle DDoS attacks and mitigate their level of damage. Some of these include reactive attack response strategies such as filtering, which allows a certain class of datagram to pass through while blocking all other datagrams.

In the case of DDoS attacks, its effects are more severe in shared wireless channels because attacks are no longer directed to a single node. Each illegitimate packet that is generated by the attacker may cause collisions at multiple neighboring nodes as well as nodes within the interference range (which can often be twice as large as the transmission range), resulting in increased retransmissions and contention for channel access.

5. DEFENSES AGAINST DDOS ATTACKS

Many observers have stated that there are currently no successful defenses against a fully distributed denial of service attack. This may be true. Nevertheless, there are numerous safety measures that a host or network can perform to make the network and neighboring networks more secure. These measures include:

- *Filtering Routers*: Filtering all packets entering and leaving the network protects the network from attacks conducted from neighboring networks, and prevents the network itself from being an unaware attacker. This measure requires installing ingress and egress packet filters on all routers.
- *Disabling IP Broadcasts:* By disabling IP broadcasts, host computers can no longer be used as amplifiers in ICMP Flood and Smurf attacks. However, to defend against this attack, all neighboring networks need to disable IP broadcasts.
- *Applying Security Patches*: To guard against denial of service attacks, host computers must be updated with the latest security patches and techniques. For example, in the case of the SYN Flood attack, there are three steps that the host computers can take to guard themselves from attacks: increase the size of the connection queue, decrease the time-out waiting for the three-way handshake, and employ vendor software patches to detect and circumvent the problem.
- *Disabling Unused Services:* If UDP echo or charger services are not required, disabling them will help to defend against the attack. In general, if network services are unneeded or unused, the services should be disabled to prevent tampering and attacks.
- *Performing Intrusion Detection:* By performing intrusion detection, a host computer and network are guarded against being a source for

an attack, as while as being a victim of an attack. Network monitoring is a very good pre-emptive way of guarding against denial of service attacks. By monitoring traffic patterns, a network can determine when it is under attack, and can take the required steps to defend itself. By inspecting host systems, a host can also prevent it from hosting an attack on another network.

6. CONCLUSION

DDoS attacks make a networked system or service unavailable to legitimate users. These attacks are an annoyance at a minimum, or can be seriously damaging if a critical system is the primary victim. Loss of network resources causes economic loss, work delays, and loss of communication between network users. Solutions must be developed to prevent these DDoS attacks.

In this paper, we discussed distributed denial of service attacks on the Internet and various taxonomies of DDoS attacks. We also discussed various defense mechanisms that could be employed by networks and hosts. It is essential, that as the Internet and Internet usage expand, more comprehensive solutions and countermeasures to DDoS attacks be developed, verified, and implemented.

REFERENCES

1. TFreak. "smurf.c", *www.phreak.org*. Oct 1997. www.phreak.org/archives/exploits/denial/smurf.c (6 May 2003).
2. Federal Computer Incident Response Center (FedCIRC), "Defense Tactics for Distributed Denial of Service Attacks". Washington, DC, 2000.
3. TFreak. "fraggle.c", *www.phreak.org*. www.phreak.org/archives/exploits/denial/fraggle.c (6 May 2003).
4. Stephen M. Specht and Ruby B. Lee; Distributed Denial of Service: Taxonomies of Attacks, Tools, and Countermeasures; Proceedings of the 17th International Conference on Parallel and Distributed Computing Systems, 2004 International Workshop on Security in Parallel and Distributed Systems, pp. 543-550; September 2004.
5. Felix Lau, Stuart H. Rubin, Michael H. Smith and Ljiljana TrajkoviC; Distributed Denial of Service Attacks; 2275-2280/2004 IEEE.
6. Andrim Piskozub; Denial of Service and Distributed Denial of Service Attacks; TCSET 2002; February 18-23, 2002; Lviv—Shavsko, Ukraine.
7. Antonio Challita, Mona El Hassan, Sabine Maalouf and Adel Zouheiry; A Survey of DDoS Defense Mechanisms; Department of Electrical and Computer Engineering American University of Beirut;asc04,mhe03,sem05,atz00}@aub.edu.lb.
8. L. Zhou and Z.J. Haas, Securing *Ad Hoc* Networks, IEEE Network Magazine, Special Issue on Network Security, Vol. 13, No. 6, 1999.
9. Y. Zhang and W. Lee, Intrusion Detection in Wireless Ad Hoc Networks, Proceedings of the 6th International Conference on Mobile Computing and Networking, Boston, Massachusetts, United States, 2000.
10. V. Gupta, S. Krishnamurthy and M. Faloutsos, Denial of Service Attacks at the MAC Layer in Wireless Ad Hoc Networks, Proceedings of the Military Communications Conference (MICOM 2002), California, Oct. 2002.
11. C. Patrikakis, M. Masikos and O. Zouraraki, Distributed Denial of Service Attacks, *The Internet Protocol Journal*, Vol. 7, No. 4, Dec. 2004.

12. J. Mirkovic and P. Reiher, A Taxonomy of DDoS Attack and DDoS Defense Mechanisms, *ACM Sigcomm Computer Communications Review*, Vol. 34, No. 2, April 2004.
13. Hwee-Xian Tan and Winston, K.G. Seah; Framework for Statistical Filtering Against DDOS Attacks in MANETs; Proceedings of the Second International Conference on Embedded Software and Systems; 2005 IEEE.
14. Xianjun Geng and Andrew, B. Whinston; Defeating Distributed Denial of Service Attacks; February 2000.
15. CERT Coordination Center, Cert Advisories: "CA-2000-01 denial-of-service developments:" ttp://www.cert.org/advisories/ CA-2000-0 1 .html; "CA-99- 17 denial-of-service tools," http://www. cert.org/advisories/CA-99- 1 7-denial-of-servicetools. html; "CA-98-1 3-tcp-denial-of-service: vulnerability in certain TCP/IP implementations," http://www.cert.org/advisories/ CA-98- 13-tcp-denial-of-ervice.1itml.

44

The RSA Optimization

Ajay Goel and Punit Soni

ABSTRACT

With the rapid progression of modern information technology, security has become important technique in many applications including virtual private network (VPN), electronic commerce and secure Internet access. RSA algorithm is most popular and well-defined security primary technique. There are many good security protocol based on RSA cryptosystem. RSA is widely used for digital signature and digital envelope, which provide privacy and authentication. However, the RSA has to take great computational cost for security consideration in order to include RSA cryptosystem efficiency in many protocols; it is desired to devise faster encryption and decryption operations. In many applications they usually select small value such as 3, 17 and 65,537 to be the public key to speed up the encryption operation. However, by the larger secret key, RSA can be speeded up by using the Chinese Remainder Theorem and using strong prime criterion of RSA, if they get the prime factors of modulus.

In fact, who holds the secret key can get factors of modulus. Hayansi proposed new modular exponentiation method to improve the efficiency of the RSA decryption operation. In this method, the modular exponential with the modulus n transforms to two substitutes operations n+1 and n+2. If modulus n+1 and n+2 can be factoring, and user can apply Chinese Remainder Theorem to these modular operations to modulus n+1 and n+2 for each. The final result can be generated by Hayansi formula.

However, n is odd number, they cannot factor n+2 easily in his method. This method is not applicable when n is odd. We implement RSA decryption operation in this paper. This method is not only based on Chinese Remainder

Theorem but also used the strong prime RSA criterion by reducing the block size. The security of RSA is based on the hardness of factoring problem. So the prime factors of modulus of RSA algorithm must be strong primes. Large exponentiation result can be generated from small exponents and modulus. The Optimized method improved the performance.

1. INTRODUCTION

Public key algorithms are designed to resist chosen plain text attacks; their security is based both on the difficulty of deducing the secret key from the public key and the difficulty of deducing plaintext from the cipher text, however most public algorithms are susceptible to a chosen-cipher text attacks. In systems where the digital signatures operation is the inverse of the encryption operation, this attack is impossible to prevent unless different keys are used for encryption and signatures [17].

The Public key cryptography has evolved as a result of an astounding break through which came into the scenario when Diffie and Hellman came up with an approach to cryptography that addressed the problems existing with symmetric encryption. The first problem associated with symmetric key cryptography is that of key distribution. The second problem that was pondered and one that is apparently unrelated to the first was that of digital signatures.

The Public key cryptography was radically different from all previous approaches to the cryptography going back over four millennia. Since then, the RSA algorithm has been accepted as the most widely accepted general-purpose approach to public key encryption.

The simple performance comparison of different RSA operations discussed by contemporary researchers illustrates the fact that the RSA decryption is slow. Also, the RSA algorithm takes greater computational cost.

The primary focus of this paper is to optimize these computational aspects like computational cost of the traditional decryption method of the RSA, the number of clock cycles taken by traditional method are to be reduced, at the same time. In a totality, the RSA is to be optimized in three ways:

1. By reducing block size,
2. Using more factorizations, and
3. Reducing its modular complications.

The performance evolution of traditional decryption *versus* optimized decryption method would be accomplished.

We have presented our innovative contribution in the form of a new method for RSA prime factoring which is based on the statistical concept of median; and to make our new factoring method efficient we have used and implemented Miler Rabin test for primality [3]. This paper is structured to provide a logical, well ordered, detailed and coherent presentation of RSA optimization and our new method for factoring. The paper consists of 7 logically and functionally separated sections. Section 2 discusses the basics of RSA. Section 3 discusses the methods of factoring. Section 4 provides the precise description of proposed schemes; computational complexity, results and analysis is performed in section 5. Section 6 concludes the paper and section 7 tells about its future scope.

2. THE RSA CRYPTOSYSTEM

One of the first public key schemes was developed in 1977 by Ron Rivest, Adi Shamir, and Len Adleman at MIT and first published in 1978. The RSA schemes has since that time reigned supreme as the most widely accepted and implemented approach to public key encryption, RSA is a block cipher in which the plaintext and ciphertext are integers between 0 and n-1 for some n. Encryption and decryption are of the following form, for some plaintext block M and ciphertext block C:

$$C = M^e \bmod n$$
$$M = C^d \bmod n = (m^e)^d \bmod n$$

Both sender and receiver must know the values of n and e, and only the receiver knows the value of d. This public key encryption algorithm is with a public key of KU = {e, n} and private key of KR= {d, n}. For this algorithm to be satisfactory for public key encryption, the following requirements must be met:

1. It is possible to find values of e, d, n such that $M^{ed} = M \bmod n$ for all $M<n$.
2. It is relatively easy to calculate M^e and C for all values of $M<n$.
3. It is infeasible to determine d given e and n.

The first two requirements are easily met. The third requirement can be met for large values of e and n.

The RSA Algorithm begins by selecting two prime numbers, p and q and calculating their product n. This is the modulus for encryption and decryption. Next, we need the quality Ø(n), referred to as Euler orient function of n, which is the number of positive integer less than n and relatively prime to Ø(n) or greatest common divisor of e and Ø(n). It can be shown that d and e have the desired prosperities.[20]

Suppose that user A has published its public key and that user B wishes to send the message M to A, then B calculates $C = M^e \bmod n$ and transmit to C. On receipt of this cipher text, user A decrypts by calculating $M = C^d \bmod n$.

The security of RSA depends critically on the inability of an adversary to compute private key from the public key. The problem of computing private key from public key is equivalent to the problem of factoring n into its prime factors. Therefore, it is important for the RSA user to select prime numbers in such a way that the problem of factoring n is computationally infeasible for an adversary. Choosing the factors as "strong primes" has been recommended as a way of maximizing the difficulty of factoring n. There are such arguments that say that strong primes are needed to protect against factoring attacks. The allied purpose of this paper is to extend this scrutiny by carefully examining the common recommendation that one should use strong primes when constructing keys for an RSA. We review the RSA security and describe that this problem can be solved using more key size, more factors or choosing strong primes numbers.

There are a few possible interpretations of "breaking RSA". The most damaging would be for an attacker to discover the private key corresponding to a given public key; this would enable the attacker both to read all messages encrypted with the public key and to forge signatures. The obvious way to do this attack is to factor the public modulus, n, into its two prime factors, p and q. From p, q, and e, the public exponent, the attacker can easily get d, the private key. The hard part is factoring n; the security of RSA depends of factoring being difficult. In fact, the task of recovering the private key is equivalent to the task of factoring the modulus: you can use d to factor n, as well as use the factorization of n to find d. It should be noted that hardware improvements alone will not weaken RSA, as long as appropriate key lengths are used; in fact, hardware improvements should increase the security of RSA[17].

3 THE RSA FACTORING

3.1 Brute Force RSA Factoring

An attacker has access to the public-key. In other words, the attacker has e and n. The attacker wants the private key. In other words the attacker wants d. To get d, n needs to be factored (which will yield p and q, which can then be used to calculate d). Factoring n is the best-known attack against RSA to date. (Attacking RSA by trying to deduce (p–1)(q–1) is no easier than factoring n, and executing an exhaustive search for values of d is harder than factoring n). Some of the algorithms [22] used for factoring are as follows:

- *Trial division*: The oldest and least efficient. Exponential running time. Try all the prime numbers less than sqrt(n).
- *Quadratic Sieve (QS)*: The fastest algorithm for numbers smaller than 110 digits.
- *Multiple Polynomial Quadratic Sieve (MPQS)*: Faster version of QS.
- Double Large Prime Variation of the MPQS: Faster still.

- *Number Field Sieve (NFS)*: Currently the fastest algorithm known for numbers larger than 110 digits, was used to factor the ninth format number.

These algorithms represent the state of the art in warfare against large composite numbers against RSA. The best algorithms have a super-polynomial or sub-exponential running time, with the NFS having an asymptotic time estimate closest to polynomial behavior.

Still, factoring of large numbers is hard. However, with the advances in number theory and computing power, it is getting easier. In 1977, Ron Rivest said that factoring a 125-digit number would take 40 quadrillion years. In 1994, RSA129 was factored using about 5000 MIPS-years of effort from idle CPU cycles on computers across the Internet for eight months. In 1995, the Blacknet key (116 digits) was factored using about 400 MIPS-years of effort (1 MIPS-year is a 1,000,000 instruction per second computer running for one year) from several dozen workstations and a MasPar for about three months. Given current trends, the key size that can be factored will only increase as time goes on.

4. COMPUTATION COMPLEXITY OPTIMIZATION

We have also performed an analysis, which reveals that the 2048 bits RSA original decryption method without any trick must take 11,79,03,360 clock cycles. The decryption method based on CRT takes 3,65,97,399 clock cycles. If we implement the same method on 512 bits, it only takes 27,15,648 clock cycles and on CRT takes 7,45,817 clock cycles. The complexity of our analyzed method is only 7% of the traditional decryption method. Our analyzed method reduces approximately 73% computational costs as compared to the decryption method based on CRT. In a word, the speed of our analyzed method is almost 4 times faster than the decryption method based on CRT only. This enhanced method can be applied to not only decryption operation but also signing phase of digital signature. This efficient decryption method can enhance and, thus, can optimize the performance of the RSA algorithm. All these contributions of this dissertation are illustrated step by step further in this chapter.

Simultaneously we, also, have performed an analysis, which reveals that the 1024 bits RSA original decryption method without any tricks must take 1,82,93,760 clock cycles. The decryption method based on CRT takes 54,34,296 clock cycles. The decryption method based on the more factoring with CRT takes 18,51,806. If we implement the same method on 2048 bits, Traditional RSA would take 1,82,93,760 clock cycles. If we implement the same method on 2048 bits, RSA Based on CRT would take 3,65,97,399 clock cycles. If we implement the same method on 2048 bits, more RSA Factoring method would take 13882307 clock cycles. If we implement the same method on 512 bits, Traditional RSA would take 27,15,648 clock cycles. If we implement the same method on 512 bits, RSA Based on CRT would take

7,45,817 clock cycles. If we implement the same method on 512 bits, more RSA Factoring method would take 2,07,417 clock cycles. The complexity of our analyzed method on 2048 bits is only 12% of the traditional decryption method. Our analyzed method reduces approximately 63% computational costs as compared to the decryption method based on CRT. In a word, the speed of our analyzed method is almost 2.9 times faster than the decryption method based on CRT only. The complexity of our analyzed method on 1024 bits is only 10% of the traditional decryption method. Our analyzed method reduces approximately 66% computational costs as compared to the decryption method based on CRT. In a word, the speed of our analyzed method is almost 3.4 times faster than the decryption method based on CRT only. The complexity of more factorized method on 512 bits is only 7% of the traditional decryption method. Our analyzed method reduces approximately 73% computational costs as compared to the decryption method based on CRT. In a word, the speed of our analyzed method is almost 4 times faster than the decryption method based on CRT only.

We define some formal notations as follows:

- MODE(y, z) denotes an operation of modular exponentiation (x^y mod z).
- M(w), A(w) and Mod(w) denote operations of multiplication, addition and modulus with the bit length of operand w.
- l(w) denotes the bit length of w.
- S denotes the shift operator.

By the addition chain method, the modulo operation c^d mod n can be expressed as:

$$\text{MODE}(d, n) = 1.5 * l(d)[M(l(n)) + 2\,\text{Mod}(l(n)) + 1].$$

The multiplication and addition operations can be expressed as follows:

$$M(w) = 3M(w/2) + 5A(w) + 2S$$
$$A(w) = w/32.$$

The modulo operation also can be expressed as the following equations based on the divide and conquer concept:

$$\text{Mod}(w) = \text{Mod}(w/2) + 4M(w/2) + 1.5A(w) + 3S.$$

Without loss of generality, we assume all of Mod(32), M(32), A(32) and S take one clock cycle. From the above equations, we get

$$\begin{aligned} M(1024) &= 3M(512) + 5A(1024) + 2S \\ &= 3M(512) + 162 \\ &= 3[3M(256) + 5A(512) + 2S] + 162 \end{aligned}$$

= 9M(256) + 408
= 9[3M(128) + 5A(256) + 2S] + 408
= 27M(128) + 786
= 27[3M(64) + 5A(128) + 2S] + 786
= 81M(64) + 1380
= 81[3M(32) + 5A(64) + 2S] + 1380
= 243M(32) + 2352
= 2595.

From the above equations, we get

Mod (1024) = Mod(512) + 4M(512) + 1.5A(1024) + 3S
= [Mod(256) + 4M(256) + 1.5A(512) + 3S] + 3295
= [Mod(128) + 4M(128) + 1.5A(256) + 3S] + 4294
= [Mod(64) + 4M(64) + 1.5A(128) + 3S] + 4577
= [Mod(32) + 4M(32) + 1.5A(64) + 3S] + 4646
= 4657

By Equation, the traditional decryption method can be repressed as:

MODE(d, n) = 1.5 * 1024[M(1024) + 2 Mod(1024)+1].

That is, the traditional decryption method should take 1,82,93,760 clock cycles.

If the decryption method based on CRT only and the bit lengths of p and q are equal, the operation of the decryption method can be repressed as

2MODE(d/2, n/2) + A(512) + 2M(512) + Mod(512).

By these calculations, the decryption method takes 54,34,296 clock cycles.

In more factorization method, p – 1, p + 1, q – 1 and q + 1 can be factored into at least three numbers. Without loss of generality, we assume the bit length of the largest prime factor is about l(n)/4 and others are l(n)/8 [6, 7, 8, 9].

The total number of operations of our analyzed method

4MODE(d/4, n/4) +8MODE(d/8, n/8) + 4[A(256) + 2M(256) + Mod(256)] + 4[A(128) + 2M(128) + Mod(128)] + 2[A(512) + M(512) + Mod(512)] + A(512) + 2M(512) + Mod(512).

It takes 18,51,806 clock cycles.

Implementation for 2048
From the above equations

M(2048) = 3M(1024)+5A(2048)+2S
= 3*2595+5*2048/32+2
= 7785+322
= 8107
Mod(2048) = Mod(1024)+4M(1024)+1.5A(2048)+3S
= 4657+4*2595+1.5*64+3
= 4657+10380+99
= 15,136

Traditional Method

MODE(d, n) = 1.5*2048[M(2048) + 2 Mod(2048)+1]
= 1.5*2048(8107+2*15136+1)
= 11,79,03,360

RSA Based on CRT only.

$2Mod_e$(d/2,n/2)+ A(1024)+2M(1024)+Mod (1024)
= 3,65,97,399
More RSA Factoring Method

4MODE(d/4, n/4) + 8MODE(d/8, n/8) + 4[A(512) + 2M(512) + Mod(512)] + 4[A(256) + 2M(256) + Mod(256)] + 2[A(256) + M(1024) + Mod(1024)] + A(1024) + 2M(1024) + Mod(1024).
= 13882307

Implementation on 512

M(512) = 3M(256)+5A(512)+2S
= 3M(256)+82
= 3(3M(128)+5A(8)+82
= 3(3M(128)+42)+82
= 9M(128)+126+82
= 9(3M(128/2)+5A(4)+2)+208
= 9(3M(64)+22)+208
= 27M(64)+406
= 27(3M(32)+5.2+2)+406
= 81*1+324+406
= 811
Mod(512) = Mod(256)+4M(256)+1.5*a(512)+3s)
=1362
The Traditional RSA Method

= 1.5*512[M(512)+2Mod(512)+1]
= 1.5*512[811+2*1367+1)
= 2715648

RSA Based on CRT

2MODE(d/2, n/2) + A(256) + 2M(256) + Mod(256).
= 745817

The More RSA Factoring Method

4MODE(d/4, n/4) + 8MODE(d/8, n/8) + 4[A(128) + 2M(128) + Mod(128)] + 4[A(64) + 2M(64) + Mod(64)] + 2[A(256) + M(256) + Mod(256)] + A(256) + 2M(256) + Mod(256).
= 207417

6. CONCLUSION

In this paper, we processed an efficient method to implement RSA decryption algorithm. This decryption method is not only based on CRT but also on the strong prime of RSA criterion. The 512 bits RSA original decryption method without any ticks must take 27,15,648 clock cycles. The decryption method based on CRT takes 7,45,817 clock cycles. By our process, the decryption method takes only 2,07,417 clock cycles. The complexity of more factorization RSA method is only 7% of the traditional decryption method. More factorized method reduces approximately 72.18% computational costs as comparing with the decryption method based on CRT. In a word, the speed of proposed method is almost 4 times faster than the decryption method based on CRT only. Our method can be applied to not only decryption operation but also signing phase of digital signature. This efficient decryption method can enhance the performance of the RSA algorithm.

7. FUTURE SCOPE

The efficiency of RSA decryption can be improved by increasing number of factors of n. n can be increased so that prime factors may be increased which can lead to more speed.

With regard to factoring as a future prospect, we may implement AKS algorithm with Miler Rabin algorithm and AKS algorithm. The logic behind this alteration is that the Miler Rabin is a probabilistic test, while AKS algorithm is a deterministic test; so if we implement AKS algorithm, we can find out much more deterministic values of p and q. It can also reduce the complexity of our new factoring method up to certain extent.

References

1. R. Rivest, A. Shamir, L. Adleman, A Method for "Obtaining Digital Signature and Public-Key Cryptosystems", Communication of the ACM, Vol. 21, No. 2, 1978, pp. 120-26.
2. B. Schneier, Applied Cryptography: Protocols, algorithms, and source Code in C, 2nd ed. John Wiley and Sons, Inc., 1996.
3. J.J. Quisquater, C. Couvreur, "Fast decipherment algorithm for RSA public-key cryptosystem", *Electronics Letters* 18, (21), 1982, pp. 905-07.
4. M. Shand, J. Vuilmin, "Fast Implementation of RSA Cryptography", Proceedings of 11th Symposium of Computer Arithmetic, 1993.
5. A. Hayashi, "A New fast Modular Multiplication Method and its Application to Modular Exponentiation-based Cryptography", *Electronics and Communications in Japan*, 83 (12), 2000, pp. 88-93.
6. M. Ogiwara, "A Method for Generating Cryptographically Strong Primes", IEICE Trans., E73, (6), 1990, pp. 985-94.
7. Ren-Junn Hwang, Feng-Fu-Su, "An Decryption Method for RSA Decryption". Proceedings of the 19th international Conference.
8. J. Gordon, "Strong RSA Keys", *Electronics Letters*, 20, (12), 1984, pp. 514-16.
9. M.J. Ganley, Note on the Generation of "Primes for RSA key sets", *Electronics Letters*, 26, (6), 1990, p. 369.
10. C.S. Lai, W.-C. Yang and C.-H. Chen, "Efficient Method for Generating Strong Primes with Constraint of Bit Length". *Electronics Letters*, 27, (20), 1991, pp. 1807-08.
11. Knuth, D.E. "The Art of Computer Programming", Vol. 2 (Semi numerical algorithms), 2nd ed. Addison-Wesley: Massachusetts, 1980.
12. Davida, G.I., Wells, D.L., Kam, J.B., "A Database Encryption System with Sub-keys", ACM Trans. On Database Systems, 6, 1981, pp. 312-28.
13. M.S. Hwang, Dynamic Participation in a Secure Conference Scheme for Mobile Communications, IEEE Trans. On Vehicular Technology, Vol. 48, No. 5, 1999, pp. 1469-74.
14. M.J.B. Robshaw, "Security Estimates for 51 2-bit RSA", RSA Laboratories 100 Marine Parkway Redwood City, CA 94065-1031.
15. C. Mclvor, M. McLoone and J.V. McCanny, "Modified Montgomery modular multiplication and RSA exponentiation techniques", p. 401.
16. Y. Yang, Z. Abid, W. Wang, Z. Zhang and C. Yang, "Efficient Multi-Prime RSA Immune against Hardware fault Attack", CF 89076-0 34.
17. Roman Popovych, "Cryptanalysis of RSA System of Enciphering with Public Dey".
18. Ronald L. Rivest, Robert D. Silvermany, "Are Strong Primes Needed for RSA", November 22, 1999.
19. S.A. Vanstone and R.J. Zuccherato, "Using Four Primes RSA With Bit Specifications", 8th December 1994.
20. Willam Stalling, "Cryptography and Network Security", 3rd Edition, published by Pearson Education.
21. http://www.cesg.gov.uk/
22. http://www.nist.gov/
23. http://wwwcryptography.com/resources/papers/
24. http://www.cs.berkely edu/~daw/peopole/crypto.htm l
25. http://www.eff.org/Privacy/Crypto_export/ITAR_FOIA/
26. Kahate Atul, "Cryptography and Network Security", Tata McGraw Hill Publishing Company, 2006.
27. The Feasibility of Breaking PGP—The PGP Attack FAQ 2/96 v.50 [beta] by infinity, daemon9@netcom.com/route@infonexus.com
28. Cohen, H., "A Course in Computational Algebraic Number Theory", Springer-Verlag Press, Berlin, 1993.
29. Van Oorschot, P.C., "A Comparison of Practical Public Key Cryptosystems-based on integer Factorization and discrete Logarithms", in Simmons, G.J. (Ed.): 'Contemporary cryptology—The science of information integrity', IEEE Press, 1991.
30. Gordon, J., "Strong RSA keys", *Electronics Letters*, 20 (12): 514-516, June 1984.

45

A Secured Password Authentication Protocol : Using Needham-Schroeder Protocol

RENU DHIR AND RAMU TANGUTURI

ABSTRACT

Password authentication protocols are important means of user authentication on network. Several password authentication protocols have been introduced each claiming to withstand to the several attacks including replay, password file compromise, denial of service, etc. Then, we present an improvement to the Needham-Schroeder protocol in order to remove two possible attacks.

1. INTRODUCTION

With the advent of e-services such as e-business, e-banking, e-commerce etc., the need for security over the World Wide Web has increased. Password Authentication Protocols (PAP), smart cards, digital signatures, and hand impressions are some of the solutions proposed, but the easiest and the most feasible solution on the network are the password authentication protocols. It can be easily implemented and provides us with simple, efficient and a secure authentication mechanism.

Password authentication protocols authenticate a user to a remote access server. A user's name and password is transmitted over a network and compared to a table of name password pairs. Typically, the passwords stored in the table are encrypted. The user uses the username as its identity and some hashed value as a *secret verifier* to verify the authentication. Earlier, the name-password pair (either encrypted or in plain text) was sent over the communication channel to login into the server. This was the most insecure scheme as once the intruder got the password he could impersonate the user. The scheme could not resist man in the middle attacks, reply attacks, denial of service attacks, stolen verifier attacks, impersonation attacks.

As a result, the concept of one-time passwords came into picture. Needham-Schroeder proposed a scheme to authenticate two users over some network. The scheme suffered with man in middle attack and stolen verifier attacks [3].

In the present paper, we discuss Needham-Schroeder protocol with possible attacks on it and propose a new scheme that will be able to remove two possible attacks.

2. NEEDHAM-SCHROEDER PROTOCOL

The term Needham-Schroeder protocol can refer to one of two communication protocols intended for use over an insecure network, both proposed by Roger Needham and Michael Schroeder [1]. Needham-Schroeder protocol is one of the earliest computer network authentication protocol designed for use on insecure networks (e.g. internet). It allows individuals communicating over a network to prove their identity to each other while also preventing eavesdropping. These are:

1. The *Needham-Schroeder Symmetric Key Protocol* is based on a symmetric encryption algorithm. It forms the basis for the Kerberos protocol. This protocol aims to establish a session key between two parties on a network, typically to protect further communication.
2. The *Needham-Schroeder Public-Key Protocol,* based on public-key cryptography. This is intended to provide mutual authentication between two parties communicating over a network, but in its proposed form it is insecure.

The symmetric protocol

Here, Alice (A) initiates the communication to Bob (B). Also,

- S is a server trusted by both parties
- K_{AS} is a symmetric key known only to A and S
- K_{BS} is a symmetric key known only to B and S
- N_A and N_B are nodes

The protocol can be specified as follows in security protocol notation:

$A \rightarrow S: A, B, N_A$

Alice sends a message to the server identifying herself and Bob, telling the server she wants to communicate with Bob.

$S \rightarrow A$:{ N_A, K_{AB} B {K_{AB}, A}$_{KBS}$}$_{KAS}$

The server generates K_{AB} and sends back to Alice a copy encrypted under K_{BS} for Alice to forward to Bob and also a copy for Alice. Since Alice may be requesting keys for several different people, the nonce assures Alice that the message is fresh and that the server is replying to that particular message and the inclusion of Bob's name tells Alice who she is to share this key with.

$A \rightarrow B$:{K_{AB}, A}$_{KBS}$

Alice forwards the key to Bob who can decrypt it with the key he shares with the server, thus authenticating the data.

$B \rightarrow A$: {N_B}$_{KAB}$

Bob sends Alice a nonce encrypted under K_{AB} to show that he has the key.

$A \rightarrow B$: {N_B–1}$_{KAB}$

Alice performs a simple operation on the nonce, re-encrypts it and sends it back verifying that she is still alive and that she holds the key.

The protocol is vulnerable to a replay attack. If an attacker records one run of this protocol, then subsequently learns the value K_{AB} used, she can then replay the message {K_{AB}, A}$_{KBS}$ to Bob, who will accept it, being unable to tell that the key is not fresh. This flaw is fixed in the Kerberos protocol by the inclusion of a timestamp.

FIG. 45.1
The Symmetric Key Protocol

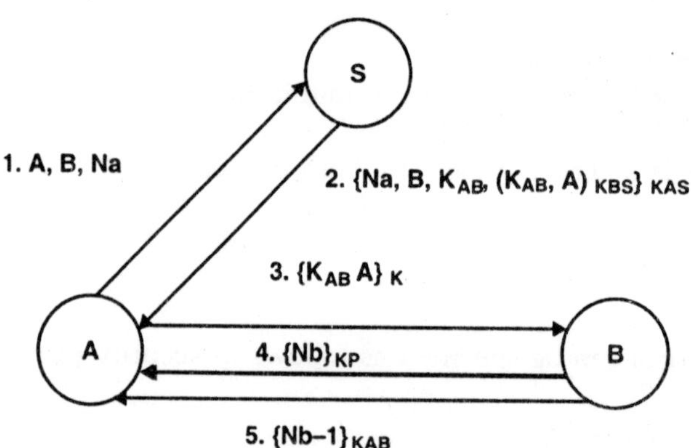

The public-key protocol

This assumes the use of a public-key encryption algorithm.

Here, Alice (A) and Bob (B) use a trusted server (S) to distribute public keys on request. These keys are:

1. K_{PA} and K_{SA}, respectively public and private halves of an encryption key-pair belonging to A.
2. K_{PB} and K_{SB}, similar belonging to B.
3. K_{PS} and K_{SS}, similar belonging to S. (Note this has the property that K_{SS} is used to *encrypt* and K_{PS} to *decrypt*).

The protocol runs as follows:

$A \rightarrow S$: A, B	A requests B's public keys from S
$S \rightarrow A$: $\{K_{PB}, B\}_{KSS}$	S responds. B's identity is placed alongside K_{PB} for confirmation.
$A \rightarrow B$: $\{N_A, A\}_{KPB}$	A invents N_A and sends it to B.
$B \rightarrow S$: B, A	B requests A's public keys.
$S \rightarrow B$: $\{K_{PA}, A\}_{KSS}$	

Server responds.

$B \rightarrow A$: $\{N_A, N_B\}_{KPA}$	B invents N_B, and sends it to A along with N_A to prove ability to decrypt with K_{SB}.
$A \rightarrow B$: $\{N_B\}_{KPB}$	A confirms N_B to B, to prove ability to decrypt with K_{SA}

At the end of the protocol, A and B know each other's identities, and know both N_A and N_B. These nonces are not known to eavesdroppers.

FIG. 45.2
The Public-Key Protocol

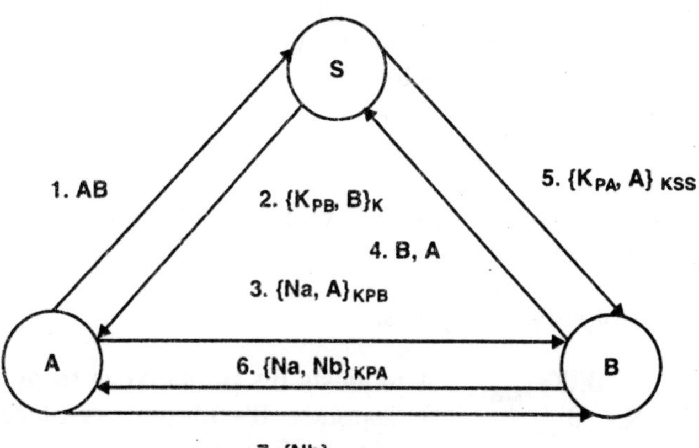

3. ATTACKS ON THE PROTOCOL

Unfortunately, this protocol is vulnerable to a man-in-the-middle attack[5]. If an impostor I can persuade A to initiate a session with him, he can relay the messages to B and convince B that he is communicating with A.

Ignoring the traffic to and from S, which is unchanged, the attack runs as follows:

$A \rightarrow I$: $\{N_A, A\}_{KPI}$	A sends N_A to I, who decrypts the message with K_{SI}
$I \rightarrow B$: $\{N_A, A\}_{KPB}$	I relay the message to B, pretending that A is communicating
$B \rightarrow I$: $\{N_A, N_B\}_{KPA}$	B sends N_B
$I \rightarrow A$: $\{N_A, N_B\}_{KPA}$	I relay it to A
$A \rightarrow I$: $\{N_B\}_{KPI}$	A decrypts N_B and confirms it to I, who learns it
$I \rightarrow B$: $\{N_B\}_{KPB}$	I re-encrypts N_B, and convinces B that he's decrypted it

At the end of the attack, B falsely believes that A is communicating with him, and that N_A and N_B are known only to A and B.

The attack was first described in a 1995 paper by Gavin Lowe. The paper also describes a fixed version of the scheme, referred to as the *Needham-Schroeder-Lowe* protocol. The fix involves the modification of message six, that is we replace:

$B \rightarrow A$: $\{N_A, N_B\}_{KPA}$ With the fixed version: $B \rightarrow A$: $\{N_A, N_B, B\}_{KPA}$

4. THE PROPOSED SCHEME

Alice (A) and Bob (B) use a trusted server (S) to distribute public keys on request. These keys are:

- K_{PA} and K_{SA}, respectively public and private halves of an encryption key-pair belonging to A
- K_{PB} and K_{SB}, similar belonging to B
- K_{PS} and K_{SS}, similar belonging to S
(Note this has the property that K_{SS} is used to *encrypt* and K_{PS} to *decrypt*)
- Ka and Kb are encryption keys belonging to respectively Alice (A) and Bob (B).

The protocol runs as follows:

$A \rightarrow S$: $\{A, B, Ka\}_{KAS}$	A requests B's public keys from S
$S \rightarrow A$: $\{K_{PB}, B\}_{Ka}$	S responds. B's identity is placed alongside K_{PB} for confirmation

$A \rightarrow B$: $\{N_A, A\}_{KPB}$	A invents N_A and sends it to B
$B \rightarrow S$: $\{B, A, Kb\}_{KBS}$	B requests A's public keys
$S \rightarrow B$: $\{K_{PA}, A\}_{KB}$	Server responds
$B \rightarrow A$: $\{N_A, N_B\}_{KPA}$	B invents N_B, and sends it to A along with N_A to prove ability to decrypt with K_{SB}
$A \rightarrow B$: $\{N_B\}_{KPB}$	A confirms N_B to B, to prove ability to decrypt with K_{SA}

At the end of the protocol, A and B know each other's identities, and know both N_A and N_B. These nonces are not known to eavesdroppers.

FIG. 45.3
The Proposed Scheme

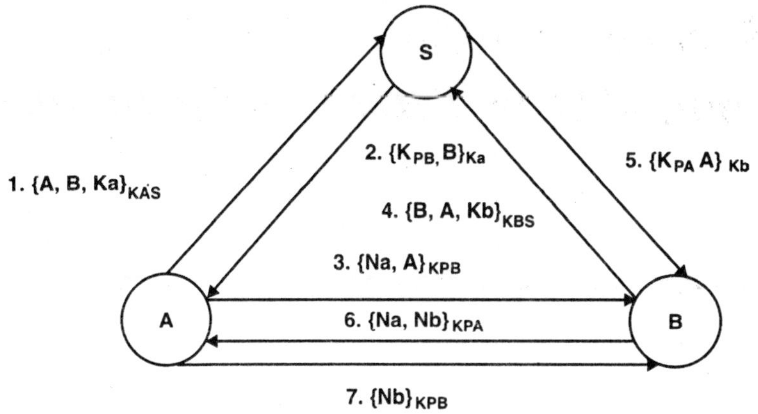

S
1. $\{A, B, Ka\}_{KAS}$
2. $\{K_{PB}, B\}_{Ka}$
3. $\{Na, A\}_{KPB}$
4. $\{B, A, Kb\}_{KBS}$
5. $\{K_{PA}\ A\}_{Kb}$
A
6. $\{Na, Nb\}_{KPA}$
B
7. $\{Nb\}_{KPB}$

5. CONCLUSION

We have shown the various attacks on Needham-Schroeder protocol, possible attacks on protocol, and the proposed scheme which can remove two possible attacks on Needham-Schroeder protocol. This scheme is vulnerable to a server spoofing attack and stolen-verifier attacks.

REFERENCES

1. Roger Needham and Michael Schroeder, "Using encryption for authentication in large networks of computers. Communications of the ACM", *Journal*, 21(12), December 1978.
2. Gavin Lowe, "An attack on the Needham-Schroeder Public Key Authentication Protocol", *Information Processing Letters*, 56(3):131-36, November 1995.
3. C.M. Chen, and W.C. Ku, "Stolen-verifier Attack on Two New Strong-password Authentication Protocol," *IEICE Transactions on Communications*, Vol. E85-B, No. 11, pp. 2519-21, November 2002.
4. Sandirigama, A. Shimizu, and M.T. Noda, "Simple and Secure Password Authentication Protocol (SAS)," *IEICE Transactions on Communications*, Vol. E83-B, pp. 1363-65, June 2000.
5. William Stallings, "Cryptography and Network Security Design and Principles".
6. John Rushby, "The Needham-Schroeder Protocol in SAL", CSL Technical Note, October 2003 (Updated June 2005).

46

Secure Communication Using Enhanced One Time Pad Technique

RENU DHIR AND AMAR ARORA

ABSTRACT

We present a new protocol through which the people can communicate to each other securely using one time pads. This protocol guarantees that even from a very small sized one time pad which is there with sender and receiver, both can communicate to each other for a very long time period. Very small one time pad is needed for both the sender and receiver and then they can have a very secure communication between them, so the server which is providing the communication between sender and receiver will also do not have any knowledge about the way to decrypt the text. This protocol is providing the secure communication by not trusting anyone except the sender and receiver which are the only one having the copy of small one time pad file.

1. INTRODUCTION

The secure communication between two persons can only be ensured secure if the key or the password used for encryption is available to only the sender and the receiver. But once this key is compromised then the communication will be no longer secure, but if the key size is equal to the size of the plain text and with the consideration that these keys are only available to sender and receiver then the secure communication is looking very much in sight, which is called as the one time pad. The one time pad cryptography technique is old, and was used during the First World War by Gilbert Vernam[1]. This technique is the only known provably secure encryption scheme in the information-theoretic sense of Shannon [2]. It is based on the concept of using a long stream of random letters (or bits) to modify the plaintext message one letter (bit) at a time. Both the sender and the receiver must have a copy of the same pad and both work through the message one letter at a time. Suppose that the sender has a sequence of bits text(i) that are to be transmitted. The sender and the receiver exchange, through some secure mechanism, a pad of random bits pad(i) so that both sender and receiver have the same pad. To transmit a message to the receiver, the sender encrypts the plaintext text(i) obtaining the encrypted message message(i) as given in the equation (1).

$$\text{message}(i) = \text{pad}(i) \text{ XOR } \text{text}(i) \tag{1}$$

and transmits the encrypted message to the receiver. The receiver can recover the plaintext byre-applying the pad and obtains the plaintext as given in equation (2).

$$\text{text}(i) = \text{message}(i) \text{ XOR } \text{pad}(i) \tag{2}$$

One time pads have a number of advantages over traditional cryptography systems. They are extremely computationally efficient both in terms of encryption and decryption. They are also unbreakable under the assumption that

1. The pad is truly random.
2. The pad is never reused.
3. The pad is secret to the two parties.

It is also interesting to note that breaking part of the message does not provide any advantage in terms of breaking the rest of the message. There is no decrypting key to guess.

2. IMPLEMENTATION OF ONE TIME PADS

The primary disadvantage with using a one time only pad is that the pad must be as large as the message to be transmitted. So, it signifies that we need a mechanism to transfer the keys with size same as size of the data securely between sender and receiver in order to have a secure communication. But, if, we would have that mechanism to transfer the keys securely, we would have transferred the data itself. Then one of the solutions suggested by Frank Rubin [3], through which moderate amount of random keys can be used to generate life time supply of keys for one time pads. Thus, with the combination of the true one time pads and using them to generate the pseudo random numbers using pseudo random number, generators can be used for making the one time pads practical to implement. In this kind of arrangement, we need not transfer the same size as the plaintext, instead once secure transfer of several number of keys can lead to a very lengthy communication. The similar kind of methodology has been suggested by Michael Jenkin and Patrick Dymond [4] for making one time pad applicable for the light weight devices in order to avoid the heavy encryption computation, which will lead to widespread use of one time pad technology. One time pads are helpful in reducing computational overheads which is required in various encryption techniques as one time pad significantly reduce encryption overhead, offering unparalleled security to even the slowest of devices [5]. But for making it possible for the light weight application, we can not think of a seed of very high length because of the computation limitation of the light weight devices and the limitation of the extendible memory of these devices. So, we have to think of a mechanism in which we can increase the complexity for the cryptanalyst without increasing the seed size.

3. ENHANCED CRYPTOGRAPHIC TECHNIQUE

For the above problem, we have to reach a solution in which with the lowest of computation we can reach maximum of complexity. That means without taking a seed of very high length we should be able to provide the complexity like the high length seed, only then we can think of providing the secure communication to variety of the devices to make this technique free from the devices constraint, then only we can be able to reach to a security protocol which will be able to transfer the data securely from sender to receiver irrespective of the devices they use. Here, instead of taking a single large true one time pad key as a seed, we have taken multiple small sized true one time pad key which is identically stored with both sender and receiver.

We are proposing the use of three random keys together to be taken from the one time pad file which is there with both sender and the receiver, and that one time pad file can be generated from any natural source random number generators such as quantis [6] and considered to be a true random numbers then they cannot be predicted. The above said file is only available to sender and receiver, not with any one else, so the service provider through which both are going to communicate will only be responsible for providing the reliable communication. We will use all the three keys one by one but together to generate the entire key stream through which we will encrypt the plaintext by one time pad technique. And once they were used, they will be removed from the one time pad file from both the sender and receiver side and will not be reused again. On the finishing of all the keys from the file, both sender and receiver should get themselves issued a new file from the server, the file which is same for both sender and receiver by some physical means like pen drive, compact disk, etc. Once the file reaches to both the users they can again start communicating again securely to a large number of sessions.

FIG. 46.1
Enhanced Cryptographic Technique for One Time Pad

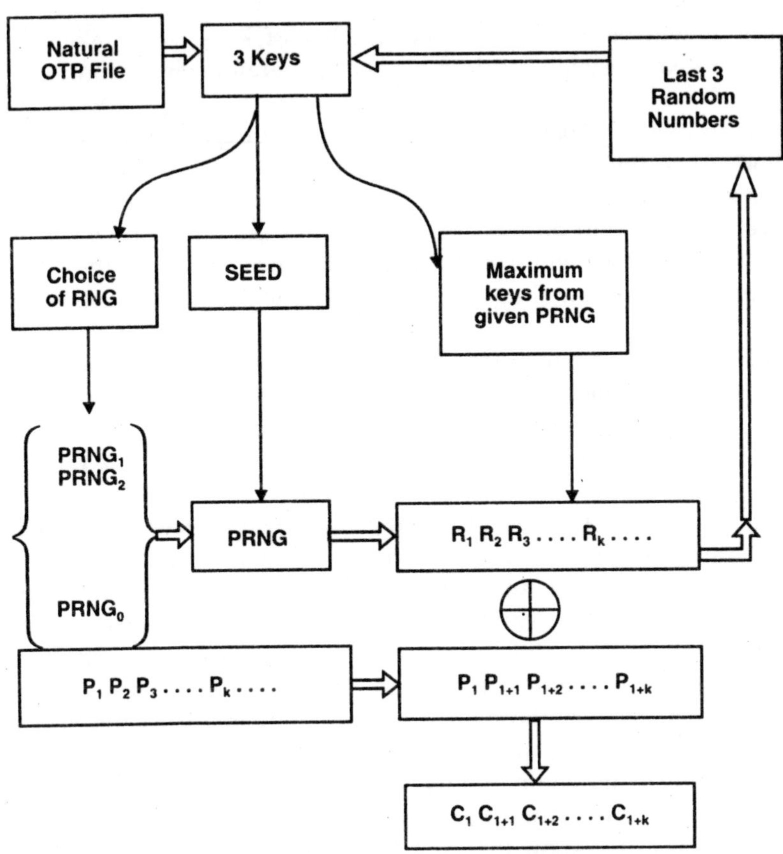

Where:

$PRNG_i$ (i=1 to n) are the choices of pseudo random number generators available for use.

R_i (i=1 to k) are the random numbers generated by particular PRNG.

P_i is the plain text individual element which is to be coded with its corresponding random number.

C_i is the cipher text individual element which has been coded from plain text element and corresponding random number.

In the Figure 46.1 we can see the overview of the new protocol for making the pads a practical solution for communication. Natural OTP (one time pad) file is available with only sender and receiver and from that both sender and receiver will take out 3 keys and will be used as given below.

The following is the description that how those random keys will be used:

(i) It will act as a seed.
(ii) It will be used to tell the choice of random number generator to be used.
(iii) It will be used to tell the number of keys to be taken from the PRNG (pseudo random number generators) in action.

As in one time pads explained above, the decryption and encryption method is just the same. So, if sender sends the data in form of the cipher text by xoring the plain text with the random numbers generated above, the receiver also have to do the same for getting the plain text back from the cipher text. Now we will explain the significance of each of the above used random keys and how they will strengthen the security of the key stream.

(i) As we know that each PRNG need some seed to produce the key stream which is totally based on the seed. If we do not change the seed then the same sequence will be produced, which can be predicted very easily, that is why we are using a true random seed to randomize the entire key stream.
(ii) If we use a single PRNG then it will be easier to guess the key stream from the various outputs we are getting as only one PRNG is involved then the above possibility cannot be ignored. Therefore, we have taken various PRNG's together in a choice format, so at every choice given by a true random number a PRNG at that particular choice will be used for that particular session for which we have taken those three random numbers. The choices of various PRNG's to be used are left to the service provider's choice to analyze its compatibility with various PRNG's and also to the device it is going to provide its service.
(iii) Now as we know that each PRNG has a period after which it starts repeating sequence then in order to avoid that and also at a larger length the prediction of PRNG sequence prediction becomes easier so we are bound to break the PRNG sequence in between and starting the process of reseeding from the last three random numbers taken from the sequence itself, it will also help in stopping the user to know about the future data if get hold of some of the data in between somehow.

In the above methodology, we can increase the complexity to a very high level as now crypt analyzer has to get the combination of three keys together and also in right sequence to break the entire code. That's not all now crypt analyzer has to work on list of various PRNG and along with their seed to get the entire key stream to decrypt the whole text. As in every session, new keys will be used all together from the Natural OTP file then, the above methodology also provide entire new key stream for each session.

4. CONCLUSION

In this paper we have proposed a new methodology through which one time pads can be practically used for communication for large range of devices. Through above methodology we will be able to decrease the key size without compromising the complexity which has come down by reduction of the key size.

By the above defined methodology we are making one time pads a practical solution between two entities which wants to communicate securely to each other, and as the one time pad file is not even with the server through which they are communicating, we are trying to remove any vulnerable point in-between. So, even if the server gets compromised, the users need not have to worry about the security of their communication.

References

1. D. Kahn. The Codebreakers. MacMillan, New York, 1967.
2. C.E. Shannon. Communication Theory of Secrecy Systems. *Bell System Tech.* J., 28:657-715, 1949.
3. Frank Rubin. One-Time Pad Cryptography, Published in *Cryptologia*, 20(4): 359-64, 1997.
4. Michael Jenkin and Patrick Dymond, Secure Communication between Lightweight Computing Devices over the Internet, Proceedings of the 35th Annual Hawaii International Conference on System Sciences, 2002.
5. Michael, E. Gruen, A Secure low-power Approach for Providing Mobile Encryption, Proceedings of the Eleventh Annual CCSC northeastern conference, 2006.
6. Id. Quantique White Paper, Version 2.0, 2004.

47

Secure Routing Protocols in Mobile Ad Hoc Networks (MANETs)

Anil Kumar

ABSTRACT

Security issues are main problem in Mobile Ad Hoc networks. A malicious attack by nodes in networks significantly affects the Quality of Service delivered by the network and disrupts the route discovery process. This problem is especially serious in mobile Ad Hoc networks (MANETs) as traditional methods created to prevent such attacks on wired networks are only partially successful when applied to mobile networks. There are some techniques to secure Mobile Ad Hoc Networks from these attacks. We take AODV as an example and develop a security mechanism to protect its routing information.

1. INTRODUCTION

Mobile Ad Hoc Networks MANET is the new emerging technology, which enables users to communicate without any physical infrastructure regardless of their geographical location, that's why it is sometimes referred to as an "infrastructure less" network such as military battlefield, emergency rescue, vehicular communication, mining operation, etc. These networks are subject to frequent link breaks, where also every node can perform the role of host as well as router, thus nodes, which are out of transmission range, can be accessed by routing through the intermediate nodes. The network topology of MANETs is always changing, as their mobile nodes are free to move around and can freely leave or join the networks. This makes Mobile Ad Hoc Networks more vulnerable to external attacks because any attacker node can easily enter the network. In addition, the constantly changing topology makes it hard to determine which node really left the network, just changed the location, or has been intercepted or blocked. Some of the characteristics of mobile Ad Hoc networks are described as follows: [2]

- MANET's constitute dynamic topology, which means that the nodes making up the network can move arbitrarily, making it very hard to predict the topology of the network at any instant of future time. Also, the optimum paths between nodes or groups of nodes (multicasting) may change continuously.
- Most of the nodes constituting a MANET may have limited power supplies and power constraints, limiting their effectiveness in routing and forwarding applications.
- Due to shared nature of the MANET networks, they are much more prone to security threats than regular fixed topology networks. Risks may include, spoofing, worm holes, denial of service attacks and many more. [3, 4]
- Also, the wireless medium of transmission has limited bandwidth capacity as well as higher rates of errors.

The paper is organized into various sections. The section 2 deals with related work done in the field of Ad Hoc networks. Section 3 explains the various functional Ad Hoc protocols that have been implemented including AODV and DSR, and the various classifications of Ad Hoc networks. Section 4 defines the various security considerations for a wireless Ad Hoc network and the various attack schemes possible. Section 5 explains the security extensions that need to be incorporated into an Ad Hoc network with the implementation model of SAODV secure routing protocol.

2. RELATED WORK

Mobile Ad Hoc Network development is in its initial stages with work going on to enhance, optimize and secure proposed designs and protocols. Enhancements include efficient utilization of bandwidth, higher throughputs, lesser per packet overheads, power consumption optimization, and security against potential threats, e.g., eaves dropping, impersonations, etc. and others. Quite a number of protocol designs have been proposed and implemented for MANET's, for example; Dynamic Source Routing (DSR), Ad Hoc On-Demand Distance Vector Routing (AODV), Destination-Sequenced Distance-Vector (DSDV) and Temporally Ordered Routing Algorithm (TORA). All of these approaches have a number of advantages and disadvantages e.g., AODV establishes routes as and when required rather than proactively searching for routes to remote hosts, therefore, utilizing bandwidth for path discovery when required. Apart from throughput, power consumption issues, overheads, optimum path discovery and other similar routing issues, security is a very important issue and integral part of reliable efficient packet routing. So, in order to address the issue of security, a number of advanced protocols have also been proposed, which solve the security problem to some extent.

Security issues for routing algorithms have been addressed in the form of extensions to existing protocol designs. These extensions work on the concept of detecting mischievous and malicious activity. But the problem is that it is likely to confuse transmission errors with malicious activity and there are no real means to guarantee the integrity and authentication of the routing messages. For example, ARAN routing protocol uses authentication and requires the use of trusted certificates. Every forwarding node must sign the control packet, which takes computing power consuming and the size of the routing message increases with each hop. Secondly, we have the SRP extension that can be used with many existing routing protocols. SRP requires that, for every route discovery, source and destination must have a security association between them. Ariadne is based on DSR. It requires clock synchronization. There are some other extensions as well, which require time synchronization between the nodes of network. In SEAD hash chains are used in combination with DSDV. At every given time each node has its own has chain. The hash chain is divided into segments; elements in a segment are used to secure hop counts. SEAD can be used with any suitable authentication and key distribution mechanism. Keeping the various requirements of a secure routing protocol in mind, we have worked on the implementations of security features inside existing routing protocol, namely AODV. We have implemented a secure version of the AODV routing protocol, SAODV. In SAODV, the main focus is on authentication and security of mutable fields, e.g., Hop Count that has to be modified by every intermediate node. AODV requires a sound key distributing system and user authentication mechanism as well as hash chains management.

3. PRACTICAL IMPLEMENTATIONS OF MANET

3.1 Designs

Mobile Ad Hoc Networks can be practically classified into two major categories, [1, 3]

1. Table-Driven (Proactive)
2. On-Demand (Reactive)

A. *A Table-Driven Routing Protocol:* Table Driven, or otherwise known as Proactive Routing protocols perform route discoveries automatically and periodically, so as to buildup a table of the network topology. [4] Therefore, routes are discovered for every mobile node of the network, without any requests for communications by the hosts. Some examples of table driven or proactive routing protocols include DSDV, WRP, CGSR and STAR.

B. *On-Demand Routing Protocols:* Apart from table driven routing protocols, there are also some reactive routing protocols, in which route discovery is performed when communication between hosts of a mobile network is required. Reactive protocols perform route discovery and path establishment by using specialized sets of packets known as control packets. Examples of Reactive routing protocols include AODV, DSR, and TORA.

C. *Dynamic Source Routing Protocol:* Dynamic source routing protocol utilizes the concept of source routing, i.e. the packet is provided with entire journey path before it is put on the link, in other words, the sender knows the complete hop-by-hop route to the destination. These routes are stored in a routing cache called the routing table. The data packets carry the source route in the packet header. The routing procedure consists of the following control packets:

- When a node in the Ad Hoc network attempts to send a data packet to a destination for which it does not already know the route, it uses a route discovery process to dynamically determine such a route. Route discovery works by flooding the network with route request (RREQ) packets.
- Each node receiving an RREQ rebroadcasts it unless it is the destination or it has a route to the destination in its routing table. Such a node replies to the RREQ with a route reply (RREP) packet that is routed back to the original source. RREQ and RREP packets are also source routed. The RREQ builds up the path traversed across the network.
- The RREP routes itself back to the source by traversing this path backward. The route carried back by the RREP packet is cached at the source for future use. If any link on a source route is broken, the source node is notified using a route error (RERR) packet. The source removes any route using this link from its cache. A new route discovery process must be initiated by the source if this route is still needed. DSR makes very aggressive use of source routing and route caching. No special mechanism to detect routing loops is needed. Also, any forwarding

node caches the source route in a packet it forwards for possible future use.

D. *Ad Hoc On-Demand Distance Vector Routing*: AODV is a practical implementation of the reactive route discovery mechanism [5]. However, AODV adopts a very different mechanism to maintain routing information. It uses traditional routing tables, one entry per destination without source routing, AODV relies on routing table entries to propagate an RREP back to the source and, subsequently, to route data packets to the destination. AODV uses sequence numbers maintained at each destination to determine freshness of routing information and to prevent routing loops. All routing packets carry these sequence numbers.

3.2 Route Discovery

1. *Route Discovery in AODV*: AODV utilizes [6] control packets such as Route Request (RREQ), Route Reply (RREP), and Route Error (RERROR) to manage routes between communicating nodes. When a node needs to determine a route to a destination node, it floods the network with a Route Request (RREQ) message. The originating node broadcasts a RREQ message to its neighboring nodes, which broadcast the message to their neighbors, and so on. To prevent cycles, each node remembers recently forwarded route requests in a route request buffer. As these requests spread through the network, intermediate nodes store reverse routes back to the originating node. Since an intermediate node could have many reverse routes, it always picks the route with the smallest hop count.
2. *Route Reply (RREP)*: When a node receiving the request either knows of a fresh route to the destination or is itself the destination, the node generates a Route Reply (RREP) message, and sends this message along the reverse path back towards the originating node. As the RREP message passes through intermediate nodes, these nodes update their routing tables so that in the future messages can be routed through these nodes to the destination.
3. *Route Errors (RERR)*: Each node periodically sends HELLO messages to its neighbors. Each node expects to periodically receive messages from each of its outgoing nodes. If a node has received no messages from some outgoing node for an extended period of time, then that node is presumed to be no longer reachable. Whenever a node determines one of its next-hops to be unreachable, it removes all affected route entries, and generates a Route Error (RERR) message [10]. This RERR message contains a list of all destinations that have become unreachable as a result of

the broken link. The node sends the RERR to each member of its precursor list. They update their routing tables, and in turn forward the RERR to their precursors, and so on. In contrast to DSR, RERR packets in AODV are intended to inform all sources using a link when a failure occurs.

4. *Route Request Buffers*: To prevent nodes from resending the same RREQs repeatedly, each node maintains a route request buffer, which contains a list of recently broadcasted route requests. Before forwarding a RREQ message, a node always checks the buffer to make sure it has not already forwarded the request. RREQ messages are also stored in the buffer by a node that originates a RREP message, so that a node does not send multiple RREPs for duplicate RREQs that may have arrived from different paths.
5. *Sequence Numbering*: Each node maintains an increasing sequence number, and every route entry includes a destination sequence number. The protocol uses sequence numbers to ensure that nodes only update routes with "newer" ones. This also ensures loop-freedom for all routes to a destination. All RREQ messages include the originator's sequence number, and its destination sequence number. Nodes receiving the RREQ update routes to the originator with the originator sequence number. If the node receives an identical RREQ message through another path, the originator sequence numbers would be the same, so the node would pick the route with the smaller hop count. If a node receiving the RREQ message has a route to the desired destination, then we use sequence numbers to determine whether this route is fresh to be used as a reply to the route request, by checking if this node's destination sequence number is at least as great as the maximum destination sequence number of all nodes through which the RREQ message has passed. If this is the case, an RREP is sent back to the originator. As with RREQ messages, RREP messages also include destination sequence numbers.
6. *Multicast Routes*: Multicast routes are set-up in a similar manner. A node wishing to join a multicast group broadcasts a RREQ with the destination IP address set to that of the multicast group and with the JOIN flag set to indicate that it would like to join the group. Any node receiving this RREQ that is a member of the multicast group that has a fresh enough sequence number for the multicast group may send a RREP. As the RREPs propagate back to the source, the nodes forwarding the message set-up pointers in their multicast route tables. As the source node receives the RREPs, it keeps track of the route with the freshest sequence number, and beyond that the smallest hop count to the next multicast group member. After the specified discovery period, the source node wills unicast a Multicast Activation (MACT) message to its selected next hop. This message serves the purpose of activating the route. A

node that does not receive this message that had set-up a multicast route pointer will timeout and delete the pointer.

7. *Precursor and Outgoing Lists*: Each node of the network keeps track of a recursor list, and an outgoing list. A precursor list is a set of nodes that route through the given node. The outgoing list is the set of nexthops that this node routes through. In networks where all routes are bi-directional, these lists are essentially the same.

4. SECURITY REQUIREMENTS IN MANET'S

One of the most distinct feature of MANET's from other static networks is the fact that each node of the networks contributes in making up routes from various sources to destinations or groups of nodes acting as destination. However, this distinct feature poses a number of serious threats to the security and privacy of the overall network as well as the individual nodes making up the network. [7, 11] The openness of Ad Hoc networks offers greater flexibility in terms of functionality, but it also provides an open path for any malicious node or intruder to gain access to the network and perform activities such as eaves dropping, spoofing, Denial of service attacks, flooding, link failure and many more. To ensure safe operation of an Ad Hoc network, the following minimum constraints should be met :

- Authentication of a node is very important so that the node can be trusted as a valid and trusted node, and malicious, eavesdropping nodes are denied access into the network.
- Data integrity is an important issue, so as to ensure the data communicated between nodes has not been tempered or altered by any malicious node.
- Privacy is also necessary to ensure that no intermediate node can access the data that is meant for the destination of that message.

4.1 Classification of Attacks in Manet

Attacks on Ad Hoc networks can be broadly classified on the basis of their origin either external or internal. [8]

- External attacks are the attacks launched by parties that are not part of the network. External attackers are not necessarily disconnected from the network though the targeted network might be a self-contained
- Internal attacks are sourced from inside a particular network. A network with internal attacker nodes is more vulnerable because a malicious node inside a network is already past the basic defense lines of a network, hence the malicious activity is very difficult to detect and curtail.

The attacks on networks can also be classified as follows:

- Passive attacks are those attacks in which a malicious node does not actively try to disrupt the network; instead, it sits silently, eavesdropping on communication and data traffic, as well as collection information about the various communicating nodes of a network.
- Active attacks are those in which a node proactively searches for flaws in the network and tries to disrupt the topology of the network by overloading it or breaking existing paths between network nodes.

4.2 Attack Types In Manet's

1. *Spoofing*: In spoofing attack [9, 12], the attacker assumes the identity of another node in the network; hence it receives the messages that are meant for that node. Usually, this type of attack is launched in order to gain access to the network so that further attacks can be launched, which could seriously cripple the network.
   Any malicious node that has enough information of the network to forge a false ID of one its member nodes can launch this type of attack and utilizing that ID and a lucrative incentive, the node can misguide other nodes to establish routes towards itself rather than towards the original node. A malicious node with this goal will most likely try to impersonate a node within the path of the data flow it requires. Modifying routing data or implying itself as a trustworthy communication partner to neighboring nodes in parallel could do it. Usually, exploiting MAC layer protocol malicious nodes could place their node between two other nodes communicating with each other (man-in-the middle attack).
2. *Denial of Service Attack*: In a denial of service attack, a malicious node may become the bottleneck for paths that are passing through it, by denying service to those paths. In this type of attack, a

FIG. 47.1
Spoofing (Man in the Middle)

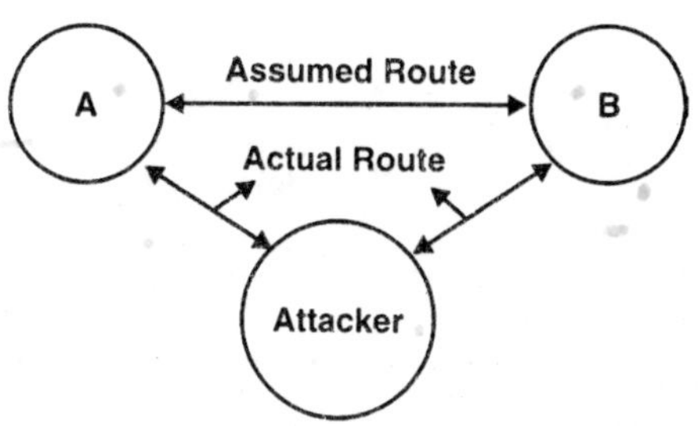

particular node, that has a single or multiple paths passing through it may stop forwarding packets, while still maintaining its presence in the networks (replying to hello packets of precursors), hence acting as a sink for data in the network.

FIG. 47.2
Denial of Service Attack

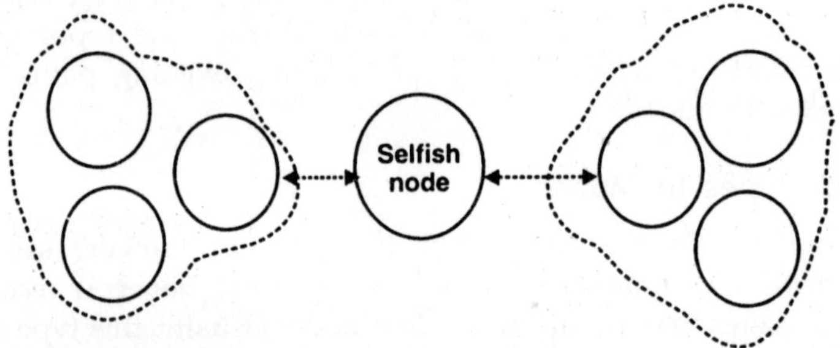

3. *Sinkholes*: In a sinkhole attack, a compromised node tries to attract the data to it from all neighboring nodes. So, practically, the node eavesdrops on all the data that is being communicated between its neighboring nodes. Sinkhole attacks can also be implemented on *Ad Hoc* networks such as AODV by using flaws such as maximizing the sequence number or minimizing the hop count, so that the path presented through the malicious node appears to be the best available route for the nodes to communicate. The problem of sinkhole attack can be much amplified if the malicious node exists within or around the center of the network so that it hears every communication happening inside the network. However, in

FIG. 47.3
Sink Hole

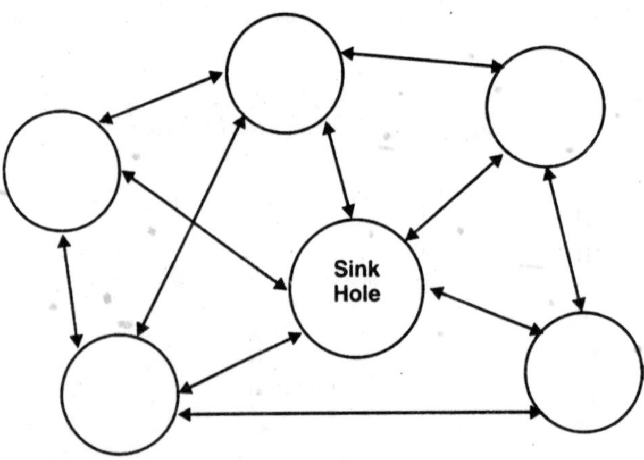

the case of multipath protocols, which send data redundantly, not relying on one path only, the problem of sinkholes can be reduced. Probabilistic protocols, which measure the trustworthiness of a network, can help detecting sinkholes within the network.

4. *Wormholes*: In a wormhole attack, a malicious node uses a path outside the network to route messages to another node at some other location. Wormholes are hard to detect because the path that is used to pass on information is usually not part of the actual network [12]. A wormhole itself does not have to be harmful; for it usually lowers the time it takes for a packet to reach its destination. But even this behavior could already damage the operation, since wormholes fake a route that is shorter than the according one within the network; this can confuse routing mechanisms, which rely on the knowledge about distance between nodes. Wormholes are dangerous because they can do damage without even knowing the network. The wormhole attack can be detected by marking each packet with timestamps and location stamps in order to detect wormhole intrusions in a system. Each packet is tagged with very precise time information of the sender node, which is then compared by the destination node to its own time and location stamps. If the comparison reveals an unrealistic distance the data took within an unrealistic amount of time, it can be assumed that there is a wormhole within the network.

FIG. 47.4
Wormholes

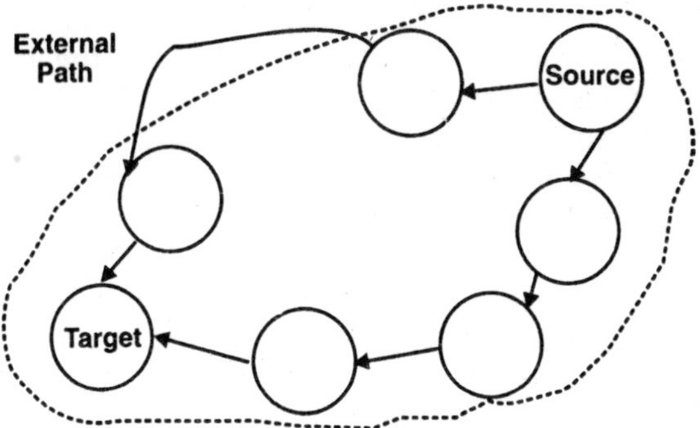

5. *Sybil Attack* : Malicious nodes in a network may not only impersonate one node, they could take up the identity of a group of nodes, this attack is called the Sybil attack. Since Ad Hoc networks depend on the communication between nodes, many systems apply redundant algorithms to ensure that the data gets from point A to point B. A consequence of this is that attackers have a harder time to destroy the integrity of information.

FIG. 47.5
The Sybil Attack

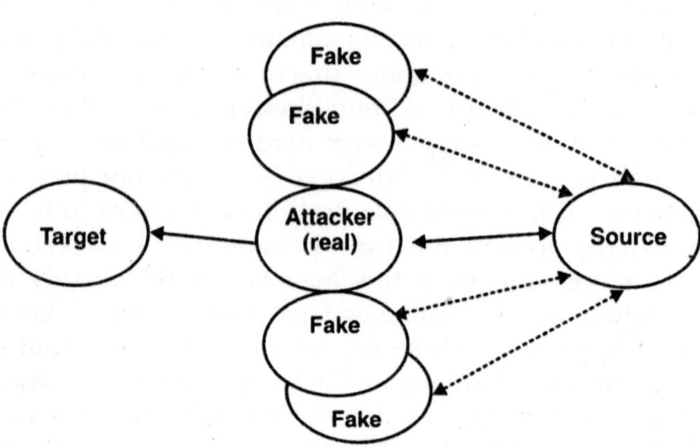

However, if a single malicious node is able to represent several other nodes, the effectiveness of these measures is significantly degraded. The attacker may get access to all the data or may alter all packets in the same transmission so that the destination node/s cannot detect the change in packets anymore. In trust-based routing environments, representing multiple identities can be used to deliver fake recommendations about the trustworthiness of a certain party, hereby attracting more traffic to it; in ideal starting point for further attacks.

6. *Flooding* : Malicious nodes may also inject false packets into the network, or create ghost packets, which loop around due to false routing information, effectively using up the bandwidth and processing resources along the way. This has especially serious effects on Ad Hoc networks, since the nodes of these usually possess only limited resources in terms of battery and computational power. Traffic may also be a monetary factor, depending on the services provided, so any flooding which blows up the traffic statistics of the network or a certain node can lead to considerable damage costs.
7. *RERR Generations* : [10] Malicious nodes can prevent communications between any two nodes by sending RERR messages to some node along the path. The RERR messages when flooded into the network may cause the breakdown of multiple paths between various nodes of the network, hence causing a no. of link failures.
8. *Attack on Mutable Fields:* In mobile Ad Hoc networks, there are a no. of fields in control and data packets that are altered along their path from one node to another. For example, the hop count field is incremented each time a node receives a RREQ control packet. So,

a malicious node can attack by modifying this mutable information e.g., by diverting all traffic through itself or by not forwarding requests, or by simply setting these fields to an infinitely high value.

References

1. http://www.acm.org/class/1998/
2. Securing *ad hoc* Routing Protocols, M. Guerrero Zapata and N. Asokan,. Proc. ACM Workshop on Wireless Security (WiSe), ACM Press, 2002.
3. An Intrusion Detection Tool for AODV-based Ad Hoc Wireless Networks, Giovanni Vigna, Sumit Gwalani Kavitha Srinivasan, Elizabeth M. Belding-Royer, Richard A. Kemmerer, Department of Computer Science, University of California, Santa Barbara.
4. Secure Routing for Vehicular Networks, SEVECOM Kickoff Workshop, 2nd February 2006, Frank Kargl.
5. Ad Hoc On-Demand Distance Vector (AODV) Routing draft-ietf-manet-aodv-13.txt, Nokia Research Center Elizabeth M. Belding-Royer University of California, Santa Barbar, Samir R. Das, University of Cincinnati.
6. Quick Guide to AODV Routing, Luke Klein-Berndt, Wireless Communications Technologies Group, National Institute of Standards and Technology.
7. A Survey of Secure Wireless Ad Hoc Routing, YIHCHUN HU University of California Berkeley, ADRIAN PERRIG Carnegie Mellon University.
8. Adaptive Secure Routing in Ad Hoc Mobile Network, Abu Raihan Mostofa Kamal, Department of Computer and Systems Science (DSV), Royal Institute of Technology (KTH), Stockholm, Sweden.
9. Ad Hoc network specific attacks, Adam Burg, Technische Universität München, 2003[10] Study of Secure Reactive Routing Protocols in, Mobile Ad Hoc Networks, Lim Sher Ee Dennis, Ee Xianhe.
10. Secure Ad Hoc On-Demand Distance Vector (SAODV) Routing, draft-guerrero-manet-saodv-06.txt, Manel Guerrero Zapata, Technical University of Catalonia (UPC).
11. Introduction to Modern Cryptography, Mihir Bellare Department of Computer Science and Engineering, University of California at San Diego, La Jolla, CA 92093, USA. mihir@cs.ucsd.edu
12. A Survey of Secure Wireless Ad Hoc Routing, YIHCHUN HU University of California, Berkeley, ADRIAN PERRIG Carnegie Mellon University.

48

Synchronous Checkpointing Protocols for Mobile Distributed Systems : A Comparative Study

SURENDER KUMAR, PARVEEN KUMAR AND R.K. CHAUHAN

ABSTRACT

Checkpointing is an efficient way of implementing fault tolerance in distributed systems. Mobile computing raises many new issues such as high mobility, lack of stable storage on Mobile Hosts (MHs), low bandwidth of wireless channels, limited battery life and disconnections that make the traditional check pointing protocols unsuitable for such systems. Minimum-process coordinated checkpointing is a preferred approach to introduce fault tolerance in mobile distributed systems transparently. This approach is domino-free, requires at most two checkpoints of each process on stable storage, and forces only interacting processes to checkpoint. Sometimes, it also requires piggybacking of information onto normal messages, blocking of the underlying computation or taking some useless checkpoints. In this paper, we point out some complexities and inconsistencies in the existing coordinated checkpointing protocols for Mobile Distributed Systems and compare them. We provide future directions for designing more efficient synchronous check pointing protocols for mobile systems.

Key words: Fault tolerance, Check Pointing, Message Logging, Independent Checkpointing, Consistent Global State, Domino Effect, coordinated Checkpointing and Mobile Systems.

1. INTRODUCTION

A mobile distributed computing system is a distributed system where some of the processes are running on Mobile Hosts (MHs). A mobile host communicates with other nodes of the distributed system via a special node called mobile support station (MSS) [1], [10]. A "cell" is a geographical area around an MSS in which it can support an MH. An MH can change its geographical position freely from one cell to another or even to an area covered by no cell. MSS has both wired and wireless links, and acts as an interface between the static network and a part of the mobile network. Static nodes are connected by a high speed wired network. A static node, that has no support to MHs, can be considered as an MSS with no MHs. Critical applications are required to execute fault-tolerantly on such systems.

In a distributed computation, an event is a spontaneous state transition by a process, or the sending or receiving of a message. A checkpoint is a local state of a process saved on stable storage. A local state of a process P_i is defined by P_i's initial state and the sequence of events that occurred at P_i. In a distributed system, since the processes do not share memory, a global state of the system is defined as a set of local states, one from each process. The state of channels corresponding to a global state is the set of messages sent but not yet received. A global state is said to be "consistent" if it contains no orphan message; i.e., a message whose receive event is recorded, but its send event is lost. The notion of consistency fits the observation that a message cannot be received before it is sent in any temporal frame of reference [4], [6]. To recover from a failure, the system restarts its execution from a previous consistent global state saved on the stable storage during fault-free execution. This saves all the computation done up to the last checkpointed state and only the computation done thereafter needs to be redone [4], [6]. In distributed systems, checkpointing can be independent (asynchronous), coordinated (synchronous), quasi-synchronous, or message logging based.

In independent checkpointing, processes do not coordinate their checkpointing activity and each process records its local checkpoint independently. After a failure, a consistent global checkpoint is established by tracking the dependencies. It may require cascaded rollbacks that may lead to the initial state due to domino-effect [12]. Multiple checkpoints need to be saved for each process. In coordinated checkpointing, the processes coordinate their checkpointing activity in such a manner that the set of local checkpoints is always consistent. The main advantage is that only one permanent checkpoint and at most one tentative checkpoint is required to be stored for a process. It suffers from the following disadvantages:

(i) If a process initiates checkpointing, all or interacting processes are required to checkpoint; if a process fails to checkpoint in an initiation, the whole checkpointing process is discarded.

(ii) In minimum-process algorithms, some useless checkpoints are taken or blocking of processes takes place.
(iii) It may require some information to be piggybacked onto computation messages.
(iv) It requires extra synchronization messages.
(v) In case of a fault, all processes need to rollback to their last committed states.

Mobile Distributed Computing Systems raise new issues such as mobility of nodes, low bandwidth of wireless channels, lack of stable storage on mobile nodes, disconnections, limited battery power and high failure rate of mobile nodes. These issues make traditional checkpointing algorithms unsuitable for checkpointing mobile systems [1], [3], [10]. A good checkpoint algorithm for mobile systems needs to have following characteristics [10]. It should impose low memory overheads on MHs and low overheads on wireless channels. The disconnection of MHs should not lead to infinite wait state. The checkpointing algorithm should avoid awakening of an MH in doze mode operation. The algorithm should be non-intrusive and minimum-process. In minimum-process checkpointing algorithm, a process takes its permanent checkpoint only if the initiator process is transitively dependent upon it. Minimum set is the set of processes which are required to checkpoint in the minimum-process algorithm.

Prakash-Singhal algorithm [10] was the first algorithm to combine min-process and non-blocking properties. It forces only minimum number of processes to take checkpoints and does not block the underlying computation. Cao and Singhal [2] have shown that the algorithm [10] can lead to inconsistencies. The authors also proved that there does not exist a non-blocking algorithm which forces only minimum number of processes to take checkpoints. Cao and Singhal [3], L. Kumar *et. al.* [8] and P. Kumar *et. al.* [9] proposed non-intrusive coordinated checkpointing algorithms where some useless checkpoints are taken. Koo and Toeg [6], and Cao and Singhal [2] proposed minimum process blocking algorithms. To maintain minimum process or non-intrusive property in coordinated checkpointing, we may require piggybacking of integer csn (checkpoint sequence number) onto normal messages [3], [5], [8], [9]. L. Kumar *et. al.* [7] proposed an all process non-intrusive checkpointing protocol for distributed systems, where just one bit is piggybacked onto normal messages. This is done by incurring extra overhead of vector transfers during checkpointing.

In message logging protocols, each process periodically records its local state and logs the messages that it receives after having recorded that state on stable storage. When a process crashes, a new process is created in its place. The new process is given the appropriate recorded local state, and then the logged messages are replayed in the order the process originally received them. All message-logging protocols require that once a crashed process recovers its recovered state, is consistent with the states of the other processes [12], [13]. Bin Yao et al. [13] describes a receiver-based message logging protocol for mobile hosts, mobile support stations and home agents in a Mobile IP environment, which guarantees independent recovery. Checkpointing is utilized to limit log size and recovery latency.

The MSSs can easily take the consistent checkpoints using synchronous checkpointing protocols [5], [6]. Since, they can communicate with each other by using the high-speed network and they have enough stable storage to store their state information. Higaki and Takizawa [11] have shown that there is a high probability that at least one MH will fail to record the checkpoint synchronously with other nodes and, thus, will render whole checkpointing effort useless. Such successive unsuccessful efforts will waste the scarce resources of mobile systems and will not allow the normal computation to proceed. They proposed a checkpointing protocol where mobile hosts checkpoint independently and fixed ones synchronously and requires blocking of processes during checkpointing. An MSS logs the messages of the MHs in its cell. If an MH fails to take its checkpoint and transfer it to the current MSS, it can try later. MSSs take checkpoints synchronously. A process on an MH can recover independently. When a process on an MH crashes, a new process is created using checkpoint of the crashed MH, and then the logged messages are replayed in the order they were originally received. When a process on an MSS fails, all processes rollback to recent synchronous checkpoint. An MH uses its recent committed checkpoint and message logs to reach to a state consistent with the synchronous checkpoint. The algorithm does not awaken an MH in doze mode operation. This algorithm suffers from the overhead of message logging for MHs.

Acharya and Badrinath [1] introduced a two-phase protocol for taking global consistent checkpoints. They proposed that checkpoints be stored on the stable storage of mobile support stations instead of on mobile hosts. In their protocol, processes alternate between two states, SEND and RECV. If a process is in the send mode and receives a message, it is forced to take a checkpoint. During recovery, the global state is reconstructed from a set of checkpoints for each process. In this algorithm, there is no control on checkpointing activity. In the worst case, the number of checkpoints is equal to the number of computation messages.

There is a tradeoff between synchronous and asynchronous checkpointing protocols for mobile systems. Some of the approaches advocate synchronous checkpointing [2], [3], [8], [9] and others advocate asynchronous checkpointing [1]. Asynchronous checkpointing in true sense is not suitable even for distributed systems due to domino effect. But, asynchronous checkpointing with message logging is quite effective for checkpointing mobile systems [11], [14].

2. NON-BLOCKING ALGORITHMS

Cao and Singhal [3] achieved non-intrusiveness in minimum-process algorithm by introducing the concept of mutable checkpoints. In their algorithm, checkpoint initiator process sends the checkpoint request to the processes on which it directly depends. Similarly, when a process receives the checkpoint request, it sends the checkpoint request to some of those processes on which it directly depends. In this way, a checkpointing tree is formed and the time taken to collect the coordinated checkpoint may be exceedingly high. During checkpointing, suppose, P_i receives m from P_j. P_i takes its mutable checkpoint before processing m, only if the following conditions are met:

(i) P_i has not taken any checkpoint in the current initiation.
(ii) P_i has sent at least one message in the current CI.
(iii) P_j has taken its checkpoint in the current initiation before sending m. The mutable checkpoint is discarded on commit if it is not the member of the minimum set. Though only minimum number of processes takes permanent checkpoints but the actual number of processes that take checkpoints may be exceedingly high in some situations.

We find the following observations in [3]:

(i) When a process P_i sends a checkpoint request to P_j, following scenarios are possible:
   (a) P_i knows that some other process has already sent the checkpoint request to P_j for the current initiation;
   (b) P_j is not transitively dependent upon the initiator process, i.e., P_j is not in the minimum set; and
   (c) P_j discards checkpoint request of P_i and P_j actually belongs to the minimum set.

(ii) When P_i sends a checkpoint request to P_j, it also piggybacks $csn_i[j]$ and a huge data structure MR[i].

L. Kumar et al [8] and P. Kumar *et. al.* [9] proposed minimum-process non-intrusive coordinated checkpointing algorithms, where number of useless checkpoints is reduced as compared to [3]. In both of these algorithms, initiator MSS collects the direct dependency vectors of all processes, computes the minimum set, and sends the checkpoint request along with the minimum set to all MSSs. In algorithm [9], during the time P_i sends its direct dependency vectors and receives the minimum set, P_i may process some messages and the fresh dependencies may be created and the computed minimum set may become incorrect. These dependencies are taken care of and the computed minimum set is updated. In algorithm [8], during the time P_i sends its direct dependency vectors and receives the minimum set, if P_i processes m which changes its own direct dependency vector, P_i takes induced checkpoint before processing m. In this way, fresh dependencies, created during checkpointing, do not alter the computed minimum set. Simulation results have shown that the number of useless checkpoints in [8] is negligible as compared to [3]. These algorithms [8], [9] are also free from problems in the algorithm [3] mentioned above at points (i) and (ii), but they suffer from the overhead of collecting dependencies, computing the minimum set and broadcasting the minimum set on the static network.

3. BLOCKING ALGORITHMS

Koo and Toeg [6] proposed a minimum-process blocking algorithm, where each process uses monotonically increasing labels in its outgoing messages. The initiator process sends the checkpoint request to P_i only if it has received m from P_i in the current CI. Similarly, P_i sends the checkpoint request to other processes. In this way, a checkpointing tree is formed and at last the leaf node processes take checkpoints. The time taken to collect coordinated checkpoint in mobile systems may be too large due to mobility, disconnections and unreliable wireless channels. The extensive blocking of processes may degrade the system performance.

Cao and Singhal [2] proposed a blocking minimum-process checkpointing algorithm for mobile systems. In this algorithm, blocking time is reduced significantly as compared to [6]. Every process maintains direct dependencies in a bit array of length n for n processes. Initiator process collects the direct dependencies and makes a set of interacting processes (S_{forced}), which need to checkpoint along with the initiator. During blocking time, processes can do their normal computations but cannot send any messages. Similarly, the algorithm [2] can ask a process, say P_1, to take the checkpoint when it is not required to checkpoint. Suppose P_2 is the checkpoint initiator and it receives m from P_1 such that P_1 has taken permanent checkpoint after sending m and P_2 receives m in the current checkpointing interval before initiation. If P_1 does not send any message to any process after taking the permanent checkpoint such that P_2 becomes dependent upon P_1, P_1 does not need to take checkpoint initiated by P_2. But, in the above situation P_2 will send the checkpoint request to P_1 unnecessarily. This problem arises because no information is piggybacked onto normal messages so that receiver process can decide whether it becomes dependent upon the sender after processing the message.

The Cao and Singhal [2] algorithm reduces blocking of processes at the extra cost of collecting dependencies, computing minimum set, and broadcasting the minimum set on the static network.

4. CONCLUSION

We have discussed challenges in coordinated checkpointing protocols for mobile computing systems. We pointed out some complexities and inconsistencies in the existing protocols and make a comparative study. We propose the following guidelines for designing such protocols for mobile systems:

(i) Exact dependencies among processes are maintained to minimize the message complexity,
(ii) Some information is piggybacked onto normal messages for the receiver to decide whether it becomes causally dependent upon the sender after processing the message, and
(iii) Concurrent initiations of the checkpointing algorithm should not lead to its concurrent executions.

References

1. Acharya, A. and Badrinath, B.R., "Checkpointing Distributed Applications on Mobile Computers," Proceedings of the 3rd International Conference on Parallel and Distributed Information Systems, pp. 73-80, September 1994.
2. Cao, G. and Singhal, M., "On the Impossibility of Min-process Non-blocking Checkpointing and an Efficient Checkpointing Algorithm for Mobile Computing Systems," Proceedings of International Conference on Parallel Processing, pp. 37-44, August 1998.
3. Cao, G. and Singhal, M., "Mutable Checkpoints: A New Checkpointing Approach for Mobile Computing systems," IEEE Transaction On Parallel and Distributed Systems, Vol. 12, No. 2, pp. 157-72, February 2001.
4. Chandy, K.M. and Lamport, L., "Distributed Snapshots: Determining Global State of Distributed Systems," ACM Transaction on Computing Systems, Vol. 3, No. 1, pp. 63-75, February 1985.
5. Elnozahy, E.N., Johnson, D.B. and Zwaenepoel, W., "The Performance of Consistent Checkpointing," Proceedings of the 11th Symposium on Reliable Distributed Systems, pp. 39-47, October 1992.
6. Koo, R. and Toueg, S., "Checkpointing and Roll-Back Recovery for Distributed Systems," IEEE Trans. on Software Engineering, Vol. 13, No. 1, pp. 23-31, January 1987.
7. Lalit Kumar, M. Misra, R.C. Joshi, "Checkpointing in Distributed Computing Systems" Book Chapter "Concurrency in Dependable Computing", pp. 273-92, 2002.
8. Lalit Kumar, M. Misra, R.C. Joshi, "Low overhead optimal checkpointing for mobile distributed systems", Proceedings of 19th International Conference on IEEE Data Engineering, pp. 686-88, 2003.
9. Parveen Kumar, Lalit Kumar, R.K. Chauhan, V.K. Gupta, "A Non-Intrusive Minimum Process Synchronous Checkpointing Protocol for Mobile Distributed Systems" Proceedings of IEEE ICPWC-2005, pp. 491-95 January 2005.
10. Prakash, R. and Singhal, M., "Low-Cost Checkpointing and Failure Recovery in Mobile Computing Systems," IEEE Transaction On Parallel and Distributed Systems, Vol. 7, No. 10, pp. 1035-48, October 1996.
11. H. Higaki and M. Takizawa, Checkpoint-recovery Protocol for Reliable Mobile Systems, Trans. of Information Processing, Japan, Vol. 40, No. 1, pp. 236-44, Jan. 1999.
12. E.N. Elnozahy, L. Alvisi, Y.M. Wang & D.B. Johnson, A Survey of Rollback-Recovery Protocols in Message-Passing Systems, ACM Computing Surveys, Vol. 34, No. 3, pp. 375-408, 2002.
13. Bin Yao, Kuo-Feng Ssu and W. Kect Fuchs, Message Logging in Mobile Computing, Proceedings of international conference on FTCS, pp. 294-301, 1999.
14. D.K. Pradhan, P.P. Krishana and N.H. Vaidya, Recovery in Mobile Wireless Environment: Design and Trade-off Analysis, Proceedings 26th International Symposium on Fault-Tolerant Computing, pp. 16-25, 1996.

49

Performance Optimization for Wi-Fi Deployment : Pre-Implementation Issues

GURVINDER SINGH, AVNIP DEORA, ROOPALI SOOD AND POOJA DHAND

ABSTRACT

Wi-Fi refers to the 802.11a/b/g wireless Ethernet standard that was designed to support wireless LANs. It has recently attracted a lot of attention and gaining popularity as a dominant platform for providing broadband wireless access to the Internet. But, establishing a wireless LANs in an organization is a crucial task because the owners of different organizations believe that these wireless networks cannot be established without spending much time and money. But, there are certain factors that help to reduce the total cost of ownership of wireless networks by eliminating costly rework that frequently occurs with measurement-based design.

Some of these pre-deployment issues for establishing Wi-Fi discussed in this paper are facility survey, topology selection, user density, applications running, access point (AP) placement, bandwidth requirement, power levels, channel assignment, total cost of ownership (TCO) and allocation of service set identifiers (SSID). A successful wireless LAN deployment is measured by how well the network meets the performance and capacity requirements of users and meeting these requirements is dependent upon the ability to properly plan, deploy, monitor, troubleshoot and security of wireless networks. One must give careful attention to requirements analysis and design to end up with an effective solution of providing quality of services (QoS).

Keywords: Deployment, Topology, Access Point, Bandwidth and Service Set Identifiers.

1. INTRODUCTION

The term 'Wireless' refers to the telecommunication technology in which radio waves, infrared waves and micro waves are used to carry a signal over the air to connect to different communication devices like cell phones, PCs, pagers, computer networks, etc. minimizing the need for wired connections. Following parameters need consideration for proper deployment of wireless networks:

1.	*Facility Survey*	A proper facility survey is required before establishing WLAN.
2.	*Topology Selection*	Which topology would be preferred for establishing WLAN?
3.	*User Density*	How many users will use WLAN resources?
4.	*Application Running*	What type of applications will run on the nodes of WLAN for bandwidth requirement?
5.	*AP Placement*	How many APs are needed to find WLAN and their optimal placement to cover dead spots or black holes?
6.	*Antenna Selection*	Which type of antenna is required for different coverage pattern?
7.	*Bandwidth Requirement*	To calculate required bandwidth for n number of users.
8.	*Power Levels*	This issue will decide transmitted power from AP to avoid congestion.
9.	*Channel Assignment*	How channels would be allocated for APs to avoid interference.
10.	*Total Cost of Ownership (TCO)*	To find out the cost involved for WLAN comparable to wired LANS.
11.	*Allocation of SSID*	How a proper SSID must be given for establishing WLAN?

1.1 Facility Survey

A Facility Survey is a step by step procedure which provides a realistic understanding of infrastructure required for wireless technology. It assists the N/W administrator by providing the essential information related to design parameters which includes RF behaviour, network capacity, roaming capabiliy, power levels and determines the appropriate placement of access points[1]. Facility survey tools like LAN Planner (Motorola), Channel Analyzer provide useful graphical illustrations of wireless network metrics, such as signal strength, response time, data rates and signal-to-noise ratio.

A Wireless Facility Survey involves the following analysis for WLANS:

- RF Behavior
- Range and Coverage Analysis
- Multi-path Fading Analysis
- Interference Analysis
- Bandwidth Requirements Analysis [2]

As radio waves do not travel the same distance in all directions because walls, doors, windows, elevator shafts and other obstacles offer varying degree of attenuation which alters the pattern of radio waves. The chart has been made which depicts the amount of attenuation involved in db for different types of infrastructure in a building [3].

TABLE 49.1
Amount of Attenuation in db

Sl. No.	*Type of Medium*	*Attenuation*
1.	Plaster board wall	3db
2.	Office window	3db
3.	Cinder lock wall	4db
4.	Glass wall with metal frame	6db
5.	Metal door	6db
6.	Metal door in brick wall	12.4db

Following steps need to be performed for an efficient Facility Survey:

- *Plotting and Inspection of facility Diagram:*
  - To start with the facility survey, a proper floor plan has to be made which depicts the location of walls, doors, windows, elevator shafts and other potential barriers (if any).
  - These facility diagrams helps in locating other potential barriers. For example, pointed glass tends to absorb more radio waves, effectively reduces signal strength and bandwidth. If the signal strength is very poor in some areas, it means RF interference is affecting the wireless and hence dead spots can be detected accordingly.

Identification of user areas: AN/W administrator must identify those areas that have high user density.

- *Determination and Verification of Preliminary Access Point Locations:* The preliminary access point locations can be determined by placing the access point and then a test can be performed to determine its coverage. This can be made possible by taking some readings about its data rates and signal readings at different points while walking through different areas of a building.

Based on these results, the access point location can be relocalized to enhance signal strength [4].

1.2 Topology Selection

Topology is the physical layout of components interacting to provide a wireless LAN that enables station mobility transparent to the higher protocol layers. The working of wireless resides physically in a radio NIC, the software interface that drives the NIC and an Access point. Topologies that define the efficient deployment of wireless networks are:

1. BSS Basic Service Set
2. IBSS Independent Basic Service Set
3. ESS Extended Service Set

A *Service set* is a logical grouping of devices and an *SSID* is the name given to wireless local area network (WLAN). All wireless devices on a WLAN must employ the same SSID in order to communicate with each other.

A. *BSS (Basic Service Set)* : It is a group of stations communicating with one another. It requires a specialized station known as an access point (AP). The AP acts as a central point of communications for all

FIG. 49.1
Basic Service Set

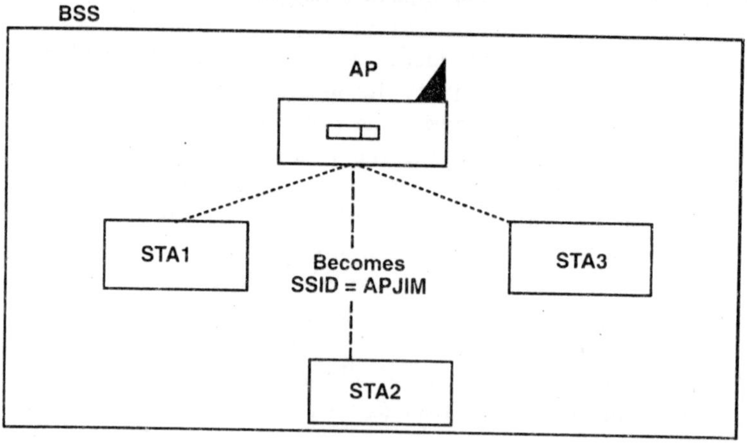

stations in BSS. The client stations communicate with AP, and the AP forwards the frames to the destination stations.

B. *IBSS (Independent Basic Service Set)* : In IBSS, a group of stations communicate directly with one another and form an independent network without the use of an access point. It is, also, referred to as an *ad-hoc* network because it is simply forms peer-to-peer WLAN. Mostly these networks are spontaneous and can be set-up rapidly.

Fig. 49.2
Independent Basic Service Set

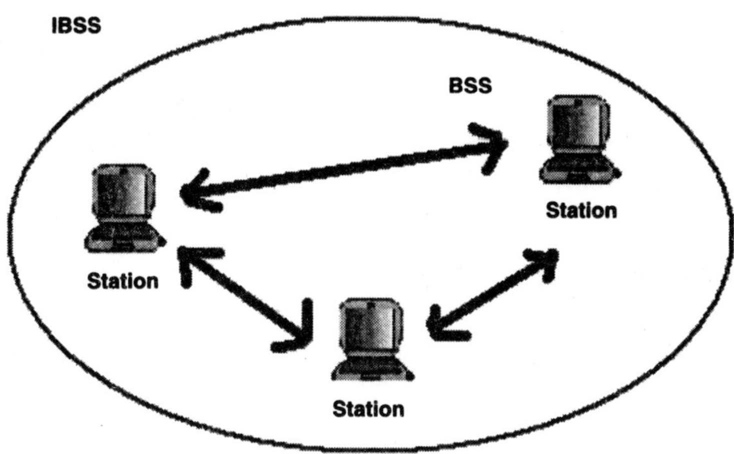

C. *ESS (Extended Service Set)* : An extended service set (ESS) is a set of connected BSSs. Access points in an ESS are connected by a distribution system. Each ESS has an ID called the SSID which is a

Fig. 49.3
Extended Service Set

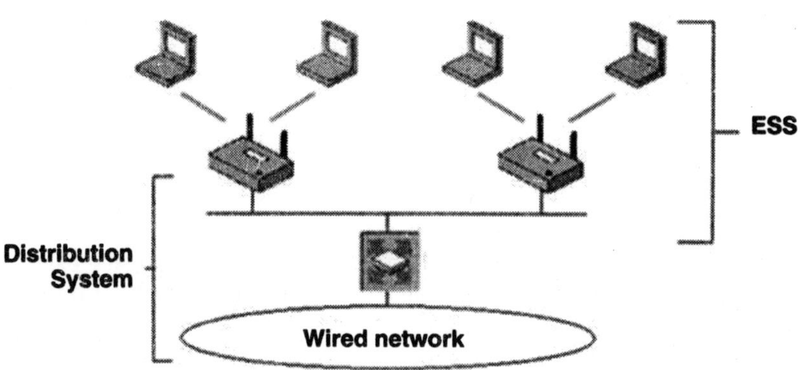

32-byte (maximum) character string. It is used to achieve greater mobility of mobile stations. This type of system is called distribution system where number of access points are used to forward traffic and facilitate the movement of mobile station within a larger area.

2. USER DENSITY

User density is the maximum number of users that can use wireless resources. As the number of clients accessing wireless resources increases, the available bandwidth decreases. So, for high user density, wireless is less appropriate, especially in case where a high bandwidth application has to be run. For the given bandwidth, wireless works best for relatively low bandwidth applications. Also, when all users are operating on the same channel, co-channel interference increases which degrades the performance. So, it is preferred to use Multi-channel RF architectures for high-density wireless requirements. These multi-channels utilize all the available channels to reduce co-channel interference.

3. APPLICATION RUNNING

There are many reasons that can make running of an application over wireless ineffective. Two main reasons are:

- Wireless LANs offer limited bandwidth.
- Wireless LANs uses shared media access and there is no traffic priority given for certain packets [5].

Due to these reasons, wireless networks have a possibility of becoming more congested and thus this congestion may be caused by running more than one application and these applications interfere with one other.

E.g. an audio/video application obtains an unfair share of the bandwidth and do not co-operate with other applications. Thus, N/W administrator should be able to obtain information of how much bandwidth each application in wireless N/W consumes. This information will enable to run other applications and allocate enough bandwidth to them. In order to run more applications effectively, it is better to prioritize packets based on 802.1P and 802.1Q standards.

- 802.1P defines how prioritization should occur within a MAC layer.
- 802.1Q defines standard for VLANs to add prioritization services in Ethernet in particular [6].

4. SELECTION AND OPTIMAL PLACEMENT OF APS

4.1 Selection

A very important factor is the selection of:

- Dual band radio access points
- Dual radio access points

Dual-band access points simultaneously support both 2.4 GHz (802.11b/g) and 5GHz (802.11a) RF bands. They are well suited to a wide range of network topologies. Whereas, Dual-radio access point is used in a building on temporary basis i.e., where there is no Ethernet connection. Moreover, Dual radio access points can provide twice the network capacity by simply setting both radios to 802.11g mode when networks do not require 802.11a mode. This approach is useful for areas with large number of users, such as adjoining classrooms or large lecture halls.

4.2 Placement

AP placement is an art, not a science. It is a major issue for proper WLAN deployment and there is a need to optimize the placement of access points. As from different analysis that has been carried out, the maximum distance between two APs should not be more than 300 feet. As the distance increases, it may degrade the effective throughput and bandwidth for the clients connected to their associated APs.

A wireless network relies on the integrated functionality of each access point to enable wireless services, authentication and security. Therefore, it is required to monitor and visualize traffic at each access point. For this, it is required to determine the idle access points as well as congested access points in a network. This information can be used for relocating the idle access points or adding more access points at the overloaded places of a network for better load sharing and adequate coverage. APs have a configuration parameter called the radio Channel that determines which part of the 802.11b bandwidth spectrum they are using. Adjacent APs should be set to different channels to maximize cross talk between them.

In last, the following adjustments must be made for strengthening the wireless signal i.e.

(a) *Increase the Number of APs*: More number of APs will increase the bandwidth but a care should be taken that they should be close enough to provide convenient wireless coverage but far enough that they do not interfere with each other.

(b) *Study the Cause of Signal Weakening*: The signal strength can be weakened because of the presence of metallic devices like doors, walls, elevators, etc. Moving such equipments and avoiding other obstacles can further enhance the signal strength.

5. ANTENNA SELECTION

The 802.11b and 802.11a standards are adaptive. In a good transmission environment close to the access point, the system uses its highest speed and best coding methods. As the distance or the noise level increases, the system successively drops the speed and coding to ensure robust communications as well as the physical coverage.

An antenna is a device used to radiate transmitted signals and capture received signals. Various types of Antennas are:

(a) *Omni-directional antenna:* It radiates signal in all directions.

FIG. 49.4
Omni-directional Antenna

AP

11 Mbps
@100 ft.

5.5 Mbps@150 ft.

2 Mbps@200 ft.

1 Mbps@300 ft.

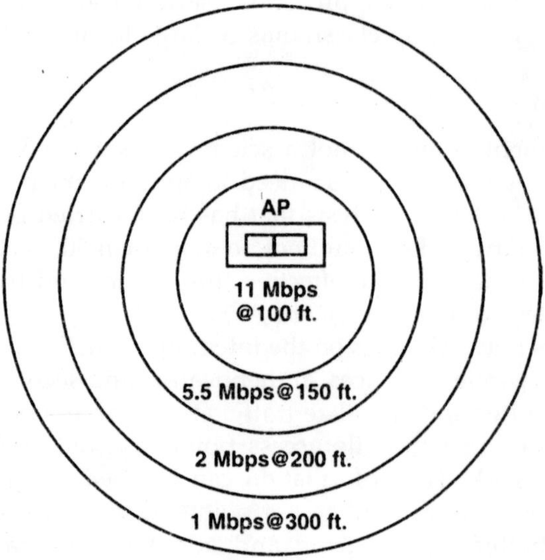

(b) *Directional antenna*: It radiates signals in specific direction, i.e. in lobes. A lobe is pattern that the radiation forms when omitted from a directional antenna as shown in Figure 49.5. The lobe can be either the main radiation lobe or side lobe. The width of the main lobe is called the bandwidth. The bandwidth of the antenna is 40 degrees.

Omnidirectional antennas are good for large coverage areas; bidirectional antennas are particularly good at covering corridors; unidirectional antennas are best at setting up point-to-point links between buildings, or even different sites. The antenna type determines its coverage pattern and radiation pattern. Depending upon this antennas are characterized by two terms:

FIG. 49.5
Antenna Lobe

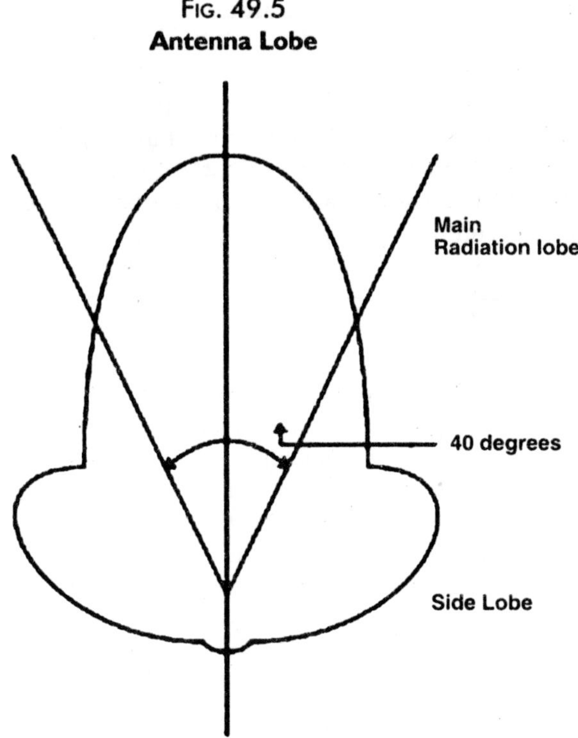

(i) *Beam Width* : It defines the coverage pattern of antennas and is measured in degrees. Antennas may have either horizontal beam width or vertical beam width. An antenna with less vertical beam width will send signal to a lesser height.

(ii) *Antenna Gain* : Gain of antenna is the effective signal power that comes out as the output. It is calculated in dB as:

$$\text{Gain} = 10 \log \frac{\text{Output Power}}{\text{Input Power}}\,.$$

Different types of antenna have different values of gain. High gain antenna can be used to improve the overall strength of a weak signal.

6. BANDWIDTH REQUIREMENT

It is important to determine the bandwidth requirement of each coverage area in wireless. No doubt that the number of users in a wireless network may change but the n/w administrator must approximate the long-term bandwidth requirement anticipated at various locations [7].

The bandwidth information can be estimated from :

- Existing wired network traffic.
- User density and their bandwidth requirement.

E.g. the bandwidth required for transmission of text-based documents is lesser as compared to the transmission of audio/video files [8]. Based on the above listed factors, a rough estimate of bandwidth per user and total number of users in coverage area is determined. A categorization of 802.11 standards has been done for various application specific environments.

7. POWER LEVELS

A primary goal of any wireless deployment is to provide proper signal coverage and bandwidth to all its users. One can extend the access point radio coverage by increasing the AP power level. The transmission power of the access point is directly proportional to the radio coverage. So, increase of power means that the radio coverage area will be larger. Government regulates the highest power level for the radio devices. There are different maximum power levels in America, Europe and Japan for different 802.11 standards. Higher frequencies need higher powers and have longer ranges. Standards with lower frequencies, like 802.11b and 802.11g have greater radio coverage. Coverage of 802.11a standard is lower because it has higher frequency.

Interference could also be the reason for reduced power on the access point. Adequate facility survey increases the transmitted power of an AP. Obstacle like building, walls; especially, steel reinforcing or some natural obstacles could even cause complete loss of signal.

A Network administrator can set-up the optimal power level on AP to get high and consistent bandwidth. The biggest impact on range of access point is the power of its transmitter. In many situation and application, radio coverage of one access point is not enough.

Following methods can be used for extension of WLAN radio coverage:

- *Repeater Mode (WDS)*: In wireless distribution system or access point in repeater mode, repeater AP is connected to the backbone over root access point to extend the wireless network range. Disadvantage is the use of repeater mode decreases overall bandwidth because AP needs to receive and send a packet on the same channel.
- *Distribute Access Points Optimally*: Distribution of access points is very important factor of the radio coverage area. It is important to determine the total number of access points needed for specific bandwidth to avoid congestion and interference. In order to make maximum radio coverage, access points can be placed to have 15% overlap among each other. Distribution of access points with minimum overlapping covers very large area with minimum cost.

Fig. 49.6
WDS

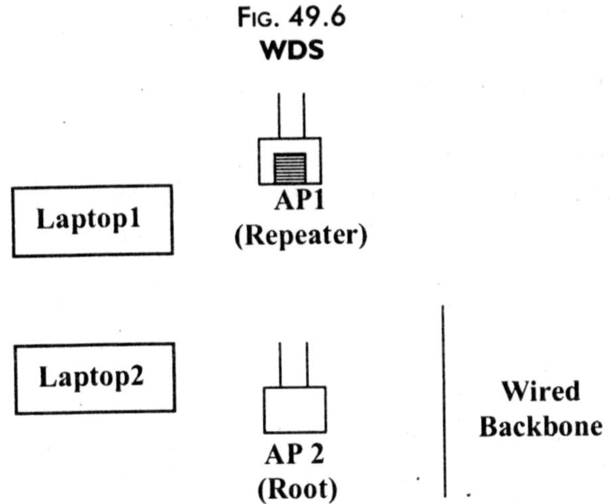

As a result, with the same SSID on all access points in an area, stations can move freely and make roaming among access points.

❖ *Use of Secondary Access Point Non-Overlapping Channels*: Use of secondary AP in access point mode with non-overlapping channels can make radio coverage much larger.

- Advantages
  - It is very easy to implement.
  - It does not require much of a configuration. Only the basic configuration on second access point is needed.
- Disadvangates
  - Wired network can reach to the secondary access point.
  - Interference would occur if two access points have overlapping channels and this leads to poor connectivity and lower bandwidth [9].
  - Congestion may occur if the distance between the two access points is not properly measured and hence, radio coverage area will be smaller.

8. CHANNEL ASSIGNMENT

The importance of channel assignment for improving the efficiency of spectrum usage in WLANs is of utmost importance. It is required to assign right channels on the access points. This will minimize the overlap of signals [10]. Access points within a range need to be configured with non-overlapping channels (i.e. 1, 6 and 11). The traffic aware channel assignment approaches could significantly improve the quality of a channel assignment in practice.

Channel assignment involves three main decision parameters:

- How to measure wireless interferences?
- How to cope with realistic wireless interference pattern?
- How to measure and predict traffic demands?

There exists many optimization metrics and efficient algorithms for channel assignment:

- *Static Channel Allocation*: Assigning channels to APs in WLANs has been a static one-time approach. Firstly, network administrator will conduct an RF site survey of the campus and determine the location and number of APs for adequate coverage. Then, the administrator manually configure the APs with 802.11's non-overlapping channels to ensure that APs operate on different channels
- *Traffic Aware Dynamic Channel Assignment*: It is found that traffic aware channel assignment is effective in real wireless network under a range of network configuration. It benefits both TCP and UDP flows. Traffic aware assignment also interacts well with multi-rate adaptation by reducing interference and allowing data communication to use higher data rates [10].

3-channels schema would be preferred for battery efficiency of WLANs over a single channel schema as shown in Figure 49.7.

FIG 49.7
Channel Assignment

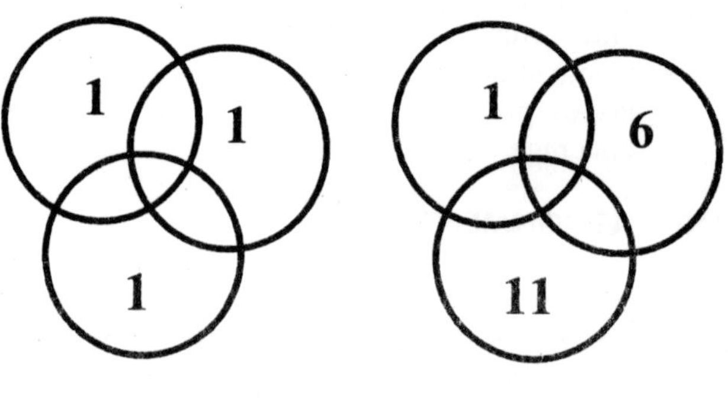

9. TOTAL COST OF OWNERSHIP

With the advancement in WLANs, there is one major issue that is coming to forefront, i.e. the cost. No doubt, the initial investment required for wireless LAN hardware is much higher than the cost of wired LAN hardware but, the overall expenses including the variable cost and life-cycle costs can be significantly lower. The proper evaluation for minimizing the cost involved for wireless LAN installation is not an easy task for engineers, network operation staff or finance departments of an organization.

The best way to control costs and manage bandwidth is to take advantage of existing wired infrastructure not only as the backbone for wireless LANs, but also as the provider of critical services for wireless LAN like security, quality of service (QoS) and management. When estimating TCO, an organization needs to plan in such a way that the overall cost involved for installing and managing WLAN should not increase the total cost of other infrastructure available. The cost elements involved in wireless networks are:

- Purchase of wireless equipments.
- Facility survey planning involves need of access points.
- Installation of the equipment i.e. mounting access points, antennas and running cables to access points.
- Service support and maintenance such as reconfiguring and upgradation of wireless LAN equipments.

Determining TCO: When making a wireless decision, it is important to consider all of the above component costs over a three-to-five year period. Because as the wireless network grows and evolves, bandwidth and

TABLE 49.2
Wireless vs. Wired TCO

	Wired LANs	*Wireless LANs*
1. Fixed Cost	Fixed Cost in wired LANs depend on following factors: • Number of nodes in LAN • Cost of Ethernet Card • Cost of Switches used	Fixed Cost in Wireless LANs depend on following factors: • Number of nodes in LAN • Cost of Access Points • Installation cost • Labour Cost • Cost of Wireless Ethernet card
2. Variable Cost	Variable Cost in wired LAN is the cost of move/change in wired port per year.	Variable Cost in Wireless LAN is the total cost of Wireless move/changes, which is equal to zero.
3. Total Expenses	Fixed Cost + Variable Cost	Fixed Cost + Variable Cost)

complexity should be factored into the TCO equation. Cisco has developed a TCO calculator which includes various models to determine the cost involved of an organization where wireless LANs need to be deployed [11]. The analysis has been made to calculate the cost involved for wired network data and wireless network data.

10. SSID AND SECURITY

Service Set Identifier (SSID) is the first level security and it is a name given to the logical group or a network. Each wireless network has an SSID to make it distinguish from other networks. Manufactures provide a default value for the SSID which remains stored in router. So, even if SSID is not broadcasted, an intruder who discovers the brand of access point or router can use the default SSID to gain access to the network. So it's better to change the default SSID name [12].

Wired equivalent privacy (WEP) [13] was the most commonly used 128-bit optional encryption standard for protecting a wireless network. But due to its weaknesses in wireless security, it has been eliminated by a new security specification called Wi-Fi Protected Access (WPA). WPA was designed to enhance the security of wireless networks.

A more secure message authentication code, i.e the encryption key is used and changed dynamically using Temporary Key Integrity Protocol (TKIP). The TKIP encryption algorithm is stronger than the one used by WEP. TKIP protocol actually has several functions.

1. First, it determines which encryption keys will be used and then verifies the client's security configuration.
2. Second, it is responsible for changing the unicast encryption key for each frame.

FIG. 49.8
Signs to Represent Nodes and it's Associated SSID

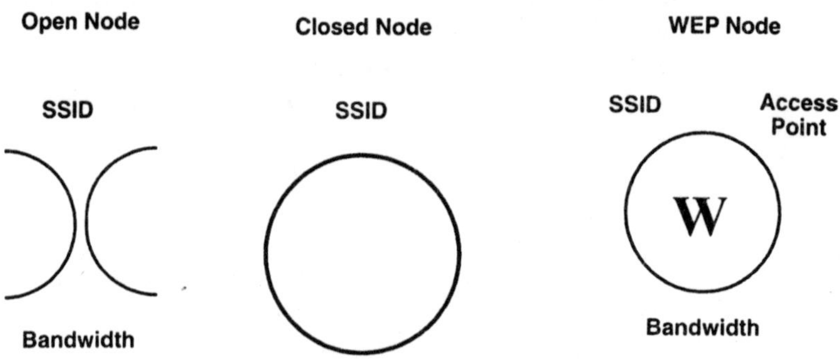

3. Finally, TKIP sets a unique starting key for each authenticated client that is using a preshared key.

There are signs, which can be used to represent the type of node in WLAN and its associated SSID.

11. CONCLUSION

Wireless LAN is an emerging technology and has grown tremendously in last few years. Employees can access data, receive/reply emails and can remain connected to their office while away from their desks. Various studies and factors studied in this paper are based on the needs of actual, large scale enterprise wireless LANs, and are essential in delivering a reliable, cost-effective and operational enterprise wireless network. The intent of this paper is to provide the researchers an overview of wireless state, motivate them and examine that how these deployment issues can be further enhanced to improve the wireless efficiency and degrade various interferences.

A wireless LAN can reduce the costs of deploying, monitoring, and managing the wired network, while simultaneously improving employee productivity through better collaboration and communication. However, to achieve these benefits, an enterprise must study pre-deployment issues of wireless LAN clearly. The enterprise of the future is one in which every employee will be a mobile user and in which every laptop and handheld device is wireless.

References

1. Wireless Site Survey: http://www.cisco.com/en/US/tech/tk722/tk809/technologies_q_and_a_item09186a00805e9a96.shtml.
2. Matthew Gast, "802.11 Wireless Networks: The Definitive Guide".
3. Jim Geier, "RF Site Survey Steps", Tutorial, May 10, 2002.
4. Eric Ouellet, Robert, "Building a Cisco Wireless LAN".
5. Tom Alexander, "Optimizing and Testing WLANs: Proven Techniques for Maximum Performance".
6. Robin Widoyo, "Measurement of Streaming Media Applications Running Over Wireless LANs".
7. Ashish Raniwala, Tzi-cker Chiueh, and Stony Brook University, "Deployment Issues in Enterprise Wireless LANs".
8. IEEE 802.11b/d3.0Wireless LAN Medium Access Control (MAC) and Physical Layer (PHY) Specification, Aug. 1999.
9. David, "Fundamentals of Wireless Communication".
10. Pejman Roshan, "802.11 Wireless LAN fundamentals".
11. www.wi-fiplanet.com
12. Brad, C. Johnson, System Experts Corporation, "Wireless 802.11 LAN Security-Understanding the Key Issues".
13. ReefEdge White Paper, "The Seven Deadly Sins of Wireless LANs".

50

Wireless Application Software Platform

RAMAN KUMAR AND HARSH KUMAR VERMA

ABSTRACT

Wireless Application Software Platform (WASP) is a software platform, which enables seamless integration of third party applications on to base band chipsets and it facilitates the high level software developers to develop hardware independent mobile applications, thus, allowing product manufacturing companies to built complete high level software in short period. It provides a standard device interface, operating system services to mobile handset applications and interface to modem.

This paper discusses the architecture, functional description and features of the wireless application software platform. It describes the three different levels of abstraction contained within its device driver software architecture—the Device Management Layer (DML), the Device Services Layer (DSL) and the Device Abstraction Layer (DAL), and also provides details about real time operating system services available through a RTOS (AOS) abstraction layer.

1. INTRODUCTION

As per the historical information retrieved yet, a semiconductor company's main aim was to sell their chipsets into the market and don't worry about the software that would make their product meaningful. It is left to the equipment manufactures to develop software, systems, debug and deliver end products to the market. Most of the software work done by these semiconductor companies was limited to just do pre-silicon and post-silicon validation of their hardware product and then support their customer while they are building their own software solution.

But, today the scenario is vastly changing because of the growing demand of the cutting edge consumer products and drastically reducing time to market requirements. Today product manufacturing companies need readymade software solutions available with chip so that they can sell their products in market on time and also add their value addition at higher levels of software functionality than worry about low level chipset drivers and their functionality, etc.

Analog Devices Inc. (ADI) is a leading semiconductor company that manufactures and provides chipsets solutions for mobile devices (cell phone industry) beside its other product lines. As the chipset owner, ADI has historically been involved in the support of customer or partner-driven development of each handset's platform software component. The customer of ADI also underwent the same problem mentioned above. To maximize the value provided to its customers and partners, ADI has recently decided to develop, package, maintain and supply its own standardized platform software as part of the customer's complete software solution. Thus, ADI came up with the software solution known as Wireless Application Software Platform (WASP). Wireless Application Software Platform (WASP) is one software solution to the above mentioned problem, which enables seamless integration of third party applications, easy migration to new chipsets and allows developing chip independent applications. [2]

2. WASP

Typically, handset software consists of platform software, modem protocol stack software, and mobile phone applications software. Platform software consists of device drivers and RTOS. Wireless Application Software Platform (WASP) provides the platform software. It acts as an interface between application software and hardware. It provides a standard device interface. OS services to mobile handset applications and interface to modem. It also provides low level access and control of chipset devices peripherals and hardware resources. [1]

Wireless Application Software Platform hides as many hardware details as possible and provides a platform on which High level software (i.e. modem software and application software) can be built. Wireless Application Software Platform permits application to use device without knowing all details of hardware. It facilitates the high level software developers to develop hardware independent mobile applications so that product manufacturing companies can built software in short period and can sell their products in market on time.

The Wireless Application Software Platform provides a foundation to the application layer by well defined standards to add, alter, remove or replace applications. It has Customizable & Extensible User Interface for easy interface and development of different applications. It also provides full freedom to replace any layer component within the Wireless Application Software Platform. It, also, provides freedom to replace RTOS.

Figure 50.1 show the architecture of software that resides in any mobile handset and how WASP resides in that architecture (shaded part indicates WASP).

FIG. 50.1
Architecture of WASP

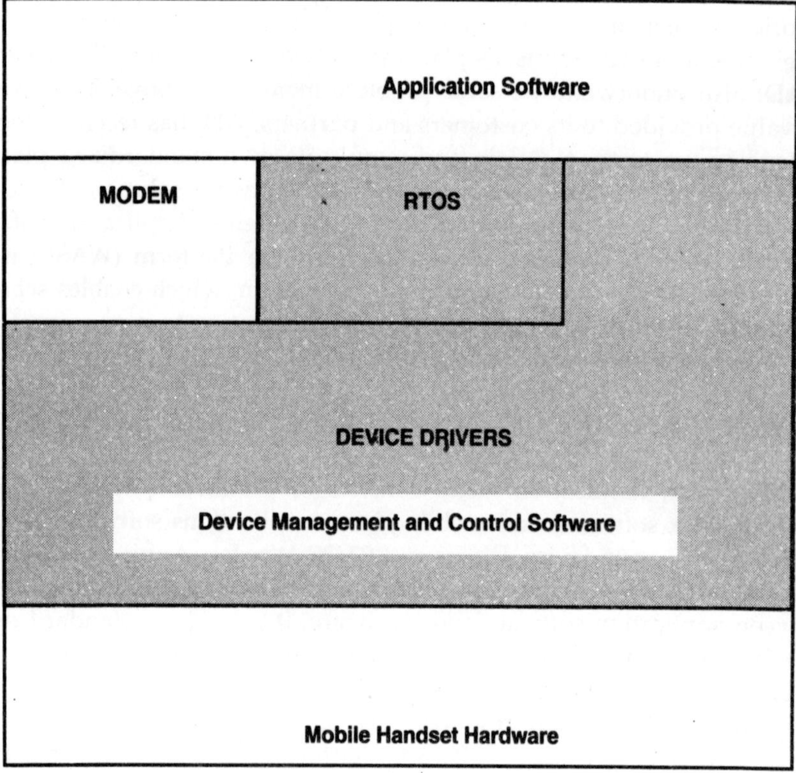

3. ARCHITECTURE OF WASP

WASP has layered architecture. The total hardware is abstracted in three layers. One layer abstracts the basic feature of real time operation system. Figure 50.2 shows the high level abstraction of WASP.

I. Device Management Layer (DMI),
II. Device Services Layer (DSL), and
III. Device Abstraction Layer (DAL).

Expose the software platform functionality at three different levels of abstraction.

3.1 Device Abstraction Layer (DAL)

This layer abstracts the underneath hardware to the upper layers. It includes a thin layer of Device definition layer which is generated automatically from the register database files. These files include the macros which write to specified layer DAL. This helps in minimizing the errors while reading/writing registers at bit level. DAL provides the independence from the architectural differences between different chipsets and provides access to upper layers through standardized APIs.

3.2 Device Services Layer (DSL)

This layer sits above the DAL layer and implements the desired services combining different DAL modules to provide a specific service to the higher layers. It also uses services of AOS layer. It has the responsibility

Fig. 50.2
High Level Overview of WASP

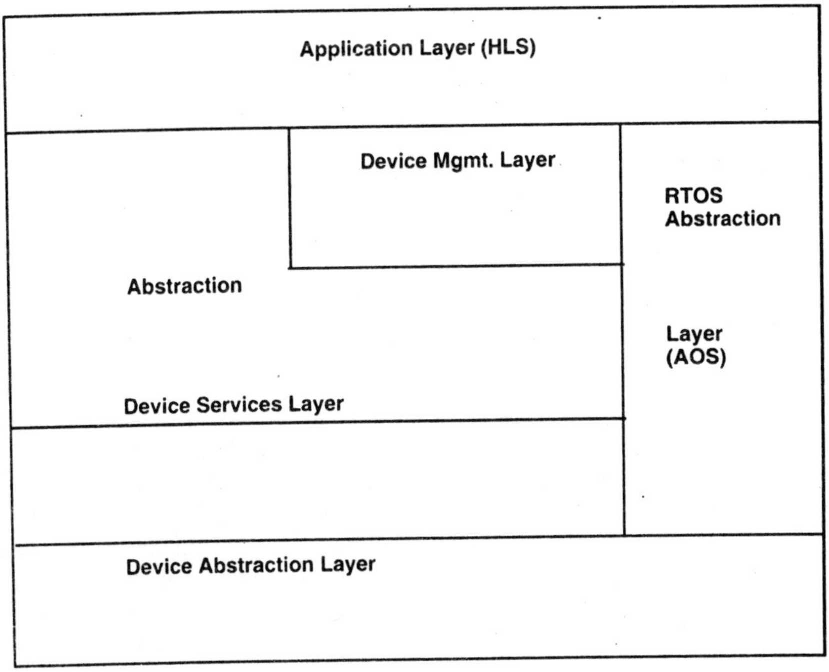

to combine services in different modules which fall under the same logical relationship. It also has well published API structures that are consistent across different hardware and DSL modules. It can make a direct function call to different lower layers and the AOS., DML (Device Management Layer).

3.3 Device Management Layer (DML)

The layer sits above DSL and DAL layers. This layer is responsible for managing different resources in the system. It has queue-based interface with HLS layer. The queue-based interface is chosen for providing synchronization between different services provided to the high layer software. The DML layer provides the feedback on the same queue based communications. Every module in the DML layer has its own queue between HSL and DML, for communication. It also provides optional API based interface with HLS if required but synchronization is not guaranteed in those services. The interface between DML & DSL, AOS is API-based only.[4]

3.4 AOS (Abstraction of Operating System)

This layer provides the basic functionality of operating system to different modules of WASP. It wraps different RTOS underneath and abstracts different services. This layer main purpose is to provide independence from different RTOS implementations and provides the independence of choosing different RTOS as per requirement. The main service from this layer includes task creation and management scheduler and data communication. The Figure 50.3 show the total architecture of WASP. It also shows the interface between the different layers of WASP and interface between wasp layers and High level Software.

4. FUNCTIONAL DESCRIPTION OF WASP

This section describes the functional outlines of modules in each layer and the implementation of modules, those comes under each layer.

4.1 DAL (Device Abstraction layer)

DAL is a set of hardware abstraction modules. DAL abstracts the hardware to the upper layers. Each module in this layer is independent of other module which provides functional independence to each module from any other module. This approach provides modularity in the architecture and causes minimum impact while porting to different platform.[3]

DAL defines a standard function call based API. APIs are defined as to provide uniform API interface across all the modules on all the platforms. All modules in DAL follow the same name, and the numbers of API that are provided to other layers are limited. This gives the consistency throughout

Fig. 50.3
WASP Architecture and Interface between Different Layers

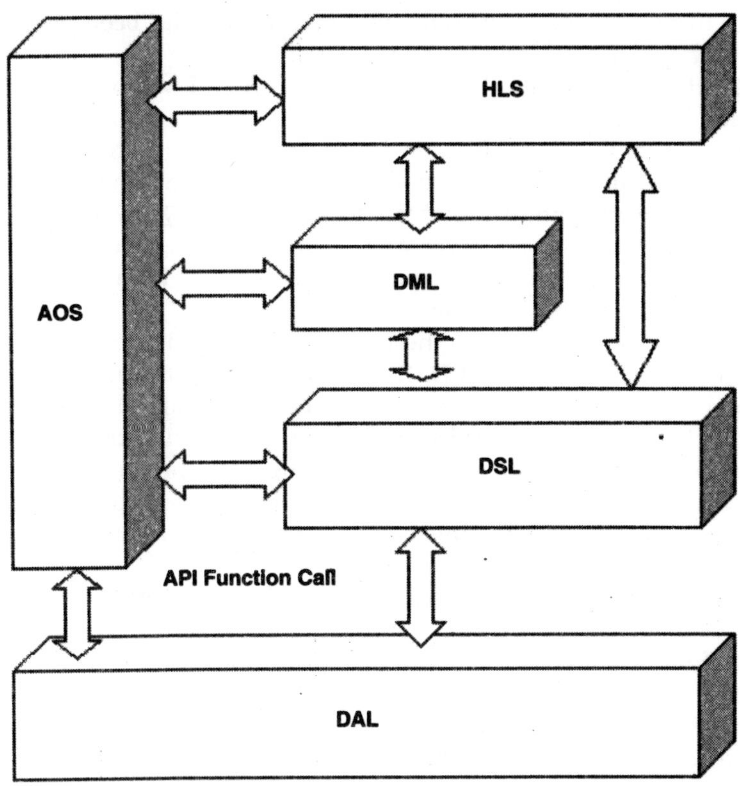

the layer and on different architecture. Only those APIs will be visible outside the module of DAL to its upper layers.

DAL provides following operations as applicable: DAL does the initialization of the hardware; it configures the devices and provides different control operations on the devices as per their functionality. It also provides interrupt handling and includes enabling, reading and clearing interrupts register. It makes sure that it hides as many hardware specific details as possible to upper layers.

DAL provides minimal device resource management in form of device open and close functionality which is based on sharing or exclusive access to devices. It also provides the critical section problems as applicable in its control and definition limits of its scope. DAL provides optimized register abstraction and access which includes consuming minimal code space and approximately zero data size.

4.2 DSL (Device Services Layer)

DSL is a set of service modules. DSL abstracts different services that logically fall in the same group of functionality. Each module in this layer is independent of other module which provides functional independence to each module from any other module. This layer makes use of different DAL modules to provide the services to other module and has been provided the intelligence which was lacking in DAL layer.

DSL defines a standard function call based API. All modules in DAL follow the same name, and the numbers of APIs that are provided to other layers are limited. These APIs are defined as to provide the uniform API interface across all the modules on all the platforms. Only these APIs will be visible outside the module of DSL to its upper layers. This gives the consistency throughout the layer and on different architecture. DSL APIs provides only control commands which can be used by high layers, thus, the API call will always be consistent.

Each service module does the following: DSL provides services to the upper layers such as HSL and DML. DSL layer hides the exposure of DAL from higher layers and is the only layer through which higher layer can access the DAL layer. The services includes the configuration of the devices together with initialization request, installing and configuring interrupts, and device specific services which are logically bound to different modules within the DSL. No DSL module can call other DSL module directly. Each module is independent from other module.

DSL module uses the services from DAL layer and AOS for its services and hides device specific details as much as possible within the context of its definition. It supports events in the ISR context via registered callback functions. This provides the ability to respond to different stimuli from the system which also includes resolution of the events depending on the priorities of the events and facilitates event driven implementation to the higher layers.[8]

4.3 DML (Device Management Layer)

DML is a set of device managers. DML layer manages the resources of the system and does the resource allocation for the HLS layer. It uses the services of DSL and AOS layer in order to provide the desired services to the upper layers. The modules in this layer allow concurrent use of itself when called by different HLS modules. DML layer defines a standard prioritized message-based APIs which are interfaces with queue. It is done in order to synchronize multiple requests from one or more HLS layer application for a particular resource. Upon receiving a message on its queue, it parses the message and provides the resources and calls desired services APIs (DSL) needed to complete the request.

Each device Manager module does the following: They provide services to HLS and other managers in DML. In this layer one module can take the services of the other modules but needs to be called through queue interface only this keeps the overall system definition consistent irrespective of internal or external calls from other layers. Also this approach provides the ability to synchronize all the requests in the system. They allows HLS to perform operations on the devices such as configuring the devices, transmit or receive data from the device if applicable, sending control commands for controlling the devices for different services.

4.4 DML Queue Interface with HLS

DML module interfaces with HLS through message-based calls and the interface with other entities in WASP is straightforward API-based calls. DML sets up communication channels between HLS and hardware which is totally transparent to HLS. It doesn't expose the complexity and implementation of underneath layers to the HLS layer. Logical channel abstracts interaction between HLS and DML. AOS services are used to provide this abstraction. Logical channel here serves as the basis of the identification number which would be given to all the individual channels which leads to the DML from the same or different applications. This logical channel is given at the time of registration of the queue and then used as a mean of basic communication entity for the particular queue channel. DML

FIG. 50.4
DML Abstraction

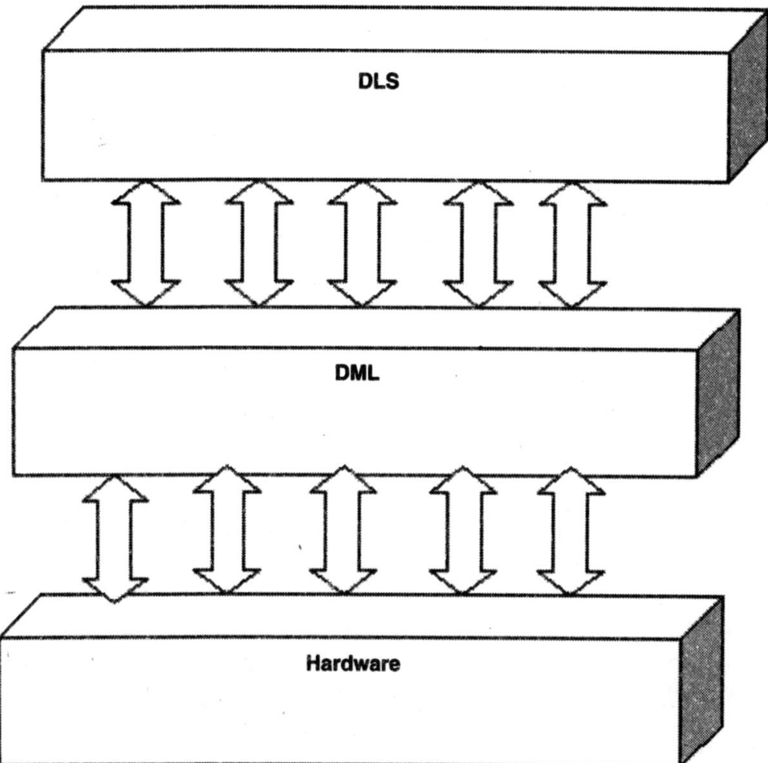

allows flexible routing of the channels by either one-to-one, one-to-many or many-to-one on logical and physical channels. This means that a queue can be used to notify or serve only one application, or more than one application, else several queues can be used to serve several different applications.[5]

4.5 AOS (Abstraction of Operating System)

The software platform employs a real-time operating system abstraction layer called AOS. The functionality AOS is to abstract the underneath RTOS services and provides consistent API interface to applications. Services are available through function call APIs. The AOS layer can house one or more RTOS under it. It also provides the communication. The AOS maps the services provided to the external interfaces with the internal RTOS services by directly calling this APIs. AOS provides the following services:

1. Error handling by providing the ISR callback functions which makes the error handling an easy task and event-based system.
2. *Memory Allocation*—It creates and initializes the stacks and heaps in the system. It also keeps track of dynamic memory allocation and freed memory.
3. *Threads*—Essentially task creation and initialization. Different task states and scheduling is provided by the RTOS.
4. Mail allocation/send/and receive for inter-task and inter-process communication such as by building mail bridge.
5. Queues for inter-task communication.
6. Semaphores and Mutexes for resource allocation such as critical region handling and resource management. Mutexees also help in synchronization.
7. Timers for timekeeping and scheduling processes, introducing delays, etc.
8. Start up and system configuration.

4.6 HLS (High Level Software)

This layer sits on the Wireless Application Software Platform and includes different applications which will use WASP services while executing on the phone. It mainly consists of third party software which includes Man Machine Interface (MMI) and application software. This layer provides the flexibility in terms of integrating third party application software, thus this platform can be used with any third party application software, thus this platform can be used with any third party and with any consumer, providing them the freedom to use their own choice of application software and allows them to customize their phone as they want[9].

5. FEATURES OF WASP

The Wireless Application Software Platform has layered Architecture which will enable developers to scale it as per the requirement and will make functionality of different modules independent of each other. Modularity of architecture, i.e. all the layers have modular components while porting to different platform. All the layers have been well-defined, published ("open") layer interfaces that avoid confusion while porting to different chipset and cater to consistent implementation. Each layer has defined, published ("open") component, interfaces to make it consistent and easy to use.

The Supplies application layer solution providers, with a software platform, upon which, a complete software application (i.e. high level software) can be developed, provides standard driver interfaces to ensure that the higher layer software will use the same interfaces irrespective of the device they are running on. Application using this interface need not to be modified when moving to a new platform, as long as the new driver provides the same interface.[6]

Provides an OS-independent API for operating system services. Thus, the platform is independent from any specific RTOS.

6. RESULTS

The Wireless Application Software Platform has been successfully implemented by Analog Devices for its GSM wireless chipsets and now it is being provided to the customers along with the GSM chip. WASP software helped Analog Devices Inc. partner meet aggressive schedules for the project. It provided significant value addition to wireless chipset customers in terms of time, cost and effort savings. Due to Wireless Application Software Platform, the customers of Analog Devices Inc. saved 6 to 8 month's time in delivering the final mobile product. Wireless Application Software Platform has a positive impact on the sales of the Analog Devices Inc.'s GSM chipsets.

7. CONCLUSION

The Wireless Application Software Platform is well-designed platform software. It is a layered, modular architecture, allows easy integration of third-party software on to Analog Devices Inc. GSM chipsets. The WASP like architecture is very much needed in the companies which have their own product lines especially in hardware industry. The requirement is also backed by the fact that the company, who has produced hardware, knows better how to utilize their hardware better compare to a third party or a customer himself. This type of architecture provides greater satisfaction from customers as their job becomes easy where they will just need to integrate their own application and as Wireless Application Software

Platform is a layered and modular architecture. It also provides customers to customize the system as per their own requirement. So, this architecture will be helpful as per the requirements of the new hardware companies

References

1. WASP Design Documents, Analog Devices Ltd.
2. Arnold, S. Berger Embedded System Design: "An Introduction to Processes, Tools and Techniques", CMP Books, 2001 Ed.
3. Geoff Huston at http://computer.org/internet/ by IEEE internet Computing.
4. M. Allman, ed., "Ongoing Research Related to Satellites", RFC 2760, Feb. 2000; available online at http://www.ietf.org/rfc/rfc2760.
5. P. Karn *et al.*, "Advice for Internet Subnet Designers", work in progress, July 2000.
6. H. Balakrishnan, V. Padmanabhan, S. Seshan, and R. Katz, "A Comparison of Mechanisms for Improving Performance Over Wireless Links" in Proceedings of ACM SIGCOMM'96, Stanford, California, Aug. 1996.
7. Wikipedia Foundation, Inc., "IEEE 802.11", Wikipedia, the free encyclopedia, http://en.wikipedia.org/wiki/802.11, December 7, 2007.
8. Jurgen, Ronald, "Automotive Electronics Handbook", McGraw-Hill, New York, NY, 2006, ISBN 0-07-034453-1.
9. Abraham Silberschatz, James L. Peterson, Peter B. Galvin, "Operating System Concepts", John Wiley & Sons, Sixth Ed.

SECTION VII

Managing a World Class IT Development

51

A Study of the Role of Information Technology in Business Process Reengineering

A.S. PANDEY

ABSTRACT

Business Process Reengineering (BPR) is a discipline in which extensive research has been carried out and numerous methodologies churned out. It has rapidly developed towards a new management philosophy. The inherent business process orientation changes the perspective of international management from a structural to a process view of headquarter-subsidiary relations. However, the re-engineering of business processes is only one aspect of the management of business processes. This paper discusses the enabling role of information technology in BPR. The BPR framework and its phases have also been discussed. The information technology depends on the character of business processes. The re-engineering of international business processes needs special attention because the multi-faceted deeper structure of business organisations increases the complexity of business processes, thus influencing the options for redesign.

1. INTRODUCTION

In 2007, the world market for consultancy in Business Process Re-engineering was about ten billion dollars and is expected to double by 2015.

Business Process Re-engineering has rapidly developed towards a new management philosophy, based upon predecessors like Total Quality Management, Overhead Value Analysis, Just-In-Time-Management. Speakers at seminars and authors use the term Business Process Re-engineering (BPR) in different ways, presenting cases of minor process improvements as well as radical changes in management philosophy and organizational structure. Most publications on BPR reflect the author's practical experience. The academic discussion is just about to start. However, both practitioners and academics have until now neglected the international dimension of business processes.

Both the characteristics of international management and the process orientation underlying the philosophy of BPR have been the reasons to present a paper at this conference.

In today's ever-changing world, the only thing that doesn't change is 'change' itself. In a world increasingly driven by the three Cs: Customer, Competition and Change, companies are on the lookout for new solutions for their business problems. Recently, some of the more successful business corporations in the world seem to have hit upon an incredible solution: *Business Process Reengineering* (BPR). BPR advocates that enterprises go back to the basics and reexamine their very roots. It doesn't believe in small improvements rather it aims at total reinvention. As for results: BPR is clearly not for companies who want a 10% improvement. It is for the ones that need a ten-fold increase. BPR focuses on processes and not on tasks, jobs or people. It endeavors to redesign the strategic and value-added processes that transcend organizational boundaries.

Definition of the Business Process Reengineering (BPR): According to Hammer and James Champy, "Reengineering is the fundamental rethinking and radical redesign of business processes to achieve dramatic improvements in critical, contemporary measures of performance, such as cost, quality, service, and speed." This definition comprises four keywords: fundamental, radical, dramatic and processes.

Fundamental: Understanding the fundamental operations of business is the first step prior to reengineering. Business people must ask the most basic questions about their companies and how they operate: Why do we do what we do? and why do we do it the way we do? Asking these basic questions lead people to understand the fundamental operations and to think why the old rules and assumptions exist. Often, these rules and assumptions are inappropriate and obsolete.

Radical: Radical redesign means disregarding all existing structures and procedures, and inventing completely new ways of accomplishing work. Reengineering is about business reinvention, begins with no assumptions and takes nothing for granted.

Dramatic: Reengineering is not about making marginal improvements or modification, but about achieving dramatic improvements in performance. There are three kinds of companies that undertake reengineering in general. First are the companies that find themselves in deep trouble. They have no choice. Second are the companies that foresee themselves in trouble because of changing economic environment. Third are companies that are in the peak conditions. They see reengineering as a chance to further their lead over their competitors.

Processes: Process is the most important concept in reengineering. In classic business structure, organizations are divided into departments, and process is separated into simplest tasks distributing across the departments. The preceding order—fulfilment example shows that the fragmented tasks—receiving the order form, picking the

FIG. 51.1
BPR Framework

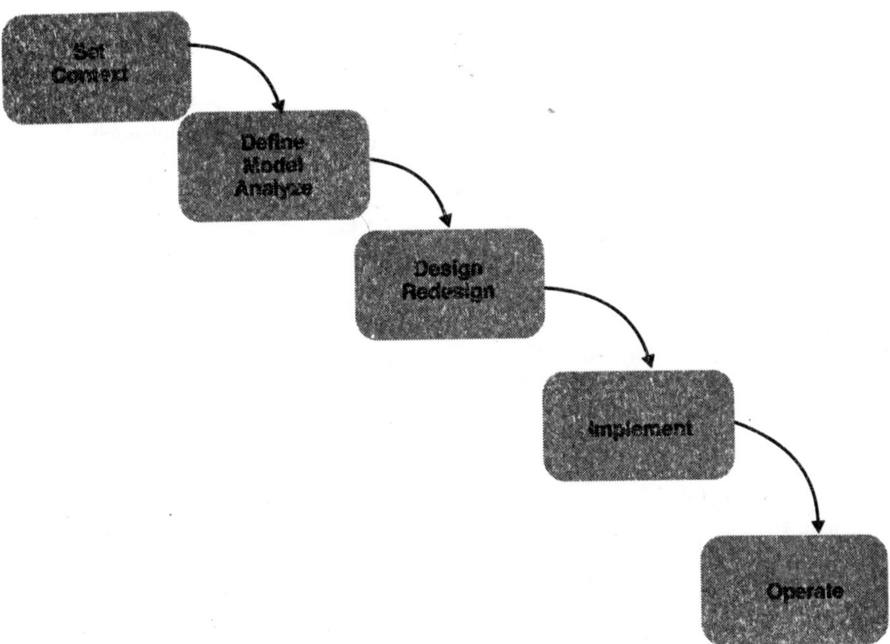

goods from the warehouses and so forth—are delayed by the artificial departmental boundaries. This type of task-based thinking needs to shift to process-based thinking in order to gain efficiency. The above example has been taken from Hammer and Champy to illustrate the characteristics of reengineering— fundamental, radical, dramatic, and especially process.

2. BPR FRAMEWORK

2.1 The Phases of BPR

There are numerous references and instructions written on the subject of improving business processes. Nearly all of them portray the BPR project as a series of steps or phases that an effort should go through to achieve good results. Although one may find a variety of labels, the ones in the figure below generally typify the process. Note that the entire process occurs in an environment where change is constantly managed and the evaluation phase is not a last step, but an ongoing activity that continually refines and adjusts the new processes.

FIG. 51.2
The Business Process Redesign Phases

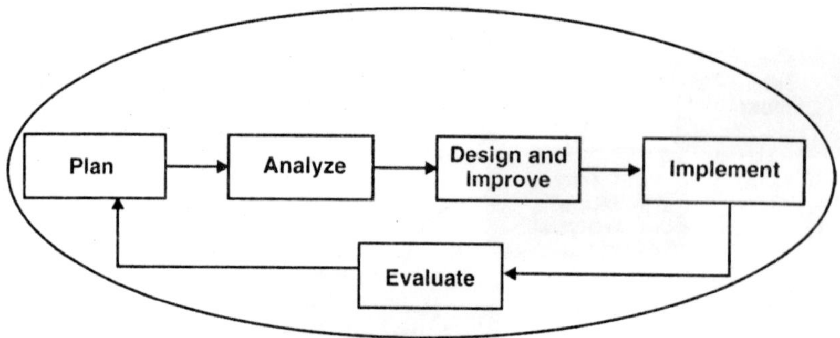

In each of the phases, effective use of collaborative methods and tools can shorten the project schedule and improve overall results.

2.2 The Enabling Role of Information Technology (IT)

The role of IT is discussed in contradictory ways. Advocates of information systems favour the view that new IT is an enabler of process re-engineering. IT has to be monitored constantly to determine whether it can generate new process designs or how it can contribute to the performance of a business process. The breakthrough of BPR is tightly connected with IT, which opens new dimensions of process reorganization. Others are convinced that first, the redesign of processes should be accomplished before IT is used to optimize the new process.

After reviewing the interviews, it is not easy to decide who is right or wrong. Business processes differ with respect to their internal structure. The proportion of information, operations and management activities varies tremendously over time between and within business processes. Consider the processes of product launch and of production: at the beginning of the product launch process, there are more information and management activities and later during the process; there are more physical operations. In contrast, production processes have a continuous flow of physical operations producing and receiving a comparatively low amount of management information. The hardware and software of IT have a spectrum of abilities to support informational or operational or, even, managerial activities with respect to the individual business processes. Therefore, it is very difficult to generalize whether IT enables or just supports BPR.

Moreover, the role of IT is influenced by those who take the initiative in process improvement or redesign. If the data processing department initiates the process change, then, IT has more of a generator function for new process redesigns. If top management sets off the change process, then, the process is first restructured and afterwards optimized through IT. In two cases, parallel change processes were reported; developing IT and process redesign simultaneously. It can not be taken for granted that IT is adapted.

2.3 Is Information Technology an Enabler or a Bottleneck?

It is reasonable to view IT as a disabler, which is never used to "challenge why things are done in a company, but instead justify the way they are done. Systems in the service sector have been used to generate more unneeded reports, speed up superfluous work steps, generate unnecessary information, encourage shoddy thinking and misdirect attention to spurious details. It has been found that the greatest improvement came when the IT group has been provided the tools, the information, and the authority to implement change, rather than by core process reengineering. The IT group was able to implement client server applications relatively early—because individuals took ownership, responsibility and accountability. Most analysts view reengineering and information technology as irrevocably linked. Walmart, for example, would not have been able to reengineer the processes used to procure and distribute mass-market retail goods without IT. Ford was able to decrease its headcount in the procurement department by 75 percent by using IT in conjunction with BPR, in another well known example.

IT can prove to be useful in the reengineering analysis and design process. Graphics software and CASE tools can produce process maps; spreadsheets and costing software allow for activity-based cost analysis; databases can track customer satisfaction and complaints; "blind" e-mail bulletin boards can be used to capture employee suggestions. In addition, e-mail and groupware can facilitate communication and coordination across geographical and organizational barriers.

During the implementation stage, companies should follow the following basic rules:

- Recognize that IT is only part of the solution: It allows managers to collect, store, analyze, communicate and distribute information better.
- Cut and paste the IT tools needed.
- Bring in internal or external IT experts: their knowledge, skills, acumen, and experience are invaluable.
- After implementation, continually monitor IT performance and keep up with new IT developments.

On the other hand, some companies have found it useful to design a technology strategy before reengineering. The "democratization" of IT from the mainframe to the PC is breaking down the communications barriers between corporate functions, suppliers, and even customers. This ability for information to be at many places at the same time—which allows companies to reap the benefits of both centralization and decentralization—is at the heart of BPR.

2.4 Reengineering Recommendations

- BPR must be accompanied by strategic planning, which must address leveraging IT as a competitive tool.
- Place the customer at the center of the reengineering effort—concentrate on reengineering fragmented processes that lead to delays or other negative impacts on customer service.
- BPR must be "owned" throughout the organization, not driven by a group of outside consultants.
- Case teams must be comprised of both managers as well as those who will actually do the work.
- The IT group should be an integral part of the reengineering team from the start.
- BPR must be sponsored by top executives, who are not about to leave or retire.
- BPR projects must have a timetable, ideally between three to six months, so that the organization is not in a state of limbo.
- BPR must not ignore corporate culture and must emphasize constant communication and feedback.

3. CONCLUSION

The reengineering profoundly changes all aspects of business and people. Part of the organisation is easy to change by reinventing a way to work. However, the other part, people, is very difficult to change. In particular, it requires not only jobs and skills change but also people's styles—the ways in which they think and behave—and their attitudes—what they believe is important about their work. These are indispensable factors to determine whether reengineering succeeds or not. Leaders must help people to cope with these changes.

An intense customer focus, superior process design and a strong and motivated leadership are vital ingredients to the recipe for the success of any business corporation. Reengineering is the key that every organization should possess to attain these prerequisites to success. BPR doesn't offer a miracle cure on a platter nor does it provide a painless quick fix. Rather it advocates strenuous hard work and instigates the people involved to not only to change what they do but targets at altering their basic way of thinking itself.

Information Technology (IT) plays a crucial role in business reengineering and is an essential enabler. However, most people misuse the technology. They look at the technology through the lens of their existing tasks, i.e. they only computerise the old existing tasks.

State of the art information technology allows to break conventional rules/assumptions of processes. These rules were designed when the processes were created. Therefore, the rules may no longer be valid nowadays.

IT should not be involved in redesign process. Redesigning process is like programming. While solving a problem, we first outline and design the solution at the top level, then implement it by a suitable language, e.g. C or Prolog. The language itself should never constrain the design. It is the same idea that specific IT should not constrained the redesign in reengineering. After the redesign, we then should seek for the best technology to implement it. Similarly, past investments in IT should not be allowed to constrain the redesign. Reengineering is about to reinvent processes. IT is just a tool.

References

1. Feldmann, Clarence G., (1998), The Practical Guide to Business Process Reengineering using IDEF0, Dorset House Publishing, New York.
2. Hammer, M. and Champy, J., (1993), Reengineering the Corporation: A Manifesto for Business Revolution, Harper Collins, London.
3. Hunt, Daniel V., (1996), Process Mapping: How to Reengineer your Business Process, John Wiley and Sons Inc., New York.
4. Manganelli, Raymond L. and Klein, Mark M., (1994), The Reengineering Handbook: A Step-by-Step Guide to Business Transformation, American Management Association, New York.
5. Martin, James, (1995), The Great Transition: Using the Seven Disciplines of Enterprise Engineering to Align People, Technology, and Strategy, American Management Association, New York.

6. Mayer, Richard J. and Dewitte, Paula, S., (1998), Delivering Results: Evolving BPR from Art to Engineering.
7. Obolensky, Nick, (1994), Practical Business Reengineering, Gulf Publishing Company, Houston.
8. Cone, Edward, Technology Chief of the Year; All the Right Moves—Tom Trainer of Reebok International Successfully Teamed Business.
9. Reengineering with Information Technology, *Information Week*, December 26, 1994; p. 35.

52

Significance of Business Process Reengineering

RAJESH VERMA AND R.K. CHAUHAN

ABSTRACT

Business Process Reengineering (BPR) is the redesign of business processes and the associated systems and organizational structures to achieve an impressive improvement in business performance. The business reasons for making such changes could include poor financial performance, external competition, and erosion of market share or emerging market opportunities. BPR is not downsizing, restructuring, reorganization, automation, new technology, etc. rather it is the examination and change of five components of the business:

1. Strategy
2. Processes
3. Technology
4. Organization
5. Culture

1. INTRODUCTION

Michael Hammer defines Business Process Reengineering (BPR) as "Fundamental rethinking and radical redesign of business processes to bring about dramatic improvements in performance."

Hammer focuses on one of the key concepts of BPR, that it is fundamental and radical. The alternative business improvement methodology is Continuous Improvement Process, which emphasizes small and measurable refinements to an organization's current processes and systems.

BPR, as a term and as a practice, has an imperfect history. Reengineering became very popular in the early 1990s. However, the methodology and approach was neither fully understood nor appreciated. Many times, improvement projects labeled with the title BPR were poorly planned and executed.

Despite this abuse of the practice and tarnished name, the practice of redesigning business processes and the associated technology and organizational structure is more popular today than ever. Companies continue to re-examine and fundamentally change the way they do business. Competitive pressures and a lethargic economy provide impetus for continued efforts to deliver more with less. Reengineering remains an effective tool for organizations for effective and efficient development.

Example of Business Process:

> The process steps are the activities that you and the store personnel do to complete the transaction. In this simple example, we have described a business process. Imagine other business processes: ordering clothes from mail order companies, requesting new telephone service from your telephone company, developing new products, administering the social security process, building a new home, etc.

Business processes are simply a set of activities that transform a set of inputs into a set of outputs (goods or services) for another person or process using people and tools. We all do them, and at one time or another play the role of customer or supplier.

You may see business processes as a set of triangles as shown Figure 52.1. The purpose of this model is to define the supplier and process inputs, your process, and the customer and associated outputs. Also shown is the feedback loop from customers.

Fig. 52.1
Business Process

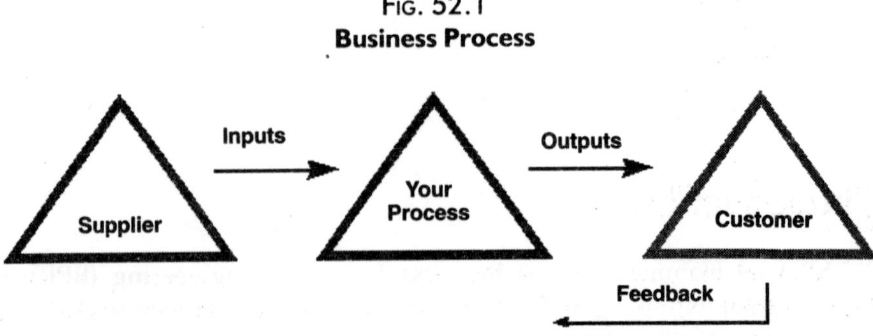

2. BUSINESS PROCESS IMPROVEMENT

Improving business processes is principal for businesses to stay competitive in today's marketplace. Over the last 10 to 15 years, companies have been forced to improve their business processes because we, as customers, are demanding better and better products and services. And, if, we do not receive what we want from one supplier, we have many options to choose (hence the competitive issue for businesses). Many companies began business process improvement with a *continuous improvement model.* This model attempts to understand and measure the current process, and make performance improvements accordingly.

The Figure 52.2 illustrates the basic steps. You begin by documenting what you do today, establish some way to measure the process based on what your customers want, do the process, measure the results, and then identify improvement opportunities based on the data you have collected. You, then, implement process improvements, and measure the performance of the new process. This loop repeats over and over again, and is called continuous process improvement. You might, also, hear it called business process improvement, functional process improvement, etc.

FIG. 52.2

Continuous Process Improvement Model

This method for improving business processes is effective to obtain gradual and incremental improvement. However, over the last 10 years, several factors have accelerated the need to improve business processes. The technologies (like internet, web) are rapidly bringing new capabilities to businesses, thereby, raising the competitive bar and the need to improve business processes dramatically. Another obvious trend is the opening of world markets and increased free trade. Such changes bring more companies into the marketplace, and competing becomes harder and harder. In today's marketplace, major changes are required just to stay. It has become a matter of survival for most of the companies.

As a result, companies need the methods for faster business process improvement. Moreover, companies want breakthrough performance changes, not just incremental changes, and they want it now. Because the rate of change has increased for everyone, few businesses can afford a slow change process. One approach for rapid change and dramatic improvement that has emerged is Business Process Reengineering (BPR).

3. BUS!NESS PROCESS REENGINEERING (BPR)

PR relies on different aspects of change than continuous process improvement. In the extreme, reengineering assumes that the current process is irrelevant because it is outdated and it does not fulfil the new requirements of customers. Such a schedule perspective enables the designers of business processes to disassociate themselves from today's process, and focus on a new process. In a manner of speaking, it is like projecting yourself into the future and asking yourself: what should the process look like? What do my customers want it to look like? What do other employees want it to look like? What might we be able to do with new technology?

FIG. 52.3
Breakthrough Reengineering Model

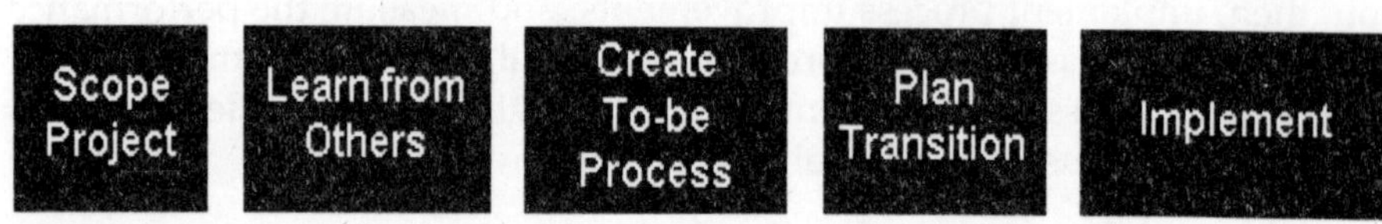

Such an approach is shown in Figure 52.3. It begins with defining the scope and objectives of your reengineering project, then going through a learning process (with your customers, your employees, your competitors and non-competitors, and with new technology). Given this knowledge-base, you can create a vision for the future and design new business processes.

In summary, the extreme contrast between continuous process improvement and business process reengineering lies in where you start, and with the magnitude and rate of resulting changes. Over time, many derivatives of radical, breakthrough improvement and continuous improvement have emerged that attempt to address the difficulties of implementing major change in corporations. It is difficult to find a single approach exactly matched to a particular company's needs, and the challenge is to know what method to use, and how to pull it off successfully such that bottom-line business results are achieved.

4. MORE PREVALENT MYTHS OF BPR

Myth #1: Business process engineering is either a relatively new concept or a passing fad. The need to transform organizations is not new and, driven by advances in technology, will only increase. What is new is the expanding discrepancy between the speed of technological innovation and organizational change responses. The tools, concepts and methodologies for transformation, the degree of innovation, the naming conventions and the manner in which they are packaged and presented will continue to vary but the need will not decline.

Myth #2: Terms such as Business Reengineering, Business Process Redesign, Total Quality Management, Business Transformation, Process Change Management are interchangeable. Although these terms as they have entered the popular lexicon, are often interchangeably used, together they represent a family of change methods that transform work processes and organizations in ways that range from incremental to radical. The more discontinuous the change required, the more likely that changes in organizational structure, strategies, business capabilities, and cultural norms will be necessary to capitalize on the business opportunities resulting from reengineering work processes. James Martin has chosen to group these various methods under a larger umbrella term known as Enterprise Engineering.

Myth #3: IT drives enterprise engineering. "Technology permits changes in work, and work must change radically in order to take advantage of technology." It is often very tempting for management to sidestep difficult but necessary decisions by seeking to reengineer an organization through systems implementation (i.e. let the system force the decisions). "Information Technology provides the infrastructure and tools, which fundamentally change organizations, but management provides the strategic business vision that transforms technology into competitive advantage" should be the mantra of every CIO and IT manager. Systems implementations make business and breakthrough process change possible and business managers should partner with IT, not the reverse. But the reality is that when there is not a clear business vision driving decisions within an organization, it is often difficult for IT to decline the leadership role in enterprise engineering efforts.

As a result, IT is often blamed for the failure to successfully transform an organization through implementation of systems when in fact, it is the lack of strategic business vision and leadership from the outset that led to the failure to achieve desired outcomes. Thus, IT managers and organizations should not accept responsibility for driving an organizational transformation without understanding the accompanying risks and only after failing to recruit the necessary business leadership and vision to lead the effort.

Myth #4: Work processes can be reengineered without significant organizational changes and organizational changes do not require changes in work processes. It is difficult to successfully reengineer existing processes to take advantage of the potential opportunities presented by technology without rethinking the existing hierarchical organizational structures and rigid processes and procedures ill-suited to meet the integrated information needs of business users. In looking for examples of dramatic breakthrough improvements achieved by organizations, more often than not you will find fundamental changes in work processes have been implemented and the organizational structure was modified to implement those changes. This is in sharp contrast to typical organizational realignments that reshuffle the upper layers of an organization but rarely impact actual work processes or the flow of information. As a result, most organizations go through multiple management reorganizations without changing work processes or technology is used to automate outdated processes, which are then forced to operate within inappropriate organizational structures.

Many of the core administrative processes in higher education institutions where new systems are being implemented in response to Y2K problems were designed before the advent of technology or designed to take advantage of centralized mainframe computing capabilities have now become obsolete. Upon closer examination, you will find that where technology exists it has been superimposed on existing work processes rather than adapting the work to take advantage of technological opportunities. Ironically, there is the real possibility that significant investments in new ERP systems, which reinforce outdated procedures, will hinder rather than enable needed change.

Myth #5: The focus of enterprise engineering is information technology. Too often people view Enterprise Engineering as associated primarily with information, digital technology, networking, and communication rather than recognizing it is primarily about people and their changing role in organizations. In many knowledge-based organizations today, expenditures associated with people represent the largest expenditure of resources. Pursuing technological potential without exploiting human potential will not yield the outcomes sought from enterprise engineering efforts. Failure to consider the human and cultural issues within an enterprise almost always results in a failure to successfully implement organizational change.

The purpose of Enterprise Engineering should be to increase the value of people whether through process or policy redesign, automation, expert systems, training, or access to information. In order to be successful, organizations will increasingly need to develop the potential of their employees, increase their knowledge and provide a work environment that facilitates learning and experimentation at every level in the organization. It is important not to lose sight of the fact that the potential of an organization represents the sum of the potential of its people.

This approach runs directly counter to the current trend in both public and private sectors to "downsize" or "right-size" organizations by reducing the number of employees instead of choosing to change the workplace and processes to increase the value of an organization's employees. Requiring people to "do more with less" is perhaps the least imaginative and effective response to competitive or resource challenges.

5. IMPACT OF BPR ON ORGANIZATIONAL PERFORMANCE

The two cornerstones of any organization are the people and the processes. If individuals are motivated and working hard, yet the business processes cumbersome and non-essential activities remain, organizational performance will be poor. Business Process Reengineering is the key to transforming how people work. What appear to be minor changes in processes can have dramatic effects on cash flow, service delivery and customer satisfaction. Even, the act of documenting business processes alone will typically improve organizational efficiency by 10 percent.

5.1 To implement a BPR project

The best way to map and improve the organization's procedures is to take a top down approach, and not undertake a project in isolation. That means:

- Starting with mission statements that define the purpose of the organization and describe what sets it apart from others in its sector or industry.
- Producing vision statements which define where the organization is going, to provide a clear picture of the desired future position.
- Build these into a clear business strategy thereby deriving the project objectives.
- Defining behaviors that will enable the organization to achieve its' aims.
- Producing key performance measures to track progress.
- Relating efficiency improvements to the culture of the organization.
- Identifying initiatives that will improve performance.

5.2 Tools to Support BPR

When a BPR project is undertaken across the organization, it can require managing a massive amount of information about the processes, data and systems. If you don't have an excellent tool to support BPR, the management of this information can become an impossible task. The use of a good BPR/documentation tool is vital in any BPR project.

The types of attributes that should be looked for in BPR software are:

- Graphical interface for fast documentation.
- "Object-oriented" technology, so that changes to data (e.g.: job titles) only need to be made in one place, and the change automatically appears throughout all the organization's procedures and documentation.
- Drag and drop facility, so that you can easily relate organizational and data objects to each step in the process.
- Customizable meta data fields, so that you can include information relating to your industry, business sector or organization in your documentation
- Analysis, such as swim-lanes to show visually how responsibilities in a process are transferred between different roles, or where data items or computer applications are used.
- Support for value stream mapping.
- CRUD or RACI reports, to provide evidence for process improvement.
- The ability to assess the processes against agreed international standards.
- Simulation software to support 'what-if' analyses during the design phase of the project to develop LEAN processes
- The production of word documents or web site versions of the procedures at the touch of a single button, so that the information can be easily maintained and updated.

6. CONCLUSION

To be successful, business process reengineering projects need to be top down, taking in the complete organization, and the full end to end processes. It needs to be supported by tools that make processes easy to track and analyze.

References

1. Martin, James, The Great Transition, Using the Seven Disciplines of Enterprise Engineering to Align People, Technology and Strategy, American Management Association, 1995.
2. Davenport, T.H. and Short, J.E. (1990 Summer), "The New Industrial Engineering: Information Technology and Business Process Redesign, *Sloan Management Review*, pp. 11-27.
3. Kerns, David and Nadler, David A., Prophets in the Dark, (Harper Business: New York, 1992). Martin, James, p. 248.
4. Harari, Oren, "Ten Reasons Why TQM Doesn't Work", *Management Review*, January 1993.
5. Usilaner, Brian, "What's the Bottom-Line Payback for TQM?", *Engineering Management Journal*, Vol. 5, No. 2, June 1993.
6. Malhotra, Yogesh (1996). Business Process Redesign: An Overview [WWW document].URL http://www.brint.com/papers/bpr.htm

7. Champy, J. and Hammer, M., Reengineering the Corporation, Harper Business: New York, 1993.
8. Nadler, D.A. and Tushman, M.L., Managing Strategic Organizational Change, New York: Delta Consulting Group, 1986.
9. King, W.R. (1994 Spring). "Process Reengineering: The Strategic Dimensions", *Information Systems Management*, 11(2), pp. 71-73.
10. Bashein, B.J., Markus, M.L. and Riley P. (1994 Spring), (Preconditions for BPR Success and How to Prevent Failures", *Information Systems Management*, 11(2), pp. 7-13.
11. Martin, James, pp. 472-89.
12. Deutsch, Claudia H., "Software That Can Make A Company Cry", *New York Times*, November 8, 1998.

53

Customer Relationship Management : A Key to Success

SEEMA KAILEY

ABSTRACT

Customer Relationship Management (CRM) is the philosophy, policy and coordinating strategy connecting different players within an organization so as to coordinate their efforts in creating an overall valuable series of experiences, products and services for the customer. It is a multifaceted process, mediated by a set of information technologies that focuses on creating two-way exchange with customers so that firms have an intimate knowledge of their needs, wants, and buying patterns. In this way, CRM helps companies to understand as well as anticipate the needs of current and potential customers. In this paper, detailed information about customers, types of customers that are internal and external, and the various players of CRM within the organization, technological considerations in which operational, analytical, collaborative CRM have been discussed. This paper also contain some objectives like acquiring new customers, optimize existing customers, retain existing customers, optimize margins, etc. Some CRM success factors are like creating a customer focused organization, know your markets and your customers, caring for existing customers, providing complete product information, implement a coordinated and customer-focused business strategy, create a CRM-friendly organizational structure, anticipate an evolutionary CRM implementation, providing services after sales, etc. have been discussed.

1. INTRODUCTION

"A LITTLE BIT OF QUALITY WILL MAKE THE CUSTOMERS SMILE AND A LITTLE BIT OF COURTESY WILL BRING THEM FROM A MILE—ANONYMOUS".

The so called typical customer no longer exists and the companies have been learning this lesson the hard way. Until very recently, business was concerned about "is" than "who". In other words, companies were focused on selling as many products as possible, without any regard to who was buying that. Maximizing profitability with low cost was the real name of the game. But with dwindling profits and increasing costs, the executives soon realized that these tactics were not enough to satisfy either the customers or the share-holders. Moreover, customers expectations rose by leaps and bounds, thereby leaving no option for the market, but to introduce flexibility and ability in their operations and practice proactive marketing strategies to smoothen their position in the market. The increased number of customer defections forced organizations into taking measures to retain its customers, thereby making way for techniques like CRM, which mainly deals with retaining customers by ensuring their *satisfaction*.

2. CUSTOMER RELATIONSHIP MANAGEMENT (CRM)

The competition driven by technology has forced the corporate world to think on new grounds for value creation, maintenance and even survival of their respective businesses. CRM is the philosophy, policy and coordinating strategy connecting different players within an organization so as to coordinate their efforts in creating an overall valuable series of experiences, products and services for the customer. It is a multifaceted process, mediated by a set of information technologies, that focuses on creating two-way exchange with customers so that firms have an intimate knowledge of their needs, wants, and buying patterns. In this way, CRM helps companies understand, as well as anticipate, the needs of current and potential customers. Functions that support this business purpose include sales, marketing, customer service training, professional development, performance management, human resource development, and compensation. Many CRM initiatives have failed because implementation was limited to software installation without alignment to a customer-centric strategy. CRM is an information industry term for methodologies, software, and usually internet capabilities that help an enterprise manage customer relationships in an organized way. For example, an enterprise might build a database about its customers that described relationships in sufficient detail so that management, salespeople, people providing service, and perhaps the customer directly could access information, match customer needs with product plans and offerings, remind customers of service requirements, know what other products a customer had purchased, and so forth. CRM consists of:

- Helping an enterprise to enable its marketing departments to identify and target their best customers, manage marketing campaigns to generate quality leads for the sales team.
- Assisting the organization to improve telesales account, and sales management by optimizing information shared by multiple employees, and streamlining existing processes (for example, taking orders using mobile devices).
- Allowing the formation of individualized relationships with customers, with the aim of improving customer satisfaction and maximizing profits; identifying the most profitable customers and providing them the highest level of service.
- Providing employees with the information and processes necessary to know their customers, understand their needs, and effectively build relationships between the company, its customer base, and distribution partners.

CRM is the broad category of concepts, tools, and processes that allows an organization to understand and serve everyone with whom it comes into contact using the internet and e-business, to provide products and services and information to customers, require that you really know and understand your customers' needs.

Who is a Customer?

Now question arises that who is the "C" in CRM? For the purposes of discussing CRM, we need to think of the customer in the broadest sense. Our definition needs to include suppliers, partners, investors, employees, and others we deal with in our definition. These are the internal customers of an organization. Each of these groups has specific and unique requirements like work environment and their satisfaction level regarding the facilities provided by the organization to them and it is the responsibility of the organization to deliver what they need so that they can do their jobs properly. If we talk about external customer, means to whom our internal customer provide the services or those outside the organization who buy the goods and services the organization sells, treating people with respect, passing on defect free work and so on is absolutely crucial if the customer is to receive excellent service, right first time. The quality of the service which reaches the customer is often determined by 'Silent Service' the quality of the service that members of the organization provide to each other. Employees will not care for their customers if they do not believe their company cares about them.

FIG. 53.1
The Internal Customer

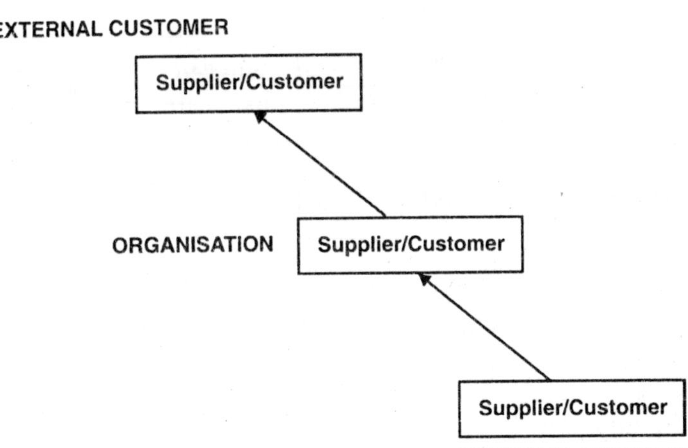

The external customer is much more likely to receive a good service if the provider of that service within the company has in turn received excellent service from his or her internal customer. When customers contact your traditional business by visiting the store or office or contacting someone personally by phone, you have the opportunity to hear their questions and offer solutions based on personal communication. If they have a misunderstanding about your product or a sales objection, you can deal with it immediately. When people visit your online business at your website, you will not even know who they are. You do not have the opportunity to ask or answer questions. It is, therefore, vitally important that you anticipate their questions and concerns and provide the needed information in a way that makes it easy for them to fully understand your offering. Customer Relationship Management is a way to get the maximum value from your e-business investment. CRM is about gathering information that is used to serve customers—basic information, such as name, address, meeting and purchase history, and service and support contacts. In a supplier relationship, it might be procurement history, terms and conditions, or contact information. This information is, then, used to better serve the client keeping in mind—the 80/20 principle—means 80% of sales come from just 20% of customer base. So, the philosophy of doing business that is developing and maintaining relationship is known as Relationship Marketing. It is all about making good and amicable relation with every partner of the organization. Based on this philosophy, CRM is evolved to build and maintain long-term valuable customer relationship. It is focused on keeping and improving existing customers as they are treated as partners of business.

FIG. 53.2
The Link Between Internal and External Customer Care

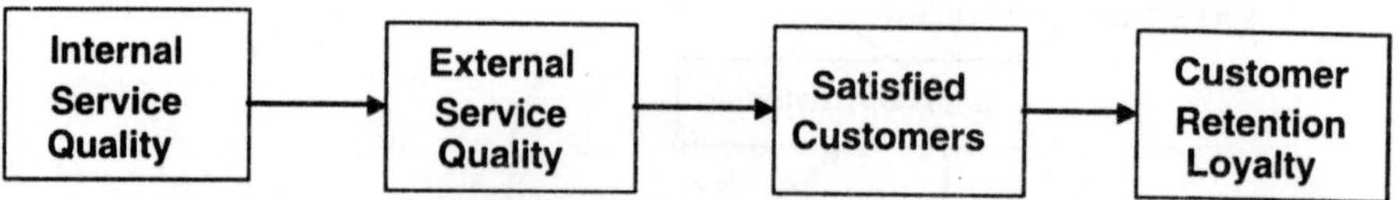

3. CUSTOMER DEVELOPMENT PROCESS

CRM is the art of one to one marketing or loyalty marketing, which involves understanding the customer individually, interacting with them and customizing the products and services to suit their needs with the ultimate aim of retaining them for a long period of time. Thus, it starts with the process of attracting customers and continuing building relations with them till the time they become an integral part of the organization.

FIG. 53.3
Customer Development Process

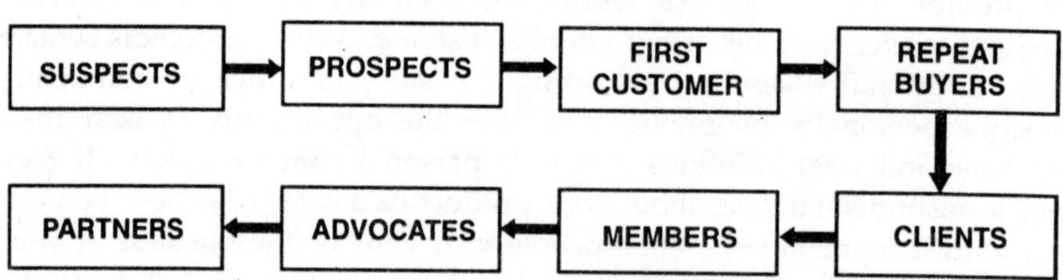

The starting point is including all the people who might conceivably buy the product or service {suspects}. From these the company determines the most likely prospects, which it hopes to convert into first time customers and then into repeat customers and then into clients—people whom the company treats very specially and knowledgeably. The next challenge is to turn clients into members by starting a membership program that offers benefits to the customers who join in and then advocates, customers who enthusiastically recommend the company and its products to others. The ultimate aim is to turn advocates into partners, people who will act as owners and will contribute in creating a niche market for organization.

4. THE FOUR KEY CRM OBJECTIVES

1. *Acquiring New Customer* : The main objective of CRM is to aquire new customers by launching new products,, prospecting and leading generation, new sales product modification, adopting new promotional techniques.

FIG. 53.4
CRM Objectives

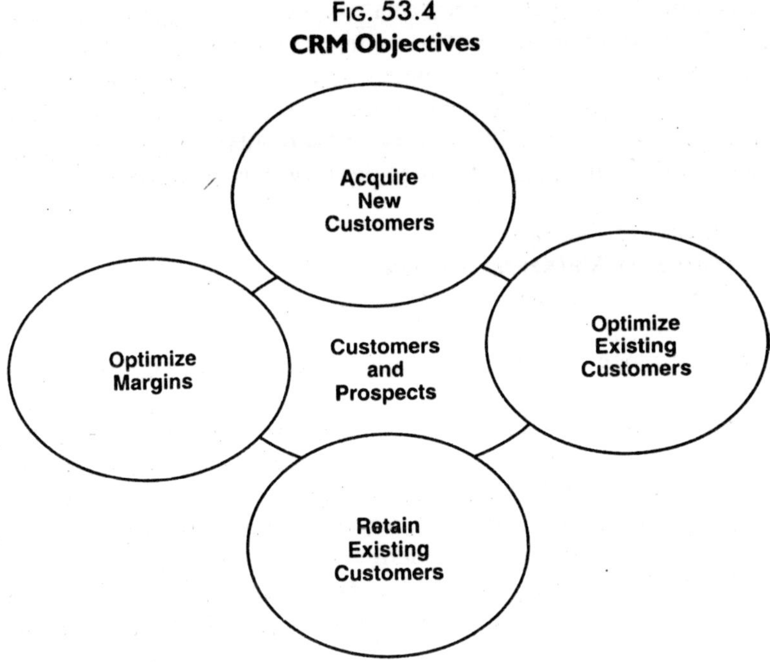

2. *Optimize Existing Customers:* The cost of acquiring new customers can be high. It takes ten times more efforts, costs, and money to attract a new customer than to keep an existing customer. To keep an existing customer the strategies can be increase product usage, discounts, product modification, etc.
3. *Retain Existing Customers:* Retaining existing customers is one of the important objective of CRM means to provide the retention, loyalty, customer care and services to existing customers.
4. *Optimize Margins:* It means channel migration, measurement of the results, product and service satisfaction.

5. TECHNOLOGY CONSIDERATIONS IN CRM

A database for customer lifecycle (time series) information about each customer and prospect and their interactions with the organization including order information, support information, requests, complaints, interviews and survey responses need to be created.

5.1 Operational CRM

Operational segment of CRM includes how data or information is being collected and used by different entities in the organization or the specific application areas of CRM system. It provides support to front office business processes including sales, marketing and service. Each interaction with a customer is generally added to a customer's contact history, and staff can retrieve information on customers from the database when necessary. One of the main benefits of this contact history is that customers can interact with different people or different contact channels in a company over time without having to describe the history of their interaction each time. Operational CRM processes customer data for a variety of purposes:

- Managing Campaigns
- Enterprise Marketing Automation
- Sales Force Automation

The three major operational or application areas of CRM system are:

- *Sales Automation*: The thrust of sales applications is automating the fudamental activities of the sales professionals that may include calender and scheduling compensation and account management, proposal generation and management, pricing and expense reporting, territory assignment and management.
- *Marketing Automation:* CRM aids marketing professionals while formulating and integrating campaigns and other marketing avtivities.
- *Service Automation:* This works for the purpose of customer retention and profitability by serving customers on better grounds.

5.2 Analytical CRM

Fig. 53.5
The Basic CRM Model

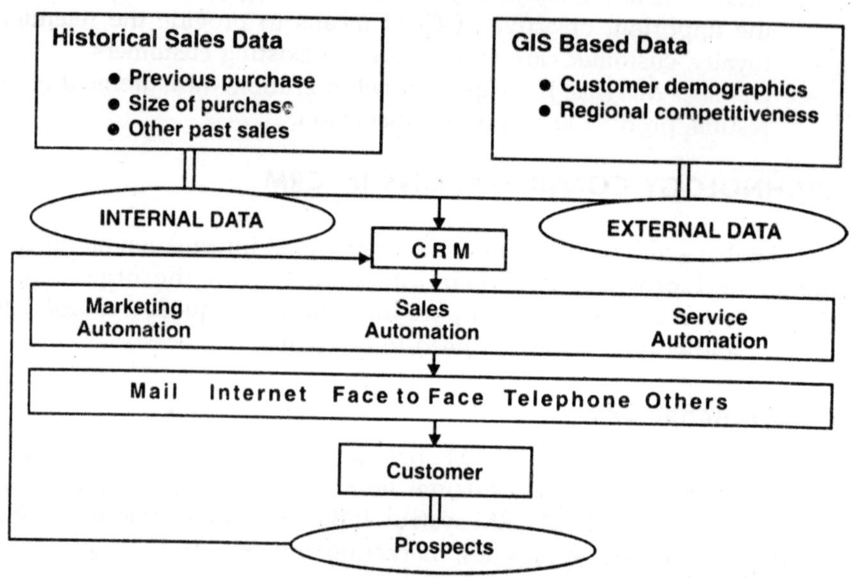

Data is fed in the CRM system taken from internal (sales history, records, etc. and the external resources through market research regarding customers demographics, competitors and Government data. This data is collected, summarized and analyzed to form meaningful information that is further used to segment the customers and build marketing compaigns for customer acquisition, extention and retention.

Analytical CRM analyzes customer data for a variety of purposes:

(a) Design and execution of targeted marketing campaigns to optimize marketing effectiveness.
(b) Design and execution of specific customer campaigns including customer acquisition, cross-selling, up-selling, retention.
(c) Analysis of customer behavior to aid product and service decision making (e.g. pricing, new product development etc.).
(d) Management decisions, e.g. financial forecasting and customer profitability analysis.
(e) Prediction of the probability of customer defection (churn analysis)
(f) Analytical CRM generally makes heavy use of data mining.

5.3 Collaborative CRM

The function of the Customer Interaction System or Collaborative Customer Relationship Management is to coordinate the multi-channel service and support customer by providing the infrastructure for responsive and effective support to customer issues, questions, complaints, etc. Collaborative CRM integrates various departments within a business, such as sales, technical support and marketing, to share the useful information that they collect from interactions with customers. Feedback from a technical support center, for example, could be used to inform marketing staffers about specific services and features requested by customers. Collaborative CRM's ultimate goal is to use information collected from all departments to improve the quality of customer service.

5.4 Geographic CRM

Geographic CRM (GCRM) is a customer relation management information system which collaborates Geographic Information System (GIS) and traditional CRM. CRM combines data collected from route of movement, types of residence, ambient trading areas and other customer and marketing information which are matched with relevant road conditions, building formations, and a floating population. Such data are conformed with a map and is regionally analyzed with OLAP (On-Line Analytical Processing) for visualization. This enables a company to examine potential customers and manage existing customers in the region.

6. CRM SUCCESS FACTORS

More and more organizations are turning to CRM solutions to drive revenue growth, productivity, and customer satisfaction. A great number of these organizations have achieved significant results. Some organizations, however, have not achieved all of the benefits they had hoped for. Instead, they have encountered problems ranging from cost overruns and integration challenges to poor user acceptance. There are several success factors to consider in CRM. The organizations that implement CRM with a strong return on investment share these characteristics.

A. Creating a Customer-focused Organization

ÇRM is about giving specialized attention to individual customers. The organizations can get success if they adopt a customer focused organization means the mantra of "The Customer is King" must be their in the organization according to which customer is always right.

- *Implement a coordinated, customer-focused business strategy*. An organization must have business strategies that promote CRM across functional boundaries. Goals that include phrases like "customer-focused" or "customer satisfaction" are indicators that CRM is important. However, if there are no underlying strategies in place that force a customer view across business functions, the organization is not likely to move far from the traditional product focus.
- *Create a CRM-friendly organizational structure*. The overall organizational structure must promote cross-functional cooperation, independent product-oriented business units, multiple marketing and sales organizations and distributed customer care centers that can inhibit an organization's ability to determine and carry out the next promotion or service activity for the customer. With the autonomy and control possessed by each business unit executive, the telecommunications company lacked the organizational structure required to implement cross department initiatives:

  - *Business Imperative and Top Team Clarity:* It is clear that unless there is a business imperative for customer retention and top management is fully committed to customer care, there is a little chance of success. Customer orientation needs to have a organization's mission, vision, value and key objectives.
  - *Listening Posts*: Organization with the best practices activity measure both internal and external customer satisfaction. They use data to make improvement and drive chance.
  - *Service Strategy and Goal:* To be successful, service-oriented

organization need to have a clear strategy and a set of specific and measurable goal for the service improvement.

- *Customer Driver Processes:* The way an organization does business with its business should match the customer needs. Technology can help as new customer channels such as the internet and contact centers have brought about new ways of doing business with the customer.
- *People Development*: An organization can benefit from training and development to enhance the employees' attitudes towards the customer' behavior, knowledge and skills. The quality of leadership in an organization often an indicator of its customer orientation.
- *Empowerment*: Giving people responsibility for decisions affecting their work encourages a customer focus and ongoing improvement.
- *Communication:* Communication among organization and customer, competitors and the best practices in customer service can help to create an impetus for change.
- *Reward and Recognition:* Organization with the best practices creates a motivating climate for their employees by recognizing and rewarding customers-oriented behavior.
- *Sustaining a customer focus:* To be more successful, the organizations recognize the need to sustain a focus on the customer at all the times.

Fig. 53.6

The Customer Focused Organization

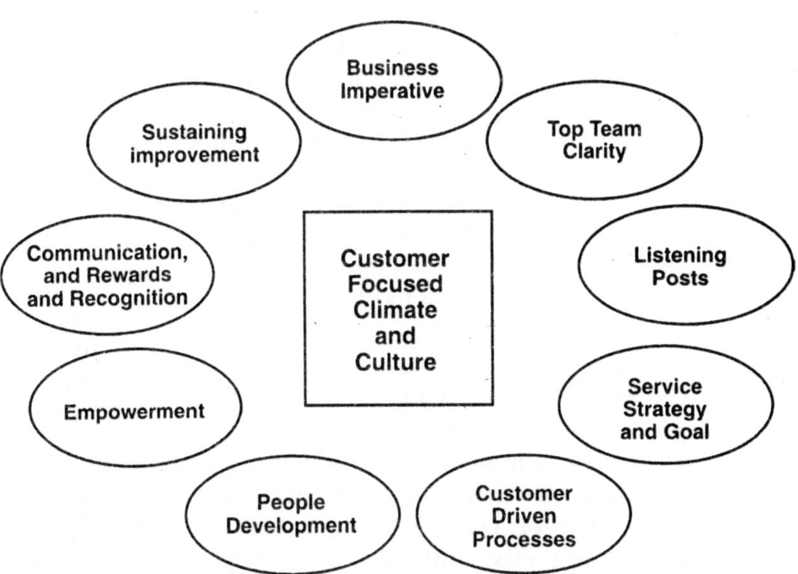

Benefits of a Customer-Centered Organization: In increasing competitive marketplaces, best practice organizations have demonstrated clear benefits of focusing on the customer. Excellent service enables a business to:

- Differentiate it from the competitors.
- Improve its image in the eyes of the customers.
- Minimize price sensitivity.
- Ensure products and services are delivered 'right first time'.
- Create a reputation for being a caring, customer-oriented company.
- Encourage employee's participation.
- Bring continuous improvements to the operation of the company.
- Achieve a maximum number of advocates for the company.
- Foster internal customer/supplier relationships.

B. Maintain a Complete, Integrated View of the Customer

An "enterprise" view of customer relationships is essential that begins with judicious technology investments. Many CRM platforms require time-consuming data aggregation and consolidation, which reduce relevance. Effective CRM requires a complete customer view, integrating demographics, purchasing behaviors, value scores, channel preferences, and communications history. This view should drive communications, personalization, timing, and content of offers. Serious economies of scale are achieved by deploying programs based on customer groups, but membership within groups must be individualized. A single view simplifies customer information management in the advent of privacy legislation, and ensures customer interaction preferences are reflected. The payback for investing in an enterprise view grows dramatically over time. Knowledge about the customers can be obtained via IT system which carries out customer value management, data warehousing and data mining. With this help, the companies are able to extract information about their customers from across the business, segment their customer base and predict individual customer behavior. There are some decisions to be taken regarding the information collection:

- *Where to get the data and information*: Generally, as the data and information become more tailored to your business and more accurate, they also become harder and expensive to obtain a list of common sources of customer information are:

  1. *Gorernment Reports*: City, country, state, and federal govt. all produce demographic based on geography that can help to know how community has changed over the years.
  2. *Private Reports*: There are many companies that provide detailed information on population based on zip code or telephone prefix unlike the Government data they will give

more precise information on education level, age, income, type of employment, etc. that can help a business pinpoint trends that could affect marketing efforts.

3. *Trade Associations*: Many trade associations conduct yearly suryey to determine trends in their industry and some other sources are employees, survey etc.

- *Putting the customer first with CRM*: Putting the customers first is a prerequisite for any successful CRM implementation. Don't wait for your customer to tell you how to do things in right way. While applying CRM, it is important to think like a customer.

C. Providing Complete Product Information

This is also a success factor in CRM because providing complete product information is a tool for the company to gain the maximum response of the new as well as existing customers. The information can be given like offering personalized products listing, sorting products by related category and providing comparison information across products.

D. Caring for Existing Customers

It takes ten times more efforts, costs, and money to attract a new customer than to keep an existing customer. This 'statistic' alone should be enough for companies to invest in CRM.

Statistic underline just how crucial retaining customers can be:

- Reducing customer defections can boost profits by 25-85 percent (Harvard Business School).
- The price of acquiring new customer can be five time greater than the cost of keeping current ones (US office of customer affairs).
- The return on investment to marketing for existing customers can be up to seven times more that to prospective customers (Ogilvy Mother Direct).

While most companies regard the acquisition of new customers as a crucial element in their sales strategy, very few of them record customers' retention rates and even fewer analyze the reasons why previously satisfied customers become dissatisfied and go. 'Frederick Reichheld' statistic states for the average retention rates in US companies 50 percent of employees are lost in a five year period. Replacement customers will not contribute to profit unless they are retained for at least three years. Only the best practice organizations such as *Toyota* have customer's retention levels higher than 70 percent. Put another way, most organizations lose significantly more than 30 percent of their customers before or at the time of repurchase decisions, mainly through poor service. The only reason market share do not drop is

FIG. 53.7
The Power of Existing Customers

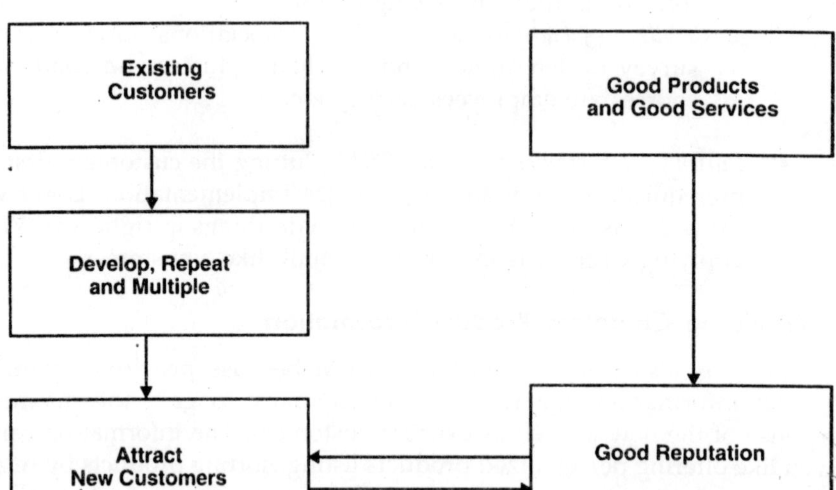

because competitors are usually in the same position and are losing customers to their competitors.

If the company can develop, repeat and multiply business relationships with existing customers, it's more able to maximize both its sales overheads and resources as above figure shows. If an organization is able to serve its existing customers, then those customers will purchase the company's products and services on regular basis that is known as loyal customer.

Reasons for developing long-term relationship with customers:

- The cost of acquiring new customers can be high.
- Loyal customers tend to spend more and cost less to serve.
- Satisfied customers are likely to recommend your products and services.
- Advocates of a company are more likely to pay premium prices to suppliers they know and trust.
- Retaining existing customers prevents competitors from gaining Market share.

E. Get Feedback from Customers

Far too often, we think we know what our customers think and want because—well, we just know, that's all. Wrong! Businesses can't be successful if they don't continue to meet the needs of their customers. There should be few activities as important as finding out what your customers want for products and services and finding out what they think of yours. Fortunately, there are a variety of practical methods that businesses can use to feedback from customers. The methods you choose and how you use them depend on what the type of feedback that you want from customers, for example, to find out their needs in products and services, what they think about your products and services, etc.

1. *Employees*: Your employees are usually the people who interact with the most with your customers. Ask them about products and services that customers are asking for. Ask employees about what the customers complain about.
2. *Comment Cards*: Provide brief, half-page comment cards on which they can answer basic questions such as: Were you satisfied with our services? How could we provide the perfect services? Are there any services you'd like to see that don't exist yet?
3. *Competitors*: What are your competitors selling? Ask people who shop there. Many people don't notice sales or major items in stores. Start coaching those around you to notice what's going on with your competition.
4. *Customers*: One of the best ways to find out what customers want is to ask them. Talk to them when they visit your facility or you visit theirs.
5. *Documentation and Records*: Notice what customers are buying and not buying from you. If you already know what customers are buying etc., then down somewhere? It should be so that you don't forget, particularly during times of stress or when trying to train personnel to help you out.
6. *Focus Groups*: Focus groups are usually 8-10 people that you gather to get their impressions of product or service or an idea.
7. *Surveys by Mail*: You might hate answering these things, but plenty of people don't—and will fill our surveys, especially, if they get something in return. Promise them a discount if they return the completed form to your facility.
8. *Telephone Surveys*: Hire summer students or part-time people for a few days every six months to do telephone surveys.

F. Anticipate an Evolutionary CRM Implementation

Don't use CRM to automate what your business already does. Be willing to redesign organizations and leverage technology to enable improved processes. It is risky to put an automation tool to work without clearly understanding the impact and having a measurement system to control it. As CRM activities expand, the technology must also accommodate a deeper understanding of customer behavior through integrated analysis, better management of the customer experience through more sophisticated communication scenarios, and tighter integration with the interaction systems for consistent communication management.

G. Providing Service after the Sales

A key to successful CRM is keeping your customer satisfied and interested after the sale this will ensure that they return in the future and recommend your product or service to others.

7. CONCLUSION

An old Chinese proverb says, "give a hundred year lease on a desert and it will become a garden; give a one year lease on a garden and it will become desert". The point is that ownership and long-term commitment makes a lot of difference when it comes to dealing with important tasks, and a customer relationship is a big deal. The field of marketing has transcended many paths from product marketing to mass marketing to niche marketing and all the way to marketing a memorable experience to customers in the form of CRM. CRM is changing the entire outlook towards running a business and is driving revenues and profitability. Today, it takes a lot of thought process and effective thinking to launch an effective and efficient CRM program. It refers to a conceptually broad phenomenon of business activity; if the phenomenon of cooperation and collaboration with customers become the dominant paradigm of marketing practice and research. CRM has the potential to emerge as the pre-dominant prospective of marketing; CRM should not be misunderstood to simply mean a software solution implementation project. Building customer relationship is a fundamental business of every enterprise and it requires a holistic strategy and process to make it successful. In short, despite the risk and cost associated with it, CRM is valuable, viable and revenue generator. CRM play an important role in the business. As from the above discussion we can say that satisfied customers cause less stress, satisfied customers take up less time and also tell others which enhance the company's reputation, brings the job satisfaction among employees that can help to provide motivation to them. There are usually four crucial elements involved in delivering quality customers care: appropriateness, consistency/reliability, timeliness and satisfying. So, without CRM a business can not even think about success.

REFERENCES

1. Greenberg, Paul, "CRM at the Speed of Light", New edition, Tata McGrow-Hill, 2nd Edition 2003.
2. Gosney, W., John, Boehm P. Thomas, "Customer Relationship Management Essentials", 2nd Edition, New Delhi, Prentice-Hall of India, 2003.
3. Cook, Sarah, "Customer care Excellence", 4th edition (New Delhi, Kogan Page India Pvt. Ltd, 2004.
4. Bee, Ronald and Frances, "Customer Care", Hyderabad, 1st edition (Universities Press India Ltd., 2000.
5. Kerr. Carol and Anderson Kristin, "Customer Relationship Management", 3rd edition, New Delhi, Tata McGraw-Hill Pubilishing Company Ltd. 2003.

6. Dawkins, P. and Reichheld, F. (1990), "Customer Retention as a Competitive Weapon", Directors and Boards, Vol. 14, No. 4, 1990.
7. Moloney, Chris X. (2006), "Winning Your Customer's Loyalty: The Best Tools, Techniques and Practices", AMA Workshop Event(s). Misc. materials distributed related to event(s). San Diego, 2006. Chris X. Moloney.
8. Stieb, James A. (2006), "Clearing Up the Egoist Difficulty with Loyalty", *Journal of Business Ethics*, Vol. 63, No. 1. Retrieved from "http://en.wikipedia.org/wiki/Loyalty_business_model".
9. IT Tool Box CRM—www.crmassist.com
10. CRM Daily.Com—www.crmdaily.com

54

CRM to CMR : A Paradigm Shift

MANDIP SAINI

ABSTRACT

The organizations world over are trying to keep a track of their customers so that they could provide them with the best of the services because retaining a customer is more cost-effective than going for a new one. Customer Relationship Management (CRM) is the most powerful tool being used for the same. But CRM is changing with the changing times. It is no longer just a tool to keep record of the information about the customer, but, is used more as a data seeker for the new leads from the existing customers.

Moreover, the organizations feel that the returns are not that great in comparison to the money and the efforts invested in the same. Another problem is from the customer view, they don't want to be managed rather they want to manage themselves, i.e. self-management. So, organizations must try to come up with such systems that could induce this in the CRM system where a customer is managing the relations with the organization. In today's tech-savvy world, information technology makes it easier to reach to far flung places and to reach more people. The motive of this study is to learn how organizations are shifting from traditional Customer Relationship Management (CRM) to Customer Managed Relationship (CMR) saga.

1. INTRODUCTION

Customer Relationship Management (CRM) is a process or methodology used to learn more about customers' needs and behaviors in order to develop stronger relationships with them. There are many technological components to CRM, but thinking about CRM primarily in technological terms is a mistake. The more useful way to think about CRM is as a process that will help bring together lots of pieces of information about customers, sales, marketing effectiveness, responsiveness and market trends. CRM helps businesses use technology and human resources to gain insight into the behavior of customers and the value of those customers. The customer is not new, relations are as old as a buyer and a seller and so is management.

CRM is considered to be a software tool and a technology solution in the information technology industry. In fact, CRM is a strategy towards achieving a holistic view of any partner engagement. CRM, which is a combination of marketing and business processes, is the basic understanding of customers and how organizations measure them. The mantra behind CRM is catering to customized needs centrally. As defined by the "gurus" of CRM—Customer Relationship Management is a business strategy to select and manage the most valuable customer relationships. CRM requires customer-centric business philosophy and culture to support effective marketing, sales and service processes. CRM software applications can enable effective customer relationship management, provided that an enterprise has the right leadership, strategy and culture.

2. WHY CRM?

Customer relationship management has become the number one focus when today's world is becoming more saturated and competitive. Now the marketing model is changing from product centric stage to customer centric stage. Customers are demanding a different relationship with the suppliers than the traditional sales model. The new database technologies enable the people to get the knowledge of who the customers are and what they bought and when they bought, and even predictions based on historical predictions, now more than ever, the ability to understand and manage a close relationship with the customer is central to delivering these business goals. This is the ultimate channel for marketing in any business. CRM helps deliver customer centric relationships. Successful companies in the future will use CRM wisely to build relationships with their customers on the level that the customers want, and will work towards developing a long-term relationship through retaining customers by delivering delight customers.

In recent years, many organizations have identified the need to get more customers facing with increased global competition. As a consequence, customer relationship management (CRM) has risen to the agenda of many organizational strategies. In 1998, global corporate expenditure on CRM was estimated to be in the region of US$1.9 billion (IDC and AMR Research, 2001). Even though CRM systems are proving an incredibly popular choice for implementation, success is proving illusive. One study of 202 CRM projects found that only 30.7 per cent of the organizations said that they had achieved improvements in the way they sell to and service customers (Dickie, 2000).

3. THE DATA WAREHOUSE

The proliferation of data warehousing technologies and applications has been widely documented among information technology consultants and vendors. According to Gartner, organizations are confronted with the challenges of managing over 30 times more data now than before in a continual effort to meet the demands associated with electronic commerce and supply-chain applications (Hochberg, 2000). Defined as a central repository used for decision support, data warehouses are integrated repositories of subject-oriented, time-variant data from whole the organization. Data related to the industry and the customers are collected over time and used to perform trend analyses, forecasting and comparative analyses. Typically, these data are not updated in real time; data are refreshed on a periodic basis from operational systems. To enable these capabilities, data warehousing implementations deploy multiple, parallel and massive processing databases well as a series of other hardware and software technologies (Wixom and Watson, 2001).

Broadly defined, CRM is a process/application that permits organizations to gather and analyze customer data rapidly while seeking to improve customer loyalty via targeted products and services (Rigby *et al.*, 2002). From a functional point of view, CRM depends upon operational integration of disparate sources of data, often in a data warehouse. The analytical functions of CRM are, typically, performed in the marketing or sales function itself, with support from a data mining or statistical analysis group.

Cooper *et. al.* (2000), in a case of First America Corporation, described analytical CRM applications as including campaign and contact management, profitability analyses and analysis of customer preferences and profiles. The data in the data warehouse must not only be the type of data necessary to support these marketing applications, but the data must also be easily accessible by the marketing function.

Prior implementation studies have offered the factors to investigate the change associated with technology adoption. In a study of 111 organizations, Wixom and Watson (2001) offered empirical findings impacting data warehousing implementations, but not in a marketing context. Few researchers, with the exception of Cooper *et. al.* (2000) and Haley *et al.* (1998), have investigated the implementation of data warehouses for the purposes of supporting specific marketing applications, such as analytical CRM, but from the point of view of upper management. While one qualitative study has focused on the data aspect of CRM implementation (Abbott *et al.*, 2001), no major studies have investigated the implementation of data warehouses for the purposes of supporting marketing applications, such as CRM focusing on the needs of marketing managers.

4. THE CRM APPROACH IN INDIA

Much has been written about customer relationship management (CRM). It has been called a strategic tool that combines business processes, technology, employees and information across an enterprise to attract and retain profitable customers. Despite this, the jury is still out on whether CRM has fulfilled its promises.

Banks and telcos still create silos of information with little scope for sharing information. All of us have received unsolicited calls and mails from financial companies and telcos asking us to buy products that we don't need and sometimes already have!

Companies, especially, those focused on retail such as banks, insurance providers and telcos, have suffered because of a lack of understanding of their clientele in terms of behavior, spending patterns, needs, and causes of dissatisfaction. Rivals, sometimes even fledgling organizations with better planned systems and processes, have grabbed some of their customers.

Has CRM in India been reduced to an empty buzzword that's tossed around so that a company appears to be keeping up with the industry? Not entirely, because organizations like Standard Chartered Bank, ICICI Lombard, BPL Telecom and Air-India have successfully used these tools and benefited. The difference lies in the way CRM has been deployed in these organizations. It is a combination of technology and process change that has worked.

So the main focus of the study is to find out the reach of CRM methodology in India. Because being a developing country, the per capita income is not high in India which is forcing the India Inc to focus on the existing customers. Baring telecom where a big chunk is added each month to the market other businesses especially the insurance and banking are feeling saturated.

Here, customer relationship management can be the trump card if implemented with the right spirit and enthusiasm, the focus of the study is more on enthusiasm as bull suggested in his study that the CRM technologies are not implemented properly nor they are used in tandem with all the departments.

5. USING ANALYTICAL CRM MODEL

The use of analytical CRM model will be a boon for insurance companies with multiple financial products and a big customer base, such as integrated insurance solution providers, will leverage their customer base to cross and up sell different financial products including insurance. Such providers will benefit from adopting analytical CRM. Market segmentation, campaign management and data mining applications will benefit them in many ways.

- *Call centre text mining*: This tool can help improve the customer experience by resolving complaints rapidly. Insurers are using these tools to mine text from call centre transcripts to identify issues faced by customers. Text mining tools also help detect and capture other useful pieces of information around a customer's life stage, financial needs and product interests. These can be used to generate leads and trigger cross-selling. However, to be fully effective, customer service representatives must be trained to probe for information that will help in cross-selling during the text mining phase. Text mining tools are leading-edge today, but are predicted to take off quickly.
- *Predictive capability to determine customer behavior*: This is an effort to study the buying or the spending pattern of the customer.
- Cross and up selling capability to provide market opportunities within an existing customer database.
- *Event-triggering and profiling*: Insurers can use event triggers to generate leads that can be acted upon quickly, usually within 24 hours. Event-triggering tools monitor incoming transaction and contact data in near-real-time to recognize changes in a customer's behavior or profile to trigger actions or alerts.
- Information regarding customer retention or attrition helps determine the likelihood of policy lapses and helps identify customers worth targeting for retention campaigns.
- Customer segmentation that leverages data to create accurate categories for use in marketing strategies.
- Market automation that combines analytics with campaign management functionality to help drive a more effective and efficient marketing campaign.

6. WHY SHIFT TO CMR?

But the spending is not worthwhile as customers don't want any one to interfere in their private life. The term CMR (Customer Managed Relationships) started to be spoken about 2 years ago but still gets little airplay. "Self-service" is a term that is more broadly used but misses the power of what customers want. It looks at the saving from a company's point of view, not the empowerment from customer's perspective.

To address these aspects of the customer behavior, you need to think in terms of a customer focused approach; hence CMR is creating a great customer experience by taking the customer view of the interaction, generating revenue by leveraging information and people through great analytics and managing costs through technology enablers.

The critical aspect is building the best set of initiatives in all three areas to suit where you need to be—a sustainable economic model that has the right balance between revenue, costs and customer experience.

So, CMR is much more than just creating self service applications on the web. It's more than good process design. It's more than successful campaign management.

CMR is :

- An ability to rethink, to reshape your organization and its knowledge so that it is at the disposal of your customers.
- Internet enabled management tools which customers use to get what they want
- An ability to react to the information being generated and used by customers in order to increase profitability.

If executed well, CMR generates three major benefits over CRM

- It is easier to implement because the customer is doing the complex stuff.
- It creates lock in since customers having invested their data with you will not move easily.
- It allows you to move faster than your competitor since you are in a trusted relationship with your customer.

7. LEVERAGING CMR

CRM has given businesses the ability to capture immense amounts of information. Few do it and of those that do, many either do it poorly or simply don't make use of it.

Many missed revenue opportunities can be avoided. These occur because of poor targeting in campaigns, poor processes that allow leakage at critical points and critically an obtuse relationship between sales and service. On top of this, there is a failure to do anything about it. What CMR drives toward is not only the more effective use of analytics but also the closing of the loop, so that the learning goes back into the business very rapidly and fixes the root causes.

The second aspect is the leverage of the skilled resources to improve operational performance. A business that understands the customer behavior drivers through the analytics is more able to predict demands on operational resources. With a greater degree of customer self-management in CMR, resources can be freed up and service levels improved. This ultimately means that the brilliant experience delivered in the self-service channels can be replicated in the live interactions, creating consistency in process, knowledge and brand.

In the telecommunications sector, where new data services have been driven by technical capabilities rather than customer demand, this is particularly key. Services are launched on an almost weekly basis with limited planning or training for front line teams. The result is that service levels suffer and service quality deteriorates. New research by Netonomy and Fujitsu has shown that around 40% of users prefer to manage the activation of these services on line. The pressure can be taken off from front line staff by ensuring the operations and marketing loop is closed, the analytical tools can predict more accurately the expected demand for the services and the contact can be driven to the self-service channels.

CMR is, also, enabled by innovative and converging technologies, CMR approach should allow customers great choice on how they blend their use of different channels to suit their situation, location or preferences. Again, taking an end to end process perspective, receiving a text message on your mobile to tell you that the stock market has crashed is almost useless if you can't do something about it. At that point, you'd be tempted to sell your Enron or Marconi shares. If you're sitting in a train, you want to be able to either send a reply text to instruct the sale, access the speech recognition system or make a follow up call to the contact centre to get more detailed information on your particular stocks before making the decision. Back to the single view, the centre agent should be aware already that you've received the text message and so know your call reason. In this example, the consequences of an action on one channel have been considered so that the customer can manage the next action their chosen way to a satisfactory outcome.

8. HERO-HONDA PASSPORT PROGRAMME—A NEW INITIATIVE IN CMR IN INDIA

Hero Honda uses a new way in which they have involved the customers in the CMR. The organization came up with an innovative idea to keep the customer along with them. The idea is very simple. Each and every customer of Hero-Honda bikes is provided with a passport by the company by way of which they become the citizens of the Hero-Honda world (currently the population is more than one billion) and the customers gets loyalty points as the credit cards provide for the purchase. Only difference is that adding points for services, parts purchase, and exchanges, etc., the one with highest purchase are rewarded each month. The customer involvement is very high as they have to get the entry made on their passport by the dealer along with an entry with the company. The people who use the passports are also invited for special events, offers and exchanges by the company. They are also informed about the upcoming products by the organization; hence future purchases could be converted easily. The effort could be refined with the use of modern day information technology and it can be more effective and closely knit relation.

9. CONCLUSION

Gone are the days when customer relationship management was adopted like an *ad-hoc* approach. Its main purpose was just to keep track of the customer and his/her demographic knowledge. The companies were not spending much on the IT aspect. But the changing economy and complexities, which are shrinking the customer base, are forcing the companies to look for the more from the existing base.

The next revolutionary step could be the interlinking of the different CRM models of various organizations so that the same customer doesn't get the call for same product from different companies. This will eliminate the number of unsuccessful efforts to reach the new customers and will also improve the conversion rate successfully. To be more effective, the companies need to come more close to the customers through programmes like CMR.

Customer Managed Relationship (CMR) is a new concept under study by business professionals. CMR aims to exploit the data from existing as well as potential customers from several channels to offer them the best service and support. It, also, aims to increase the effectiveness of marketing. Its principle is to have the company concentrate its efforts and money on allowing the customer to manage and control information related to his characteristics and wishes. In other words, the complexity of the data management is off-loaded to the customer. CMR, thus, functions as a mechanism of valuation of customers, and can select the ones that are advantageous, potential and unlikely. The company can, then, refrain from directing efforts towards the unlikely ones.

REFERENCES

1. Yu Yurong, "Adopting Customer Relationship Technology" (2002).
2. Bull Christopher, "Strategic issues in customer relationship implementation" (2003), Available on www.emerald insight.com
3. ThuyUyen, H. Nguyen, Joseph S. Sheriff and Michael Newby, "Strategies for successful CRM implementation".
4. Fay Cobb Payton, Debra Zahay "Why doesn't Marketing use the Corporate Data Warehouse? The Role of Trust and Quality in Adoption of Data-warehousing Technology for CRM Applications".
5. Lyndon Simkin "Marketing is marketing—maybe", The Research Register for this Journal is Available at http://www.mcbup.com/research_registers/mkt.asp
6. Neylor, D., "The shifting balance of power-getting Results in Customer Managed World", www.limebridge.com\CRM\CMR Customer Managed Relationships.htm
7. www.crm2day.com/cmr.

55

Serving Customers Intelligently through IT Enabled CRM

Sanjeev Singh and Yogita Sharma

ABSTRACT

Customer Relationship Management (CRM) is a process of knowing about customers' needs and behaviors in order to develop stronger relationships with them. The main goal of CRM is to optimize revenue through improved customer satisfaction via improved interactions at each customer touch point. This can be accomplished by a better understanding of customers, based on their purchasing patterns and demographics, and better information empowerment at all customer touch points. There are many technological components to CRM.

The more useful way to think about CRM is as a process that will help bring together lots of pieces of information about customers, sales, marketing effectiveness, responsiveness and market trends. With CRM, a small business or large corporations can know what its customer wants; thus, it can provide the service or product the client wants, keeping them as a repeat customer and gaining greater sales volumes.

There are different forms of CRM like—Operational CRM, Analytical CRM, Collaborative CRM, Geographic CRM etc., which have their separate functional approach. In modern age of service management, retail sector has made a vast platform, where business people have to re-think about Customer Relation Management.

The paper discusses about different aspects of CRM and IT enabled approach and tools to manage and control it.

1. INTRODUCTION

Customer Relationship Management (CRM) is a business strategy. It is a broad term that covers concepts used by companies to manage their relationships with customers, including capture, storage and analysis of customer, vendor, partner and internal process information. The goal of CRM is to make companies more profitable by serving customers more intelligently.

The beauty of CRM is that it benefits both the customer and the business or service provider. Customers receive a higher level of customer service because their needs are met and anticipated, allowing them to relax through transactions that are often much quicker than they are used to.

The business gets benefit through improved sales, higher customer confidence and satisfaction, and a more effective work environment. With CRM, a small business or large corporations can know what its customer wants; thus, it can provide the service or product the client wants, keeping them as a repeat customer and gaining greater sales volumes.

CRM offers the opportunity to develop, maintain, and leverage a consistent, accurate and timely set of customer, product, and service information across the customer-facing. marketing, sales, service, support, and product development units of the enterprise. Its ability to directly increase corporate revenues explains its mainstream popularity. Indeed, enterprises implementing CRM can, and, if necessary in real time, quantify their investment in CRM in terms of increased revenue, lower costs, enhanced customer satisfaction/retention, new business development and improved profitability.

2. FORMS OF CRM

2.1 Operational CRM

Operational CRM provides support to front office business processes including sales, marketing and service. Each interaction with a customer is generally added to a customer's contact history, and staff can retrieve information on customers from the database whenever necessary. Operational CRM processes customer data for a variety of purposes:

- Managing campaigns
- Enterprise marketing automation
- Sales force automation

2.2 Analytical CRM

Analytical CRM analyzes customer data for a variety of purposes:

- Designing and execution of targeted marketing campaigns to optimize marketing effectiveness

- Design and execution of specific customer campaigns including customer acquisition.
- Analysis of customer behavior to aid product and service decision-making, management decisions and prediction of the probability of customer defection.

2.3 Collaborative CRM

The function of the collaborative customer relationship management is to coordinate the multi-channel service and support given to the customer by providing the infrastructure for responsive and effective support to customer issues, questions, complaints, etc.

2.4 Geographic CRM

Geographic CRM (GCRM) is a customer relationship management information system which collaborate geographic information system and traditional CRM. It combines data collected from route of movement, types of residence, ambient trading areas and other customer and marketing information which are matched with relevant road conditions, building formations and a floating population. Such data are conformed to a map and is regionally analyzed with OLAP (On-Line Analytical Processing) for visualization. This enables a company to examine potential customers and manage existing customers in the region.

2.5 Support for Biggest Asset: Customers

CRM applications, also known as front-office applications, help organizations manage critical customer relationships by supporting all customer-centric processes within an enterprise including marketing, sales, and customer support.

3. KEY FUNCTIONALITIES OF CRM

A typical CRM system can be sub-divided into three basic sub-modules:

1. Marketing
2. Sales
3. Service

3.1 Marketing

Marketing sub-module primarily deals with providing functionalities of long-term planning and short-term execution of marketing-related activities within an organization.

3.2 Sales

Sales functionalities are focused on helping the sales team to execute and manage the presales process better and in an organized manner. Sales team is responsible for regularly capturing key customer interactions, any leads or opportunities they are working on etc., in CRM system. The system helps by processing this data, monitoring against the targets and proactively alerting the sales person with recommending further actions based on company's sales policy.

3.3 Service

Service-related functionalities are focused on effectively managing the customer service (planned or unplanned), avoid "leakage" of warranty-based services, avoid "penalties" arising due to non-conformity of SLA (Service Level Agreements), and provide first and second level support to customers. All the three CRM sub-modules (Marketing, Sales and Service) can be executed across these Communication channels. Based on these criteria, CRM offerings can be further sub-divided into Table 55.1.

Table 55.1
CRM Sub-modules

Communication Channel/CRM Module	*Direct*	*Internet*	*Call Centre*
Marketing	Online Marketing	Web Marketing	Tele Marketing
Sales	Web Shop	Tele Sales	
Service	Online Service	Customer Self-Service Portal	Tele Service

4. RELATIONSHIP MANAGEMENT IN RETAIL

At a top retail company, it may appear that a CEO or CFO is in complete command of the information being produced throughout the company, but the reality is often quite different. Spreadsheets produced within individual business units can easily become islands of information creating a lost opportunity to leverage critical reporting and analysis tasks. Companies don't need 100 different analysts doing different things with the data; they need analysts who have access to a single set of data, and who can base their decision-making and collaboration efforts on a common platform.

Ultimately, retailers must empower all users of the technology to become strategic analysts, not mere data gatherers and imputers. This does not require reinventing the wheel; we all know spreadsheets are not going to disappear. But retailers must integrate spreadsheets into an environment that provides a more secure and complete system for the data repository, business rules and analytics—the key performance indicators that governs and drives the company.

In recent years, retail competition has generally been intensified due to the consequences of new technologies, more sophisticated management practices and the internet. TV, digital billboards and catalogues have all commonly been used in the advertising sector. These communication instruments have an effect on consumers' shopping attitudes in an increasingly competitive marketplace.

Retailers of all sizes have made impressive gains in managing and responding to customer demand, from Point-Of-Sale (POS) promotions to merchandise flow. The rapid shift from running cash register tapes to using data from the sophisticated POS computers in today's stores clearly illustrates how comprehensive collection and use of information can increase sales and promote efficiencies.

Unfortunately, while retailers have excelled at capturing vast amounts of data, they have often overlooked the fundamental need to make sense of it all. While many retail organizations have invested significant capital to implement unified, enterprise-wide platforms for their operational systems, they have often neglected to provide an equivalent unified platform for their Business Intelligence (BI) solutions. Even, the largest retailers still face barriers in using all this information for strategic planning and deployment of resources beyond the current quarter.

The crux of the problem is that many of these retail organizations lack an integrated BI approach that can take data from disparate information systems, combine it in a centralized, easy-to-access repository, and enable reporting, analysis and collaboration based on common business rules. A basic definition of BI, defined as "any information that pertains to the history, current status or future projections of an organization", illustrates the problem. Retailers have a strong command of sales history, but where future projections are concerned, even the best chains often depend on straight-line projections and guesswork.

The extent to which Indian retailers are able to deliver a positive shopping experience will determine the degree of customer satisfaction and customer loyalty that they engender and will be the ultimate driver of improved sales and profitability. That is one of the reasons which has drastically changed the role of relationship Manager who is the

Table 55.2

Changing Role of the Relationship Manager

Traditional Role	*Change Role*
• Polite behaviour with customers	• Gaining insights into customer's needs
• Selling the product	• Offering the complete solution
• Representing the sales department	• Representing the entire company
• Focus on the immediate transaction	• Focus on the customer's lifetime value

representative of a company to end consumer. The Table 2 shows the changing role of Relationship Manager.

Common sense dictates that it's cheaper to generate more revenue from existing customers than to acquire new ones. According to surveys, the cost of finding new customers is estimated at three to five times the cost of customer retention. Retaining customers isn't easy though. The internet has lowered the cost of switching and made markets more price-sensitive.

Customers increasingly are asking for custom solutions to their problems, using comparative shopping services and freely available rating systems to pit companies against each other. In this increasingly competitive environment, businesses must differentiate not only their products, but their customer experience. In fact, customer experience is emerging as the most important competitive differentiator between vendors in many markets. The focused ability to anticipate and respond to customer needs will separate market leaders from also-rans.

5. BARE FACTS OF CRM

When Monster.com rolled out a customer relationship management (CRM) program in 1998, it was sure it had a new money-making strategy on its hands. The Massachusetts-based job-listings company had invested over $1 million in customized software and integrated all its computer systems in an attempt to boost the efficiency of its sales force. These CRM applications had been specially developed to allow Monster.com's sales representatives instant access to data for prospective customers. However, the new system proved to be frighteningly slow so slow, in fact, that salespeople in the field found themselves unable to download customer information from the company's databases onto their laptops. Every time they tried, their machines froze. Eventually, Monster.com was forced to rebuild the entire system. It lost millions of dollars along the way, not to mention the goodwill of both customers and employees.

The promise of customer relationship management is captivating, but in practice, it can be perilous. When it works, CRM allows companies to gather customer data swiftly, identify the most valuable customers over time, and increase customer loyalty by providing customized products and services. It, also, reduces the costs of serving these customers and makes it easier to acquire similar customers down the road. But when CRM doesn't work—which is often—it can lead to Monster-like (and monster-sized) debacles.

Consider this: 55% of all CRM projects don't produce results, according to Gartner group, a research and advisory firm. Also consider this: According to Bain's 2001 survey of management tools, which tracks corporate use of, and satisfaction with management techniques, CRM has been ranked in the bottom three for satisfaction out of 25 popular tools. In fact, according to last year's survey of 451 senior executives, one in every five users reported that their CRM initiatives not only had failed to deliver profitable growth but also had damaged long-standing customer relationships. One manufacturer retailer, for instance, invested $30 million in a CRM solution in 1999 only to scrap the entire project in early 2001. The company abandoned the project because customers had become increasingly irritated instead of loyal, as did the employees trying to deal with them. And while the company was struggling with CRM deployment, its rivals steadily moved into stronger market positions.

6. COMMUNICATION GAP IN BUSINESS INTELLIGENCE

Retailers have become accustomed to investing millions of dollars in the latest software and hardware systems to support mission critical operational systems. In fact, the logistical side of most successful retail information solutions reflects top-notch thought and organization. These organizations have implemented highly sophisticated systems that control the flow of merchandise throughout the enterprise, and also feature planning, budgeting, forecasting and reporting systems.

Most have sophisticated merchandising systems that support a vast number of internal buyers and the vendors they buy from. Store transactions are also well covered, with new Point-Of-Sale (POS) systems sitting on store counters collecting enormous amounts of data. Many retail chains have also spent millions of dollars on Enterprise Resource Planning (ERP) systems that improve accounts payable, general ledger and other accounting functions.

Yet, these systems generally operate on different IT platforms that do not communicate with each other. At most companies, the information in these systems is not effectively integrated into a common "analytical layer" that utilizes common databases and information delivery mechanisms. As a result, even at the biggest retail chains, the larger dimensions of business intelligence—analytics, applications and platforms—can be surprisingly archaic.

By focusing on a business intelligence architecture that utilizes common databases and end-user applications, it is possible for today's retail organizations to address the various information needs of their different departments. From a technical perspective, this architecture would lay above the transactional systems that feed it with the appropriate information. The architecture would typically consist of three layers:

- A relational database layer, that supports meta-data and more granular-level information for more detailed analysis.
- An On Line Analytical Processing (OLAP) database layer, that provides speed-of-thought access to more summarized information with read-write capabilities to support modelling and planning.
- A delivery layer, that consists of common interfaces across the

enterprise, capable of easily communicating with the underlying databases that support them.

The Figure 55.1 shows transfer of data as input from various sources to output to different departments.

FIG. 55.1
Use of Database Management for CRM

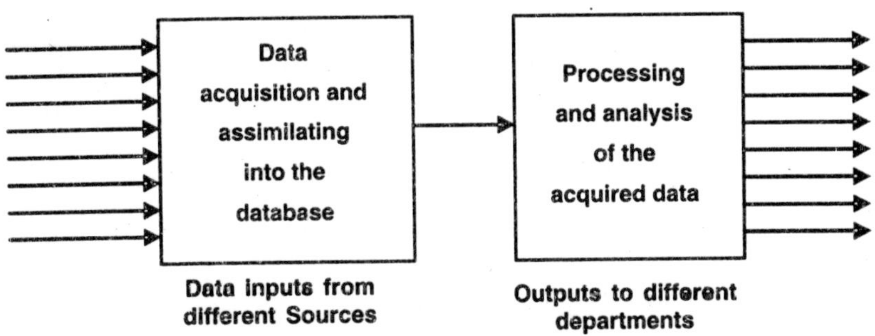

6.1 From Data Gatherers to Strategic Analysts

An integrated business intelligence solution can also have a positive effect on the employees who use it. A typical employee doesn't want to be a "spreadsheet jockey" for his or her whole life. Deploying new technology, that makes basic tasks easier and more rewarding, is a great way to keep people motivated and retained. In addition, their skill sets will be enhanced as they learn how to use the new technology. An ideal business intelligence solution constantly evolves as the company and the retail industry evolves. This creates an exciting environment for the employees who grow and change with the system, as they will depend on it to meet their analytical needs.

6.2 Privacy and Data Security

The data gathered as part of CRM must consider customer privacy and data security. Customers want the assurance that their data is not shared with third parties without their consent and not accessed illegally by third parties.

Customers also want their data used by companies to provide a benefit for them. For instance, an increase in unsolicited telemarketing calls is generally resented by customers, while, a small number of relevant offers is generally appreciated by customers.

6.3 Click Stream Analysis

On a Website, clickstream analysis is the process of collecting, analyzing, and reporting aggregate data about which pages visitors visit in what order—which are the result of the succession of mouse clicks each visitor makes. There are two levels of clickstream analysis, traffic analysis and e-commerce analysis.

Traffic analysis operates at the server level by collecting clickstream data related to the path the user takes when navigating through the site. The analysis tracks how many pages are served to the user, how long it takes pages to load, how often the user hits the browser's back or stop button, and how much data is transmitted before a user moves on.

E-commerce-based analysis uses clickstream data to determine the effectiveness of the site as a channel-to-market by quantifying the user's behavior while on the web site. It is used to keep track of what pages the user lingers on, what the user puts in or takes out of their shopping cart, and what items the user purchases.

Because a large volume of data can be gathered through clickstream analysis, many e-businesses rely on pre-programmed applications to help interpret the data and generate reports on specific areas of interest. Clickstream analysis is considered to be most effective when used in conjunction with other, more traditional, market evaluation resources.

7. APPLICATION OF IT SYSTEMS FOR BETTER CRM

The IT systems need to be of use to CRM, otherwise the investments and the initiatives that organisation initiates for CRM becomes unfruitful. The company should properly plan the entire use of systems to ensure attaining desired objectives. Some major uses that IT systems might include are:

1. Selecting profitable customers
2. Insight of customer preferences
3. Estimation of life time value of customers
4. Enhance profitability by maintaining relationship

7.1 Tools for IT enabled CRM

The entire process of CRM would necessitate the performance of various function that would require particular systems. These systems should be carefully planned to ensure that they complement the CRM tool that has been chosen. Also, the technical details of the sub-components comprising the system should ensure that there is cohesive functioning when all the sub-components are integrated to create the total system. The system can also be segregated on the basis of:

1. Hardware (comprising of the computers, display systems, handheld devices, etc.)
2. Software (the programmes that would be used by the hard and enable functionality).

3. Networking (the connectivity tools like leased lines, hubs, routers, etc.).

7.2 Cost Assessment in CRM

Customer acquisition cost is the cost associated with convincing a consumer to buy your product or service, including research, marketing, and advertising costs. Customer acquisition cost should be considered along with other data, especially, the value of the customer to the company and the resulting Return On Investment (ROI) of acquisition. The calculation helps a company decide how much of its resources can be profitably spent on a particular customer.

Generally, companies frequently ignore such calculations in their pursuit of growth. For example, according to Optimize Magazine, at one point, amount spent on online relationship management was about $40 to acquire each customer, although the average lifetime value of a customer to them was only about $25. The Optimize article suggests that it is not good business sense to spend more acquiring a customer than the amount that customer will net the company in return.

We can, finally, say that CRM systems support business growth in two critical ways:

1. They enable sales and support personnel to gather detailed information about individual customer needs, enabling them to offer custom products and services the customer can't find anywhere else.
2. Analytics provide insight about customer behaviour on a broad scale. So analytics and data mining can reveal hidden information about customer behaviour that can greatly benefit the business.

References

1. Mukherjee, Kaushik "Customer Relationship Management—Strategic Approach to Marketing", PHI, New Delhi, 2007, pp. 88-100.
2. Mukherjee, Kaushik "Customer Relationship Management—Strategic Approach to Marketing", PHI, New Delhi, 2007, pp. 102-14.
3. Campbell, Alexandera J., "Creating Customer Knowledge Competence: Managing Customer Relationship Management Programs Strategically", *Industrial Marketing Management*, 32 (5:2003, pp. 375-83).
4. Godin, Seth (1999): Permission Marketing: Turning Strangers into Friends and Friends into Customers, New York: Simon and Schuster, 1999.
5. Kimball, Ralph; Merz, Richard (1996): The Data Web house Toolkit: Building the Web-Enabled Data Warehouse, New York: Wiley and Sons, 1996.
6. Pine, James (1993): Mass Customization: The New Frontier in Business Competition, Boston: Harvard Business School Press, 1993.
7. Schubert, Petra; Ginsburg, Mark (2000): Virtual Communities of Transaction: The Role of Personalization in Electronic Commerce, in: *Electronic Markets Journal*, Vol. 10, No. 1, 2000.

56

Changing the Winds of Information Security : Role of Modern Business Organizations

SURESHRAMANA MAYYA AND SHREEMATHI S. MAYYA

ABSTRACT

All the businesses spend a major portion of their annual budgets on high-tech computer security. But the firewalls, security gates, locks, software security can be pierced by attackers targeting untrained, uninformed or unmonitored users. It is very difficult to address the human element of information security. Often, this is one area that spills sensitive information. Many a times, experts who use deceptive and manipulative tactics to gain unauthorized access to information use them for their personal gains. No system is immune to human ingenuity. Effective information security must be culturally ingrained and backed by strategies and processes that are continually tested, taught, measured and refined.

1. INTRODUCTION

In past, data and information were confined to a particular location and it was relatively easy to protect it from falling in the hands of those who should not have it. Now, the business has grown globally, we have started processing the information in a central location, there is necessity of ensuring that it was readily accessible to authorized personnel. Europol, the European Police agency, observed in its 2003 report on EU organized crime:

the establishment of worldwide financial markets, economic globalization, and the creation of the EU common market has provided good opportunities for organized crime groups. Thus, maintaining confidentiality, integrity and availability were the main tenants for managing information security. At the same time Dhillon & Backhouse (2000) felt, the emphasis should be on establishing responsibility, integrity of people, trustworthiness and ethicality.

Networked computer systems have become important not only for conventional commercial and financial transactions, but for informal and social interactions. These are the two uses of network infrastructures. They represent the two ends of a range of possible ways in which these infrastructures are being appropriated and utilized. Social engineering attacks are so common, through which the confidential information is gathered. Some of the best tools for fighting social engineering attacks are security awareness training and social engineering testing. The effectiveness of these controls will vary based on the quality of their implementation, including follow-up and retraining. Social engineering testing, by its very nature, can be difficult to conduct without third-party assistance. One option is to engage an information security organization to conduct testing. The testing can uncover areas in which an organization is most vulnerable so that risk can be assessed and mitigation strategies can be formulated and implemented (Stephen Lineberry, 2007).

According to Calder, Alan (2005), threats in the digital world originate with people. These people fall into five groups:

- Criminals (thieves, fraudsters, organized crime);
- Malefactors (hackers, vandals, terrorists, cyber-warriors, some ex-employees and other disgruntled or vengeful individuals);
- Spies (commercial and governmental);
- Undesirables (scam artists, spammers, 'ethical' hackers and nerds); and
- The incompetent, or the simply unaware (staff, contractors, customers and other third parties).

Above attacks disturb individuals and businesses indiscriminately. In most cases, they target big business firms. Attackers dwell inside or outside of the organization. Incompetence, lack of awareness and lack of skill are some of the problems facilitating these attacks. The types of attacks are:

- Criminal Attacks (fraud, theft and grand larceny, identity theft, hacking, extortion, intellectual property (IFR) and copyright theft, piracy, brand theft, 'spoofing');
- Destructive attacks (cyber-terrorism, hackers, ex-employees, vengeful individuals, cyber war, cyber-vandals, anarchists, viruses);
- Nerd attacks (denial of service attacks, publicity hounds, adware); and
- Espionage attacks (data and IPR theft, spy ware).

2. IMPACT OF INFORMATION SECURITY BREACHES

The seventh annual Information Security Breaches Survey (ISBS, 2004), managed by Pricewaterhouse-Coopers (www.security-survey.gov.uk) identified the following symptoms:

- One-third of large businesses and two-thirds of all companies still have no information security policy;
- Processes for keeping anti-virus software up to date are often weak;
- Only half of all wireless networks have security controls in place
- Spam is a growing issue (probably now 80 per cent of all e-mail, two-thirds of UK businesses had at least one malicious security breach in the last year, an increase from just under half two years earlier);
- Over a quarter of businesses suffered a significant incident arising from accidental systems failure or data corruption; and
- The average UK business now has one security incident a month.

3. FUTURE PROBLEMS

Distributed computing is becoming common today. Computing power has migrated from centralized mainframe computers and data processing centres. The use of digital cameras, laptop computers, Personal Digital Assistants (PDAs), mobile phones, portable projectors and MP3 players has made possible working from home. They have created security problems also. They have created many remote access points and made the system vulnerable to security risks.

The increasing importance of internet has created more acute problems. No doubt, this is immediate and powerful method of communication. Some of the problems are:

- Technologically superior hacker tools are available every day. These tools are improved regularly and, increasingly technologically proficient criminals—and computer literate terrorists have been creating more problems to networks.
- Hackers, virus writers and spam operators have been finding newer ways of spreading more spam. They have found that direct e-mail marketing of dodgy products is lucrative. Phishing and other internet fraud activity will continue evolving and will become an ever bigger problem.
- Sophisticated technology mechanisms, particularly around user authorization and authentication, will drive an increase in social engineering-derived hacker attacks.
- While most people today have computer skills, the next generation is growing up with a level of familiarity with computers that will enable them to develop and deploy an entirely new range of threats.

- WiFi or Bluetooth makes information and the internet available cheaply and easily from virtually anywhere, thereby potentially reducing the perceived value and importance of information and, certainly, exposing confidential and sensitive information more and more to casual access. This has created more difficult problem.

4. EMAIL PROBLEM

Email is vulnerable to hackers. Email has developed from its early days as an efficient and cost-effective way of communicating short messages across computer networks. It is now a critical business application that can be deployed for numerous purposes over and above the simple relay of information. As an integral part of everyday business, email applications serve multiple roles. For example, in some cases, employees are so reliant on their email applications as scheduling tools, address books and work archives, that their work virtually comes to a halt if ever the system goes out of commission.

This article considers the main sources of email security risk and means of addressing it, the problems associated with passwords, firewalls, spywares and other security issues with particular reference to the creation and deployment of email security policies, at a time, when lapses in email security have demanded attention in the media. It draws on primary research conducted with two sets of data subject:

1. Email security experts and computer experts; and
2. End-users in a consultancy firm that is heavily dependent on email in its daily business.

The article concludes with a consideration of key elements that should be addressed when considering issues of computer security.

Concerns about email now focus on the security (or insecurity) of the medium. A heightened awareness of email danger, especially in the light of cases that have been well publicized in the media, has prompted businesses to review how their employees handle email. They seek means of ensuring that employee email practices do not jeopardise organisational interests. Hence, there is information risk issue, business information professionals have an interest in the role of technologies, policies and user education in determining how email is safely deployed in the office environment (Zoe Kelleher and Hazel, 2005).

5. ORIGIN OF EMAIL SECURITY PROBLEMS

The email is vulnerable and its interception and alteration causes security problems. According to experts, the major source of interception is from outside the organization. Breaches of email security are most readily associated with malicious sources from outside the organization. Third parties often gain unauthorized access to information. Even many viruses like Love Letter, Nimda and Code Red have caused billions of pounds worth of damage to business (Know your enemy, 2003, p. 4). In 2003, it was estimated that by the end of the year, viruses would cost businesses £907 billion worldwide (Know your enemy, 2003, p. 4). The previous year, 70 per cent of SMEs in the UK had received a viruses and suffered losses in revenue, data and productivity as a consequence (Virus Attacks, 2002, p. 2). The problems created by virus are multifarious and far-reaching causing lot of inconvenience hampered the relationships with clients and parties. A research study has indicated that representatives of 58 per cent of UK companies, subjected to viruses as a result of interactions with other organisations, would not open emails from same source. Additionally, 17 per cent said that such incidents eroded trust in business relationships (Virus attacks, 2002, p. 11).

A significant aspect of email security risk relates to the personal use of the system, especially in cases where what is communicated is inappropriate material. A 1999 survey of 800 email users revealed that 30 per cent sent private company information in personal emails, and 64 per cent received or sent offensive personal emails. Equally, an 'ethics' survey conducted in 2001 reported that 36 per cent of employees surveyed admitted to sending racist, sexist or pornographic material via their work email accounts (Corbelli, 2002, p. 26). Such imprudent use of email is particularly precarious in large organisations where people share similar names: a Dell employee in France was sacked for forwarding pornography to a senior manager in the US. The email had been intended for a local colleague with a very similar name (Bentley, 2001, p. 44). Even if every care is taken to ensure that the recipients' names are correct, there is no way of controlling what recipients do with email after they receive it (Flynn, 2002, p. 1).

6. METHODS OF ADDRESSING EMAIL RISKS

All the organizations are required to take precautionary measures to guard against email security risks. External threats, including hackers or viruses, are addressed through the use of technology such as firewalls and encryption software — provided that it is deployed effectively. For local use, technical solutions include scanning and monitoring software.

7. FORMS OF COMPUTER FILE ACCESS

It is imperative that executives must learn about electronic modes of communication—how to use them and how to protect them. If we are not careful, our computers could end up in the public domain. What are the forms of computer file access? The following are some of the forms of computer file access as indicated by Karen, D.G., and Kathleen, J.S. (2006).

8. HACKING

That is how easy it was to hack into a computer network. The most prominent definition of hacking is the act of gaining access without legal authorization to a computer or computer network. A hacker first attacks an easy target, and then uses it to hide his or her traces for launching attacks at more secure sites. The goal of an attack is to gain complete control of the system (so you can edit, delete, install, or execute any file in any user's directory), often by gaining access to a "super-user" account. This will allow both maximum access and the ability to hide your presence. Hacking is:

- Unauthorized or illegal
- Attempts to bypass security mechanisms of information systems or networks
- Usually to destroy or disrupt computer systems or commit illegal activities

Computer Forensic Analysis (CFA)

- Authorized recovery, analysis, and presentation of computer-based material for court use

Examiner and Hacker Goals

- Discover, recover, or uncover data/documents
- Interpret hidden and recovered data
- Determine employee activity (e-mail use and misuse of resources, theft of information)
- Restore deleted or password-protected files
- Re-create chain of events through files, gaps, erasures.

Who might want Data or Evidence?

- Attorneys
- Business owners
- Chief executives or executive
- Directors Consultants Data "Salespersons"
- Disgruntled employees
- Police departments
- Private investigators
- Relatives Reporters
- Researchers
- Supervisors
- You

Why search for Evidence or Data?

- Background check (i.e., arrest, financial, residency, employment records)
- Client information (i.e., identity, social security, medical history)
- Defamation
- Divorce proceedings
- Information-related crimes committed by an angry employee
- Intellectual property theft

- Medical malpractice suit
- Spoliation of an evidence
- Personal injury
- Pornography
- Research
- Trade secrets
- Wage and injury claims
- Workplace sexual harassment

What can be Found?

- Correspondence
- Web sites visited
- Piles
- Files downloaded
- Timing of files last accessed
- Attempts to conceal or destroy
- Evidence attempts to fabricate evidence

Sources of Evidence and Data

- Computer hard drives
- "Flash", "jump", or thumb drives (portable hard drives the size of one's thumb)
- Floppy disks Handheld computers
- Personal Digital Assistants (PDAs)
- Blackberries
- Car cell phones
- Fax machines

9. GENERIC COMPUTER SECURITY ISSUES (CSIS)

- Invasion of privacy
- Theft and destruction of documents
- Theft and destruction of program and research databases
- Monitoring personal use of workplace equipment
- Client, legal, employee, employer charges

Security Enhancement

- Protect your computer at all times.
- Shut it down when not in use
- Use programs that require an identification and password
- Beware of vulnerability when using wireless router system
- Limit and monitor access to organizational hardware and server system(s)

Causes of Security Breaches

- Lack of strong password
- "Vulnerable" (easily guessed) password

- Viruses
- Spyware
- Hijackers

Password

- Confidential authentication
- Information made up of a string of case sensitive characters

Purpose of Passwords

- To protect your computer from intrusion
- To prevent access to critical information

Precautions

- Choose a password that is easy for you to remember. Strong passwords: 8+ characters; 3+ of the 8 are numbers or symbols
- Use numbers, punctuation marks, upper and lowercase letters
- Change the password periodically
- Use password-protected screen-savers: locks after specified "idle" time
- Do not use a password easy for someone to guess (i.e., your name, spouse's name, date of birth, child's name, social security number, etc.)
- Do not write your password down where someone can see it (i.e., on a post-it stuck to your monitor, on a card in your desk).
- Do not give your password(s) to anyone

Challenges

- Forgetting passwords
- Disgruntled employees who change passwords

Available Password Software Programs

- Passware: Go to www.lostpassword.com
- Password Re coven* Tool Kit: Go to www.accessdata.com
- Password Tools: Go to www.PasswordTools.com

Computer Virus

- A program or piece of computer code installed or executed onto any computing device without the knowledge of the owner
- Runs against owner wishes, often disrupts or alters normal operation of infected computer often destructive, permanently damaging data files or programs on a computer

Antivirus Software

- Prevents viruses from attacking your computer

- Treats and cleans viruses that are present
- Download virus detection program updates frequently
- For example, Norton Anti-Virus, McAfee Antivirus

Cookies

- Short pieces of data
- Used by Web servers
- Help identify Web users
- Are on your computer's hard drive
- Make all Internet actions "trackable" by Web site sponsors who use cookies.

How to Remove Cookies?

- Right click on "Internet Explorer" icon
- Click on "properties"
- Click on "delete cookies" and select "OK"
- Click on "delete files"
- Check off "Delete all off-line content"
- Click "OK"
- Click on "clear history" and say "yes"

Spyware

- Software that tracks Internet use
- Sends that information to third party
- May be in programs downloaded from Internet
- May be disguised as pop-up advertisements (see below)

Programs That Clean Spyware-Infected Systems

- *Ad-Aware*: Go to www. lavasoftusa.com
- *Spybot*: Go to www.safernetworking.org

Hijacking

- Software that steals your browser Web connections for its own purpose
- Malicious software
- Changes Internet Explorer settings
- Changes your home page
- Adds new "favorite" sites of "dubious content"
- Can cause home page to revert to unwanted site even if manually changed
- May block access to certain Web pages (i.e., site of antispyware software manufacturer)
- Known to disable antivirus and antispyware software

Avoiding Hijackers

- Use common sense

- Use and update an antivirus program regularly
- Use antivirus "auto protection"
- Keep an anti-hijack "toolkit" for emergencies
- Change your Internet Explorer security settings
- Try an alternate browser

To probe Inside your Computer

- Belarc Advisor™ tells what is happening inside your computer—its guts
- Easy to use
- Gives summary of all software and hardware on your system (Jives operating system running and how much memory is in the machine
- Save the results on a disk, CD, or a hard copy for future reference. (This information is needed when you call tech support.) Free copy: Go to http://www.belarc.com/freedownload.html

Other Protection Tips

- Install Firewalls for Software and Hardware
- Gateway programs that limit access between networks according to local security policy
- Restrict traffic for internal and external users
- Should be updated annually
- Back Up Your Files
- Keep additional copies of all files
- Develop habit of backing up regularly (on floppy disk, CD, DVD, server, or tape system)
- Keep back up files in a secure location
- Use Metadata Removal Tools
- Metadata is nothing but the facts about data hidden within the file "Metadata Assistant" or "Microsoft
- Office—Remove Hidden Data in Word or WordPerfect documents
- File metadata may reveal:

    o Who the author is
    o Who else contributed to it
    o Creation and modification dates
    o Changes or edits to the document
    o Text that was removed from the final printed version

Self-Regulation

This is one of the most effective method of regulation rather than poling of cyberspace. The efforts of government of legal measures are not effective. There is realization that although legislation and enforcement can go a long way in helping to curb cyber crimes, they are not going to eradicate cyber crimes. It should be taken as one of a combination of measures that must be carried out together. Probably one of the most effective prevention techniques is to give users enough autonomy to self-regulate themselves, each taking on the responsibility to the degree and level of control and regulation that best suits his or her needs and environment.

Take Care about Hard Disk

At the time of disposing or dismantling the computer, care should be taken so that no body can have access to that hard disk. It has to be dismantled completely. Never put anything in an e-mail you would not want to seen on the front page of a newspaper.

10. USER EDUCATION

In cases, where appropriate technologies and policies are in place to protect the organisation from information risk associated with inappropriate computer usage practice, they are often useless unless supported by a programme of adequate user education. Numerous reported examples show how users hold inaccurate perceptions of computer security. There is a lack of awareness regarding the implications of sending emails containing libellous or offensive materials, and the degree to which an email, as a written document, is legally binding. Such cases highlight the need for companies to have in place a strict policy outlining what is an acceptable and unacceptable use of email. They also indicate that employees need to be aware of, and adhere to, an email security policy. User education involves teaching as many people as possible the values of security, responsible use of computer technology, how to handle security incidents, how to recover from security incidents, how to deal with the evidence if legal actions are to be followed, and how to report security incidents.

References

1. Backhouse, J., and Dhillon, G. (1995), Managing Computer Crime: A Research Outlook. *Computers and Security*, 14(7), 645-51.
2. Bentley, R. (2001), 'Don't Let email Gaffes Put You in Court', *Computer Weekly* 2, August, p. 44.
3. Calder, Alan (2005), Business Guide to Information Security, Kogan Page.
4. Corbelli, M. (2002), 'Set an email Policy', *Computer Weekly*, 18 April, p. 26.
5. Flynn, N. (2002), A Cautionary Tale in the Age of email: the eLove note read around the globe. Retrieved 25 June 2004 from: www.epolicyinstitute.com/press/articles/sink.html
6. *Hall Business Information Review* 22; 46.
7. Health Promotion Practice, (July 2006), Published by Society for Public Health Education, Vol. 7, No. 3, 27-79.
8. Know Your Enemy—Part Two: viruses (2003), Retrieved 25 April 2008 from: www.iwks.com/features/default.asp?pagetypeid=2&articleid=16243&subsectionid=655& subsubsectionid=0
9. Stephen Lineberry (2007), The Human Element: The Weakest Link in Information Security, *Journal of Accountancy;* Nov., 2004, 5; ABI/INFORM Global, p. 44.
10. Virus Attacks Cost UK Businesses Money, Time and Trust (2002) 20 November. Retrieved 19 May 2008 from: www.pressbox.oo.uk/Det-ailed/8111.html
11. Zoe Kelleher and Hazel (2005), Response to Risk: Experts and End-user Perspectives on email Security, and the Role of the Business Information Professional in Policy Development.

57

Indian SMEs and their Attitude Towards Information and Communication Technology (ICT)

NAVJOTE KHARA, BALRAM DOGRA AND SUKHMEET SINGH

ABSTRACT

Despite the increasing role of ICT in today's business scenario, little research is available on its adoption by small and medium firms in India. This article offers analysis of the ICT awareness among Indian firms and the extent of its adoption. The study was conducted on sixty Small and Medium Enterprises (SMEs) in Punjab using personal interview. The study that reveals there is poor awareness regarding ecommerce and electronic data interchange in the firms. The primary use of ICT is in e-mailing, use of internet, information search, intra-company communication and browsing pages. The primary factors affecting adoption of e-commerce in India is marketing, competitiveness and for entry into new markets.

1. INTRODUCTION

Firms are trying to grapple with the new emerging market scenario, which is characterized by increased competition from foreign firms. With increasing globalisation, knowledge and technological processes have become central to realization of economic prosperity in an integrated world economy. Information and knowledge are revolutionizing the behaviour of enterprises by altering management and production processes, product innovation, supply chain relationship between firms, demand conditions and regulations. Information and Communication Technologies (ICT) offers these firms ways to improve their competitiveness. They provide access to new market opportunities and specialized information services (Fulantelli and Allegra, 2003). Organizations can exchange real-time information and build closer relationships with their customers, suppliers and business partners; immediate customer feedback allows companies to react fast to changing customer demands and recognizing new market niches. Organizations that are able to exploit the potentials offered by ICT can handle innovative processes, such as Supply Chain Management, Customer Relationship Management, Knowledge Management, more effectively. In fact, the success of firms, and national economies as a whole, is ever more reliant upon their effectiveness in gathering and utilizing knowledge.

Globally, it is recognized that 80 percent of economic growth comes from SMEs (Jutla *et. al.*, 2002). A total of 99 percent of all businesses in North America and Europe are SMEs (Adam *et. al.*, 1999). Therefore, governments in developed nations sees ICT and e-business as the keys to the knowledge-based economy and the assured competitive advantage of their economies. There is increasing pressure for SMEs to fully embrace ICT and e-business techniques because, in aggregate, they are big buyers, big sellers, big innovators and, most important politically, big employers (Taylor and Murphy, 2004). Despite their size, small businesses are seen as significant contributors to the prosperity of national economies. For instance, in India, Small Scale Industries (SSIs) account for 95 per cent of the country's industrial units, 40 per cent of its industrial output, 80 per cent of employment in the industrial sector, 35 per cent of value added by the manufacturing sector and 7 per cent of net domestic product. The European Commission views small businesses as the backbone of the European economy (Europa, 2003). Similarly, the Australian government recognises that small businesses are a "powerhouse" of economic potential, whose employees account for almost five million members of the workforce (NOIE, 2002) making them a major source of jobs.

It has been suggested that SMEs adoption of internet technologies follows a sequence of stages (Martin and Matlay, 2001). These staged models imply that businesses move in stages from basic use of the internet (as an e-mail or marketing tool) to more sophisticated usage that redesigns business processes and integrates business systems. It is assumed that greater benefits will be obtained when a company engages in a process of business transformation. Within these models, the early stages of internet adoption are typically characterized by organisations gaining access to the internet followed by the use of relatively simple technologies (e.g. e-mail) to exchange information. Subsequent stages relate to the establishment of a simple static home page containing basic information. Later, the business starts to publish a wider range of information and attempts to market its products and perhaps provide some after-sales support. E-commerce deployment is next, allowing the users of the site to order and/or pay for products and services. In the most mature stages, the company web site is fully integrated with the various back office systems such as Enterprise Resource Planning (ERP), Customer Relationship Management (CRM), and integrated Supply Chain Management (SCM) applications.

SMEs are not a homogeneous set of businesses. They vary significantly by size, age, sector, motivation, mode of organisation, ethnic background, location, knowledge base, power and control of resources, innovative capacity and so on (Taylor and Murphy, 2004). It is also difficult to explain the extent to which SMEs are engaged with ICT and e-business techniques due to level of generalisation involved and the different ways that statistics have been compiled.

Information and Communication Technologies (ICT) enable new means to provide services for customers. However, in majority cases, ICT is used only for basic functionalities, and not to improve internal and external communication, or to activate new information services (Fulantelli and Allegra, 2003). E-commerce involves the application of web-based information technologies towards automating business processes, transactions and workflows, and buying and selling information, products, and services using computer networks (Kalakota and Whinston, 1997). E-commerce technology has the potential to become a major source of competitive advantage to small businesses because it is a cost effective way of reaching customers globally and competing on par with larger counterparts. In contrast, to large firms, the rate of e-commerce adoption in the small business sector has remained relatively low (Magnusson, 2001; Poon and Swatman, 1998; Van Akkeren and Cavaye, 1999).

Despite government support and the exponential growth of e-commerce, it is mainly the larger businesses that have reaped the benefits of this technology (Riquelme, 2002). Small businesses have fewer resources and expertise available to them (Blili and Raymond, 1993; Cragg and King, 1993) and have less control over their external environment (Hill and Stewart, 2000). Lack of initial capital and staff support for implementation and the lack of availability of training services and products (concerning both the technology and its application for enterprises) have been indicated as the main barriers (Fulantelli and Allegra, 2003). High costs associated with implementing e-commerce, the complexity of e-commerce technology and the difficulty of measuring the return on investment, also, act as a major impediment to adopt it. Some of the major non-technical limitations that slowdown the spread of internet-based e-commerce among SMEs high startup costs include connection costs to the internet, the cost of adequate hardware/software, set-up and maintenance costs.

2. LITERATURE REVIEW

Fulantelli and Allegra (2003) on a study of attitude of small firms regarding Information and Communication Technology (ICT) solutions concluded that forcing the introduction of technology is one of the main reasons behind the failure of SMEs to use ICT effectively for new services. The introduction of ICT-based processes should take into account the specific culture of the company: the background of the entrepreneur and/or the managers is important as well as their openness to innovation. Another important aspect is that ICT-based solutions should be introduced gradually because with sudden transformations there is risk to fail against unaware and unready business organizations. Further, adequate training and support is essential to successful implementation.

Thomas and Bridgewater (2004) have studied the impact of internet on exporting; and identified the factors that influence firm's success in using internet as a virtual export channel (VEC) in export markets. The findings of this paper show strong support for the existence of network effects. The more other firms are linked to the internet, the more information can be accessed using search engines and communication. However, the experience of using the internet specifically increases the likely success of the VEC. Providing information, transacting or building relationships effectively—with rich web sites – has an impact on the successful creation of VECs. This is an important suggestion for those setting up internet sites to serve export markets, as it relates to the way in which firms provide information, build relationships or transact. Greater returns are gained by regular and intensive exporters who can use VECs not only for revenue generation, but also to improve their business processes. However, this paper suggests that firms with less export experience succeed better with VECs, because firms with lower levels of experience are more committed to internet technology and devote more of their energies to making VECs work.

Kaynak *et. al.* (2005) have identified the factors influencing adoption of ecommerce in SMEs based on a study of more than 200 Turkish firms. The major benefits of internet based ecommerce are 24-hour accessibility, low-cost communication, easy access to international, markets, easy access to potential customers, gathering information about potential markets, enhancing the company image and creating a global image. The benefits have been classified into four factors, viz. market development, efficiency of sales and promotion, ease of accessibility, and cost reduction.

MacGregor and Vrazalic (2005) investigated the e-commerce barriers in small businesses. The study was conducted on firms in Sweden and Australia. They opine that the barriers can be grouped as "too difficult" and "unsuitable". The "Too Difficult" factor is related to the barriers which make e-commerce complicated to implement, including barriers such as the complexity of e-commerce implementation techniques, the difficulty in deciding which standard to implement because of the large range of e-commerce options, the difficulty of obtaining funds to implement e-commerce, the lack of technical knowledge and the difficulty of finding time to implement e-commerce. The "Unsuitable" factor is related to the perceived unsuitability of e-commerce to small businesses. The barriers in this group include the unsuitability of e-commerce to the organisation's products/services, its way of doing business, and its client's way of doing business, as well as the lack of perceived advantages of e-commerce implementation.

Gregory *et. al.* (2007) in their study have described how e-commerce drivers affect export marketing strategy of firms. They have identified four major e-commerce drivers, both internal and external, in terms of their relevance to export marketing strategy. The internal e-commerce drivers include product online transferability and e-commerce assets, whereas, the external drivers include e-commerce infrastructure and demand for e-commerce. *Product online transferability* is the extent to which a product can be digitized for transfer over the Internet. A firm's *e-commerce assets* are defined as allocated technology and human resources in the service of e-commerce activities. As for external e-commerce drivers, export market *e-commerce infrastructure* is defined as the set of resources that enable reliable and affordable access to all parties involved in e-commerce transactions in the export market. The survey was conducted on 340 Australian exporters and the unit of analysis used is individual product-market export venture of the firm. The study shows that product online transferability has a direct, positive effect on four of the six dimensions of export venture marketing strategy: promotion adaptation, communication efficiency, distribution support, and distribution efficiency. Further, e-commerce assets have a positive, significant effect on five dimensions of export venture marketing strategy: promotion adaptation, communication efficiency, distribution support, distribution efficiency, and price competitiveness. The findings also reveal that the demand for e-commerce has a positive, direct impact on three export marketing strategy dimensions: communication efficiency, distribution efficiency, and price competitiveness. The export market e-commerce infrastructure enhances the effects of e-commerce export experience on both distribution efficiency and price competitiveness. An important finding is that e-commerce assets moderate the management commitment–export strategy relationship in four strategy dimensions: communication and distribution efficiency, distribution support, and price competitiveness.

3. METHODOLOGY

3.1 Research Design

This research is based on an empirical study of Indian Small And Medium Enterprises (SMEs). The main objective of the study was to understand the attitude of the Indian SMEs towards Information Communication technology. Consequently, a cross-sectional survey was conducted in Jalandhar (India) to collect primary data from the sixty SME firms, based in the north Indian state of Punjab.

The major steps followed to accomplish the research objectives are briefly outlined as follows. A structured questionnaire was developed using a multistage process to conduct the survey. First, prior studies on exporting were reviewed to identify the previously used measures in export marketing. Second, based on the identified measures, a list of items was assembled and liker-type statements were used. Third, to ensure the content validity of the questionnaire, it was pre-tested in two stages.

In stage one; the questionnaire was evaluated by three professors from international marketing and marketing research. Based on their feedback, some items as well as scales were added, modified and deleted. In stage two, the questionnaire was administered to nine sports goods exporters using personal interviews. The interviews lasted for one hour and the objective was:

(a) To study the awareness of firms towards ICT,
(b) To study the extent of adoption of ICT by the firms, and
(c) To analyse the factors influencing SME adoption of e-commerce.

3.2 Sample and Data Collection

After finalising the questionnaire, the method of data collection used was that of personal interviews with the Managing Director of the firms. The sampling unit consisted of the small and medium sized firms based in the Jalandhar in the northern state of Punjab. The unit of analysis was an Indian firm that is engaged in manufacturing and is considered as a SME. A total of sixty firms responded to the survey and their results are illustrated in the next section.

4. RESULTS AND FINDINGS

The responses obtained from the sports goods exporters formed the basis of statistical analysis carried out using SPSS. A profile of the survey respondents is given in Table 57.1. The investment figures are given in Indian Rupees (Rs.).

4.1 Awareness Regarding ICT

Table 57.2 reveals the awareness of the firms regarding ICT. The results show that all the exporters are fully aware regarding PC with LAN, Email and internet as a tool for ICT, which is expected.

4.2 Use of ICT Components

Table 57.3 shows the ICT components being used by the small and medium enterprises. As the Table 57.3 depicts all the SMEs are using the email and the internet as a medium of business, whereas e-commerce and EDI has seen limited adoption.

TABLE 57.1
Profile of the Survey Respondents

Characteristics	*Number of Firms*	*Percent of Firms*
Market Focus		
Local	26	43.3
Regional	16	26.7
National	14	23.3
International	4	6.7
Number of Employees		
<9	16	26.7
10-29	26	43.3
30-49	11	18.3
< 50	7	11.7
Age of Firm (Years)		
<5	10	16.7
6-10	18	30.0
11-15	10	16.7
>15	22	36.7
Level of Investment (Rs. Million)		
<2	13	21.7
2-4	18	20.0
4-6	15	25.0
6-8	9	15.0
>8	5	8.3

TABLE 57.2
SME Awareness Regarding ICT

ICT Components	*Minimum*	*Maximum*	*Mean*	*SD*
Internet	1	1	1.00	.00
E-mail	1	2	1.02	.13
PC with LAN	1	3	1.13	.43
Ecommerce	1	3	1.88	.83
Electronic Data Interchange	1	3	2.42	.72

Note : The mean is the average on a scale of 1 = Fully Aware, 2 = Partially Aware, 3 = Not Aware, SD = Standard Deviation; Number of respondents = 60.

TABLE 57.3
SME Adoption of ICT

ICT Component	*Respondents Using (%)*
Internet	100
E-mail	96.7
LAN	85
E-commerce	30
EDI	10

Note : Number of respondents=60.

4.3 Extent of Adoption of ICT

The extent of internet based EC adoption for the SMEs based on the mean measure of usage frequency across 13 EC applications, is shown in Table 57.4. Scores are significantly different on the friedman two way ANOVA test (p<0.001). For the 13 EC applications, the first group of EC applications with the largest frequency of usage is as follows: "e-mailing" (1.3), "usenet" (1.47), "information search" (1.45), "intra-company communication" (1.48) and "browsing pages" (1.62).

The second group of EC applications (those ranked 6-8) is "exchange of information with clients" (1.83), "exchange of information with suppliers" (1.85), "market and product research" (1.85).

TABLE 57.4
Extent of Adoption of ICT by SMEs

EC Applications	*Rank*	*Mean*	*SD*
E-mail	1	1.30	0.5
Information search	2	1.45	0.57
Usenet	3	1.47	0.75
Intra-company communication	4	1.48	0.72
Browsing Company Homepages	5	1.62	0.61
Exchange of information with clients	6	1.83	0.64
Exchange of information with suppliers	7	1.85	0.61
Market and product research	8	1.85	0.66
Recieving orders from clients	9	2.05	0.62
Placing orders to suppliers	10	2.12	0.61
Medium of payment	11	2.15	0.76
Placing job recruitment advertisement	12	2.65	0.55
Video-conference	13	2.88	0.37

Note : The mean is the average on a scale of 1=Frequent use, 2=Seldom use, 3=Never use; SD=Standard Deviation; scores are significantly different on Friedman two-way ANOVA test (p<0.001); Number of respondents=60.

The third group used seldom (9-11) is "receiving orders from clients" (2.05), "placing order to suppliers" (2.12) and "medium of payment" (2.15).

The fourth and lowest ranked group (12-13) consists of applications related to job requirement. The applications of "Placing job recruitment advertisement" (2.65) and "video conference" (2.88) are rarely used.

4.4 Frequency of Use of ICT

The extent of internet based EC adoption for the SMEs based on the mean measure of usage frequency across 6 EC applications, is shown in Table 57.5. Scores are significantly different on the Friedman two way ANOVA test ($p<0.001$). For the 6 EC applications, the first group of EC applications with the largest frequency of usage (once a week) is as follows: "e-mailing" (1.6). The second group which is used once a week consists of "internal communication" (2.22), and "using for information search" (2.35).

The third group of EC applications is with the frequency of usage (several times a week) are "communicating with suppliers" (3.03) and "communication with customers" (3.08).

The fourth group of EC applications is with the least frequency of usage (once a month) is "market and product research" (3.45).

TABLE 57.5
Frequency of Use of ICT by SMEs

ICT Component	*Mean*
E-mail	1.60
Internal Communication	2.22
Using for Information Search	2.35
Communicating with Supplier	3.03
Communicating with Customer	3.08
Market and Product Research	3.45

Note : The mean is the average on a scale of 1=Daily, 2=Once a week, 3=Several times a week, 4=Once a month, 5=Several times a month, 6=Never access. Number of respondents=60.

4.5 Perception Regarding Purpose of Website

From the sixty firms surveyed, only eight firms (13.3%) mentioned that they were using the website. The purpose for having a website is set out in rank order in Table 57.6. As is clear from the table; "promotion of company" (1.87) is the highest ranked purpose for the company maintaining a website, followed by "status symbol" (2.40), website as a "online purchase" (2.45), "showcase products to potential customers" (2.47), "inter-office functions" (2.47), "collect visitor's database" (2.92).

TABLE 57.6
Perception regarding Purpose of Website

ICT Components	*Mean*	*SD*
Promotion of Company	1.87	.57
Status Symbol	2.40	.81
Online Purchase	2.45	.83
Showcase Products to Potential Customers	2.47	.95
Inter-office Function	2.47	1.03
Collect Visitor's Database	2.92	1.00

Note : The mean is the average on a scale of 1=Fully Aware, 2=Partially Aware, 3=Not Aware, SD=Standard Deviation; Number of respondents=60.

4.6 Factors Influencing EC Adoption

Eleven of the most common benefits of EC were identified from literature. The respondents were asked to rate the importance of those factors in their decision to adopt EC on a five point Liker type scale (where 1=Very Unimportant, 2=Unimportant, 3=Neutral, 4=Important, 5=Very Important). Table 57.7 shows the descriptives of the sample.

TABLE 57.7
Descriptives of Factors Influencing EC Adoption

Factors	*Minimum*	*Maximum*	*Mean*	*SD*
For New Products	2	4	2.26	.65
Access to Markets	1	5	2.16	.96
Reduce Cost	1	4	2.05	.62
Improve Services	1	4	1.95	.71
Target New Customers	1	3	1.89	.57
Links to Customers	1	4	1.89	.66
Promotion	1	4	1.84	.76
Company's Reputation	1	3	1.84	.50
Competitive Advantage	1	3	1.84	.60
Information Transfer	1	3	1.84	.50
Links to Suppliers	1	3	1.84	.50

Note : Number of respondents=13, SD is Standard Deviation.

The scales of measurement were tested using Cronbach á reliability test. Cronbach á was 0.8228 which is satisfactory level of construct reliability. The correlations between the factors were then examined and it appears that correlations exist between certain factors. These findings suggested the use of factor analysis to investigate any separate underlying factors and to reduce the redundancy of certain barriers indicated in the correlation matrices. Principle Components Analysis was chosen as the method of extraction in order to account for maximum variance in the data using a minimum number of factors.

TABLE 57.8
Factors Influencing EC Adoption

Factors	*Loadings*	*Eigen Value*	*Percentage of Variance Explained*	*Cumulative Variance*
Marketing		4.812	43.744	43.744
Link to Suppliers	.752			
Link to Customers	.862			
Develop New Products for Existing Customers	.610			
Effective Promotion	.909			
Competitiveness		2.393	31.762	65.503
Company Reputation	.909			
Reduce Costs	.677			
Competitive Advantage	.690			
Improve Services to Customers and Suppliers	.778			
Access/Entry to New Market		1.198	17.867	76.392
Target New Customers	.768			
Easy Access to Markets	.731			
Facilitate Information Transfer	.791			

The default solution (eigenvalues > 1) resulted in three factors being extracted. A three-factor solution was extracted with eigenvalues of 4.812, 2.393 and 1.198. These three factors accounted for 76.392 per cent of the total variance. Table 57.8 summarizes the orthogonal solution resulting from a principal components/varimax rotation of the original five measures.

The factor 1 variables: "Links to suppliers", "Links to Customers", "Developing new products/services for existing customers", "Effective Promotion" are interpreted under the construct *Marketing*. Factor 2 was named as *Competitiveness* and includes the variables "Easy Access to Markets", "Reduce Costs", "Competitive Advantage" and "Company Reputation". Factor 3 was named as *Access/entry to New Market* and includes variables "Access to Market", "Information Transfer" and "Target New Customers".

5. DISCUSSION AND IMPLICATIONS

The result of the above study reveals that the SMEs are fully aware of internet and email, whereas there is partial awareness for ecommerce and poor awareness regarding Electronic Data Interchange (EDI). Consequently, almost all the firms are using e-mail and internet in their business whereas only thirty and ten percent firms use ecommerce and EDI respectively.

Study on the extent of adoption of the various ecommerce (EC) components reveals that depending on their usage, the ecommerce applications can be divided into four groups. Group one has maximum usage frequency, comprises of "E-mail", "Information search", "Usenet", "Intra-company communication", which were ranked one, two, there and four respectively. The second group of EC applications "exchange of information with clients", "exchange of information with suppliers", "market and product research", were given ranks six, seven and eight respectively. The third group of EC applications, that is used seldom, is "receiving orders from clients", "placing order to suppliers" and "medium of payment", were ranked nine, ten and eleven respectively. The fourth and lowest ranked group, rarely used, consists of applications related to "job recruitment advertisement" and "video conference", which were ranked twelve and thirteen respectively.

The extent of internet-based EC adoption for the SMEs based on the mean measure of usage frequency across six EC applications again is divided into four groups. For the six EC applications, the first group of EC applications with the largest frequency of usage (once a week) is "e-mailing". The second group, which is used once a week, consists of "internal communication" and "using for information search". The third group of EC applications based on the frequency of usage (several times a week) consists of "communicating with suppliers" and "communication with customers". The fourth group of EC applications with the least frequency of usage (once a month) is "market and product research".

Regarding use of website, "promotion of company" is the highest ranked purpose for the company maintaining a website, followed by "status symbol", "online purchase", "showcase products to potential customers", "inter-office functions" and "collect visitor's database".

The results of the study are significant to various organisations that are promoting the use of technology as a medium of doing business. Awareness needs to be improved regarding the components of ecommerce and EDI to the SMEs. They need to be made aware of the benefits and use of these ICT components in their business. ICT-related firms can accordingly market their products to these firms. Government organisations and public policy-makers need to create awareness among the small firms towards various ICT tools and possibly provide training to them regarding its use.

References

1. Blili, S. and Raymond, L. (1993), "Threats and Opportunities for Small and Medium-Sized Enterprises", *International Journal of Information Management*, Vol. 13, pp. 439-48.
2. Cragg, P.B. and King, M. (1993), "Small-Firm Computing: Motivators and Inhibitors", *MIS Quarterly*, Vol. 17, No. 1, pp. 47-60.
3. Europa—The European Commission (2003), "SMEs definition", available at: http://europa.eu.int/comm/enterprise/ enterprise_ policy/sme_definition/index_en.htm .
4. Fulantelli, G. and Allegra, M. (2003), "Small Company Attitude Towards Ict-based Solutions: Some Key-Elements To Improve It", *Educational Technology & Society*, Volume 6, No. 1, pp. 45-49.
5. Gregory, G., Karavdic, M. and Zou, S. (2007). "The Effects of E-Commerce Drivers on Export Marketing Strategy". *Journal of International Marketing*, 15(2): 30–57
6. Hill, R. and Stewart, J. (2000), "Human Resource Development In Small Organisations", *Journal of European Industrial Training*, Vol. 24, Nos. 2/3/4, pp. 105-17.
7. Jutla, D., Bodrick, P. and Dhaliwal, J. (2002), "Internet Research: Electronic Networking Applications and Policy", Volume 12, No. 2.
8. Kalakota, R. and Whinston, A. (1997), *"Electronic Commerce: A Manager's Guide"*, Addison-Wesley, Reading, MA.
9. Kaynak, E., Tatoglu, E. and Kula, V. (2005), An Analysis of the Factors Affecting The Adoption of Electronic Commerce by SMEs: Evidence from an Emerging Market. *International Marketing Review*, 22(6): 623-640.
10. MacGregor, R.C. and Vrazalic, L. (2005). A Basic Model of Electronic Commerce Adoption Barriers: A Study of Regional Small Businesses in Sweden and Australia. *Journal of Small Business and Enterprise Development*, 12(4): 510-27.
11. Magnusson, M. (2001), *"E-commerce in Small Businesses—Focusing on Adoption and Implementation"*, Proceedings of the First Nordic Workshop on Electronic Commerce, Halmstad, 28-29 May.
12. Martin, L. and Matlay, H. (2001), "Blanket' Approaches To Promoting Ict In Small Firms: Some Lessons From The Dti Ladder Adoption Model In The UK", *Internet Research: Electronic Networking Applications and Policy*, Vol. 11, No. 5, pp. 399-410.
13. NOIE (2002), *"E-Business For Small Business"*, The National Office for the Information Economy, available at: www.noie.gov.au/projects/ebusiness/Advancing.
14. Poon, S. and Swatman, P.M.C. (1998), *"Small Business Internet Commerce Experiences: A Longitudinal Study"*, Proceedings of the 11th International Bled Electronic Commerce Conference, Bled, 8-10 June.
15. Riquelme, H. (2002), "Commercial Internet Adoption in China: Comparing the Experience of Small, Medium and Large Businesses", *Internet Research: Electronic Networking Applications and Policy*, Vol. 12, No. 3, pp. 276-86.
16. Taylor, M. and Murphy, A. (2004), "SMEs and e-business", *Journal of Small Business and Enterprise Development*, Volume 11, Number 3, pp. 280-89.
17. Thomas, A.M. and Bridgewater, S. (2004), Internet and Exporting: Determinants of Success in Virtual Export Channels. *International Marketing Review*, 21(4/5): 393-408.
18. Van Akkeren, J. and Cavaye, A.L.M. (1999), *"Factors Affecting Entry-Level Internet Technology Adoption By Small Business In Australia: An Empirical Study"*, Proceedings of the Tenth Australasian Conference on Information Systems, Wellington.

58

Information Technology and Rural Development in India : Today and Tomorrow

AKHILESH KUMAR BHARDWAJ AND AMIT JAIN

ABSTRACT

Our maximum population lives in rural parts of India and if we want to be in the domain of developed countries; it should be our prior goal to empower the rural India. Here, IT can play a significant role. Information Communication Technology (ICT) like telecom services and internet services can play a very vital role for the rural development. This paper pays attention to how can IT contribute to the up lift meant of rural India? And, also, it watches that only IT can produce the desired results? How suitably can IT empower them to lead India to the developed country?

1. DESCRIPTION OF RURAL DEVELOPMENT PROJECTS

Gyandoot Project: District of Dhar, Madhya Pradesh—An ICT Initiative

Gyandoot means messenger of knowledge, is a Government-to-citizen intranet-based service portal, instituted in the state of Madhya Pradesh in district of Dhar in India in January Y2K. The Dhar district has a population of 2.0 million, 54% of whom are tribal and 40% are below poverty line (BPL).

The aim of designing the project was to extend the benefits of information technology (IT) to the people in rural parts by directly linking the state government and villagers through the information centers. These information centers or information hubs are named as KIOSKS. A Kiosk is generally a small room equipped with a computer, an internet connection, a printer, an UPS, furniture and stationary. The kiosks enable villagers to apply for different services and file complaints online by sending e-mails in Hindi or regional language to the district headquarters. E-mails received by the district headquarters are forwarded to the concerned department. These kiosks are located in government buildings or at prominent locations such as markets, or along main roads. The central hub is located in the district administrative headquarter. The information on the portal is in the local language, Hindi.

Warana Project in Maharashtra

The project Warana was a joint venture of National Informatics Centre (NIC—on behalf of Central Government), State Government of Maharashtra and Warana Vibhag Shikshan Mandal initiated in Kolhapur and Sangli District of Maharashtra in 1998. The project is a tool to *Bridge the Digital Divide* in the rural areas and has used information technology to access distinguished services. This project was started with an initial fund of 2.6 crores out of which 40% was chipped in by the Government of Maharashtra, 50% by Central Government and rest 10% by Warana Vibhag Shikshan Mandal. The project was launched with 6 business centres, 6 IT centers and 70 village kiosks. The project made the local administration transparent to the villagers especially in case of land-related matters and created a geographical information system (GIS) around 70 villages. The villagers could get the benefits of 6 web-based applications from the kiosks.

iKisan project

This project was a startup of Nagarjuna group of companies in Andhra Pradesh and Tamilnadu. iKisan project was started with the objective to provide need based agricultural information to the villagers by using two components ikisan.com and technical centers (kiosks). Knowledge seeker farmers can become the members of these kiosks by paying Rs. 100 per annum or Rs. 20 per month and can get the information offered by the project. The unique feature of this project is that the kiosk operators (soochaks) are agricultural graduates and have the knowledge of ICT, that's why they are able to diagnose, analyze and advise about diseases and can work better as the interface between computer networks and farmers. The Soochaks (the organizers of Kiosks) can get the information from both online (www.ikisan.com) and offline media (CD-ROM) and pass to the framers.

2. PROCESS AND IMPACTS

1. The *Gyandoot* project was started up with 39 kiosks (20 governments owned and 19 privately owned) and with a budget of 2.5 million. The project provides services in 9 blocks of Dhar District, each kiosk serving 25 to 30 villages, with a population of 20,000 to 30,000. Each kiosk consists of a computer, a printer, an uninterrupted power supply, furniture, stationery. For connectivity, 32 kiosks use fiber optics and other have wireless in local loop (WILL). The project has a server with Windows, some customized softwares and DBMS installed on it in Hindi language. The information provided to the farmers are collected by the project staff from different departments and magazines. The time elapsing between new information being received by the project staff and the average member of the farming community receiving it, ranges from one day to one week. The villagers can use the services provided by the project by paying a fee of Rs. 10 to 20 per service. More than 6000 email-complaints were filed by the villagers in first year of this project, which shows the success of this project and the inefficiency of the district administration. Lots of work have been done by this project for the rural youth like more than 120 rural youth were trained in kiosks. Computer training centres were established in various high schools. Impressed by the success of this project, a member of parliament has allocated Rs. 25,00,000 to develop a new model of e-education by setting up kiosks in 30 schools. After recognizing the interest of people in ICT, Indira Gandhi National Open University (IGNOU) has started a study centre for UG and PG courses on computer applications.
2. The *Warana* project was started with 70 kiosks at village level with a budget of 25 million. But after some time, the number has reduced to 56 active kiosks. These kiosks provide the services to many villages of Sangli and Kolhapur district in Maharashtra. To support this project, 25 co-operative societies were formed. To provide the agricultural information to the farmers, an independent agriculture development department has been set up by these societies. Each kiosk consists of a computer, networking hardware, associated softwares (in regional language) and some customized softwares. Each kiosk is facilitated with power supply and furniture. For network connectivity, 10 mbps intranet and internet (by telephone line) and 2 mbps WLL (Wireless in Local Loop) were used. Information could be accessed from three types of DBMS namely Application server, Internet and Mail-server. The time interval between the information being received by the project staff and farmers receiving it ranges from 1 to 2 days. The major sources of the information for the project staff were various

development departments and magazines. ICT as the information gathering tool was not so much popular.

3. The *iKisan* project started off with 9 information centers or kiosks in Andhra Pradesh, but this had increased to 18 by the time of the investigation. The project used two servers (external memory 40 GB each, NT server Operating System) with three database servers namely Application server, Internet server and Mail sever. For network connectivity, a leased line of 100 mbps is used. There are 3 hub centres, each connected by 10 terminals (with windows-98). The major sources of information for project staff was www.ikisan.com, Nagarajuna reports, Acharya NG Ranga Agricultural university's agricultural experts and magazines. The time taken for the information received at the kiosk to reach the farmers ranged from one day to seven days. Project staff used ICT as an information-gathering tool very rarely.

Comparative Study of Three Projects

1. It was very encouraging that so many villagers had taken the benefits of these projects, but unfortunately the graph of the number of villagers using the services of these projects is following top-down approach.
2. *Age Factor* of the *users* of these projects played very important role in the success of these projects; the participation of the youth is negligible.

3. PROJECT STAFF

An attempt has been made to understand the functional characteristics of the ICT-based three projects.

A. Educational Qualifications

Interesting differences have been found out when comparative analysis of qualifications took place.

In Gyandoot project 50% of the staff had completed their secondary education or intermediates, but not up to the degree level (83% of them having computer basics).

In Warana project 50% of staff was graduate (70% of them having computer basics) and in iKisan project, 57% were agriculture graduates (17% of them having computer degree). In Gyandoot, matriculates were encouraged to become Soochaks. In Warana project, co-operative members were kiosk operators while in iKisan project technically qualified people were preferred. Thus, the staff of the Gyandoot project appears to be well qualified technically.

B. Training Parameters

In Gyandoot project, 87% of the staff has received a one month training course. During that they had a good exposure to the philosophy, approach, objectives, procedures and activities of the project. After that, they received individual guidance per week and a full day meeting every month for all the soochaks. 97% of the staff in Warana project pursued training (7 to 10 days) on joining the project including collection and printing online payment slips and giving them to farmers, providing solution of the problems of the farmers, sending e-mails to head office etc. 90% staff of iKisan project pursued training.

TABLE 58.1
Comparative Training Parameters

Training %	*GYANDOOT*	*WARANA*	*IKISAN*
Training received	86.66	96.60	90.11
Training not received	13.33	3.33	10.00

C. Interest in ICT

Favorable use of ICT was 33% in Gyandoot project, 26.6% in Warana project and 70% in iKisan project.

D. Faith in People

In Gyandoot project, 73% staff showed a moderate level of faith and 13% showed a low level of faith.

In warana, 60% staff showed a moderate level of faith and 23% showed a high level of faith.

In iKisan, 53% showed a moderate level and 23% showed low level faith.

4. LIMITATIONS AND CHALLENGES AHEAD

It is proved that the implementation of ICT is relatively significant for the development of rural areas but instead of one way effort by the Government/Corporate sectors or NGOs, we need simply two way dynamic communications between the organizers and the villagers. This is practically not shown in the early projects.

Causes may be—

1. Illiteracy deadlocks rural people to understand and utilize the impact of ICT.
2. Proper training, feedback policy and review structure is not followed professionally.

3. Poor infrastructure and transportation facilities.
4. Villagers focus on basic survival needs rather than welcoming the new concepts and technologies.
5. Participation percentage of corporate sectors is not up to the mark.
6. Negligible participation of women and youngsters.

5. CONCLUSION AND IDEAS

Although every project starts with enthusiasm and research work but due to limitations, it fails or misses the desired success rate. *Implementing ICT is not the single solution but making the knowledge a part itself, technology may bring the revolution for rural India.*

1. *Government should re-orient* its policies according to the needs of the people and geographic conditions from time to time.
2. *Vocational training courses* for the economic and social growth of rural students and farmers using user friendly softwares, GUIs and pictorial information.
3. *Technical institutions* (Engineering colleges/Polytechnics/ITIs) in rural parts, regional university centers, rural post offices, railway stations, panchayat offices and schools may be developed as the information hubs or knowledge parks for providing agricultural, health and educational services.
4. *Private media channels and News service* providers could play a major role for the rural development in India.
5. A *Rapid survey and awareness* campaigning before establishing the project can create faith in community (in case of Gyandoot project, 60% of villagers did not use Gyandoot due to unawareness).
6. *Mobile-based information* centers could do better than PC-based kiosks in the initial phase of the project. They are cheap and easy to handle.
7. *Focus* on a particular class of service rather than mixing the service pattern.
8. *Corporate giants in IT, media and agriculture* and infrastructure sector could combine their efforts to use multidimensional skills for rural development.
9. *Improvement* needed in rural telecom services.

Some Projects at a Glance—

- Land record computerization (BHOOMI) in Karnataka (grant/aid driven).
- www.tarahaat.com-Uttar Pradesh and Punjab (grant/aid driven).
- SRISTI (society for research and initiative) in Gujarat runs project entitled knowledge network for grass-root innovations (grant/aid driven).

- Jai-kisan project in Uttaranchal (initiated by a NGO).
- Rural e-Seva project (district Godavari, stare A.P.).
- INFO-VILLAGE by MSSRF in Pondicherry.

Few agricultural portals—

- www.krishiworld.net
- www.acqachopal.com
- www.agriwatch.com
- www.soyachopal.com

References

1. GOI (2001), 'Report of Prime Minister's Task Force on India as Knowledge Superpower'. Planning Commission, Government of India, New Delhi.
2. Meera, S.N. (2002), A Critical Analysis of Information Technology in Agricultural Development: Impact and Implications. Unpublished Ph.D. thesis, IARI, New Delhi
3. Swami Nathan, M.S. (1993) (ed.), *Information technology: Reaching the Inreached.* Chennai: Macmillan India.
4. Gomez, R., and B. Casadiego, 2002, Letter to Aunt Ofelia: Seven Proposals for Human Development using New Information and Communications Technologies. A Publication of the International Development Research Centre, Available [Online]: http://www.web.idrc.ca/en/ev-8199-201-1-DOTOPIC. html.
5. Kiri, K. and D. Menon. 2006, "For Profit Rural Kiosks in India: Achievements and Challenges" in Information for Development. Information Technologies for Development Last accessed: 22 August 2006. Address: http://www.i4donline.net/articles/currentarticle.asp?articleid=700&typ=Features.
6. Madon, S., 2004, Evaluating the Developmental Impact of E-Governance Initiatives: An exploratory framework. Edited by M.P. Gupta, In Towards E-Government,. New Delhi: Tata McGraw-Hill.
7. Menon, D., K. Kiri, and K. Toyama, 2006, Rural PC-Kiosks: Who Benefits and How? Paper read at Indian Telecentre Forum 2006, at New Delhi.
8. Mission 2007. 2006. Every Village a Knowledge Centre. Last accessed: 29 September 2006. Address: http://www.mission2007.org/.
9. Prakash Naveen, "Evaluating the Impacts of the Gyandoot Project", Regional Development Dialog, Volume 24, Autumn 2002 (United Nations Center for Regional Development).
10. Info-Change: IT and Development, "Netsurfing in a Dhar Village: An Intranet Network Brings the Administration Closer to Village India." URL: <http://www.infochangeindia.org/ItanddIstory.jsp?recordno=183§ion_idv=9>.
11. Jafri, Anwar, Amithabh Dongre, V.N. Tripathi, Aparajita Aggarwal, Shashi Shrivastava. 2002, "Information Communication Technology and Governance:
12. The Gyandoot Experiment in Dhar District of Madhya Pradesh, India", London: Overseas Development.
13. Institute. URL: http://www.odi.org.uk/publications/working_papers/wp160.pdf
14. Madhya Pradesh Agency for Promotion of Information Technology. URL: http://www.mapit.gov.in/GDhome.htm

59

Applications of Simulation in Business Process Modelling : Potential Barriers and Advantages

ASHU GUPTA, KAWALJEET SINGH AND RAJESH VERMA

ABSTRACT

As organisations need to adapt to new business conditions and respond to competitive pressures, various change management approaches have been developed. Many studies suggest that the success of business change projects could be increased by developing dynamic models of business processes prior to their radical change. This paper investigates a potential of simulation modelling to be used for modelling business processes. It is postulated that discrete-event simulation can be considered as a missing link between change management approaches such as Just in Time (JIT), Total Quality Management (TQM) or Business Process Re-engineering (BPR). The usability of simulation modelling for evaluating alternative business process strategies is investigated, and the guidelines for achieving more widespread use of business process simulation are proposed.

1. INTRODUCTION

Simulation modelling is being widely used for modelling and analysis of systems in various application areas such as manufacturing, construction, transport, logistics, communication networks, health care, military, etc.

Another, gradually emerging application area of simulation is business process modelling (BPM).

Many organisations have to implement some sort of change management approach in order to survive in competitive business environments. Examples of such approaches include Total Quality Management (TQM), Just in Time (JIT), Business Process Re-engineering (BPR), Process Innovation (PI) and Knowledge Management (KM). Any change brings substantial risk as it is usually difficult to predict the outcome of changes before they are put into practice, and it is evident that the failure rates of business process change related project are high. For example, it is estimated that the failure rate of BPR projects is over 50% (Hammer and Champy, 1993).

It seems reasonable to claim that simulation modelling could offer a great potential in modelling and analysing business processes, and therefore reduce the risk associated with business process change. For example, these models can dynamically model different samples of parameter values such as arrival rates or service intervals which can help discovering process bottlenecks and investigating suitable business alternatives. Simulation models can provide a graphical display of process models that can be interactively edited and animated to show process dynamics. Most importantly, such models enable conducting of "what if" analysis that can be used to evaluate the consequences of changes before they are implemented.

This paper investigates a potential of simulation modelling to be used for modelling business processes and demonstrates the supporting role of simulation for business process change projects. It is argued that there is a need for a wider use of simulation techniques by business community. The paper is structured as follows. Following a discussion on the business process modelling methods and tools, the suitability of discrete-event simulation for business process modelling is investigated. Several management innovation and change programs including TQM, JIT, BPR, PI and KM are then presented, and a discussion on how simulation modelling could increase their effectiveness is provided. It is argued that simulation could be viewed as a missing link between these approaches. Furthermore, some guidelines on achieving more extensive use of simulation for business process modelling within the business community are proposed. Finally, the conclusions outline the main findings of this research.

2. BUSINESS PROCESS MODELLING METHODS AND TOOLS

The increasing business and academic interest in organisational change has resulted in a multitude of approaches, methodologies, and techniques to support these design efforts (Wastell *et al.*, 1994; Harrison and Pratt, 1993). Kettinger *et al.* (1997) conducted an empirical review of existing methodologies, tools, and techniques for business process change and developed a reference framework to assist positioning of tools and techniques that help in re-engineering strategy, people, management, structure, and technology dimensions of business processes.

Although simulation is mentioned as one of the modelling methods in a survey conducted by Kettinger *et al.* (1997), the authors identified a need for more user-friendly multimedia process capture and simulation software packages that could allow easy visualisation of business processes and enable team members to actively participate in modelling efforts.

Business process modelling tools are continuously being released in the software market. Many of these tools represent business processes by graphical symbols, where individual activities within the process are shown as a series of rectangles and arrows. A majority of software tools for business process modelling have an origin in a variety of process mapping tools that provide user a static view of the processes being studied. Some of these tools provide basic calculations of process times. Other, more sophisticated, tools allow some attributes to be assigned to activities and enable some sort of process analysis. However, most of these tools are not able to conduct "what if " analysis and show a dynamic change of business processes and evaluate the effects of stochastic events and random behaviour of resources which is possible by using simulation models of business processes. Simulation software tools are able to model dynamics of the processes such as the build up of queues and show it visually, which, then, can enhance generating the creative ideas on how to redesign the existing business processes.

It is apparent that there is a lack of a comprehensive, scientifically established design methodology to structure, guide, and improve business process modelling efforts. Many authors argue that one of the major problems that contribute to the failure of business process change projects is a lack of tools for evaluating the effects of designed solutions before implementation (Paolucci *et al.* 1997; Tumay 1995). However, the lack of modelling tools is only a part of the problem. Perhaps, even more important obstacle for more widespread use of simulation for business process modelling is a lack of awareness of simulation within the business community.

3. THE SUITABILITY OF DISCRETE-EVENT SIMULATION FOR BUSINESS PROCESS MODELLING

Simulation models of business processes can help overcome the inherent complexities of studying and analysing businesses and, therefore, contribute to a higher level of understanding and improving these processes. In terms of the business environment, simulation models usually focus on the analysis of specific aspects of an organisation, such as manufacturing or finance.

There are relatively few examples of using simulation for business process modelling available in the literature. A majority of these publications were written by simulation modelling practitioners rather than business analysis specialists. In one of the articles related to business process simulation, authors (Tumay, 1995) discovered that over 80% of BPR projects used static flowcharting tools for business process modelling. Static modelling tools, that are predominately used, are deterministic and do not enable evaluating alternative re-designed processes. The use of business process modelling tools is usually focused on modelling current business process without a systematic approach to evaluate business processes alternatives. On the other hand, simulation models can incorporate and depict dynamic and random behaviour of process entities and resources. A physical layout and interdependencies of resources used in processes under consideration can be shown visually and the flow of entities among resources can be animated using simulation as a modelling tool.

Simulation models provide quantitative information that can be used for decision-making and can be regarded as problem understanding rather than problem-solving tools. There are several characteristics of simulation that make it suitable for business process modeling. For example, a simulation model can be easily modified to follow changes in the real system and as such can be used as a decision support tool for continuous process improvement. Furthermore, a process-based approach (world view) in simulation modeling terminology relates to a time-ordered sequence of interrelated events which describes the entire experience of entity as it flows through the system.

The visual interactive features of many simulation packages available in the market enable a graphical display of dynamic behavior of model entities, showing dynamic changes in state within processes. Simulation model can incorporate the stochastic nature of business processes and the random behavior of their resources. Finally, simulation models can capture the behavior of both human and technical resources in the system.

Simulating the effects of redesigned processes before implementation improves the chances of getting the processes right at the first attempt. Visual interactive simulation models, together with a variety of graphical output reports, can demonstrate the benefits of redesigned processes which is useful for business process re-engineering approval. Simulation could also be useful for focusing 'brainstorming' meetings, where various new ideas can be tested using a simulation model, and informed decisions can be made on the basis of model results.

To summarise, there are several characteristics of discrete-event simulation that make it suitable for business process modelling (Hlupic, 1998):

- A simulation model can be easily modified to follow changes in the real system and as such can be used as a decision support tool for continuous process improvement.

- A process-based approach (world view) in simulation modelling terminology relates to a time-ordered sequence of interrelated events which describes the entire experience of entity as it flows through the system.
- The flow of information within and between business processes can be modelled as the flow of temporary entities between processing stations.
- A simulation model of non-existing business processes can be developed and used for process design (rather than for redesign).
- Simulation models can capture the behaviour of both human and technical resources in the system.
- The visual interactive features of many simulation packages available in the market enable a graphical display of dynamic behaviour of model entities, showing dynamic changes in state within processes.
- Simulation model can incorporate the stochastic nature of business processes and the random behaviour of their resources.

4. DISCRETE-EVENT SIMULATION: A SUPPORT FOR CHANGE MANAGEMENT PROGRAMS

It is important to address the supporting role of simulation for various business process change management approaches in the context of business process modelling. Five well known change management approaches are considered in this research: *Total Quality Management* (related to company-wide quality improvement initiatives), *Just-in-Time* (focused on inventory reduction), *Business Process Re-engineering* (involving a radical change of business processes in order to achieve better business performance), *Process Innovation* (focused on radical change of business processes and innovation of core processes) and *Knowledge Management* (related to systematic generation, codification and transfer of company knowledge). Table 59.1 demonstrates how simulation can support these approaches and help increase their effectiveness.

It is apparent that simulation modelling could play an important role in supporting all five approaches. Simulation models could provide a graphical display of physical elements and/or business processes, and capture dynamic changes. These models could be used as communication tools to help people understand the current processes using AS-IS models, and evaluate the impact of changes using TO-BE models. Random behaviour of system elements can be simulated by models as well as changes to the layout of systems, priorities, sequencing of tasks and human resource management.

A major difference between change management approaches in the context of simulation is that models that support TQM and JIT are usually manufacturing oriented. They tend to represent the flow of physical objects (for example, the movement of parts between work centres). But models

TABLE 59.1

A Comparison of Five Innovation and Change Programs

Concept	*The Role of Simulation*
Total Quality Management (TQM)	Decision support system for continuous improvement, graphical display of physical elements, simulating dynamic changes of the system, communication tool, problem understanding tool, AS-IS *vs*. TO-BE models, random behaviour of system elements captured in models, manufacturing-oriented models, models usually represent the flow of physical objects
Just-In-Time (JIT)	Decision support system for continuous improvement, graphical display of physical elements, simulating dynamic changes of the system, communication tool, problem understanding tool, AS-IS *vs*. TO-BE models, random behaviour of system elements captured in models, manufacturing-oriented models, models usually represent the flow of physical objects
Business Process Re-engineering (BPR)	One off study for evaluating strategy for radical change, graphical display of business processes, simulating dynamic changes of the system, communication tool, problem understanding tool, AS-IS *vs*. TO-BE models, random behaviour of system elements captured in models, 'people'-oriented models, models usually represent the flow of information
Process Innovation	One off study for evaluating innovation to core processes, graphical display of business processes, simulating dynamic changes of the system, communication tool, problem understanding tool, AS-IS *vs*. TO-BE models, random behaviour of system elements captured in models, 'people' oriented models, models usually represent the flow of information
Knowledge Management	Simulation models can be used to investigate knowledge management processes, to simulate missing data needed for knowledge management, and to evaluate alternative models of knowledge management strategies. One off or continuous study for evaluating knowledge management processes, graphical display of business processes, communication tool, AS-IS *vs*. TO-BE models, 'people' and information-oriented models, models usually represent the flow of information/knowledge.

that support BPR, Process Innovation and Knowledge Management, normally, deal with the flow of information and how resources may be re-deployed. These models are usually 'people-oriented' as business processes normally involve human resources.

In the context of TQM, simulation models can incorporate business activities undertaken by employees and provide a graphical display of tasks undertaken by different workers, their duration and sequence, dynamic changes of activities and any potential bottlenecks could be discovered. As such, simulation models could be used regularly as decision support tools for continuous improvement. For example, a simulation model of a production system could be used for investigating operating strategies that would reduce the size of inventory, machine cycle times, assess various scheduling rules, or reduce the level of faults. By doing this, any changes to be done to the real system could be tested on the model to avoid risks of inadequate decisions, and business activities could then be better understood. When changes tested on the model are implemented in the real system, effectiveness of the system should be improved as well as the competitiveness of an organisation.

Whilst JIT has been viewed as a management philosophy of integrated manufacturing, planning and control in Japan, the western countries often see JIT in the narrow context of inventory control (Currie and Hlupic, 2000). Simulation modelling can support both approaches to JIT. Real-time models of an integrated manufacturing system could incorporate models of inventory control systems, production design, and resource planning and scheduling. In addition, detailed models of inventory control systems can be used regularly to assess the impact of various JIT strategies, the inventory re-ordering policies, optimal levels of inventory and so on.

In the context of BPR, it is apparent that mistakes brought about by BPR can only be realized once the redesigned processes are implemented, when it is too late, costly and probably impossible to easily correct such errors. Although the evaluation of alternative solutions may be difficult, this may reduce some of the risks associated with BPR projects. For example, Hlupic *et al.* (2000) presented a business process model of a telephony system of a large multinational company that has been used for determining business processes that needed to be radically changed. The impact of these changes was investigated using the model before the real system was changed.

Like BPR, the essence of Process Innovation is to radically reshape or even transform key business processes to enhance business performance. This approach emphasizes innovation and not just improvement. The focus is on one-time change. Here, simulation models may be developed to investigate key processes to determine innovation strategies, to develop a vision of new processes and to evaluate alternative models of new processes.

In the context of knowledge management, simulation models can be used to investigate knowledge management processes, to simulate missing data needed for knowledge management, or to evaluate alternative models of knowledge management strategies. Simulation projects usually relate to one-off or continuous study for evaluating knowledge management processes. Models are normally 'people' and information-oriented, as they models usually represent the flow of information and knowledge, or could show the effects of new knowledge management practices on business processes. Such models could incorporate human resources and their involvement with knowledge management, and they are not concerned with movements of physical objects within the system.

5. GUIDELINES FOR MORE EXTENSIVE USE OF BUSINESS PROCESS MODELLING

So far, the paper has argued for the need to use discrete-event simulation for business process modelling, in order to reduce the risk associated with business process change projects. However, it is apparent that the potential of simulation for business process modelling is yet to be recognised within the business community. Relatively few publications on business process change and simulation were mainly written by simulation specialists and there is little evidence about the awareness of simulation within the business community. For example, the ProSci's 1997 Benchmarking Study (ProSci, 1997) analysed over 60 large international organisations that went through BPR exercise. The study has analysed the issues such as the reasons for redesigning business processes, methodology and modelling tools used, applying change management concepts, and the role of managers within BPR teams. It is interesting to note that the study revealed that only less than 10% of the companies used simulation software as a modelling tool. Other tools used include flowcharting tools, spreadsheet, project management tools, word processors and database development tools.

A survey on the use of simulation software (Hlupic, 2000) revealed that only about 6% of the survey participant used discrete-event simulation packages for business process modelling.

There are many ways to increase the awareness of simulation potential in business process modelling arena. Some of the guidelines and strategies that could be employed include:

- More widespread teaching of simulation in business and management courses both at undergraduate and postgraduate level,
- Increasing the awareness of top management about the potential benefits of business process modelling,
- Wide dissemination of the information about successful BPM case studies,
- Introducing special journals on BPM,
- Providing more books on BPM, and
- Providing better software tools for BPM.

6. CONCLUSION

This paper has investigated the potential benefits and obstacles in using discrete-event simulation for business process modelling. It is apparent that whilst simulation can support business process change related projects and reduce the risk associated with such projects, it is still not being widely used as a business process modelling method within the business community. Regardless of precise estimations, it is apparent that a more widespread use of simulation for business process modelling can increase the rate of success of business process change projects, which should then result in savings of resources and better service provided to the customers.

It has been demonstrated that discrete-event simulation can support five most popular change management approaches. It could be claimed that modelling provides an important means of discovering the essential aspects of the organisational system where improvements will make a real difference in performance as well as providing a sound basis for managing the consequences of the agreed actions (Ackermann *et al.*, 1999).

There are many reasons why simulation modelling should be used as a process modelling tool. For example, a new business process might involve a decision about capital investment that is difficult to reverse. It is, usually, too expensive to experiment with the real business processes, especially, if this involves large scale organisational change. In many cases, the variables and resources for new processes are not determined or understood. The process of simulation model development can facilitate a deeper understanding of some of these issues. The value of simulation depends on the model validity and the likelihood that the results of model experimentation may be replicated and implemented in the real processes.

In addition to modelling business processes to support BPR, Process Innovation and Knowledge Management approaches, simulation modelling could be (and has been) used in a manufacturing sector to support TQM and JIT strategies. In conclusion, it could be claimed that simulation modelling could be viewed as the missing link between these change management approaches, particularly as it may help to delineate the boundaries between them and how they may work in practice. In addition, another important benefit of simulation is its ability to provide continuity to change management in companies where the fads seem to come and go.

References

1. Ackermann, F., Walls, L. and Borman, M., 1999, Taking a strategic view of BPR to develop a multidisciplinary framework. *Journal of the Operational Research Society*, 50: 195-204.
2. Currie, W. and Hlupic, V., 2000, Change Management Panaceas and the Supporting Role of Simulation Modelling. Proceedings of the WSC'2000, Orlando, USA, 2022-28.
3. Hammer, M. and Champy, J., 1993, Reengineering the Corporation, New York: Harper Collins Books.
4. Harrison, B.D. and Pratt, M.D., 1993, A Methodology for Reengineering Businesses, *Planning Review* 21(2): 6-11.

5. Hlupic, V., 1998, Business Process Re-engineering and Simulation: Bridging the Gap. Proceedings of the European Simulation Multiconference ESM'98, Manchester, United Kingdom, 641-45.
6. Hlupic, V., Choudrie, J. and Patel, N., 2000, The REBUS Approach to Business Process Re-engineering. *Cognition, Technology and Workplace,* 2(2): 89-96.
7. Hlupic, V., 2000, Simulation Software: An Operational Research Society Survey of Academic and Industrial Users. Proceedings of the WSC'2000, Orlando, USA, 1676-83.
8. Kettinger, W.J., Teng, J.T.C. and Guha S., 1997, Business Process Change: A Study of Methodologies, Techniques, and Tools, *MIS Quarterly,* 55-80.
9. Paolucci, E., Bonci, F. and Russi, V., 1997, Redesigning organisations through business process re-engineering and object-orientation. Proceedings of the European Conference on Information Systems, Cork, Ireland, 587-601.
10. ProSci's 1997 Benchmarking Study—Best Practicess in Business Process Re-engineering and Process Design, 1997, ProSci.
11. Tumay, K., 1995. Business process simulation. Proceedings of the WSC'95—Winter Simulation Conference, Washington DC, USA, 55-60.
12. Wastell, G.W., White, P. and Kawalek, P., 1994, A Methodology for Business Redesign: Experience and Issues, *Journal of Strategic Information Systems,* 3(1): 5-22.

60

Impact of Information Technology in Training Methodologies : A Case Study of Cement Industry

S. BANERJEE AND RINKU SANJEEV

ABSTRACT

India today ranks second in the world, next only to china, in annual installed capacity and production of cement. However the per capita cement consumption at 130 kg, against the world average of 355 kg is in the lowest group in the world ranking falling much behind developing countries like Brazil (191 kgm), Thailand (366 Kgm)). The cement industry has achieved spectacular result by adding values to its HRD programs through the utilization of innovation in information technology. New training initiatives are required with effective training methodologies to update the manpower to meet the future challenges in cement industry.

In this paper, authors briefly discuss the impact of information technology in training area in Indian cement industry. This is resulting in increased learning, reduced learning time, reduced cost of training, increased employee productions, increased management efficiency, up gradation of skill at all levels and changes in attitude of work force. Today, the cement industry personnel are better equipped; they work with confidence and with better approach. There is no doubt that cement industry in India is going to has a bright future in the days to come.

Keywords: Information Technology, Training Methodology, Cement Industry, Future Challenges

1. INTRODUCTION

The world today is in transition from industrial age to information age. The information technology revolution is making tremendous impact on the industry and trade by relentless technology innovators, massive growth in computer power, world-wide networking.

The cement industry in India has been most responsive and performed well since 80s when it was put on liberalization phase. Cement industry has seen tremendous changes in terms of modernization and expansion over past decades. To keep pace with the modern technological advancements, this necessarily requires updation of knowledge and improvement of the skills of personnel at all levels already working in the industry.

Training is considered to be an important function contributing directly to the development of human resources. From survey carried, it is observed that a large number of Indian organization do not spend even 0.1 percent of their budget on training, thus it is neglected in most of the organizations. With the rapid changing technical scenario the role of training managers also changes, for example, cement industry has seen tremendous changes in terms of modernization and expansion.

Training recognizes the scientific and technological orientation its application, and at the same time, it percolates into a person for dignity, self reliance freedom and more responsibility, to achieve total participation and conviction. (1)

Information Technology (*IT*), as defined by the Information Technology Association of America (ITAA), is "the study, design, development, implementation, support or management of computer-based information systems, particularly software applications and computer hardware." In Information Technology (IT) as a whole, it is noted that the use of computers and information are associated. (2)

Information technology as per UNESCO has been defined as the scientific, technological and engineerining disciplines and the management techniques used in information handling and processing their application which facilitate interaction with man and machine and associated social, economic and cultural matters. (3)

From this definition, we can understand that the convergence of three stands of technologies such as computers, micro-electronics and communication constitute the information technology (IT) for the purpose of acquisition, process storage and dissemination of vocal, pictorial, textural and numeric information.

2. CHANGING SCENARIO IN HRD IN CEMENT INDUSTRY

India today ranks second in the world, next only to china, in annual installed capacity and production of cement. However, the per capita cement consumption at 130 kg., against the world average of 355 kg. is the lowest group in world ranking falling much behind developing countries like Brazil (191 kg), Thailand (366 kg). The Indian cement industry, presently is growing at around 9% annual CAGR and poised for quantum jumps in more than 100 million tones capacity addition in the span of a few years, is currently jettisoned by infrastructure bottlenecks at each stage of project implementation. (4)

Human resource base and skill development of workers to cope with quantitative and qualitative demands of a fast expanding industry and changing technologies need continuous up-gradation at all levels. The projected fast track cement capacity growth to reach 298 mn tones by 2011-12 faces a threat of acute shortage of high skilled and technological manpower, if, one goes by the present disposition of their availability and slow increment growth in India. To fulfil this objective, better HRM strategy has to be planned.

3. TRAINER'S. ROLE USING INFORMATION TECHNOLOGY (IT)

Training Managers at all levels are acquiring skills to use more IT to their advantages from systematic information handling to streamlining the

FIG. 60.1

Participation Profile of Trainees in Cement Technology Based Training

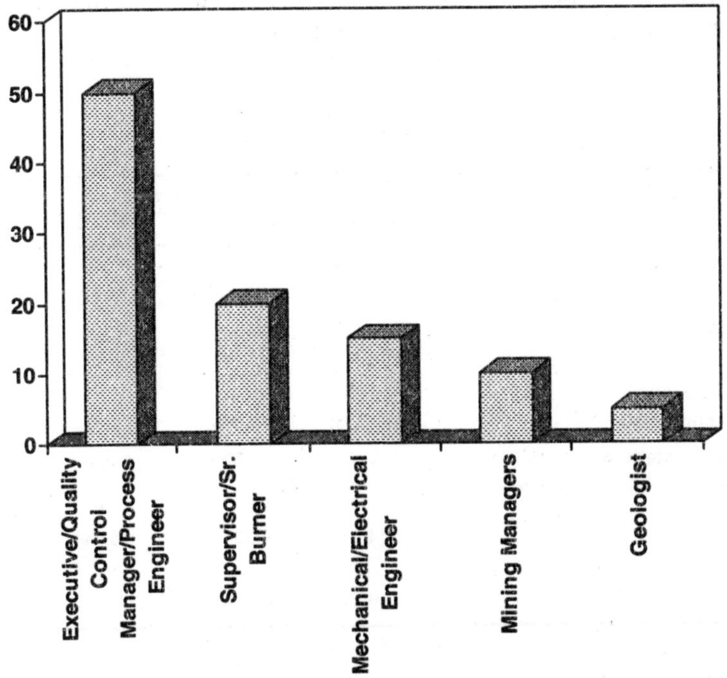

Top Management Middle management Supervisors	General Managers, Production Managers, Process Engineers, Mechanical, Chemical, Electrical Engineers, Senior Burners, Burners, Testers, Gangers, etc.

decision-making process and to disseminate the information to the advantage of others. A trainer's main objective is to transfer his or her knowledge and skills to the trainees. A class room session is not complete with out some relevant material provided to the trainees with extensive graphics, power point presentation, and better interaction between trainers and trainees and among the trainees themselves. Now there are LCD projection systems in most of the classrooms.

A survey was organized in leading training centre, where all the major cement plant personal participated in cement based training courses. The Figure 60.1 shows that Training programme attracts the existing professionals in the cement industry (from the 113 numbers of cement plants in India) which can be classified(5).

4. IMPACT OF IT IN TRAINING METHODOLOGIES AND INTERACTIVE LEARNING

The training courses encompasses the training methods like lectures, case studies group discussion, role playing using computers-based training (CBTS) packages. Training methodology is a determining factor and has a crucial role in training process. In the survey, trainees stated that they frequently uses lecture method, case study, group discussion, laboratory demonstrators hands on practices; and other methods like role playing, business games were rarely used. (Table 60.1)

TABLE 60.1
Training Methodology

Sl. No.	*Training Methods*	*Responses*			
		Frequent	*Occasionally*	*Rarely*	*Total*
1.	Lecture Method	102 (100%)	0 (0%)	0 (0%)	102 (100%)
2.	Group Discussion	96 (94.1%)	6 (5.9%)	0 (0%)	102 (100%)
3.	Laboratory Demonstration	98 (96.1%)	4 (3.9%)	0 (0%)	102 (100%)
4.	Other Methods—Role Playing, Business Games	4 (4%)	32 (32%)	64 (64%)	100* *2 Not respond (100%)
5.	CBT—Package	0 (0%)	68 (66.7%)	30 (33.3%)	102 (100%)

Now a days emphasis is gaining ground in interaction learning and computer-based training. Packages (CBTs) are being developed. CBT refers to specified software and other training material created exclusively for the purpose of training which can be loaded on a PC and operated. The Trainees are led to successive display of screen of information visuals and even audio information (multimedia) by pressing a key on the key board or clicking the mouse in various captions on the screen and, thus, the trainees can acquire the necessary skills and knowledge Thus, the CBT is useful for self-learning and in situations where trainers are scared or are tide up with other preoccupations.

The most important advantage of CBT is that a trainer can learn at his own pace whenever he is free from his scheduled work.

5. SIMULATOR BASED TRAINING

Now with the advancement of information technology (IT), simulator trainer is used in cement technology-based training courses. It has functions like process value manipulation. This technique enables to break the common barrier associated with the traditional student teacher relationship. Cement industry training contains the following systems for providing training:

1. Vertical Roller Mills for raw material coal as well as cement grinding.
2. Roller press-ball system for raw material and cement grinding.
3. Closed circuit ball mill for raw material coal and cement grinding.
4. Separate line Calciner (SLC)/in-line Calciner (ILC) kiln with 4/5/6 stage preheater and conventional/modern grate cooler.

6. CORPORATE BLOGGING : AN INTERACTIVE TOOL IN HRM

Corporate Blogging is an on-line plate form providing opportunities for active participation of employees at all levels, to read, to write and to communicate with each other on organizational issues, thereby, create open communication and suggest ways and means to improve upon them. Corporate blog is a corporate website, which is continuously updated as a corporate dairy, news outlet, text, links, audio/video and pictures can go into it. Blogging is an extremely cost effective way to build people management functions with newer contracts and opportunities. In modern day management, blogs are prerequisite for successful handling of people management. (6)

7. CORPORATE BLOGGING IN TRAINING AND DEVELOPMENT

"Corporate blogs can be used for training and development of employees in the organization. Training refers to the process of imparting specific skills, and development refers to the learning opportunities designed to help employee grow." (7)

The e-learning also known as "distributed learning" or "distance learning" or "technology-enabled learning" and on line learning, is a form of learning that uses a network of delivery, interactive or facilitation. The network may include Local Area Network (LAN) or Wide Area Network (WAN) and Internet or Intranet.

The management of any organization needs to initiate modern innovative process in HRM. The practices of traditional processes in HR are to the assessed and replaced with the process that has complete knowledge and close proximity to modern day employees at all levels. Many HR process needs lot of human interactions. With the changing lines today, free and open interaction with employees is paramount in a competitive world.

Hence corporate blogging will definitely help management come closer to employees and create a culture of trust, and develop a transparent communication in the organization. This is a future need of learning in the industry. The benefits are shown in Figure 60.2.

FIG. 60.2
Benefits of Multimedia Technology

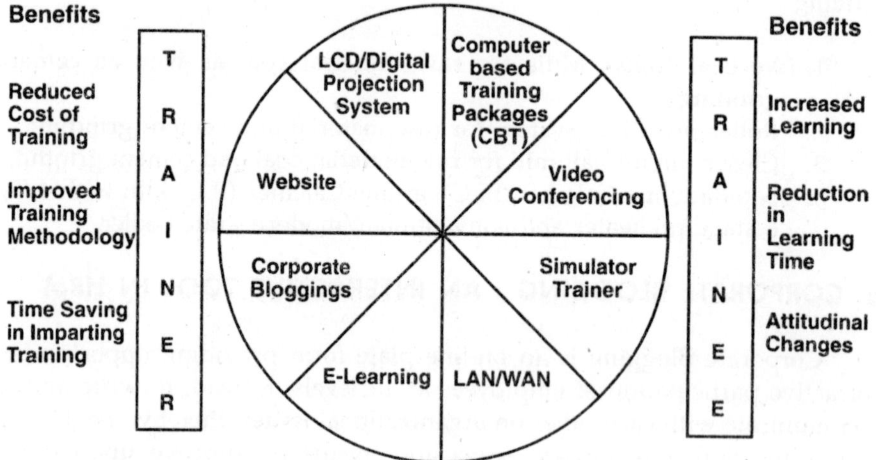

8. ARTIFICIAL INTELLIGENCE AND EXPERT SYSTEM

Artificial intelligence is that part of computer science that is concerned with developing intelligent computer programme. An intelligent computer program can in some sense think, i.e. solve problem in a way that would be considered intelligent if done by a human. Application area of Artificial intelligence (AI) includes game playing, theorem proving, general problem solving, perception, natural language understanding. Expert-System or "Knowledge Based System" is the most significant among the applications of AI. Expert System (ES) is an "intelligent "compute program that solves problem in a specialized domain by using knowledge acquired from experts. It has a great deal of domain specific knowledge embedded in it, the size and quality of which determines its success. It is capable of explaining its reasoning, which is essential since users will not accept results from a computer unless they are convinced of the accuracy of the reasoning process that produced the results.

The direct benefits of incorporating interactive training methodologies and multimedia technology in teaching/learning process include—

- Increase learning
- Reduction in learning time
- Reduced Cost of Training
- Increased Employee Productivity
- Increased Management Efficiency

9. CONCLUSION

Information technology has revolutionized the training methodologies of the Cement Industry in India. The cement Industry of today has achieved spectacular result by adding values to its HRD programs through interactive methodologies, i.e. utilization of innovations in information technology. This has resulted in increased learning, reduction in learning times, reduced cost of training, increased management efficiency, up-gradation of skill at all levels, changes in attitude of work force and increased management efficiency. This has brought new initiatives in training methodologies in cement Industry.

Today, India cement industry personnel are better equipped; they work with more confidence and with analytical approach. They have, now, a new outlook in achieving their objectives and goals. All this has been possible with the information technology revolution and by active support of the management of cement industry to adopt IT in their work culture, in order to have a competitive edge in international market.

There is no doubt that the cement industry in India is going to see a bright future in days to come. It is truly said that, if we are information rich we will naturally be in better position to compete with others.

References

1. Lynton, R.P. and Pareek, U., Training for Development, Vista Publication, New Delhi 1990.
2. www.wikipedia.com
3. Kankachary, M., "Information Technology *vis-a-vis* the Libraries—New vistas in Library and Information Science", Raju *et. al.*, Vikas Publication, p. 423, (1995).
4. S.P. Ghosh, G.Y. Narayana, Indian Cement Industry—Growth Trends and Future Perspectives, NCB Cement Manufacturers' Association—Special Publication, Delhi, Nov. 2007.
5. S. Banerjee, Trainer's Perception towards Training Process, *The Indian Concrete Journal*, Vol. 74, No. 9, September 2000.
6. G.C. Nag, Corporate Blogging, *HRM Review*, ICFAI University Press Vol. VIII Issue IV, April 2008, p. 40.
7. Aswathappa, K., Human Resource and Personnel Management—Text and Cases, New Delhi, Tata McGraw Hill Publishing Company, Fourth Edition, p. 194.

61

Deriving Business Value from ERP—A Case Illustration

ASHWANI KUMAR AND S.K. BANSAL

ABSTRACT

Increased globalization and ever escalating costs have placed continuous pressure on manufacturers to optimize resources, meet tighter delivery schedules, and improve overall responsiveness. These demands are driving change and forcing many companies to consider ERP strategies. Almost all organizations are turning to ERP package as a solution to their information management problems. ERP packages, if chosen correctly, implemented judiciously and used efficiently, have the ability to raise productivity and profits of the company. ERP software is no longer the legacies of big companies such as SAP, BAAN and JD Edwards, even local and indigenous software companies are also entering the foray.

The present paper highlights the concept of ERP and its functionality. A case study of an auto component manufacturer, deriving benefits by implementing Nuron ERP software has been presented. Nuron software is a Punjab-based Software company catering to the needs of mid and small sized companies.

1. INTRODUCTION

An ERP (Enterprise Resource Planning) system is a multi-module computer application which is designed to support all of the key activities of an enterprise in an integrated fashion. This includes managing the key elements of the supply chain operation—product planning, purchasing, production control, inventory control, interaction with suppliers and customers, delivery of customer service and keeping track of orders. It may also include HR modules which maintain a central database of the organization's people, which is critical to production and staff scheduling functions, and to staff payments.

An ERP is regarded as central to an organization's ambition to survive and prosper in today's business environment. It often replaces a myriad of individual systems including accounting systems, production planning and inventory control systems. It can be a much more effective way of providing computer support to the business functions. It is particularly relevant in case of large complex businesses or where it is necessary to rationalize and integrate systems, and operations in complex situations. It also allows for significantly greater efficiencies in managing the supply chain. Customers have become more dependent on faster delivery of products and tighter lead times. Safety stocks can almost disappear and JIT (just-in-time) philosophies dominate. In effect, ERP has the effect of making an enterprise more time-sensitive and consequently, more vulnerable to the impact of time delays.

The History of ERP

The history of ERP is about 50 years old. It has emerged as a strategic tool because of continuous improvement in the available techniques to manage business and the fast growth of information technology. The focus of manufacturing systems in the 1960's was on inventory control. Most of the software packages, then, (usually customized) were designed to handle inventory based on traditional inventory concepts. In the 1970's, the focus shifted to MRP (Material Requirement Planning) systems that translated the master schedule built for the end items into time-phased net requirements for the sub-assemblies, components and raw materials planning and procurement. In the 1980's, the concept of MRP-II (Manufacturing Resources Planning) evolved which was an extension of MRP to shop floor and distribution management activities. In the early 1990's, MRP-II was further extended to cover areas like Engineering, Finance, Human Resources, Projects Management, etc. i.e. the complete gamut of activities within any business enterprise. Hence, the term ERP (Enterprise Resource Planning) was coined. Originally, ERP packages were targeted at the manufacturing industry, and consisted of mainly functions for planning and managing core businesses such as sales management, production management, accounting and financial affairs, etc. However, in recent years, adaptations have been made to process and service industries also.

ERP (Heart of SCM): The term ERP was coined by the Gartner Group of Stanford, Connecticut. It ensures that a firm's manufacturing decisions are not made without taking into account their impact on the total supply chain. Implementation of ERP systems offers homogenous transactional databases that serves as the medium for accomplishing the integration of the decision-making process by automating every department in the company (Garg and Venkitakrishnan, 2005). An ERP is an integrated transaction processing and reporting system. The different software applications and forms of ERP support 'business process engineering'. ERP systems add 'process logic' to an organizational information system and create a fundamental discipline in business processes (Monczka *et. al.*, 1998).

"ERP is a planning philosophy enabled with software that attempts to integrate all the business processes of different departments and functions across a company onto a single computer system that can serve particular needs of the different departments."

The domain of ERP (Figure 61.1) covers finance, human resources, manufacturing, and distribution activities. It has undergone a series of improvements over the years. In the 1980s, ERP covered basic business functions such as purchase, sales, finance, manufacturing, quality control, plant maintenance, etc. During 1990s, some companies (Seibel and Clarify) integrated suppliers and customers databases into ERP packages through the Web, which were known as Extended ERP (EERP)/ERP II package. Later, some software vendors like COGNOS and Brio incorporated Business Intelligence, Auditor Information System and Transfer Pricing as standard modules; such an integrated package may be called Intelligent Enterprise Management System (IEMS) or ERP III.

FIG. 61.1
ERP Systems

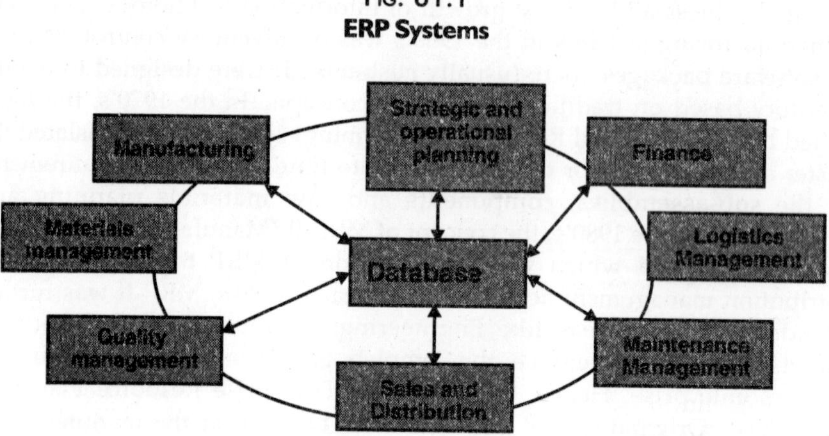

The new phase of collaboration has increased the significance of ERP systems as well as the need for a new generation of systems that support internal and external integration. The ability to expand processes and capabilities outside the company requires improved internal processes as well new capabilities that the first-generation of ERP systems lack. It has given birth to a new system called ERP II, a term coined by the Gartner Group. The ERP II application and deployment strategy is different from the ERP system in the ways given in Table 61.1.

TABLE 61.1
ERP vs. ERP II

Role	*ERP*	*ERP II*
Role	Enterprise Optimization	Collaborative Commerce and Supply Chain Management
Domain	Focus on Manufacturing and Distribution	Supply Chain, Customer-Facing, and Supplier Facing Systems
Function	Internal Processes such as Finance, Manufacturing, and Distribution	Cross-industry and specific Industry Concepts
Process	Internal and Hidden	External and Open
Architecture	Closed and Monolithic	Web-based, Open and Component-based Environment
Data	Internally Generated and Consumed	Internally and Externally Published and Subscribed

Source : Garg and Venkitakrishnan, 2005.

Covisint is an innovative vehicle founded by DaimlerChrysler, Ford, General Motors, Nissan, Renault, CommerceOne, Oracle and PSA Peugeot. Its main purpose is to connect the auto industry in a virtual environment to give momentum to decision-making, waste elimination, and cost reduction while supporting common business processes between manufacturers and their supply chain. It makes the information accessible and visible within a secure online environment. Covisint functions as the central hub where OEM (original equipment manufacturers) and suppliers join together to do business in a single business environment using one user ID and password.

2. BRIEF LITERATURE REVIEW

Vokurka et al., (2001) present an approach to improve the effectiveness of DRP (Distribution Requirement Planning) in an ERP environment with a case study of SPL Company. It was found that the company is not using this module effectively. DRP can improve the outbound logistics of the company without incurring additional costs. They have quantified the DRP benefits and the impact of these benefits has been projected on corporate profitability using ROI as the performance measure.

Chaturvedi and Gupta (2005) have presented a case study giving a detailed account of the failure of supply and demand planning software implementation at Nike, a leading footwear and apparel company. It traces the history of supply chain and ERP software implementation, and also details the circumstances that led to the SCM software implementation failure. Finally, the case explores how Nike was able to use the learning from the failure to its advantage and emerge successful with the SAP implementation, a part of the Nike supply chain project.

Aberdeen research (2007) has shown that cost of software, services, and maintenance are those factors which are most often measured and considered when evaluating software or measuring the return on investment of ERP implementation. Costs vary significantly as companies grow in size.

Basu and Siems (2007) found evidence that the impact of e-business technologies on supply chain operations have resulted in a reduced 'bullwhip effect', lower inventory, reduced logistics costs and streamlined procurement processes. These improvements, in turn, have likely helped to lower inflation, reduce economic volatility and strengthen productivity growth.

In another research in 2008, it was observed that rigid regulations and compliance requirements are a reality for manufacturers in process-related sectors. This places unique demands on ERP implementations and the quality management functions within the organization.

Reasons for the Growth of ERP

According to Jakovljevic (2006), ERP is becoming a necessary condition for globalization. It provides the competitive advantage by revitalizing organizations to bring agility in production and enabling management of supply chain demand. They are of the view that organizations need solid information system that supports all aspects of business with power and flexibility, and ERP provides such operational, managerial and strategic information for improving productivity, quality and competitiveness in a supply chain.

The ERP market is having a significant impact on the implementation strategies and execution plans of manufacturers. In addition, continued pressure on manufacturers to optimize resources, meet tighter delivery schedules, and improve overall responsiveness is driving change and forcing many companies to re-evaluate their ERP strategies. It is beyond doubt that ERP systems are in great demand today. Corporate pundits are expecting a growth rate of more than 50% in the next ten years. The following are the major drivers of ERP growth (Altekar, 2005):

1. To enable improved business performance through—
   - Cycle time reduction
   - Increased business agility
   - Reduction in inventory
   - Order fulfilment improvement
2. To support business growth requirements
   - New products/product lines, new customers
   - Global requirements

3. To provide flexible, integrated and real time decision support—
   - Improve responsiveness across the organization
4. To eliminate the limitations of legacy system—
   - Century dating issues
   - Fragmentation of data and processing
   - Inflexibility to change
   - Insupportable technologies
5. To take advantage of untapped mid-market—
   - Increased functionality at a reasonable cost
   - Client server/open systems technology
   - Vertical Market solutions

These are some of the reasons for the growth of ERP markets and ERP vendors. As more and more companies are entering the arena, the focus is also shifting from big companies to mid-size and small-size companies. The Table 61.2 shows the top ERP vendors and the aspiring ERP vendors.

TABLE 61.2
List of Latest ERP Vendors

Top 20 ERP Vendors	SAP, Oracle, Infor/SSA Global, Lawson/intentia, Microsoft Dynamics, Sage group, Epicor, Exact, IFS, Glovia, CDC Ross, QAD, JDA, CINCOM, American Software, SoftBrands, SYSPRO, Made2manage, ProfitKey, Intuitive.
Aspiring ERP players	iQMS, NetSuite, Tech Group, Beach Access Software, Deacom, Adonix, Blue Agave, Mincom, xERP, Software 21, Activant, Abacus Data Systems, Enterprise Logix, TTW, Friedman, Verticent, Foresight Software, OpenMfg, Ramco, Global Shop Solutions.

Source : Benchmarking ERP in Manufacturing, 2006, www.aberdeen.com

The future will see fierce battle for market share and mergers & acquisition for strategic and competitive advantage (Leon, 2000). Few years ago, ERP companies struggled hard for relative positioning on the "Top 50" list published annually by Manufacturing Systems Magazine (now MBT Magazine). Later, the list was expanded to top 100, so that aspiring market leaders could also get their share of focus. But now the list has shrunk to 15 vendors. Over 130 ERP products and extensions have been acquired over the years. Many of the market leaders of 80s and 90s such as Baan, Peoplesoft, JD Edwards, ASK, Cullinet and Panasophic have all been acquired by competitors. As a result, many ERP users may know the name of the product but are ignorant about the vendors. The following table shows genealogy of the top ERP vendors' solutions:

Table 61.3
ERP Solutions

Company	*Acquisition*	*Product*
(1)	*(2)*	*(3)*
Chinadotcom www.cdccorporation.net	Ross	Ross Enterprise
Cincom www.cincom.com		Cincom Manufacturing Business Solutions
Consona www.consona.com	• Made2manage • DTRPlastics • Cimnet • Axis • ÉnCompix • Intuitive	Made2manage, DTRPlastics,Cimnet, EnCompix, Axis, Intuitive
Epicor www.epicor.com	• Scala • Dataworks • DCD • Dataflow • Manfact	Enterprise, iScala, vantage, Vista, Dataflo, Manfact
Exact Software www.exactamerica.com	• Macola • Kewill	Macula, Kewill ERP, MAX, jobBoss
Glovia (Xerox Computer Systems) www.glovia.com		Glovia (Xerox Chess)
IFS www.ifsworld.com	• SSA Global • InterBiz of CA • ASK • Cullinet • Panasophic • Software International • Infinium • Marcam • Baan • Lilly • Future Three • Brain • Mapics • Frontstep (Symix) • Pivotpoint (Spectrum)	COM, BPCS, ERP LN, ERP LX, MANMAN, MK Manufactuirng, KBM, MAXCIM, CAS, PRMS, Masterpiece, Infinium, Prism, Protean, BAAN,Visual, TRANS4M, Expert, XA, Syteline, Adage, System 21, A+, FACTS, SX.e. Anael, Sun Systems, and Varial

(*Contd.*)

Table 61.3 (Contd.)

(1)	(2)	(3)
	• SCT • Geac • JBA • Extensity • Systems Union Group	
IQMS www.iqms.com	Enterprise IQ ERP	
Lawson www.iqms.com	• Intentia	S3, M3 (Movex)
Microsoft Dynamics www.microsoft.com/ dynamics	• Axapta • Great Plains • Navision • Solomon	Microsoft Dynamics AX, Microsoft Dynamics GP, Microsoft Dynamics NAV, Microsoft Dynamics SL
NetSuite www.netsuite.com		NetSuite
Oracle www.oracle.com	• Siebel • People soft • JD Edwards • Vantive • Redpepper	E-Business Suite, Peoplesoft Enterprise, JD Edwards EnterpriseOne, JD Edwards World
Plexus Online www.plex.com		Plexus Online
QAD www.qad.com		QAD Enterprise Applications 2007 (MFGPRO)
The Sage Group www.sage.com	• ACCPAC • Adonix • State of the Art	Sage PFW ERP, Sage Pro ERP, ACCPAC 90/?200/500
SAP www.sap.com		R/3, mySAP Business Suite, SAP Business One, SAP All-in-one
SYSPRO www.syspro.com		SYSPRO
Visibility www.visibiliuty.com		Visibility ERP3

Source : ERP In Manufacturing, 2007, www.aberdeen.com

3. ERP IN MANUFACTURING INDUSTRIES

Though, ERP strategies in manufacturing are mainly driven by global competition and response to accelerated growth, but it has also been revealed that majority of the companies view ERP as a strategic weapon to streamline and automate business processes in order to improve efficiencies. As a result, companies are prompted to take a holistic approach to ERP and to standardize both business processes and ERP implementations. This view has made them to achieve better control over inventory and manufacturing schedules and reduce time to month-end close. Table 61.4 shows the specific ERP vendors catering to the needs of various manufacturing industries:

TABLE 61.4

ERP Solutions for Manufacturing Industries

ERP vendor	*Manufacturing Industries Served*
Cincom www.cincom.com	Aerospace and Defense, Communications and Telecommunications, Industrial Products, Transport Equipment
Consona www.consona.com	Industrial and Commercial Machinery, Electronics, Furniture, Industrial equipments, Food machines
Epicor www.epicor.com	Aerospace, Automotive, Capital Equipment, Electronics, Medical devices, Machine Builders, Rubber and Plastics
Exact Software www.exactamerica.com	The Macola is a horizontal solution targeting mid-size manufacturers and the jobBOSS is suitable for job shops, custom manufacturers, and high tech shops
Glovia and Glovia www.glovia.com	Automotive, Capital Equipment, and Electronics
IFS www.ifsworld.com	Aerospace and defense, Automotive, Construction, Process Industries, Utilities and telecom
Infor www.infor.com	Automotive, Process Industries, Distribution, Industrial equipment, High tech and electronics
IQMS www.iqms.com	Plastics, Automotives, Consumer products, Medical, Appliances, Electronics and Computers
Lawson www.lawson.com	Fashion, Food and beverages, Wholesale distribution, Asset intensive industries, General manufacturing
Microsoft Dynamics www.microsoft.com	Automotive, Chemicals, Consumer packaged goods, Oil and gas, Utilities, and manufacturing
Oracle www.oracle.com	Industrial manufacturing, Hi-tech, Consumer packaged goods, Life sciences, communication, Engineering and Construction
Plexus Online www.plex.com	Automotive, Aerospace and defense, Medical devices
QAD www.qad.com	Automotive, Consumer packaged goods, Electronics, Industrial manufacturing, Life sciences
SAP www.sap.com	Aerospace, Automotive, Chemicals, Consumer products, High-tech, Life sciences, Mill products, Mining oil and gas
SYSPRO www.syspro.com	Aerospace, Automotive, Chemicals, Computer, Machinery, Medical devices, Services, Wholesale distribution, Consumer products

4. ERP IN PROCESS INDUSTRIES

Process manufacturers face some unique challenges in their business processes, potentially dealing with rigid regulations, compliance requirements, and tight control over manufacturing processes. The ERP efforts in these industries are targeted on the need to standardize and accelerate front office sales and support functions, through the manufacturing process, to shipping and logistics, as well as back office financial accounting. The multi-channel environment and increased global competition force such companies to reach beyond the traditional boundaries of ERP to include special features and extended functionalities. Aberdeen hypothesizes (Table 61.5) that profitable growth is the key enabler of ERP strategies for process industries. Yet, in order to achieve Best-in-Class performance, process manufacturers must also improve customer service and response times.

TABLE 61.5
Best-in-Class PACE Hypothesis

Pressures	*Actions*	*Capabilities*	*Enablers*
• Shareholder expectations of profitable growth	• Standardize and accelerate non-manufacturing processes (Order management, finance, administrative functions)	• Standardize enterprise wide procedures for order management, procurement, production planning and execution, cash collection and financial reconciliation	• Integrated ERP, integrated order entry, procurement, production, and financial management applications
	• Provide visibility to business processes across functions and departments	• Manufacturing operations are integrated and coordinated with customer service	• Industry specific ERP features
		• 100% able to comply with process manufacturing industry regulations	• Formula or recipe-based management, laboratory , and sample management
		• Able to measure both product and customer profitability	• Applications to support yield and inventory optimization

The following performance metrics were used to determine the best-in-Class:

- Reduced level of inventory

- Inventory accuracy
- Manufacturing schedule compliance
- Percent on-time and complete shipments
- Number of days to close a month

Some other metrics were also considered:

- Reduction in manufacturing operational costs and administrative costs
- Improvement in complete and on-time shipments
- Improvement in manufacturing schedule compliance
- Improvement in order-to-delivery cycle time
- Perfect order time

It was proved that with the passage of time, ERP has crossed the boundaries of core functionality. The number of modules and the extent of functionality have grown tremendously over the last two decades. The specific functionality required for process manufacturing is not fulfilled even by the largest ERP vendor. The following Table 61.6 shows the list of ERP vendors with process specific functionality:

TABLE 61.6
ERP Vendor Landscape

Company	*Selected Process Industries*
(1)	*(2)*
3i Infotech www.3i-infotech.com	Chemicals, Food and Beverages, Pharmaceuticals
Batchmaster www.batchmaster.com	Chemicals, Cosmetics, Food and Beverages, Paints and Coatings
Adonix www.adonix.com	Chemicals, Foods and Beverages, Life Sciences
CDC/Ross Systems www.cdcsoftware.com	Chemicals, Foods and Beverages, Pharmaceuticals
Deacom www.deacom.com	Pharmaceuticals, Foods and Beverages, Cosmetics, Adhesives, Paints
Fullscope www.fullscope.com	Foods and Beverages, Life Sciences, Primary metals, Pulp and Paper
Infor www.infor.com	Foods and Beverages, Chemicals, Pharmaceuticals, Life Sciences
Lawson www.lawson.com	Foods and Beverages, Chemicals, Pharmaceuticals, Life Sciences, Paints, Metals and Plastics
Oracle www.oracle.com	Chemicals, Life Sciences, Natural Resources, Foods and Beverages

(Contd.)

TABLE 61.6 (Contd.)

(1)	(2)
ProcessPro ewebpro.innovations.com	Foods and Beverages, Chemicals, Pharmaceuticals, Life Sciences
QAD www.qad.com	Foods and Beverages, Chemicals, Consumer goods, Life Sciences
Ramco www.ramco.com	Foods and Beverages, Chemicals, Pharmaceuticals, Life Sciences
Sage www.sagesoftware.com	Foods and Beverages, Chemicals, Pharmaceuticals, Life Sciences, Metals, Paints and Adhesives, Pulp and paper
Seradex www.seradex.com	Foods and Beverages, Chemicals, Pharmaceuticals, Life Sciences, paints, Metals and plastics
SAP www.sap.com	Home and Personal Care, Chemicals, Pulp and Paper
Technology Group International www.tgiltd.com	Foods and beverages, Chemicals, Pulp and paper

Source : ERP Plus in Process industries, 2008, www.Aberdeen.com

5. DERIVING BUSINESS VALUE FROM INFORMATION TECHNOLOGY IN AN AUTO COMPONENT FIRM

5.1 A Case Study—Nuron Software Technologies Pvt. Ltd.

Nuron is a leading provider of ERP solutions for Small and Medium Manufacturing Organizations (www.nuronsoftware.com).

Overview

Nuron develops and delivers a fully integrated suite of e-business & Enterprise Resource Planning (ERP) and Customer Relationship Management (CRM) applications designed to help small-to-midsize businesses (SMBs) to quickly respond to customers, suppliers, partners and employees around the world. *Nuron Infiniti* ERP is a flexible and affordable solution that offers to effectively streamline business processes across an organization, while providing tight integration and transparency of information. It allows staying on top of the business by providing a true and unified picture of critical, up-to-the minute business information across an organization. Although, Infiniti offers functionality, Nuron Infiniti—ERP software offers the solution to optimize and increase the productivity unlike other single-source suite of business applications. Infiniti consists of:

- Business and Accounting Software
- E-commerce and Distribution Modules
- Manufacturing and Payroll Systems
- Advanced Customization Tools

With a firm technical foundation and commitment to excellence in performance, Infiniti provides the required functionality and reliability.

SMB Makeover Program

Intel designed its SMB IT makeover program specifically for businesses in emerging markets. The program helps SMBs understand how to gain business benefits by investing in IT. Experts from Intel IT work with technology solution suppliers (such as ISVs, original equipment manufacturers [OEMs], and channel partners), to understand an SMB's current and future business needs. The team, then, designs an appropriate IT solution to create business value. Based on its knowledge, experience, and best practices, Intel IT provides unique insight into deploying IT for business value and works with the SMB after solution deployment to help it understand the quantitative business benefits created by the IT investment using an IT Business Value (ITBV) model. The makeover program creates shareable best practices, deployment guides, usage models, and case studies for specific solution sets, which can then be leveraged by the ISVs, OEMs, and channel partners to help their customers achieve measurable value from IT.

Nuron Software's Definition of ERP: ERP, the industry acronym for Enterprise Resource Planning, refers to the broad set of activities that multi-module application software supports. It aims to serve as a backbone for whole business and management process to facilitate the flow of information between all functions within your organization. ERP helps businesses manage important functions such as product planning, parts purchasing, maintaining inventories, interacting with suppliers, providing customer service, and tracking orders. The software needs to communicate across functions (with minimum of human intervention and paperwork). ERP aims to replicate business processes.

Select Customer List

Nuron is working on a wide variety of projects for clients whose processes, company culture, and development needs are completely different. The following are some of the clients for Nuron ERP:

Engineering and Auto Components

- Deepak Fasteners Ltd., Focal Point, Ludhiana (Unbrako-Fasteners)
- G.S. Radiators, G.T. Road, Ludhiana (Manufacturer of Automotive Radiators)
- JVR Forgings Ltd., Dhandari Kalan, Ludhiana (Engineering)
- Kay Jay Forgings, Focal Point, Ludhiana (Manufacturer & Exporter of Machined Components)
- Mehta Engineers Limited, Focal Point, Ludhiana (Original Equipment Manufacturer & Suppliers)

- Munish Forge, Focal Point, Ludhiana (Government of India Recognized Export House)
- New Swan Enterprises, Industrial Area B, Ludhiana (Manufacturer and Exporter of Automotive Components)
- New Swan Auto Comp, Focal Point, Ludhiana (Manufacturer and Exporter of Automotive Components)
- Shiv Forgings, Industrial Area B, Ludhiana (Hand Tools)
- Vira Scooters, Focal Point, Ludhiana (Automotive Components)
- Zodix Auto Pvt. Ltd., Gill Road, Ludhiana (Auto Parts)

Apparel and Garments

- Bhandari Hosiery Ltd., Rahon Road, Ludhiana (Apparels)
- Oswal Woollen Mills Ltd. (Unit # 5), Industrial Area A, Ludhiana (Readymade Garments)

Agri and Foods

- Cremica Agro Foods Limited, Una, HP (Manufacturers and Exporters of Bakery Products)
- Kashmir Apiaries Exports/Little Bee, Doraha (Leading Beekeeper and Exporter of Honey in India)
- Mrs. Bector's Specialites Ltd., Phillaur, Jallandhar (Manufacturers and Exporters of Bakery Products)

Chemicals and Paints

- Rajit Paints Ltd., Ludhiana (Manufacturer of Industrial Paints)

Brief Overview of Nuron Software

Today, thousands of small & medium businesses need a practical, user-friendly and quick-to-implement business solution, at an affordable price. Current breed of ERP solutions, designed for small businesses, are not only cost prohibitive but also are unable to meet complex and ever changing requirements of growing small businesses. Infiniti ERP solution offers functionality similar to mid-market solutions, yet it comes at a price that is even lower than a small business solution. Also, as it comes with revolutionary customization toolkit *eDeveloper*, it can be extensively customized to suit each customer's individual requirement. Nuron's Partner Program is intended for companies that desire to sell and/or implement Nuron's ERP solutions in small & medium business market similar to midsize business solutions, yet it comes at a surprisingly low price. Nuron undertakes the following e-business:

- *Custom Application Development*: "Web services-oriented" architecture applications for PCs, Wireless and Mobile devices.
- *eBusiness consulting*: Helps businesses of all sizes build a

commanding presence in the rapidly expanding world of business-to-business and business-to-consumer internet commerce on Microsoft.NET platform.

- *Enterprise Application Integration*: Helps to automate business processes by integrating internal applications with business partners over the internet, using XML and web services.
- *Collaboration and Workflow*: Helps to implement workflow automation software which eliminates manual and paper-based processes by capturing, routing and tracking information using computer-based e-forms.

5.2. A Case Study—New Swan Autocomp. Pvt. Ltd.

New Swan Autocomp. Pvt. Ltd., a components manufacturer in Punjab, India, realized that it needed to streamline business processes and leverage IT in order to deal with global players in the automotive industry. Manual and *ad hoc* processes affected productivity and blocked visibility into the business, forcing managers to spend all their time overseeing day-to-day operations. To manage growth, create new customers, and align its IT infrastructure with global practices, New Swan needed an IT makeover. *Intel IT and Nuron*, a local independent software vendor (ISV), analyzed New Swan's business processes.

The Opportunity

India's auto components industry is growing at a very fast pace. A number of global companies such as General Motors, Delphi, DaimlerChrysler, Toyota, and MICO/Bosch have operations there, opening up big opportunities for local SMBs. New Swan Autocomp. Pvt. Ltd. is one such company. Based in Ludhiana, an industrial city in the north Indian state of Punjab, New Swan is ambitious and wants to grow big and grow fast. The company commenced operations in April 2003 and currently manufactures and exports 250 fine blanked components and high-precision automotive assemblies for clients worldwide. It wants to rapidly expand its portfolio to remain competitive and to address new market segments, growing into an INR 980 crores (USD 22 million) revenue company by 2008 from the current level of INR 134 crores (USD 3 million).

Problem Identification

Within a short time, New Swan's top management found itself grappling with issues such as lack of data (reports detailing inventory in stock, orders with sub-contractors, and so on were not readily available), faulty employee attendance records, delayed receivables, and duplicate payments to vendors. These bottlenecks left management without time to innovate or acquire new customers. Before it could embark on its ambitious growth plan, New Swan had to implement standard practices to eliminate *ad-hoc* processes and create an infrastructure for operational efficiency and transparency. Additionally, to do business with target clients—large domestic and overseas companies—it needed a compatible IT infrastructure to pass stringent client audits.

Taking all these inefficiencies together, the company was losing business, money, and manpower. Even, finalizing vendors became a problem in the absence of performance and comparison reports. The company also faced problems with payables and receivables. Additionally, New Swan was unable to install 3-D software for product design on their old systems and needed to upgrade to a high-performance, scalable platform.

IT Requirements

New Swan needed an affordable and reliable enterprise solution, based on streamlined business processes, to eliminate internal inefficiencies, acquire new customers, and grow rapidly. To meet these goals, the company worked with Intel's *SMB IT Makeover program,* which helps companies gain business value through technology investments. Intel IT teamed with Nuron, a local ISV, to study New Swan's business processes and identify solution requirements, which included the following:

- Make information easily available for decision-making by bringing visibility into business processes
- Control business processes to streamline payables, receivables, and inventory management
- Enable traveling executives to access business data to make decisions
- Automate routine processes to allow management to focus on business development
- Profile vendors by using past data
- Bring IT infrastructure in line with customer systems
- Capture new opportunities by implementing 3-D design software on a dependable platform

Intel IT translated these business requirements into application functionality and then identified specific modules within Nuron's Small and Medium Business ERP solution, Infiniti*, to implement:

- Inventory management
- Purchase management
- Sales and distribution management
- Finance and accounts
- Payroll (machine-based attendance)

The Solution

The team from Intel IT and Nuron worked together to provide New Swan with an efficient and affordable solution. Finally, Intel IT carried out an in-depth study and generated an IT Business Value (ITBV) model to quantify gains and provide a rationale for IT investments. The model gave New Swan a way to calculate potential returns on strategic IT investments, spread over a five year period. Based on Intel IT best practices, the team streamlined manual business processes into application functionalities, and then recommended Nuron Infiniti*, an ERP solution for SMBs. Next, they mapped the IT infrastructure to the new business processes and deployed one Intel® Xeon® processor-based server and ten Intel® Pentium® 4 processor-based client machines for specific tasks. The team also recommended two Intel ® Centrino® mobile technology, based laptops to help keep senior managers in touch with their teams and customers while traveling. Additionally, Intel provided New Swan with a roadmap for future technology purchases to optimize returns on current IT investments and maximize business benefits.

Post Implementation Benefits

The system has been running with very good uptime and the complete hardware and software cost them just around INR 4,49,569 (USD 10,000). New Swan started enjoying the benefits of its IT deployment almost immediately, because managers had real-time visibility into business processes. Decision-making has become smart and quick because of this makeover. People in the office no longer have to wait for the presence of senior managers to resolve issues and they can now send queries and get responses by e-mail. The following further benefits were observed after the implementation of ERP software:

1. *Inventory:* Inventory management improved remarkably, with inventory levels reduced to 19 days, from 30 days. With the help of Nuron Infiniti* inventory management module the company experienced better inventory planning and demand forecasting.
2. *Office Automation*: Delays and errors in billing are a thing of the past. The application generates automatic alerts whenever bills are due and helps New Swan better manage its cash flow. All records and information from past transactions are maintained on the server and managers have access to information about vendors, based on their past performance and rate quotes. The company can also automatically capture attendance records and manage payroll.
3. *Productivity*: New Swan saw a 15 percent productivity increase for non-factory employees.
4. *Design:* After upgrading to a high-performance, scalable platform, the company has also deployed a 3-D design application to tap

growing market demands and to better manage its product portfolio.

5. *Client Relationships:* Company also feels more confident in dealing with overseas clients, because it knows it can meet and exceed expectations. The management feels that it was essential to align the IT infrastructure with customers systems to efficiently manage activities like inventory, purchasing, finance and accounts, sales, and distribution. New customers also want manufacturers to have a compatible IT infrastructure to facilitate product review at all levels and enhance internal capabilities.
6. *New business:* Within four months of deploying new technology, New Swan acquired two customer orders worth INR 98 lacs (USD 2.2 million). It is a remarkable feat for a company whose turnover was INR 134 lacs (USD 3 million) in 2004-05. "Customers visited our factory for a rigorous audit of our technology and processes before they gave us orders to manufacture auto parts for them," says a company official. Now, New Swan is looking at further increasing exports.

The Company is expecting a benefit of INR 96 lacs (USD 209,000), with an investment of INR 964 lacs (USD 21,000) over the next five years.

Business Value Tool

To help companies justify their IT investments and then forecast the business benefits of these investments based on quantifiable business metrics, Intel IT developed an IT Business Value (ITBV) tool. The tool, specifically designed for SMBs, is based on Intel's own best practices in making IT investment decisions and measuring the success of internal IT projects. It uses a standardized, systematic, asset-based methodology to assess the annual lifecycle cost of an IT investment and the returns to the business. This integrated tool has a cost derivation section to holistically assess IT costs and payback over asset lifecycles, while the business value section helps to visualize benefit using a set of business value categories (for example, increased revenue, reduced inventory, better productivity, and so on). Results allow businesses to make data-driven decisions, prioritize their investment options, and demonstrate direct financial benefits. With the ability to align IT investments with business performance, management can make better investment decisions that create competitive advantage for their companies.

6. CONCLUSION

The ERP market has become one of the fastest growing segments of the IT market worldwide over the last few years, and will continue to grow in the coming years.

The present case study shows that with the right management decisions and actions, through the simultaneous and coordinated projects of business process reengineering and the development of the integral information system, the poor effects of the listed problems can be minimized or eliminated, which is clear from the tangible and intangible benefits outlined in this case study.

References

1. Altekar, Rahul V. (2005), ERP Theory and Practice, Prentice Hall of India, New Delhi.
2. Basu, Amit and Siems, Thomas F. (2007), The Impact of E-Business Technologies on Supply Chain Operations: A Macro-economic Perspective, Federal Reserve Bank of Dallas, Research Department Working paper 0404.
3. Chaturvedi, Ruchi and Gupta, Vivek (2005), "SCM and ERP Software Implementation at Nike-From failure to success, www.icmindia.org
4. Garg, Vinod and Venkitakrishnan, N.K. (2002), ERPWARE—ERP Implementation Framework, Prentice Hall of India, New Delhi.
5. Monczka, Robert; Trent, Robert and Handfield, Robert (1998), *Purchasing and Supply Chain Management*, Cincinnati: South-Western College Publishing.
6. Vokurka, Robert J., Lummus, Rhonda R. and Krumweide, Dennis (2007), "Improving Manufacturing Flexibility: The Enduring Value of JIT and TQM", *Sam Advanced Management Journal*, Winter, pp. 14-21.
7. Wu, Nesa L'abbe (2002), SCM, ERP and the Internet, *Productivity*, Vol. 42(4), pp. 535-38.
8. www.sap.com
9. www.intel.com/IT
10. www.swnindia.com/swan-auto/index
11. www.su-kam.com
12. www.nuronsoftware.com
13. www.aberdeen.com
    - Common ERP Beliefs: Fact or Myth, 2007.
    - ERP in Manufacturing, 2007.
    - Benchmarking ERP In Manufacturing, 2006.
    - Can ERP Simplify Complex Manufacturing, 2007.
    - ERP Plus in Process Industries, 2008.
    - Quality Management: The Plus Side of ERP Plus, 2008.
    - The Cost of ERP Functionality, 2007.
    - The Total cost of ERP Ownership in Large Companies, 2007.

Index